بسم الله الرحمن الرحيم

حاشية الموفق على لمعة الموفق

Ḥāshiyah̤ al-Muwaffaq ʻalā Lumʻah̤ al-Muwaffaq

A commentary by
Shaykh Muwaffaq al-Dīn Yūsuf b. Ṣādiq al-Ḥanbalī

Compiled and edited by
Mūsā Abū Khuzaymah̤

Reviewed and edited by
Abū Yaḥyā Naveed Raza & Abū Ibrāhīm

المدرسة الحنبلية
AL-MADRASAH
AL-HANBALIYYAH

Ḥāshiyaḧ al-Muwaffaq ʻalā Lum'aḧ al-Muwaffaq

2nd Edition
Sha'ban 1446H / February 2025
ISBN: 978-967-170 20

Published by:
Apologia PLT (LLP0019412-LGN)
No.2 Tingkat 1 Jalan Pangkur
off Jalan Tun Razak, 50400 Kuala Lumpur
apologiaplt@gmail.com

Cover design by:
Sayyid Abdul Rahman al-Junaid

Cover illustration:
Painting of the Grand Umayyad Mosque
by Gustave Bauernfeind, 1890

Typesetting by:
Noorulzaman Abdul Kadir

Transliteration Chart

ء	°	ر	r	ف	f
ا	a, ā	ز	z	ق	q
ب	b	س	s	ك	k
ت	t	ش	sh	ل	l
ث	th	ص	ṣ	م	m
ج	j	ض	ḍ	ن	n
ح	ḥ	ط	ṭ	ه	h
خ	kh	ظ	ẓ	و	w, ū
د	d	ع	‘	ي	y, ī
ذ	dh	غ	gh	ة	ḧ

ّ represented by double letters

CONTENTS

الحمد لله الذي هو كما أثنى على نفسه فالعبد لا يحصي

ثناءًا على ربه

والصلاة والسلام على أفضل خلقه محمد وآله وصحبه

All praise is for Allāh as He praised Himself due to the servant's inability to enumerate praise upon his Lord, and prayers and peace upon the best of the creation, the Prophet Muḥammad ﷺ his followers and companions.

IMĀM IBN QUDĀMAẗ AL-MAQDISĪ

His name, lineage and title

He is Muwaffaq al-Dīn Abū Muḥammad, 'Abd Allāh b. Aḥmad b. Muḥammad b. Qudāmaẗ b. Miqdām b. Nāṣir b. 'Abd Allāh al-Maqdisī; a descendant of 'Umar b. al-Khaṭṭāb. For the Ḥanābilaẗ he is Shaykh al-Madhhab, while they also refer to him as one of the Shaykhān; the other being Majd al-Dīn (d. 652H), the grandfather of Taqī al-Dīn Ibn Taymiyyaẗ.

His birth, early years, seeking knowledge and death

He was born in Sha'bān in the year 541H., in the village of Jammā'īl, Jabal Nāblus. For the first ten years of his life he remained with his family in Palestine, and began his memorization of the Qurān. In 551H, he and his family made hijraẗ to Damascus, due to the Christian invasion of their lands. Whilst in Damascus, Ibn Qudāmaẗ completed his memorization of the Qurān, and in addition memorized a large number of narrations. Furthermore he memorized *Mukhtaṣar al- Khiraqī*; one of the primary texts concerning the fiqh of Imām Aḥmad. He remained in Damascus for ten years and began to journey the Islamic lands in search of knowledge around his twenties. In 561H, he travelled to Baghdad, which was considered at that time to be one of the main cities of knowledge; being the residing place of many luminaries of the time. On his journey to Baghdad he was accompanied by his maternal cousin al-Ḥāfiẓ 'Abd al-Ghanī al-Maqdisī (d. 600H); while he inclined towards the study of fiqh, his cousin inclined towards the study of hadith, nevertheless, they accompanied each other to lessons and acquired both. Ibn Qudāmaẗ remained in Baghdād for four years, and again studied *Mukhtaṣar al-Khiraqī*, but this time under the tutelage of Shaykh 'Abd al-Qādir al-Jīlānī (d. 561H). However, Allāh willed for the death of Shaykh 'Abd al-Qādir, only fifty nights after Ibn Qudāmaẗ's arrival. He later studied under Ibn al-Jawzī (d. 597H); then remained with Ibn al-Manniyy (d. 583H). Under the guidance of his teachers he learned the fiqh of the Ḥanābilaẗ and its principles, excelling in them. He then returned to Damascus, before again embarking on travels to Baghdad as well as Mecca in 573H in order to perform Ḥajj and meet other people of knowledge. After performing Ḥajj he returned to Baghdad where he remained for a year before returning to Damascus where he settled and began to author beneficial works in many branches of knowledge, one of the most famous being *al-Mughnī*. Muwaffaq al-Dīn b. Qudāmah passed away on Saturday, during the day of ʿĪd al-Fiṭr in 620H.

Statements of the scholars about him

He was known for his vast knowledge, wisdom, good manners and wit. He was renowned as the Scholar of the people of al-Shām of his time. Although an independent work can be dedicated to his character and knowledge, this is not the proper place to embark on such an endeavour. Here, it is sufficient to mention a few statements of the scholars regarding him.

A close relative, and scholar in his own right, Diyā° al-Dīn (d. 643H) said about him:

> 'He was of good manners, he would hardly be seen except that he was smiling, he would tell stories and joke. I heard Bahā° al-Dīn (d. 624H). say; "the Shaykh, during readings would joke with us and be at ease. Once they complained to him about some children who worked with him, so he said; "They are children, they have to play and you used to be just like them."'[1]

Ibn al-Najjār (d. 643H) describes him as:

> 'The Imām of the Ḥanābilah in the congregational Mosque (in Damascus), trustworthy, a proof, noble of figure, extremely generous, complete in intelligences, intense in worship, always composed, well-mannered, decent, pious, worshipping upon the statute of the Salaf, his face emitting light, and he was endowed with dignity and prestige. One would benefit from the sight of him, before even hearing his speech!'[2]

Ibn Taymiyyah (d. 728H), born only forty years after the death of Ibn Qudāmah, said: 'No one possessing more understanding of the religion entered al-Shām after al-Awzāʿī (d. 157H) other than al-Shaykh al-Muwaffaq.'[3]

---

[1] Al-Dhahabī, *Siyār A'lam al-Nubulā*, vol. 22, p. 171

[2] Ibn Rajab, *Dhayl 'alā Ṭabaqāt al-Ḥanābilah*, vol. 3, p. 284

[3] Ibn Rajab, *Dhayl 'alā Ṭabaqāt al-Ḥanābilah*, vol. 3, p. 286

His writings

Ibn Qudāmah possessed a great amount of knowledge, deep understanding, and was a prolific writer. Due to these combined characteristics, his plentiful works; some single and others consisting of multiple volumes reached the level of excellence in knowledge; full of deep insight, contemplation and clear love for the words of Allāh the Exalted, and His Messenger ﷺ.

Ibn Rajab (d. 795H) remarks concerning this:

> 'Al-Shaykh al-Muwaffaq wrote many beneficial works about the (Ḥanbalī) Madhhab; it's principles and branches, in (the sciences of) hadith, language, asceticism and heart softeners. His writings in uṣūl al-dīn reach a level of high quality. Many of them (i.e. his books) being on the path of the muḥaddithīn, full of narrations from the Prophet ﷺ and reports from the Salaf and chains of narration. This was the way of Imām Aḥmad and the scholars of Narrations.'[4]

Lastly, some of his more famously known books will be enumerated in relation to the specific field of Islamic science. In fiqh he wrote: *al-Mughnī, al-Kāfī, al-Muqni'* and *al-'Umdah*. In uṣūl al-fiqh he wrote: Rawḍah al-Nāẓir. In admonition, heart-softeners (raqā°iq), purification of the self (tazkiyah al-nafs) and taṣawwuf, he wrote: *al-Riqqah wa al- Bukā, al-Tawwābīn*, and *Dhamm mā 'alayhi Mudda'ū al-Taṣawwuf*. Here it should be pointed out that Ibn Qudāmah did not author the well- known book *Mukhtaṣar Minhāj al-Qāṣidīn*, as is wrongfully stated by certain publishers. This book was authored by Imām Aḥmad b Muḥammad b. 'Abd al-Raḥmān b. Qudāmah al-Maqdisī, who died in 682H. Although, he was related to Muwaffaq al-Dīn Ibn Qudāmah (the author of *al-Lum'ah*) he died some 60 years later. In 'ilm al-ḥadīth he wrote: *Mukhtaṣar al-'Ilāl al-Ḥadīth lī al-Khallāl*. With regards to 'aqīdah, it is said that he was a stern proponent of the Atharī 'aqīdah and during his time he was one of its central figures. He penned many beneficial works elucidating and defending the Atharī 'aqīdah. Including, but not limited to:

- *Al-Burhān fī Mas°alāh al-Qurān,*
- *Al-Ṣirāṭ al-Mustaqīm fī Bayān al-Ḥarf al-Qadīm,*
- *Lum'ah al-I'tiqād,*

[4] Ibn Rajab, *Dhayl 'alā Ṭabaqāt al-Ḥanābilah*, vol. 3, p. 291

- *Ṣifaḧ al-‘Uluww,*
- *Dhamm al-Ta°wīl,*
- *Taḥrīm al-Naẓar fī Kutub Ahl al-Kalām,*
- *Faḍā°il al-Ṣaḥābaḧ.*

SHAYKH YŪSUF BIN ṢĀDIQ Al-ḤANBALĪ

His name, kunyaḧ and laqab

He is Shaykh Yūsuf Muḥammad b. Ṣādiq al-Ḥanbalī. His kunya is Abū Muslim and his laqab is Muwaffaq al-Dīn.

Some of the scholars he studied under

Shaykh Yūsuf b. Ṣādiq studied under scholars from both al-Azhar University (Jāmi'aḧ al-Azhar al-Sharīf) and scholars outside of it; from Egypt as well as other countries. The most important of the scholars he studies under is the Grand Shaykh of the Ḥanābilaḧ, Shaykh Dr. Muḥammad Sayyid al-Ḥanbalī, the main teacher of the Ḥanbalī madhhab in Jāmi' al-Azhar al-Sharīf. Shaykh Yūsuf also studied under Shaykh Aḥmad Ma'bad 'Abd al-Karīm, Shaykh Aḥmad 'Umar Hāshim and Shaykh Ḥasan al-Shāfi'ī; all three being from the Higher Committee of scholars of al-Azhar al-Sharīf. He also studied under Shaykh Ashraf Makkawī, Shaykh Ḥazim al-Kilānī and Shaykh Jamāl Farūq al-Daqāq, Shaykh 'Alī Ṣāliḥ al-Azharī, Shaykh Rabī' al-Ghafīr, Shaykh Fatḥī Ḥijāzī, Shaykh Muḥammad Ḥasan 'Uthmān and Shaykh Sa'd Sa'd Jāwīsh. From outside of Egypt, Shaykh Yūsuf studied with the Pakistan based muḥaddith Shaykh Muḥammad b. 'Abd Allāh al-Shujā' Ābādī. The Shaykh also studied wordily sciences at the Misr International University, in the faculty of Humanities/al-Alsun; combining the study of linguistics, translation and English literature, the latter being the focus of his graduation thesis.

Some of the sciences and books he studied

Shaykh Yūsuf b. Ṣādiq studied various books and branches of Islamic knowledges under the aforementioned scholars. What follows is a general, yet far from complete summary. Under Shaykh Dr. Muḥammad Sayyid al-Ḥanbalī he studied *Sharḥ al-Kawkab al-Munīr* in uṣūl al-fiqh (he also studied this book with Shaykh Ashraf Makkāwī), and in Ḥanbalī fiqh he studied *Bidāyaḧ al-'Ābid, Akhṣār al-Mukhtaṣarāt, Hidāyaḧ al- Rāghib Sharḥ 'Umdaḧ al-Ṭālib, Kashshāf al-Qinā'*. In ḥadīth, he studied *Musnad Imām Aḥmad* with Shaykh Dr. Muḥammad Sayyid al-Ḥanbalī, as well as *Sharḥ al-Kharīdah al-Bahiyyah* in 'ilm al-kalām, and *Lum'aḧ al-I'tiqād* and *Qalā°id al-Iqyān* in Ḥanbalī 'aqīdaḧ, and also grammar (nahw), rhetoric (balāghaḧ) and logic (mantiq). Shaykh Yūsuf also studied logic under

Shaykh Hazim al-Kilānī and Shaykh Ḥasan al-Shāfi'ī, who taught him from *Mi'yār al-'Ilm*. The latter also taught him ḥadīth and taṣawwuf. With Shaykh Aḥmad Ma'bad 'Abd al-Karīm he studied *Tadrīb al-Rāwī* in muṣtalāḥ al-ḥadīth, as well as *Fatḥ al-Mughīt Sharḥ Alfiyyaḧ al-ḥadīth*. With Shaykh Jamāl Farūq al-Daqāq he studied 'ilm al-kalām. Under Shaykh Muḥammad b. 'Abd Allāh al-Shujā' Ābādī he studied *Musnad al-Shāfi'ī* and *al-Muwaṭṭa°* in ḥadīth. He also studied ḥadīth under Shaykh Sa'd Sa'd Jāwīsh. Apart from studying grammar with Shaykh Dr. Muḥammad Sayyid al-Ḥanbalī, Shaykh Yūsuf also studied *al-Ajrumiyyaḧ, Sharḥ al-Makūdī* and parts of *Qaṭr al-Nadā* under Shaykh 'Alī Ṣāliḥ al-Azharī, as well as *Sharḥ Ibn 'Aqīl 'alā Alfiyyaḧ Ibn Mālik* under Shaykh Rabī' al-Ghafīr. Other books in grammar and morphology (ṣarf) were studied under Shaykh Muḥammad Ḥasan 'Uthmān.

His ijāzāt

Apart from having specific ijāzāt in various books, Shaykh Yūsuf b. Ṣādiq also holds general ijāzāt in the Ḥanbalī madhhab, which he received from Shaykh Dr. Muḥammad Sayyid al-Ḥanbalī[5] and Shaykh Dr. Walīd al-Manīsī al-Ḥanbalī[6], the president of the Islamic University of Minnesota and a senior member of the Permanent Fatwa Committee of the Assembly of Muslim Jurists in America (AMJA). Shaykh Yusuf b. Ṣādiq also received general ijāzāt[7] from the Grand Shaykh of the Shāfi'ī madhhab, 'Abd al-'Azīz al-Shahāwī, Shaykh Muḥammad Mahanā, Shaykh Muḥaddith Ismā'īl al-Daftār and Shaykh Mu'awaḍ 'Awaḍ Ibrāhīm; who was a hundred-and-four years of age, may the *Raḥmaḧ* of Allāh be upon him.

---

[5] Shaykh Dr. Muḥammad Sayyid al-Ḥanbalī himself holds various general ijāzāt in the Ḥanbalī madhhab. He received ijāzāt from the late Saudi Shaykh of the Ḥanābilaḧ 'Abd Allāh b. 'Aqīl al-Ḥanbalī, as well as the muftī of the Ḥanābilaḧ in Duma Syria, Shaykh Aḥmad al-Dūmī and the Egyptian scholar Shaykh 'Abd al-Razzāq Khafājah al-Ḥanbalī.

[6] For more information on Shaykh Dr. Walīd al-Manīsī, visit: https://www.amjaonline.org/scholars/dr-waleed-al-maneese-ph-d/

[7] An ijāzah is a license given by someone who possesses authority in a specific text, subject, branch of knowledge, to someone who studied under him; indicating that this person is authorized to transmit and teach a certain text or subject. When one holds a general ijāzah in a madhhab, it means that someone is deemed overall qualified, by someone who himself possesses both authority and general qualification, to teach and transmit from every branch of knowledge and book within that particular madhhab. Thereby, his knowledge is considered of such high standard that he can transmit and teach without him having necessarily studied each and every book.

His teaching posts

Shaykh Yūsuf b. Ṣādiq holds an official teaching post at Madrasah Shaykh al-'Amūd, teaching various Islamic sciences such as Ḥanbalī fiqh, ḥadīth and tafsīr. He is also the main teacher of the Ḥanbalī Madrasaḧ online platform, which provides both short and long-term online courses, in both the Arabic and English languages, in subjects such as uṣūl al-fiqh, fiqh, 'aqīdaḧ and ḥadīth. Outside teaching, the shaykh has also worked as an English interpreter. His Islamic and worldly studies, coupled with his work and fluency in Arabic and English mean he is aptly qualified to teach the Islamic sciences to an English-speaking audience.

GENERAL INTRODUCTION

Remarks on al-Lum'aẗ: themes, organization and contextualization

The book *Lum'aẗ al-I'tiqād*, which is by far the most widely known contribution of Ibn Qudāmaẗ to the field of 'aqīdaẗ, is the main focus of this work. It deals with various topics of 'aqīdaẗ, such as sunnaẗ in opposition to bid'aẗ (innovation), qaḍā° (Divine decree) and qadar (pre-ordainment), issues concerning imān (faith), the ru°yaẗ (seeing) of Allāh, the Messenger ﷺ and his Companions (Ṣaḥābaẗ), interaction with rulers, orthodoxy in opposition to heterodoxy, and the relationship between ijtihād and taqlīd. Apart from these themes, this work is for the larger part dedicated to elucidating the correct belief with regards to two main topics. The first being Allāh and His Attributes (ṣifāt)[8] and the correct approach to the texts that make mention of these Attributes, the enumeration of some of these texts, and the stance and approach that luminaries of the first generations took in this regard. The second being, the *Kalām*[9] of Allāh and the reality of the Qurān. Approximately half of *al-Lum'aẗ* is concerned with these two topics and others directly related to them.

When browsing through *al-Lum'aẗ*, it becomes apparent that the topics contained within it are not the most well-organised, especially when compared with more structured books of 'aqīdaẗ. For example, the author inserts a discussion on the People of the Qiblaẗ, and the continuous nature of Ḥajj and Jihād in between a passage relating to the companions and the wives of the Prophet ﷺ. It could be argued that these issues would be better suited in the section concerned with obedience to the ruler and leadership. The organisation of the book however, does not detract from the content and the importance of the book whatsoever, and it remains to this day succinct and easy to understand. It is written in a straightforward manner, absent of difficult theological

[8] A conscious choice has been made to only transliterate the Attributes of Allāh, and their related verbal forms, into English, instead of substituting them with the English translation; this is in order to obey the prohibition to do so. It must be stressed however, that the proposed translations given, are only related to the Arabic word in the context of human speech and their understanding. Therefore, the proposed English word is not to be understood as a direct translation of the Attribute of Allāh, as the meaning in relation to Allāh is unknown.

[9] Kalām can be translated as 'speech'.

terminologies, clearly informing the reader what is required to be known in order for one to be truly upon the orthodox Ḥanbalī- Atharī ʻaqīdaḧ.

Most books concerned with the Atharī ʻaqīdaḧ up to the time of Ibn Qudāmaḧ, discuss the same topics as mentioned above with little variation. However, this must not be taken to mean that the author of a particular work only holds the beliefs mentioned in his book or that he differs in belief with another author who mentioned different issues. On the contrary, most books of ʻaqīdaḧ were written as a reaction to erroneous beliefs prevalent during the time of the author, or in order to provide answers to questions put forward to the author by individuals and groups. Therefore, books of ʻaqīdaḧ present not only the ʻaqīdaḧ that their authors found to be correct, but also shine light upon the historical context in which the books were written. This subsequently resulted in the variation found in works of ʻaqīdaḧ and in the importance each author allocated to a particular issue, and it is in this context that the books on Atharī ʻaqīdaḧ must be viewed and understood. In the time of Ibn Qudāmaḧ there was fierce opposition between different schools of thought resulting in debates, exclusive behaviour and even clashes between individuals and groups of opposing schools. The tone was often harsh and polarizing and in some cases driven by political motives and this poured over into the written works as well. It is extremely important to keep this context in mind when reading classical books of ʻaqīdaḧ, regardless of the author or school of thought the book belongs to. An appreciation of this context means that not all the statements of an author, regarding other groups and individuals, can or should be applied uncritically in the modern day; and this approach should also be taken into account when studying *al-Lumʻaḧ*.

The revival of al-Lumʻaḧ: a new commentary

The nature of the book is such that it is not in need of a detailed or lengthy explanation (sharḥ) which attempts to clarify difficult concepts or terminologies. Hence a short, to-the-point commentary (ḥāshiyaḧ) suffices in order to grasp the full meaning of the book. Especially, a commentary which seeks to convey and expound the intent of the original author; i.e. a concise commentary from a Ḥanbalī-Atharī perspective, that explains this classical Ḥanbalī-Atharī text in such a way that will aid the original author in conveying his message, while facilitating the reader with getting acquainted with the text. This text is by no means in need of a commentary that aims to present or promote ideas and convictions that the author did not hold, nor is the original work of the author in need of being used as a mere tool or springboard to establish such goals. Unfortunately, this is exactly what has been the case with most translations and commentaries of the book, especially during recent times. Various Salafī groups have tried, on more than one occasion, to explain the book in a way that does not agree with what Ibn Qudāmaḧ wanted to convey.

What is striking is that in general, these groups and individuals appreciate and follow what Shaykh al-Islām Ibn Taymiyyaḧ and Ibn Qayyim (d. 751H) stated, yet, they fail to understand and follow a very important point that the latter put forward regarding the method of explaining texts. In *I'lām al-Muwaq'īn*, he states on more than one occasion that when an author states something in his books(s), and one (e.g. the translator or explanator) knows that the author meant a certain thing by it, he or she should not attempt to change that particular meaning by explaining away the authors intended meaning or changing it to something that fits his own personal opinion or agenda. Rather, one should try to keep as close to what the author stated as possible. Following other than this method of explaining texts, is a form of intellectual dishonesty. If someone disagrees with an author he should either author an original work himself, in which he can convey what he wants, or, when explaining a particular point in which one disagrees with the author, the point should be kept intact and transmitted honestly, and only afterwards should the disagreement be mentioned along with its reasoning. This can be placed either in the text of the commentary, whilst making it clearly distinct from the original text, or by use of footnotes. However, he should leave the original text and its intended meaning, in all cases, intact.

A number of Salafī oriented commentaries of *Lum'aḧ al-I'tiqād*, currently on the market, which have been translated into English and other languages, do not adhere to this concept of respecting the authors intentions. What one ends up with is a book which used to contain the original Ḥanbalī-Atharī 'aqīdaḧ, that is changed and distorted through its commentary and is eventually presented as Salafī 'aqīdaḧ. To confuse the general reader even more, even the term Atharī 'aqīdaḧ is hijacked to make the work appear authentic, although in reality the Atharī 'aqīdaḧ is not synonymous with Salafī 'aqīdaḧ. In contrast to this, it is the intent of this current work to present the true Ḥanbalī-Atharī 'aqīdaḧ put forward in *al-Lum'aḧ*, and accompany it with a commentary that will facilitate and aid the reader in better understanding the text from this perspective, as explained by one of the qualified Ḥanbalī scholars of Egypt. It is hoped that with this effort, Muslims will rediscover *al- Lum'aḧ*, as intended by the author himself i.e. from a Ḥanbalī and Atharī perspective.

Text and commentary: the structure of the book

In order to stay as true as possible to the original text, the following structure is maintained. Firstly, for complete transparency and to aid those intending to memorize the text, the reader is presented with the vowelized Arabic text. In order to keep footnotes at a minimum, no references have been given for the Arabic text. Secondly, after each passage from the Arabic text, the English translation is presented. As the aim is to minimize usage of footnotes in the Arabic and its translation, only references to the Qurānic āyāt have been given. Finally, the commentary is presented according to a traditional ḥāshiyaḧ-style, and this is done to break away from the usual structure of English commentaries of Arabic texts, which rely on masses of footnotes which can, in some cases, exceed several pages and surpass the length of the original text. These footnotes detract from the reading experience and cause it to be fragmented rather than flowing naturally through the text and commentary. This style has also been selected to pay homage to the classical method of explaining Islamic texts, which apart from being an intellectual endeavour, also endowed the texts with an aesthetic dimension present throughout the whole work, which included rhyming titles, organic and easy-flowing text with commentary, and adornments in margins. With the ḥāshiayḧ-style, the commentary is made an integral part of the text and in this work differentiating the commentary from the actual text is done simply by presenting the original text in **bold** and inserting the commentary between brackets [...].

In presenting the commentary, the intention is to make it flow naturally with the text it explains, by using additional words at times. Only in some instances is there a clear distinction between the original text and the commentary. While a conscious choice was made to avoid the use of footnotes for the Arabic and translation, full notes are given for the commentary. These include references for all āyāt, narrations and quotations. Only in rare cases could a reference to a specific source not be found, however these have been indicated where necessary. Some additional information is also given in the footnotes regarding particular points, but only when it was felt that doing so would improve the reader's understanding.

Before commencing with the actual text and its commentary, a few points must be mentioned in order to further contextualise the work and give a general outline of the science of 'aqīdaḧ, providing the student a clear perspective while reading and studying the text. Due to their importance, these points will be discussed as four separate chapters.

AN IMPORTANT DISCUSSION CONCERNING THE SALAF AL-ṢĀLIḤ AND AHL AL-ḤADĪTH

The Salaf al-Ṣāliḥ (the Pious Predecessors) are the three preferred generations that where praised by the Prophet ﷺ in his statements: *'The best people are those of my generation, then those who come after them, then those who come after them. Then, there will come people after them whose testimony precedes their oaths and their oaths precede their testimony.'*[10] Although this statement appears to be clear, there has however been scholarly discussion regarding who exactly is included within the 'best generations'. This, mostly stems from disagreement surrounding the definition of the word 'generation' (qarn). It has led some to consider a generation to be a period of time spanning a hundred years. Subsequently, this group of scholars considered the Salaf al-Ṣāliḥ as those who lived within the first three hundred years of Islamic history i.e. from 0 to 300 hijri; and this opened up the possibility of more than three individuals succeeding each other. Others defined generation more conventionally, i.e. a number of people succeeding those before them, and therefore considered a generation as one individual or a specific group of individuals.

Although, the former definition is good, as it includes all the famous imāms like Abū Ḥanīfaḧ (d. 150H), Mālik (d. 179H), al-Shāfi'ī (d. 204H) and Aḥmad (d. 241H), it must be noted however, that amongst the people living during these three generations, were innovators and deviants. For example, those who persecuted and tortured Imām Aḥmad (i.e. the Mu'tazilaḧ), such as Ibn Abī Du°ād (d. 240H). An additional problem is that various people and groups seek to include or exclude others from this definition. For example, some will try to include 'Uthmān al-Dārimī (d. 280H) from amongst the Salaf al-Ṣāliḥ, yet according to others he was a mujassim[11]11. It therefore appears that there is a problem with the practicality of this definition as the criteria for including someone from among the Salaf al-Ṣāliḥ varies from one group to another, and as a result, who the Salaf al-Ṣāliḥ actually are may vary from people to people. Therefore, it is better to keep the term Salaf al-Ṣāliḥ away from the discussion

---

[10] Al-Bukhārī no. 6429 / Muslim no. 2533

[11] A mujasim is someone who has fallen into anthropomorphism and regards or depicts Allāh in such fashion. For example, one who holds the belief that Allāh is actually seated on the Throne, or that Allāh is a body comprising of different parts i.e. resembling created bodies.

related to ʻaqīdaḧ, and not use the term ʻaqīdaḧ al-Salaf al- Ṣāliḥ, or even ʻaqīdaḧ Salafiyyah for that matter, but instead use the term ʻaqīdaḧ Ahl al-Ḥadīth instead. Thus, it is clear that developing a single definition by which one can determine who the salaf are is problematic and results in disputes.

Unfortunately, this term and its variations are often used argumentatively to force a certain belief on someone out of guilt and make one's opponent fear any disagreement. When it is said that such- and-such is the opinion of the Salaf, the majority of people would fear to disagree with it, and as a result simply submit to it. However, as previously pointed out, the Salaf consists of a range of different individuals, with some being trustworthy (thiqah) and upright (ādil), while others were weak (daʻīf) and even corrupt or open sinners (fusāq). According to the science of ḥadīth, all the of the companions were upright and trustworthy, however the same is not the case with those who came after them. Therefore, anyone from the subsequent generations is individually assessed to determine whether he or she is trustworthy or not.

As previously stated, use of the term Ahl al-Ḥadīth is more appropriate than the term Salaf al-Salih and therefore we are concerned here with the ʻaqīdaḧ of Ahl al-Ḥadīth, or more specifically the Atharī ʻaqīdaḧ. When looking at prominent individuals who belong to Ahl al- Ḥadīth, the best representative is surely Imām Aḥmad b. Ḥanbal. During the time of the miḥnaḧ (inquisition)[12], there was a dispute between two parties namely the Muʻtazilaḧ, represented by Ibn Abī Duʻād, and Ahl al- Sunnaḧ, represented by Imām Aḥmad b. Ḥanbal. There were of course others who stood against the Muʻtazilaḧ, but ultimately it was only Imām Aḥmad who did not submit to the demands of the inquisitors, and as a result endured physical and mental torture at the hands of his persecutors. The ordeal that he experienced cemented his role as the leader and defender of the ʻaqīdaḧ of Ahl al-Ḥadīth; and naturally this was carried by his direct students and the ones who followed them, eventually this ʻaqīdaḧ became known as the Ḥanbalī or Atharī ʻaqīdaḧ. For this reason, in some prominent Ashʻarī books such as *al-Mawāqif* and *al-Maqāṣid*, there is found reference to a group of people they call Ahl al-Ḥadīth al-Ḥanābilaḧ. This indicates that it is possible that one can be Shāfiʻī in fiqh, yet Ḥanbalī in ʻaqīdaḧ (if they ascribe themselves to the Atharī ʻaqīdaḧ). Furthermore, this proves that the Ḥanābilaḧ are Ahl al- Ḥadīth, for even the Ashāʻiraḧ who disagreed with them consider them to be Ahl al-Ḥadīth. If this

---

[12] It refers to the period of state-imposed inquisition, which started in 218H, lasting around fifteen years and ended in 233H.

is understood, it is known that when ‘aqīdaḧ al-Ḥanābilaḧ is mentioned, it refers to the ‘aqīdaḧ of Aḥmad b. Ḥanbal who is the best representative of Ahl al-Ḥadīth, and it is synonymous with the Atharī ‘aqīdaḧ.

DETAILING THE ‘AQĪDAḦ OF THE ḤANĀBILAḦ

Various books can be consulted and studied in order to obtain the authentic ‘aqīdaḧ al-Ḥanābilaḧ (or Atharī ‘aqīdaḧ). From the classical books of the early (mutaqaddimīn) phase of the Ḥanābilaḧ, the most important is: *Uṣūl al-Sunnaḧ* authored by Imām Aḥmad b. Ḥanbal himself[13]. In addition, *Sharḥ al-Sunnaḧ* by al-Barbahārī (d. 329H) and *al-Hā°iyaḧ* by Ibn Abī Dawūd (d. 316H) can be consulted. The latter should perhaps best be studied with the explanation of Al-Safārīnī (d. 1188H), titled *Lawā°iḥ al-Anwār al-Saniyyaḧ*. However, due to its advanced nature it should not be engaged with during the beginning or intermediate level of study. Al-Qāḍī Abū Ya‘lā (d. 458H), considered to be the last of the early phase, also authored important works on ‘aqīdaḧ, such as *Mukhtaṣar al-Mu‘tamad fi Uṣūl al-Dīn* and *Ibṭāl al-Ta°wīlāt*.

From the middle (mutawassiṭīn) phase the poem *al-Qaṣīdaḧ al- Dāliyyaḧ* by al-Kalwadhānī (d. 510H) and *al-Iqtiṣād fī al-I‘tiqād* by ‘Abd al-Ghanī al-Maqdisī are considered sound and important reference materials. Also, from this period is the famous *al-Lum‘aḧ* of Ibn Qudāmaḧ which is considered a well-established starting point[14].

Books from the later (muta°akhkhirīn) phase include *al-‘Ayn wa al- Athar* by ‘Abd Al-Bāqī (d. 1071H) and *Qalā°id al-Iqyān* by Ibn Balbān (d. 1083H), which is the summary of *Nihāyaḧ al-Mubtadī°īn* by Ibn Ḥamdān (d. 695H) whose book in ‘aqīdaḧ is an important work in its own right. More advanced level books include those of al-Safārīnī, such as *Lawāmi‘ al-Anwār* and *Lawā°iḥ al-Anwār* (which is

[13] Most other books on the ‘aqīdaḧ of Imām Aḥmad are attributed to him only, and his authorship of them is not firmly established. While some scholars do regard them as being his, others question his authorship. Therefore, it is best to limit oneself to the aforementioned book (i.e. *Uṣūl al-Sunnaḧ*). In line with this, the authenticity of *Kitāb al-Sunnaḧ* of ‘Abd Allāh b. Aḥmad has also been called into question and should not be used as a primary source for studying the Ḥanbalī ‘aqīdaḧ. It should be pointed out that this does not mean that these are books deprived of benefit as they do contain sound material. Yet, they should be used with caution, and it perhaps may be more pertinent to use them as secondary study materials.

[14] The works on ‘aqīdaḧ authored by Ibn al-Jawzī (d. 597H), who is considered to be a scholar from the middle phase of the Madhhab, do not represent the correct Ḥanbalī ‘aqīdaḧ, as he is not consistent in his approach, mixing between the ‘aqīdaḧ of the Ḥanābilaḧ and Ashā‘iraḧ. Also, one should not concern himself with the books of Ibn Taymiyyaḧ (and his student Ibn al-Qayyim and others who propagated their school of thought in matters of ‘aqīdaḧ) when studying in order to grasp the official Ḥanbalī ‘aqīdaḧ. Although, considered one of the four major Ḥanbalī scholars in fiqh (i.e. Ibn Qudāmaḧ, Majd al-Dīn, Ibn Taymiyyaḧ and Ibn Rajab al-Ḥanbalī), his opinions in ‘aqīdaḧ are not decisive and are only selectively considered. Therefore, one should best take from other sources such as Ibn Qudāmaḧ and al-Kalwadhānī, or the later day scholars who are in line with them, such as Ibn Balbān and ‘Abd al-Bāqī.

the aforementioned commentary of *al-Hā°iyaḧ*)[15], however his books are very advanced containing difficult, and sometimes vague phraseology and laborious terminology. Therefore, it is perhaps best to not engage with these works until a thorough grasp of the subject matter has been attained, and instead it may be more beneficial to engage with the more accessible summary authored by Ḥasan al-Shaṭṭī (d. 1348H); entitled *Mukhtaṣar Lawāmi' al-Anwār.* Another advanced level text is the book *al-Aqāwīl al- Thiqāt* by Mar'ī b. Yūsuf al-Karmī (d. 1033H).

[15] These two books should not be confused, although they have very similar titles. *Al-Lawāmi'* is the explanation of al-Safārīnī to his own shorter poem in 'aqīdaḧ, titled *al-Durraḧ al- Maḍiyyaḧ*: while *al-Lawā°iḥ* is his explanation to the poem of Ibn Abī Dawūd.

DIFFERENCES BETWEEN THE SCHOOLS OF 'AQĪDAḦ

Many scholars from the latter generations state that Ahl al-Sunnaḧ wa al-Jamā'aḧ comprises of the Ḥanābilaḧ, Ashā'iraḧ and Māturīdīyaḧ. This is plainly stated by the Ḥanbalī scholars 'Abd al-Bāqī in *al-'Ayn wa al-Athar* and al-Safārīnī in *Lawāmi' al-Anwār*[16]. However, during earlier phases of Hanbali scholarship, e.g. the time of Ibn Qudāmaḧ, this was not the case. Ibn Qudāmaḧ did not consider the Ashā'iraḧ from Ahl al- Sunnaḧ, and he spoke very harshly against them, this being evident in *al-Lum'aḧ* and other works. It is understood however, that the social and political circumstances in which he lived played a critical role in shaping the way scholars from different theological schools interacted with each other. The domain of 'aqīdaḧ was often characterised by fierce debates, mutually exclusive attitudes and hostilities between partisans from different theological schools, e.g. the Ashā'iraḧ and the Ḥanābilaḧ. With changes in these underlying factors, especially in later times, there was also a change in the mutual interaction and tolerance towards one another, resulting in more and more Ḥanbalī scholars disagreeing with the strict approach of Ibn Qudāmaḧ and others towards the Ashā'iraḧ.

In general, the Ashā'iraḧ accept the 'aqīdaḧ of the Ḥanābilaḧ and vice versa, except for a disagreement concerning the Attributes of Allāh and the concept of *ta°wīl* relating to them, which the Ḥanābilaḧ strongly reject. Apart from this, they disagree with the Ḥanābilaḧ on some other issues, although these are less severe in nature. This however, is not the place to delve into these, at times nuanced, differences, for the main focus is explaining the text of *al-Lum'aḧ* and providing a proper exposition of the Atharī 'aqīdaḧ[17]. With regards to the Ashā'iraḧ and the

---

[16] Abd al-Bāqī in *al-'Ayn wa al-Athar*, p. 53 / al-Safārīnī in *Lawāmi' al-Anwār al-Bahiyyaḧ*, vol. 1, p. 292

[17] This commentary is geared towards the novice and intermediate or general Muslim who wants to grasp the Atharī 'aqīdaḧ and its basic tenets. At this level one should avoid delving into the differences between various groups and their representations of issues in 'aqīdaḧ. One should also avoid occupying himself with studying more than the basic issues of the 'aqīdaḧ he is committed to. This also means that at times the way an issue is handled and presented in the commentary is less nuanced than it actually is, as the aim of this work is to provide a general understanding or framework. Once a student has grasped the basics, the study can be advanced by adding more detailed issues, nuances and differences of opinions to his understanding. This progressive method is a tried and tested method of studying that ensures the student is gradually exposed to more advanced and often complex issues. This approach to studying is applied across the board, holding true for various Islamic sciences such as: 'aqīdaḧ, fiqh and ḥadīth. Finally, and perhaps an obvious point, the study of 'aqīdaḧ, or any other science for that matter, should be carried out under the supervision of a qualified teacher. It should in no way be an individual undertaking as studying without a qualified teacher inevitably leads to errors in one's understanding.

Māturīdīyah and the differences between their positions in 'aqīdah; these are less in number and even more nuanced when compared to the differences between the Ḥanābilah and the Ashā'irah (and the Māturīdīyah for that matter). Their differences, however, are too advance to be discussed here and are outside the intent of the present commentary. Thus, for the sake of simplicity, these theological schools will be considered as one. Therefore, when it is said in this commentary that the Ḥanābilah disagree with the Ashā'irah, it is implied that they generally disagree with the Māturīdīyah also. However, if a particular position of the Ashā'irah is stated, it does not necessarily mean that the position is shared with the Māturīdīyah. Furthermore, this book should not be used as a reference for the differences between the Ḥanābilah and the Māturīdīyah, as the latter were never the main focus of the Ḥanābilah unlike the Ashā'irah who have always represented the larger and more prevalent group from the various schools of Kalām.

It is important to note that the Ḥanbalī 'aqīdah, which has historically been called the Atharī 'aqīdah, is not synonymous with the contemporary Salafī 'aqīdah which is often erroneously labelled as such. The Salafi 'aqīdah as is the case with the other theological schools, has a distinct approach when it comes to the Attributes of Allāh. Additionally, they too disagree with the positions of the Ḥanābilah on other points of 'aqīdah. However, as stated previously, expounding these differences is not the focus of this work.

IJTIHĀD VS TAQLĪD

Allāh said: *'and ask the people of knowledge...'*[18], indicating that taqlīd in matters of fiqh is permissible. However, where matters of 'aqīdaḧare concerned, one has to acquire Shahādaḧ (belief with evidence) and attain certain knowledge (yaqīn). Taqlīd,in this case, would only give probable knowledge (ẓan) and results in one following the opinion of another without knowing the evidence behind it. Simply put, there is no taqlīd in matters of 'aqīdaḧ.

This is contrary to what most of the modern-day Salafī groups propagate, by claiming that there is taqlīd in 'aqīdaḧ and ijtihād in fiqh. Furthermore, it is stressed that everyone is required to believe according to his own ijtihād in the primary issues of 'aqīdaḧ, such as the oneness of Allāh, Him having no children, partners or parents, and Him having created and originated all of creation. In all these basic issues there is no excuse for someone to resolve to taqlīd, instead ijtihād should be resorted to in order to arrive at certain belief based on evidences. However, particular issues that Allāh did not require his creation to know, are not included and ijtihad in these matters is not required; instead making taqlid of a qualified scholar in such a case is sufficient and can be resorted to.

With the above stated, one might wonder how a relied upon position (mu'tamad) can exist in Ḥanbali 'aqīdaḧ when taqlid in primary matter has already been censured. The answer to this is that the relied upon position did not originate from taqlīd, instead it developed through the individual ijtihād of prominent scholars of the Ḥanābilaḧ, who eventually reached the same conclusions. This is illustrated by al-Suyūṭī (d. 911H), when he mentioned that he never followed al-Shāfi'ī (d. 204H) (i.e. he did not do taqlīd of the Shāfi'ī madhhab) instead he performed ijtihād and found himself agreeing with the Imām in all but a few issues.

Hence, there is a clear difference between agreeing on something after the process of ijtihād, leading one to a particular conclusion, and following an opinion without knowing the evidence behind it (i.e. taqlīd). Making ijtihad in 'aqīdaḧ and reaching the same conclusions Imām Aḥmad reached is not particularly difficult,

[18] Qurān 16:43

as the number of issues related to ʻaqīdah are relatively few when compared to fiqh and therefore the probability of arriving at the same result is much higher.

فضيلة العلامة شيخ الحنابلة محمد السيد الحنبلي قال:

ومن فوائد التلقي على الشيوخ لا من الصحف إحياء سنة التلقي وسنة الإسناد ومعرفة آبائك في العلم واختصار الوقت وتعلم الأدب وتسديد الفهم فإذا خلصت نيتك في تعليم العلم بعد هذا أو ناظرت صاحب بدعة أو قمت لأمر من أمور الشريعة فتحركت تحركت معك سلسلة الشيوخ غيرة على ابنهم البار ونصرة الوريث النبوة وما يعقلها إلا العالمون.

The virtuous Shaykh, the 'allāmaḧ, Shaykh al-Ḥanābilaḧ Muḥammad al-Sayyid al-Ḥanbalī said:

'From the benefits of takingknowledge from shuyūkh instead of books is: the revival of the sunnaḧ of taking knowledge from a shaykh and the sunnaḧ of the chain (of narrators), knowing your fathers in knowledge[19], shortening time spent, learning manners and correcting understanding. Then, if you have a sincere intention to teach knowledge after this (i.e. having learned and obtained a chain), or debate an innovator, or start doing things from the sharī'aḧ matters, and move towards this, then the chain of shuyūkh, with solicitude for their good son,

[19] Shaykh Muḥammad Sayyid is referring to the famous and well-known notion amongst scholars, in which they express that a student may consider, and refer to his teacher/shaykh as his father. In this sense, the chain of scholars is seen as a chain of father figures one has, connecting him to each subsequent scholar in the chain before him; so one's shaykh is his father, and his shaykh is the grandfather, and the shaykh before that is the great grandfather, and so on, going back to a particular scholar or even the Prophet ﷺ himself. Saying such a thing is not considered an innovation or the speech of Sufis, for Allāh has stated in the Qurān: *'The Prophet is more worthy of the believers than themselves, and his wives are their mothers'* (Qurān: 33:6), and this makes the Prophet ﷺ their father, in a figurative sense. In addition, the Prophet ﷺ himself has stated with regards to knowledge that he is as a father, for he said: *'I am to you like a father; I teach you.'*, as narrated by Abū Dawūd, no. 8, and others. All this however, does not mean that a real tie of kinship is established or laws of inheritance are applied.

supporting him, moves with you[20], because he is the heir of prophethood[21] and no one understands this except the intelligent.'

With these beautiful and beneficial words in mind, what follows is the presentation of the complete Ḥanbalī chain of *Lum'aḧ al-I'tiqād* as narrated from Shaykh Muwaffaq al-Dīn Abū Muslim Yūsuf b. Ṣādiq al- Ḥanbalī; and he said:

أخبرني الشيخ حاتم الأنصاري الحنبلي قال أخبرني شيخ الحنابلة محمد السيد الحنبلي أخبرنا الشيخ عبدالله بن محمود بن محمد السيد الدومي الشاذلي الحنبلي، قال : حدثنا به والدي المحدث الفقيه الشيخ محمود السيد بن محمد السيد الدومي الحنبلي، عن شيخه مصطفى بن أحمد الشطي الحنبلي، عن أبيه أحمد الشطي الحنبلي، عن العلامة حسن بن عمر الشطي الحنبلي، عن مصطفى بن سعد الرحيباني الحنبلي، عن محدث الشام محمد بن أحمد السفاريني الحنبلي عن شيخه التغلبي عن قدوة الحنابلة في زمانه علما وعملا أبي عبد الله محمد بن بدر الدين البلباني الصالحي في الصالحية من الشام صاحب قلائد العقيان وكتب سلسلته فقال: أروي الفقه والطريقة القادرية وغيرهما مما يجوز لي وعني روايته عن شيخ الإسلام الشهاب أحمد بن علي الوفائي المفلحي عن شرف الدين موسى بن سالم الحجاوي وعن القاضي برهان الدين بن مفلح وهما عن والده نجم الدين بن مفلح عن والده القاضي شمس الدين صاحب الفروع عن الشيخ تقي الدين بن تيمية عن شمس الدين ابن أبي عمر عن عمه شيخ الإسلام موفق الدين ابن قدامة المقدسي.

---

[20] The possessor of the chain should envision this 'moving of the chain of shuyūkh' when he is debating, teaching or doing something from the sharī'aḧ, as if his fathers are present with him, backing him, supporting him, and strengthening him.

[21] Abū Dawūd, no. 3641, al-Tirmidhī, 2683, and others narrated that the Prophet ﷺ said: *'The scholars are the heirs of the Prophets, and the Prophets leave neither dinar nor dirham, leaving only knowledge, and he who takes it takes an abundant portion.'*

حاشية الموفق على لمعة الموفق

Ḥāshiyah al-Muwaffaq ‘alā Lum‘ah al-Muwaffaq

THE AUTHOR'S INTRODUCTION

قَالَ الشَّيخُ الإِمَامُ مُوَفَّقُ الدِّينِ أَبُو مُحَمَّد عَبدِ اللهِ بنِ أَحْمَدَ بنِ مُحَمَّد بن قُدَامَةَ المقدسي رحمه الله تعالى:

Imām Muwaffaq al-Dīn Abū Muḥammad 'Abd Allāh b. Aḥmad b. Muḥammad b. Qudāmah al-Maqdisī, may Allāh, the Exalted, have mercy on him, said:

بسم الله الرحمن الرحيم

الحَمْدُ لله المحمود بِكُلِّ لِسانِ المعبودِ فِي كُلِّ زَمَانٍ، الَّذِي لَا يَخْلُو مِنْ عِلْمِهِ مكانٍ، ولا يَشْغَلُهُ شَأْنٌ عَن شَانٍ، جَلَّ عَن الأشباه والأَنْدادِ، وَتَنَزَّهَ عَنِ الصَّاحِبَةِ والأولاد، ونَفَذَ حُكمُهُ في جَمِيعِ العِبادِ، لا تُمَثِّلُهُ العُقولُ بِالتَّفكير، ولا تَتَوَهَّمُهُ القُلوبُ بِالتَّصْوِيرِ، لَيْسَ كَمِثْلِهِ شَيْءٌ وَهُوَ السَّمِيعُ البَصِيرُ، لَهُ الْأَسْمَاءُ الْحُسْنَى والصِّفاتُ العُلى، الرَّحْمَنُ عَلَى الْعَرْشِ اسْتَوَى * لَهُ مَا فِي السَّمَوَاتِ وَمَا فِي الْأَرْضِ وَمَا بَيْنَهُمَا وَمَا تَحْتَ الثَّرَى * وَإِن تَجْهَرْ بِالْقَوْلِ فَإِنَّهُ يَعْلَمُ السِّرَّ وَأَخْفَى ، أَحَاطَ بِكُلِّ شَيْءٍ عِلْمًا، وقَهَرَ كلَّ مَخْلوقٍ عِزَّةً وحُكْمًا ، وَوَسِعَ كُلَّ شَيْءٍ رَحْمَةً وَعِلْمًا، يَعْلَمُ مَا بَيْنَ أَيْدِيهِمْ وَمَا خَلْفَهُمْ وَلَا يُحِيطُونَ بِهِ عِلْمًا ، مَوْصوفٌ بِما وَصَفَ بِهِ نَفْسَهُ فِي كِتَابِهِ العظيمِ، وعلى لسانِ نبيهِ الكريمِ.

In the name of Allāh, *al-Raḥmān, al-Raḥīm*.

All praise is due to Allāh, the one praised by every tongue, worshipped at every time, there is no place that is free from His *'Ilm*, nor does one affair preoccupy Him over another. He is far beyond any equal or rival, as well as being free of the need for a wife or children. His rule is executed over all of His servants. No intellect can derive an example of Him with pondering, nor can the heart attempt to depict Him. *'There is nothing equal to Him, and He is al-Samī, al-Baṣīr'*[22]. To Him belong the best of Names and most exalted Attributes. *'al-*

[22] Qurān 42:11

Raḥmān did istawā over the Throne. To Him belongs what is in the heavens and the earth, and what is between them, and what is under the ground. And if you speak aloud, then verily, He ya'lamu the secret and that which is yet more hidden. Allāh, there is no god but He. To Him belong the best of Names.'[23] His *'Ilm* encompasses everything. He subjugates all creatures by His *'Izza* and rule, and His *Raḥmaḧ* and *'Ilm* encompass everything. *'He ya'lamu what is before them, and what is behind them, while they do not encompass it with knowledge.'*[24] He is described with what He has attributed to Himself in His Magnificent Book and upon the tongue of His honourable Prophet.

Commentary: The Author's Introduction

In the name of Allāh, ***al-Raḥmān***[25], ***al-Raḥīm***[26]

All praise is due to Allāh, the one praised by every tongue, worshipped at every time, there is no place that is free from His *'Ilm*[27] [meaning: His *'Ilm* is everywhere. Yet, while His *'Ilm* is everywhere, He, *bi-Dhātihi*[28], is not everywhere. Saying He is everywhere *bi-Dhātihi,* is a grave mistake and leads one to anthropomorphism (tajsīm), and this may be kufr (disbelief)[29]. So, when asked where Allāh is, the correct response is to say: Allāh is fī al-samā[30], while He is everywhere with His *'Ilm*], **nor does one affair preoccupy Him over another. He is far beyond any equal or rival, as well as being free of the need for a wife or children. His rule is executed over all of His servants. No intellect can derive an example of Him with pondering, nor can the heart attempt to depict Him** [for one cannot ever imagine how Allāh is. All Muslims are agreed upon the reality of His *Dhāt*[31] being unknown. Hence, if this is the reality of His *Dhāt*, then it must also be the reality of His Attributes. For, it is known that attributes are related to

---

23 Qurān 20:5-8

24 Qurān 20:110

25 Raḥmān can be translated as 'merciful'.

26 Raḥīm can be translated as 'compassionate'.

27 Ilm can be translated 'knowledge'.

28 Bi-dhātihi is often translated as 'with his essence'.

29 It must be pointed out that an innovation (bid'aḧ) leading to kufr (disbelief) may instead be fisq (abhorrent sin). This is dependent upon the one committing the act or holding a belief being a mujtahid or a muqallid. If one's ijtihād leads him to such an act or belief, it is kufr; when done out of following a mujtahid, it is considered fisq.

30 Fī al-samā° is often translated as: above the Heavens, however, this must not be understood as Allāh being in a physical direction, nor should it be taken in such a way that the heavens encompass Him by translating it as 'in'. Allāh's refuge is sought from that. It is better in all cases to stick to the Arabic wording: Allāh is fī al-samā° or Allāh fī al-samā°; as per the text

31 Dhāt can be translated as 'essence (of something)'.

the essence of something that they are attributed to. Therefore, when one does not know the reality of the essence, one does not know the reality of the attribute(s) either. It is however possible that a result or something related to a particular attribute is understood, for example the *Raḥmah*[32] of Allāh indicates that He will forgive and not punish. Yet, the reality of the attribute itself (e.g. *Raḥmah*) cannot be described or defined, for it cannot even be imagined in the mind]. ***'There is nothing equal to Him*** [in His comparison], ***and He is al-Samī', al-Baṣīr'***[33] [restricting oneself to saying *al-Samī'*[34], *al-Baṣīr*[35] as it is prohibited to translate Allāh's Names or Attributes[36]. Consequently, one should use the Arabic words such as: *Yad*[37], *Wajh*[38], *Sam'*[39] and *Baṣr*[40] and avoid the use of their translations in other languages, instead resorting only to transliteration. **To Him belong the best of Names and most exalted Attributes. *'al-Raḥmān istawā*[41] *over the Throne. To Him belongs what is in the heavens and the earth, and what is between them, and what is under the ground. And if you speak aloud, then verily, He ya'lamu*[42] *the secret and that which is yet more hidden. Allāh, there is no god but He. To Him belong the best of Names.'*[43] His *'Ilm* encompasses everything. He subjugates all creatures by His *'Izzah*[44] and rule, and His *Raḥmah* and *'Ilm* encompass everything. *'He ya'lamu what is before them, and what is behind them, while they do not encompass it with knowledge.'*[45] He is described with what He has attributed to Himself in His Magnificent Book and upon the tongue of His honourable Prophet.**

---

[32] Raḥmah can be translated as 'mercy'.

[33] Qurān 42:11

[34] Samī' can be translated as 'hearing'.

[35] Baṣīr can be translated as 'seeing'.

[36] See, 'Abd al-'Azīz al-Zimzimī, *Manẓūmah al-tafsīr wa 'ulūm al-Qurān*, lines 15-16. These lines are concerned with the Qurān in general. If this is the case with the Qurān in general, then it is even more applicable to the Attributes in particular. The prohibition of translating the Attributes of Allāh is the chosen opinion of Shaykh Yūsuf b. Ṣādiq al-Ḥanbalī.

[37] Yad can be translated as 'hand'.

[38] Wajh can be translated as 'face'.

[39] Sam' can be translated as 'hearing'.

[40] Baṣr can be translated as 'sight'.

[41] Istawa can be translated '(he) rose'.

[42] Ya'lamu can be translated '(he) knows'.

[43] Qurān 20:5-8

[44] Izza can be translated as 'might/power'.

[45] Qurān 20:110

THE OBLIGATION TO ACCEPT THE ĀYĀT AND AḤĀDĪTH RELATED TO ALLĀH'S ATTRIBUTES

وَكُلُّ ما جاءَ في القُرْآنِ أَوْ صَحَّ عَنِ المُصْطَفَى عَليهِ السَّلامُ مِنْ صِفَاتِ الرَّحْمَنِ وَجَبَ الإيمانُ بِهِ وَتَلَقِّيه بالتسليم والقَبُولِ، وَتَرْكُ التَّعَرُّضِ لَهُ بالرَّدِّ والتَّأْوِيلِ، والتَّشْبيهِ والتَّمْثِيلِ. وما أَشْكَلَ مِنْ ذَلِكَ وَجَبَ إِثْبَاتُهُ لَفْظاً ، وتَرْكُ التَّعَرُّضِ لِمَعْنَاهُ، ونَرُدُّ عِلْمَهُ إِلَى قَائِلِه، وَنَجْعَلُ عُهْدَتَهُ عَلَى نَاقِلِهِ، اتّباعاً لِطَرِيقِ الرَّاسِخِينَ فِي العِلْمِ الَّذينَ أَثْنَى اللَّهُ عَلَيْهِم فِي كِتَابِهِ المُبِينِ بِقَوْلِهِ سُبْحَانَهُ وَتَعَالَى : ﴿وَالرَّاسِخُونَ فِي الْعِلْمِ يَقُولُونَ آمَنَّا بِهِ كُلٌّ مِّنْ عِندِ رَبِّنَا﴾، وقال في ذَمِّ مُبْتَغِي التَّأْوِيلِ المُتَشَابِهِ تَنْزِيلِهِ: ﴿فَأَمَّا الَّذِينَ فِي قُلُوبِهِمْ زَيْغٌ فَيَتَّبِعُونَ مَا تَشَابَهَ مِنْهُ ابْتِغَاءِ الْفِتْنَةِ وَابتِغاء تَأْوِيلِهِ وَمَا يَعْلَمُ تَأْوِيلَهُ إِلا اللَّهُ﴾، فَجَعَلَ ابْتِغَاءَ التَّأْوِيلِ عَلَامَةً عَلَى الزَّيْغِ وقَرَنَهُ بِابْتِغَاءِ الفِتْنَةِ فِي الذَّمِّ ، ثُمَّ حَجَبَهُم عَمَّا أَمَّلُوهُ، وَقَطَعَ أَطْمَاعَهُم عَمَّا قَصَدُوهُ، بِقَوْلِهِ سُبْحَانَهُ: ﴿وَمَا يَعْلَمُ تَأْوِيلَهُ إِلَّا اللَّهُ﴾

Everything that has come in the Qurān and that is authentically narrated from al-Muṣṭafā ﷺ concerning the Attributes of *al-Raḥmān*; it is obligatory to have faith in it and receive it with submission and total acceptance. We must abandon opposing it with rejection (al-radd), false interpretation (ta°wil), comparison (tashbīḥ) and making examples (tamthīl). As for what appears unclear, then we are obligated to affirm its wording and abandon opposing to its meaning. And we refer knowledge thereof to the One who stated it, and we entrust it to the one who transmitted it, following the example of those who are firmly grounded in knowledge; those whom Allāh has praised in His manifest Book, with His saying, free of imperfections and Exalted is He: *'And those who are firmly grounded in knowledge say: We believe in it; the whole of it is from our Lord.'*[46] And Allāh says, while blaming and criticizing those who seek interpretation of the unclear *āyāt* of His revelation: *'As for those in whose hearts there is a deviation, they follow that which is not entirely clear thereof, seeking mischief (fitnah) and seeking for its hidden meanings, but no one knows its hidden*

[46] Qurān 3:7

meaning except Allāh'[47]. Thus, Allāh made the seeking of hidden meanings a sign of deviation. And He has, in dispraise of it, equated it with seeking after mischief. Then, He placed a barrier between them and that which they aspire to, and He cuts off their ambition from what they seek after, by His saying, free of imperfections is He: *'but no one knows its hidden meaning except Allāh.'*[48]

Commentary: The Obligation to Accept the Āyāt and Aḥādīth related to Allāh's Attributes

Everything that has come in the Qurān is accepted by Muslims, for it has come by way of mutawātir aḥādīth; meaning, it is narrated by such a large number of individuals that it is inconceivable that they would have agreed upon a lie. This, from the perspective of the sharī'ah gives certainty] **and that is authentically narrated from al- Muṣṭafā** ﷺ [regarding this, Najm al-Dīn al-Ṭūfī (d. 716H) stated that: 'the texts (i.e. the Qurān and ḥadīth) concerning the Attributes are of three levels: 1) authentic (ṣaḥīḥ), whose authenticity is agreed upon by the scholars of ḥadīth; 2) weak (da'īf), whose weakness is agreed upon (by the aforementioned scholars); 3) those that are differed over with regards to their acceptance (i.e. some considering them weak while other considering them authentic). With respect to the first, it is with what the Attributes can be affirmed with; while the second and third are not considered in this issue'[49]. Thus, anything authentically reported from the Prophet ﷺ that gives certainty must be accepted, for in primary matters of 'aqīdah there is no reliance on that which does not give certainty. This however does not mean that only the mutawātir aḥādīth give certainty, thereby excluding the *āḥād* narrations. For the latter can give certainty, if certain conditions are met such as: the acceptance by the vast majority of scholars (e.g. *āḥād* narrations mentioned in the *Ṣaḥīḥ* works of al-Bukhārī and Muslim), or the narrators in its chain being of very high standing (e.g. a ḥadīth narrated by Aḥmad b. Ḥanbal, from al-Shāfi'ī, from Mālik, from Nāfi' (d. 117H), from Ibn 'Umar (d. 83H). Also, when the narration is well-known (mashūr) according to its technical meaning[50], it may lead to certainty, although this is not necessarily the case. These are additional traits, amongst others, that could give

[47] Qurān 3:7

[48] Qurān 3:7

[49] Al-Ṭūfī, *Al-Intisārāt al-Islāmiyyah*, vol. 2, p. 702.

[50] It should be pointed out that there is a difference between the technical (iṣtilāḥī) and non- technical (ghayr iṣtilāḥī) meaning of well-known (mashhūr). The technical meaning, which is assigned by the scholars of ḥadīth is: the report that has three or more narrators at every level of its chain. Shaykh Yūsuf favours the opinion that it should be at least four narrators on every level.

certainty, or may let it reach that level; however, since the primary concern of this work is 'aqīdah, further and more detailed discussion regarding the sciences of hadith are not appropriate here. It is sufficient to know in general that *āḥād* aḥādīth should be further investigated to ascertain whether certain characteristics are present in order to determine whether certainty can be established through them, and if they are therefore suitable to be used in primary issues of 'aqīdah] **concerning the Attributes of *al-Raḥmān***[51] [from the specific

---

[51] Ibn 'Aqīl (d. 513H) stated with regards to the Attributes (and the original text is in **bold**, while the commentary of Shaykh Muwaffaq al-Dīn Yūsuf b. Ṣādiq is between brackets [...]):

One does not affirm an Attribute, upon which one's belief is, except by decisive (clear-cut) evidence, (that is) either: 1) a text from the Book of Allāh; 2) or the mutawātir Sunnah of His Messenger; [and in what follows Ibn 'Aqīlgives examples of tawāṭurtransmission] **which the Muslims** [meaning, the scholars] **have agreed on transmitting** [although, practically it is nearly impossible to find this type of tawāṭu]r,. Nonetheless, theoretically, this would be the highest level of tawāṭu]r, or the majority of them (agreed [i.e. the scholars. And this type is below the aforementioned level, and more commonly occurring, such as the ḥadīt'h: *Whosoever tells a lie against me intentionally then surely let him occupy his seat in the Hellfire.'*, and it was reported by more than one- hundred Companions; and the scholars from all eras], **or those who are not allowed to lie - from amongst the trustworthy (thiqāt)**[the righteous individuals who have a good memorization] **whose 'aqīdah is sound** [having the trustworthy as reporters in the chain is not a condition for tawāṭu.r So, if a disbeliever relates something, and the number is overwhelming, to the extent that it is impossible for them to have agreed upon a lie, then the statement is accepted; due to it being mutawātir. Although, it is as if Ibn 'Aqīl,through this specific statement of his, wants to convey that he does not accept this fact with regards to 'aqīdah. Thus, matters of 'aqīdah are only accepted when it comes from those who are thiqah and have sound 'aqīdah]; **or 3) the of the Ummah about evidence that they were certain about** [and consensus is of two types: the first is the type that takes its value from the agreement of all the scholars on a specific thing; and the second is the type of consensus that takes its value from the Qurān and Sunnah. For example, the obligation of prayer, and it is not obligatory due to the consensus of scholars (which is the first type of consensus that is mentioned), but instead it is obligatory because evidences from the Qurān and Sunnah indicate its obligation clearly; and Ibn 'Aqīl referred to this second type of consensus] **or 4) logical proof (which gives certainty)** [when it comes to matters of 'aqīdah, one requires certainty, and this is gained by each one of the four mentioned evidences; including logical proofs. By logical proof it is meant, one ponders and considers the universe and reaches the conclusion that Allāh exists; that He is the One whose existence is obligatory and necessary (wājib al-wujūd). And if He is as such, than He is *al-'Alīm*, and *al-Ḥayy*; and these are in fact Attributes. The mind can independently conclude these Attributes amongst others, without the need for a text, yet it cannot independently conclude and know that He is *Samī'* or has a *Yad* or a *Wajh*, as with regards to these Attributes, which are often termed the reported Attributes (ṣifāt khabariyyah), the mind is dependent on the Qurān and Sunnah]. **By other than these (aforementioned) ways, it is not possible to affirm an Attribute of Allāh, Exalted is He.** [Thus it is impermissible to affirm them] **through analogy (qiyās); the opinion of one of the companions; or the opinion of some scholars in an era, while other scholars did not approve; or a āḥād report, that has not been received by the whole Ummah of scholars with acceptance** [meaning, they did not approve of it and did not accept it as evidence]. **Rather, it is like that (which we have stated), because other than these four types of evidence, meaning: 1) the Book of Allāh, 2) the mutawātir Sunnah of His Messenger, 3) consensus of the Ummah and 4) logical proof, do not give certainty nor are they decisive (clear-cut); rather they establish probable practices** [which are related to fiqh, and uṣūl of 'aqīdah is not a part of this]. **The Attributes of Allāh, Exalted is He, cannot be affirmed based on probability or preponderance of probability (ghalabah al-ẓann); as is the case with His *Dhāt*, Exalted is He** [and the speech concerning His Attributes, is a branch of the speech concerning His *Dhāt*. Which in essence means, that which is true for the *Dhāt*, is also true for His Attributes. For example, if His *Dhāt* is pre-existent (qadīm), then His Attributes are also pre-existent as well. So, if the existence of Allāh cannot be accepted based on probability (ẓann), then likewise it is not accepted for His Attributes] **which cannot be affirmed with this** [meaning, these ways other than the four approved ways mentioned above].

wording used by the author, it is understood that he specifically meant issues concerning the Attributes of Allāh. So, these reports need to be authentic and give certainty. In other issues of 'aqīdah one may accept something which does not give (complete) certainty. For example, describing details regarding Paradise using aḥādīth that are less than authentic, i.e. not reaching the level of certainty. Consequently, belief in Paradise and some of its blessings are proven with certainty, while other blessing and specific details may not be]; **it is obligatory to have faith in it and receive it with submission and total acceptance** [because it contains things which cannot be understood as Allāh did not allow us to understand it fully[52]. In this regard Ibn 'Abbās said: *'There is nothing in this life similar to what is in paradise, except by the names'*[53]; meaning, when one enters paradise, one will not find anything other than the names of things. For example, one will see things that are called milk (laban) or honey ('asl), yet they will be completely different from what one knew to be milk and honey in this worldly life. If our knowledge and realisation is insufficient to know and understand things in Paradise which are created, then this is even more the case when it concerns knowing and understanding Allāh and His Attributes. Therefore, willing submission and total acceptance regarding the Attributes is required; and everyone is obligated to believe, submit and accept, from the layman who cannot read and write to the erudite scholar]. **We must abandon opposing it with rejection (al-radd), false interpretation (ta°wil), comparison (tashbīḥ) and making examples (tamthīl). As for what appears unclear** [meaning, what is unclear or not obvious (mutashābiḥ) in its meaning[54]], **then we are obligated to**

It is not permissible (and possible) to establish (and proof) it [i.e. His *Dhāt* and Attributes] **with this** [i.e. probable evidence (dalīl al-ẓannī)].

[52] In *Taḥrīm al-Naẓar*, p. 51, Ibn Qudāmah says: 'We do not need to know the meanings of what was intended by Allāh, the Exalted, from His Attributes, Mighty and Majestic (is he). Indeed, He did not intend regarding them any action, nor did He connect to them any responsibility aside from believing in them. The belief in them, without knowledge of their meaning is possible; and, indeed, belief with ignorance is correct. Certainly, Allāh, the Exalted, ordered belief in His angels, His books, and His messengers, and what is revealed to them; even if we do not know from that except the names.'

[53] Al-Ṭabarī, *Jāmi' al-Bayān*, vol. 1, p. 416, under the explanation of Qurān: 2: 25.

[54] Ibn Qudāmah mentions in his book in uṣūl al-fiqh, titled *Rawḍah al-Nāẓir*, vol. 1, p. 215, that the āyāt of the Attributes are from the category of the mutashābiḥ (ambiguous/unclear). He sates: 'And the correct opinion is that the mutashābiḥ āyāt, that had been revealed concerning the Attributes of Allāh, Glorified is He, are obligatory to believe in and it is prohibited to seek their interpretation, such as statement of Allāh, the Exalted: *'al-Raḥmān did is istawā over the Throne'* (Qurān, 20:5), *'Rather, His Yadā are widely outstretched'* (Qurān, 5:64), *'...which I created with My Yadayy...'* (Qurān, 38:75), *'And there will remain the Wajh of your Lord'* (Qurān, 55:27), *'Sailing under Our A'yun'* (Qurān, 54:14) and similar to them. The Salaf, may Allāh have mercy upon them, agreed on affirming them, passing over them as they came, and leaving the interpretation of them. For, indeed Allāh, Glorified is He, has censured the seekers of their interpretation and paired them, in His censuring, with those who seek discord and named them 'the People of Deviation.'

affirm its wording and abandon opposing to its meaning [by explaining it or giving a meaning to it. Thus, the author says that when there is something that appears unclear or difficult to understand, one should approve of the wording and abandon exposing oneself to the meaning[55]. One should not expose himself to the trial of explaining it, and in the case one feels confused about something due to its being unclear, then the right course of action is to believe in the wording, refer the knowledge of its meaning to Allāh, and move on]. **And we refer knowledge thereof** [it must be stressed that this does not mean that the Ḥanābilaḧ say that these words do not have a meaning. On the contrary, they do have a meaning, although it is not known to us. The idea that 'referring knowledge back to Allāh', or what is commonly understood as relegation and in Arabic is termed tafwīḍ, implies that one is convinced that these words do not have meaning and are like a random collection of letters is erroneous. No scholar ever claimed that this is he intended meaning of tafwīḍ, except for Ibn Taymiyyaḧ, who perhaps misunderstood the madhhab of certain scholars in this regard. He conceived this incorrect understanding and contemporary Salafī scholars unfortunately followed him in this. However, it is not as he states, for the word *Yad* has a meaning; but it is not the literal meaning of the word that is known to men, and the meaning is only known by Allāh.

It is important here to address the difference between the tafwīḍ approach as propagated by the Ḥanābilaḧ, and the ta°wīl approach of the Ashā'iraḧ. These two different approaches to the Attributes of Allāh essentially reject the claim that one should understand and affirm the literal meanings or the actual realities of the specific words denoting Allāh's Attributes. This claim is problematic, for if one sticks to the literal meanings of these words, or their actual realities, it would result in assigning qualities of created beings to Allāh; and this is prohibited. The Ḥanābilaḧ refute anyone who approves and claims that the literal meanings of these words, in the various āyāt and aḥādīth, are Attributes of Allāh. With this in mind, the crucial question remains: 'what did Allāh then mean by words like *Yad* and *Wajh*?'.

[55] With the phrase: 'we are obligated to affirm its wording and to abandon opposing to its meaning', the author states quite clearly that the affirmation of the Attributes of Allāh is upon their wording and that their meanings are consigned to Allāh. In footnote 52, a quote from Ibn Qudāmaḧ has been mentioned that states that the meanings are unknown, indicating that the meaning should be referred back to Allāh. This all helps to qualify what the author meant whenever he states (throughout his books) that the Attributes are to be considered upon their apparentness (ẓāhir)). It appears that his intent with this word 'apparent' is the 'apparent wording' and not the 'apparent meaning'.

One would assume that an answer to such a crucial question is complex and intricate, yet the opposite is true. The position of the Ḥanābilaĥ concerning these matters is simply that they do not know what is meant by them. However, there are certain groups from the Ashā'iraĥ and other groups and sects, who state the opposite. They claim to know what Allāh intended with these specific words, and assign meanings to them. Although, the Ḥanābilaĥ say one cannot know for sure what is meant by these specific words, they do say there is a probability that Allāh meant such-and-such with an *āyaĥ*; thereby understanding the general meaning of the āyaĥ as a whole. For instance, regarding the Attribute of *Yad*, Allāh says: *'Nay, both His Yadā are widely outstretched'*[56]. The Ḥanābilaĥ believe in this without knowing the meaning of what Allāh intended by the word *Yad*; all the while rejecting the literal meaning of it, and not assigning and specifying a metaphorical meaning. Nonetheless, they understand that the whole *āyaĥ* indicates that Allāh owns everything, to the extent that Allāh can give anyone whatever he wants and needs.

This approach, which is the approach of the Ḥanābilaĥ, is also one of the opinions found within the madhhab of the Ashā'iraĥ. Another famous approach held by the Ashā'iraĥ, which is most common amongst them now, is the usage of ta°wīl tafṣilī, i.e. detailed interpretation, with regards to the words denoting the Attributes[57], and this is the type of ta°wīl that the Ḥanābilaĥ deem prohibited. In this approach the Ashā'iraĥ will say, for example, that by *Yad*, Allāh meant His *Qudraĥ*[58] or His *Irādaĥ*[59], depending on the context in which it is said. Thus, they will not confine themselves to the approach of the Ḥanābilaĥ (i.e. tafwīḍ), and assign a probable meaning of which they admit they are not sure whether it is the right one or not.

---

[56] Qurān: 5:64

[57] As is clear from the above explanation, it is incorrect to view the Ashā'iraĥ as a madhhab that only propagates one specific approach to the Attributes. In its broadest sense there is a clear visible historical dichotomy, dividing the Ash'arī madhhab into an early and later school of thought. Within these two schools there is a clear difference in the approach to the Attributes of Allāh, whereby the latter school made ta°wīl tafṣilī (detailed interpretation), i.e. the mainstream approach of their school. Despite this view being mainstream amongst the Ashā'iraĥ, there still exists variations in approach to the Attributes within their school, ranging from using only tafwīḍ, to mixing between tafwīḍ and ta°wīl tafṣilī depending on the Attribute in question, to using ta°wīl tafṣilī exclusively. For the sake of brevity, only the two main approaches within the Ash'arī madhhab are presented. One should keep in mind that this is a very generalised and basic presentation of the Ash'arī madhhab;

[58] Qudraĥ can be translated as 'ability.

[59] Irādaĥ can be translated as 'will'.

Thus, when it comes to the different approaches concerning the Attributes; there are in reality two types of ta°wīl. The first type is ta°wīl ijmalī, i.e. general interpretation, which is the same as tafwīḍ. It is rejecting the literal meaning of an attribute, affirming that the word in that specific context denoting the Attribute has a metaphorical meaning, and stating that the metaphorical meaning is unknown; therefore, one should refrain from specifying or assigning it. Moreover, stating that it has a metaphorical meaning, means on the one hand that it is not merely a meaningless word, while on the other hand it rejects the literal meaning[60]. For, if the literal meaning is rejected, and it is not meaningless (i.e. random letters put together), then it should be a metaphorical meaning because there is no other viable option left. The second type is ta°wīl tafṣilī, and it is rejecting the literal meaning of an attribute, affirming that the word in that specific context denoting the attribute has a metaphorical meaning, which is then further specified (based on its context)[61]. This latter type of ta°wīl is favoured by a large number of Ash'arī scholars, whilst being strongly prohibited by the Ḥanābilaḧ] **to the One** [meaning, Allāh] **who stated it** [so, He knows best], **and we entrust it to the one** [meaning, the Prophet ﷺ] **who transmitted it** [and even he ﷺ did not know the reality of Allāh and His Attributes, and this is because he ﷺ is a part of the creation, and his nature is different from the nature of the Creator. A question may be asked whether the reality of Allāh and His Attributes will eventually be known in paradise; however, the answer to this question is in the negative. There are many things that will eventually be known in paradise, in addition to what we know now, yet, because our 'nature' will not change in paradise (i.e. we still be a part of the creation), there still exists a fundamental difference between the creation and the Creator. For as long as this difference remains, we will not know and understand the reality of Allāh, and in extension His Attributes as well; for the created cannot encompass the Creator], **following the example of those who are firmly grounded in knowledge; those whom Allāh has praised in His manifest Book, with His saying, free of imperfections and exalted is He: *'And those who are firmly grounded in knowledge say: We believe***

---

[60] the literal meaning would be the meaning as related to created beings, i.e. the meaning of a word as understood in the context of the created world, and this has preceded earlier in the commentary.

[61] Ibn Qudāmaḧ wrote a small treatise titled *Dhamm al-Ta°wīl* in which he brought many narrations from the Salaf, as well as his own arguments, in condemnation of this detailed type of ta°wīl. It should not be understood from the title of this booklet, that Ibn Qudāmaḧ condemned ta°wīl in general, for he only targeted those groups and individuals who used ta°wīl to give a specific meaning to the Attributes.

in it [meaning the clear and unclear āyāt]; ***the whole of it is from our Lord.'***[62-63] **And Allāh says, while blaming and criticizing those who seeks interpretation of the unclear āyāt of His revelation: *'As for those in whose hearts there is a deviation, they follow that which is not entirely clear thereof, seeking mischief (fitnaḧ) and seeking for its hidden meanings, but no one knows its hidden meaning except Allāh'***[64] [this *āyaḧ* effectively blocks any hope that one may have with regards to knowing the meanings of the Attributes of Allāh. Furthermore, this also implies that it is prohibited to translate the Attributes of Allāh into other languages. As, when translating, one is essentially interpreting, and therefore attempting to understand the (hidden) meaning. Such a person is blamed and criticized by Allāh, as is mentioned in the above āyaḧ. It should however be noted that translating the Qurān is a matter of scholarly dispute: some stating permissibility, whilst others prohibiting it. However, when it concerns the Attributes of Allāh specifically it should be unequivocally prohibited and no one should oppose this, as Allāh's Attributes are something that we do not understand.

Essentially, there are two different reasons for the prohibition of translation. The prohibition to translate the Qurān in general, because one is comparing his own way with the way of the Qurān, by giving an interpretation of the meaning of an āyaḧ. When it comes to the Attributes specifically, it is not permitted to translate, because the science of translation does not allow the translation of something without understanding the source language (and that which is translated). Yes, the source language is Arabic but the reality of Allāh and His Attributes are not known in that language, therefore they cannot be translated into another language]. **Thus, Allāh made the seeking of hidden meanings** [for example, by saying *Yad* means His *Qudraḧ*] **a sign of deviation. And He has, in dispraise of it, equated it with seeking after mischief. Then He placed a barrier between them and that which they aspire to, and He cuts off their ambition**

---

[62] Qurān: 3:7

[63] Ibn Rajab al-Ḥanbalī (d.795H) stated something similar to Ibn Qudāmaḧ in *Ikhtiyār al-Ūlā*, p. 40-41: 'As for what the Prophet ﷺ attributed to his Lord, Mighty and Majestic is He, with what he described Him with; then everything the Prophet ﷺ attributed to his Lord, Mighty and Majestic is He, is true and sincere; it is obligatory to believe in and confirm it, just like what Allāh attributed to himself; accompanied with the negation of making examples for it. Whoever finds difficulty in understanding something of this and finds them confusing should say like those praised by Allāh, the Exalted; the firmly rooted in knowledge; about whom it is reported (in the Qurān) that they say concerning the mutashābih āyāt: '*We believe in it, all of it is from our Lord*'. Just as it was said by the Prophet ﷺ with regards to the Qurān: *'Whatever you are ignorant of, then leave it to its knower'*. Narrated by Imām Aḥmad, al-Nasā°ī, and other then them.'

[64] Qurān: 3:7

from what they seek after, by His saying, free of imperfections is He: *'but no one knows its hidden meaning except Allāh.'*[65]

[65] Qurān: 3:7

THE WAY OF THE IMĀMS OF THE SALAF CONCERNING ALLĀH'S ATTRIBUTES

قال الإمام أبو عَبْدِ اللَّهِ أَحْمَدُ بْنُ مُحَمَّدِ بْنِ حَنْبَلٍ رَضِيَ اللَّهُ عَنْهُ فِي قَولِ النَّبِيِّ صَلَّى اللَّهُ عَلَيْهِ وَسَلَّمَ : ((إنَّ اللَّهَ يَنْزِلُ إِلَى سَمَاءِ الدُّنْيَا)) و ((إنَّ اللَّهَ يُرى في القِيامَةِ)) : وما أَشْبَه هَذِهِ الأحاديثِ : (نُؤْمِنُ بِها ونُصَدِّقُ بِها لا كَيْفَ ولا مَعْنَى ولا نَرُدُّ شَيْئاً مِنْها، ونَعْلَمُ أَنَّ مَا جَاءَ بِهِ الرَّسُولُ حَقٌّ ، ولا نَرُدُّ على رسولِ اللَّهِ صَلَّى اللَّهُ عَلَيْهِ وَسَلَّمَ، ولا نَصِفُ اللَّهَ بِأَكْثَرَ مِمَّا وَصَفَ بِهِ نَفْسَهُ ، بِلا حَدَّ ولا غايَةٍ، ﴿ لَيْسَ كَمِثْلِهِ شَيْءٌ وَهُوَ السَّمِيعُ البَصِيرُ ﴾. ونقولُ كما قالَ، وَنَصِفُهُ بِما وَصَفَ بِهِ نَفْسَهُ، لَا نَتَعَدَّى ذَلِكَ، ولا يَبْلُغُهُ وَصْفُ الوَاصِفِينَ، نُؤْمِنُ بِالقُرْآنِ كُلِّهِ مُحْكَمِهِ ومُتَشَابِهِهِ، وَلَا نُزِيلُ عَنْهُ صِفَةً مِنْ صِفَاتِهِ لِشَنَاعَةٍ شُنِّعَتْ، ولا نَتَعَدَّى القُرْآنَ والحَديثَ، ولا نَعْلَمُ كَيْفَ ذَلِكَ إِلَّا بِتَصْدِيقِ الرَّسُولِ صَلَّى اللَّهُ عَلَيْهِ وَسَلَّمَ وَتَثْبِيتِ القُرْآنِ).

Imām Abū 'Abd Allāh Aḥmad b, Ḥanbal, may Allāh have mercy on him, said concerning the saying of the Prophet ﷺ: *'Verily, Allāh yanzilu to the heaven of this world (i.e. the lowest heaven)'* and *'Verily, Allāh will be seen on the Day of Resurrection'* and what is similar to these narrations: 'We believe in it and testify to the truthfulness of it, without explaining 'how' and without 'meaning', nor do we reject anything of it. We know that whatever the Messenger ﷺ came with is the truth; we do not reject anything from the Messenger of Allāh ﷺ, nor do we describe Allāh with more than what He has described Himself with, without any limit nor any boundaries. *'There is nothing equal to Him, and He is al-Samī', al-Baṣīr.'*[66] We say as He said and describe Him with what He described Himself with, nor do we go beyond this. The descriptions of those who attempt to describe Him cannot grasp Him. We believe in all of the Qurān, the muḥkam (clear and decisive) and mutashābiḥ (unclear). We do not reject any of His Attributes due to them appearing repulsive. We do not go beyond the Qurān and the narrations, and we do not know how to understand them, except through the truthfulness of the Messenger ﷺ, and the affirmation of the Qurān.'

---

[66] Qurān: 42:11

قالَ الإمامُ أَبو عَبْدِ اللَّهِ مُحَمَّدُ بْنُ إِدْرِيسَ الشَّافِعِيُّ رَضِيَ اللَّهُ عَنْهُ : (آمَنْتُ بِاللَّهِ وَبِمَا جَاءَ عَنِ اللَّهِ عَلَى مُرادِ اللَّهِ، وَآمَنْتُ بِرَسولِ اللَّهِ وبما جاءَ عَن رَسُولِ اللَّهِ عَلَى مُرادِ رَسولِ اللَّهِ).

Imām Abū 'Abd Allāh Muḥammad b. Idrīs al-Shāfi'ī, may Allāh be pleased with him, said: 'I believe in Allāh and what has come from Allāh, in accordance with the meaning that Allāh intended. And I believe in the Messenger of Allāh ﷺ and what has come from the Messenger of Allāh ﷺ, in accordance with the meaning that the Messenger of Allāh ﷺ intended.'

وعلى هذا دَرَجَ السَّلَفُ وأَئِمَّةُ الخَلَفِ رَضِيَ اللَّهُ عَنْهُم، كُلُّهُمْ مُتَّفِقُونَ عَلَى الإِقْرَارِ، والإمْرارِ والإِثْبَاتِ لِما وَرَدَ مِنَ الصِّفاتِ في كِتابِ اللهِ وسُنَّةِ رَسُولِهِ صَلَّى اللَّهُ عَلَيْهِ وَسَلَّمَ، مِنْ غَيْرِ تَعَرُّضٍ لِتَأْوِيلِهِ.

This was the way pursued by Salaf as well as the imāms of the Khalaf (later generations), may Allāh be pleased with them. All of them being in agreement with acknowledgement (iqrār), passing over (imrār), and affirming (ithbāt) what has been mentioned in the Book of Allāh and the Sunnah of His Messenger ﷺ concerning the Attributes, without turning to ta°wīl.

Commentary: The Way of the Imāms of the Salaf concerning Allāh's Attributes

Imām Abū 'Abd Allāh Aḥmad b, Ḥanbal (d. 241 H), may Allāh have mercy on him, said concerning the saying of the Prophet ﷺ: *'Verily, Allāh yanzilu to the heaven of this world (i.e. the lowest heaven)' and 'Verily, Allāh will be seen on the Day of Resurrection'* and what is similar to these narrations: 'We believe in it and testify to the truthfulness of it, without explaining 'how' and without 'meaning' [this is a famous saying of Imām Aḥmad. He, like the rest of the pious Salaf, did not delve into the details of matters that should just be believed in and not be deeply questioned or discussed. That is to say, Imām Aḥmad would refuse to give any 'meaning' or 'howness' in matters concerning the Attributes. A simple way of explaining the statement of Imām Aḥmad 'no how and no meaning' (lā kayf, wa lā ma'nā) would be that he refused to give the 'howness' because he did not know the 'meaning'. In truth, the statement by Imām Aḥmad is very clear and to say that by 'no meaning' he meant: 'no meaning other than the meaning that is known', then this is ta°wil and the intentional twisting of his words], **nor do we reject anything of it. We know that whatever the Messenger ﷺ came with is the truth; we do not reject anything from the Messenger of Allāh ﷺ, nor do we describe Allāh with more than what He has described Himself with** [therefore, if Allāh attributed *Yad* and *Wajh* to Himself, than one ought to believe in it and leave it at that. This is in itself a clear rejection of the Ash'arī method of ta°wīl tafṣīlī for Allāh did not state that His *Yad* meant *Qudrah*, otherwise He would have made this clear], **without any limit nor any boundaries. *'There is nothing equal to Him, and He is al-Samī', al-Baṣī'*[67] We say as He said and describe Him with what He described Himself with nor do we go beyond this. The descriptions of those who attempt to describe Him cannot grasp Him. We believe in all of the Qurān, the muḥkam (decisive)** [meaning, which is clear and self-explanatory] **and mutashābiḥ (unclear)** [meaning, that which may have more than one possible meaning, like the āyāt that mention Attributes]. **We do not reject any of His Attributes due to them appearing repulsive** [one has to believe in the Attributes as Allāh meant, believing in the meaning that is known to Allāh alone and not known to anyone other than Him]. **We do not go beyond the Qurān and the narrations** [meaning, one does not seek knowledge and understanding of the Attributes of Allāh elsewhere, for example through ijtihād, logic or philosophy], **and we do not know how to understand them** [meaning, the Attributes], **except through the truthfulness of the Messenger ﷺ, and the affirmation of the Qurān.**'[68]

Imām Abū 'Abd Allāh Muḥammad b. Idrīs al-Shāfi'ī, may Allāh be pleased with him, said: 'I believe in Allāh and what has come from Allāh [meaning the Qurān, and relating to this chapter, the Attributes of Allāh in particular], **in accordance with the meaning that Allāh intended** [thereby rejecting any other interpretation or meaning that may be given to it by way of ta°wīl tafṣīlī, distortion (taḥrīf), logical or philosophical deduction, and the like]. **And I believe in the Messenger of Allāh ﷺ and what has come from the Messenger of Allāh ﷺ** [meaning, the aḥādīth], **in accordance with the meaning that the Messenger of**

---

[67] Qurān: 42:11

[68] This saying of Imām Aḥmad: 'We believe in it and testify to the truthfulness of it, without explaining 'how' and without 'meaning...', is narrated from Ḥanbal b. Isḥāq (d. 273H). Although well-known, it has some variation; some are longer than others, and some have slightly different wording; yet all carry the same meaning. They are mentioned by Ibn Qudāmah in *Dhamm al-ta°wīl*, no. 33; Qaḍı Abu Ya'lā in *Ibṭāl al-ta°wilāt*, vol. 1, no. 9; and Ibn Baṭṭah al-'Ukbarī (d. 387H) in *al-Ibānah*, vol. 7, no. 50, who reports it via 'Abd Allāh b. Ḥanbal (d. 290H), instead of Ḥanbal b. Isḥāq. Another version of the narration of Ḥanbal b. Isḥāq, that slightly differs in wording, is mentioned by al-Lālikā°ī (d. 418H) in *Sharḥ Uṣūl I'tiqād*, vol. 2, no. 777, stating: *'bilā kayf, wa lā ḥadd.*

Allāh ﷻ intended'[69] [in these statements there is a clear refutation of those who reject and resort to ta°wīl tafṣīlī, comparison, negation (ta°ṭīl) and making examples].

This was the way pursued by Salaf[70] [meaning, the great imāms from amongst them, for 'Salaf' is a general and broad term including people from different ranks and standing as was discussed in the general introduction] **as well as the imām of the Khalaf (later generations), may Allāh be pleased with them. All of them being in agreement with acknowledgement (iqrār), passing over it (imrār)** [meaning, one should accept these narrations and take them at face value, saying *Yad* not *Qudraḧ*. This also includes sticking and limiting oneself to the use of the Arabic wording. Therefore, one should not translate them to hand, face, essence etc.[71] Al-Shīrāzī (d. 468H) stated that Imām Aḥmad said concerning the reported Attributes (akhbār al-ṣifāt): 'pass over them, as they come' (amrūhā kamā jā°a)[72]. A man asked Imām Aḥmad concerning the statement: *'Verily, Allāh*

---

[69] The same is also mentioned by Ibn Qudāmaḧ in, *Dhamm al-Ta°wīl*, no. 89, and in his *Ithbāt Ṣifaḧ al-'Uluww*, p. 24.

[70] In his small treatise *Dhamm al-Ta°wīl*, p. 9, no. 6-8, he says regarding the madhhab of the Salaf: 'The madhhab of the Salaf, Allāh's *Raḥmaḧ* be upon them, is belief in the Attributes of Allāh, the Exalted, and His Names, with what He described Himself with in His āyāt and His revelation; or (with what he was described with) on the tongue of His messenger; without adding to them, nor detracting from them, nor exceeding them, nor giving them explanation or interpretation with that which opposes their apparentness, nor comparing them with the attributes of the creation nor with the features of contingencies (al-muḥdathīn). On the contrary, (they) passed over them, as they came (amrūhā kamā jā°at) and referred knowledge of it (back) to the One who stated them, and its meaning (back) to the one who spoke with it [...] and they knew that the one (i.e. Allāh or the Prophet ﷺ) who spoke with them was truthful, (there being) no doubt in his sincerity; therefore, they believed Him. They did not know the reality of their meaning, thus they remained silent concerning that which they did not know. And the later and the first (from them) took this and cautioned each other with the good of following and stopping where the first of them stopped; and they warned from exceeding them, and straying from their path, and they made their way and doctrine clear for them. We hope that Allāh, the Exalted, will make us from amongst those who imitate them in elucidating what they elucidated, and travel the path they travelled.'

In *Tahrīm al-Naẓar*, p. 54, he says concerning their way: 'It is the believe in the wording, the ayāt and reports, with the meaning that was intended by Allāh, the Exalted; and silence concerning what we do not know from its meanings; to abandon searching for what we were not burdened with by Allāh; and (to abandon) searching for their explanation and what He did not inform us about from His *'Ilm;* and to follow the way of the firmly-grounded in knowledge; those praised by Allāh in His manifest Book, when He said: *'We believe in it. All [of it] is from our Lord...'* (Qurān: 3:7).'

[71] The words: hand, face and essence given above are only used as a way of providing examples. They are not to be understood as valid translations for specific Attributes of Allāh.

[72] And this statement (pass over it, as it comes), has been reported from Imām Aḥmad in a variety of forms. In *Uṣūl al-Sunnaḧ,* from Imām Aḥmad himself, p. 8, he states concerning the aḥādīth of 'the seeing' (ru°yaḧ) of Allāh, and similar narrations: 'we believe in it as it has come' (nu°min bihi kamā jā°at). Al-Khallāl (d. 311H) reports in *al-Sunnaḧ,* no. 283, by way of Abū Bakr al-Marūdhī (d. 275H) that Imām Aḥmad said a similar thing; as did al-Ājurrī (d. 360H) in *al-Sharī'aḧ*, no. 726. Ibn Baṭṭaḧ reports the same in *al-Ibānaḧ,* vol. 7, no. 50, and by way of al-Marūdhī, albeit with regards to the aḥādīth of the Attributes, vol. 7, no. 253.

yanzilu[73] *every night to the heaven of this world (i.e. the lowest heaven)'*, and he (i.e. Imām Aḥmad) said: 'this ḥadīth is authentic (ṣaḥīḥ).' The man asked 'does His *Qudrah* or He himself *yanzilu*? Imām Aḥmad responded: 'Woe to you (you are doomed), what is this!' Pass the ḥadīth on as is has come' (i.e. as it has been narrated)[74], and upon us are the reports of the Salaf and they are an excellent example to follow.[75]] ***and affirming (ithbāt) what has been mentioned in the Book of Allāh and the Sunnah of His Messenger ﷺ concerning the Attributes, without turning to ta°wīl*** [whenever ta°wīl is mentioned without specification, it most often refers to ta°wīl tafṣilī. Only when one needs to make a distinction between the two forms of ta°wīl, are they made specific from each other].

---

[73] Yanzilu can be translated as '(he) descends'

[74] Understanding the specific phrases: *kamā jā°at, 'alā ẓāhiri, 'alā ḥaqīqati.*

- *Wa al-ḥadīth 'indanā 'alā ẓāhiri kamā jā°at:* 'and the narration with us are taken upon their apparentness, as they have come'.
- *nu°minu bihi kamā jā°at 'alā ẓāhiri* 'we believe in it as they have come, upon their apparentness.

This means, one accepts and takes the narration(s) as they are, with those wordings, not changing or interpreting anything of them whether one understands their meaning of or not. Therefore, concerning the texts containing Attributes of Allāh, one should just accept their wording, leave them as they are, and consign the meaning back to Allāh. With regards to texts which can be understood, such as those that contains a certain ruling or a description of paradise, an individual may or may not understand their apparent meaning.

There are two possibilities: either one understands the meaning of a text and believes in it, or if the meaning is problematic then one does tafwīḍ or resorts to ijtihād in understanding the intended meaning, however, in the case of the Attributes one should be careful and only resort to tafwīḍ; as speaking about Allāh without knowledge is prohibited.

- *'Alā ḥaqīqati* 'upon the literal (meaning)'.

This term *ḥaqīqī* is problematic. When used it should be investigated to see what is meant by it, for it can be used in different ways. It can be used as a term that comes close to the proper way of handling the Attributes of Allāh or, it can also be used in a way as to indicate comparison (tashbīḥ) and anthropomorphization (tajsīm). In the latter case, it is unacceptable and prohibited because it describes Allāh in the way of His creation. In the former case, when the term 'the literal meaning' (al-ma'nā al-ḥaqīqī) is used, it denotes that the meaning of a particular word, which is unknown to us, is also an actual meaning. So, in accordance with this usage there are two actual meanings for the same word, such as in the case with the word 'ayn. One actual meaning of 'ayn is 'an eye', however another is 'a spy'. The word ḥājib means both 'eyebrow' and 'doorkeeper'. There may also be more than two actual meanings for the same word. Although, this outlook may be incorrect, it nevertheless still results in tanzīḥ (the transcendence) of Allāh and His Attributes. Amongst the Ḥanābilah who stated that the Attributes are literal (ḥaqīqiyyah) was Najm al-Dīn al-Ṭūfī; see, *Ḥalāl al- 'Uqd fī Bayan Aḥkām al-Mu'taqad* (p. 32-33).

[75] The specific rendition of this report from Imām Aḥmad is found in *Al-Tabṣirah fī Uṣūl al-Dīn*, p. 146, by al-Shīrāzī. Older works such as *Ibṭāl al-Ta°wīlāt*, no. 260, by Qāḍī Abī Ya'lā, and *Sharḥ Uṣūl I'tiqād*, vol. 2, no. 777, by al-Lālikā°ī report a narration, by way of Ḥanbal b. Isḥāq, that shares similarities to what is found in *al-Tabṣirah*.

THE ORDER TO FOLLOW THE SUNNAḦ AND A WARNING AGAINST INNOVATION

وقَدْ أُمِرْنا بِاقْتِفَاءِ آثَارِهِمْ والاهْتِدَاءِ بِمَنارِهِم، وحُذِّرْنا المُحْدَثَاتِ، وَأُخْبِرْنَا أَنَّهَا مِنَ الضَّلالاتِ، فَقَالَ النَّبِيُّ صَلَّى اللَّهُ عَلَيْهِ وَسَلَّمَ :((عَلَيْكُم بِسُنَّتِي وَسُنَّةِ الْخُلَفَاءِ الرَّاشِدِينَ المَهْدِيِّينَ مِنْ بَعْدِي، عَضُّوا عَلَيْهَا بِالنَّوَاجِذِ، وَإِيَّاكُمْ وَمُحْدَثَاتِ الأُمُورِ، فَإِنَّ كُلَّ مُحْدَثَةٍ بِدْعَةٌ، وَكُلَّ بِدْعَةٍ ضَلَالَةٌ)).

We have been ordered to follow their way and to be guided by their example. We have been warned of innovations and we have been informed that they are from the things that lead astray. The Prophet ﷺ said: *'upon you is my Sunnaḧ and the sunnaḧ of the rightly-guided caliphs after me, bite on to it with your molar teeth and beware of newly invented matters. Verily, every newly invented matter is an innovation, and every innovation is a misguidance.'*

وقالَ عَبْدُ اللَّهِ بْنُ مَسْعودٍ رَضِيَ اللَّهُ عَنْهُ: (اتَّبِعُوا ولا تَبْتَدِعُوا فَقَد كُفِيتُمْ)

'Abd Allāh b. Mas'ūd, may Allāh be pleased with him, said: 'Follow and do not innovate! For indeed you have been sufficed.'

وقالَ عُمَرُ بْنُ عَبْدِ العَزيزِ رَضِيَ اللَّهُ عَنْهُ كَلامًا مَعْناهُ: (قِفْ حَيْثُ وَقَفَ القَوْمُ، فَإِنَّهُم عَن عِلْمٍ وَقَفُوا، وبِبَصَرٍ نافِذٍ كَفُّوا، وَلَهُمْ عَلى كَشْفِها كانوا أقْوى، وبِالفَضْلِ لَوْ كانَ فيها أحْرَى، فَلَئِنْ قُلْتُمْ: حَدَثَ بَعْدَهُم. فَما أَحْدَثَهُ إلَّا مَنْ خَالَفَ هَدْيَهُمْ، وَرَغِبَ عَن سُنَّتِهِمْ، وقَدْ وَصَفُوا مِنْهُ ما يَشْفِي، وتَكَلَّمُوا مِنْهُ بِما يَكْفي، فَما فَوْقَهُم مُحَسِّرٌ، وما دُوْنَهم مُقَصِّرٌ، لَقَدْ قَصَّرَ عَنْهُم قَوْمٌ فَجَفَوْا، وَتَجاوَزَهُمْ آخَرُونَ فَغَلَوْا، و إِنَّهُمْ فِيما بَيْنَ ذَلِكَ لَعَلى هُدًى مُسْتَقيمٍ.)

'Umar b. 'Abd al-'Azīz, may Allāh be pleased with him, said, with the meaning of: 'Stop where the people have stopped! For indeed, they have stopped upon knowledge. The clear evidences would suffice them and they were the strongest at manifesting it. If there were any additions, they would have done them first. If you say: 'it was introduced after them', then no one has introduced it except the one who opposed their guidance and desires other than their example. For they have certainly described from it what satisfies, and have spoken about it with what suffices. Consequently, whatever is above them is excessiveness, and what is below them is inadequacy. Indeed, some people have fallen short of them and were removed, while others went beyond them and fell into extremism. And they were between these; upon straight guidance.'

وقالَ الإمامُ أبو عَمْرٍو الأَوْزاعِيُّ رَضِيَ اللَّهُ عَنْهُ: (عَلَيْكَ بِآثارِ مَنْ سَلَفَ و إنْ رَفَضَكَ النّاسُ، و إيّاكَ وآراءَ الرِّجالِ و إنْ زَخْرَفُوهُ لَكَ بالقَوْلِ)

Imām Abū 'Amr al-Awzā'ī, may Allāh be pleased with him, said: 'Adhere to the narrations of those who came before you, even if the people avoid you and reject you. And beware of the opinions of men, even if they beautify them for you with their speech.'

وقالَ مُحَمَّدُ بْنُ عِبْدِ الرَّحْمَنِ الأَدْرَمِيُّ لِرَجُلٍ تَكَلَّمَ بِبِدْعَةٍ وَدَعَا النَّاسَ إلَيْها: (هَلْ عَلِمَها رَسولُ اللَّهِ صَلَّى اللَّهُ عَلَيْهِ وَسَلَّمَ وأبو بَكْرٍ وعُمَرُ وعُثْمانُ وعَلِيٌّ أَوْ لَمْ يَعْلَموها؟ قالَ: لَمْ يَعْلَموها، قالَ: فَشَيْءٌ لَمْ يَعْلَمْهُ هَؤُلاءِ عَلِمْتَهُ أنْتَ؟ قالَ الرَّجُلُ: فَإنِّي أقولُ قَدْ عَلِمُوها!، قالَ: أفَوَسِعَهُمْ أنْ لا يَتَكَلَّمُوا بِهِ ولا يَدْعُوا النَّاسَ إلَيْهِ، أمْ لَمْ يَسَعْهُمْ؟ قالَ: بَلْ وَسِعَهُمْ، قالَ: فَشَيْءٌ وَسِعَ رَسولَ اللَّهِ صَلَّى اللَّهُ عَلَيْهِ وَسَلَّمَ وخُلَفاءَهُ، لا يَسَعُكَ أنْتَ؟ فَانْقَطَعَ الرَّجُلُ، فَقالَ الخَليفَةُ، وكانَ حاضِراً: لا وَسَّعَ اللَّه عَلى مَنْ لَمْ يَسَعْهُ ما وَسِعَهُمْ)!

Muḥammad b. 'Abd al-Raḥmān al-Adramī said to a man – who was speaking of an innovation and calling people to it: 'Did the Messenger of Allah, Abū Bakr, 'Umar, 'Uthmān and 'Alī have knowledge of this or did they not have knowledge of if?' The man replied: 'They did not have knowledge of it'. He (al-Adramī) said: 'So, something which they had no knowledge of, you know?!' The man responded: 'Then I say that they did know of it'. He (al-Adramī) said: 'Was it sufficient for them that they did not speak about it nor call the people towards it, or was it not sufficient for them?' The man replied: 'Of course it was sufficient for them'. He (al- Adramī): 'So, something which was sufficient for the Messenger of Allāh and his caliphs is not sufficient for you?!' So, the man refrained (from continuing the debate) and the caliph who was present said, 'May Allāh not suffice the one who is not satisfied by what they found sufficient.''

وهَكَذا مَنْ لَمْ يَسَعْهُ ما وَسِعَ رَسولَ اللَّهِ صَلَّى اللَّهُ عَلَيْهِ وَسَلَّمَ وأَصْحابَهُ والتَّابِعينَ لَهُمْ بِإِحْسانٍ، والأَئِمَّةَ مِنْ بَعْدِهِم، والرّاسِخينَ في العِلْمِ، مِنْ تِلاوَةِ آياتِ الصِّفاتِ وقِراءَةِ أَخْبارِها، و إِمْرارِها كَما جاءَتْ، فَلا وَسَّعَ اللَّهُ عَلَيْهِ

Likewise, May Allāh not suffice whoever is not sufficed by that what sufficed the Messenger, his Companions, their followers who followed them in righteousness, and the imāms that came after them, as well as those firmly grounded in knowledge; concerning recitation of the āyāt of the Attributes, and reading of their reports, and passing over them as they came.

Commentary: The Order to Follow the Sunnaḧ and a Warning against Innovation

We have been ordered to follow their way [i.e. the way of the Prophet ﷺ, his companions and the great imāms from the Salaf who followed them] **and to be guided by their example** [Ibn Hubayraḧ (d. 560H) said: 'It is not the madhhab of Aḥmad, except for following, categorically, what the Salaf said. He said as they said, and what they were silent about, he was silent about. To the extent that he rejected to say: "my utterance of the Qurān is created, or uncreated"; because they did not say it. He said concerning āyāt of the Attributes: pass them on, as they came'[76]]. **We have been warned of innovations and we have been informed that they are from the things that lead astray. The Prophet ﷺ said** [in a famous narration]: ***'upon you is*** [to follow] ***my Sunnaḧ and*** [to follow] ***the sunnaḧ of the rightly-guided caliphs after me, bite on to it with your molar teeth*** [being a metaphor for firmly sticking to something without leaving it] ***and beware of newly invented matters. Verily, every newly invented matter is an innovation, and every innovation is a misguidance.***'[77]

'Abd Allāh b. Mas'ūd (d. 32H), may Allāh be pleased with him, said: 'Follow [the Sunnaḧ strictly, without adding to it or omitting from it] **and do not**

[76] Ibn Rajab, *Dhayl 'alā Ṭabaqāt al-Ḥanābilaḧ*, vol. 2, p. 155.

[77] Imām Aḥmad, *al-Musnad*, no. 17145 / Abū Dawūd, no. 4607 / Al-Tirmidhī no. 2676.

innovate! Because you have been sufficed'[78] [with the perfection of the religion in the era before you. So, if they did not speak about a certain thing, then do not speak about it, unless there is a very serious innovation that needs to be refuted. In that case, one is forced to speak about something they did not speak about. Otherwise, one should keep his approach as simple as they did and remain silent[79]].

'Umar b. 'Abd al-'Azīz (d. 101H), may Allāh be pleased with him, said with the meaning of: 'Stop where the people have stopped! For indeed, they have stopped upon knowledge [meaning, they did not stop because they were ignorant, instead they stopped because they were knowledgeable. This affirms that the Salaf were more knowledgeable than the Khalaf[80]]. **The clear evidences would suffice them and they were the strongest at manifesting it. If there were any additions, they would have done them first** [the Salaf refrained from going beyond the Sunnaĥ even though they were more capable of uncovering additional benefits and more deserving of any extra virtue, yet they did not find exceeding the Sunnaĥ to be a good thing. **If you say: 'it was introduced after them', then no one has introduced it except the one who opposed their guidance** [as their guidance is to not delve into certain matters] **and desires other than their example. For they have certainly described from it** [i.e. the religion] **what satisfies, and have spoken about it** [i.e. the religion] **with what suffices** [for, they passed on everything and did not hold anything back or keep it secret]. **Consequently, whatever is above them** [meaning, doing or saying more than what they did] **is excessiveness, and what is below them** [meaning, doing or saying less than what they did] **is inadequacy. Indeed, some people have fallen short of them and were removed** [from the Sunnaĥ], **while others went beyond them and fell into extremism. And they** [the companions and the imāms of the

---

[78] Various successors (tabi'īn) reported it from Ibn Mas'ūd. For example, al-Nakha'ī, as found in *Kitāb al-'Ilm*, no. 54, by al-Khaythamaĥ (d. 234H); and in the *Musnad* of (Abū Muḥammad 'Abd Allāh) al-Dārimī (d. 255H), no. 224, it is found as a report from al-Sulamī (d. 75H).

[79] With regards to remaining silent when it comes to the Attributes, Ibn Qudāmaĥ states in *Taḥrīm al-Naẓar* (p. 54): 'And if fault is found in (the approach of) silence with respect to explanation, this is a mistake! Because, we do not know its explanation. It is obligatory for whoever does not know anything, to be silent concerning it and it is prohibited for him to speak regarding it. Allāh, Exalted is He, said: *'do not pursue that of which you have no knowledge...'* (Qurān: 17:36) and Allāh, Exalted is He, mentioned concerning the prohibitions: *'to say about Allāh what you do not know.'* (Qurān: 2:169). Also, if this position is found erroneous, then the Prophet ﷺ is erroneous (as well). Indeed, he believed in Allāh and His words, and he did not explain anything of it, nor did he expound on their meanings.'

[80] Ibn Rajab al-Ḥanbalī wrote concerning the superiority of the Salaf over the Khalaf, titled *Bayān Faḍl 'Ilm al-Salaf*. On p. 93, He said: 'Whether it is their words in the foundation of the religion (uṣūl al-dīn) or its branches (furū'), in tafsīr in ascetism (zuhd), heart-softeners (raqā°iq), points of wisdom and exhortation, and other than these of what they spoke of; then whoever travels upon their path, he is indeed guided.'

Salaf] **were between these** [meaning, between the deviations of excessiveness and inadequacy.

So, from amongst those who have deviated to different degrees are: the Mu'tazilah, the Ashā'irah and the Salafiyyah. The Ashā'irah as a group are still considered from Ahl al-Sunnah, because from amongst their different approaches towards the Attributes, is an approach similar to that of the Ḥanābilah. Ultimately, they believe in the tanzīh[81] of Allāh and therefore should be included in Ahl al-Sunnah[82]]; **upon straight guidance.'**[83]

Imām Abū 'Amr al-Awzā'ī (d 157H), may Allāh be pleased with him, said: 'Adhere to the narrations of those who come before you [meaning, the way of the Companions and the ones who followed them], **even if the people avoid you and reject you. And beware of the** [baseless] **opinions of men** [meaning, the opinions that are not based on the Sunnah, but instead on personal preferences and desires], **even if they beautify them for you with their speech'**[84] [for one may use a beautiful way of speaking or (irrelevant) Qurānic verses or aḥādīth to support one's argument, and people with a poor mentality or understanding

[81] Tanzīḥ: often translated as 'transcendence'. It could be rendered as: to declare something or someone pure and free of something else. Relating to Allāh and His Attributes, it is defined as Allāh being declared incomparable with anything of His creation. In this regard it is juxtaposed with the concept of tashbīḥ; which is to make resemblance between Allāh and anything of His creation in general - and to humans in particular.

[82] Throughout the course of history, the Ḥanābilah and Ashā'irah have always exchanged harsh words and critique, evident from works of the scholars from the early times; and even past the time of Ibn Qudāmah (e.g. the various clashes between Ibn Taymiyyah and his Ash'arī contemporaries which occurred more than hundred years after the death of Ibn Qudāmah). It has already been mentioned that this negative and hostile attitude towards the Ashā'irah is evident from the words of Ibn Qudāmah himself throughout his various works.

This attitude however must be contextualised, and thought must be given to the socio-political context at the time in which these scholars lived. Most probably it should be understood that (harsh) criticism from the Ḥanābilah was directed to certain aspects of the Ash'arī madhhab and/or specific individuals, rather than at the school and its beliefs as a whole. For example, in *Taḥrīm al-Naẓar*, Ibn Qudāmah censures Ibn 'Aqīl, and the Ash'arī tendencies that he had. In a similar fashion, passages of the famous book *Talbīs Iblīs* by Ibn al- Jawzī are not seeking to critique or refute the ideas and practices of the Ṣufiyyah in general, but is directed only towards certain specific aspects that he found problematic.

In recent times, the hostilities between the Ḥanābilah and Ashā'irah seem to have decreased, and in the last few centuries, there has emerged amongst the scholars of the Ḥanābilah the opinion that the Ashā'irah are to be considered from Ahl al-Sunnah. Further details can be found in the 'aqīdah works of Ibn al-Bāqī and al-Safārīnī.

[83] It appears to be the saying of 'Abd al-'Azīz b. Abī Salamah al-Mājishūn (d. 164H), as is apparent from *Burhān fi Bayān al-Qurān*, p. 88-89, in which Ibn Qudāmah transmits it from him with minor differences. Although in *al-Burhān, al-Munāẓarah* (p. 79) and *al-Lum'ah*, Ibn Qudāmah points to 'Umar b. 'Abd al-'Azīz as having said something similar in meaning. Perhaps he was referring to that which is reported from 'Umar b. 'Abd al-'Azīz concerning his reply to a question regarding al-qadar, which is o.a. reported by Abū Dawūd, no. 4612 / Abū Nu'aym in *al-Ḥilyah al-Awliyā°*, vol. 5, p. 338.

[84] Reported by al-Ājurrī in *Kitāb al-Sharī'ah*, vol. 1, no. 127.

could easily be convinced that it is a good claim or opinion. Therefore, when it comes to the claims and opinion of men one should always check whether the arguments and evidences are relevant to the claim that is being made. If this is done in fiqh, then how about in matters of 'aqīdaḧ where one should be more critical towards the claims and opinions of men!

Muḥammad b. 'Abd al-Raḥmān al-Adramī[85] [a scholar from the third century] **said to a man**[86] **who was speaking of an innovation** [which was the innovation of the created nature of the Qurān (fitnaḧ khalq al-Qurān)] **and calling people to it: 'Did the Messenger of Allāh, Abū Bakr, 'Umar, 'Uthmān and 'Alī have knowledge of this** [innovation] **or did they not have knowledge of if?' The man replied: 'They did not have knowledge of it'. He (al-Adramī) said: 'So, something which they had no knowledge of, you know?!' The man responded: 'Then I say that they did know of it'. He (al-Adramī) said: 'Was it sufficient for them that they did not speak about it nor call the people towards it, or was it not sufficient for them?'** [so, the innovator had two options: 1) either to say they had known it but did not inform people about it (i.e. the Messenger, Abū Bakr, 'Umar and 'Ali kept it a secret), or 2) they told people what they knew. In the latter case, one should ask for proof in the form of a report containing this specific knowledge (i.e. that the Qurān is created) - and such narration does not exist]. **The man replied: 'Of course it was sufficient for them'. He (al-Adramī) said: 'So, something which was sufficient for the Messenger of Allāh and his caliphs is not sufficient for you?!'**[87] **So, the man refrained (from continuing the debate) and the caliph** [Wāthiq bi-Allāh (d. 232H), the grandson of the caliph Harūn al-Rashīd (d. 193H)[88]] **who was present** [as these debates regularly took

---

[85] It appears that the name is misspelled, as it should be al-Ādharmī (as is found in the various reports of the story). Also, some versions of *al-Lum'ah* mention al-Ādharmī instead of al- Adramī. See the edition of *al-Lum'aḧ* by al-Farḥān, titled *Risālaḧ al-I'tiqād*, p. 75, footnote 3; in which he compares the differences in the various texts of *al-Lum'aḧ*.

[86] He is al-Qāḍī Ibn Abī Du'ād; the chief investigator of the Mu'tazilī inquisition.

[87] In *Taḥrīm al-Naẓar*, p. 51, Ibn Qudāmaḧ uses a similar line of argumentation to establish that there is no need, and in fact no way, to know the meaning of the Attributes, because it was not known to the Prophet ﷺ and his Companions. If he ﷺ knew it, he would have explained it to them, and they to the subsequent generation and so forth. So, he says: 'If explanation was an obligation, the Prophet ﷺ would have clarified it to his Ummaḧ; because it is not permitted to delay an explanation from its time. If it was an obligation for us to do the interpretation, then it would be an obligation for the Prophet ﷺ (i.e. he would have to do the same); because he is an equivalent to us with regards to the rulings. If it was an obligation for him to do so, he would not be deficient in it. And because he ﷺ was keen and careful for his Ummaḧ, he would not hide anything from them that Allāh ordered him with. Indeed, Allāh has said: *'O Messenger, announce that which has been revealed to you from your Lord, and if you do not, then you have not conveyed His message...'* (Qurān: 5:67).'

[88] The story is told through 'al-Muhtadī' (d. 256H), who is the son of al-Wāthiq. Ibn al-Jawzī mentions in *Manāqib al-Imām Aḥmad*, p. 481, that caliph Wāthiq recanted his view that the Qurān was created, and

place in the court of the caliph who often attended himself] **said, 'May Allāh not suffice the one who is not satisfied by what they** [meaning, the Messenger and his companions] found sufficient.''[89]

Likewise, May Allāh not suffice whoever is not sufficed by that what sufficed the Messenger, his Companions, their followers who followed them in righteousness, and the imāms that came after them, as well as those firmly grounded in knowledge; concerning recitation of the āyāt of the Attributes, and reading of their reports [meaning, it is sufficient to just recite these āyāt and aḥādīth] **and passing over them as they came** [meaning, leaving these reports just as they were transmitted, without re-interpreting them; and all who were mentioned above found sufficiency in this. Ibn al-Jawzī[90] said, while explaining the ḥadīth: *'Allāh yaḍhak[91] at the two men'*: 'The majority of the Salaf did not do ta°wil when it came to this (i.e. the reports which mention the Attributes), and they passed over it as it came, and imrār should be taken into consideration in this: (it is) the belief that the Attributes of Allāh do not resemble (or do not have any similarities with) the attributes of the creation. The meaning of al-imrār is: having no knowledge of the intended meaning of it (i.e. the Attributes), accompanied with the belief of tanzīḥ.'[92] Ibn al-Jawzī is accurate in saying 'the majority of the Salaf, as it has been explained earlier that the Salaf are not one homogenous group who all agreed on, and said, the same thing. It is therefore correct to say, 'the majority of the Salaf' instead of claiming ijmā' or saying 'they all said such-and-such'.

The exposition of Ibn al-Jawzī concerning imrār is beneficial, as imrār is usually explained according to its linguistic meaning, i.e. to pass over something

---

repented. It seems that this debate was the reason for his recantation. Another version of the story is also related by al-Khaṭīb al-Baghdādī (d. 463H) in *Tārīkh (Baghdād) Madīnah al-Salām*, vol. 11, no. 5142.

[89] Ibn al-Jawzī relates two versions of the story in *Manāqib al-Imām Aḥmad*, p. 475-481, one being short and the other considerably longer. Ibn Qudāmah paraphrases the short version in *al-Lum'ah*. The longer version is reported o.a. by al-Ājurrī in *Kitāb al-Sharī'ah*, no. 193.

[90] When it comes to statements of Ibn al-Jawzī on issues of 'aqīdah, and in particular the Attributes of Allāh, the Ḥanābilah take a critical approach. To state it in simple terms: Ibn al-Jawzī does not represent the Ḥanbalī madhhab. He has his own opinions, at times he considers some Attributes as the Ḥanābilah do, while other times he opts for a different approach (and resorts to ta°wil tafṣīlī), yet in other instances he does not consider some Attributes to be Attributes at all. At times he himself is confused concerning the issue of the Attributes, and is often confusing to understand. This was all mentioned in the larger works of Ḥanbalī 'aqīdah, authored by scholars such as: al-Safārīnī and Mar'ī al-Karmī. In all, the scholars of the Ḥanābilah have assessed the different statements of Ibn al-Jawzī and taken from them what they appreciated and found in agreement with the Ḥanbalī madhhab, such as the statement mentioned in this hāshiyah.

[91] Yaḍḥak can be translated as '(he) laughs'.

[92] Ibn Hajar Al-'Asqalānī, *Fatḥ al-Bārī*, vol 9, p. 76, no. 2826.

without discussing it. In this way it is explained according to the consequences of 'passing over' something. However, Ibn al-Jawzī explains the technical definition, i.e. having no knowledge of the intended meaning of that which one passes over, in this context being the Attributes of Allāh, while being accompanied with the belief of tanzīḥ].

ĀYĀT AND AḤĀDĪTH CONCERNING ALLĀH'S ATTRIBUTES

فَمِمَّا جاءَ مِنْ آياتِ الصِّفاتِ قَولُ اللَّهِ عَزَّ وجَل: ﴿وَيَبْقَى وَجْهُ رَبِّكَ﴾، وقولُه سُبحانَهُ وَتَعَالَى: ﴿بَلْ يَدَاهُ مَبْسُوطَتَانِ﴾، وقولُهُ تعالى إخْبارًا عَن عِيسَى عَلَيْهِ السَّلامُ أَنَّهُ قال ﴿تَعْلَمُ مَا فِي نَفْسِي وَلَا أَعْلَمُ مَا فِي نَفْسِكَ﴾، وقولُهُ سُبْحانَهُ: ﴿وَجَآءَ رَبُّكَ﴾، وقولُهُ تَعالى: ﴿هَلْ يَنظُرُونَ إِلَّا أَن يَأْتِيَهُمُ اللَّهُ﴾، وقولُهُ: ﴿رَضِيَ اللَّهُ عَنْهُمْ وَرَضُوا عَنْهُ﴾. وقولُهُ تَعالى: ﴿يُحِبُّهُمْ وَيُحِبُّونَهُ﴾، وقولُهُ تعالى في الكُفّارِ: ﴿غَضِبَ اللَّهُ عَلَيْهِمْ﴾، وقولُهُ تَعالى: ﴿اتَّبَعُوا مَا أَسْخَطَ اللَّهَ﴾، وقولُهُ تَعالى: ﴿كَرِهَ اللَّهُ انبِعَاثَهُمْ﴾

From what has come in the āyāt concerning the Attributes, is the statement of Allāh, the Mighty and Majestic: *'And the Wajh of Your Lord, full of Majesty and Honour, will abide forever.'*[93] His saying, free of imperfections and Exalted is He: *'On the contrary, His Yadāhu are widely outstretched'*[94]. His statement, Exalted is He, in which He informs us that 'Isa b. Maryam, peace be upon him, said: *'You know what is in my inner-self, though I do not know what is in Your Nafs.'*[95] And His statement, free of imperfections is He: *'And your Lord jā°a'.*[96] His statement, Exalted is He: *'Do they then wait for anything other than that Allāh ya°tiya to them'*[97]. And His statement: *'Allāh is raḍiyā with them, and they are pleased with Him.'*[98] And His statement, Exalted is He: *'He will yuḥibu them, and they will love Him.'*[99] And His saying, Exalted is He, concerning the disbelievers: *'and the ghaḍab of Allāh is upon them.'*[100] His saying, Exalted is He: *'That is because they*

---

[93] Qurān: 55:27

[94] Qurān: 5:64

[95] Qurān: 5:116

[96] Qurān: 89:22

[97] Qurān: 2:210

[98] Qurān: 5:119

[99] Qurān: 5:54

[100] Qurān: 48:6

followed what askhaṭa Allāh.'[101] And His saying, Exalted is He: *'Allāh kariha their being sent forth.'*[102]

ومِنَ السُّنَّةِ قَوْلُ النَّبِيِّ صَلَّى اللَّهُ عَلَيْهِ وَسَلَّمَ: ((يَنْزِلُ رَبُّنا تبارك وتعالى كُلَّ لَيْلَةٍ إلى سَماءِ الدُّنْيا، وقولُهُ: ((يَعْجَبُ ربكَّ مِنَ الشَّابِّ لَيْسَتْ لَهُ صَبْوَةٌ))، وقولُهُ: ((يَضْحَكُ اللَّهُ إلى رَجُلَيْنِ قَتَلَ أَحَدُهُما الآخَرَ ثُمَّ يَدْخُلانِ الجَنَّةَ))

From the Sunnah is the statement of the Prophet ﷺ: *'Our Lord, may He be Blessed and Exalted, yanzilu to the lowest heaven every night'*. He ﷺ said: *'Your Lord ya'jibu by the youth who does not possess childish manners.'*, and his statement ﷺ: *'Allāh yaḍḥak at two men, one of whom kills the other and they both enter Paradise'.'*

فَهَذا وما أَشْبَهَهُ مِمّا صَحَّ سَنَدُهُ، وعُدِّلَتْ رُواتُهُ، نُؤْمِنُ بِهِ، ولا نَرُدُّهُ، ولا نَجْحَدُهُ، ولا نَتَأَوَّلُهُ بِتَأْوِيلٍ يُخالِفُ ظاهِرَهُ، ولا نُشَبِّهُهُ بِصِفاتِ المَخْلوقينَ، ولا بِسِماتِ المُحْدَثِينَ ونَعْلَمُ أَنَّ اللَّهَ سُبْحَانَهُ وَتَعَالَى لا شَبيهَ لَهُ، ولا نَظيرَ: ﴿لَيْسَ كَمِثْلِهِ شَيْءٌ وَهُوَ السَّمِيعُ الْبَصِيرُ﴾، وكُلُّ ما تُخُيِّلَ في الذِّهْنِ أَوْ خَطَرَ بِالبَالِ، فَإِنَّ اللَّهَ تَعالى بِخِلافِهِ.

This and others similar to it from those whose chain of narration are authentic, and whose reporters are acceptable; We believe in it, and do not reject it, nor deny it, nor do we (re)interpret it with interpretation which contradicts its obvious meaning. We do not make comparisons with the attributes of creation, nor do we use the names (given) by the innovators. And we know that Allāh, Glorified and Exalted is He, has no similar or equal: *'There is nothing whatsoever like Him. And He is al-Samī', al-Baṣīr.'*[103] Hence, everything that is imagined by the mind or produced in ones thought, then surely Allāh is different from it.

ومِنْ ذَلِكَ قَوْلُهُ تَعالى: ﴿الرَّحْمَنُ عَلَى الْعَرْشِ اسْتَوَى﴾. وقَوْلُهُ تَعالى: ﴿ءَأَمِنتُم مَّن فِي السَّمَاءِ﴾، وقولُ النَّبِيِّ صَلَّى اللَّهُ عَلَيْهِ وَسَلَّمَ: ((رَبُّنَا اللَّهُ الَّذِي في السَّماءِ تَقَدَّسَ اسْمُكَ)).وقالَ لِلْجارِيَةِ: ((أَيْنَ اللَّهُ؟))، قالَتْ: في السَّماءِ قالَ: ((أَعْتِقْها فإنَّها

[101] Qurān: 47:28

[102] Qurān: 9:46

[103] Qurān: 42:11

مُؤْمِنةٌ)) رَواهُ مَالِكُ بْنُ أَنَسٍ ومُسْلِمٌ وغَيْرُهما مِنَ الأَئِمَّةِ. وقالَ النَّبِيُّ صَلَّى اللَّهُ عَلَيْهِ وَسَلَّمَ لِحُصَيْنٍ: ((كَمْ إِلَهًا تَعْبُدُ؟)) قالَ: سَبْعَةً: سِتَّةٌ في الأَرْضِ وواحِدًا في السَّماءِ، قالَ ((مَنْ لِرَغْبَتِكَ وَرَهْبَتِكَ؟))، قالَ: الَّذي في السَّماءِ، قالَ: ((فَاتْرُكِ السِّتَّةَ وَاعْبُدِ الَّذي في السَّماءِ وَ أَنَا أُعَلِّمُكَ دَعْوَتَيْنِ))، فَأَسْلَمَ وَعَلَّمَهُ النَّبِيُّ صَلَّى اللَّهُ عَلَيْهِ وَسَلَّمَ أَنْ يَقُولَ: ((اللَّهُمَّ أَلْهِمْني رُشْدِي وَقِني شَرَّ نَفْسِي)) وَفيمَا نُقِلَ مِنْ عَلاماتِ النَّبِيِّ صَلَّى اللَّهُ عَلَيْهِ وَسَلَّمَ وأَصْحابِهِ في الكُتُبِ المتَقَدِّمَةِ أَنَّهُم يَسْجُدونَ بِالأَرْضِ، ويَزْعُمونَ أَنَّ إِلَهَهُم في السَّماءِ. وَرَوَى أبو داوُدَ في سُنَنِهِ أَنَّ النَّبِيَّ صَلَّى اللَّهُ عَلَيْهِ وَسَلَّمَ قالَ: ((إِنَّ مَا بَيْنَ سماءٍ إِلَى سَمَاءٍ مَسِيرَةَ كذَا وكَذَا)) - وذَكَرَ الخَبَرَ إلى قَوْلِهِ: ((وَفَوْقَ ذَلِكَ العَرْشُ وَاللَّهُ سُبْحَانَهُ فَوْقَ ذَلِكَ.))

And from this is His statement, Exalted is He: *'al-Raḥmān istawā over the Throne'*[104], and His statement, Exalted is He: *'Do you feel secure that He who is fī al-samā°'*[105]. And the statement of the Prophet: *'Our Lord is Allah, who is fī al-samā°! Sanctified be Your Name.'* Also His ﷺ saying to the slave-girl: *'Where is Allāh? She said: 'fī al-samā°' So he said: 'Set her free, for indeed she is a believer.'*; as reported by Muslim and Mālik b. Anas and others from the imāms. The Prophet ﷺ said to Ḥusayn (b. 'Imrān): *'How many gods do you worship? He said: 'seven; six in the earth and one fī al-samā°. He ﷺ said: 'Who is it that you hope in and fear?' He said: 'The One that fī al-samā°.' He ﷺ said: 'Then abandon the six and worship the One who fī al-samā°, and I will teach you two supplications.' So, he accepted Islām and the Prophet ﷺ taught him to say: 'Oh Allāh, Grant me guidance and save me from the evil of myself.'* What was reported in the previously revealed books, concerning the signs of the Prophet ﷺ and his Companions, is that: they prostrate on the earth while they claim that their god is fī al-samā°. Abū Dawūd reported in his *Sunan* that the Prophet ﷺ said: *'Indeed, what is between one level of heaven and (another) level of heaven is a distance of such and such...'* He ﷺ continued until he mentioned: *'And above that is the Throne. And Allāh, the One free of all defects, is above that.'*

---

[104] 104 Qurān: 20:5

[105] Qurān: 67:16

فَهَذَا وَمَا أَشْبَهَهُ مِمَّا أَجْمَعَ السَّلَفُ رَحِمَهُمُ اللَّهُ عَلَى نَقْلِهِ وقَبُولِهِ ولَمْ يَتَعَرَّضُوا لِرَدِّهِ ولا تَأْوِيلِهِ ولا تَشْبِيهِهِ ولا تَمْثِيلِهِ

This and similar to it from what the Salaf, may Allāh have mercy on them, have agreed upon concerning transmission and accepting, and not subjecting it to outright rejection nor distortion, comparison or making example for it.

سُئِلَ الإمامُ مَالِكُ بْنُ أَنَسٍ رَحِمَهُ اللَّهُ فَقِيلَ: (يا أَبَا عَبدِ اللَّهِ: ﴿الرَّحْمَنُ عَلَى الْعَرْشِ اسْتَوَى﴾ كَيْفَ اسْتَوَى؟ فَقالَ: الاسْتِواءُ غَيْرُ مَجْهولٍ، والكَيْفُ غَيْرُ مَعْقولٍ، والإِيمانُ بِهِ واجِبٌ والسُّؤالُ عَنْهُ بِدْعَةٌ، ثُمَّ أَمَرَ بِالرَّجُلِ فَأُخْرِجَ).

Imām Mālik b. Anas was once questioned, and it was said to him: 'O Abā 'Abd Allāh! The most Merciful *istawā* over the Throne. How is the *istiwā*?' So, he responded: 'The *istiwā* is not unknown. The 'how' is incomprehensible. Believing in it is an obligation. And asking concerning it is an innovation.' Then he commanded someone, and he was thrown out.'

Commentary: Āyāt and Aḥādīth concerning Allāh's Attributes

[In the following two chapters the author will list various āyāt and aḥādīth regarding the Attributes. As previously mentioned on more than one occasion, giving a specific meaning (or explanation) to an Attribute of Allāh is categorically prohibited. For this reason, the commentary will not expound on these āyāt and aḥādīth in great detail, sufficing only with mentioning the general meanings of particular āyāt and aḥādīth. It is stressed that the general meanings that are given for these āyāt and aḥādīth should not to be confused for specific interpretations for the Attributes themselves. Therefore, when it is said that from the āyah *'His Yadāhu*[106] *are widely outstretched'* it is generally understood to mean that Allāh is generous and can do whatever he wants. This does not mean that *'His Yadāhu'* means 'His Generosity'. Giving a general explanation to a whole text differs from giving a specific interpretation or explanation of a specific Attribute that is mentioned in an āyah or ḥadīth.]

From what has come in the āyāt concerning the Attributes, is the statement of Allāh, The Mighty and Majestic: *'And the Wajh of Your Lord, full of Majesty*

[106] Yadāhu can be translated as 'both his hands'.

and Honour, will abide forever.'[107] [the general meaning being, that Allāh has no end and likewise no beginning]. **His saying, free of imperfections and Exalted is He: *'On the contrary, His Yadāhu are widely outstretched.'***[108] [and the general meaning is, that Allāh has the full ability and *Irādah* to do anything and nothing can stop Him from doing what he wants. He is the most generous]. **His statement, Exalted is He, in which He informs us that 'Isa b. Maryam, peace be upon him, said: *'You know what is in my inner- self, though I do not know what is in Your Nafs.'***[109-110] [the general meaning being, Allāh knows everything that a person keeps in his mind, yet we do not know and cannot comprehend the *'Ilm* of Allah]. And His statement, free of imperfections is He: ***'And your Lord jā°a'***[111-112] [with the angels in rows. This āyah is concerned with two things: 1) the coming of the angels on the Day of Judgement, and 2) Allāh will be attendant on that day. One should not ask whether Allāh is with the angels, i.e. being physically with or accompanying them and similar such questions, for these are erroneous things that should not be discussed. On the contrary, one should stick to what Allāh said: *'And your Lord jā°a and the angels in rows'*. The general meaning being, that we know that Allah will be attendant on that day, and we may somehow be able to see Him on that day]. **His statement, Exalted is He: *'Do they then wait for anything other than that Allāh ya°tiya*[113] *to them'***[114] [this āyah is different from the previous āyāt, because Allāh is criticizing the people who are waiting for Allāh and the angels to come to them; as if Allāh is going to descend from the clouds to them. Allāh rejects this faulty idea and disproves it]. **And His statement: *'Allāh is raḍiyā*[115] *with them, and they are pleased with Him***[116] [the general meaning being, Allāh will reward those people]. **And His statement, Exalted is He: *'He will yuḥibu*[117] *them, and they will love Him***[118] [the general meaning of this āyah is identical to the previous one, i.e. He will reward those people and will grant them paradise. The meaning of ḥubb and its translation as 'love' is problematic as it is

---

[107] Qurān: 55:27

[108] Qurān: 5:64

[109] Nafs can be translated as '(inner)self'.

[110] Qurān: 5:116

[111] Jā°a can be translated as '(he) comes'.

[112] Qurān: 89:22

[113] Ya°tiya can be translated as '(he) should come'.

[114] Qurān: 2:210

[115] Raḍiyā can be translated as '(he) is pleased'.

[116] Qurān: 5:119

[117] Yuḥibu can be translated as '(he) will love'.

[118] Qurān: 5:54

something that happens in the heart, and comprises of feelings and emotions]. **And His saying, Exalted is He, concerning the disbelievers: *'and the ghaḍab*[119] *of Allāh is upon them'*[120]** [*ghaḍab* is defined as 'the boiling of the heart out of anger', and here this actual meaning does not suit Allāh and it should therefore not be translated as 'anger'. The general understanding of the āyaḧ is that those people mentioned will be punished by Allāh]. **His saying, Exalted is He: *'That is because they followed what askhaṭa*[121] *Allāh.'*[122] And His saying, Exalted is He: *'Allāh kariha*[123] *their being sent forth'*[124]** [the general meaning of these āyāt is similar to what is mentioned with regards to the āyaḧ concerning the *Ghaḍab* of Allah].

From the Sunnaḧ is the statement of the Prophet ﷺ: *'Our Lord, may He be Blessed and Exalted, yanzilu*[125] *to the lowest heaven every night.'*[126] [the common English translation is 'He descends to the lowest heavens', and Allāh is the only one who's help is sought! This implies that Allāh is limited and restricted by the boundaries of the lowest heaven, in that it contains Him. If one says 'yes, this is true', then he is at least being honest, however gravely mistaken in his conviction. If one would say 'no, this is not true' then the reply should be: 'why then, would you say such a thing?' The Ḥanābilaḧ, contrary to what they say, simply state it as the Prophet ﷺ did, without explanation or translation, i.e. *'Yanzilu rabunā ilā al-samā°i al-dunya'*. They believe in the wording of the ḥadīth, although they do not believe He actually descends to the lowest heaven. Ibn al-Bannā° al-Ḥanbalī (d. 471 H) stated clearly, when explaining the Attribute of *Nuzūl*[127]: 'And this and what resembles it; then taking *al- Nuzūl* to be descending to empty space, occupying space and movement, is kufr. To carry it upon its apparentness (ẓāhirihi) is permissible.'[128] Apart from it being very clearly stated that *Nuzūl* should not be understood as 'movement', it is also an important statement for it contains proof that the usage of '(its) apparentness', does not mean the literal meaning of the word in this context (i.e. in relation to Allāh and

---

[119] Ghaḍab can be translated as 'anger'.

[120] Qurān: 48:6

[121] Askhaṭa can be translated as '(he) discontented'.

[122] Qurān: 47:28

[123] Kariha can be translated as '(he) disliked'.

[124] Qurān: 9:46

[125] Yanzilu can be translated as '(he) descends'.

[126] Narrated by Imām Aḥmad in *al-Musnad*, no. 7592 / al-Bukhārī, no. 1145 / Muslim, no. 758.

[127] Nuzūl can be translated as 'descend'.

[128] Ibn al-Bannā°, *Al-Uṣūl al-Mujarradaḧ*, p. 47.

His Attributes); for, Ibn al-Bannā° first rejected the literal meaning (i.e. moving from one place to another), and only later stated that 'to carry it upon its apparent' (ḥamlaha 'alā ẓāhirihi) is permissible; indicating that when the word 'apparent' (ẓāhir) is used, it refers to the wording of the āyaḧ or ḥadīth and not the literal meaning of the word itself[129].

Certainly, both *yanzilu* and *Nuzūl* have meanings, but they are unknown to us, and Allāh knows best! The general meaning of the āyaḧ indicates that Allāh will have more *Raḥmaḧ* with the people at that time, and will reward them more during it, and the last part of this narration actually implies this general understanding[130]]. **He ﷺ said: *'Your Lord ya'jibu*[131] *by the youth who does not possess childish manners.'***[132] [and this is one of the cases in which it is not entirely clear what the intended overall meaning should be. It could be said that the general meaning of the ḥadīth points to Allāh rewarding such a person and elevating him in rank and status. However, there are other general meanings available for it], **and his statement ﷺ: *'Allāh yaḍḥak at two men, one of whom kills the other and they both enter Paradise'.'***[133]

This and others [i.e. other āyāt and aḥādīth] **similar to it, from those whose chain of narration is authentic** [and give certainty], **and whose reporters are acceptable; We believe in it , and do not reject it , nor deny it, nor do we (re)interpret it with interpretation which contradicts its obvious meaning** [meaning, which contradicts the obvious meaning of the whole āyaḧ or narration. Thus, Ibn Qudāmaḧ is talking about understanding the obvious meaning of the whole āyaḧ or narration and not the specific Attribute only. Consequently, twisting the whole meaning of the āyaḧ or ḥadīth to a different meaning is impermissible and unacceptable. Furthermore, the obvious meanings of these narrations are something that most people can understand. Yet, as for the Attributes themselves that are contained in these narrations, then only Allāh knows best what they actually mean]. **We do not make comparisons with the attributes of creations, nor do we use the names** [meanings, features or traits]

---

[129] A similar conclusion based on the words of Ibn Qudāmaḧ was reached in footnote 55.

[130] The last part being: *'Is there anyone to invoke Me so that I may respond to his invocation? Is there anyone to ask Me, so that I may grant him his request? Is there anyone seeking My forgiveness so that I may forgive him?'*

[131] Ya'jibu can be translated as '(he) is amazed'.

[132] This wording is transmitted by al-Qaḍā'ī in *Musnad al-Shihāb*, vol. 1, no. 576 / Imām Aḥmad reported something similar in *al-Musnad*, no. 17371, albeit with a slightly different wording. A different, yet stronger ḥadīth which affirms this Attribute, is transmitted by al- Bukhārī in his *Ṣaḥīḥ*, no. 488.

[133] Imām Aḥmad in *al-Musnad*, no. 7326 / al-Bukhārī, no. 2826 / Muslim, no. 1890.

(given) **by the innovators** [and consequently, when the innovators say something concerning Allāh and His Attributes, the Ḥanābilaĥ do not accept it. For example, calling Allāh *(al-sāni'aĥ)*, meaning 'the manufacturer'. Although, this innovated term might not be wrong per se, using it and others similar to it is prohibited]. **And we know that Allāh, Glorified and Exalted is He, has no similar and equal: *'There is nothing whatsoever like Him. And He is al-Samī'*[134] *al-Baṣīr*[135].'[136] Hence, everything that is imagined by the mind or produced in ones thought, then surely Allāh is different from it** [so, all the imaginations that the human intellect can produce are inherently nothing like Allah].

And from this is His statement, Exalted is He: *'al-Raḥmān istawā over the Throne'*[137] [in a manner that suits His Majesty[138]], **and His statement, Exalted is He: *'Do you feel secure that He who fī al-samā°'*[139]** [*istawā* is something that one must believe in, and when it is said that Allāh is over the heavens one should believe it that. One should definitely not believe that Allāh is physically above the heavens or that there is some kind of distance between Him and the heavens, or something to that effect. The general meaning of these āyāt is to show the greatness of Allāh in relation to His creation. For, the 'Arsh is the biggest creation of all created things, yet Allāh is above that]. **And the statement of the Prophet:**

---

[134] Samī' can be translated as 'hearing'.

[135] Baṣīr can be translated as 'seeing'.

[136] Qurān: 42:11

[137] Qurān: 20:5

[138] In some 'aqīdaĥ works by sects who claim and affirm the literal meanings for the Attributes of Allāh, often the addition 'as it suits His Majesty' (or similar phrases) is found, after first having stated that the Attribute is taken on its literal meaning. They use this additional phrase to avoid falling into anthropomorphism. However, this addition is problematic and does not help in attaining the goal they set out to reach, which is avoiding anthropomorphism. On the contrary, it only further complicates the matter for the 'literal meaning' is always something that is related to the physical created world and comprises of created materials. For example, every yad is comprised of flesh and bones and other created materials. When it is said that this meaning is not intended, then this means that the Attribute is in fact not taken on its 'literal meaning' at all, but on a metaphorical one instead. Thus, when one takes an Attribute of Allāh on its literal meaning it implies linking it to, or resembling it with, the creation. Although differences in shared attributes do occur amongst various creatures, such as the difference between a human hand, the hand of an ape, or the hand of another animal, they do share common factors such as: all being created things and using the hand as a 'tool'. Therefore, the addition 'as it suits His Majesty' does not help to avoid anthropomorphism, comparison and making examples. In actuality, it only further complicates the matter. Such a person, in essence, says that Allāh shares in something with the creation, yet His Attribute is different from the creation because it suits His Majesty, and this is a clear contradiction. Furthermore, Allāh says that 'nothing whatsoever is like Him', and this alone should be enough to divert the Attribute(s) away from their literal meanings. The phrase 'as it suits His Majesty' is on its own not problematic, but only in combination with affirming the literal meaning does it result in a self-contradictory and messy statement.

[139] Qurān: 67:16

'Our Lord is Allah, who is fī al-samā°! Sanctified be Your Name.'[140] [another general meaning one could understand from this is that Allāh is not physically with His creation], **also His ﷺ saying to the slave-girl: *'Where is Allāh? She said: 'fī al-samā°' So he said: 'Set her free, for indeed she is a believer.'*; as reported by Muslim and Mālik b. Anas and others from the imāms**[141]**. The Prophet ﷺ said to Ḥusayn (b. 'Imrān): *'How many gods do you worship? He said: 'seven; six in the earth and one fī al-samā°. He ﷺ said: 'Who is it that you hope in and fear?' He said: 'The One that is fī al-samā°.' He ﷺ said: 'Then abandon the six and worship the One who is fī al-samā°, and I will teach you two supplications.' So, he accepted Islām and the Prophet ﷺ taught him to say: 'Oh Allāh, Grant me guidance and save me from the evil of myself.'*[142] What was reported in the previously revealed books, concerning the signs of the Prophet ﷺ and his Companions, is that: They prostrate on the earth while they claim that their god is *fī al-samā°.*[143] Abū Dawūd (d. 275H) reported in his *Sunan* that the Prophet ﷺ said: *'Indeed, what is between one level of heaven and (another) level of heaven is a distance of such and such...'* He ﷺ continued until he mentioned: *'And above that is the Throne. And Allāh, the One free of all defects, is above that.'***[144] [yet, He is not physically above that, as He is not confined to place or time].

This and similar to it from what the Salaf, may Allāh have mercy on them, have agreed upon concerning transmission and accepting [of these reports], **and not subjecting it to outright rejection nor distorting, comparing or making examples for it** [with the characteristics of the creation].

Imām Mālik b. Anas was once questioned, and it was said to him: 'O Abā 'Abd Allāh! The most Merciful *istawā* over the Throne. How is the *istawā?'* So, he [i.e. imām Malik] **responded: 'The istawā is not unknown** [meaning, that the word is known in the Arabic language. When it is spoken in Arabic, an Arabic speaker will understand what is meant by it; and it means to 'ascend']. **The 'how' is incomprehensible** [meaning, the mind cannot comprehend how this is with regards to Allāh]. **Believing in it is an obligation. And asking concerning it**

---

[140] Imām Aḥmad in *al-Musnad*, no. 23957 / Abū Dawūd, no. 3892.

[141] Muslim, no. 537 / Imām Mālik in *al-Muwaṭṭa°*, no. 2251/ and others, like: Imām Aḥmad in *al-Musnad*, no. 23762 / Abū Dawūd, no. 930 / Al-Nasā°ī, no. 1218.

[142] Al-Tirmidhī, no. 3483.

[143] It is based on the report that Ibn Qudāmah mentions in *Ithbāt Sifah al-'Uluww*, p. 78.

[144] The whole version of the ḥadīth is narrated by Imām Aḥmad in *al-Musnad*, no. 1770 / Abū Dawūd, no. 4723.

[meaning, asking about its kayfiyyah (i.e. how it is), its reality or meaning] **is an innovation.' Then he commanded someone** [to throw out the questioner], **and he was thrown out.'**[145]

[145] This is a famous and authentic saying from Imām Mālik, and it is narrated through various reporters, with assorted wordings. An early source for the exact wording mentioned by Ibn Qudāmaḧ is *'Aqīdaḧ al-Salaf Asḥāb al-Ḥadīth* by al-Ṣābūnī (d. 449H), p. 180-181, and even earlier by Abī al-Shaykh al-Aṣbahānī (d. 369H) in *Ṭabaqāt al-Muḥaddathīn*, vol. 2, p. 214. One of the earliest sources that mentions the report of Imām Mālik is *al-Radd 'alā al-Jaymiyyah*, no. 104, by 'Uthmān b. Sa'īd al-Dārimī (d. 280H); with a slight difference in the order of phrases.

ومِنْ صِفاتِ اللَّهِ تَعالى أَنَّهُ مُتَكَلِّمٌ بِكَلامٍ قَديمٍ، يَسْمَعُهُ مِنْهُ مَنْ شاءَ مِنْ خَلْقِهِ. سَمِعَهُ مُوسَى عَلَيْهِ السَّلامُ مِنْهُ مِنْ غَيْرِ وَاسِطَةٍ، وسَمِعَهُ جِبْرِيلُ عَلَيْهِ السَّلامُ، وَمَنْ أَذِنَ لَهُ مِنْ مَلائِكَتِهِ، وَرُسُلِهِ. وأَنَّهُ سُبْحَانَهُ يُكَلِّمُ المُؤْمِنينَ في الآخِرَةِ، ويُكَلِّمُونَهُ، ويَأْذَنُ لَهُمْ فَيَزُورُونَهُ، قالَ اللَّهُ تَعالى: ﴿وَكَلَّمَ اللَّهُ مُوسَى تَكْلِيمًا﴾، وقالَ سُبْحانَهُ: ﴿يَا مُوسَى إِنِّي اصْطَفَيْتُكَ عَلَى النَّاسِ بِرِسَالاتِي وَبِكَلامِي﴾، وقالَ سُبْحانَهُ: ﴿مِنْهُمْ مَنْ كَلَّمَ اللَّهُ﴾، وقالَ سُبْحانَهُ: ﴿وَمَا كَانَ لِبَشَرٍ أَنْ يُكَلِّمَهُ اللَّهُ إِلا وَحْيًا أَوْ مِنْ وَرَاءِ حِجَابٍ﴾، وقالَ سُبْحانَهُ: ﴿فَلَمَّا أَتَاهَا نُودِيَ يَا مُوسَى * إِنِّي أَنَا رَبُّكَ﴾، وقالَ سُبْحانَهُ: ﴿ إِنَّنِي أَنَا اللَّهُ لا إِلَهَ إِلا أَنَا فَاعْبُدْنِي﴾ وغَيْرُ جائِزٍ أَنْ يَقولَ هَذا إِلَّا اللَّهُ.

From the Attributes of Allāh is that He is *mutakalim* with *Kalām* that is pre-existent. He causes whomsoever He wills to hear it. Mūsā, peace upon him, heard it from Him without a medium in between. Jibrīl, peace upon him, heard it, as well as whomsoever He permitted from His angels and messengers. He, the One free from all defects, *yukallimu* to the believers in the Hereafter and they will speak to Him. And He will give permission to them, so that they will visit Him. Allāh, Exalted is He, says: *'and Allāh kallama to Mūsā, with actual speech.'*[146] And He, free from imperfections, says: *'He said, O Mūsā, I have chosen you above men by My Messages, and by my Kalām.'*[147] And He, free of imperfections, says: *'Allāh kallama to some of them.'*[148] Allāh, free of imperfections, says: *'It is not for any human being that Allāh yukallima to him unless by Revelation, or from behind a veil.'*[149] And Allāh, free of imperfections, says: *'And when he came to it, he was called by name: O Musa, Verily, I am your Lord...'*[150] Allāh, free of imperfections, also says: *'Verily, I am Allāh, None has the right to be worshipped except I, so*

146 Qurān: 4:164

147 Qurān: 7:144

148 Qurān: 2:253

149 Qurān: 42:51

150 Qurān: 20:11-12

worship me, and establish the Prayer for My remembrance.'[151] It is not permissible for anyone to say this is other than Allāh.

وقالَ عَبْدُ اللَّهِ بْنُ مَسْعودٍ رَضِيَ اللَّهُ عَنْهُ: إِذَا تَكَلَّمَ اللَّهُ بِالوَحْيِ سَمِعَ صَوْتَهُ أَهْلُ السَّماءِ، ورُوِيَ ذَلِكَ عَنِ النَّبِيِّ صَلَّى اللَّهُ عَلَيْهِ وَسَلَّمَ. ورَوى عَبْدُ اللَّهِ بْنُ أُنَيْسٍ عَنِ النَّبِيِّ صَلَّى اللَّهُ عَلَيْهِ وَسَلَّمَ أَنَّهُ قالَ: ((يَحْشُرُ اللَّهُ الخَلائِقَ يَوْمَ القِيامَةِ عُراةً حُفاةً بُهْمًا فَيُنادِيهِمْ بِصَوْتٍ يَسْمَعُهُ مَنْ بَعُدَ، كَمَا يَسْمَعُهُ مَنْ قَرُبَ: أَنَا المَلِكُ، أَنَا الدَّيَّانُ)) رواه الأئِمَّةُ واسْتَشْهَدَ بِهِ البُخارِيُّ.

'Abd Allāh b. Mas'ūd said, *'When Allāh takallama through revelation, the inhabitants of the Heavens hear His Ṣawt'*. He narrated this from the Prophet ﷺ. Also, 'Abd Allāh b. Anīs reported that the Prophet ﷺ said: *'Allāh will gather the creatures on the Day of Judgement, naked, barefooted, uncircumcised having nothing with them. He will call to them with a Ṣawt, that those who are far as well as those who are near will hear, (saying:) 'I am al-Mālik, I am al-Dayyān.'* As narrated by the imāms, and quoted by al-Bukhārī.

وفي بعْضِ الآثارِ أَنَّ مُوسَى عَلَيْهِ السَّلامُ لَيْلَةَ رَأى النّارَ فَهالَتْهُ، وفَزِعَ مِنْها، فَنَاداهُ رَبُّهُ يا مُوسَى! فَأَجابَ سَريعًا اسْتِئْناسًا بِالصَّوْتِ، فَقَالَ: لَبَّيْكَ لَبَّيْكَ! أَسْمَعُ صَوْتَكَ ولا أَرَى مَكانَكَ، فَأَيْنَ أَنْتَ؟ فَقالَ: أَنا فَوْقَكَ، وَ أَمامَكَ، وعَنْ يَمِينِكَ، وعَنْ شِمَالِكَ، فَعَلِمَ أَنَّ هَذِهِ الصِّفَةَ لا تَنْبَغِي إِلَّا للَّهِ تَعالى. قالَ: كَذَلِكَ أَنْتَ يَا إِلَهِي! أَفَكَلامَكَ أَسْمَعُ أَمْ كَلامَ رَسولِكَ؟ قالَ: بَلْ كَلامِي يا مُوسَى.

In some narrations, it mentions that: *'one night Mūsā, peace upon him, saw the fire and it overthrew him, so he became frightened by it. Then his Lord called to him, 'O Mūsā!' So, he responded quickly, being familiar with the Ṣawt 'Here I am to serve you! Here I am! I hear Your Ṣawt but I do not see your place. Where are you?' He said, 'I am above you, and I am in front of you, on your left and on your right.' So, he realized that this attribute did not befit anyone except Allāh. He then said, 'You are just as You say, my Lord. Do I hear Your Kalām or the speech of one of Your Messengers? He said, 'No, rather My Kalām, O Mūsā.''*

[151] Qurān: 20:14

From the Attributes of Allāh is that He is *mutakalim*[152] with *Kalām*[153] that is pre-existent. He causes whomsoever He wills to hear it [yet, this does not mean that when one hears something that Allāh said, that He has just said it at that particular time. On the contrary, it means that He causes whoever He wills from amongst His creation to hear His *Kalām*]. **Mūsā, peace upon him, heard it from Him without a medium in between. Jibrīl, peace upon him, heard it, as well as whomsoever He permitted from His angels and messengers** [here the author establishes two important points. The first being that his *Kalām* is pre-existent, it has no beginning, just as the rest of His Attributes as the governing principle[154] dictates that: 'Allāh has no beginning, therefore His Attributes have no beginning'. The second being that His *Kalām* can be heard by whoever He chooses, without the need of a medium]. **He, the One free from all defects, *yukallimu*[155] to the believers in the Hereafter** [meaning, that they will hear his *Kalām*. It does not mean that He initiates new *Kalām* at that particular moment in time] **and they will speak to Him. And He will give permission to them, so that they will visit Him. Allāh, Exalted is He, says: *'and Allāh kallama*[156] *to Mūsā, with actual speech.'***[157] [meaning that it is actual kalām (*kalām* ḥaqīqī) which can be heard by His creation. This is contrary to the view that what people hear is the creation of speech (in something else created) brought about by Allāh. How this actual *Kalām* happens, and what the reality of it is or even how it sounds, is unknown and is consigned to the knowledge of Allah. There is however an accepted narration in which there is mention of a sound resembling a chain being dragged across a rock.[158] Yet, to understand from this that His *Kalām* makes this sound, or that these chains are His *Ṣawt*[159] is incorrect. It is merely understood from the narration that this sound is what the angels hear, and it is something that accompanies His actual *Kalām*] **And He, free from imperfections, says: *'He said, O Mūsā, I have chosen you above men by My Messages, and by my***

[152] Mutakalim can be translated as 'speaking'.

[153] Kalām can be translated as 'speech.

[154] It was mentioned previously that attributes are related to the essence of something that they are attributed to.

[155] Kallimu can be translated as '(he will) speak'.

[156] Kallama can be translated as '(he) spoke'.

[157] Qurān: 4:164

[158] Abū Dawūd in his *Sunan*, no. 4738.

[159] Ṣawt can be translated as 'voice' or 'sound' depending on the context.

***Kalām.*'**[160] [and this shows that His *Kalām* is actually audible, for what would be the advantage of Mūsā hearing the *Kalām* of Allāh, if it was just something that He created in a tree or in something else? If it was not His actual *Kalām*, there would be no difference between prophet Mūsā and a person who recites Qurān and through this act hears some of the *Kalām* of Allāh; as in both cases it would be related to something created, i.e. hearing His *Kalām* through the created sounds of the reciter, or hearing His *Kalām* through it being created in a tree. Therefore, the advantage of Mūsā over other men, was by means of him hearing and being directly addressed by His actual *Kalām*. This does not mean he was the only one who was preferred in this way, for the Prophet ﷺ did hear the *Kalām* of Allāh directly on particular occasions, and he ﷺ saw Allāh according to the relied upon position of the Ḥanbalī madhhab] **And He, free of imperfections, says: *'Allāh kallama to some of them.'*[161] Allāh, free of imperfections, says: *'It is not for any human being that Allāh yukallima to him unless by Revelation, or from behind a veil.'*[162] And Allāh, free of imperfections, says: *'And when he came to it, he was called by name: O Musa, Verily, I am your Lord...'*[163] Allāh, free of imperfections, also says: *'Verily, I am Allāh, None has the right to be worshipped except I, so worship me, and establish the Prayer for My remembrance.'*[164]** [indicating His *Kalām* is actual speech with actual words] **It is not permissible for anyone to say this** [i.e. this previously mentioned āyaḧ] **other than Allāh.**

'Abd Allāh b. Mas'ūd said, *'When Allāh takallama through revelation, the inhabitants of the Heavens hear His Ṣawt'*[165] [or a clanking sound like the dragging of steel chains. This 'clanking' sound is what they hear, and it is not necessarily what comes from Allāh. How would someone understand something from a clanking sound? This is not a language; therefore, it must be something other than His *Ṣawt*. When Allāh *kallama* with the Qurān and the inhabitants of the Heavens heard it, did they translate or convert it into Arabic? Certainly this is not the case, and it is in contradiction to what is mentioned in the Qurān,

---

[160] Qurān: 7:144

[161] Qurān: 2:253

[162] Qurān: 42:51

[163] Qurān: 20:11-12

[164] Qurān: 20:14

[165] 'Abd Allāh b. Aḥmad in his *Kitāb al-Sunnaḧ*, no. 536; and this particular wording is also transmitted by Abū Bakr al-Najād (d. 348H) in *al-Radd 'alā man Yaqūl al-Qurān Makhlūq*, no. 5 / al-Sijzī (d. 444H) in *Risālah ilā Ahl Zabīd*, p. 166. Other versions of this narration, with slightly different wordings, i.e. not containing the word '*His Ṣawt*', are transmitted o.a. by Abū Dawūd in his *Sunan*, no. 4738 / al-Dārimī in *al-Radd 'alā al-Jahmiyyaḧ*, no. 308 / and Ibn Khuzaymaḧ (d. 311H) in *Kitāb al-Tawhīd*, p. 350-357.

regarding it being in 'clear Arabic' ('arabiyyin mubīn). Therefore, this 'clanking' sound is not His *Ṣawt*)].' **He narrated this from the Prophet ﷺ. Also, 'Abd Allāh b. Unays reported that the Prophet ﷺ said: *'Allāh will gather the creatures on the Day of Judgement, naked, barefooted, uncircumcised having nothing with them. He will call to them with a Ṣawt, that those who are far as well as those who are near will hear, (saying:) 'I am al-Mālik*[166]*, I am al-Dayyān*[167]*.'*[168] As narrated by the imāms**[169]**, and quoted by al-Bukhārī.**[170] [From these aḥādīth one understands that Allāh has the Attribute of Kalām. It also points to another Attribute, namely His *Ṣawt*, and both are related to each other as the *Kalām* of Allāh is with a *Ṣawt (Kalām Allāh bi-Ṣawt)*. It is also understood from this that His *Kalām* is actual *Kalām* and that He has a Ṣawt that can be heard, although how it actually is or how one may hear it is unknown].

In some narrations, it mentions that [and this particular wording used by the author shows that the narration following it is weak[171], although it does not harm to cite such a narration to support the main idea concerning the *Kalām*, i.e. it being actual *Kalām* with a *Ṣawt* that can be heard. Still, it is redundant to do so because stronger evidences have already been presented]: ***'one night Mūās, peace upon him, saw the fire and it overthrew him, so he became frightened by it. Then his Lord called to him, 'O Mūās!' S,ohe responded quickly, being familiar with the Ṣawt, 'Here I am to serve you! Here I am! I hear Your Ṣawt but I do not see your place. Where are you?' He said, 'I am above you, and I am in front of you, on your left and on your right.' o, he realized that this attribute did not befit anyone except Allāh. He*** [i.e. Mūsā] ***then said, 'You are just as You say, my***

---

[166] Malik can be translated as 'king'.

[167] Dayān can be translated as 'recompencer'.

[168] Imām Aḥmad in his *Musnad*, no. 16042.

[169] Amongst others: Ibn Abū 'Āṣim (d. 287H) in *Kitāb al-Sunnah*, no. 514 / and al-Ḥākim (d. 405H) in *al-Mustadrak*, no. 8778; with a slightly different wording.

[170] *Ṣaḥīḥ al-Bukhārī*, bk. 97, ch. 32.

[171] At certain places in *al-Lum'ah*, and also in other books of 'aqīdah in general, the author cites weak (da'īf) aḥādīth to support or illustrate a particular issue. The citing of a weak ḥadīth does not necessarily mean that the specific issues is baseless if the particular weak ḥadīth was non-existent. In the majority of instances, when a weak ḥadīth is used it means that the meaning it conveys is at least correct. Therefore, these weak ḥadīth should not be dismissed, categorically, because they can convey correct meanings. It is also possible that a stronger ḥadīth was transmitted but not mentioned by the author (due to various reasons).

Lord. Do I hear Your Kalām or the speech of one of Your Messengers [i.e. angels]***? He said, 'No, rather My Kalām, OMūās.'***"[172]

[172] Imām Aḥmad in *Kitāb al-Zuhd*, no. 342, p. 54-56, narrates the complete story about prophet Mūsā; and it is from the Isra°iliyāt. Ibn Qudāmaȟ quotes only a small part of it; as did al- Sijzī in *Risālah ilā Ahl Zabīd*, p. 163.

THE QURĀN IS THE KALĀM OF ALLĀH

ومِنْ كَلامِ اللَّهِ سُبْحانَهُ: القُرْآنُ العَظيمُ، وهُوَ كِتابُ اللَّهِ المُبينُ، وحَبْلُهُ المَتينُ، وصِراطُهُ المُسْتَقيمُ، وتَنْزِيلُ رَبِّ العَالَمِينَ، نَزَلَ بِهِ الرُّوحُ الأمِينُ، عَلى قَلْبِ سَيِّدِ المرْسَلِين بِلِسانٍ عَرَبِيٍّ مُبِينٍ، مُنَزَّلٌ غَيْرُ مَخْلوقٍ، مِنْهُ بَدَأ و إلَيْهِ يَعُودُ.

From the Kalām of Allāh, is the Glorious Qurān. It is the clear Book of Allāh and His firm Rope. It is His Straight Path and the revelation of the Lord of the universe. The most honourable spirit descended with it to the heart of the best of the Messengers, in a clear Arabic language. It was revealed and not created. From Him it began and to Him it will return.

وهُوَ سُوَرٌ مُحْكَمَاتٌ، وآياتٌ بَيِّنَاتٌ، وحُرُوفٌ وكَلِماتٌ مَنْ قَرَأَهُ فَأَعْرَبَهُ فَلَهُ بِكُلِّ حَرْفٍ عَشْرُ حَسَناتٍ. لَهُ أَوَّلٌ وآخِرٌ، وأَجْزاءٌ وأَبْعاضٌ، مَتْلُوٌّ بِالأَلْسِنَةِ مَحْفوظٌ في الصُّدورِ مَسْمُوعٌ بَالآذانِ، مَكْتوبٌ في المصاحِفِ.

It consists of decisive ṣūrahs, clear āyāt, letters and words. Whoever recites it and does so properly, will have ten good deeds for every letter he recites. It has a beginning and an end, and it consists of specific sections and parts. It is that which is recited by the tongues, memorized in the hearts, listened to by the ears and written in the maṣāḥif.

فِيهِ مُحْكَمٌ ومُتَشابِهٌ، ونَاسِخٌ ومَنْسُوخٌ، وخاصٌّ وعامٌّ، وأمْرٌ ونَهْيٌ ﴿لا يَأْتِيهِ الْبَاطِلُ مِن بَيْنِ يَدَيْهِ وَلا مِنْ خَلْفِهِ تنزيلٌ مِنْ حَكِيمٍ حَمِيدٍ﴾، ﴿قُلْ لَّئِنِ اجْتَمَعَتِ الإِنسُ وَالْجِنُّ عَلَى أن يَأْتُواْ بِمِثْلِ هَذَا الْقُرْآنِ لاَ يَأْتُونَ بِمِثْلِهِ وَلَوْ كَانَ بَعْضُهُمْ لِبَعْضٍ ظَهِيرًا﴾

In it are āyāt which are muḥkam (clear) and āyāt which are mutashābiḥ (ambiguous), that which is abrogating and that which is abrogated, that which is specific and that which is general and that which contains obligation and that which contains prohibition. *'Falsehood cannot approach it from before it or behind. It is sent down by al-Ḥakīm, al-Ḥamīd.'*[173], *'Say; If mankind and jinn were*

[173] Qurān: 41:42

to gather together to produce the likes of this Qurān, they could not produce the likes thereof, even if they helped one another.'[174]

وهُوَ هَذَا الكِتابُ العَرَبيُّ الَّذي قالَ فِيهِ الذِينَ كَفَرُوا: ﴿لَن نُّؤْمِنَ بِهَذَا الْقُرْآنِ﴾، وقالَ بَعْضُهُم: ﴿ إِنْ هَذَا إِلا قَوْلُ الْبَشَرِ﴾، فَقالَ اللَّهُ سُبْحانَهُ: ﴿سَأُصْلِيهِ سَقَرَ﴾، وقالَ بَعْضُهُم: هُوَ شِعْرٌ. فَقالَ اللَّهُ تَعالى: ﴿وَمَا عَلَّمْنَاهُ الشِّعْرَ وَمَا يَنْبَغِي لَهُ إِنْ هُوَ إِلا ذِكْرٌ وَقُرْآنٌ مُبِينٌ﴾ فَلَمَّا نَفى اللَّهُ عَنْهُ أَنَّهُ شِعْرٌ وأَثْبَتَهُ قُرْآناً لَمْ يَبْقَ شُبْهَةٌ لِذِي لُبٍّ في أَنَّ القُرْآنَ هُوَ هَذا الكِتابُ العَرَبيُّ الَّذي هُوَ كَلِماتٌ، وحُرُوفٌ وآياتٌ؛ لِأَنَّ ما لَيْسَ كَذلِكَ لا يَقُولُ أَحَدٌ: إِنَّهُ شِعْرٌ.

This is the Arabic Book of which the disbelievers said concerning it: '*We will never believe in this Qurān.'*[175] *And some of them said: 'This is nothing but the word of a human being.'*[176] So, Allāh, free from imperfections, said: *'I will cast him into the Hellfire.'*[177] Some of them said that it was poetry, so, Allāh, Exalted is he, said: *'And We have not taught him poetry, nor it is suitable for him. This is only a reminder and a plain Qurān.'*[178] Thus, when Allāh denies that it is poetry and confirms that it is Qurān, there should not remain any doubt for the one possessing intellect, that the Qurān is that Arabic Book which is composed of words, letters and āyāt. This is because if it were not so, then they would not have claimed it was poetry.

وقالَ عَزَّ وجَلَ: ﴿وَ إِنْ كُنتُمْ فِي رَيْبٍ مِّمَّا نَزَّلْنَا عَلَى عَبْدِنَا فَأْتُوا بِسُورَةٍ مِّن مِّثْلِهِ وَادْعُوا شُهَدَاءَكُم مِّن دُونِ اللَّهِ﴾، ولا يَجُوزُ أَنْ يَتَحَدَّاهُمْ بالإِتْيانِ بِمِثْلِ ما لا يُدْرَى ما هُوَ ولا يُعْقَلُ.

Allāh, The Mighty and The Sublime, says: *'And if you are in doubt concerning what We have sent down to Our Slave, then produce a ṣūrah the like thereof and*

[174] Qurān: 17:88
[175] Qurān: 43:31
[176] Qurān: 74:25
[177] Qurān: 74:26
[178] Qurān: 36:69

call your witnesses besides Allāh.'[179] It is not right for Him to challenge them with producing something that they neither know nor understand.

وقالَ تَعالى: ﴿وَ إِذَا تُتْلَى عَلَيْهِمْ آيَاتُنَا بَيِّنَاتٍ قَالَ الَّذِينَ لا يَرْجُونَ لِقَاءَنَا ائْتِ بِقُرْآنٍ غَيْرِ هَذَا أَوْ بَدِّلْهُ قُلْ مَا يَكُونُ لِي أَنْ أُبَدِّلَهُ مِنْ تِلْقَاءِ نَفْسِي﴾، فَأَثْبَتَ أَنَّ القُرْآنَ هُوَ الآياتُ الَّتي تُتْلَى عَلَيْهِمْ. وقالَ تعالى: ﴿بَلْ هُوَ آيَاتٌ بَيِّنَاتٌ فِي صُدُورِ الَّذِينَ أُوتُوا الْعِلْمَ﴾

Allāh, Exalted is He, says; *'And when Our clear āyāt are recited unto them, those who not hope for the meeting with Us, say; Bring us a Qurān other than this, or change it.' Say; It is not for me to change it of my own accord. I only follow that which is revealed unto me.'*[180] This confirmed that the Qurān consists of āyāt, which are recited unto them. And He, Exalted is He, says: *'No, but they are clear āyāt that are preserved in the breasts of those who have been given knowledge.'*[181]

وقالَ تعالى: ﴿ إِنَّهُ لَقُرْآنٌ كَرِيمٌ * فِي كِتَابٍ مَكْنُونٍ * لا يَمَسُّهُ إِلا الْمُطَهَّرُونَ﴾، بَعْدَ أَنْ أَقْسَمَ عَلَى ذَلِكَ

And He, the Exalted, says after having sworn upon it: *'That is indeed an honourable Qurān. In a Book well-guarded, which none can touch, except the purified.'*[182]

وقالَ تَعالى: ﴿كهيعص﴾، ﴿حم * عسق﴾ ، وافْتَتَحَ تِسْعًا وعِشْرينَ سُورةً بِالحُروفِ المُقَطَّعَةِ. وقالَ النَّبِيُّ صَلَّى اللَّهُ عَلَيْهِ وَسَلَّمَ: ((مَنْ قَرَأَ القُرْآنَ فَأَعْرَبَهُ فَلَهُ بِكُلِّ حَرْفٍ مِنْهُ عَشْرُ حَسَنَاتٍ، وَمَنْ قَرَأَهُ وَلَحَنَ فِيهِ فَلَهُ بِكُلِّ حَرْفٍ حَسَنَةٌ))، حَديثٌ صَحيحٌ وقالَ عَلَيْهِ الصَّلاةُ والسَّلامُ: ((اقْرَؤُوا القُرْآنَ قَبْلَ أَنْ يَأْتِيَ قَوْمٌ يُقِيمُونَ حُرُوفَهُ إِقامَةَ السَّهْمِ لا يُجَاوِزُ تَرَاقِيَهُمْ يَتَعَجَّلُونَ أَجْرَهُ وَلا يَتَأَجَّلُونَهُ)). وقَالَ أَبُو بَكْرٍ وعُمَرُ رضيَ اللَّهُ عنهما

[179] Qurān: 2:23

[180] Qurān: 10:15

[181] Qurān: 29:49

[182] Qurān: 56:77-79

(إِعْرابُ القُرْآنِ أحَبُّ إِلَيْنا مِنْ حِفْظِ بَعْضِ حُرُوفِهِ). وقالَ عَلِيٌّ رَضِيَ اللَّهُ عَنْهُ: (مَنْ كَفَرَ بِحَرْفٍ مِنْهُ فَقَدْ كَفَرَ بِهِ كُلِّهُ).

And Allāh, Exalted is He, says: *'Kāf Ha Ya 'Ayn Ṣād.'*[183] And: *'Ḥa Mīm 'Āyn Sīn Qāf.'*[184] He begins twenty-nine ṣūrahs of the Qurān with individually separated letters. The Prophet ﷺ said in an authentic narration: *'Whoever recites the Qurān and recites it properly, there will be ten good deeds for him, for every letter from it. And whoever recites the Qurān and he recites it improperly, there will be one good deed for him for every letter.'* and this is an authentic ḥadīth. And he ﷺ said: *'Read the Qurān before there comes to you a people who will straighten its letters like an arrow is straightened; yet, it will not pass their throats. Their reward will be hastened and not postponed.'* Abū Bakr and 'Umar said: 'To make 'irāb of the Qurān is more beloved to us than to memorize some of its letters.' 'Alī said: 'Whoever disbelieves in one letter from it; then he has disbelieved in all of it.'

واتَّفَقَ المُسْلِمونَ عَلى عَدِّ سُوَرِ القُرْآنِ وآياتِهِ وكَلِماتِهِ وحُروفِهِ. ولا خِلافَ بَيْنَ المُسْلِمينَ في أنَّ مَنْ جَحَدَ مِنَ القُرْآنِ سُورَةً أوْ آيَةً أوْ كَلِمَةً أوْ حَرْفاً مُتَّفَقاً عَلَيْهِ أنَّهُ كافِرٌ، وفي هَذا حُجَّةٌ قاطِعَةٌ على أنَّهُ حُروفٌ.

The Muslims have agreed on the number of ṣūrahs, āyāt, words and letters of the Qurān. There is no disagreement amongst the Muslims concerning the disbelief of the one who denies a ṣūrah, āyah, word or letter from the Qurān, which has been agreed upon. In conclusion, this is conclusive proof that the Qurān consists of huroof.

Commentary: The Qurān is the Kalām of Allāh

From the *Kalām* of Allāh, is the Glorious Qurān [as mentioned in the previous section, Allāh is attributed with *Kalām*, and as is the case with Him and all of His Attributes, it follows that we do not have a full realisation of His *Kalām*. There are two important issues related to His *Kalām*. Firstly, the totality of Allāh's *Kalām* is pre-existent and someone being able to hear it depends upon His *Will*. Secondly, although we do not know everything about His *Kalām*, we can know for sure that the Qurān is from His *Kalām*; as mentioned by the author]. **It is the**

---

[183] Qurān: 19:1

[184] Qurān: 41:1

clear Book of Allāh and His firm Rope. It is His Straight Path and the revelation of the Lord of the universe. The most honourable spirit [i.e. Jibrīl] **descended with it to the heart of the best of the Messengers** [and creatures], **in a clear Arabic language** [therefore, all the general meanings of the Qurān are known]. **It was revealed and not created** [thus, Allāh did not create the Qurān, but *kallama* with it, and He does not need a tool to be able to speak]. **From Him it began and to Him it will return** [and the author is referring to an event that will happen before the Day of Judgement. At some point, the Qurān will be taken from the hearts of people and the maṣāḥif[185] and will return back to Allāh such that all the maṣāḥif will be left blank and no one will remember it by heart[186]].

It consists of decisive ṣūrahs, clear āyāt, letters and words [meaning, these ṣūrahs, āyāt and words are understandable, some in a specific way and some only in general. The words and letters are known in the Arabic language, and can they be looked up for example in a dictionary]. **Whoever recites it and does so properly** [meaning, with 'irāb], **will have ten good deeds for every letter he recites**[187] [understanding what one says is not a condition for receiving these good deeds as is apparent from the narrations. Merely reciting properly, without understanding, will reward one these good deeds. Something to this effect has been mentioned by Imām Aḥmad[188]]. **It has a beginning and an end, and it consists of specific sections and parts. It is that which is recited by the tongues** [thus, the Qurān that Allāh *takallama* with is the same Qurān that is recited by people. However, this does not mean that it can be said that the pronunciation

---

[185] The Musḥaf refers to the compiled written Qurān.

[186] A narration with this meaning has been transmitted by al-Dārimī in his *Sunan*, no. 3661, 3663: *"Recite the Qurān much before it is taken away.' They said, 'These maṣāḥif will be taken away! What about that which is (memorized) in men's hearts?' He said: 'Something will come and take it one night, and in the morning, they will wake up without it. They will forget the phrase 'lā ilāha ilā Allāh' and they will start to recite the sayings and poetry of the Jāhiliyyah. That is when the Word will be fulfilled against them."*

A similar narration has been transmitted by al-Ṭabarānī in *Mu'jam al-Kabīr*, no. 8698: *'This Qurān will most certainly be taken away from amongst you. He was asked: 'Oh, Abū 'Abd al-Raḥmān, how will it be taken away when it is so firmly rooted in our hearts and it is written in our maṣāḥif?' He said: 'Something will come to it at night, then there will be nothing left of it in people's hearts or in the musḥaf, and the next morning the people will be like animals.' Then he recited the āyah: 'And if We willed, We could surely, take away that which We have revealed to you. Then you would find no protector against Us in that respect'.'*

[187] Al-Tirmidhī in his *Sunan*, no. 2910: *'Whoever recites a letter from Allah's Book, then he receives the reward from it, and the reward of ten the like of it. I do not say that Alif Lam Mim is a letter, but Alif is a letter, Lam is a letter and Mim is a letter.'*

[188] Ibn al-Jawzī in *Manāqib al-Imām Aḥmad*, p. 583-584, and the source is al-Khallāl in *al-Majālis al-'Ashrah*, no. 50: 'Abd Allāh b. Aḥmad said: 'I heard my father saying: 'I saw the Lord of Might, Mighty and Majestic is He, in my sleep. I said: 'O Lord, what is the best thing that those who wish to get closer to you can do?' He said: 'To recite my word (Qurān).' I said: 'O Lord, with or without understanding it?' He said: 'Yes, with or without understanding.''.

of someone who recites it is the same as when Allāh *takallama* with it, as people pronounce and their pronunciation of it is created, and Allāh does not pronounce like this. Yet, the words people recite are from the *Kalām* of Allāh which is one of His Attributes], **memorized in the hearts, listened to by the ears and written in the maṣāḥif.**

In it are āyāt which are muḥkam (clear) and āyāt which are mutashābiḥ (ambiguous), that which is abrogating and that which is abrogated, that which is specific and that which is general and that which contains command and that which contains prohibition. ***'Falsehood cannot approach it from before it or behind. It is sent down by al-Ḥakīm[189], al-Ḥamīd[190-191]*** ***'Say; If mankind and jinn were to gather together to produce the likes of this Qurān, they could not produce the likes thereof, even if they helped one another.'***[192] [and this is the real miracle of the Qurān].

This is the Arabic Book of which the disbelievers said concerning it; ***'We will never believe in this Qurān.'***[193] **And some of them said:** ***' his is nothing but the word of a human being.''***[194] **So, Allāh, free from imperfections, said: 'I will cast him into the Hellfire.'**[195] **Some of them said that it was poetry, so, Allāh, Exalted is He, said:** ***'And We have not taught him*** [i.e. Prophet Muḥammad ﷺ] ***poetry, nor is i suitable for him. his is only a reminder and a plain Qurān.'***[196] **Thus, when Allāh denies that it is poetry and confirms that it is Qurān, there should not remain any doubt for the one possessing intellect, that the Qurān is that Arabic Book which is composed of words, letters, and āyāt. This is because if it were not so, then they** [i.e. the disbelievers] **would not have claimed it was poetry** [if it was in fact poetry, or something created, then the disbelievers would not have had a problem with it. They only claimed it was such because they objected to it being from Allāh, as a part of His *Kalām*. Consequently, Allāh refutes them by saying it is in fact Qurān from Allāh and not something created such as poetry].

Allāh, The Mighty and The Sublime says; ***'And if you*** [i.e. the disbelievers] ***are in doubt concerning what We have sent down to Our Slave*** [i.e. Muḥammad

---

[189] Ḥakīm can be translated as 'wise.

[190] Ḥamīd can be translated as 'one who is praised a lot'.

[191] Qurān: 41:42

[192] Qurān: 17:88

[193] Qurān: 43:31

[194] Qurān: 74:25

[195] Qurān: 74:26

[196] Qurān: 36: 69

ﷺ], *then produce a ṣūrah the like thereof and call your witnesses besides Allāh.'*[197] [indicating the real miracle of the Qurān is the inability to produce something or even a small part like it, which is understood and known to people] **It is not possible for Him to challenge them with producing something that they neither know nor understand** [it is not likely for Allāh to challenge human beings with producing something that is neither known or impossible to be understood by the intellect and herein lies the essence of the miracle. For, if one challenges another to do something oneself did, then it must be something that is known or understood by the other person. Otherwise, it is an not a challenge. Furthermore this proves that we can understand all of the Qurān although not necessarily every single word, and Allah's Attributes are from those words that are not necessarily understood, even though one can understand enough from them. An example of this is how we can generally understand from Allāh being *al-Khāliq*, that He created the world. Similarly, it is understood from His Attribute *Raḥmaḧ* that by it, people will go to Paradise or will be saved from the torment of Hell. Yet, the literal meanings and realities of these Attributes are unknown].

Allāh, Exalted is He, says; *'And when Our clear āyāt are recited unto them, those who do not hope for the meeting with Us, say; Bring us a Qurān other than this, or change it.' Say; It is not for me to change it on my own accord. I only follow that which is revealed unto me.'*[198] This confirmed that the Qurān consists of [amongst others, those] **āyāt, which are recited unto them** [meaning, the disbelievers, as they responded to parts of the Qurān being recited to them]. **And He, Exalted is He, says: *'No, but they are clear āyāt that are preserved in the breasts of those who have been given knowledge.'*[199]**

And He, the Exalted, says after having sworn upon it: *'That is indeed an honourable Qurān. In a Book well-guarded, which none can touch, except the purified.'*[200]

And Allāh, Exalted is He, says: *'Kāf Ha Ya 'Ayn Ṣād.'*[201] And: *'Ḥa Mīm 'Āyn Sīn Qāf.'*[202] He begins twenty-nine ṣūrahs of the Qurān with individually separated letters. The Prophet ﷺ said in an authentic narration: *'Whoever*

[197] Qurān: 2:23

[198] Qurān: 10:15

[199] Qurān: 29:49

[200] Qurān: 56:77-79

[201] Qurān: 19:1

[202] Qurān: 41:1

recites the Qurān and recites it properly, there will be ten good deeds for him, for every letter from it [and the letters are described as being from the Qurān. Consequently, the Ḥanābilaĥ hold that the *Kalām* of Allāh is with *Ṣawt* and ḥarf and they do nor base this on personal ijtihād, but rather because there is textual evidence (i.e. naṣṣ) which points to this fact]. ***And whoever recites the Qurān and he recites it improperly, there will be one good deed for him for every letter'***[203] ***and this is an authentic hadith.*** **And he ﷺ said:** ***'Read the Qurān before there comes to you a people who will straighten its letters like an arrow is straightened; yet, it will not pass their throats*** [meaning, they will recite it beautifully, yet what they recite will not reach their hearts and minds (i.e. they do not ponder over its meanings, nor are their hearts affected by it)]. ***Their reward will be hasten and not postpone.'***[204] **Abū Bakr and 'Umar said: 'To make 'irāb** [meaning, to recite it properly according to the rules of recitation] **of the Qurān is more beloved to us than to memorize some of its letters.'**[205] [indicating that good and correct recitation is better than mere memorisation]. **'Alī said: 'Whoever disbelieves in one letter from it; then he has disbelieved in all of it.'**[206] [and the one who denies a single letter of the Qurān becomes a disbeliever immediately. In addition to this, the differences in the authentic qirā°āt should not be used to say that the Qurān is not agreed upon. On the contrary, the statement that the Qurān is agreed upon means that all the authentic qirā°āt are agreed upon, and are mutawātir when it comes to their chains of transmission. The differences between the various qirā°āt originated from the Prophet ﷺ, who received these differences from Jibrīl who in turn received them from Allāh, free of any imperfections and Exalted is He. Furthermore, the different styles of recitation should not be mixed. If there is, for example, an obligatory madd

---

[203] Ibn Qudāmaĥ reported it with this specific wording. Al-Ṭabarānī (d. 260H) transmits in *al-Awsaṭ*, vol. 7, no. 7574, a ḥadīth with a slightly different wording, and perhaps this is the source of that which Ibn Qudāmaĥ transmits. Although, Ibn Qudāmaĥ said regarding it: 'authentic', It is classed as 'very weak' by other scholars. It must be pointed out that a similar, yet more reliable ḥadīth is transmitted by al-Tirmidhī; albeit with a slightly different wording (see. footnote. 184). Therefore, the meaning of the narration that Ibn Qudāmaĥ transmits seems to have a basis.

[204] Ibn Abī Shaybaĥ (d. 235H) in *al-Musnad*, no. 98, transmits a narration that comes close to the wording used by Ibn Qudāmaĥ. Similar narrations are also transmitted by Imām Aḥmad, *al- Musnad*, no. 14855 / Abū Dawūd, *al-Sunan*, no. 830; all, with variations in wording.

[205] Ibn al-Anbārī (d. 328H) in *Īḍāḥ al-Waqf wa al-Ibtidā*, vol. 1, no. 16, 22, transmits it with a slightly different wording.

[206] Ibn Qudāmaĥ reports it as a statement from 'Alī b. Abī Ṭālib. It is found as such in his *Manāziraĥ fī al-Qurān*, no. 36. Al-Harawī (d. 481H) reports a similar statement from Ibn Mas'ūd in *Dhamm al-Kalām wa Ahlih*, vol. 2, no. 186; as well as various other statements - to the same effect - from other than him. This version from Ibn Mas'ūd is also found in *al- Muṣannaf*, no. 16963 of 'Abd al-Razzāq (d. 211H). Ibn Abī Shaybaĥ (d. 235H) reports this statement in his *Muṣanaf*, vol. 10, no. 30715, from Ibrāhīm al-Nakha'ī (d. 96H). It appears such a statement was not uncommon from the Companions and their Followers.

(lengthening of the vowel) in one qirā°aḧ, it cannot be shortened according to another recitation; and if this is the case when it comes to tajwīd, then how about the cases of different letters, words or pronunciations? With regards to the inauthentic qirā°āt, they cannot be used for recitation in the Prayer unless they are mutawātir, nor can they be used for general recitation because they are not considered to be Qurān. According to the relied upon position of the Ḥanābilaḧ, they may be used in tafsīr, as a way of explanation and elucidation.]

The Muslims have agreed upon the number of ṣūrahs, āyāt, words and letters of the Qurān [and this is correct from the angle of each mode of recitation (qirā°aḧ) independently, as this depends on which mode is being used. Different modes may have different words, numbers of āyāt, and variations, yet these differences are insignificant and do not detract from the magnificence of the Qurān. There exist some narrations in which Ibn Mas'ūd stated that he did not include the last two ṣūrahs (Mu'awwidhatayn), i.e. ṣūrah al-Falaq and ṣūrah al-Nās, in his version of the Qurān, or that he erased them[207]. However, 'not including' is not synonymous with, or understood as, him disagreeing with them being from the Qurān. Regarding the narration which states that he 'erased' them, it is shādhdh (anomalous), and contradicts that which is established through mutawātir narrations]. **There is no disagreement amongst the Muslims concerning the disbelief of the one who denies a ṣūrah, āyaḧ, word or letter from the Qurān, which has been agreed upon. In conclusion, this is conclusive proof that the Qurān is made of huroof.**

[207] Aḥmad in his *Musnad*, no. 21186, 21188.

والمؤْمِنونَ يَرَوْنَ رَبَّهُمْ فِي الآخِرَةِ بِأَبْصارِهِم، ويَزُورُونَهُ، ويُكَلِّمُهُم ويُكَلِّمُونَهُ، قالَ اللَّهُ تَعالى: ﴿وُجُوهٌ يَوْمَئِذٍ نَاضِرَةٌ * إِلَى رَبِّهَا نَاظِرَةٌ﴾.

The believers will see their Lord in the Hereafter with their own eyes and they will visit Him. He will speak to them and they will speak to Him. Allāh, Exalted is He, says: *'(Some) faces on the day will be shiny and radiant. Looking at their Lord.'*[208]

وقالَ تَعالى: ﴿كَلا إِنَّهُمْ عَنْ رَبِّهِمْ يَوْمَئِذٍ لَمَحْجُوبُونَ﴾، فَلَمَّا حَجَبَ أُولَئِكَ في حالِ السُّخْطِ دَلَّ عَلى أَنَّ المُؤْمِنينَ يَرَوْنَهُ في حالِ الرِّضَى، و إِلَّا لَمْ يَكُنْ بَيْنَهُمَا فَرْقٌ.

And, Exalted is He, says: *"Nay! Surely, they will be veiled from seeing their Lord that Day."*[209]209 If Allāh is screened from these people during a state in which they are in discontentment, then this indicates that the believers will see Him while being in (the opposite); a state of pleasure. If this were not so, there would be no distinction between the two.

وقالَ النَّبِيُّ صَلَّى اللَّهُ عَلَيْهِ وَسَلَّمَ: ((إِنَّكُمْ سَتَرَوْنَ رَبَّكُمْ كَمَا تَرَوْنَ هَذَا الْقَمَرَ، لا تُضَامّونَ في رُؤْيَتِهِ)). حَديثٌ صَحيحٌ مُتَّفَقٌ عَليْهِ. وهَذا تَشْبيهٌ لِلرُّؤْيَةِ بِالرُّؤْيَةِ لا لِلمَرْئيِّ بِالمرْئيِّ، فَإِنَّ اللَّهَ تَعالى لا شَبيهَ لَهُ ولا نَظيرَ.

The Prophet ﷺ said: *'Indeed, you will see your Lord, just as you see this moon. There is no difficulty in your seeing it.'* The ḥadīth is authentic and agreed upon. This statement is a comparison between one manner of seeing and another manner of seeing. It is not a comparison between what is being seen and something else that is being seen, for indeed Allāh has neither comparisons nor equals.

---

[208] Qurān: 75:22-23

[209] Qurān: 83:15

The believers will see their Lord in the Hereafter with their own eyes[210] **and they will visit Him. He will speak to them and they will speak to Him. Allāh, Exalted is He, says: *'(Some) faces on the day will be shiny and radiant. Looking at their Lord.'***[211]

And, Exalted is He, says: *"Nay! Surely, they* [i.e. the evil-doers] ***will be veiled from seeing their Lord that Day."***[212] **If Allāh is screened from these people** [i.e. the evil-doers] **during a state in which they are in discontentment, then this indicates that the believers will see Him while being in (the opposite); a state of pleasure** [and as a reward]. **If this were not so, there would be no distinction between the two** [meaning, if this was the case, the believers and the disbelievers would be the same in this regard, because they would both not see their Lord. And if this was so, why would 'not seeing Him' be expressed as a punishment? This logical evidence shows that 'not seeing Him' is a punishment, and means that 'seeing Him' is due to believers being rewarded].

The Prophet ﷺ said: *'Indeed, you will see your Lord, just as you see this moon. There is no difficulty in your seeing it.'*[213] **The ḥadīth is authentic and agreed upon. This statement is a comparison between one manner of seeing and another manner of seeing. It is not a comparison between what is being seen and something else that is being seen, for indeed Allāh has neither comparisons nor equals** [Allāh will be seen very clearly, but this does not mean nor necessitate Him being seen as He is in reality. For, everything that can be seen in this world, is not necessarily seen as it actually is in reality. And when something in this world is seen, as it is in reality, it is not necessarily fully grasped nor understood in its totality.

---

[210] With regards to the seeing of Allāh by the believers, some related issues include:

1. Can Allāh be seen in this world? The Ḥanābilaĥ say that He cannot be seen in this world, as is apparent from the story of Mūsā.
2. Did the Prophet see Allāh during the nightly journey and heavenly ascent? According to the relied upon position of the Madhhab, he did see Allāh with his eyes, and not as some say: 'with his heart'.
3. Can one see Allāh in a dream? According to the Ḥanābilaĥ one can see Allāh in a dream; yet, one cannot see Him as He actually is. This is apparent from the dream of Imām Aḥmad in which he saw Allāh; and it has preceded, and similar narrations are transmitted from other scholars of the Salaf.

[211] Qurān: 75:22-23

[212] Qurān: 83:15

[213] Imām Aḥmad, *al-Musnad*, no. 19190 / Al-Bukhārī, no. 573 / Muslim, no. 633.

The notion that Allah will be seen should not be objected to by claiming it is erroneous because it means one will be able to realise everything about Allāh, and see Him how he actually is. This line of thought is incorrect, for saying that Allāh will be seen, does not necessitate the above conclusion of the objector. Man is a part of creation, thus created and newly occurring (ḥādith), while Allāh is pre-existent. Mankind moving from this world to the next does not bring about a change in this origin. Consequently, man's knowledge will always be restricted and limited and will never be able to comprehend all things or have access to ultimate knowledge i.e. Allāh's *'Ilm*. Therefore, it will never be possible to see Allāh as He is in reality, for this requires ultimate knowledge which cannot be attained by His creation.

With regards to the seeing of Allāh, the Exalted, (by His creation), it is impossible according to the Mu'tazilaḧ, as Allāh does not exist in a direction for this is something related to bodies (i.e. created beings). However, the Ḥanābilaḧ say that seeing Allāh does not necessarily mean that 'the seeing' is in a specific direction. As is known, the event is authentically narrated from the Prophet ﷺ, and the Ḥanābilaḧ believe in it as such. How this 'seeing of Allāh' will take place is something man should not concern himself with, as it is related to Allāh and He is not confined nor is He related to limits or directions as opposed to His creation which is confined to such things].

THE QAḌĀ° (DIVINE DECREE) AND QADAR (PREORDAINMENT)

ومِنْ صِفاتِ اللّهِ تَعالى أَنَّهُ الفَعَّالُ لِما يُرِيدُ، لا يَكُونُ شَيءٌ إلَّا بِإرادَتِهِ، وَلا يَخْرُجُ شَيءٌ عَن مَشِيئَتِهِ، وَلَيْسَ في العالَمِ شيْءٌ يَخْرُجُ عَن تَقْدِيرِهِ، وَلا يَصْدُرُ إلَّا عَن تدْبِيرِهِ، ولا مَحِيدَ عَن القَدَرِ المَقْدورِ، ولا يَتَجاوَزُ ما خُطَّ لَهُ في اللَّوْحِ المَسْطورِ، أرادَ ما العالَمُ فاعِلوهُ، وَلَوْ عَصَمَهُمْ لَمَا خالَفوهُ، وَلَوْ شاءَ أنْ يُطِيعُوهُ جَمِيعًا لَأَطاعُوهُ، خَلَقَ الخَلْقَ وأفْعالَهُمْ، وقَدَّرَ أرْزاقَهُمْ وآجالَهُمْ، يَهْدِي مَنْ يَشاءُ بِرَحْمَتِهِ، وَيُضِلُّ مَنْ يَشاءُ بِحِكْمَتِهِ، قالَ اللّهُ تعالى: ﴿لا يُسْأَلُ عَمَّا يَفْعَلُ وَهُمْ يُسْأَلُونَ﴾

From the Attributes of Allāh, is that He does whatever He wants. Nothing comes to pass, except by His *Irādah* and nothing escapes His *Mashī°ah*. There is nothing in this world that escapes from His qadar (preordainment) and nothing comes to pass except with His administration. No one can escape what has been written for him in the Preserved Tablet (al-lawḥ al-masṭūr or al-lawḥ al-maḥfuẓ). He wills all that the creation does. Had He made them infallible, they would not disobey Him, and had He willed that they all obey Him, then they would surely obey Him. He created the creation and their actions and He determined their provisions and life-spans. He guides whom He wills by His *Ḥikmah*. Allāh, Exalted is He, says: *'He cannot be questioned as to what He does, while they will be questioned.'*[214]

وقالَ اللّهُ تَعالى: ﴿ إِنَّا كُلَّ شَيْءٍ خَلَقْنَاهُ بِقَدَرٍ﴾، وقالَ تَعالى: ﴿وَخَلَقَ كُلَّ شَيْءٍ فَقَدَّرَهُ تَقْدِيرًا﴾، وقالَ تَعالى: ﴿مَا أَصَابَ مِنْ مُصِيبَةٍ فِي الأَرْضِ وَلا فِي أَنْفُسِكُمْ إلا فِي كِتَابٍ مِنْ قَبْلِ أَنْ نَبْرَأَهَا﴾، وقالَ تَعالى: ﴿فَمَنْ يُرِدْ اللّهُ أَنْ يَهْدِيَهُ يَشْرَحْ صَدْرَهُ لِلإِسْلامِ وَمَنْ يُرِدْ أَنْ يُضِلَّهُ يَجْعَلْ صَدْرَهُ ضَيِّقًا حَرَجًا﴾.

Allāh, Exalted is He, says: *'Verily, We have created all things with qadar.'*[215] And He, the Exalted, says: *'He has created everything; and has measured it*

[214] Qurān: 21:23

[215] Qurān: 54:49

exactly according to its due measurements.'[216] Also He, the Exalted, says: *'No calamity befalls on the earth or in yourselves, except that it is in a book; before We bring it into existence.'*[217] And He, the Exalted, says: *'Whoever Allāh wills to guide, he opens his breast to Islām. And whoever He wills to send astray, he makes his breast closed and constricted.'*[218]

وروى ابْنُ عُمَرَ أنَّ جِبْرِيلَ عَلَيْهِ السَّلامُ قالَ لِلنَّبِيِّ صَلَّى اللَّهُ عَلَيْهِ وَسَلَّمَ: ما الإِيمانُ قالَ: ((أنْ تُؤْمِنَ بِاللَّهِ وَمَلائِكَتِهِ وَكُتُبِهِ وَرُسُلِهِ وَاليَوْمِ الآخِرِ، وبِالْقَدَرِ خَيْرِهِ وَشَرِّهِ))، فَقالَ جِبْرِيلُ: صَدَقْتَ. انْفَرَدَ مُسْلِمٌ بِإِخْراجِهِ. وقالَ النَّبِيُّ صَلَّى اللَّهُ عَلَيْهِ وَسَلَّمَ: ((آمَنْتُ بِالقَدَرِ خَيْرِهِ وَشَرِّهِ، وَحُلْوِهِ وَمُرِّهِ)). ومِنْ دُعَاءِ النَّبِيِّ صَلَّى اللَّهُ عَلَيْهِ وَسَلَّمَ الَّذي عَلَّمَهُ الحَسَنَ بْنَ عَلِيٍّ يَدْعُو بِهِ في قُنُوتِ الوِتْرِ: ((وقِنِي شَرَّ مَا قَضَيْتَ)).

Ibn 'Umar reported that Jibrīl the Prophet ﷺ what imān was, so he responded: *''To Believe in Allāh, His Angels, His Books, His Messengers, the Last Day and the qadar, the good of it and the bad of it.' So, Jibrīl told him ﷺ: 'You have spoken truthfully.''*[219] as narrated by Muslim. And the Prophet ﷺ said: *'I believe in the qadar, the good of it and the bad of it, the sweet of it and the bitter of it.'*[220] One of the supplications that the Prophet ﷺ taught al-Ḥasan b. 'Alī, and which he himself used to supplicate with during the qunūt of witr was: *'And save me from the bad of what You have ordained.'*[221]

ولاَ نَجْعَلُ قَضاءَ اللَّهِ وقَدَرَهُ حُجَّةً لَنا في تَرْكِ أوامِرِهِ وارْتِكابِ نَوَاهِيهِ، بَلْ يَجِبُ أنْ نُؤْمِنَ ونَعْلَمَ أنَّ للَّهِ الحُجَّةَ عَلَيْنا بِإِنْزالِ الكُتُبِ، وبَعْثَةِ الرُّسُلِ، قالَ اللَّهُ تَعالى: ﴿لِئَلا يَكُونَ لِلنَّاسِ عَلَى اللَّهِ حُجَّةٌ بَعْدَ الرُّسُلِ﴾.

We do not use the qaḍā° (Divine decree) of Allāh and His qadar as an excuse for us to abandon following His commandments or failing to observe His prohibitions. On the contrary, we are obligated to believe in (it) and know that

---

[216] Qurān: 25:2

[217] Qurān: 57:22

[218] Qurān: 6:125

[219] Al-Bukhārī, no. 50 / Muslim, no. 8.

[220] Al-Ḥākim in *Ma'rifah 'Ulūm al-Ḥadīth*, no. 60, and it is 'weak'. Although, the meaning is established by the preceding narrations of al-Bukhārī and Muslim.

[221] Abū Dawūd, no. 1425 / Al-Tirmidhī, no. 464.

Allāh has established proof against us by revealing the Scriptures and sending the Messengers. Allāh, Exalted is He, says: *'In order that mankind shall have no excuses against Allāh after the Messengers.'*[222]

ونَعْلَمُ أنَّ اللَّهَ سُبْحَانَهُ ما أمَرَ ونَهى إلَّا المُسْتَطِيعَ لِلْفِعْلِ والتَّرْكِ، وأنَّهُ لَمْ يُجْبِرْ أحَداً على مَعْصِيَةٍ، ولا اضْطَرَّهُ إلى تَرْكِ طَاعَةٍ، وقالَ اللَّهُ تعالى: ﴿لا يُكَلِّفُ اللَّهُ نَفْسًا إلا وُسْعَهَا﴾، وقالَ تَعالى: ﴿فَاتَّقُوا اللَّهَ مَا اسْتَطَعْتُمْ﴾

We know that Allāh, the One free of imperfections, did not command or forbid anyone, except the one who is capable to do what is commended or avoid what is forbidden. He did not compel anyone to commit acts of disobedience (to Him) nor has He forced anyone to abandon obedience to Him. Allāh, Exalted is He, says: *'Allāh has not given any soul a responsibility, except that He has given it the ability (to carry it out).'*[223] And He, the Exalted, says: *'So fear Allāh as much as you are able.'*[224]

وقالَ تَعالى: ﴿الْيَوْمَ تُجْزَى كُلُّ نَفْسٍ بِمَا كَسَبَتْ لا ظُلْمَ الْيَوْمَ﴾. فَدَلَّ عَلى أنَّ لِلْعَبْدِ فِعْلا وكَسْبًا يُجْزَى عَلى حَسَنِهِ بِالثَّوَابِ، وعَلى سَيِّئِهِ بِالعِقابِ، وهُوَ واقِعٌ بِقَضاءِ اللَّهِ وقَدَرِهِ.

And He, the Exalted, says: *'This Day every person will be recompensed for what he earned. There will be no injustice (upon anybody in their judgement) on that Day.'*[225] This indicated that every servant possesses actions and earnings; he will be recompensed for his good deeds with reward and for his bad deeds with punishment. This will occur by the qaḍā° of Allāh and His qadar.

Commentary: The Qaḍā (Divine Decree) and Qadar (Preordainment)

From the Attributes of Allāh, is that He does whatever He wants. Nothing comes to pass, except by His *Irādah*[226] and nothing escapes His *Mashī°ah*[227]. There is nothing in this world that escapes from His qadar (preordainment) and

[222] Qurān: 4:165

[223] Qurān: 2:286

[224] Qurān: 64:16

[225] Qurān: 40:17

[226] Irādah can be translated as the 'desire (to do something)'.

[227] Mashī°ah can be translated as 'will'.

nothing comes to pass except with His administration. No one can escape what has been written for him in the Preserved Tablet (al-lawḥ al-masṭūr or al-lawḥ al- maḥfuẓ) [at this point it is appropriate to mention that the scholars discussed and differentiated between two things: 1) Allāh's *'Ilm* that such-and-such will happen, and 2) His Divine Decree that such-and- such a thing will happen.

With regards to preordainment, there is a ḥadīth which states that it may be possible for a supplication to alter the preordainment of Allāh.[228] A question arises regarding how this can be understood. It must be known that sometimes the qaḍā° and qadar are written (on the preserved tablet) in a particular way, yet Allāh knows it will change. Therefore, it appears that in essence there are two types of qadar: 1) a type that will never be changed, and 2) a type that can change. It must be stressed that this does not mean His *'Ilm* changes from a state of not- knowing or ignorance to knowing, when a particular event occurs. Or, that He knew something and then what He knew changed. Allāh is far exalted above this. His *'Ilm* is absolute in that He knows everything in detail before and as it occurs, and even if something, by His will, did not occur, He knows what would have happened if it did occur. His 'Ilm is nothing like our knowledge, which is related to our senses and is in fact fallible. For example, if someone is in a desert and sees water from a distance, only to realise later when moving closer that there was no water. Allah's *'Ilm* is not like this, He does not make mistakes in His *'Ilm*, nor does He learn new things as events unfold; meaning His *'Ilm* does not update. Returning to the type of qadar that may change, that may be written in al-lawḥ al-maḥfuẓ or may be given to some angels, such as the angel of Death. This angel knew what was in the qadar of prophet Mūsā, yet when he went to Mūsā he could not take his soul, and this indicates that there is another preordainment according to Allāh and this took the form of the choice that was given to prophet Mūsā by which he was allowed to pass his hand over the back of an ox, and to live one extra year for every hair that he touched on the ox's back.

In summary, there is one type of qaḍā° and two types of qadar. One should also know that with regards to the lawḥ al-maḥfuẓ; not everything that will happen has been written in it, as this would imply that something created is able to contain and limit one of Allāh's Attributes, in this case His *'Ilm*, which is

---

[228] Al-Tirmidhī in his *Sunan*, no. 2139: *'Nothing turns back the Decree except supplication, and nothing increases the life-span except righteousness.'* Also, al-Bukhārī, no. 2067, and Muslim, no. 2557, both transmit a ḥadīth in which it states that keeping good relations with one's family will have one's provision and life extended, which may also indicate the preordainment being changed.

impossible]. **He wills all that the creation does** [e.g. He wills that someone goes on a vacation, or that a baby cries, or that someone's car is in a good or bad state, or that someone gets sick or dies. For this reason, the great Ḥanbalī scholar al-Kalwadhānī (d. 510H) says, in a beautiful poem: 'if Allāh did not will something, yet that thing happened; it would be a deficiency (in Him)'[229], as this would result in questioning Him as a God. For, how can He not will something yet it still happens, and vice versa. Allāh is far removed from this type of deficiency. This erroneous position was held by the Mu'tazilah who stated that people create their own evil actions and that these are not willed by Allāh. We seek refuge with Allāh from this type of speech]. **Had He made them infallible, they would not disobey Him, and had He willed that they all obey Him, then they would surely obey Him. He created the creation and their actions and He determined their provisions and life-spans. He guides whom He wills by His *ḥikmah*[230]. Allāh, Exalted is He, says: *'He cannot be questioned as to what He does, while they will be questioned.'*[231]** [therefore, one may not question Allāh's decisions and determinations, by saying 'why did Allāh decide to do so-and-so'. However, it is permissible to ask why a certain thing happened. Regarding the permissible type of questions, it must be pointed out that in relation to the issue of cause and effect, there is a difference between the 'metaphorical reason' and the 'real reason'. Reasons, other than 'Allah willed it' that may be given in response to the question of why something happened, are only of a metaphoric nature, however in all cases and in reality, the real reason is always that is was the will of Allāh. For example, when someone is sick and takes medication to cure him or herself, the medication that is taken is the metaphorical reason, while the real reason for the cure is in fact and reality that Allāh cures. In the same way, it is in reality not the fire that burns, but Allāh that burns, and it is not the knife that cuts, but Allāh that cuts. Therefore, the knife may be as sharp as it can be, it will not cut anything as long as Allāh does not will it to cut. It would however be very confusing and chaotic for people if fire randomly burned or did not burn, or a very sharp knife cuts at one time yet is not able to cut at other times, and so Allāh created and assigned patterns in these things, and this is from the Sunnah of Allāh (i.e. His way or His pattern) in His created universe. Allāh said in the Qurān that His Sunnah is not changeable[232]. So, fire will always (or as expected) burn, and a sharp knife will always (or as expected) cut. If there is an exception, it may be

---

[229] Al-Kalwadhānī, *al-Qaṣīdah al-Dāliyyah*, line 29.

[230] Ḥikmah can be translated as 'wisdom'.

[231] Qurān: 21:23

[232] See ṣūrah Fāṭir (Qurān: 35:43): *'but you will not find any alteration in the way of Allāh...'*.

called a miracle, such as when Allāh ordered the fire to be gentle to prophet Ibrāhīm, and it did not burn him when he was cast into it as was mentioned in the Qurān[233].

Lastly, with regards to things that Allāh willed to happen, the Ḥanābilaḧ state that not all of His actions necessitate benefit of some sort. In this the Ḥanābilaḧ again opposed the Mu'tazilaḧ, who stated that Allāh is obligated to do the best or the most beneficial thing. On the contrary, it is as the author mentioned, Allāh does whatever He wants]. **Allāh, Exalted is He, says: *'Verily, We have created all things with qadar.'*[234] And He, the Exalted, says: *'He has created everything; and has measured it exactly according to its due measurements.'*[235]** [and only Allāh knows its measurements, for they are His measurements. The measurements and standards other than His are not taken into consideration. Some of the measurements of Allāh are known to certain degrees and can be utilised by His creation, such as His sharī'aḧ. Yet, the knowledge of His measurements is extremely limited] **Also He, the Exalted, says: *'No calamity befalls on the earth or in yourselves, except that it is in a book; before We bring it into existence.'*[236] And He, the Exalted, says: *'Whoever Allāh wills to guide, he opens his heart to Islām. And whoever He wills to send astray, he makes his breast closed and constricted.'*[237]**

Ibn 'Umar reported that Jibrīl asked the Prophet ﷺ what imān (faith) was, so he responded: *"To Believe in Allāh, His Angels, His Books, His Messengers, The Last Day and the qadar, the good of it and the bad of it.' So, Jibrīl told him ﷺ: 'You have spoken truthfully."*[238] as narrated by Muslim. And the Prophet ﷺ said: *'I believe in the qadar, the good of it and the bad of it, the sweet of it and the bitter of it.'*[239] One of the supplications that the Prophet ﷺ taught al-Ḥasan b. 'Alī (d. 51H), and which he himself used to supplicate with during the qunūt of witr was: *'And save me from the bad of what You have ordained.'*[240]

---

[233] See ṣūrah al-Anbiyā° (Qurān: 21:69): *'O fire! be coolness and safety upon Abraham...'*.

[234] Qurān: 54:49

[235] Qurān: 25:2

[236] Qurān: 57:22

[237] Qurān: 6:125

[238] Imām Aḥmad, *al-Musnad*, no. 191 / Al-Bukhārī, no. 50 / Muslim, no. 8.

[239] al-Ḥākim in *Ma'rifaḧ 'Ulūm al-Ḥadīth*, no. 60 / al-Ṭabarānī in *al-Mu'jam al-Kabīr*, no. 13581; it is 'weak'. Although, the meaning has a basis in the preceding narrations.

[240] Imām Aḥmad, *al-Musnad*, no. 1717 / Abū Dawūd, no. 1425 / Al-Tirmidhī, no. 464.

We do not use the qaḍā° (Divine Decree) of Allāh and His qadar as an excuse for us to abandon following His commandments [by saying, for example, Allāh willed that I did not pray 'Asr] **or failing to observe His prohibitions** [by saying, for example, Allāh willed that I commit this sin]. **On the contrary, we are obligated to believe in (it) and know that Allāh has established proof against us by revealing the Scriptures and sending the Messengers. Allāh, Exalted is He, says: *'In order that mankind shall have no excuses against Allāh after the Messengers.'***

We know that Allāh, the One free of imperfections, did not command or forbid anyone, except the one who is capable to do what is commanded or avoid what is forbidden. He did not compel anyone to commit acts of disobedience (to Him) nor has He forced anyone to abandon obedience to Him[241]. Allāh, Exalted is He, says: *'Allāh has not given any soul a responsibility, except that He has given it the ability (to carry it out).'*[242] And He, the Exalted, says: *'So fear Allāh as much as you are able.'*[243]

And He, the Exalted, says: *'This Day every person will be recompensed for what he earned. There will be no injustice (upon anybody in their judgement) on that Day.'*[244] This indicates that every servant possesses actions [meaning, one can do things according to one's choice. Therefore, one cannot say 'I did not do, but, Allāh did'. Of course, ultimately it was Allāh's doing, but according to ones doing and choice[245]] **and earnings** [meaning, one deserved a particular thing to happen according to his action]; **he will be recompensed for his good deeds**

---

[241] It can be mentioned here that the *Irādah* of Allāh is of two types: 1) universal *Irādah (kawnī)* and legislative *Irādah (shar'ī)*. The difference between both types is that the former necessitates that what is decreed by Allāh will occur, yet it does not necessarily mean that it is something beloved to Him. While the later type is that which is desired and loved by Allāh, yet this does not mean that it will necessarily occur. To give an example of the universal *Irādah* would be His saying: *'And whoever Allāh desires (i.e. wills) to guide, He opens his breast to Islām. And whoever He desires (i.e. wills) to send astray, He makes his breast closed and constricted'* (Qurān: 6:125). Or, the fact that He created Shaytān, yet He hates him (i.e. Shaytān). An example of the legislative type would be His saying: *'Allāh desires (i.e. loves) to accept your repentance'* (Qurān 4:27). Him desiring this repentance, does not necessitates that everybody repents, for people may or may not repent. Likewise, his command to pray, yet, people may or may not pray based on their obedience or disobedience.

[242] Qurān: 2:286

[243] Qurān: 64:16

[244] Qurān: 40:17

[245] It must be stressed that this does not mean Allāh only acted after or at the same time one made the choice to act. On the contrary, Allāh already knows the choices and doings of every person before they choose and do it.

with reward and for his bad deeds with punishment. This will occur by the qaḍā° of Allāh and His Qadar.

والإيمانُ قَوْلٌ بِاللِّسانِ وعَمَلٌ بِالأَرْكانِ وعَقْدٌ بِالجَنَانِ، يَزِيدُ بِالطَّاعَةِ ويَنْقُصُ بِالعِصْيانِ قالَ اللَّهُ تَعالى: ﴿وَمَا أُمِرُوا إِلا لِيَعْبُدُوا اللَّهَ مُخْلِصِينَ لَهُ الدِّينَ حُنَفَاءَ وَيُقِيمُوا الصَّلاةَ وَيُؤْتُوا الزَّكَاةَ وَذَلِكَ دِينُ الْقَيِّمَةِ﴾، فَجَعَلَ عِبادَةَ اللَّهِ تَعالى و إِخْلاصَ القَلْبِ، و إِقامَ الصَّلاةِ، و إِيتاءَ الزَّكاةِ، كُلَّهُ مِنَ الدِّينِ

Imān (faith) is a statement on the tongue, an action of the limbs and belief in the heart. It increases with obedience and decreases with disobedience. Allāh, the Exalted, says: *'And they were commanded not, except that they should worship Allāh alone, making the Religion sincere to Him, and establish the Prayer, and give the Zakāt, and that is the right religion.'*[246] So, He made the worship of Allāh the Exalted, the sincerity of the heart, the establishment of prayer and the giving of Zakāh, all as being from the Religion.

وقالَ رَسولُ اللَّهِ صَلَّى اللَّهُ عَلَيْهِ وَسَلَّمَ: ((الإِيمَانُ بِضْعٌ وَسَبْعُونَ شُعْبَةً، أَعْلاهَا شَهَادَةُ أَنْ لاَ إِلَهَ إِلَّا اللَّه، وَ أَدْنَاهَا إِمَاطَةُ الأَذَى عَنِ الطَّرِيقِ)). فَجَعَلَ القَوْلَ والعَمَلَ مِنَ الإِيمانِ وقالَ تَعالى: ﴿فَزَادَهُمْ إِيمَانًا﴾، وقالَ: ﴿لِيَزْدَادُوا إِيمَانًا﴾. وقالَ رَسولُ اللَّهِ صَلَّى اللَّهُ عَلَيْهِ وَسَلَّمَ: ((يَخْرُجُ مِنَ النَّارِ مَنْ قالَ: لا إِلَهَ إِلَّا اللَّهُ. وَفِي قَلْبِهِ مِثْقالُ بُرَّةٍ أَوْ خَرْدَلَةٍ أَوْ ذَرَّةٍ مِنَ الإِيمانِ)) فَجَعَلَهُ مُتَفاضِلاً.

The Messenger of Allāh ﷺ said: *'Imān consists of more than seventy branches. The highest of them is to testify that: 'None has the right to be worshipped but Allāh'. And the lowest of them is removing a harmful object from the road.'* The Prophet ﷺ made speech and action part of Imān. Allāh, the Exalted, says: *'it has increased their imān'*[247] And He says: *'In order that may grow more in imān.'*[248] The Messenger of Allāh ﷺ said: *'Whoever says, 'None has the right to be worshipped but Allāh' and he has in his heart imān, the weight of a wheat grain,*

[246] Qurān: 98:5

[247] Qurān: 9:124

[248] Qurān: 48:4

or a mustard seed or an atom, will be extracted from the Hellfire.' Therefore, he made it of different levels.

Commentary: The Reality of Imān

Imān (faith) is a statement on the tongue, an action of the limbs and belief in the heart [for the Ḥanābilah imān is threefold: speech, actions and belief. Yet, it must be pointed out that imān does not rely on three pillars. In essence its pillars are the belief in the heart and the uttering of the testimony of faith (shahādah), as long as there is nothing that prevents one from saying it. Furthermore, the discussion concerning actions being a pillar of imān, meaning one becomes a disbeliever unless one performs actions, is an innovation in itself, regardless of the conclusion that is reached. Apart from this, it is correct to say, as is stated by Ibn Qudāmah and other scholars, that imān manifests itself in three ways: 1) belief in the heart, 2) utterance on the tongue and 3) actions of the limb. So, it does in fact consist of three realities.

Thus, the pillars of imān are: 1) the belief in the heart, and 2) the testimony of faith upon the tongue, and this should translate into actions. However, action itself is not a pillar of imān and does not determine whether one is a believer or a disbeliever. Naturally, some actions will have this effect, for example, intentionally desecrating the Qurān by throwing it into a toilet, or the action of apostasy or rejecting the Prayer (provided certain conditions are met). Although, in reality what determines kufr, is the intention that preceded the act even if it is not followed by the actual action itself. This shows that the matter wholly concerns what is in the heart, and although action is a part of imān, it is not a condition for, or a pillar of it]. **It increases with obedience and decreases with disobedience** [and this is the Ḥanbalī 'aqīdah, that is found with its scholars, and is line what Imām Aḥmad said[249]]. **Allāh, the Exalted, says: *'And they were commanded not, except that they should worship Allāh alone, making the Religion sincere to Him, and establish the Prayer, and give the Zakāt, and that is the right religion.'*[250] So, He made the worship of Allāh the Exalted, the sincerity of the heart, the establishment of prayer and the giving of Zakāt, all as being from the Religion** [so, action is required even if it be slight. And even the one who does not pray can be a Muslim, because there is no takfīr before he is called to pray by the ruler or his deputy, which can be a qualified judge or

---

[249] See *Uṣūl al-Sunnah* by Imām Aḥmad b. Ḥanbal, p. 9. / al-Khallāl, *al-Sunnah*, no. 1002, 1010.

[250] Qurān: 98:5

someone with religious authority licensed by the ruler. If he refuses, there are particular implications according to the laws of fiqh[251], but he may in fact still be considered Muslim according to Allāh, even if he was announced to be a disbeliever by the judge. It is important to keep in mind that there is a difference between the ruling of Allāh in fact and reality, and the worldly ruling applied by and between people].

The Messenger of Allāh ﷺ said: 'Imān consists of more than seventy branches. The highest of them is to testify that: 'None has the right to be worshipped but Allāh'. And the lowest of them is removing a harmful object from the road.'[252] [and this means that imān can be translated into actions (i.e. actions can indicate the existence of faith)] **The Prophet ﷺ made speech and action part of imān. Allāh, the Exalted, says: 'it has increased their imān.'**[253] **And He says: 'In order that they may grow more in imān.'**[254] **The Messenger of Allāh ﷺ said: 'Whoever says, 'None has the right to be worshipped but Allāh' and he has in his heart imān, the weight of a wheat grain, or a mustard seed or an**

---

[251] In the commentary to *'Umdah al-Ṭālib*, Shaykh Yūsuf b. Ṣādiq states the following (the original text is **bold**, and its commentary is given between brackets [...]):

If someone rejects its obligation [meaning, insists on rejecting the obligation of the Prayer, by saying it is only recommended or merely something good to do; or, when someone actually prays all of the prescribed prayers, yet maintains they are not obligatory], **he has disbelieved** [however, this verdict is only given by scholars and should not be carried out by layman; for the person in question may have an excuse which should be dealt with first. Furthermore, when this person eventually becomes a disbeliever, it does not mean he is executed immediately, for it may be that this person has not even become a Muslim yet, as he may not be aware of essential information which led him to the original rejection. Only when this person has no excuse and insists in rejecting the obligation of prayer does he become an apostate-disbeliever; but this should be established by a competent judge] **also a person who leaves it** [i.e. prayer] **out of laziness** [or indifference], **when he is called by the imām** [meaning, the caliph or ruler] **or his deputy and he rejects until the second** [prayer] **time** [meaning, the person who is called by the ruler or his deputy to pray, for example, Ẓuhr prayer; but he does not pray it during its time period. Then 'Asr time enters and during it he still does not pray Ẓuhr; until the remaining time of the 'Asr is too short to include both prayers. In other words, this person is kept until the second prayer's time becomes too short to be able to pray the two prayers. If this is the case, then the ruler or his deputy may announce this person to be a disbeliever and imprison him for three days and nights], **and** [during it] **he** [the one who rejects the obligation of prayer or the one who leaves it (i.e. does not perform it)] **is called to repent for three days** [during these days scholars are sent to him in order to convince him to repent and he is called to prayer every time the prayer time enters. His repentance is by praying, either in public or in private, depending on the situation. Qāḍī Abū Ya'lā stated that a way to convince someone may be by beating him. Consequently, if he does not repent and does not pray within these three days, a state execution may occur].

[252] This version is from Ibn Ḥibbān, *Ṣaḥīḥ*, no. 193 / other versions are narrated o.a. by Imān Aḥmad, *al-Musnad*, no. 9748 / al-Tirmidhī, no. 2614.

[253] Qurān: 9:124

[254] Qurān: 48:4

atom, he will be extracted from the Hellfire.'[255] Therefore, he made it [meaning, imān] of different levels.

[255] Imām Aḥmad, *al-Musnad*, no. 12772 / al-Bukhārī, no. 44 / Muslim, no. 193.

THE OBLIGATION TO BELIEVE IN WHAT THE MESSENGER HAS INFORMED US OF

ويَجِبُ الإيمانُ بِكُلِّ مَا أَخْبَرَ بِهِ النَّبِيُّ صَلَّى اللَّهُ عَلَيْهِ وَسَلَّمَ وصَحَّ بِهِ النَّقْلُ عَنْهُ فيما شَاهَدْناهُ أوْ غابَ عَنّا، نَعْلَمُ أَنَّهُ حَقٌّ وصِدْقٌ، وسَواءٌ في ذَلكَ ما عَقَلْناهُ وجَهِلْناهُ، ولَمْ نَطَّلِعْ عَلى حَقيقَةِ مَعْناهُ، مِثْلُ حَديثِ الإسْراءِ والمِعْراجِ وكانَ يَقَظَةً لا مَنامًا، فَإِنَّ قُرَيْشًا أَنْكَرَتْهُ وأَكْبَرَتْهُ ولَمْ تَكُنْ تُنْكِرُ المَناماتِ. ومِنْ ذَلِكَ أَنَّ مَلَكَ المَوْتِ لمَّا جاءَ إلى مُوسَى عَلَيْهِ السَّلامُ لِيَقْبِضَ رَوْحَهُ لَطَمَهُ فَفَقَأَ عَيْنَهُ، فَرَجَعَ إلى رَبِّهِ فَرَدَّ عَلَيْهِ عَيْنَهُ.

We are obligated to have faith in everything that the Prophet ﷺ informed us of and in what has been authentically transmitted from him, concerning that which we ourselves witnessed or that which we were absent from. We know that it is reality and truth. There is no difference in these matters between that which we can understand and that which we may be ignorant of and have not come to know the reality of its meaning. An example of this is the narration concerning the Isrā° and Mi'rāj (Nightly Journey and Heavenly Ascension), during which he was awake and not dreaming; for indeed Quraysh denied it and considered it something incredible, and they did not deny dreams. Another example is when the Angel of Death approached Mūsā, peace upon him, in order to take his soul. He struck him and gouged out his eye, so he returned to his Lord who gave him his eye back.

ومِنْ ذَلِكَ أَشْراطُ السّاعَةِ، مِثْلُ خُروجِ الدَّجّالِ، ونُزولِ عِيسَى بْنِ مَرْيَمَ عَلَيْهِ السَّلامُ فَيَقْتُلُهُ، وخُروجِ يَأْجوجَ ومَأْجوجَ، وخُروجِ الدَّابَّةِ، وطُلُوعِ الشَّمْسِ مِنْ مَغْرِبِهَا، وأَشْباهِ ذَلِكَ ممّا صَحَّ بِهِ النَّقْلُ.

And from those things are the Signs of the Hour, such as: the emergence of the Dajjāl; the decent of 'Īsā b. Maryam, peace upon him, who will then kill him; the emergence of Ya°jūj and Ma°jūj; the emergence of the Beast; the rising of the sun from the West, and what is similar to these things from what has been authentically reported.

وعَذابُ القَبْرِ ونَعيمُهُ حَقٌّ، وقَدِ اسْتَعاذَ النَّبِيُّ صَلَّى اللَّهُ عَلَيْهِ وَسَلَّمَ مِنْهُ، وأمَرَ بِهِ في كُلِّ صَلاةٍ. وفِتْنَةُ القَبْرِ حَقٌّ، وسُؤالُ مُنْكَرٍ ونَكيرٍ حَقٌّ، والبَعْثُ بَعْدَ المَوْتِ حَقٌّ وذَلِكَ حينَ يَنْفُخُ إسْرافيلُ عَلَيْهِ السَّلامُ في الصُّورِ: ﴿فَإِذَا هُمْ مِنَ الأَجْدَاثِ إِلَى رَبِّهِمْ يَنسِلُونَ﴾.

The Punishment and Pleasure of the grave are true. The Prophet ﷺ would seek refuge from it, and he commanded that this be done in every prayer. The fitnah (Trial) of the grave is true. The questions of Munkar and Nakīr are true. The Resurrection after death is true and it will occur when Isrāfīl, peace upon him, blows the Trumpet: *'And behold from the graves they will come out quickly to their Lord.'*[256]

ويُحْشَرُ النّاسُ يَوْمَ القَيامَةِ حُفاةً عُراةً غُرْلاً بُهْمًا فيَقِفونَ في مَوْقِفِ القِيامَةِ، حَتَّى يَشْفَعَ فيهِمْ نَبِيُّنا مُحَمَّدٌ صَلَّى اللَّهُ عَلَيْهِ وَسَلَّمَ، ويُحاسِبُهُم اللَّهُ تَبارَكَ وتَعالى، وتُنْصَبُ المَوازينُ، وتُنْشَرُ الدَّواوينُ، وتَتَطايَرُ صَحائِفُ الأَعْمالِ إلى الأَيْمانِ والشَّمائِلِ ﴿فَأَمَّا مَنْ أُوتِيَ كِتَابَهُ بِيَمِينِهِ * فَسَوْفَ يُحَاسَبُ حِسَابًا يَسِيرًا * وَيَنقَلِبُ إِلَى أَهْلِهِ مَسْرُورًا * وَ أَمَّا مَنْ أُوتِيَ كِتَابَهُ وَرَاءَ ظَهْرِهِ * فَسَوْفَ يَدْعُو ثُبُورًا * وَيَصْلَى سَعِيرًا﴾.

Mankind will be gathered on the Day of Judgement, barefoot, naked, uncircumcised, and having nothing with them. They will stop at the final place of standing, until our Prophet ﷺ intercedes for them and Allāh, blessed and exalted is He, calls them all to give account for their deeds; then the Scales will be erected, the records will be distributed and the books of the deeds will be dispersed into the right and left hands: *'Then as for him who will be given his record in his right hand, he surely will receive an easy reckoning. And will return back to his family in joy! But whoever is given his record behind his back (or in his right hand), he will invoke (for his) destruction. And he shall enter the Blazing Fire and (he shall be) made to taste its burning flames.'*[257]

والميزانُ لَهُ كِفَّتانِ ولِسانٌ، تُوزَنُ بِهِ أعْمالُ العِبادِ ﴿فَمَنْ ثَقُلَتْ مَوَازِينُهُ فَأُولَئِكَ هُمُ الْمُفْلِحُونَ * وَمَنْ خَفَّتْ مَوَازِينُهُ فَأُولَئِكَ الَّذِينَ خَسِرُوا أَنفُسَهُمْ فِي جَهَنَّمَ خَالِدُونَ﴾

[256] Qurān: 36:51

[257] Qurān: 84:7-12

The mizān (Balance) has two scales and a tongue, by which the deeds are weighed: *'Then those whose Balance (of good deeds) are heavy, they are the successful. And those whose Balance (of good deeds) are light, they are those who lose their own selves, in Hell will they abide (forever).'*[258]

ولِنَبِيِّنا مُحَمَدٍ صَلَّى اللَّهُ عَلَيْهِ وَسَلَّمَ حَوْضٌ في القِيامَةِ ماؤُهُ أشَدُّ بَياضًا مِنَ اللَّبَنِ، وأحْلَى مِنَ العَسَلِ، وأبَارِيقُهُ عَدَدُ نُجُومِ السَّماءِ، مَنْ شَرِبَ مِنْهُ شَرْبَةً لَمْ يَظْمَأْ بَعْدَها أبَدًا.

For our Prophet ﷺ is the ḥawḍ (Basin) on the Day of Resurrection; its water is whiter than milk and sweeter than honey. Its drinking vessels are as numerous as the stars in the sky. Whoever drinks of it, will never again experience thirst.

والصِّراطُ حَقٌّ يَجُوزُهُ الأَبْرارُ، ويَزِلُّ عَنْهُ الفُجَّارُ.

The ṣirāṭ (Bridge) is true. The righteous people will cross it and the evil ones will fall from it.

ويَشْفَعُ نَبِيُّنا صَلَّى اللَّهُ عَلَيْهِ وَسَلَّمَ فيمَنْ دَخَلَ النّارَ مِنْ أُمَّتِهِ مِنْ أهْلِ الكَبَائِرِ فيَخْرُجونَ بِشَفاعَتِهِ بَعْدَمَا احْتَرَقُوا وصارُوا فَحْمًا وحُمَمًا، فيَدْخُلونَ الجَنَّةَ بِشَفاعَتِهِ. ولِسائِرِ الأَنْبِيَاءِ والمُؤْمِنينَ والمَلائِكَةِ شَفاعاتٌ، قالَ تَعالى: ﴿وَلا يَشْفَعُونَ إلا لِمَنِ ارْتَضَى وَهُم مِنْ خَشْيَتِهِ مُشْفِقُونَ﴾. ولا تَنْفَعُ الكافِرَ شَفاعَةُ الشّافِعينَ.

Our Prophet ﷺ will intercede for whoever enters the Fire from the people of his Ummah who have committed major sins. They will come out of it due to his shafā'ah (Intercession), but only after having been burned until they became ashes and charcoal. They will then enter Paradise due to his intercession. Intercession will also be done by the rest of the Prophets, believers and Angels. Allāh, Exalted is He, says: *'And they cannot intercede except for him with whom He is pleased. And they stand in awe for fear of Him.'*[259] The intercession of the intercessors will be of no avail to the disbelievers.

[258] Qurān: 23:102-103

[259] Qurān: 21:28

والجَنَّةُ والنّارُ مَخْلوقَتانِ لا تَفْنَيانِ، فَالجَنَّةُ مَأْوى أوْلِيائِهِ، والنّارُ عِقابٌ لِأَعْدائِهِ، وأَهْلُ الجَنَّةِ فيها مُخَلَّدونَ. ﴿إِنَّ الْمُجْرِمِينَ فِي عَذَابِ جَهَنَّمَ خَالِدُونَ * لا يُفَتَّرُ عَنْهُمْ وَهُمْ فِيهِ مُبْلِسُونَ﴾.

Jannah and Nār (Paradise and Hellfire) are two creations that will not cease to exist. Paradise is the final resting place of the awliyā° of Allāh, while the Hellfire is the place of punishment for His enemies. The inhabitants of Paradise will remain therein eternally: *'Verily, the sinful evildoers will be in the punishment of Hell to remain in it eternally, (their torment) will not be lightened for them, and they will be plunged into destruction with deep regret and sorrow.'*[260]

ويُؤْتَى بِالمَوْتِ في صورَةِ كَبْشٍ أَمْلَحَ، فيُذْبَحُ بَيْنَ الجَنَّةِ والنّارِ، ثُمَّ يُقالُ: (يا أَهْلَ الجَنَّةِ خُلودٌ ولا مَوْتَ، ويا أَهْلَ النَّارِ خُلودٌ ولا مَوْتَ).

Death will be brought in the form of a sturdy ram and slaughtered between Paradise and Hellfire. Then it will be said: *'O inhabitants of Paradise! Eternity for you and no (more) death! O inhabitants of Hell! Eternity for you and no (more) death!'*

Commentary: The Obligation to Believe in what the Messenger has Informed us of

We are obligated to have faith in everything that the Prophet ﷺ informed us of and in what has been authentically transmitted from him, concerning that which we ourselves witnessed [through our senses] **or that which we were absent from**[261]**. We know that it is reality and truth** [especially when something is authentically transmitted]. **There is no difference in these matters between that which we can understand and that which we may be ignorant of and have not come to know the reality of its meaning. An example of this is the narration concerning the Isrā° and Mi'rāj (Nightly Journey and Heavenly Ascension)**[262]**,**

---

[260] Qurān: 43:74-75

[261] This chapter is concerned with al-sama'iyāt (auditory reports). It is everything that is affirmed through hearing (i.e. Divine Legislation). One's intellect has no part in these matters, and therefore one should believe in and submit to them.

[262] The primary source for this event is the Qurān, in which Allāh says: *'Glorified is He who took his servant for a journey by night from al-masjid al-Ḥarām to al-masjid al-Aqṣā°'* (Qurān: 17:1). The aḥādīth provide further detail regarding this event, See for example, al-Bukhārī, no. 349, 7517 / al-Nasā°ī, no. 450.

during which he was awake and not dreaming [and this is the mu'tamad of the Madhhab. He ﷺ was awake during these events and saw Allāh with his eyes]; **for indeed Quraysh denied it and considered it something incredible** [and unbelievable], **and they did not deny dreams** [for, if someone went to them with a dream in which such-and-such happened, they would not bother to refute or deny the dream. However, what the Prophet ﷺ said bothered them, because he claimed it happened to him in reality (i.e. while being awake)]. **Another example is when the Angel of Death approached Mūsā, peace upon him, in order to take his soul. He** [i.e. Mūsā] **struck him and gouged out his eye, so he returned to his Lord who gave him his eye back**[263] [and it may be difficult for some to understand and believe that this has happened in reality, but it has been authentically reported from the Prophet ﷺ and one should submit to and believe in it accordingly].

And from those things [that one is required to accept and have faith in] **are the Signs of the Hour** [i.e. the Day of Judgment], **such as: the emergence of the Dajjāl**[264]**; the descent of 'Īsā b. Maryam, peace upon him,** [and this does not contradict with the claim that the Prophet Muḥammad ﷺ is the last prophet, for 'Īsāwill not descend as a prophet or a messenger. Instead, he will descend as a servant of Allāh with particular task to carry out (i.e. kill the Dajjāl). Furthermore, he will follow the sharī'ah of Muḥammad and not his own. According to some narrations he will pray behind a Muslim imām[265]], **who will then kill him**[266] [i.e. the Dajjāl]; **the emergence of Ya°jūj and Ma°jūj**[267]**; the emergence of the**

---

[263] See footnote no. 182.

[264] See for example, al-Bukhārī, no. 1882: *'Allāh's Messenger ﷺ told us a long narrative about al-Dajjāl, and among the many things he mentioned, was his saying: 'al-Dajjāl will come...''*

[265] See for example, Muslim, no. 156: *'A section of my people will not cease fighting for the Truth and will prevail till the Day of Resurrection. He said: 'Īsā b. Maryam would then descend and their commander would invite him to come and lead them in prayer, but he would say: No, some amongst you are commanders over some (amongst you). This is the honour from Allah for this Ummah.'*

[266] See for example, Abū Dawūd, nr 4321: *'Then prophet 'Isā b. Maryam will descend at the white minaret to the east of Damascus. He will then catch him up at the gate of Ludd and kill him (i.e. al-Dajjāl)'*

[267] The primary source for this event is the Qurān, in which Allāh says: *'Until, when Ya°jūj and Ma°jūj are let, and they swiftly swarm from every mound'* (Qurān: 96:97). And, what is mentioned in ṣūrah al-Kahf (Qurān: 18:93-99) of the story of Dhu al-Qarnayn.

Also, see Muslim, no. 2937: *'And then Allah would send Ya°jūj and Ma°jūj and they would swarm down from every slope. The first of them would pass the lake of Tiberias and drink out of it. And when the last of them would pass, he would say: There was once water there.'*, and it is part of a very long ḥadīth concerning other signs of the Hour.

Beast[268]**; the rising of the sun from the West**[269]**, and what is similar to these things from what has been authentically reported**[270] [these examples are supported by numerous authentic narrations].

The Punishment and Pleasure [or reward] **of the grave are true. The Prophet ﷺ would seek refuge from it** [meaning, from the punishment and torment], **and he commanded that this be done in every prayer** [Ibn 'Abbās reported that he ﷺ taught his companions to say this supplication, just like he taught them ṣūrahs from the Qurān), instructing them to say: *'O Allah, I seek refuge with You from the torment of hell. And I seek refuge with You from the torment of the grave, and I seek refuge with You from the trial of al-Masīḥ al-Dajjāl, and I seek refuge with You from the trial of life and death.'*[271] The relied upon position in the Ḥanbalī madhhab is that it is recommended to say the aforementioned supplication in every prayer, while the other opinion in the Ḥanbalī madhhab is that it is obligatory. 'Obligation' means that if it is left out intentionally, the Prayer becomes invalid immediately, and if it is left out due to forgetfulness or ignorance, one must perform the prostration of forgetfulness. The justification for this later position (i.e. including the performance of this supplication amongst the obligatory aspects (wājibāt)) is that it was the habit of the Prophet ﷺ to say it during the Prayer, and he did not leave its performance. Although an obligatory aspect has to be supported by clear evidence, this was included nonetheless because the Prophet ﷺ never left it out. Additionally, to say that the four things mentioned in this supplication are mere metaphors is kufr[272]]. **The fitnah (Trial) of the grave is true**[273]**. The questions of Munkar and Nakīr are true**[274]**. The Resurrection after death is true and will occur when**

---

[268] The primary source for this event is the Qurān, in which Allāh says: *'And when the Word is fulfilled against them (the unjust), we shall produce from the earth a beast for them, to speak to them'* (Qurān: 27:82).

Also, see Muslim, no. 2901 in which ten signs of the Last Hour are mentioned, one of them being the coming of the Beast.'

[269] Al-Bukhārī, no. 7121: *'Till the sun rises from the West. So, when the sun will rise and the people will see it...'*

[270] Like the coming of al-Mahdī. As is transmitted by Abū Dawūd, no. 4283, in his *Sunan* in book 38: *'If only one day of this time (world) remained, Allah would raise up a man from my family who would fill this earth with justice as it has been filled with oppression.'*

[271] Reported by Muslim, no. 590.

[272] A general principle is: something is only taken as a metaphor if there is evidence to indicate this, or there is evidence that the literal meaning cannot be intended.

[273] A long narration detailing the trials of the grave, such as the questioning, punishment and pleasure is transmitted by al-Tirmidhī in his Sunan, no. 4753.

[274] Al-Tirmidhī, no. 1071: *'When the deceased, or he said when one of you, is buried, two angels, black and blue come to him. One of them is called al-Munkar, and the other al-Nakīr. They say: 'What did you used*

Isrāfīl[275], peace upon him, blows the Trumpet[276] [there is some disagreement amongst the scholars whether there are two or three bowings of the Trumpet. The relied upon position of the Ḥanbalī madhhab states that it is three, and one can refer to *Lawāmi' al- Anwar* by al-Safārīnī and its Mukhtaṣar by al-Shaṭṭī. The first blowing is called the nafkhaḧ al-fazā' (blowing of terror), and it will terrify the creation of Allāh. The second is called the nafkhaḧ al-ṣa'qaḧ (blowing of the shock), and it will cause every living thing to die. The third is the nafkhaḧ al-qiyām li-rabb al-'ālamīn (blowing of the standing before the Lord of the worlds) and it causes the Resurrection and standing before Allāh at the dawn of the Day of Judgement. The second blowing can also be described as the nafkhaḧ al-mawt (blowing of death), while the third may also be called the nafkhaḧ al-ba'th wa al-nushūr (blowing of the Resurrection and standing) as the first blowing will cause all people to die. With regards to the second blowing of the Trumpet, Allāh, the Exalted, says]: ***'And behold from the graves they will come out quickly totheirLord.'***[277]

Mankind will be gathered on the Day of Judgement, barefoot, naked, uncircumcised, and having nothing with them. They will stop at the final place of standing, until our Prophet ﷺ intercedes for them [and this is al-shafā'aḧ al-'uẓmā (the Great Intercession)[278]] **and Allāh, blessed and exalted is He, calls them all to give account for their deeds; then the Scales will be erected, the records will be distributed and the books of the deeds will be dispersed into**

---

to say about this man?' So, he says what he was saying (before death): 'He is Allah's slave and His Messenger. I testify that none has the right to be worshipped but Allāh and that Muḥammad is His slave and His Messenger.'

[275] Ibn Hajar al-'Asqalānī mentions in *Fatḥ al-Bārī*, vol. 20, p. 295-297, various aḥādīth which mention Isrāfīl as the angels that is designated to blow the Trumpet. One of these aḥādīth is transmitted by Abū al-Shaykh al-Aṣbahānī in *Kitāb al-'Aẓamaḧ*, no. 389: *'Then He (Allāh) said: 'Be!' and Isrāfīl was (created)... and he was commanded to take the Trumpet, and he took it.'* This and other aḥādīth are also mentioned by al-Bayhaqī in *al-Ba'th wa al- Nushūr* (p. 336-339).

[276] There will be two distinct trumpet blows. The first is the 'blowing of terror' (nafkhaḧ al-faza') which will alarm and frighten mankind, after which they will fall dead. The second is the 'blowing of resurrection' (nafkhaḧ al-ba'th), which will resurrect mankind and causes them to rise from their graves. As is mentioned in ṣūrah al-Zumar: *'And the Trumpet will be blown, and all who are in the heavens and all who are on earth will swoon away, except whom Allāh wills (to remain). Then it will be blown a second time and behold, they will be standing, looking on'* (Qurān: 39:68).

[277] Qurān: 36:51

[278] Linguistically 'intercession' means 'to make an odd number (al-witr) even (shaf'an)'. Technically it means 'to act on someone's behalf to gain some benefit or to prevent some harm'.

The Intercession (al-shafā'aḧ) on the Day of Judgement is divided into two types:

1) the specific (al-khās) intercession, meaning that which is specific only to the Prophet Muḥammad ﷺ, and 2) the general (al-'āmm) intercession, meaning that which is general for the Prophet ﷺ as well as for others.

the right and left hands [and all of these things are from the ghābiyāt (unseen); they are all real and true]: ***'Then as for him who will be given his record in his right hand, he surely will receive an easy reckoning. And will return back to his family in joy! But whoever is given his record behind his back (or in his right hand), he will invoke (for his) destruction. And he shall enter the Blazing Fire and (he shall be) made to taste its burning flames.'***[279]

The mizān (Balance) has two scales and a tongue, by which the deeds are weighted [and it is real, existing with certain characteristics]: ***'Then those whose Balance (of good deeds) are heavy, they are the successful. And those whose Balance (of good deeds) are light, they are those who lose their own selves, in Hell will they abide (forever).'***[280]

For our Prophet Muḥammad ﷺ is the ḥawd (Basin)[281] **on the Day of Resurrection; its water is whiter than milk and sweeter than honey. Its drinking vessels are as numerous as the stars in the sky. Whoever drinks of it, will never again experience thirst**[282]. [The ru°yah, shafā'aḧ and ḥawḍ, are established in mutawātir narration of the highest degree and are real and not metaphoric.].

The ṣirāṭ (Bridge) is true. The righteous people will cross it [in various ways; some will crawl or walk over it, whilst other will pass over it quickly] **and the evil ones will fall from it**[283] [therefore crossing the ṣirāṭ depends on one's deeds].

Our Prophet ﷺ will intercede for whoever enters the Fire from the people of his Ummaḧ who have committed major sins. They will come out of it due to his shafā'aḧ (Intercession), but only after having been burned until they became ashes and charcoal. They will then enter Paradise due to his intercession. Intercession will also be done by the rest of the Prophets, believers and Angels[284] [thus, the shafa'aḧ is not limited to the Prophet Muḥammad ﷺ only, although his intercession is the greatest and reserved for him alone[285].

---

[279] Qurān: 84:7-12

[280] Qurān: 23:102-103

[281] Al-ḥawd, is also often translated as 'the Fountain

[282] Al-Bukhārī, no. 6579 / Muslim, no. 2292.

[283] Al-Bukhārī, no. 7439 / Muslim, no. 183.

[284] See footnote no. 231

[285] The following are the various types of shafā'aḧ (intercession) that are affirmed for Prophet Muḥammad ﷺ:

Other groups amongst the creation may intercede after they have been given permission from Allāh to do so, such as the intercession of the martyr[286]]. **Allāh Exalted is He, says: *'And they cannot intercede except for him with whom He is pleased. And they stand in awe for fear of Him.'*[287] The intercession of the intercessors will be of no avail to the disbelievers** [thus, the disbelievers will not benefit from intercession, except that intercession can be made for them to lighten their punishment and torment in Hell. For example, the intercession of the Prophet ﷺ for his uncle Abū Ṭālib, which will be for the lightning of his punishment. Regarding this type of intercession one can argue whether it is an actual intercession or not, as one might say it is Allāh's mercy instead. However, the majority have understood it as a type of intercession].

Jannaḧ and Nār (Paradise and Hellfire) are two creations that will not cease to exist [and both are already existent, for the Prophet ﷺ saw them in reality. The 'aqīdaḧ of the Ḥanābilaḧ is that the Hellfire, just as Paradise, will remain forever, and will not cease to exist at some point. Someone who insists on the idea of Paradise or Hellfire ceasing to exist at some point, becomes an innovator on account of his statement. However, labelling such a person as a disbeliever would be a step too far, as he still believes in paradise and the hellfire. If he is shown the evidences which do not agree with his view, and he still insists, then he has abandoned the clear āyāt from the Qurān, which state that Paradise and Hellfire will remain forever, in favour of ambiguous text and erroneous

---

1. The great intercession (al-shafā'aḧ al-'uẓmā) which is specifically for the Prophet ﷺ, and this is his intercession for the coming of Allāh in order for the Judgement to begin.
2. His intercession for people whose good and bad deeds are equal, he will intercede for them to enter Paradise.
3. His intercession for another group of people for whom the Fire had been ordered, so he will intercede that they do not enter it.
4. His intercession for the raising of the ranks of those who have entered Paradise, that their rank be raised to one greater than what the reward for their actions would have given them.
5. His intercession for a people to be entered into Paradise without reckoning.
6. His intercession for the lightening of the punishment for those who deserve it, such as his intercession for his uncle Abū Ṭālib that his punishment be lightened.
7. His intercession for permission to be granted for all the Believers to enter Paradise.
8. His intercession for the people who committed major sins, amongst those who entered the Fire, that they may be brought out of it. This type is al-'ām (generally for the Prophet Muḥammad ﷺ, the angels, the other prophets, and the believers)].

[286] Al-Tirmidhī (no. 1663): *'There are six things with Allāh for the martyr. He is forgiven with the first flow of blood (he suffers), he is shown his place in Paradise, he is protected from punishment in the grave, secured from the greatest terror, the crown of dignity is placed upon his head -and its gems are better than the world and what is in it, he is married to seventy two wives from the Ḥūr al-'Ayn, and he may intercede for seventy of his close relatives.'*

[287] Qurān: 21:28

arguments, and he becomes an innovator on this account. The Prophet ﷺ will be the first to open the gates of Paradise, and the first one who will enter it. Therefore, the rest of the people will only enter after he ﷺ does. People who die will remain in their graves until the Day of Resurrection, and will not physically enter Paradise or Hell before that day, although they will be shown their final abodes while being in their graves.]. **Paradise is the final resting place of the awliyā°288 of Allah, while the Hellfire is the place of punishment for His enemies. The inhabitants of Paradise will remain therein eternally: *'Verily, the sinful evildoers will be in the punishment of Hell to remain in it eternally, (their torment) will not be lightened for them, and they will be plunged into destruction with deep regrets and sorrows.'*** [289] [and the author did not say 'the inhabitants of the Hellfire', as he did with regards to Paradise; yet, he said 'the sinful evildoers', meaning the believers who have sinned will eventually be taken out of the Hellfire and their duration in it will vary.

Death will be brought in the form of a sturdy ram and slaughtered between Paradise and Hellfire. Then it will be said: *'O inhabitants of Paradise! Eternity for you and no (more) death! O inhabitants of Hell! Eternity for you and no (more) death!'* [290] [so, death will be brought forward in a materialistic form and will be slaughtered; which means there will be no more death after this event and everyone will remain eternally in their final abode. This slaughtering will take place only after all the believers have been removed from the Hellfire and have entered Paradise].

---

[288] Awliyā° is often translated as 'close friend' although it is not an accurate translation. It might be that the term 'ally' is more appropriate, however, a 'one word' translation in this case will not suffice and does injustice to the Arabic word.

[289] Qurān: 43:74-75

[290] Al-Bukhārī, no. 4730 / Muslim, no. 2849

ومُحَمَّدٌ رَسولُ اللهِ صَلَّى اللَّهُ عَلَيْهِ وَسَلَّمَ خاتَمُ النَّبِيِّينَ وسَيِّدُ المُرْسَلينَ، لا يَصِحُّ إيمانُ عَبْدٍ حَتَّى يُؤمِنَ برِسالَتِهِ، ويَشْهَدَ بِنُبُوَّتِهِ، ولا يُقْضَى بَيْنَ النَّاسِ في يَوْمِ القِيامَةِ إلَّا بِشَفاعَتِهِ، ولاَ يَدْخُلُ الجَنَّةَ أُمَّةٌ إلَّا بَعْدَ دُخولِ أُمَّتِهِ. صاحِبُ لِواءِ الحَمْدِ، والمَقامِ المَحْمودِ، والحَوْضِ المَوْرودِ، وهُوَ إمامُ النَّبِيِّينَ، وخَطِيبُهُم، وصاحِبُ شَفاعَتِهِم، أُمَّتُهُ خَيْرُ الأُمَمِ وأَصْحابُهُ خَيْرُ أَصْحابِ الأَنْبِياءِ عَلَيْهِمُ السَّلامُ.

Muḥammad is the Messenger of Allāh ﷺ, the Seal of the Prophets and the leader of those sent by Allāh. The imān of a servant is not valid until he believes in his message and bears witness to his Prophethood. Mankind will not be judged on the Day of Resurrection except with his intercession. No nation will enter Paradise until his nation has entered it. He is the possessor of the Banner of Praise (al-lawā°i al-ḥamd), the most Praiseworthy Station (al-maqām al-maḥmūd) and the ḥawḍ. He is the leader of the Prophets, their spokesman and the one who possesses their intercession. His Ummah is the best of nations and his companions are the best of those who accompanied Prophets.

وأَفْضَلُ أُمَّتِهِ أبو بَكْرٍ الصِّديقُ، ثُمَّ عُمَرُ الفاروقُ، ثُمَّ عُثْمانُ ذو النُّورَينِ، ثُمَّ عَلِيٌّ المُرْتَضَى رَضِيَ اللَّهُ عَنْهُم أَجْمَعِينَ. لِمَا رَوى عَبْدُ اللَّهِ بْنُ عُمَرَ رَضِيَ اللَّهُ عَنْهُما قالَ: (كُنَّا نَقولُ والنَّبِيُّ صَلَّى اللَّهُ عَلَيْهِ وَسَلَّمَ حَيٌّ: أبو بَكْرٍ، ثُمَّ عُمَرُ، ثُمَّ عُثْمانُ. فَيَبْلُغُ ذَلِكَ النَّبِيَّ صَلَّى اللَّهُ عَلَيْهِ وَسَلَّمَ فَلا يُنْكِرُهُ). وصَحَّتِ الرِّوايَةُ عَن عَلِيٍّ رَضِيَ اللَّهُ عَنْهُ أَنَّهُ قالَ: (خَيْرُ هَذِهِ الأُمَّةِ بَعْدَ نَبِيِّها أبو بَكْرٍ ثُمَّ عُمَرُ، ولَوْ شِئْتُ سَمَّيْتُ الثَّالِثَ). ورَوى أبو الدَّرْداءِ عَنِ النَّبِيِّ صَلَّى اللَّهُ عَلَيْهِ وَسَلَّمَ أَنَّهُ قالَ: ((مَا طَلَعَتِ الشَّمْسُ وَلاَ غَرَبَتْ بَعْدَ النَّبِيِّينَ والمُرْسَلِينَ عَلَى أفْضَلَ مِنْ أَبِي بَكْرٍ)). وَهُوَ أَحَقُّ خَلْقِ اللَّهِ بِالخِلافَةِ بَعْدَ النَّبِيِّ صَلَّى اللَّهُ عَلَيْهِ وَسَلَّمَ؛ لِفَضْلِهِ وسَابِقَتِهِ، وتَقْدِيمِ النَّبِيِّ صَلَّى اللَّهُ عَلَيْهِ وَسَلَّمَ لَهُ في الصَّلاةِ عَلى جَمِيعِ الصَّحابَةِ رَضِيَ اللَّهُ عَنْهُم، و إجْماعِ الصَّحابَةِ عَلى تَقْديمِهِ

ومُبايَعَتِهِ، ولَمْ يَكُنِ اللَّهُ لِيَجْمَعَهُم عَلى ضَلالَةٍ. ثُمَّ مِنْ بَعْدِهِ عُمَرُ؛ لِفَضْلِهِ وعَهْدِ أبي بَكْرٍ إليْهِ. ثُمَّ عُثْمانُ رَضِيَ اللَّهُ عَنْهُ؛ لِتَقْديمِ أهْلِ الشُّورى لَهُ. ثُمَّ عَليٌّ رَضِيَ اللَّهُ عَنْهُ؛ لِفَضْلِهِ و إجْماعِ أهْلِ عَصْرِهِ عَلَيْهِ. وهَؤُلاءِ الخُلَفاءُ الرَّاشِدونَ المَهْدِيُّونَ الَّذينَ قالَ رَسولُ اللَّهِ صَلَّى اللَّهُ عَلَيْهِ وَسَلَّمَ فيهِم: ((عَلَيْكُمْ بِسُنَّتِي وَسُنَّةِ الْخُلَفاءِ الرَّاشِدِينَ الْمَهْدِيِّينَ مِنْ بَعْدِي، عَضُّوا عَلَيْهَا بِالنَّوَاجِذِ)). وقالَ صَلَّى اللَّهُ عَلَيْهِ وَسَلَّمَ: ((الخِلافَةُ مِنْ بَعْدِي ثَلاثُونَ سَنَةً)) فَكانَ آخِرَها خِلافَةُ عَلِيٍّ رَضِيَ اللَّهُ عَنْهُ.

The best of his Ummaḧ was Abū Bakr al-Ṣiddīq (the truthful one), then ʿUmar al-Farūq (the distinguisher), then ʿUthmān Dhū al-Nūrayn (Possessor of the two lights) and then ʿAlī al-Murtaḍā (the one who attained Allah's pleasure), may Allāh be pleased with all of them. This is based upon what has been reported by ʿAbd Allāh b. ʿUmar, Allāh be pleased with him, that he said: *'We used to say, while the Prophet ﷺ was alive; Abū Bakr, then 'Umar, then 'Uthmān. This would reach the Prophet ﷺ and he would not deny it.'* It is reported on the authority of ʿAlī, Allāh be pleased with him, that he said: *'The best of this Ummaḧ after its Prophet is Abū Bakr, then 'Umar. And if I wanted to, I would have named a third.'* Abū al-Dardā° reported that the Prophet ﷺ said: *'The sun does not rise nor does it set upon anyone better, after the Prophets and the Messengers, than Abū Bakr.'* He had the most right to the caliphate from all of the creation of Allāh, after the Prophet ﷺ; and this is due to his merits and his precedence, and also due to the Prophet ﷺ preferring him over all of his companions, may Allāh be pleased with them, to lead the prayer. It is also due to the ijmāʿ of the companions in recognising his superiority and giving the pledge of allegiance to him. And Allāh would not have united them upon misguidance. Then after him was ʿUmar, due to his merits and Abū Bakr's delegation of it to him. Then ʿUthmān, Allāh be pleased with him, due to him being chosen by the members of the shūrā (council). Then ʿAlī, Allāh be pleased with him, due to his merits and the ijmāʿ of the people of his time. These are the rightly guided caliphs about whom the Messenger of Allāh ﷺ said: *'Stick to my Sunnaḧ and the sunnaḧ of the rightly-guided caliphs after me. Bite onto it with your molar teeth.'* The Prophet ﷺ said: *'The caliphate after me will endure for thirty years.'* The last part of it occurred with the caliphate of ʿAlī, Allāh be pleased with him.

ونَشْهَدُ لِلعَشَرَةِ بِالجَنَّةِ، كَما شَهِدَ لَهُمُ النَّبِيُّ صَلَّى اللَّهُ عَلَيْهِ وَسَلَّمَ فَقالَ: ((أَبُو بَكْرٍ في الجَنَّةِ، وعُمَرُ فِي الجَنَّةِ، وعُثْمَانُ في الجَنَّةِ، وعَلِيٌّ في الجَنَّةِ، وطَلْحَةُ فِي الجَنَّةِ، والزُّبَيْرُ فِي الجَنَّةِ، وسَعْدٌ فِي الجَنَّةِ، وسَعِيدٌ في الجَنَّةِ، وعَبْدُ الرَّحْمنِ بْنُ عَوْفٍ في الجَنَّةِ، وأَبُو عُبَيْدَةَ بْنُ الجَرَّاحِ في الجَنَّةِ)). وكُلُّ مَنْ شَهِدَ لَهُ النَّبِيُّ صَلَّى اللَّهُ عَلَيْهِ وَسَلَّمَ بِالجَنَّةِ شَهِدْنَا لهُ بِها، كَقَوْلِهِ: ((الحَسَنُ والحُسَيْنُ سَيِّدَا شَبَابِ أَهْلِ الجَنَّةِ))، وقَوْلِهِ لثَابِتِ بْنِ قيَسٍ: ((إِنَّهُ مِنْ أَهْلِ الجَنَّةِ)).

We testify for the ten who will be in Paradise, just as the Prophet ﷺ testified for them, when he said: *'Abū Bakr is in Paradise, 'Umar is in Paradise, 'Uthmān is in Paradise, 'Alī is in Paradise, Ṭalḥa is in Paradise, al- Zubayr is in Paradise, Sa'd is in Paradise, Sa'īd is in Paradise, 'Abd al-Raḥmān b. 'Awf is in Paradise, Abū 'Ubaydah b. al-Jarrāḥ is in Paradise.'* As for everyone else whom the Prophet ﷺ has testified will be in Paradise, then we bear witness to that. Such as his statement: *'Al-Ḥasan and al-Ḥusayn are the leaders of the youth in Paradise.'* And his statement to Thābit b. Qays: *'Indeed, he is from the inhabitants of paradise.'*

ولا نَجْزِمُ لِأَحَدٍ مِنْ أَهْلِ القِبلَةَ بِجَنةٍّ ولا نارٍ إلاَّ مَنْ جَزَمَ لَهُ الرَّسُولُ صَليَّ اللَّهُ عَلَيْهِ وَسَلَّمَ لَكِنَّا نَرْجو لِلْمُحْسِنِ ونَخَافُ عَلى المُسِيءِ.ولاَ نُكَفِّرُ أَحَدًا مِنْ أَهْلِ القِبْلَةِ بِذَنْبٍ، ولاَ نُخْرِجُهُ عَنِ الإِسْلامِ بِعَمَلٍ

We do not confirm for anyone from the People of the Qiblah that he will be in Paradise or Hellfire, except for the one whom the Messenger has confirmed it for. However, we hope for the one who does good, and we fear for the one who does evil. We do not declare anyone from the people of the Qiblah a disbeliever because of a sin, nor do we expel him out of Islām because of an action or deed.

ونَرَى الحَجَّ والجِهَادَ ماضِياً مَعَ طاعَةِ كُلِّ إمامٍ بَرًّا كانَ أَوْ فَاجِرًا، وصَلاةُ الجُمُعَةِ خَلْفَهُم جائِزَةٌ. قالَ أَنَسٌ: قالَ النَّبِيُّ صَلَّى اللَّهُ عَلَيْهِ وَسَلَّمَ: ((ثلاَثٌ مِنْ أَصْلِ الإِيمَانِ: الكَفُّ عَمَّنْ قَالَ: لاَ إِلَهَ إِلَّا اللَّهُ. وَلا نُكَفِّرُهُ بِذَنْبٍ، وَلاَ نُخْرِجُهُ مِنَ الإِسْلاَمِ بِعَمَلٍ.

وَالْجِهَادُ مَاضٍ مُنْذُ بَعَثَنِي اللَّهُ عَزَّ وجَلَّ حَتَّى يُقَاتِلَ آخِرُ أُمَّتِي الدَّجَّالَ، لا يُبْطِلُهُ جَوْرُ جَائِرٍ وَلا عَدْلُ عَادِلٍ، وَالإِيمَانُ بِالأَقْدَارِ)). رَوَاهُ أبو داوُدَ.

We hold that Ḥajj and Jihād are continuous along with the obedience to every Muslim leader, whether he is righteous or wicked. And the congregational prayer behind them is permissible. Anas reported that the Prophet ﷺ said: *'Three thing are from the foundation of imān; refraining from (harming) anyone who says 'None has the right to be worshipped but Allāh'. We do not declare him a disbeliever due to a sin (which he has committed), nor do we expel him out of Islām due to an action (he has done). Jihād is everlasting from the time Allāh sent me to the time when the last part of my Ummah will fight the Dajjal. It will not be invalidated by the oppression of the oppressor, or the justice of the just. And (the third is) the belief in al- qadar.'* Narrated by Abū Dawūd.

ومِنَ السُّنَّةِ تَوَلِّي أَصْحابِ رَسولِ اللَّهِ صَلَّى اللَّهُ عَلَيْهِ وَسَلَّمَ ومَحَبَّتُهُم، وذِكْرُ مَحاسِنِهِم والتَّرَحُّمُ عَلَيْهِمْ، والاِسْتِغْفارُ لَهُم، والكَفُّ عَن ذِكْرِ مَسَاوِئِهِم، ومَا شَجَرَ بَيْنَهُم، واعْتِقادُ فَضْلِهِم، ومَعْرِفَةُ سابِقَتِهِم. قالَ اللَّه تَعالى: ﴿وَالَّذِينَ جَاءُوا مِنْ بَعْدِهِمْ يَقُولُونَ رَبَّنَا اغْفِرْ لَنَا وَلِإِخْوَانِنَا الَّذِينَ سَبَقُونَا بِالْإِيمان وَلا تَجْعَلْ فِي قُلُوبِنَا غِلاًّ لِلَّذِينَ آمَنُوا﴾، وقالَ تَعالى ﴿مُحَمَّدٌ رَسُولُ اللَّهِ وَالَّذِينَ مَعَهُ أَشِدَّاءُ عَلَى الْكُفَّارِ رُحَمَاءُ بَيْنَهُمْ﴾. وقالَ النَّبِيُّ صَلَّى اللَّهُ عَلَيْهِ وَسَلَّمَ: ((لا تَسُبُّوا أَصْحابي، فَإِنَّ أَحَدَكُمْ لَوْ أَنْفَقَ مِثْلَ أُحُدٍ ذَهَباً ما بَلَغَ مُدَّ أَحَدِهِمْ ولا نَصيفَهُ))

From the Sunnah is; loyalty to the companions, to love them, mention their good qualities, and to ask Allāh to grant them mercy and to forgive them. And (also) refraining from mentioning their shortcomings and what they differed in, believing in their virtues and acknowledging their superiority. Allāh, the Exalted, says: *'And those who come after them say; 'our Lord! Forgive us and our brothers who preceded us in Faith. And put not in our hearts any hatred against those who have believed.'*[291] And He, the Exalted, says: *'Muḥammad is the Messenger of Allāh. And those who are with him are severe against the disbelievers, while being merciful among themselves'*[292] The Prophet ﷺ said: *'Do not revile my companions,*

[291] Qurān: 59:10

[292] Qurān: 48:29

for indeed if one you were to give in charity, the equivalent of the mount of Uḥud in gold, it would not reach a mudd of one of them, not even half (of what they gave).'

وَمِنَ السُّنَّةِ التَّرَضِّي عَنْ أَزْوَاجِ رَسُولِ اللَّهِ صَلَّى اللَّهُ عَلَيْهِ وَسَلَّمَ، أُمَّهَاتِ الْمُؤْمِنِينَ الْمُطَهَّرَاتِ، الْمُبَرَّآتِ مِنْ كُلِّ سُوءٍ، أَفْضَلُهُنَّ خَدِيجَةُ بِنْتُ خُوَيْلِدٍ وَعَائِشَةُ الصِّدِّيقَةُ بِنْتُ الصِّدِّيقِ الَّتِي بَرَّأَهَا اللَّهُ فِي كِتَابِهِ، زَوْجُ النَّبِيِّ صَلَّى اللَّهُ عَلَيْهِ وَسَلَّمَ فِي الدُّنْيَا وَالْآخِرَةِ فَمَنْ قَذَفَهَا بِمَا بَرَّأَهَا اللَّهُ مِنْهُ فَقَدْ كَفَرَ بِاللَّهِ الْعَظِيمِ.

From the Sunnaĥ is; being pleased with the wives of the Messenger of Allāh ﷺ, the Mothers of the Believers, the pure ones free of every type of evil. The best of them were Khadījaĥ b. Khuwaylid and 'Āᵓishaĥ b. al- Ṣiddīq, whom Allāh declared free in His Book (from the false accusations against her). She is the wife of the Prophet ﷺ in this world and the next. Whosoever falsely accuses her with that which Allāh declared her free of, has disbelieved in Allāh, the Most Great.

وَمُعَاوِيَةُ خَالُ الْمُؤْمِنِينَ، وَكَاتِبُ وَحْيِ اللَّهِ، وَأَحَدُ خُلَفَاءِ الْمُسْلِمِينَ رَضِيَ اللَّهُ عَنْهُم

Mu'āwiyaĥ is the uncle of the Believers, and one of those who wrote the Revelation of Allāh. He was one of the caliphs of the Muslims, Allāh be pleased with them.

Commentary: The Prophet ﷺ and his Companions

Muḥammad is the Messenger of Allāh ﷺ, the Seal of the Prophets and the leader of those sent by Allāh [additionally he is also the best of creation, and in that regard, he is better than the Throne ('arsh). His burial place is the best place on earth, even better than the Ka'baĥ, although Mecca in general is better than Medina, likewise the Sacred Mosque (i.e. Masjid al-Ḥarām) is considered better than the mosque of the Prophet g. And this is according to the mu'tamad position of the Madhhab]. **The imān of a servant is not valid until he believes in his message and bears witness to his Prophethood. Mankind will not be judged on the Day of Judgement except with his intercession. And no nation will enter Paradise, until his nation has entered it. He is the possessor of the Banner of Praise (al-lawāᵓi al-ḥamd), the Praiseworthy Station (al-maqām al-maḥmūd) and the ḥawḍ. He is the leader of the Prophets, their spokesman and the one who possesses their intercession. His Ummaĥ is the best of nations and his**

companions are the best of those who accompanied Prophets. The best of his Ummaĥ was Abū Bakr al-Ṣiddīq (the truthful one), then 'Umar al-Farūq (the distinguisher), then 'Uthmān Dhū al-Nūrayn (Possessor of the two lights) and then 'Alī al-Murtaḍā (the one who attained Allah's pleasure), may Allāh be pleased with all of them. This is based upon what has been reported by 'Abd Allāh b. 'Umar, that he said: *'We used to say, while the Prophet ﷺ was alive; Abū Bakr, then 'Umar, then 'Uthmān. This would reach the Prophet ﷺ and he would not deny it.'*[293] It is reported on the authority of 'Alī, that he said: *'The best of this Ummaĥ after its Prophet is Abū Bakr, then 'Umar. And if I wanted to, I would have named a third.'*[294] Abū al-Dardā° reported that the Prophet ﷺ said: *'The sun does not rise nor does it set upon anyone better, after the Prophets and the Messengers, than Abū Bakr.'*[295] He had the most right to the caliphate from all of the creation of Allāh, after the Prophet ﷺ; and this is due to his merits and his precedence, and also due to the Prophet ﷺ preferring him over all of his companions, may Allāh be pleased with them, to lead the prayer. It is also due to the ijmā' of the companions in recognising his superiority and giving the pledge of allegiance to him. And Allāh would not have united them upon misguidance [and this is mentioned in the books of uṣūl al-fiqh; that the ijmā' has strength, because, the Prophet ﷺ mentioned that this Ummaĥ can never gather upon something that is incorrect, and this narration is almost mutawātir[296]]. **Then after him was 'Umar, due to his merits and Abū Bakr's delegation of it** [meaning, the caliphate] **to him** [before he died]. **Then 'Uthmān, Allāh be pleased with him, due to him being chosen by the members of the shūrā (council). Then 'Alī, Allāh be pleased with him, due to his merits and the ijmā' of the people of his time on it** [meaning, he was the most deserving of the caliphate from amongst his peers, according to them]. **These are the rightly guided caliphs about whom the Messenger of Allāh ﷺ said: *'Stick to my Sunnaĥ and the sunnaĥ of the rightly-guided caliphs after me. Bite onto it*** [i.e. His ﷺ Sunnaĥ and those of the rightly-guided caliphs] ***with your molar teeth.'***[297] [And this means one should follow it very strictly, and not diverge from it]. **The**

[293] Al-Bukhārī, no. 3655 /Abū Dawūd, no. 4628 / al-Tirmidhī, no. 3707, and these narrations all stop after mentioning 'Uthmān. Imām Aḥmad does transmit a report in *al-Musnad*, no. 4797, that mentions 'Alī as the third in line, based on certain qualities. However, this appears to be a weak report. Perhaps, Ibn Qudāmaĥ combined between these reports. Whatever the case may be, the names and order mentioned by Ibn Qudāmaĥ are generally accepted as being correct.

[294] Imām Aḥmad in *al-Musnad*, no. 1060 / *Faḍā°il al-Ṣaḥābaĥ*, no. 397.

[295] Imām Aḥmad in *Faḍā°il al-Ṣaḥābaĥ*, no. 135.

[296] Al-Tirmidhī, no. 2167.

[297] Imām Aḥmad, *al-Musnad*, no. 17145 / Abū Dawūd, no. 4607 / al-Tirmidhī, no. 2676.

Prophet ﷺ said: *'The caliphate after me will endure for thirty years.'*[298] The last part of it occurred with the caliphate of 'Alī, Allāh be pleased with him [yet, from the last six months of this specific time period was the rule of al- Ḥassan b. 'Alī, before he handed it over to Mu'āwiyah b. Abī Sufyān who's rule fell outside of the time mentioned in the aforementioned prophetic narration. Therefore, al-Ḥasan b. 'Alī may also be considered from the rightly-guided caliphs[299]].

We testify for the ten who will be in Paradise, just as the Prophet ﷺ testified for them, when he said: *'Abū Bakr is in Paradise, 'Umar is in Paradise, 'Uthmān is in Paradise, 'Alī is in Paradise, Ṭalḥa is in Paradise, al-Zubayr is in Paradise, Sa'd is in Paradise, Sa'īd is in Paradise, 'Abd al-Raḥmān b. 'Awf is in Paradise, Abū 'Ubaydah b. al- Jarrāḥ is in Paradise.'*[300] As for everyone else whom the Prophet ﷺ has testified will be in Paradise, then we bear witness to that. Such as his statement: *'Al-Ḥasan and al-Ḥusayn are the leaders of the youth in Paradise.'*[301] And his statement to Thābit b. Qays: *'Indeed, he is from the inhabitants of Paradise.'*[302]

We do not confirm [with certainty] **for anyone from the People of the Qiblah that he will be in Paradise or the Hellfire, except for the one whom the Messenger has confirmed it for. However, we hope for the one who does good** [that he shall enter Paradise], **and we fear for the one who does evil** [that he will enter Hellfire. So, whether Muslim or a disbeliever, their final abode (i.e. Paradise or Hellfire) is not determined at all by people. Maybe a person was in fact the opposite of what people said, for only Allāh knows the true reality of a person. However, in general it can be said that the disbeliever will go to the hellfire, and the Muslim will enter paradise]. **We do not declare anyone from the People of the Qiblah a disbeliever because of a sin** [he has committed, like leaving the Prayer for example, until he is tried and tested], **nor do we expel him out of Islām because of an action or deed** [that he has done, until it is confirmed what he meant by it. The trying and judging of a person is performed by the ruler, his

---

[298] Abū Dawūd, no. 4646 / al-Tirmidhī, no. 2226.

[299] The Prophet ﷺ died in 11H, which means that the period of the caliphate he mentioned would endure until 41H. Al-Ḥasan b. 'Alī took over the caliphate after his father 'Alī died (40H). He subsequently held this position for seven months, after which he surrendered his reign to Mu'āwiyah in the year 41H. This shows that his reign was within the period of the rightly-guided caliphs, as described by the prophet ﷺ.

[300] Imām Aḥmad, *al-Musnad*, no. 1675 / al-Tirmidhī, no. 3747.

[301] Imām Aḥmad, *al-Musnad*, no. 10999 / al-Tirmidhī, no. 3768.

[302] Imām Aḥmad, *al-Musnad*, no. 12399 / al-Bukhārī, no. 3613 / Muslim, no. 119.

deputies and the scholars, and further details regarding this can be found in the books of fiqh.]

We hold that Ḥajj and Jihād are continuous along with the obedience to every Muslim leader, whether he is righteous or wicked [as long as he applies the sharī'ah]. **And the congregational prayer behind them is permissible** [unless they are open sinners, which will make the congregational prayer impermissible behind them according to the relied upon opinion in the Ḥanbalī madhhab]. **Anas reported that the Prophet ﷺ said:** ***'Three thing are from the foundation of imān; refraining from (harming) anyone who say 'None has the right to be worshipped but Allāh'. We do not declare him a disbeliever due to a sin (which he has committed), nor do we expel him out of Islām due to an action (he has done). The Jihād is everlasting from the time that Allāh sent me to the time when the last part of my Ummah will fight the Dajjal. It will not be invalidated by the oppression of the oppressor, or the justice of the just*** [although, the kufr of the disbeliever will invalidate it]. ***And (the third is) the belief in the qadar.'*** **Narrated by Abū Dawūd**[303] [however this narration is not authentic].

From the Sunnah is; loyalty to the companions, to love them, mention their good qualities [and to show kindness and respect to them], **and to ask Allāh to grant them mercy and to forgive them. And (also) to refrain from mentioning their shortcomings and what they differed in** [for example, what happened during the first fitnah between Mu'āwiyah and 'Alī], **believing in their virtues and acknowledging their superiority** [and acknowledging that they preceded us in Islām; meaning, they are better than the rest]. **Allāh, the Exalted, says:** ***'And those who come after them say; 'our Lord! Forgive us and our brothers who preceded us in Faith. And put not in our hearts any hatred against those who have believed.'***[304] **And He, the Exalted, says:** ***'Muḥammad is the Messenger of Allāh. And those who are with him are severe against the disbelievers, while being merciful among themselves'***[305] **The Prophet ﷺ said:** ***'Do not revile my companions, for indeed if one you were to give in charity, the equivalent of the mount of Uḥud in gold, it would not reach a mudd*** [a type of measurement commonly used in the time of the Prophet ﷺ] ***of one of them, not even half (of what they give).'***[306]

---

[303] Abū Dawūd, no. 2532.

[304] Qurān: 59:10

[305] Qurān: 48:29

[306] Imām Aḥmad, *al-Musnad*, no. 11079 / al-Bukhārī, no. 3673 and Muslim, no. 2541

From the Sunnah is; being pleased with the wives of the Messenger of Allāh ﷺ, the Mothers of the Believers, the pure ones free from every type of evil. The best of them were Khadījah b. Khuwaylid and 'Ā°ishah b. al-Ṣiddīq, whom Allāh declared free in His Book (from the false accusations against her) [and this is regarding the story of the necklace and the slander (al-ifk)[307]]. **She is the wife of the Prophet ﷺ in this world and the next. Whosoever falsely accuses her with that which Allāh declared her free of, has disbelieved in Allāh, the Most Great** [because he has disbelieved in the Qurān. A general principle in the Madhhab states that such a person becomes a disbeliever, if the accusing is the result of ijtihād. However, if it is the result of taqlīd, then such a person becomes an open sinner, yet, he is not to be regarded as a disbeliever. Therefore, one should not generalize and label all the Shī'ah as disbelievers, because of what they say and do although, one should hate those things. To conclude, one should be careful regarding making takfir of other Muslims.]

Mu'āwiyah is the [maternal] **uncle of the Believers** [as he is the brother of Umm Ḥabībah, who was one of the Prophet's wives], **and one of those who wrote the Revelation of Allāh. He was one of the caliphs of the Muslims** [who came straight after the period of the rightly-guided caliphs], **Allāh be pleased with him.**

[307] al-Bukhārī, no. 4141; in a very long ḥadīth narrated by 'Ā°ishah.

ومِنَ السُّنَّةِ السَّمْعُ والطَّاعَةُ لِأَئِمَّةِ المُسْلِمِينَ وأُمَرَاءِ المُؤْمِنِينَ بَرِّهِمْ وفَاجِرِهِمْ، ما لَمْ يَأْمُروا بِمَعْصِيَةِ اللَّهِ، فَإِنَّهُ لا طاعَةَ لِأَحَدٍ في مَعْصِيَةِ اللَّهِ.

From the Sunnah is; hearing and obeying the Muslim leaders and the leaders of the believers, the righteous from amongst them as well as the unrighteous ones as long as they do not order disobedience to Allāh. Verily, there is no obedience to anyone if it involves disobedience to Allāh.

ومَنْ ولِي الخِلافَةَ، واجْتَمَعَ عَلَيْهِ النَّاسُ ورَضُوا بِهِ، أَوْ غَلَبَهُمْ بِسَيْفِهِ حَتى صارَ خَليفَةً، وسُمِّيَ أميرَ المُؤْمِنينَ، وَجَبَتْ طاعَتُهُ، وحَرُمَتْ مُخَالَفَتُهُ والخُروجُ عَلَيْهِ وشَقُّ عَصا المُسْلِمينَ.

It is obligatory to obey whosoever is given the caliphate while the people are united in his selection and are pleased with him, or whoever became the caliph by overpowering the people with his sword and is called Leader of the Believers. Opposing him, revolting against him and sowing the seeds of dissension among the Muslim against him is forbidden.

Commentary: Obeying the Muslim leader

From the Sunnah is; hearing and obeying the Muslim leaders and the rulers of the believers, the righteous from among them as well as the unrighteous ones as long as they do not order the disobedience to Allāh [so, when he rules with something other than the sharī'ah he orders disobedience. In this case he is not to be followed or obeyed]. **Verily, there is no obedience to anyone if it involves disobedience to Allāh** [and this ruler should be disobeyed and can even be fought in some cases, but this is related to the maṣlaḥah (public interest and benefit). For example, if fighting the ruler leads to widespread bloodshed or worsens the affairs of the Muslims, then it should be avoided and not fighting him will be considered the lesser of the two evils. It is important to emphasize that the scholars should be consulted for a ruling regarding fighting the ruler or not.].

It is obligatory to obey whosoever is given the caliphate while the people are united in his selection and are pleased with him, or whoever became the caliph by overcoming the people with his sword [the act of 'overpowering people with the sword' by using armed force might be prohibited, however, it being prohibited is irrelevant to the issue of keeping Muslims safe, and stopping any bloodshed by obeying this person as long as he keeps the religion safe] **and is called Leader of the Believers** [it is not necessary that the people and/or scholars proclaim him leader of the believers. He himself can proclaim to be leader of the believers as he has the position and army to support his claim. If there is a case where two parties proclaim themselves to be the rightful caliph, then the one who proclaimed it first is to be followed[308]]. **Opposing him, revolting against him and sowing the seeds of dissension among the Muslims against him** [thereby, breaking their unity], **is forbidden.**

---

[308] In his regard Muslim transmitted in his *Ṣaḥīḥ*, no. 1853: *'When oath of allegiance has been taken for two caliphs, kill the one for whom the oath was taken later.'*

ومِنَ السُّنَّةِ هِجْرانُ أَهْلِ البِدَعِ ومُبَايَنَتُهُمْ، وتَرْكُ الجِدَالِ والخُصُومَاتِ في الدِّينِ، وتَرْكُ النَّظَرِ في كُتُبِ المبْتَدِعَةِ والإِصْغاءِ إلى كَلامِهِمْ، وكُلُّ مُحْدَثَةٍ في الدِّينِ بِدْعَةٌ.

And from the Sunnaħ is; abandoning of the People of Innovations (Ahl al-Bid'aħ) and distinguishing oneself from them, leaving arguing and disputing in the religion, and not looking into the books of the innovators or listening attentively to their speech. And every newly invented matter in the religion is an innovation.

وكُلُّ مُتَّسِمٍ بِغَيْرِ الإِسْلامِ والسُّنَّةِ مُبْتَدِعٌ: كَالرَّافِضَةِ، والجَهْمِيَّةِ، والخَوارِجِ، والقَدَرِيَّةِ والمُرْجِئَةِ، والمُعْتَزِلَةِ، والكَرَّامِيَّةِ، والكُلَّابِيَّةِ، ونَظَائِرِهِم، فَهَذِهِ فِرَقُ الضَّلالِ وطَوَائِفُ البِدَعِ أَعَاذَنَا اللَّهُ مِنْها.

Anyone who names himself with other than Islām and the Sunnaħ is an innovator, such as the Rāfiḍaħ, the Jahmiyyaħ, the Khawārij, the Qadariyyaħ, the Murji°aħ, the Mu'tazilaħ, the Karrāmiyyaħ, the Kullābiyyaħ and those similar to them. These are sects of misguidance and parties of innovation. May Allāh grant us refuge from them.

Commentary: Abandoning the People of Innovation

And from the Sunnaħ is; abandoning of the People of Innovations (Ahl al-Bid'aħ) and distinguishing oneself from them [it is an obligation to abandon innovators, in order for their hearts to be reminded of their corrupted ways and to compel them to cease their innovation. Additionally, when it is known that a certain individual or group should be abandoned or boycotted, then this act of abandonment helps to make others aware of their erroneous and abhorrent positions. The evidence for the abandonment of the innovator is what has been narrated by Ibn 'Umar from the Prophet ﷺ, that he said: *'The Qadariyyaħ are the Magians of this community. If they are ill, do not visit them, and if they die, do not attend their funerals.'*[309]

[309] Abū Dawūd, no. 4691.

Furthermore, individuals are either scholars or layman. Concerning the scholar, if he befriends an innovator, agrees with his innovations and believes their kufr, then this scholar will be accused with regards to his aqīdaħ. With regards to the layman, if he befriends the innovators and gets along with them, then the innovators own position will strengthen due to the layman's ignorance. With all this in mind, it becomes clear that it is an obligation to reject innovators and their innovations by abandonment of them and their innovations which may actually be, or lead to kufr in certain cases], **leaving arguing and disputing in religion, and not looking into the books of the innovators and listening attentively to their speech** [and this is in general for all Muslims, although the scholars are subject to different rulings as at times they need to argue and dispute with innovators and look into their books in order to refute them so as to protect the religion]. **And every newly invented matter in the Religion** [itself] **is an innovation**[310] [it concerns innovations into the religion itself, not innovations related to the religion because all of one's life is related to the religion. So, to classify everything that is newly invented as an innovation would be highly problematic for one's life. For example, when one has a job and works to earn money to buy books in order to study the Religion, then in that case his job is related to the religion. When something is newly invented in this job, it is not classified as an innovation. However, when it is something newly invented in the religion itself such an extra type of prayer or fast and the like, then it is classified as an innovation].

Anyone who names himself with other than Islām and the Sunnaħ is an innovator, such as the Rāfiḍaħ, the Jahmiyyaħ, the Khawārij, the Qadariyyaħ, the Murji°aħ, the Mu'tazilaħ, the Karrāmiyyaħ, the Kullābiyyaħ and those similar to them. These are sects of misguidance and parties of innovation [in a general sense; including all of their branches. The author did not mention the Ashā'iraħ and the Māturīdīyaħ specifically, indicating perhaps that he did not certainly consider them from amongst the sects of misguidance and innovation, categorically; even though he spoke harshly of the Ashā'iraħ in his other books such as *Taḥrīm al-Naẓar*. Therefore, it may be understood that his critique, including his harsh words, regarding the Ashā'iraħ is more specific and is directed at particular opinions and methods of theirs. This ties in with what was mentioned earlier with regards to their two opinions regarding the Attributes of

---

310 Abū Dawūd, no. 4607 / al-Nasā°ī, no. 1578: *'...every newly-invented matter is an innovation...'*

Allāh; one opinion being rejected by the Ḥanābilaḧ while they both agree on the other (i.e. tafwīḍ or general ta°wīl]. **May Allāh grant us refuge from them.**

وأمَّا النِّسْبَةِ إلى إمامٍ في فُروعِ الدِّينِ كَالطَّوائِفِ الأَرْبَعِ فَلَيْسَ بِمَذْمُومٍ، فَإِنَّ الاخْتِلافَ في الفُروعِ رَحْمَةٌ، وَالمُخْتَلِفونَ فيهِ مَحْمُودُونَ في اخْتِلافِهِمْ، مُثابُونَ في اجْتِهادِهِمْ، وَاخْتِلافُهُمْ رَحْمَةٌ واسِعَةٌ، وَاتِّفاقُهُمْ حُجَّةٌ قاطِعَةٌ.

As for ascribing oneself to an imām in the subsidiary issues of religion, such as the four madhhāhib, then this is not something blameworthy. For indeed, the differing in the subsidiary issues of religion is a mercy and those who differ in it, are praiseworthy in their differing; and they will be rewarded for their ijtihād. Their differing is a vast mercy and their agreement is a decisive proof.

Commentary: Concerning Taqlīd and Ijtihād

As for ascribing oneself to an imām in the subsidiary issues of Religion [meaning, issues of fiqh], **such as the four Madhāhib** [by referring to oneself as Ḥanbalī, Mālikī, Shāfi'ī or Ḥanafī], **then this is not something blameworthy** [and the words of the author indicate something that is more general than taqlīd for a mujtahid can also ascribe himself to a particular madhhab, always agreeing in his ijtihād with the positions of the scholars of that madhhab. This is what al-Suyūṭī mentions about himself, saying: 'I never followed al-Shāfi'ī, but whenever I did ijtihād I reached the same conclusion (as him)']. **For indeed, the differing in the subsidiary issues of religion is a mercy and those who differ in it, are praiseworthy in their differing** [meaning, it is not the actual differing between the scholars that is praiseworthy, but it is the reaching of different opinions through their ijtihād that is praiseworthy and they will be rewarded even if they were wrong.]; **and they will be rewarded for their ijtihād. Their differing is a vast mercy and their agreement is a decisive proof.**

CLOSING REMARKS

نَسْأَلُ اللَّهَ أنْ يَعْصِمَنا مِنَ الْبِدَعِ وَالْفِتْنَةِ، وَيُحْيِينَا عَلى الإِسْلامِ وَالسُّنَّةِ، وَيَجْعَلَنَا مِمَّنْ يَتَّبِعُ رَسولَ اللَّهِ صَلَّى اللهُ عَلَيْهِ وَسَلَّمَ في الحَياةِ، وَيَحْشُرَنَا في زُمْرَتِهِ بَعْدَ المَمَاتِ بِرَحْمَتِهِ وَفَضْلِهِ آمِينَ.

We ask Allāh that he protects us from innovation and trials and that He causes us to live upon Islām and the Sunnaĥ. And that He makes us from among those who strictly follow the Messenger of Allāh ﷺ when alive and that He resurrects us in his company after death, through His *Raḥmaĥ* and His *Faḍl*. Āmīn.

وَهَذَا آخِرُ المُعْتَقَدِ. وَالحَمْدُ للهِ وَحْدَهُ، وَصلَّى اللَّهُ عَلى سَيِّدِنَا مُحَمَّدٍ وَ آلِهِ وَصَحْبِهِ وَسَلَّمَ تَسْلِيمًا.

This is the end of the ʻaqīdaĥ. All Praise is due to Allāh alone, and may Allāh's peace and blessing be upon our leader Muḥammad, his family and his Companions.

This was written by one in need of the pardon of his Lord al-Ghanī, Muwaffaq al-Dīn, Yūsuf b. Ṣādiq al-Ḥanbalī, and it was finished on the night of the 1st of the month of Rajab, 1441AH/February 25, 2020.

And all praise is due to Allāh.

May the peace and blessing of Allāh be upon our master Muḥammad and his followers and companions.

BIBLIOGRAPHY

For the six canonical works of ḥadīth: al-Bukhārī, Muslim, Abū Dawūd, al-Tirmidhī and al-Nasāºī, the reference (ch., no.) is used as provided by sunnaḧ.com: https://sunnaḧ.com

Abū al-Shaykh, Muḥammad. (1992). *Ṭabaqāt al-Muḥaddathīn bi-Aṣbahān*, Beirut: Muºasasaḧ al-Risālaḧ.
— (1996). *Kitāb al-ʻAẓamaḧ* (vol. 5). Riyad: Dār al-ʻĀsimaḧ.

Abū Khaythamaḧ, Zahīr b. Harb. (2001). *Kitāb al-ʻIlm*, Riyad: Maktabaḧ al-Maʻārif

Abū Jaʻfar al-Ḥanbalī, al-Ḥajj. (2018). *The Creed and Way of Muslim Orthodoxy*. (n.p.): HTS Publications.

Al-Ājurī, Abū Bakr. (1997). *Kitāb al-Sharīʻaḧ*. (vol. 1, 3). Riyad: Dār al-Waṭan.

Al-Anbārī, Abū Bakr. (1971). *Īḍāḥ al-Waqt wa al-Ibtidāº fi Kitāb Allāh Azza wa Jall* (vol. 1). Damascus: Maṭbūʻāt Majmaʻ al-Lughaḧ al-ʻArabiyyaḧ

Al-Aṣbahānī, Abū Nuʻaym, ʻAbd Allāh. (1987). *Ḥilyaḧ al-Awliyāº wa al- Ṭabaqāt al-Aṣfiyāº* (vol. 1). Beirut: Dār al-Fikr.

Al-ʻAsqalānī, Ibn Hajar. (2013). *Fatḥ al-Bārī Sharḥ Ṣaḥīḥ al-Bukhārī* (vol. 20). Beirut: Dār al-Risālaḧ al-ʻĀlamiyyaḧ.

Al-Bayhaqī, Abū Bakr. (1986). *al-Baʻth wa al-Nushūr*. Beirut: Markaz al- Khudumāt wa al-Abhāth al-Thaqāfiyyah.

Al-Dārimī, Abū Muḥammad. (2013). *Al-Musnad al-Jāmiʻ*. Beirut: Dār al- Bashāºir al-Islāmiyyaḧ.

Al-Dārimī, ʻUthmān b. Saʻīd. (1985). *Al-Radd ʻalā al-Jahmiyyaḧ*. Kuwait: al-Dār al-Salafiyyaḧ.

Al-Dhahabī, Shams al-Dīn. (1986). *Siyār Aʻlām al-Nubulāº* (vol. 11, 22). Beirut: Muºasasaḧ al-Risālaḧ.

Al-Ḥākim, Muḥammad b. ʻAbd Allāh. (1997). *Al-Mustadrak ʻalā al- Ṣaḥīḥayn* (vol. 5). Cairo: Dār al-Ḥaramayn.
— (2003). *Maʻrifaḧ ʻUlūm al-Ḥadīth*. Beirut: Dār Ibn Ḥazm.

Al-Harawī, Abū Ismā'īl. (2003). *Dhamm al-Kalām wa Ahlih* (vol. 2), (n.p.): Maktabaḧ al-Ghurabā° al-Athariyyaḧ

Al-Kalwadānī, Abū al-Khaṭṭāb. (n.d.). *Dāliyyaḧ al-Imām Abū al-Khaṭṭāb Al-Kalwadānī fi al-Sunnaḧ.* Retrieved September 29, 2019, from: http://amribnhaiman.blogspot.com/2019/03/pdf_69.html

Al-Khallāl, Ḥasan b. Muḥammad. (1990). *Al-Majālis al-'Ashraḧ al-Amāl.* (n.p.): Dār al-Ṣaḥābaḧ

—. (1994). Al-Sunnaḧ (vol. 1), Riyad: Dār al-Rāyaḧ.

Al-Khaṭīb al-Baghdādī, Abū Bakr. (2001). *Tārīkh Madīnaḧ al-Salām* (vol. 11), Beirut: Dār al-Gharb al-Islāmī

Al-Lālikā°ī, Abū Qāsim (2003). *Sharḥ Uṣūl I'tiqād Ahl al-Sunnaḧ wa al- Jamā'aḧ* (vol. 2). Riyad: Dār Ṭaybaḧ.

Al-Najād, Abū Bakr Ibn. (n.d.). *al-Radd 'alā man yaqūl al-Qurān Makhlūq*. Kuwait: Maktabaḧ al-Ṣaḥābaḧ al-Islamiyyaḧ

Al-Quḍāī, Aḥmad 'Abd Allāh. (1986). *Musnad al-Shihāb* (vol. 1). Beirut: Mu°asasaḧ al-Riasālaḧ.

Al-Ṣābūnī, Ibn 'Uthmān. (1998). *'Aqīdaḧ al-Salaf Aṣḥāb al-Ḥadīth,* Riyad: Dār al-'Āṣimaḧ

Al-Safārīnī, Muḥammad b. Aḥmad. (2016). *Lawāmi' al-Anwār al- Bahiyyaḧ wa Sawāṭi' al-Asrār al-Athariyyaḧ* (vol. 1). Riyad: Dār al-Tawḥīd li-al-Nasr.

Al-Ṣan'ānī, *'Abd al-Razzāq. (2015). Al-Muṣannaf* (vol. 7). Cairo: Dār al-Ta°ṣīl.

Al-Sijzī, Abū Nasr. (1994). *Risālaḧ al-Sijzī ilā Ahl Zabīd,* Riyad: Dār al-Rāyaḧ

Al-Ṭabarānī, Abū al-Qāsim. (1994). *Al-Mu'jam al-Kabīr* (vol. 9). Cairo: Maktabaḧ Ibn Taymiyyaḧ

—. (1995). *Al-Mu'jam al-Awsaṭ* (vol. 7). Cairo: Dār al-Ḥaramayn.

Al-Ṭabarī, Muḥammad b. Jarīr. (2001). *Tafsīr al-Ṭabarī* (vol. 1). Cairo: Dār Hajr.

Al-Ṭūfī, Najm al-Dīn. (1999), *Al-Intisārāt al-Islāmiyyaḧ* (vol. 2). Riyad: Maktabaḧ al-'Abīkān.

Al-'Ukbarī, Ibn Baṭṭaḧ. (1994). *Al-Ibānaḧ 'an Sharī'aḧ al-Firqaḧ al- Nājiyaḧ,* (vol. 7). Riyad: Dār al-Rāyah.

Al-Zimzimī, 'Abd al-'Azīz. (n.d.). *Manẓūmaḧ al-Zimzimī*. Retrieved from: https://saaid.net/Anshatah/dorah/5.pdf

Ibn 'Abd Al-Qādir, 'Abd al-Bāqī. (1987). *Al-'Ayn wa al-Athar fī 'Aqā°id Ahl al-Athar*. Beirut: Dār al-Mā°mūn al-Turāth.

Ibn Abū 'Āṣim, Abū Bakr. (1980). *Kitāb al-Sunnaḧ* (vol. 1), Beirut: al- Maktab al-Islāmī.

Ibn Abī Shaybaḧ, Abū Bakr. (2008). *Musannaf Ibn Abī Shaybaḧ* (vol. 10). Cairo: al-Fārūq al-Ḥadīthaḧ.

Ibn Aḥmad, 'Abd Allāh. (1996). *Kitāb al-Sunnaḧ* (vol. 1), Riyad: Dār 'Ālam al-Kutub.

Ibn al-Bannā°, al-Ḥasan b. Aḥmad. (2007). *Al-Uṣūl al-Mujarradaḧ 'alā Tartīb al-Qaṣīdaḧ al-Mujawwadaḧ*, Damascus: Dār Ṭaybaḧ.

Ibn Anas, Mālik. (1997). *Al-Muwaṭṭa°* (vol. 2), Beirut: Dār al-Gharb al-Islāmī

Ibn al-Farā°, Abū Ya'lā. (n.d.). *Ibṭāl al-Ta°wilāt* (vol. 1). Kuwait: Dār Īlāf al-Dawliyaḧ.

Ibn al-Jawzī, 'Abd al-Raḥmān. (2008). *Manāqib al-Imām Aḥmad*. Cairo: Dār al-Hajr.

Ibn Ḥanbal, Aḥmad. (1999). *Musnad Imām Aḥmad Ibn Ḥanbal*. Beirut: Mu°asasaḧ al-Risālaḧ.
—. (1999). *Al-Zuhd*, Beirut: Dār al-Kutub al-'Ilmiyyaḧ.
—. (1999). *Faḍā°il al-Ṣaḥābaḧ* (vol. 1), Dammam: Dār Ibn al-Jawzī.
—. (2012). *Uṣūl al-Sunnaḧ*, Beirut: Dār al-Kutub al-'Ilmiyyaḧ.

Ibn Khuzaymaḧ, Abū Bakr. (1988). *Kitāb al-Tawhīd wa Ithbāt Ṣifāt al- Rabb 'Azza wa Jalla* (vol. 1), Riyad: Dār al-Rushaykh

Ibn Qudāmaḧ, Muwaffaq al-Dīn. (1988). *Burhān fi Bayān al-Qurān*. Port Said: Maktabah al-Hadiyy al-Nabawī al-Islamiyyah
—. (1988). *Ithbāt Ṣifaḧ al-'Uluww*. Madīnaḧ: Maktabaḧ al-'Ulūm wa al Ḥikam
—. (1990). *Munāẓaraḧ fī al-Qurān al-'Aẓīm*. Kuwait: Maktabaḧ Ibn Taymiyyaḧ
—. (1990). *Taḥrīm al-Naẓar fī Kutub al-Kalām*. Riyad: Dār 'Ālam al-Kutub
—. (1994). *Dhamm al-Ta°wīl*. Sharjah: Dār al-Fatḥ.
—. (1998). *Rawḍaḧ al-Nāẓir wa Jannaḧ al-Manāẓir* (vol. 1). Beirut: Mu°asasah al-Riyān
—. (2019). *Lum'aḧ al-I'tiqād al-Hādī ilā Sabīl al-Rashād*. Riyad: Dār al-Rakā°iz

Ibn Rajab, Zayn al-Dīn. (1985). *Bayān Faḍl ʻIlm al-Salaf ʻalā ʻIlm al-Khalaf*. Riyad: Dār al-Ṣamīʻī.
—. (2005). *Dhayl ʻalā Ṭabaqāt al-Ḥanābilaḧ* (vol. 2, 3). Mecca: Maktabaḧ ʻAbīkān.
—. (2008). *Ikhtiyār al-Ūlā fī Sharḥ ḥadīth Ikhtiṣām al-Mal°a al-Aʻlā*. Kuwait: Dār al-Aqṣā°.

MARIA'S Common Law BATTLE

A Novel

JEFFREY MORRIS

VISTASTAR
PUBLISHING

Vistastar Publishing
Toronto, Canada
vistastar.com

Book design by Alex Lubertozzi
Cover design by David Drummond

ISBN 978-0-9731657-3-9 (paperback)
ISBN 978-0-9731657-4-6 (ebook)

To Adrienne—whose love and care lift me through each day, and to whom I hope to give back even a fraction of the light she brings into my life

PART I

– 1 –

MAYA CARSON eased herself into a white wooden deck chair, her bare feet resting on the cool, moist grass, hardly aware of the gentle waves of the ocean below. The same persistent, nagging decision circled in her mind. After seven long years in an unwed union with Julian Barrett, the act of leaving felt like liberation.

He dodged every effort to discuss her ticking biological clock at the age of thirty-four. A child, not now and perhaps not ever—with him.

Her blonde hair hung loose over her shoulders, and a light summer dress clung softly to her frame. The sun found the freckles across her cheeks and nose, a constellation that gave her an almost girlish air, though her eyes—clear, blue, and watchful—belonged to someone older, someone who had learned when to stay guarded.

A seagull's cry pierced the air as it swooped down, startling her and disrupting her thoughts.

Resolve hit. Nope, it's time to move on.

As she breathed in the salt air, the memory of last night's fight drifted back. Maya rarely lost her composure, but last night was an exception. He had driven her past the breaking point—one excuse piled on top of another. His artwork was gathering dust, not selling. The economy was in shambles. People just weren't buying. His father's estate was a tangled mess.

Maya spent her nights tossing and turning, unable to find peace. The endless replay of conversations left her in turmoil, unresolved and drifting, as if her life was stuck in a loop, never truly beginning or moving forward.

He boldly suggested, "Let's wait another year," as if that settled everything, as though he believed he had the ultimate say.

"Don't you walk away, Julian!"

"What?" he called back, already near his studio down the hall, moving out of reach.

She stood in the dimly lit hallway, her hands clenched into fists at her sides. Her voice pierced the air as she called out to the room where Julian stood, absorbed in his newest painting.

"I'm so sick and tired. Last year it was your father's passing, now it's the mess he left, and now we're drowning in the chaos he left behind. You and your brother have done nothing to tackle this overwhelming disaster!"

Julian marched back from the studio, his voice filled with intensity, teetering on the edge of a full-blown yell.

"Well, that's the reality, Maya! What don't you get? This isn't the right moment to begin a family."

"It never is with you! Life will never be perfect, Julian. You'll keep delaying this indefinitely. I need an answer. Is it yes or no?"

Julian paused, unsure of himself. She noticed the brief moment of doubt in his expression, marked by the tension in his jaw.

"Maya, I need time to figure this out."

Maya's eyes widened, her heart thumping hard. She clenched her fists in her lap. "Answer me—yes or no. Right now!"

Even though she tried to keep her voice steady, the words emerged louder and more sharply than intended. She battled to suppress the erupting anger within, wishing Julian would finally recognize her mounting frustration.

He nearly shouted, "No, for now," but managed to lower his voice just in time.

"Then go. I need time. Get some things and go to your father's house for the night. I want to be alone. Go sleep there."

He obeyed and left quietly, not uttering another word. The house fell silent, leaving her with his response—and her choice to drive him away. A decision she both regretted and stood by.

Maya sat in the white deck chair, her feet buried in the wet grass. The argument from the previous night hung in the air, fading away with the arrival of morning. Sunlight shimmered on the water. The scent of salt filled the air. Rain was on its way. The ocean waves rolled in beneath, with a calm and steady rhythm. The day was starting. The sea's horizon held her gaze.

Her legs draped over the chair's edge; with two toes, she plucked a new dandelion.

A gull circled high. Waves quieted her mind. Problems drifted away in the open air—clarity formed just by breathing it in.

Memories came, one after another—Julian's slow hands moving up her thigh, his laugh, the days they painted and redecorated the living room together. Maya ran her brush down the wall, drawing a crude stick-man portrait of him right in the centre. Julian grinned, told her she could be an artist too, if she wanted.

But that wasn't it. Maya didn't want to be an artist. She wanted a family. She wanted something of her own—something that would last. She wanted to stop waiting.

Maya shut her eyes, enveloped by the silence. As she stood on the front lawn, the wind pushing at her, the chill of it threading through the thin fabric of her dress. The sea's murmur drifted up from below, steady but distant, just out of reach.

After some time, she turned around. Inside, her life awaited her—silent rooms, morning light casting shadows on the floor, and the remnants of yesterday's argument still resonating within the walls.

The kitchen was a mess. Julian's dirty painting rags lay beside the sink. Canvases were stacked three deep against the far wall, each one a silent story waiting to be told, their surfaces splattered with vibrant hues and abstract patterns. Old bills with their torn edges were tucked haphazardly under the fruit bowl, peeking out as reminders of tough times. Last night's emptied wine bottle. The cork by the sink tap. The courage it gave her to speak her mind.

Things just left, not tidy.

She remembered the first days in the house, about five years ago—how old and worn it had felt. The kitchen linoleum curled at the edges; the bathroom fixtures belonged to another era. Maya spent nearly a year sanding floors and woodwork, selecting paint colours, and doing most of the work herself. Even after all the changes, something of the old house lingered—history in the floorboards, the faint trace of Barrett family chaos in every room. Julian's father, Howard Barrett, had passed almost a year before, and the mess he left behind continued to widen.

There was that day—before the family issues arose—around a year after Maya had settled into the old, rundown cottage the Barretts called the Beach House. Julian had spent his childhood there, before Howard built a new, luxurious home down the road at the height of his success.

Howard showed up, arms wrapped around a plain cardboard box, a spark in his eyes she hadn't seen before. Maya had tracked down the Jean-Paul Riopelle painting herself, found it in a quiet Halifax estate, half-forgotten, amazed that something so important could be hidden so close to home. Howard, ever the art collector, had pounced the moment she called.

He carried the package through the front door, cradling it as if it were breakable, set it on the kitchen table, and took a long breath. The box was sealed tight with layers of transparent tape, wrapped in an old wool blanket that smelled of cedar and dust. Not a professional job, but careful. Maya watched as he worked the tape loose, slow and steady, each rip echoing in the quiet house. When he opened the box, colour burst on the canvas—thick, bold, unmistakable.

Howard looked at Maya then, proud and boyish, pleased by what they'd managed to bring home. He was gone now, but she still saw him there, steady hands unfolding the blanket and beaming with joy.

Using two hangers, Howard placed the Riopelle above the fireplace on the pink wall of the Beach House living room. At that time, the property was jointly owned by Howard and Julian—a sign of trust, or perhaps just practicality. Although Maya had moved in and handled most of the renovations, she never insisted on having her name on the title.

Standing behind Howard, she pondered issues like insurance and inheritance, questioning whether the painting or Beach House would ever truly belong to her. She never dared to voice this question, leaving it lingering in the air, unresolved—something she now regretted.

The Riopelle was both sculpture and painting—thick ridges of oil rising and folding, with pigment squeezed directly from the tube. Black, white, red, yellow, and blue collided in chance and colour. The surface was shaped by gravity, not just brush or palette knife. Depending on the light, you might see a wing, a river's bend, or a storm's edge. Other times, it was pure colour, battling on the canvas, resisting a single meaning.

Each time Maya passed, something changed—a branch, a glint, a memory. Riopelle never explained it; you just had to let it move through you.

Time to get a move on; the morning is slipping away. She picked up her mug, poured more coffee, and walked through the living room—pink walls, faded now. She stepped around Julian's latest unfinished canvas. The floor creaked. The Riopelle above the mantel—bright colour in a pink room. She looked at it, then looked away.

In the bathroom, she splashed water on her face and observed the droplets slide down the porcelain sink. Her reflection in the mirror revealed an older appearance, marked by lines around her mouth and weariness under her eyes. She dried her face, smoothed her hair, and stared at herself, anticipating an emotion that never came. Checking her teeth, she attempted a small smile, which felt unfamiliar.

Maya put on her jeans, tied her hair back, and removed the sheets from the bed, leaving them in the hallway. The bed seemed too large. She paused in the doorway, embracing the silence, before heading to the kitchen to make toast. She ate it standing, watching the yard, as butter dripped onto her hand.

She reached for her phone, her thumb hovering over Julian's name. She didn't type anything or erase any previous messages. No text was sent. Her heart ached, pulling her toward him with a longing she couldn't completely suppress. Perhaps she was making a mistake—should she let him return, or should she make the separation final? She wiped her hands, placed the phone face down, and resisted the urge to look at it again.

At ten o'clock, the front door opened to a brighter morning. The sun was higher now, the air warmer, sharp with the scent of salt. Maya turned back towards the front steps, a bundle of yesterday's mail clutched tight in one hand—mostly fliers and bills. The faint sea sounded from behind the cottage, road quiet but for the far-off thrum of a lawnmower. Maya paused, waiting outside the door.

Greta approached along the lane, her elderly black Lab trotting beside her, its muzzle grey and pace slow. Greta was tall and slender, with a windbreaker zipped up to her chin and short, white hair. She stopped in front of Maya, as steady as a rock, her eyes bright behind wire-rimmed glasses.

"Morning, Maya." Greta lifted her hand in a small, fluttering wave.

"Morning," Maya replied.

Greta loosened the leash, allowing the dog to sniff around in the grass. "I saw Julian on his dad's porch last night while I was taking Sam for a late walk. Is everything all right?"

Maya felt a quick pang in her chest. "Just needed some time alone. Nothing major."

Greta gave a slight smile. "You're welcome to talk or come over for some wine anytime."

Maya tried to make sense of it all—torn, uncertain about Julian, still so unsure about a future together. Greta watched her, her eyes gentle and patient, waiting. Maya suppressed her feelings, thinking it best not to reveal them in public. She wasn't even sure about what she truly wanted.

"Thanks, Greta. I might take you up on that."

Greta nodded, and as the dog tugged, they continued down the lane, leaving the yard feeling emptier.

Maya strolled along the garden's perimeter. Tall weeds choked the lilies. She crouched, yanking out roots until her nails were filthy, working until her back throbbed. Sweat trickled down her forehead as the sun burned away the last of the fog.

After a while, she made her way inside. The front door slammed behind her, making her heart jump—but it was only the wind. In the kitchen, she rinsed her mug under the hot tap, feeling the sting on her hands, and wiped them on her jeans. The house was quiet, except for the fridge's gentle hum.

She wiped the counter and made a list—groceries, laundry, maybe revise her will.

Near ten, she opened her laptop to find a new email.

Forwarded by Julian. Written by his brother, Lucas.

Lucas's message was terse. No greeting.

> **Subject: Fwd: Riopelle**
>
> Tell Maya to bring the Riopelle to Howard's house. It belongs to the estate. IT'S TIME TO SELL!

She read it twice. Her jaw tightened, heat rising in her chest. Bring the Riopelle? None of it made sense.

She fired off a response to Julian:

> What the hell?? No. I need to know what's going on. Get here now.

Sent.

She sat at the table, hands flat, gripping the edge, fingernails digging in.

Morning light spilled through the window. Heat pressed against her back.

That was it—the bastards.

– 2 –

JULIAN LINGERED at the window, coffee steaming in his mug, watching the realtor's sign sway in the breeze. He caught his reflection in the glass—tall, a little over six feet, narrow through the shoulders, still carrying the easy frame of youth. His hair, dark and slightly overgrown, curled at the ends and brushed his collar, a touch of boyish grace he'd never quite lost. The sunlight illuminated the bold red letters, FOR SALE, loud in the morning light—a kind of silent plea. Selling his parents' home wouldn't solve anything; it was heavily mortgaged.

Instead, just one more thing slipping away. Julian wanted to move on, start fresh, break free from Maya and everything his family's house stood for. But standing there, the place felt safe, familiar. He couldn't quite let go, not yet.

The grass out front was high and unruly. Julian thought about cutting it, then let the chore drift—no word from the realtor, no buyers lined up, the market slow, and no sale coming soon. It could wait.

Howard's house was emptier than ever. His brother, Lucas, had visited with empty boxes, taking away cherished items to sell. Every room felt plundered, as if someone had slipped in while he slept and made off with anything that mattered. The night before, he'd wandered from room to room, trying to find a place that felt right. So many things gone. Memories erased, the rooms vacant and still. The silence was suffocating, weighing down like an anchor.

He tried his old bedroom first. The mattress sagged deeply in the centre—a dip he used to slide into unconsciously. Now, he despised it, the way his back sank with no support underneath. He needed something firmer, something that wouldn't give way in the night.

Julian decided to check Howard's room instead. The large TV was gone. The walls showed pale outlines where paintings once hung, ghosts in the paint. The mattress was newer—too firm, never like his own. But the bedroom set was a wedding present, his parents' first. Lying back, he could feel his mother there, moving through the woodwork, dusting and polishing. Though she had been gone for a long time, a part of her still lingered in the room. It was enough to comfort him, at least for the night.

Further down the corridor, the realtor had tried to fill the empty spaces with Walmart prints: cheap frames, tulips too bright, Paris cafés with cartoon faces—pictures that didn't belong in this house. Julian thought about taking them down, hanging his work instead. But the will wouldn't come. He stood in the hallway, emptiness stretching around him, the rooms waiting for something that wasn't coming back.

In the pale light of dawn, he pondered once more why the realtor had permitted Lucas to strip the house so completely. Why remove the art and sell off everything that gave the home its lived-in feel? Yet even before he finished the thought, he knew the answer. Lucas did whatever he pleased—never asking, just acting. If he saw a way to pocket a little extra or speed things along, he'd do it. Impulsive, restless, always in need of money, and never patient. The realtor went along with it, eager for a quick sale, content to cover the empty walls with whatever prints were on hand.

He heard Lucas before he saw him—the old Ferrari rumbling up the drive, a door slammed harder than needed. The front door swung open, cool air following him in. Lucas never knocked. He filled the doorway—tall, fit, every movement crisp and certain. His hair was cut close, dark blond with a few silver threads showing through, and his skin carried the faint polish of moneyed leisure, a tan that looked maintained rather than earned. The clothes were perfect, as always—pressed polo, leather loafers, watch glinting in the light—yet the face told another story. The lines around his eyes had deepened, and something jittered just beneath the surface, a small tremor that betrayed too many sleepless nights. His smile could dazzle, but his eyes stayed cold, measuring the room. He clomped across the hardwood in his shoes, ignoring the mat. Their mother never allowed shoes in the house. Lucas never went along with anything that even looked like respect.

His voice cut through the quiet, steady and assured. "Jules? You in here?"

"In here." Julian's answer was low, dull. He kept his eyes on the pine kitchen table, drumming his fingers along the mug's chipped rim—the same chip, he remembered, from the night Maya dropped it.

He heard the scrape of Lucas's empty duffel bag sliding across the kitchen floor, zipper already open—ready to swallow up whatever was left. Julian felt a tug in his chest, picturing Maya's keys on the windowsill at the Beach House, her shoes lined up by the door and wondered if he could really ask her to leave the home they'd built there. The Beach House was his, on paper. But nothing else felt like it belonged to him.

Lucas glanced around the vast kitchen, never still. His gaze swept over the canvases and half-finished panels propped against the empty wall where their mother's cherished hutch had once been. The pungent scent of turpentine hung in the air.

"It smells like a hardware store in here," he muttered. "If we have a potential buyer coming, make sure to clean this up. Nobody wants to buy an art supply depot."

Without looking at Julian, Lucas sat down at the kitchen table and flipped through the short stack of new mail, tossing junk aside, searching for the bills he had to pay—just enough to keep the lights and water on.

The other stacks—legacy debt—remained untouched, the kind that sits in your gut like bad food: designer clothes Howard bought on credit, a new furnace his father couldn't afford but needed anyway.

Lucas grabbed the realtor's folder and waved it. "You know the listing is almost expired. Only two showings—pathetic. We should try Jane Fitzsimmons; she says she moves places like this. Do you think? Otherwise, it's just going to sit. And if I let you stay here, at least keep it tidy, will you?"

Julian didn't look up. He traced a hairline crack in his cup, thumb back and forth, a quiet rhythm.

"It's your call," he said, voice flat. "You're in charge." He didn't bother to ask why Lucas wanted his opinion. Lucas always did what he wanted. Julian's views never really mattered.

Lucas grunted. His phone pinged—once, then again. He glanced at the screen, didn't bother to reply, just dropped it onto a pile of mail.

"Dad's company is fucked. If we're lucky, selling the last three units from the Bridgewater condo project might let us pay off the loans—at best, we break even. But I need cash flow now. We've got no choice but to sell the Beach House and the vacant lot. Both, right away. The Riopelle has to go too—I need Dad's investment back for new projects. The vacant lot, we'll list with a custom build. That's where the real profit is."

Julian felt sick. He pictured her hands gripping the kitchen sink, the silence when he told her. He owned the house, but could he turn her out?

Lucas wouldn't let up. "Julian, face reality. It's over between you two. Maya will be fine—she can move back to Halifax, closer to the gallery. That commute was insane. You're doing her a favour. Get it done. Now."

Julian stared into his empty mug. Enough already.

Lucas leaned back in his chair, voice sharp. "I've got two deals lined up—new build in Herring Cove, duplex reno in Dartmouth. If you keep stalling, we both drown in Dad's mess. You hold it up; you choke us both.

"I'm not waiting, Julian. Now, now, now." He slapped the table as he spoke, three times in quick succession.

Julian shifted in his chair. He set his mug down, then picked it up again, leaving a faint ring of cold coffee on the table.

Lucas's gaze sharpened. He stood, pushing his chair back to the table, not looking at his brother.

"You can't keep dragging things out with Maya. If you're not ready for marriage, for a family, you need to be fair and let her go. Make a clean break. Be a grown-up for once—settle up and move her out. You own the house. You have all the power."

Julian knew it was true, but basic decency meant giving her time and treating her gently with respect.

"Yeah, but I'm not throwing her out. Not like that."

"Oh my God. Fair—you are so soft. Jesus."

Lucas wandered into the living room, searching for something valuable but finding nothing. He lifted a framed family picture, a beach scene: their father, Howard; their mother; Julian; and himself, all squinting in the sunlight. His mother's hand rested on Howard's arm. Lucas was already focusing on the camera, and Julian seemed poised to step out of the frame. The glass had become cloudy with age, the ceramic border chipped.

Lucas called out, "You should pack this photo and keep a few of Mom's trinkets too."

Back in the kitchen, with the photo frame in hand, Lucas put it face down and then picked up a manila envelope, tugging out a spreadsheet and pushing it across the table.

"When Dad put the title to the Beach House in both your names as joint tenants, his goal was to make it harder for creditors to go after it. But he still wanted to keep control for himself. The truth is, he never intended for you to get the house automatically if he died—it just worked out that way, because he probably didn't think he'd ever die. All the money for the Beach House renovations came from his company. I need that money back ASAP."

"No, Maya put in about fifty grand," Julian protested.

Lucas shrugged. "You didn't put in a dime, so it doesn't matter. And anyway, the mortgage was tiny—she got nearly free living for years."

After a pause, Lucas put it coldly: "The estate should get back ownership of the Beach House and the vacant lot. Since we're both equal beneficiaries, you'll still inherit half the value."

Julian shook his head. "Dad meant the Beach House for me. You got plenty of cash over the years, and I think he was trying to even things out by making sure I got the house. The vacant lot, fine—we split it. But what about Maya's share?"

Lucas's eyes narrowed, jaw tightening. "That's bullshit—I never got more than you. It's fifty-fifty, that's the law. Maya owns nothing. Pay her what you can prove she spent. The rest is fantasy."

"She won't accept that. She put in a ton of work fixing the place up."

"You're weak. We need the money."

Julian looked at him, voice flat. "No. You always need money."

Lucas felt defensive and snapped back, "Just as much as you do. The will states that everything is divided equally. However, the renovation money sunk into the Beach House—two hundred grand—was from the company. That should be returned off the top."

Julian blinked. His chest tightened. Lucas said it like it was simple, but it wasn't.

"I thought I would own the Beach House. Maybe not the vacant lot." Julian's voice betrayed him—it came out more like a question than a claim.

"Nope. You didn't pay for it. Dad put it in your name to keep it clear of creditors. The estate's lawyer says you were just holding it in trust for Dad. You weren't the true owner. And besides, the company advanced $200,000 of reno money and paid the contractor directly—that shows Dad meant to stay the real owner. The lawyer says it doesn't matter that the title ended up in your name. Dad didn't mean to die and let that stand."

Lucas tapped the spreadsheet with growing impatience. "Do the math, Jules. Deduct two hundred grand to repay the company. The place is worth about seven hundred thousand in this market. So, subtract the two hundred thousand company reno loan and the one hundred thousand mortgage balance—what's left is your half."

"So, what do I get?" Julian asked, scratching his head.

"Two hundred thousand, straight up. That's your share from the Beach House. Then I'll buy your half of the vacant lot. Are we agreed?" Lucas's tone had a salesman's flair.

It sounded easy. Julian looked at the numbers and didn't trust them. He never could. Lucas owned the company now—on paper, anyway—even if the whole mess was underwater. But two hundred grand off the top, that would be Lucas's win, not his.

Julian tried to find his footing. "Let me think about it. But we still haven't settled on what to do about Maya."

Lucas's mouth went crooked. "Maya?" He sounded tired of the whole subject. "She's not on title, not in the will, not anywhere that matters. She's not a beneficiary. Not a partner. Not legally."

Julian shook his head. "She paid the mortgage, put her savings in. Did the work—real work. You know that matters. We can't just—"

Lucas cut him off and shrugged, checking his phone. "Pay her out of your share, if you're that soft. It's your problem, not mine."

A text buzzed on Lucas's phone. He scanned it, then slid the phone into his back pocket.

"Painters want their money. I've got to pay them or they'll lien the condo project in Bridgewater. Then I'm finished if that happens. The lender will take it over. If you keep dragging this out, it's only getting worse."

Julian stared at the numbers again. "I just can't—push her out, not like this. She deserves more."

Lucas tightened his jaw and pressed his lips together firmly. "Look, the Beach House will sell faster than this place. Plus, there's no equity in this house. I have no idea where Dad spent all that borrowed money. The real estate market is declining. If we wait, we'll both end up losing. I also want to list the vacant lot with a custom build—it's easily worth a million."

"Okay." Julian pressed his face into his hands and rubbed at his eyes.

Lucas lowered his voice. "The Riopelle painting belongs to the company. Its value has skyrocketed. There's a Fine Art auction in Toronto this September. The lawyer insists it needs to be relocated—for safekeeping—to my house. Get it packed and bring it over."

He was busy texting again, not waiting around. "The auction requires confirmation. It's three months away. Don't disappoint me, Julian."

"I know it's the estate's," Julian muttered, but the words had no weight.

Lucas looked up sharply. "No, it's the company's property. Dad sent the money to buy the Riopelle right out of the company account—direct to the gallery."

"Dad left you the company, so are you claiming the Riopelle is yours?" Julian exclaimed, clutching the table's edge as his knuckles turned white. In Julian's mind, he envisioned the painting with its raised oil textures, Howard's pride, and Maya standing in the pink living room, arms crossed and head tilted, seeing something he never could. The Beach House with its vibrant hues, her laughter on a rainy morning, and the feel of her hand on his back were now gone, yet never truly distant.

Lucas pressed on, relentless. "Let's just say I'm open to a discussion on the Riopelle. My lawyer is looking at that. In the meantime, you dragging your feet just makes it harder for everyone. Maya is claiming things that don't belong to her. That's not her painting, not her house. You want to lose out because you're too soft to get it done?"

Julian shook his head, small, almost invisible.

Lucas slapped the realtor's valuation down—a fat sheaf, notes in blue ink scrawled everywhere. "Sell the Beach House, we'll split it. I'll keep the lot and pay you your half of its value. The lot is the only empty one left on the peninsula. Dad would've done the same."

He adjusted his jacket and tucked the phone into his pocket. He gave Julian one final, expressionless glance. "Dad would've wanted us to be fair. Everything to be split evenly between us. I'm not trying to take more."

But that was a lie, and Julian felt it in his gut. If the Riopelle belonged to the Company, Lucas owned it all—a dead business until you remembered the painting. Suddenly, it meant everything.

And now the Beach House and the lot, both currently in Julian's name alone, Lucas clawing them back into the estate and calling it fairness. Fifty-fifty, he said. But it was Julian who kept losing ground.

All those years, Lucas took money from Howard—nobody counted that. Why wasn't it in the math?

Lucas's footsteps resonated through the corridor, firm and purposeful. The front door closed with a swing, the aged brass latch clicking into place. Silence flooded the space—saturating the kitchen, seeping through the empty living room, and ascending the stairs. The entire house seemed to be holding its breath.

Julian didn't move for a long while. The house grew dim, the light pooling low on the floor, stretching the shape of the table legs. He picked up the family photo, wiped the cloudy glass with his shirt, and set it on the kitchen table. The faces stared past one another—everyone half-turned, as if caught on their way out.

He fetched the battered moving box from the closet, set it by the kitchen door, and hovered, hands ready but unable to fold the flaps shut. The box waited. He waited. Nothing moved.

Julian returned to the kitchen table and examined the spreadsheet, noticing Lucas's notes written in bold blue ink—*half for you, half for me, Maya—nothing*. Lucas had suggested that the Riopelle might be the sole property of the company, which was now under his ownership. Julian folded the paper in half twice and tucked it beneath a stack of Howard's old bills.

The wind battered the kitchen windows, making the glass shudder in its frame. Above the beach, gulls wheeled and vanished into the grey.

Julian spread his palm on the table, feeling where the varnish had worn to raw wood—his father's rings had left shallow grooves, Maya's coffee stains never quite scrubbed clean.

With his eyes shut, he focused on the sounds of the house creaking and settling. In his imagination, he saw the Beach House clearly—the hammock at the back gently swaying in the breeze, the garden overrun with growth, and the Riopelle painting adding a splash of colour above the fireplace.

He imagined Maya there, not quite ready to let go.

Julian stayed there as the day slipped away, the house holding every silence, every decision left hanging in the air.

What could he say to Maya—what truth would she hear, if he managed to say it?

He kept searching for the words, but nothing came.

– 3 –

JULIAN'S RESTLESS mind wouldn't quiet, never letting him fall into anything close to real sleep. He tossed and turned, shifting between states of consciousness, always feeling the elusive edge of sleep slip further out of reach. The more he realized he couldn't settle, the more agitated he became.

The night pressed in, hot and close. The room at Howard's felt heavy with muggy air, the damp sheets clinging to his back while the weight of it settled on his skin.

At one in the morning, Julian strained to hear through the open window. Somewhere beyond the hedges, laughter and shouting drifted in on the breeze. Maybe teens were partying at the vacant lot next to the Beach House again, a Saturday night ritual.

The vacant lot sat between the Beach House to the north and Howard's house to the south, its beachfront a stretch of white, pristine sand. The high tide never quite cleansed the commotion of the prior night, but it washed over it all the same. Julian often found himself picking up beer bottles half-filled with water, dragging wet, blackened logs back to the scrub—remnants from the teens' midnight fires. With Howard gone, he was the last one left to look after the property.

"Yes, I'm certain they're there," he murmured under his breath, pushing the linen top sheet aside. Anxiety began to creep in—how could he possibly prevent the community from trespassing on his land to access the beach, holding bonfires, and swimming past midnight? Every fence was pushed down. Every private property sign was knocked off. He vowed—again—to be more vigilant. But the worry stayed with him, and sleep would not return.

By three in the morning, the noise had faded. The world felt hushed. Julian lay still, his mind finally quiet. He slipped under for a while, and when he woke four and a half hours later, it was as if he'd finally caught a handful of real sleep.

The dreams, when they came, were fractured. He heard Maya's laugh far off, caught in a breeze through a window he couldn't see. Sometimes her voice sounded hopeful, teasing him about the life they could still have. Sometimes it was already resigned, her face slipping away as he reached for her.

But half awake all night, he kept rehearsing the conversation. He could see her across a table, serious and wary. He tried to explain how much he loved their life, the possibilities, the freedom they shared. He wanted to convince her, maybe one last time, that happiness was what you make of it, not that it must be this way or that. That love could last and be enough, even if it meant just the two of them.

But the words changed every time. Sometimes he promised nothing, just asked for more time. Other times, he almost believed he could say yes, that he could give her the future she wanted—family and all. Then the doubt returned, honest and clear: he knew he couldn't promise a family, not now. He couldn't lie, not to her, not to himself, not even to make things easier. The future flickered—open, then closed, then open again—until all that remained was the ache of wanting, and the certainty that whatever he said, she would hear only what she needed to hear.

The script played on, half-waking and half-dreaming. We could travel. See Madrid, study in Florence, and walk the ruins of Athens together. Wander through galleries, stand quietly in front of paintings, and lose ourselves in the colour and light. Take a week in Montreal, just a vacation, painting in the mornings and searching out new exhibits in the afternoons. Why rush? We could build a life on what we both love.

He could hear her answer, see her face, but it changed with each loop. Sometimes she smiled, agreeing. Sometimes she turned away, shaking her head, already out of the room. Julian felt both hope and grief, the sweet ache of wanting something that might still be possible.

He rolled over, blinked at the glowing numbers on the bedside clock—7:28 A.M. He rose, barefoot on the cool floorboards, though the room was still warm and damp, stepping onto the colder bathroom tiles. The mirror showed his face: stubble, rugged, a smudge of blue-green paint on his chin. He splashed water on his cheeks, pressed his hands to his eyes, and leaned for a long moment into the cool porcelain, staring blankly at his reflection, the script still running in his head.

It doesn't have to be all or nothing, Maya. I love you. I want us. Let's give ourselves time. We don't have to know everything right now. A year isn't long—not really. We can wait, see where we are then. The world won't close in on us if we don't decide today.

He poured himself a cup of coffee and drank most of it, letting the rest go cold. He set his pencil to the starch-white canvas, trying to draw something—anything—but the first lines came out hesitant and wrong, as if they didn't belong to him. The pencil felt heavy, uncooperative, resisting the day. He erased his false starts, working them back to white, but faint graphite smudges lingered, evidence of indecision that wouldn't quite vanish.

When he looked up again, the canvas was empty except for a ghost trace where he'd pressed too hard and lost his nerve. No vision. More than an hour was wasted. Just the blank weight of wanting, and the outline of a future he couldn't see his way into.

He thought about Maya, waiting at the Beach House. He imagined her by the window, possibly strong and hopeful, leaving room for him to explain. Or perhaps she was exhausted, ready to call it quits. Either way, something would break today. He couldn't delay any longer.

He took out his phone and typed a message.

Can we talk this morning?

He stared at the screen, holding his breath. The response came quickly.

You can come over. When?

Julian typed back:

As soon as I get dressed.

Julian paused for a moment, letting Maya's response linger in his mind. Her words were neutral, offering no clue about her feelings, leaving him even more uncertain. He put on his khaki shorts and a muscle shirt, then changed into a cleaner one without paint. Bag slung over his shoulder, he looked around Howard's empty house. The air was heavy with lingering heat and the sharp scent of old paint and brush cleaner. He locked the door behind him and stepped out into the morning.

By nine-thirty, the day was already warm. He put on his sunglasses, squinting in the bright sunlight. While he strolled down the gravel road towards the Beach House, a sharp stone slipped into his sandal. He removed it with his index finger.

He glanced to his right and noticed a family cutting across his empty lot, the grass and dirt trampled flat from previous trespassers. They were lugging a cooler and a striped umbrella, the father holding the metal post like a flagpole. They showed no hesitation and didn't bother to check if anyone at the Beach House minded them crossing private land to reach the beach.

The children dashed off, giggling and rolling down the sandy slope, abandoning their sandals and towels as they went. Their thrilled voices reverberated up the hill, excited and eager for the water. He watched the cooler hit the ground with a thud, leaving a new mark in the sand. His hand clenched tighter around his bag strap. The happy cries persisted, cutting through the heat, each one as sharp as the stone that had jabbed his heel.

It wasn't only the noise that irritated him. It was also how they strolled through his property as if they owned the place. Entitled, he mused. Disrespectful. He bent down, removed another pebble from his sandal, and felt the smooth leather with his finger. He couldn't comprehend how parents could tolerate such a racket, the screaming, and the incessant need to supervise them. He observed them for another moment, feeling the heat on his neck, then turned away and continued on his way.

He arrived at the Beach House, where the garden was tidy and vibrant, its colours lining the stone path. The porch swing gently moved on its chain. Julian paused on the porch, his hand resting on the rail that was still slightly sticky from fresh paint, then he ascended the steps.

The front door stuck momentarily before opening. Inside, the air was filled with the faint aroma of baking, perhaps bread or muffins. Maya's bathing suit was draped over a chair in the dining area, her shoes were placed by the front door, and a mug with a heart design sat on the entryway shelf, bearing red lipstick marks on its rim. The grandfather clock ticked, slowing the moment, allowing him to collect his thoughts and strategize. Julian put his bag down and wiped his sweaty palms on his khakis. The Beach House was crowded with her, with the memories of their life together, one he had lived almost without noticing.

He lingered in the living room, his hand brushing against the couch, feeling the soft, floral cotton fabric. The Riopelle painting hung above the mantel, a burst of colour in the bright window light, its wild strokes appearing even more pronounced and lively now.

"I'm here," he called softly, hoping for a response.

He heard Maya upstairs—the quiet patter of bare feet on the wooden floor, the bathroom door opening, then shutting again. A few minutes later, she descended the stairs, her hair tied up, face bare, eyes slightly swollen, and an expression of sombreness. She was wearing shorts, an old T-shirt, and his bracelet from an early Christmas, dangling on her wrist. They moved together to the kitchen, exchanged brief pleasantries, nothing more, then each pulled out a chair, sitting at opposite ends of the rectangular table from one another.

They did not speak at first. Julian twiddled his thumbs while Maya crossed her arms, closing and protecting. The only sound was the fridge humming, and then a seagull, then nothing.

He began with what he hoped was enough truth. "I couldn't sleep," he admitted. "I kept thinking about you. About us. I want to be with you, Maya. I love you. But to be honest, I'm not in a position to promise anything about starting a family right now. Everything's a mess."

Maya gazed at him for a while, her expression cold and devoid of warmth. "So, nothing's changed since our argument."

He nodded. "Not really. I'm willing to discuss it in the future, and I think that should be enough for us to continue together."

She tightened her lips and looked at the floor. "Then this is the end. We need to make this separation final. I'm not going to invest in something that leads nowhere. I've told you many times, I'm ready for commitment and a family. No more delays, no more empty promises that are just a maybe."

He nodded, a flicker of uncertainty flashing in his thoughts; perhaps he didn't love her as deeply as he'd believed, which might explain his reluctance to commit to a family and a lasting future.

"I love our life. I like it just the way it is and don't want to jeopardize that. So, I can't commit to promises I might not be able to keep."

She allowed the silence to linger, the house remaining still and suspended in that moment.

"I can't keep waiting for you to make up your mind; it's been years," she stated. "I've had enough of waiting. I want a family. I want a life. I deserve it, and I want a man who wants the same. Do you understand?"

He nodded once more. "I do."

There was nothing left to discuss. The silence lingered, making the situation and its inevitable outcome clear.

Eventually, Julian spoke up, "Lucas is pressuring me about the house and the painting. He insists that the Beach House should be sold, along with the Riopelle. If we're going our separate ways, you might want to consider relocating closer to your job."

Maya's head jerked up, anger racing across her face. "What does Lucas have to do with our house? With the painting? Howard gave those to us. Lucas doesn't have a say, we decide what happens to our home and our painting."

Julian sighed, rubbing his forehead. "Lucas is the trustee of the estate. He claims that even though the house and the empty lot are under my name, they actually belong to my dad's estate."

She exhaled deeply. "I don't get it. I've invested a lot of effort into this place—my money went into the renovations, and I've covered the mortgage and taxes. Are you saying that doesn't matter?"

He looked away, his voice shaky, yet he continued, "Lucas claims that because I didn't purchase the property myself, I never actually owned it. According to him, Dad arranged it that way to shield it from his business creditors. Nevertheless,

I still receive half in the end because if the estate owns it, then it gets divided equally between Lucas and me according to Dad's will."

Maya turned away, repulsed at this news. "And where does that leave me exactly?"

"We'll need to work that out."

Maya gestured towards the living room. "Are you seriously going to let him walk away with the Riopelle?"

Julian let out a deep sigh. "It's not about what I want. Lucas claims the painting was purchased using the company's funds. He's involved the lawyer, and the creditors need to be settled. Do you recall how Howard paid your gallery for the painting? Was it truly bought by the company?"

"I'll look tomorrow. In the meantime, you could try telling him to go fuck himself. Just for once!" Maya's voice was sharp enough to surprise even herself.

Julian shook his head with a half-smile that always tempted her to throw something. "You know what will happen if I do that. He'll haul me into court."

He rested his elbows on the table and cradled his face in his hands. "I'm sorry. I should have given you a heads-up. Lucas needs money to keep the company going and to finance two new projects. He says selling the Riopelle could help the company survive—"

Maya interrupted him, "And what about my survival? What about my investment in the Beach House?"

Julian looked at her for a long moment, and she saw the first flicker of real anger in his eyes. "You're not the only one who feels fucked over, Maya. I just lost my dad. I just lost everything."

She let out a low, humourless laugh. "Lost everything? You still have your inheritance. I invested in a house, secured an incredible deal on a painting intended for us and our future, and now you're asking me to give it all to Lucas and the lawyers."

"You don't get it," Julian explained. "Lucas is persuasive. He insists that the painting isn't truly mine or yours. It's all a façade—to conceal assets. Think back to when my dad split from Janet. That's when he put the Beach House title in my name too. That's why he left the painting there. She was never aware of it. Lucas claims it was never intended for us but to keep it hidden from his ex-wife."

"That's ridiculous," Maya exclaimed, clenching her fists. "You're letting Lucas take advantage of you, just like your father used to do to everyone. Lucas is utterly deceitful."

Julian sat silently, gazing out the window at the diving swoop of a gull. "Maybe I'm just tired of fighting. I'm not going to take him on," he admitted.

She resisted the impulse to grab him and jolt him into action, instead keeping her voice calm. "Then I'll fight for both of us," she declared.

He turned to her, studying her intently as if noticing something unfamiliar or threatening. "What do you plan to do?" he asked.

Maya paused before responding. "I'm not giving it up. Not without a fight. You tell Lucas that if he wants it, he can come here and explain to my face why I don't matter. I have receipts, I have emails, I have every scrap of evidence about what I put into this house and how I found this painting. Didn't Howard tell you the Riopelle was ours?"

Julian glanced down. "I can't tell what's real and what I've imagined. He said something like, 'You hold onto it, but return it when I need it.'"

Maya stared at him with wide eyes, "What on earth does that mean? You only returned the painting to his place for grand parties to wow his fancy friends. Have you consulted a lawyer? Surely, we have some rights in this situation."

"Not yet. Maybe I should, and perhaps you should too. He might be mistaken," Julian said, raising his hands to suggest it was a possibility.

She leaned forward, pressing her hands firmly on the table. "Lucas always got his way. Howard gave him a lot of money, probably used for drugs. I believe Howard was trying to balance things between you two. The house and the painting should belong to you—or to us! After all the money given to Lucas, this house and the painting—I assumed they were meant for us. You never mentioned any strings attached. Why didn't you?"

Julian shrugged. "Well, my dad would say all sorts of things when he was drunk. And I have to agree with you. We need to figure this out. I apologize. I don't really want to argue with Lucas. You know how difficult he can be."

Maya's breathing steadied as she lowered her gaze to the table. "You never fight. Not for me. Not for yourself. I'm glad this is over. You are not the man I want. You are not the kind of guy I'd even want to father my kids."

Julian felt like he'd been hit in the stomach. "Whoa, that's harsh. Can't we keep this civil? We should try to make the best out of a bad situation here. It would be better if we worked together against Lucas. Don't you think?"

"Yes, I agree. Fine, but you need to fight for my rights. You can't just bulldoze over me." He nodded.

She sprang to her feet and hurried off. "I need to use the bathroom," she said, jogging up the stairwell and slamming the bathroom door shut behind her.

"Are you all right?" he shouted, but there was no response.

Maya sat on the toilet, tears streaming down her cheeks, her heart heavy with the pain of the breakup, but even more so from the sting of unfairness and betrayal.

"Hey Maya, are you all right?" Julian called out.

"Just give me a few minutes!" she yelled in response.

Julian remained in the kitchen, his heart racing and his thoughts overwhelming him. It was all too much for both of them to handle.

Moving quietly, he entered the living room. The Riopelle loomed above, wild with colour and texture, but Julian barely noticed. After a moment's hesitation, he reached up and lifted the painting from the wall, surprised by its weight. In the dining room, he found a faded beach towel from his childhood, folded neatly in the laundry basket. He wrapped it around the frame once, then carried the painting by one hand as he headed out of the Beach House.

There was no pause for a final look back. The photo of him and Maya, arm in arm—possibly from his birthday—sat unseen on the coffee table. He passed the old spot on the floor where he used to paint while she cooked, walking with purpose, mind fixed on leaving quickly. Self-preservation mattered more now than old memories of quieter, happier days.

He exited through the front door with the painting tucked under his arm, not glancing back. As Julian walked down the road, guilt weighed on him, and he wished he could turn around to apologize and set things right. He glanced back toward the Beach House, where he saw the door open and Maya peering out, searching for him. Quickly, he moved closer to the hedges to stay hidden.

Julian paused briefly in a clearing by the roadside, feeling immobilized. He started back toward Maya, then stopped again. In that moment, a stark truth surfaced: people act out of self-interest, choosing what benefits them, even at the expense of others.

He turned and continued his retreat toward Howard's house, cementing his decision to put his well-being first.

Inside, Maya was quietly mystified. How could Julian walk out like that? Yes, she'd said some harsh things, but did that justify leaving without a word?

She considered sending him a text to apologize and ask him to return so that they could part on a more positive note. With that in mind, Maya headed to the living room, settled onto the sofa, and began typing a message of reconciliation on her phone.

As she pondered her words, she lifted her eyes and froze. The area above the fireplace mantel was now empty, a bare rectangle of wall where the Riopelle had once been. She gazed at the spot, scanning left, right, up, and down. It was unmistakably gone. Her mind raced to comprehend the absence, a tightness forming in her chest.

Then the realization struck her—he had taken it.

That was the reason he slipped away. A surge of anger erupted within her—a powerful, overwhelming sensation. She seized the potpourri jar from the coffee table and flung it against the empty wall. It shattered, sending shards of glass, along with lavender and rose petals, scattering in every direction.

"What a bastard!" she yelled.

She picked up her phone, hands shaking, and typed:

> MOTHERFUCKER. BRING BACK THE PAINTING.
> NOW. GET OVER HERE.

She flung the phone onto the couch and collapsed onto the floor, pulling her knees up to her chest. The scent of lavender was both sweet and piercing in the air, with shattered glass scattered everywhere. She cried, hugging her shins tightly.

Maya sat quietly, absorbing the situation.

She had just broken the jar, but he had shattered her trust.

He hadn't replied to her message, leaving her with nothing to do but start planning and get busy with packing and organising—tasks she was excellent at and could immerse herself in.

She was eager to leave the chaos behind and return to a tidy life, where she was in control and everything was orderly.

Moving to the kitchen, she opened her computer and searched for apartments for rent in Halifax, contemplating how close she should live to work.

She was strong and could easily sever ties with her old life.

She was now in control of her destiny, which felt reassuring and even comforting.

– 4 –

MAYA CARSON spent the hour-long drive from Halifax to Chester that Monday evening letting the coastline and winding road untangle last weekend's turmoil. The day at the gallery had been slow—just one customer all afternoon, plenty of quiet to replay every argument in her head. The betrayal burned, and trusting Julian felt impossible. She didn't deserve that. Throughout the workday, Maya maintained a composed demeanour, concealing her anger beneath a professional calmness.

As Maya curved into the Beach House driveway, at least it looked in order. The old cottage stood tidy and elegant, a compact cedar-shingled cottage painted a grey blue that seemed to blend into the ocean backdrop and sky, with crisp white shutters and garden beds edged and blooming along the porch.

The day following the betrayal, on Sunday, the porch was first swept and then thoroughly mopped. The garden beds were tidied and trimmed precisely. Her hands were red and rough from all the scrubbing, packing, and repairing. Maya's nails were bitten down to the quick, and she had a cut from chopping large, tough potatoes. She ticked off her rituals: the kitchen counters wiped, the bed made, the mug with the lipstick stain scoured with baking soda, then put at the back of the shelf. No mess left behind. Nothing for anyone to point to and say, "This is where she lost it."

The day before, she had considered calling her father. However, she knew he wouldn't understand or genuinely want to hear about her heartbreak. He already had enough to deal with, given her mother's alcoholism and constant raging. They remained together out of financial necessity and routine. Maya resembled her father—reserved and enduring—but much like a steam engine, she could only take so much before she erupted. She promised herself she would never turn out like her mother, who was always critical and seemed to think the world revolved around her as though she were the only person who mattered. No, reaching out to her parents would offer her no comfort. The weather was the only topic she could discuss with them.

She had no one to turn to for guidance. How was she supposed to manage the meeting with Julian and Lucas that evening to sort out specifics, such as her moving date and the return of her investment? Should she argue for a share of the value of the Riopelle or the vacant lot? Perhaps consulting a lawyer about her legal standing would have been wise. Everything seemed so uncertain.

At five minutes to eight in the evening, just before her meeting, Maya began her walk down the gravel road. To her right, the sun was setting, casting a warm glow over the west, while the Beach House slowly disappeared behind her.

Maya moved quickly, her sandals scuffing against the gravel, her right hand clenched tightly. Anxiety and fear of what lay ahead filled her. She noticed the tender area inside her lip, a result of her frequent biting from the day-long tension. Determined not to glance back at the Beach House, she pressed forward. Each step felt like an act of atonement, as if she could somehow escape the shame she carried, believing it was all her fault. Nearly thirty-five, without a home, a relationship, or a family, her life felt like a chaotic mess, reminiscent of her childhood, as she always strove to prevent everything from unravelling.

Maya continued onward, her chest constricted and her breathing quick. She focused on clearing her mind. Walking along the gravel in the fading light, she transitioned into the mindset she relied on the most—organising and bringing order. Chaos unsettled her; she craved everything to be in its proper place, every issue resolved. Whatever awaited her at the meeting with Julian and Lucas, she was determined to address it and set things right.

The road extended a brief distance between the two Barrett properties, with a long, narrow vacant lot in between—approximately four hundred feet from the old Beach House to Howard Barrett's newer build.

To her left, the old wire fence bordered the vacant lot, standing mostly upright except for a section near the well-trodden path, where it lay flat from people stepping over it to reach the shore. The muddy trail from the fence to the ocean's edge was visible, slicing through the tall, wild grass, dotted with wildflowers and dandelions.

The PRIVATE PROPERTY sign had been knocked over into the bush—likely on purpose, she assumed—with the words partially obscured but still noticeable to anyone paying attention. The grass was littered with fast food wrappers, beer cans, and plastic bottles, evidence of people using the shortcut to get to the beach. She thought the entire area desperately needed a cleanup. It was so untidy.

Just a short distance away, Howard Barrett's house stood prominently behind a row of aging birch and spruce trees. Despite being built in 1962, the house's broad porch and steeply sloped roof remained striking, reflecting an era when families showcased their status with grand homes. Although the landscaping was neglected and the paint was peeling, the house still hinted at former prosperity, before Howard faced difficulties in recent years. The adjacent vacant lot added to the property's estate-like ambiance, and Maya thought it would be unfortunate if it were ever developed. The vacant lot also provided the Beach House with a cherished sense of privacy she had always appreciated.

She gazed past the hilltop and saw the deserted beach below. From her vantage point, the sound of waves crashing fiercely and rising under the constant wind was clear. Her sundress fluttered, and she held it down as the cool ocean breeze brushed against her legs, starkly contrasting the lingering warmth of the day. Goosebumps appeared where the sun had shone, the last remnants of heat dissipating as she made her way towards the front steps of Howard's house, the weight of it all settling in.

The driveway was bordered by wild grass creeping in from the sides, making the Ferrari hard to overlook. The dimming sunlight muted its vibrant red colour. The car was haphazardly parked across the path, and Maya sighed softly. Lucas, as usual, ignored any sense of order, parking wherever he liked, as though rules applied to everyone but him.

She checked her phone but found no new messages or alerts from Julian. Maya's eyes shifted to the Ferrari parked in the driveway, and her heart rate increased. Lucas was notorious for being late, often taking pride in making others wait. Seeing him arrive early was unsettling. She couldn't shake the concern that he might have gotten to Julian ahead of her, potentially plotting against her interests.

Maya quietly entered through the unlocked door. The air was a mix of cool and musty, with a strong aroma of brush cleaner and paint varnish. Beneath these scents was a subtle hint of something more intense, perhaps garlic or fried onions from Julian's meal. From the back, Julian's voice could be heard, calling out, "We're in here."

Maya traced Julian's voice down the hallway, her sandal heels softly tapping on the wooden floor. Keeping them on was her subtle act of defiance. Shoes made her feel more confident and grown-up, while socks made her feel juvenile. It was a small thing, but wearing her sandals made her feel more self-assured as she entered the dining room.

The elegant mahogany dining set was gone, probably sold to raise some desperately needed money. Instead, an old oval pine table with four mismatched chairs now occupied the space, each chair resembling an antique from a different era. The room felt as though it had been prepared for an auction, devoid of its previous air of formality. The early evening light from the north window cast long shadows across the floor, highlighting the dust and empty corners.

Lucas was already seated at the head of the table, his sunglasses pushed up into his hair, wearing a high-end track jacket over shorts, and flipping through a thick stack of papers, entirely at ease, playing the part of the boss. Julian sat to his right, hunched, thumb tracing circles on the tabletop, his hair as wild as ever. Maya paused just inside the doorway, taking in the two of them, neither looking up at first.

No one spoke for a moment. Maya hovered at the edge of the dining room, feeling the edge of things—the emptiness of the house, the tension in the air. Julian caught her eye and offered a small, friendly smile, almost apologetic. Lucas didn't look up. He sat back in his chair, elbows wide, radiating impatience.

Lucas broke the silence. "Let's get this over with." His voice was clipped, practiced, and pitched to fill the room. He slid a file across the table—not quite toward Julian, not quite toward Maya—making it clear he was in charge, and everyone was on his clock.

"We all know why we're here," Lucas said, tone flat but eyes calculating. "Time to put this mess to bed."

Maya kept her face still. She wasn't giving him anything. Julian just nodded, the motion small, uncertain.

Lucas opened the file and clicked his pen. "First, the Beach House. It's going up for sale—the realtor should be Jane Fitzsimmons. Listing goes active within ten days. I'd say we list for an asking price of $739,000 and aim to get at least $700,000. That does not include the vacant lot; it only refers to the Beach House. So, get it ready to market. Vacant possession by September 15, if it sells."

"So, I've got roughly sixty days to clear out," Maya said, matter-of-factly.

"Only if it sells right away, but we'll agree to set a closing within sixty days of a signed agreement."

Maya saw no reason to argue this point. She was already scouting apartments and condos in Halifax. Buy if she got a decent settlement; rent if things stayed uncertain.

Julian seemed fine if Maya was.

"Lucas, I'm assuming I can also stay at Dad's house until it sells, right?" Julian asked his older brother.

"Sure, but you should take care of the utilities. The estate has been paying all of it. Why should you get a free pass?" Lucas scoffed.

Julian glanced down, contemplating where he could find the funds. Life had been much simpler when he relied on Maya's income from her position as a gallery manager.

Lucas seemed pleased he'd landed his first demands. His tone stayed firm. "Out of the proceeds, after realtor's commission and fees, the company gets repaid for the $200,000 it put into the Beach House renovations. Plus, 10 percent interest, close to market rate—since the date of that investment, almost six years ago. Maya gets reimbursed for every receipt she can produce—paint, light fixtures, whatever. Dollar for dollar, nothing more. Then, what's left is split fifty-fifty between Julian and me, as per Dad's will. That's roughly $150,000 each after the mortgage is paid off and the loans are repaid."

He paused, letting the numbers hang in the air.

Maya bristled but said nothing. She totalled receipts of around $40,000. It was an absolute scam. He hadn't even offered to compensate for the countless hours spent painting, stripping woodwork, working on the deck, all the landscaping, and more.

Turning to a new page, Lucas looked at his notes. "The vacant lot is being transferred to the company. Julian, you'll receive $250,000 for your share—it's a decent offer. The company plans to develop as a new build and sell it."

Maya interrupted, "Julian said the property might be worth about a million. So why just $250,000? His portion should be $500,000." Julian perked up, impressed by her quick calculations and foresight. He nodded, grateful for her financial savvy in their relationship.

Lucas flicked his eyes to Julian, then back to Maya.

"I'm being more than fair. A million is a maybe in a strong market, so who knows what it's worth. I'm taking all the risk and giving Julian hard cash, a quarter of a million, tax free. He should jump at that."

Maya appeared sceptical, but Julian thought a quarter million was a reasonable amount. He seemed okay with it.

"So how are you managing to pay Julian and me all this money? I was under the impression the company was broke." Maya leaned back in her chair, wanting to understand the whole situation.

"The Riopelle sale is clearly where the funds come from," he asserted, his voice growing louder. "That painting belongs to the company, and neither of you has any legal claim to it. I want it now. If you hesitate, my lawyer will take legal action against you. Just hand it over today and spare yourselves the trouble."

Maya's fingers splayed on the wooden surface, her grip so tight that her knuckles turned pale. Her pulse throbbed insistently in her throat, a relentless drumbeat against her skin.

The room was silent, except for the loud ticking of the old wall clock.

"How convenient, Lucas. Your dad leaves you shares in a company that are worthless and you make a money grab for the Riopelle. Prove to me the company owns it. It was a gift to Julian and me. Howard hung it up in the Beach House, our home."

Julian nodded, supporting her logic.

Lucas retorted, "Verify with the gallery's bank. You'll find that the wire transfer for the Riopelle acquisition in 2019 was made straight from the company's bank account to the gallery. It's absolutely clear—the company owns it. Case closed."

Maya didn't have a logical defense to that.

Instead, she said, accusingly, "That's not just insulting, Lucas. That's theft. Howard gave that painting to us. It was his to give—he owned the company at the time."

Lucas responded, "Provide me with evidence of that, Maya. It simply doesn't exist." Rising to his feet, Lucas faced Maya and stated, "That's it, we're finished."

Maya sat still; her voice was low and steady. "No, we are not done. Your offer on the Beach House is unfair. I've been paying the mortgage and taxes for years and invested a lot of effort to make that house beautiful. Howard transferred it to Julian's name for a reason. Do you really think I'll give it all up for a few receipts and some spare change?"

Lucas shrugged, his gaze remaining icy. "You want to fight, Maya? Be my guest. But you'll come out on the losing end. You're not listed on the title; you were just staying there like a tenant. You don't have anything in writing. I've got the paperwork backing me up, and the company's lawyer will bury you."

Julian looked down at his hands, turning his ring. "Can't we just—"

Lucas cut him off. "No more debates. I need the painting, Julian. Where is it?"

Maya jumped up, causing her chair to scrape loudly across the floor. "You're not getting the painting." With that, she spun around and left, the screen door slamming shut behind her.

Julian sat for a moment, head bowed. Lucas glared. "Get her back in here. This isn't a game, Julian."

Julian stood, forced himself to look Lucas in the eye. "Sit tight. I'll talk to her."

He followed Maya outside, squinting in the sudden brightness. She was halfway down the porch steps, fists clenched, pacing in the shade. He stood behind her, unsure, feeling the pull of loyalty in two directions.

"He's trying to scare you," Julian said softly. "That's always his way. We don't have to take his deal."

Maya spun on him. "He'll screw you, too, if I'm not here. You can't just let him dictate some rotten deal. This is your chance to stand up for yourself, Julian. For both of us."

Julian shrugged, looking away. "What do we do?"

Maya spoke fast, counting off on her fingers. "You're on title to the Beach House and the vacant lot. That has to matter.

For the Beach House, the company gets its $200,000 back—no interest. Then whatever's left splits fifty-fifty, you and me. The vacant lot is worth at least a million. If he wants it, fine, but he pays what it's worth. We'll talk about splitting that, but you won't get screwed. And the Riopelle stays with us until there's a real deal or a judge says otherwise. Howard wanted you to have something equal. Lucas already got the company. He got a ton of money over the years. He doesn't get everything."

Julian let out a shaky breath. "You'll have to explain it." The math still swirled in his head, but he trusted she knew what she was doing. She negotiated at the gallery every day.

Maya shook her head. "He plays hardball, but we need to play hardball back."

She squared her shoulders. They went back inside together.

Lucas was pacing by the window, phone in hand, face tight with anger.

Maya stood across from him. "Here's our counter. Beach House sells, company gets $200,000 back, no interest. Remaining proceeds split fifty-fifty—Julian and me. The vacant lot goes for fair market value—one million. If the company wants to develop it, that's your business, not ours. The Riopelle stays with us until this is sorted. I say it's ours. Howard meant for it to be ours. We only ever lent it to him for parties; it always came back to us. Don't they say possession is nine-tenths of the law?"

Lucas's eyes narrowed, his businesslike mask slipping for a flash, teeth bared. "Your offer is ridiculous. Never in a million years would I consider something like that. Besides, the company's broke. I need the Riopelle money to pay out Julian for the vacant lot and fund the Company projects. You two think you can screw me? Give me the painting, Julian. Now."

He pushed by Julian, angrily moving through the lower floor before heading upstairs. Doors swung open and slammed shut. The handle of the central bedroom closet jiggled—it was locked. The Riopelle was secure inside, just as Julian had placed it hours ago, with the key safely tucked in his pocket. A wave of relief washed over him; at least he had managed that correctly. Lucas's footsteps echoed as he descended the stairs again.

Lucas's footsteps pounded back down the stairs.

"Where is it? In the closet?"

Julian shrugged, hands up, voice mild. "Locked up safe."

Lucas then looked at Maya. "Do you have it?"

She met his glare without blinking. "It's in my gallery vault. It's not going anywhere until this is resolved." A lie, but safer than the truth. If Lucas thought the painting was at the gallery, there wasn't much he could do.

Lucas glared at Julian. "You let her take it?"

Julian just held his hands open, palms out. "Sorry, bro."

Lucas's face darkened. "You're both going to regret this. I'm calling my lawyer first thing in the morning."

He stalked to the door, pausing to turn back one last time. "Oh, and Julian, one more thing. You're out of Howard's house. Pack your things. You stab me in the back, you're finished."

He slammed the front door so hard that the old glass rattled.

Silence took over the house. Maya and Julian stood in the bare dining room, light shifting on the floor. A breeze sent the screen door creaking.

Julian slumped into a chair, head in his hands.

Maya didn't move, just let herself breathe, her pulse slowing, one heartbeat at a time.

"I'm leaving too." Maya followed Lucas out the door a minute later, making sure the Ferrari roar was gone before she went down the steps.

She walked back to the Beach House, her sandals scuffing against the gravel. The empty lot next to the Beach House was silent except for the wind rustling through the grass and the faint sound of waves crashing in the distance. Once inside, she locked the door behind her and placed her bag on the table. The blank space on the wall, where the painting used to hang, irritated her. She hadn't forgiven Julian for that betrayal, but for now, she had managed to prevent Lucas from getting his hands on the Riopelle. Julian had solemnly promised her that he wouldn't touch the Riopelle, assuring her it would remain locked in the closet, while keeping Lucas under the impression that it was still in her gallery vault.

She started gathering evidence—old receipts, emails, photos of repairs, garden beds she'd built herself, paint swatches with her handwriting. She scanned and labeled every scrap. She felt herself hardening, bit by bit.

Maya looked at her phone, thinking. Yes, she needed to call Robin back—the one person who would know how to proceed.

She found Robin's name from her recent call list and waited while it rang. The kitchen felt cavernous and silent around her as she waited.

Robin picked up almost immediately. "Hey, how did it go?" Her voice was warm, but there was an edge—she knew this wasn't a social call.

Maya let out a breath. "Honestly? I need a good lawyer. Did your dad have anyone in mind?"

Robin didn't hesitate. "He does. I gave him the basics earlier. He asked his assistant, and she checked with Terrance Leeworthy—he's a partner at Dad's law firm, does property and estate stuff, especially messy breakups. She said Terrance can meet you Wednesday at ten, if that works. I'll text you the address."

Maya nodded, even though Robin couldn't see her. "Perfect. I'm just organising my stuff—receipts, emails, all of it."

"Good plan. Bring everything. You'll want to walk him through the whole mess from the start," Robin said, her voice growing steadier, practical.

"Yeah," Maya said. "Thanks, Robin. For real."

"Anytime. Text me if you want to talk later."

"I might," Maya said. She managed the faintest smile. "Talk soon."

After they hung up, Maya stood still for a moment, letting the quiet settle around her. Then she set her phone down, crossed the kitchen, and pulled the battered shoebox of receipts from the cupboard. The fight wasn't over. But at least now she'd have someone who could call bullshit on Lucas.

– 5 –

MAYA STOPPED at the curb, watching as the morning traffic inched along the Halifax waterfront. Across the street, the granite buildings of Historic Properties lined the water, renovated and lively, their old stones bright in the sun, windows set with new displays. Mannequins gazed out from behind the glass, dressed in crisp linen and bright summer colours, ready for tourists with money to spend.

In the window, Maya caught her faint reflection—a pale outline, hair pulled tight, lips pressed and colourless, looking nothing like the glossy figures behind the glass. She shifted her bag, her shoulders tightening under the burden of what was to come.

The battle over the house, the sense of betrayal, and the uncertainty about what lay ahead felt overwhelming, almost unbearable. For a brief moment, she questioned how she would navigate through it all. As the traffic light changed, Maya stepped off the sidewalk, her heart pounding but her determination strengthening. What other option did she have?

Fight or risk losing it all. In the crosswalk, people on both sides brushed past her, the city continuing, indifferent to the mess she carried alone.

She found the alley, narrow and tucked between the buildings, easy to miss unless you knew where to look. The Old Red Store sign swung above her, some paint peeling, the Canadian flag flapping. The air smelled of coffee and seaweed, hinting at the harbour just beyond. The shingles were grey and weathered; the shutters were wide open to the light. Red awnings cast their colour over the Carpenter Shop, baskets of petunias and ivy softening the wood.

Maya walked through shadows and sunlight, her heels clicking against the cobblestones. She passed a black cannonball beside blooming geraniums. Overhead, string lights reminded her that the area was for late-night laughter as much as for quiet mornings.

The lane widened as it neared the waterfront. A couple lounged in red and yellow Adirondack chairs, sunlight flashing off the man's glasses as he leaned in, smiling. Their dog, a mix of black and white, lay sprawled at their feet, tail sweeping the pavement. The woman laughed and rested her hand on the man's knee. Maya slowed, heart clenching. The sense of isolation came fast, familiar, sharp. She blinked, wiped at a tear, and kept moving. Their laughter echoed behind her, undisturbed by her passing.

Maya checked her watch and quickened her steps. She arrived at the law office, noticing the clean yet aged white trim and the brass plaque beside the solid door. Inside, her footsteps were muffled by the thick green carpet. Near the reception area, mahogany chairs with brass tacks were lined up neatly, their leather polished, the air carrying a subtle lemon scent. Behind the desk, the panelled walls displayed framed degrees and antique map prints. A clock with pewter hands ticked softly above the wainscoting.

Terrance Leeworthy emerged, one hand on a file, the other extended in greeting. He looked to be in his late thirties, hair thinning, lines around his eyes, stocky build. His smile was simple and honest—no performance. Although he wasn't tall, he had a solid, reliable presence. He seemed like someone who had spent countless hours with people facing difficulties, cultivating a patient demeanour. When he shook her hand, his grip was firm and reassuring.

She relaxed a little. He came across as genuine and reliable, someone who spoke with sincerity. He guided her from the foyer into the boardroom, where the daylight streamed in, softened by the half-open beige blinds.

The boardroom was cool and quiet, with leather chairs arranged around a polished table, and papers stacked neatly. Maya set down her folders, every edge lined up. She gazed through the window at the blue harbour, where boats gently swayed and gulls flew overhead, while a distant container ship slowly moved past after departing the terminal. Maya placed her hands on the edge of the table and took a moment to calm her breathing. Outside, life continued. Inside, she prepared for what was to come.

Terry sat across from her, silver pen ready, his legal pad already scrawled with questions. He started at the beginning. When had she moved in with Julian? That was the easiest question.

"Why was ownership of the Beach House and vacant lot only registered under Julian's name and his father's? Why did Julian not add your name too?"

"Julian was brutally honest. He explained that his father, Howard, was gifting us the Beach House, but if we ever split up, he wanted to avoid any legal complications. He said my name would be added to the deed later, but that never happened, and I foolishly never insisted on it."

"Complications, how did you interpret that?" Terry touched the pen top to his lip.

"That it wouldn't lead to a messy breakup, but I still thought I'd be compensated for my share and reno investment."

"And what did you believe was your share?"

"Well, maybe half and I thought at the time we were going to get married. So I knew that eventually I'd be protected as his spouse, you know. Don't things get split down the middle in a divorce?"

"Yes, often, but not always, it depends." Terry pursed his lips and tilted his face left, then right, signifying it was more complicated.

"And what did you contribute to the renovations to the Beach House?" Terry asked.

"It was essentially a rundown old cottage," Maya recalled, glancing at the ceiling. "We completely renovated it—new plumbing, wiring, kitchen, bathroom, roof, everything."

She recounted spending weekends painting by herself, staying up late, sanding floors, and working on the old window trim and staircase. She chose a light pine stain, her hands bearing calluses and splashes of colour as proof of her hard work. She arranged for the kitchen, which she financed herself, and the decking surrounding the house, along with all the paint, stain, and paint stripper, maxing out her credit cards in the process.

"Probably forty grand, I'd say. Maybe two hundred hours of labour or more."

She showed Terry the spreadsheet. Every purchase, every receipt. It summarized all the late nights spent renovating the cottage after long days at the gallery. Hours upon hours were dedicated to stripping away layers of old paint, applying two fresh coats of stain to the exposed wood doors and trim, constructing the deck, and planting shrubs along the perimeter and in the garden to ensure it would blossom by late June. She never referred to it as a sacrifice; to her, it was about building a life together.

Terry scribbled each point down. "Who had paid the mortgage and taxes?"

She gave a short, humourless chuckle. "Almost 100 percent me. Julian rarely sold a painting, and when he did, I gave him a cheque from the gallery and he put it in his own bank account."

"Sorry, I am not sure I follow?"

"Oh, I should have mentioned, I met Julian when he visited the gallery where I was employed. We took him on as one of our artists. I acted as his constant advocate at the gallery, struggling to prevent my boss from kicking him out, as Julian's artwork simply wasn't selling. Julian had a new sale every three or four months, at most. The majority of our customers preferred ocean-themed art or vibrant colours for their home decor. Although his abstract pieces are interesting compositions, they are better suited for fine art venues, such as museums or serious collectors, rather than our usual clientele. I recommended that he sell his work in Montreal galleries, but he never really followed up on that suggestion.

"And what did he do with that money?"

"Oh, he bought his own clothes, wine and pot sometimes, art supplies, art online subscriptions, an expensive racing bike, oh, a high-end turntable, speakers, tons of records and stuff like that, all for himself."

Then Maya listed everything she'd bought for the Beach House: the carpets, the new sofa and chair, the queen mattress, the main bedroom furniture, and more. She'd paid for it all—for them.

"I see," said Terry, writing faster.

The money from her paycheck and year-end bonus was always deposited into the joint account and spent on mortgage payments, taxes, power bills, heating oil bills, repairs, groceries, and everything else. Julian's name was on the account, but the only deposits were hers. She had the bank statements to prove it.

"I probably put in $100,000 more than Julian for mortgage and bills."

Terry listened, underlining "joint account," circling "paid all living expenses," his finger pausing on the total column of the spreadsheet.

"You are meticulous," Terry said. A compliment, he noticed all the folders with coloured tabs, organised by sub ject matter.

"Any debts?"

"We each had a Visa card, but I was the one who always paid off the credit card bills in full and on time, covering both his expenses and mine. I could see what he bought, and occasionally he would give me cash from his own account. For instance, when he bought his racing bike, he gave me two thousand dollars, which was from the sale of one of his better paintings."

"So, the mortgage was under Julian and Howard's names, I assume? Yet you were the one who paid it?"

"Yes, I feel like an idiot now. You've reminded me. Julian mentioned that the property needed to remain in both his and his father's names because he couldn't show enough income on his own to secure a mortgage. His father's signature and co-signing were necessary to obtain the loan. That mortgage funded half of the renovations, and on top of that, his dad contributed an additional $200,000. I took care of the remaining expenses."

"You mean the $40,000 you paid for the cottage renovations?" Terry asked to verify the numbers.

"Correct. He said his dad had to be on title too, according to what the bank wanted. But I made the mortgage payments every month. I can show you." She tapped the folder, already open to the right page.

Terry's eyes flicked up. "So you covered the mortgage, taxes, upkeep…"

She nodded, "Utilities, insurance, every repair—dishwasher, water heater, septic pump-out. If it needed fixing, I did it or paid for it."

"And the car?" He pointed to a line item in the spreadsheet.

"Yup, me too. I took out a bank loan myself; I needed a car to commute from Chester to my job at the gallery, I put on 200 kilometres a day."

"All right, I have two more questions. You mentioned there's an empty lot beside your house—do you know who owns it?"

"Yes, it was originally under Julian and his dad's name. However, after his dad passed away suddenly last year, everything, including the house property, was transferred solely to Julian. I can't quite remember the legal term for it."

"Joint tenancy," Terry voiced, "it means the title passes automatically to the survivor of the joint owners, so Julian is the sole owner now."

"But according to his brother Lucas, his father's estate owns the Beach House and vacant lot!"

"I know his argument, and what his lawyer will say. They'll claim that since Julian didn't purchase the properties, he was merely holding them in trust for his father, the rightful owner. The estate is now claiming it back."

"Is that the law? Can't he gift it to us, or at least to Julian?"

"It depends; each case is decided on its own facts. We need more details on that. It's complicated."

"I forgot to mention, I do know that Howard's company paid the contractor for the Beach House renovations, about $200,000 or so and Lucas wants that paid back with 10 percent interest."

Terry shifted back in his chair, noting this added another layer of complexity.

"Lucas says the Beach House needs to be sold, and that loan is paid back first, then what's left is split between Lucas and Julian. They said they would pay me back for these receipts," she said, pointing at the receipt folder, overflowing and scattered on the table.

"Maya, I think that we can get you more. I am of the opinion that you have a legitimate trust claim on the estate and Julian's share."

Maya smiled softly.

"And what about the Riopelle, our painting? Can I get a share of that?"

"You told me Howard's company did pay for it, $452,000 and that was wired to the gallery's bank account."

"That's right, I verified it with our bank. Howard gave it to us, and it always stayed at the Beach House. The only time it wasn't there was when Howard wanted to show it off at his big parties. Julian would take it for the event but return it the following day."

"I understand," Terry thought, trying to figure out how to craft a legal argument that would capture Maya's interest. "Typically, we'd argue that the painting was a gift meant for both you and Julian, but since the Company paid for it, that complicates things."

She wrote a single word in the margin—gift?—and let her pen fall still.

Across the table, Terry's voice kept going, but Maya's eyes drifted to the neat lines of the wainscoting—straight, ordered, no room for doubt.

"What do you think the painting is worth now?"

Maya hesitated. "The market for Jean-Paul Riopelle has strengthened considerably in recent years. His major canvases are now commanding prices well beyond previous estimates—particularly in London and Paris. I'd expect a work of this calibre to achieve well over a million, provided it's offered at the right sale and properly presented."

Terry's hand wrote in big letters, "A MILLION AT LEAST—PAINTING."

After clearing his throat, Terry asked, "Riopelle—Jean-Paul, right? French artist?"

She smiled. "Close—Canadian, actually. He's about as famous here as you can get. Big in abstract—lots of wild colour, thick paint, wild landscapes."

"All right, leave it with me. I'll draft a letter to Lucas—setting out your position and your claim. I'll send you a copy to review before it goes out."

Maya nodded, letting the words settle. For the first time all morning, she felt someone was on her side.

"Oh, I forgot to ask. Do you know if Julian has a lawyer?"

"Not yet, but I will make sure he gets a copy. Will you be asking for his share."

"Not directly, you are my client, but your rights flow through him, in part, so we need to build the best-case scenario. Basically, he owns the Beach House and vacant lot. You have a trust claim for those assets. Additionally, you and Julian are co-owners of the Riopelle, as it was legally gifted to both of you. Howard, as the Company's owner, could still transfer it to you, even though the Company funded it."

"Terry, I'm not exactly sure what this is, but I went through Julian's cluttered drawer full of papers and pencil sketches and came across this."

Her lawyer scanned the paper, "Whose handwriting is this on the yellow sticky?"

"Howard's, I would guess," she shrugged, but confidently.

"It is a copy of the property transfer papers to Julian and his dad as co-owners. But the yellow sticky seems to read: 'Julian's when I pass away, does not go through the estate. Company to Lucas under the will.'"

"This was back in 2019, when Howard's company was still doing really well," Maya commented.

"Yes, this could be useful. I'll make a copy."

"Excellent!" Maya stood up and shook Terry's hand.

– 6 –

THE HARBOURFRONT Grill opened just after sunrise, though Julian was still asleep. The coffee came out strong and black, always hot, with a trace of chocolate if you noticed. The servers topped off every cup without asking. The regulars sipped and read the paper, no rush.

Nothing changed here. The cracked tile by the cash register still rocked underfoot. The menus were made of thick plastic, with soft corners. The radio by the kitchen stayed on Q104. Oldies—Bryan Adams, Sting, Tom Petty—rolled out of the speakers in the ceiling, mixing with the clatter of dishes and the low voices at the tables.

Julian pedalled along Queen Street on his racing bike, his legs weighed down by a week of poor sleep. When he reached the iron railing, he took the lock out of his backpack and wrapped it twice around the graphite frame of his matte-black Cervélo, the priciest item he owned outright. He observed the morning hustle, noting the local man in a yellow jacket walking his aged dog along the hedge. Satisfied, he turned back and twisted the dial until the lock clicked securely closed. Chester was a safe place, but you couldn't be too careful with a bike like that.

He trotted up the steps to the porch. The Grill's siding was a blue-grey hue, just enough to catch the first rays of sunlight. Strips of paint had peeled away, revealing the wood near the gutter. The white trim was streaked with rust where the metal flagpole dripped. Umbrellas—white, cracked, a little off-kilter—cut the porch into triangles of shadow and light. He bent down to pass beneath one, his shoes tapping on the worn wooden planks, and the edge of a "Best Ice Cream" sign flopped beside the entrance. The chalkboard still displayed the previous evening's specials, though the writing had smudged in the fog from the night before.

Inside, the place was already filling up. Tom Petty's "Free Fallin'" played softly on the radio; its opening chords just audible above the clinking of dishes and the quiet chatter of early morning conversations. The floorboards were broad and worn to a pine finish, each step emitting a slight creak. The walls and ceiling were also made of rough, unfinished light pine, with beams that sat low and slightly uneven. The stone fireplace dominated half of the wall, unused during the summer, with the hearth swept clean and a few patterned cushions neatly placed to one side.

The tables and chairs were a mix of styles—some had rattan armchairs with blue and yellow cushions, while others had spindle-backed wooden chairs. Despite the lack of uniformity, everything seemed to be in perfect order. The corners held a few old oars, a faded map in a frame, and houseplants doing their best to stay green in the filtered light from the windows. The place smelled of toast, coffee, and whatever someone was frying on the back grill. It felt like it always had a local, practical, almost home-like quality.

Julian settled into his usual spot at the table, which had two chairs positioned against the back wall. He placed his helmet on the other chair, avoiding looking at it. The vacant seat was hard to miss. It had been more than three weeks since they parted ways. Julian's thumb traced a dent on the table's edge, a spot where Maya used to tap when the food service was slow. Sunlight flooded the wooden table, highlighting the coffee rings and a persistent stain that remained despite efforts to remove it. Julian briefly remembered her tracing the most prominent ring with her finger until her omelet arrived.

Rosie approached with the coffee pot in hand. She had been working there for longer than Julian could recall. A robust woman in her late fifties, with hair dyed a bold yellow and a red floral apron stained at the front, she paused with the coffee pot ready.

Her eyes flicked to the empty chair, then returned to him. Keeping the pot steady, she leaned in slightly, chin tucked. "Expecting anyone?" Her voice had a subtle edge, as if she were trying to solve a puzzle.

Julian shook his head. "No, just me."

"All right love, the usual?"

He nodded.

She poured his coffee, well-acquainted with his regular order, and went on with her duties. He watched the steam swirl up from the cup, with the seat across from him empty except for his helmet.

For a brief moment, he imagined Maya there—her posture upright, gaze fixed on the window, hands clasping her mug. The vision lingered briefly before fading. Julian looked around the room through an artist's eyes, noticing how the morning light brightened the blue walls and how the shadows under the tables created a feeling of warmth and intimacy. Sunlight streamed through the glass, casting rectangles on the worn floorboards, softening as it fell over the jacket on the rack and the small drift of old newspapers.

The restaurant was almost at capacity, except for a large table that had a "reserved" sign on it. An older adult wearing a baseball cap was engrossed in a newspaper. Close by, two workers in T-shirts splattered with paint were leaning over their coffee, laughing together about something amusing. By the window, a pair of tourists, identifiable by their matching Yankees caps, were seated.

A little before nine, the front door opened, and a group entered, making their way to the round reserved table near the entrance. Vivienne, his aunt, stood out immediately with her navy wool jacket, sharply cut silver hair, and pearl studs that gleamed in the dim light. She wore no makeup and always seemed overdressed for breakfast, especially in this setting. She didn't notice Julian as she chose the seat facing the window, her back turned to the rest of the room—and to him.

What drew his focus was the group accompanying her: four other locals, mostly older, not part of her usual bridge companions. Among them was a woman with red glasses from the Heritage Society, a retired school principal with a buzzcut, a man with a perpetual scowl and a drooping left eyelid like a broken blind, and finally, a thin man in a tweed jacket who seemed out of place until he started speaking—his voice was loud and booming, easily filling the room. Julian recognized him from the last election—Richard Mosher, who had run for the NDP and finished third behind the Tory. Despite his loss, Mosher carried himself with the confidence of a union leader, always speaking as if victory were already his. The defeat hadn't fazed him at all.

Vivienne's table exuded an air of seriousness. There was no laughter or casual conversation. Each person took turns speaking, leaning forward, and keeping their voices hushed. Restless hands were busy folding napkins, curling their edges, or tapping on the sides of the cups. The man in the tweed jacket was the most vocal, speaking rapidly and with assurance, while the others either nodded or frowned, carefully considering each point he made.

Occasionally, the waitress would stop by to clear away dishes and refill coffee cups. No one expressed gratitude or even glanced her way. There was a palpable tension at the table, as if the group couldn't agree on their discussion topic.

Vivienne stood up and headed to the restroom, noticing Julian as she did. She gave a small, somewhat sheepish wave, as if caught doing something awkward, then disappeared down the hallway. Julian found the entire scenario peculiar. If Vivienne wanted to chat, she would have approached him.

He devoured his meal quickly—pancakes with bacon, drenched in syrup and slathered with too much butter. He needed the fuel for the 20-kilometre bike ride he planned to take after eating. From Vivienne's table, he tried to pick up bits of a conversation—the politician mentioned terms like "notice," "right-of-way," "municipality," and "beach"—all partially overheard amid the clatter of dishes and the radio playing Tom Cochrane's "Life Is a Highway."

Julian took his last gulp of coffee just as the politician shook hands with Vivienne and departed. The principal followed suit, signalling for the check. The waitress refilled Julian's mug until it was full. Once Vivienne was alone at her table, the waitress removed the remaining cups. Vivienne then stood up, holding her coffee mug, and headed directly to Julian's small table.

He gave a slight smile when she took her seat, though she remained expressionless. She clasped her hands together, sitting upright, and the subtle, crisp scent of citrus from her perfume lingered on her jacket.

"Morning, Julian. I heard about Maya. I'm sorry—it must be tough."

He placed his cup down carefully. "Yeah. It's tough. You must have spoken to Lucas."

"He called. Asked about the vacant lot and what the communities plans were. You know the old grapevine, news travels quickly around here."

"Well, I haven't heard any news." His words were honest.

A brief expression flitted across her face before disappearing. "I can tell you everything."

"Please, don't leave me hanging. Go ahead and share."

The waitress hovered. Vivienne's cup was filled again with black coffee. She nodded at Julian. "You're jittery. Too much caffeine."

Julian held her gaze. "Was that an NDP meeting? You running next time?" He nodded toward the empty table. "Their last guy had no chance to win it—too far to the left, if you ask me."

Vivienne traced the rim of her cup. "Chester has more rebels than you'd think. When property values get this high, everyone's looking for a piece of the pie. We all want our share."

Julian shrugged. "You're not wrong."

Her head tipped, watching him. "We all heard there's a plan to sell the vacant lot and the Beach House. Lucas wants to offer the lot for a new home build. Shame, really—it's a beautiful piece of land. Your grandfather had a knack for real estate."

Julian blinked, cautious. "Who told you that news?"

Vivienne's mouth twisted, not quite a smile. "Please. In Chester, secrets leak faster than rain through an old roof. Lucas was talking to a few local realtors about property values and how the market is doing."

He nodded, resigned. "Lucas says the lot's hitting the market soon. He's got an architect drawing up plans. Says it'll be a big place, someday. His call—not mine."

Vivienne's eyes narrowed. "It matters to the village—especially that lot. People are going to push back."

He shrugged it off casually. "This is our land. Why should it concern any of you?"

She went serious, almost scolding. "You know that's not true, Julian. That lot's been the only way to the beach since the '40s, when our family bought it. You remember—bonfires, picnics, kids swimming. A lot of folks think that beach is theirs."

"Maybe the beach is public," Julian emphasized. "But the vacant lot is ours. Private property. They never respected that."

She tapped her mug and said, "Exactly. If people have been using it for decades, they might establish a right-of-way. Legally, it's called a public easement, which is based on continuous use. Even if the land is privately owned, the path might be permanently protected."

He shifted, feeling the trouble rise. "That means nobody's building on it, not with a footpath right through the middle. Lucas will fight it, and it'll get ugly."

Vivienne nodded in agreement. "Yes, we're aware. That's why we formed a community group to support a lawsuit, aiming to have the right-of-way acknowledged by the court. It could take years, but no one will purchase that lot with a pending lawsuit."

He shook his head. "Definitely. That's the reason Lucas contacted you, right? You're the ringleader? Dad would have labeled you a traitor."

"My brother was a true capitalist. Me, yes, a socialist. We were like night and day, but I still miss him."

It seemed she was conspiring with the community to secure public access to the Barrett vacant lot, much to the Lucas's dismay. Julian speculated whether her actions were driven by political motives or lingering resentment over the family inheritance. Her younger brother, Howard, had received the entire Chester waterfront property, while she was left with just a modest cash gift from their grandfather. This was her opportunity to even the odds and settle old grievances.

Vivienne took a slow, steady breath, weighing how much to say. "Eight of us are hiring a local lawyer. Lawrence Graham, Q.C.—his daughter was in your grade. He's going to file the lawsuit to establish the right-of-way. You're correct;

once that's underway, no one will be willing to pay a million dollars for a lot where construction isn't possible, especially with a public path and half the village accessing the beach right out front."

"You told Lucas about this?" Julian asked.

She gave a slight smile. "Not yet, I was vague. Let him get the lawsuit. I just said the community would try to stop the build. He told me we'd lose."

Julian exhaled slowly, his brow furrowed with worry. "This will cause chaos, not just for him," he said, his voice laced with frustration. "I was counting on that payout for half of the vacant lot. He promised to buy out my share," Julian explained, his eyes narrowing as he imagined the consequences. "If you go through with this, he'll offer me next to nothing."

Vivienne's expression was tight; her lips pressed into a thin line. "I know. I'm sorry, Jules," she said, her voice carrying a hint of regret. "But Howard bulldozed his way through this town for decades. He commercialized the shoreline, turned over houses like they were playing cards, and forced every zoning variance no matter the outcome. Maybe it's time to give something back."

He gazed out the window. "Dad caused you trouble as well, didn't he? He lost your money in those sugar and coffee trades. A lot of your money disappeared too."

Vivienne shrugged, eyes cold but honest. "He lost a hundred thousand of mine. It hurt, but it didn't kill me. The millions he lost of his own money sunk him, though. I still can't believe how reckless he was. I cared about him, not the money. But I care about Chester too."

He truly saw her then, perhaps for the first time in years—the delicate lines etched into her face, each one a testament to the life she had led, and the unwavering spine of principle she had never surrendered. He had always thought of her as a persistent thorn in his father's side, but maybe, just maybe, she was the only one left who still held any semblance of decency.

"If you win, what happens?" he asked, swallowing the last of his coffee.

"The lot remains empty, and the path to the beach might even get paved. The town could transform it into a park with picnic tables, swings, and a community beach. They can name it Barrett Park if they choose, though I won't propose it. This way, our family name endures. If it can't be developed, then it has little value. Then the town can either purchase it from Howard's estate or expropriate it, and then we can gather private donations to create a park. Though we may eventually leave that place, something beneficial for the community will remain."

Julian nearly chuckled. "Lucas is going to be furious when he finds out. Even Dad—he's likely rolling over in his grave at this moment."

Vivienne's gaze mellowed. "It has to be done. Are you going to join us, or are you siding with Lucas? You've never been one to chase after the almighty dollar."

He looked down at his empty cup, silent, not sure.

"Don't be angry with me, Julian. It's for the good of the village."

His stomach churned with a mix of apprehension and determination, caught between the old dread of a fight lost before it even began and a flicker of hope that this time might be different.

He remained silent. Vivienne got up, gently rested a hand on his shoulder—her version of a hug—and departed with a determination that showed she meant everything she said.

Julian stayed seated, observing the door as it closed, burdened by the question she had left hanging in the air. The room remained the same, yet something inside him had altered. For the first time, he was uncertain about where his loyalties lay.

– 7 –

JULIAN STEPPED out into warm air, where the ocean breeze was growing stronger. He thumbed the bike lock open and took one last look at the Grill's porch—sun whitening the blue-grey boards, umbrellas swaying in a gust.

Rolling onto Queen Street, tires bumping down the curb, Julian paused, weighing which way to ride. As he traveled south, the post office and the old art gallery flashed by in vibrant blocks of colour and form. His artist's eye lingered on the angles created by the light, the bright red of a mailbox, and the sharp darkness of a spruce tree at the corner.

He waited at the stop sign, listening to the deep rumble of the cement truck as it changed gears, with a white Ford pickup truck trailing closely behind. At the bottom of the main road, the harbour opened up, sailboats swaying in their moorings and the water sparkling with white-tipped waves.

Vivienne's words lingered in his mind. He envisioned the vacant lot not as a legacy but as a park, with picnic tables, swings, children running along the old path, and teenagers drinking beneath the stars. In this space, everyone, including him, could discover a bit of happiness.

This time, it didn't hurt—not really. The money, he told himself, wouldn't buy happiness. It couldn't touch the hollow ache in his gut from breaking up with Maya. No, the vacant lot was something else entirely. Maybe, if he was honest, it was the only thing that offered even a hint of relief. Helping someone else brought a kind of comfort, a feeling that, for a brief moment, he could make things right, even if only in small ways.

He slowed at the bend at the harbour's edge, letting the possibility settle. If the park happens, that cash vanished. However, if he could recoup it by selling the Beach House, the Riopelle, it wouldn't be a complete loss. He realized he had to confront Lucas and strike a much better deal. But how could he achieve that? In that moment, he concluded he needed to hire a decent lawyer.

At the road's end by the harbour, a gleaming black monument was erected near the former home of Rear Admiral Desmond Piers. After years spent at sea—escorting convoys and participating in D-Day—the Rear Admiral returned to Chester. The village honoured him with this monument, inscribed with his name, medals, and the traditional navy motto at its base: READY AYE READY.

Julian slowed as he passed. For years, he had seen those words without pausing to reflect on them. *Aye*—naval slang for "yes" or "always." Ready, always ready. Not just prepared, but unwavering. Constantly vigilant. A commitment to remain steadfast, no matter what challenges might arise.

He pondered what it required to live under constant threat from U-boats and torpedoes, every single day, never knowing if you'd make it back home. The monument helped him see his problems in a new light. He experienced a calm sense of relief, almost gratitude, as if the load he bore was just one of life's minor burdens, not something overwhelming.

Julian realized how effortlessly the minor challenges of life—such as financial struggles, setbacks, and ego—could expand until they overshadowed everything else. The real risk involved one's own life. Genuine sacrifice meant offering one's life for a cause greater than oneself, such as freedom, the protection of others, or the aspiration for peace. Such bravery couldn't be quantified in numbers; it was assessed by the lives it affected and the legacy it left.

Most of what we fear is only a shadow of reality. Most day-to-day storms, however fierce, break and end with time. Riding on, Julian carried the old motto with him—a quiet reminder that when you set your troubles beside the actual stakes of life and death, their weight lessens, and what matters most endures.

Vivienne's words came back to him, more distinctly now than when they had discussed it at the table. A park, not a financial gain. Something to leave as a legacy. She wanted him to understand that the real importance lay not in the money, but in what remained afterward.

At the restaurant, he clung to his need for security, especially now that Howard was gone and Maya was no longer his anchor. He questioned whether he could manage on his own. But after visiting the monument, something in him shifted. Vivienne had always looked beyond the money. She cherished what lasted: children running barefoot, bonfires lighting the night, a narrow path worn down by years of simple joy. She wanted the land to be shared, so that laughter and memories would endure, outlasting any promise of financial gain.

Julian envisioned the vacant lot—wild grass, a trail worn by countless generations, and the faint echoes of happy voices. It wasn't merely a piece of land; it held the potential to enrich the lives of those who came after. The Rear Admiral's monument communicated that sacrifice was the highest calling. For the first time, he comprehended Vivienne's words.

He reached the top of the hill, his legs aching and his breath laboured. Below him, the road stretched out, with houses receding toward the shoreline. Julian pushed himself more, allowing the physical pain to drown out the chaos in his mind. As he coasted downhill toward home, the tension dissipated. He felt an emptiness, yet a soothing lightness spread through his muscles.

When Julian arrived at Howard's house, he saw the big structure with its partially closed blinds and a garden worn down by the years of neglect. After parking his bike in the garage, Julian stepped onto the porch and paused, observing a gull lazily circling beyond the point, persistent and seeking something to claim. For the moment, he felt at peace.

Julian paused on the porch and noticed a folded newspaper by the door. He bent to pick it up, brushing off a bit of grit before opening it. The *Masthead News*, the local Chester newspaper, always featured a headline on its homepage, such as the latest council meeting summary or a bake sale in need of pies. However, this morning, just a day after Julian had talked with Vivienne at the restaurant, the leading story was prominently featured at the top of the page, right above the classified ads and the fishing cartoon:

COMMUNITY GROUP FIGHTS FOR 'BARRETT PARK'

The story began with a quote from Richard Mosher, a two-time losing NDP candidate who was now the group's spokesperson. Mosher called it "a vital strip of heritage coastline, threatened by speculative development and corporate greed." The article featured a photo of six residents standing by the vacant lot, with a cardboard sign stuck in the grass that read SAVE OUR BEACH! Vivienne was front and centre, hand on the sign's top right corner. The newspaper named the Barretts, talked about a right-of-way dating back generations, and detailed the legal action to keep it public.

The only quote from Lucas came by email. His reply to the reporter? "No comment. It's in the hands of my lawyer."

By noon, everyone in Chester had seen it. Realtors called the vacant lot a ship on the rocks, sinking fast. At the Harbourfront Grill, the talk spun in familiar circles—everyone knew Lucas wouldn't give up without a fight. He stood alone now, with council and community lined up on the other side, holding their ground. It was still private property, and Lucas wanted a million. But the general sense was that if the public won access, the lot might be worth only $20,000. Vivienne and her group now had the town behind them. Lucas had lost most of his allies, though few would say so out loud.

In Howard's kitchen, Julian was making a smoothie when his phone buzzed—Lucas's name lit up the cracked display.

"Did you see the newspaper story?" Lucas barked, skipping any greeting.

"Yeah," Julian said, keeping his tone even. "Even Chuck sent me a message about it."

"They expect us to give away a million-dollar property. Are they fuckin' kidding? It's disgusting—those leftist crazies. Vivienne and her little sidekick, that pathetic politician—they won't ruin me. Or us. Are you on board?"

Julian hesitated, the blender still running in the background. "It could hurt us both, sure. But maybe we should consider it. Money isn't the only thing that matters."

Lucas scoffed. "Are you serious? Turn it into a park? Some lousy benches, dog shit everywhere? Dad would be furious. It's our property—they can't just take it. They need to pay what it's worth. That's final. Don't be an idiot."

Julian let the silence work in his favour. "It's under my name. Shouldn't I have a say?"

Lucas's breathing sharpened. Then he laughed, a short, empty sound. "It belongs to the estate. Dad put it in your name to protect it, not to give it away. It's not yours. It's ours. And I say no. I'm the executor. I decide. We fight."

Julian sighed, letting the old habit take over. "Fine. I'd like to see some money out of it too, honestly."

That did it—Lucas was satisfied. He hung up without another word.

A minute later, Lucas was already thumbing a message to Vivienne:

TRAITOR!!!!

Then another:

> Hope you choke on it, you old fuckin bitch. IT'S NEVER GOING TO BE "YOUR" PARK.

—

WHILE SITTING at her desk in the Halifax gallery, Maya heard her phone chime with a text from Greta.

"Check this out," Greta said, along with a link.

Maya went over the article twice, feeling a wave of satisfaction. For once, Lucas wasn't in control. For once, he wouldn't get his way.

Greta's next message arrived: "How about dinner at my house after work?"

As Maya drove from Halifax to Chester, her thoughts wandered from her argument with Julian about her fair share back to the passing landscape. The coastline blurred past—a blend of coves, pine trees, and glimpses of open water.

As Chester approached, the familiar tension surged within her, a torrent of old questions crashing in: where did she belong now, with the Beach House, her longing to start a family, and the nagging doubt about whether breaking up with Julian had been a mistake. Could she truly find someone new, someone who ticked all the right boxes?

Her mind swirled with uncertainty; torn between the path she chose and the possibilities she might have left behind.

Greta's news intensified the situation, escalating the conflict with the community. Maya hoped for Lucas's defeat, but this only heightened her risk—Lucas and Julian would resist her more fiercely over the Beach House and the Riopelle if they anticipated losing a million on the empty lot.

She walked up the road from the Beach House, taking around ten minutes, passing by leaning, aged mailboxes and neatly trimmed hedges, until she reached Greta's charming little cottage. It lacked an ocean view and wasn't particularly valuable, but it offered privacy, surrounded by tall oaks and pines. Greta emerged behind the screen door, her hair as frizzy and full as always, holding two glasses of white wine. "Read the news I sent you?" Greta said.

Maya shook her finger at Greta, feigning outrage. "I might not have asked you to keep quiet about my fight with Julian and Lucas, but you definitely stirred up trouble by spilling everything to Vivienne."

Greta let out a small smile. "Dear, you know where my loyalty is. That path to the beach has been used for decades. I can't imagine not walking Sam down there. We have rights now," she said, in the confident tone of a former librarian who'd researched the law online. "Twenty years, Maya. Once a path's been used that long, Lucas can't stop us. The beach is crown land—it's not even part of his lot. I had to get Vivienne involved, before Lucas sold it off to some unsuspecting buyer. This isn't fiction. We have real rights here."

Maya nodded and took a long swallow of wine. They sat in the kitchen, the window cracked open to the ocean breeze, ferns draping the sill, their roots tangled in old wooden planters.

Maya traced her glass with her thumb. "Do you think the community can win?"

Greta only smiled. "Depends on what stories get told. Howard made deals—some on paper, some with handshakes. Folks remember the handshakes longer. Maybe proof turns up, maybe it doesn't. That's Chester for you."

Maya's thoughts drifted to the paperwork she'd found in Julian's drawer—maybe evidence, maybe nothing. "Are you in the lawsuit?"

Greta shook her head. "No. But people talk to me. They remember more than they say. I might get called. Who knows what I'll remember in court, at eighty and still sharp."

Maya grinned. Greta was as sharp as ever.

They let the conversation wander. When Maya left, Greta handed her a fresh sprig of fern from the window planter. "Put it where it gets light. Don't drown it."

Maya headed home with the fern tucked in her pocket—a tiny, living piece to nurture, carrying traces from Greta's realm. Her spirits lifted slightly. Yet the thought of those old documents lingered in her mind, a secret she hadn't revealed. She had to scan them and forward them to her lawyer. If they contained what she suspected—evidence no one else possessed—they had the potential to alter everything. Perhaps this time, she finally had the true game changer.

– 8 –

THE NEXT day, Lucas sat at his cluttered kitchen desk, nestled in the alcove by the counter. The empty bottle of 21-year-old Macallan scotch still stood on the floor near the trash, awaiting its turn in the recycling, exactly where he'd left it. He held a steaming espresso, enjoying its fragrance, though his hand shook slightly as he placed the cup back down.

Blinking to clear his mind, Lucas hesitated before opening his iPad, already bracing for what waited there. The thought of facing his morning emails filled him with dread—each day brought another round of stress, another tightening of the vise. As he scanned his inbox, the usual barrage hit him: irate vendors demanding immediate attention, overdue loans piling up, and a fresh legal threat from the painter's lawyer—one he planned to ignore until after his second espresso.

Each subject line felt like a personal attack, with his name tied to warnings like "failure to pay" or "urgent action required." It was overwhelming. What gnawed at him most was the memory of his father's massive losses in commodities trading—how could Howard have risked Lucas's future like that?

For a fleeting moment, he wondered if his father had felt the same—a slow, creeping realization that his efforts couldn't mend past financial mistakes. Lucas tried to shut down reality internally, yearning for an escape from this relentless cycle.

Lucas struggled to focus on his emails; his mind kept drifting to Howard's last years. Over five years, everything seemed to unravel—first his business, then his second marriage, and finally his father's health. Howard's drinking began as a nighttime habit but grew into all-day binges.

After the market losses, he was a regular at the liquor store, buying rye, vodka, and coffee liqueur for Russians—White or Black, depending on the day. Lucas remembered how his father seemed to shrink, shirts hanging loose at the collar, skin washed out except for the red, broken veins spreading across his nose and cheeks. By the end, Howard looked empty—his voice slurred, eyes puffy and bloodshot, always complaining about chest pain but never taking it seriously.

Lucas learned to track his father's moods by the space in the whisky bottle—three inches below the top, and the day would stay smooth, but as the bottle dipped lower, Howard grew combative, quick to raise his voice. Working for him was chaos; Howard expected miracles. Sell more units. Secure the next site. Nothing was ever good enough. Howard would vanish into his study, skipping dinner, letting the phone ring endlessly on the other side of the door, pouring himself "one last drink."

At first, Lucas tried to talk to his father, asking careful questions, offering quiet suggestions, hoping things might change. But every time, Howard answered with criticism, or worse, the two of them ended up in liquor-fuelled fights that left both raw and silent for days.

Lucas knew better, but he could never keep himself from getting pulled into his father's storms. When Howard changed—when the drink took over—he became like someone else entirely: mean, ugly, impossible to reason with. Lucas shot back, trading insults like old rivals, each argument twisting until words cut deep. The kitchen became a ring, love and anger tangled together, leaving only exhaustion and shame. Neither ever walked away for good. They circled back, bound by wounds they couldn't name, hurting each other just to let the pain out. If there was love, it was scarred and stubborn, holding on even as it kept breaking them both.

So Lucas changed his approach. When Howard became critical, Lucas grew louder, making jokes, devising plans, and doing whatever he could to get noticed. When praise ran dry, he tried harder: bigger sales, riskier schemes, always pushing for more. In their house, it felt like love only showed up for the bold, so Lucas made himself as large as he could.

Lucas carried that strategy into the rest of his life, even after his father had passed away. Now, alone in his house with an empty bottle by the garbage, he caught himself talking, arguing, proving himself—even when no one was there to listen. He told himself he wasn't like his father. But most nights, in the quiet, he felt the truth: the old shame of failure—of losing what should have been his—along with all the destructive cycles handed down from one generation to the next.

Whenever the anxiety threatened to engulf him, Lucas turned to numbers. He'd lose himself for hours in complicated spreadsheets, building columns of expenses and income, sketching out projections for the Beach House, the Riopelle, the vacant lot. He recalculated his expected payout if everything went as planned with Julian, then mapped out his cash needs for the projects and his living expenses, item by item. The painting's market value, his half of the Beach House, the vacant lot—a question mark in the spreadsheet cell beside it. He highlighted and adjusted each number, double-checked the formulas, and recalculated the totals repeatedly. Well over $2 million, less what was due to Julian. His younger brother would have to figure out Maya's share. Lucas called the lawyer and left a voicemail.

By noon, the heat made the stair banister sticky. Lucas ran his palm along the wood as he came down from his bedroom, phone pressed to his ear, listening to the lawyer's voicemail greeting for the third time. He left a sharper, shorter message, then set the phone on the table and paced the length of the kitchen. He poured himself a quick shot, keeping it controlled during the day, then wiped his mouth with the back of his cotton sleeve. He sat with his hands flat on the table, waiting for the lawyer to call back.

The lawyer, Phil Jenkins, called back within ten minutes. Lucas pressed the speaker and listened, eyes on the yard where the Ferrari was parked in the shade under the maple.

"The legal action is ready," the lawyer said. "We're ready to issue and effect service of the action as soon as you review and approve."

"Three parties? Who else besides Maya and Julian?"

"I'll explain. We had to name both Maya and Julian. The claim is against Julian as the legal owner of the Beach House and the vacant lot. It's also against Maya, on the grounds that she's holding assets improperly—you said the Riopelle is in her gallery's vault. So we had to name the gallery as well, to cover that issue. We'll scan and send you the draft for approval."

Lucas took a deep breath. His heart thudded in his chest. He tried to keep his voice steady, but it came out fast and thin, pitched a little too high. One shot hadn't calmed him.

"I trust you, Phil. Just issue the papers. You know what to say. I don't."

Phil Jenkins's tone shifted to a more somber note. "All right, the next matter—we were served with the legal action by the community group. They are pursuing a permanent right-of-way through the vacant lot to access the beach. They've included Julian, as well as you, the estate, and your company in the lawsuit."

"Those bastards. Damn bastards." Lucas hissed through gritted teeth, his jaw so tense that a vein throbbed at his temple. He clenched his hand into a fist on the table.

"We need to prepare a defence. Start reaching out to people—anyone in the community who might have information. I need names. Go through your dad's records—look for anything: notes, letters, photos, whatever—about the vacant lot and how it was used. If you find anything showing that Howard or your family ever allowed people to use the path to the beach, that's important.

"Okay, I'll have a look through Howard's files."

"And put any plans to sell on hold. No one will buy the lot while this right-of-way dispute is unresolved."

"But I don't understand how these people can cross my property; it's friggin' private property. It makes no sense."

Philip paused, "Let me explain in simple terms. They can get rights under the 'doctrine of Lost Modern Grant.' It sounds like something out of a history book, but it's a very practical, judge-created tool that's relevant to your situation.

"Think of it like this: if you've used a path across someone's land for a long, long time without anyone stopping you, the law can step in and say your right to use that path is now legally protected. Specifically, the court will presume that, way back when the use started, there was an actual formal, written legal paper giving you that right, but that piece of paper has been lost to time."

"That's legal bullshit. How many years again do they have to be using the path to get these legal rights?"

"To win in court, they must prove a few things. First, they need to demonstrate that the use of the pathway has been ongoing for a continuous twenty-year period. The use also needs to be 'open and notorious'—meaning it should not be done in secret. Most importantly, this use must have been 'without permission.' This is a key detail. If Howard or his family gave people express permission to cross his land, then they cannot claim a permanent right-of-way over your lot. They need to use the path for those twenty years without permission."

"What is permission, how is it given?" Lucas said, following the logic.

"Permission is like your father saying, 'Yes, you have my consent to cross my land.'

"But if your father knows people are using the path, sees it happening, but doesn't do anything to stop them, and lets it continue, that's a big problem for your case."

"But they have to prove they went over my property to get to the Beach for twenty years without any permission from our family?" said Lucas.

"Exactly, that's it," Philip replied emphatically. "If they can prove open, uninterrupted use for twenty years, without the owner's permission, the court will grant them a permanent right of access by saying the original, formal permission was granted decades ago, and the document just got lost. Again, it's a legal fiction, but that's how it works."

"Well how do we prove we gave people permission, to defeat their claim?" Lucas asked.

"Listen, they have the burden of proving to the court that they crossed without permission, for twenty years or more. You just need to cast enough doubt, where they can't prove that. You, as owner, must point to specific 'positive acts' that either expressly or impliedly granted that permission," Philip said confidently, knowing what he was talking about.

"But Vivienne is on their side, she's backing them up. She'll say Howard never gave permission, nor anyone else."

"That's a big problem. We need to attack her credibility; show she's not telling the true story. I get to examine her under oath to hear what she's going to say."

"You know, Teddy Haliburton used to tie up his speed boat at the dock by the beach. Dad and Teddy used to go fishing all the time. Teddy would park in front of the lot, come down across it, and head out. He'd back us up—he'd say he always had permission to cross the land and that Howard let everyone cross. You know, Howard would be down at the beach too, drinking with people, all the time."

"That's the kind of evidence we need. Can you call Teddy and tell him to call me, I want to talk to him. I would like to obtain a written statement from him sooner than later, before Vivienne's lawyer gets to him first. She'll remember that he tied up his boat there too, that'll hurt their case."

"I'll call him now."

"Great, talk soon." Philip's advice was clear. Permission, they all had permission.

Lucas paced the house, kicked aside a pair of shoes near his desk, and dialled Teddy's number.

"Hello?" Teddy's voice, old and soft, held the easy rasp of a seventy-one-year-old fisherman—a man who liked his pipe and building ship models.

"It's Lucas. Howard's son."

"Yes, yes, Lucas, how's it going?"

"Listen, I need your help. Can you call Phil Jenkins? We're in a bind. A bunch of locals—my aunt Vivienne, Richard Mosher, you know that socialist nutcase—are trying to steal my vacant lot, the one between Howard's place and the Beach House."

"They can't do that. What the hell's going on?"

"It's this thing called adverse possession. If people crossed our land for twenty years and nobody stopped them, they get to use the path forever. No one can ever build there. They want to turn it into a park."

"Left wingers, always after something. Your family bought that land. What do you need from me?"

"I need you to tell Phil that Howard always gave you permission to tie up your boat and walk across the lot whenever you needed. For others too. You need to say he always consented to people crossing."

"Well, he didn't really say it, we were just friends, that's all."

Lucas exhaled sharply. "No, say he permitted you to go from your car, across the lot, down to the dock. That's what we need."

Teddy paused. "Okay, I'll tell Phil. They won't get your land, buddy. I'm here for your dad; may his soul rest in peace."

"Good. And say Howard did the same for everyone else—he'd wave, say hello, tell people to have a great day at the beach. Things like that."

"Well, I'm not sure I saw all that. Howard did put up a private property sign."

"Don't mention that. It got knocked down anyway. Just tell Phil what I said—Howard was fine with people crossing, gave them the okay. Got it?"

"Got it."

Lucas hung up, already thinking who to call next. His dad's old foreman, Willy, used to bring his kids down to the beach. Willy had permission. He could say Howard permitted others as well. He'd call. Willy would know what to say.

– 9 –

MAYA TAPPED the elevator button for the sixteenth floor, eager to find out if the condo's view matched the online photo. Beside her, the agent, Gwen, wearing a white dress and grey jacket, verified the unit number on her printout.

As the doors opened, Gwen remarked, "Sixteen-twelve, to the right. I think you're going to love this, Maya. Lots of calls and interest—it won't last long."

Maya felt a flicker of suspicion. Was this merely typical realtor talk, or was there genuine interest in the property?

"Could you remind me of the monthly rent?" she inquired.

"Twenty-six hundred."

Maya walked behind Gwen as they passed by three identical off-white doors, halting at unit 1612. Gwen inserted the key, and with a clunk from the lock, the door swung open.

The condo was flooded with light, featuring open spaces, sleek lines, light-coloured walls, and a kitchen shining with stainless steel and polished slate. Their footsteps echoed on the dark hardwood floors. However, it was the view that made

Maya pause. Two expansive windows spanned the wall, offering a breathtaking view of the city and harbour, with sunlight shimmering on the blue water. In the distance, Georges Island crouched green and low, the pale lighthouse catching the sun. The glare was bright enough to make Maya blink.

"I know," Gwen said, her voice softening as she crossed the room. "The view up here is something else. You get the sky, the water, the bridge—even the tugs and navy ships sometimes. On clear days, isn't this a little piece of heaven?"

"Honestly, that's exactly what I need right now." Maya wanted to shout how much she loved it but tamped down her excitement. No reason to let the realtor know how badly she wanted the place—not if she was going to negotiate.

Even so, she could envision living here. Just a ten-minute walk to the gallery, eliminating the lengthy commutes from Chester. No more retrieving paintbrushes from the kitchen sink or finding Julian's red and green paint smudges on the light switch. She could start her day with an espresso, enjoying the sunrise.

"How long has this place been for rent?" she inquired casually, aiming to gather some information.

Gwen grinned. "Just around six weeks. The owners are investors from Toronto, so they're willing to wait for the perfect tenant."

Six weeks, Maya thought.

She pressed her fingers into the fridge's stainless front—no prints. Not rented. Overpriced. Too much for me.

Maya tried to imagine breakfast here with her mug instead of Julian's chipped blue one, using a single plate, and only having her crumbs to clean up afterward. She imagined herself resting against the window, watching as ships set sail from the harbour into the expansive ocean, gliding through the fog beyond Georges Island, cloaked in mist and filled with stories. For almost two hundred years, it had housed Acadian prisoners, English troops, quarantine facilities, and even a lighthouse keeper—a secret world existing right in the heart of the city's harbour.

Gwen broke Maya's thoughts, "Do you want to see the bedrooms?"

"Please."

The tour continued, two bedrooms, one smaller, that could be set up as an office, but with a view that almost matched the living room. The main bedroom had a large window, angled toward the harbour bridge. Maya opened the closet, felt the soft roll of the doors, and closed them again. Everything was so new, but she liked the blankness—no one's past lingering in the air. She glanced back at the living room, drawn by the brightness. The condo felt clean, unburdened. Hers, maybe.

They returned to the kitchen. Gwen leaned against the main countertop.

"Do you have any questions?" Gwen asked.

"A few," Maya said, and found herself smiling.

She slowed her questions, not wanting to miss any expense, trying to make it work.

Maya started with the practical: heat, parking, and storage locker. Gwen's eyes darted to her phone at a ping, then looked back up and focused on Maya.

They both understood what was about to happen. Maya inhaled deeply and maintained a casual tone. "And is the monthly rent negotiable? Twenty-six hundred per month is high for me. I researched other units in the building, lower floors, but they were about $400-$500 less per month."

Gwen's smile became strained, uncomfortable with where things were heading. "But you're on the top floor. You'll be paying a premium, for the view."

Maya nodded, tracing the water's edge with her eyes.

"It's beautiful. But my budget was $2,200. What do you recommend?"

Gwen crossed her arms, signalling her discomfort with the conversation. "Yes, the price does appear a bit higher than the market average. However, properties with this waterfront location and view are rare. Plus, this one is brand new—no renovations or redecorating required."

Maya leaned in, palms pushing on the counter. "Still, it's over-budget. I was thinking of offering $2,250, just slightly higher than I want to pay. If I did that, how do you think the owners would feel about that type of offer?"

She observed as Gwen clenched her jaw and crossed her arms tightly over her chest. For a moment, Gwen's eyes flicked toward the window, blinking hard, then back.

"I could present that, but I know the owners want something closer to minimum of $2,500."

Not so firm after all. Maya felt the progress and shrugged. "Would they be offended with my $2,250 offer? I might continue searching for another place within that budget. I really like the space, but I'm not in a rush. I understand the market, and this seems a bit expensive, don't you agree?"

"Fine—but let's put in a written offer." Gwen wanted a commitment before presenting a low offer and filled out the paperwork.

"Let me talk to the owner, see where we stand. Can you wait here a minute?" Gwen began walking down the hallway and made a call.

"Of course."

The empty bedroom door shut.

As the agent stepped away, Maya returned her gaze to the water. Far off, the midday ferry left a white wake behind it, while the sun gleamed on the glass windows across the harbour.

She allowed her purse to slide off her shoulder and moved closer to the window, trying hard to take in the entire view.

No sense trying to move anything large from the Beach House. She didn't want to have that discussion with Julian—how to split the contents. Most were on her credit card but were long paid for and well-worn. The coffee table bore white rubber streaks from his sneakers. Maya envisioned where her books might be placed. A plant could sit on the windowsill. The Riopelle would look fantastic above the couch, although she realized she would never win that contest.

Gwen returned, face composed but guarded. "They countered—$2,450. That's a big drop, but I feel it's as far as they're willing to go. There weren't too happy, and it took a lot for me to talk them into it."

Maya let out a breath, slow, buying herself a second. "It's decent movement down. I do appreciate it. But it's still over my price range."

Gwen looked at Maya with a blank stare—she wasn't used to renters pushing so hard. "You might lose this deal," the realtor threatened.

Maya lifted a hand, calm. "I know my budget. If it doesn't work, that's okay. But I can't overpay, beautiful view or not." She crossed her arms, no emotion, and then silence.

The agent wavered, not knowing where to go.

Maya threw out an idea, just a thought, not a command. "Well, I'm at $2,250 and they're at $2,450. Would you be willing to see if they might meet in the middle, at $2,350?"

"I'm not sure they'll go for that."

Maya pushed, "Give them a call and suggest to them that if they can get to that rental number, you think you can move me there too. Could you float that trial balloon?"

Maya smiled, her face composed, but her heart beating faster. Last try to land this.

Gwen shrugged her shoulders. "Well, it's worth a try, but I'm not sure this is going to get it done." She disappeared back down the hallway.

Maya glanced out the window once more. Far below, a family congregated by the water, their dog pulling on its leash before they headed back to a park bench. Life continued with boats gliding by, seagulls and birds soaring through the air, and Georges Island basking in the summer sun. For a brief moment, she allowed herself to imagine the future—a new home, her name on a lease, and a different kind of morning light.

The bedroom door softly thudded open, and Gwen marched in. "Done deal, congratulations, they'll meet you in the middle at $2,350. I'm a little surprised. Let's put some initials on the price change."

Maya was elated at first. However, she soon had to inform Julian that she would be leaving in just over two weeks. Wasn't this what they wanted all along, for her to vacate and relinquish any claim to the Beach House, the lot, and Riopelle? But she reminded herself that wasn't going to happen; she'd fight for her fair share.

With a final look out the window, the harbour transformed, lighting up as the clouds drifted away from Dartmouth, the city across the water that Maya would greet each day with her morning coffee.

She stepped out into the corridor, light following her out. The elevator doors opened, moving her to the city below—the traffic moving, workers going back to the office after lunch. For the first time in weeks, she felt unanchored and free.

The sun shone brightly as Lower Water Street buzzed with tourists and the sounds of the city, the air carrying the scent of the sea and a warm breeze from the harbour. Just down the block, the Maritime Museum's famous *Titanic* exhibit always drew a crowd—people came to see the deck chair, fragments of wood, and the tiny shoes of the "Unknown Child," Sidney Goodwin, one of the youngest to perish. Halifax has the most *Titanic* graves in the world, with 121 located at Fairview Lawn Cemetery. Visitors continue to leave flowers and teddy bears in memory of the child buried there.

Sometimes, standing near the museum, Maya thought about all those lives pulled from the water, their stories still echoing.

Maya turned the corner and looked up George Street toward Citadel Hill, the old fort still holding its ground above Halifax Harbour. At the base stood the Old Town Clock, its white octagonal tower bright against the grass, Roman numerals sharp against the blue, the hands just past one. She loved the way it caught the afternoon sun, casting a faint shadow down toward the water. To her, it was the city's heartbeat, marking the hours for generations of Haligonians, garrison soldiers, and sailors from distant ports.

Walking up the steep hill to the gallery, Maya pushed through the glass door. Inside, it was quiet. The city noise fell away—pale wood floors. Clear light. The air was cold enough for Maya to pick up the sweater on the back of her desk chair. She checked for messages. Nothing urgent. Then she moved into the main room, her heels echoing in the quiet.

Paintings hung close and tight in neat lines—landscapes mostly, the Atlantic in a dozen moods, big sky, battered wharves, islands rising pale and blue. There was a cluster of folk art in the centre: a carved yellow heron, a wooden fisherman, a little girl with a painted red coat and wild black hair. The walls were bright with frames—some worn and cracked, some gold-leaf, a few grey and modern. Maya liked the mix, not caring if they weren't matching.

At 1:30, Maya was expecting a buyer for the Brymner—Morning Sails, Île d'Orléans—the second of two paintings the artist had made of the same wharf. This one caught the early light, the schooner's sails bone white against the low green hills, a handful of men talking on the dock.

The owner paid $19,000 at auction four years ago. Now he wanted to break even after Maya's cut, and the painting needed to be priced at $34,000. That was the arrangement—the gallery received its portion for providing the space, attracting clients, and handling sales. The owner priced the artwork high enough to account for these costs. In this market, merely breaking even was still improbable.

The bell activated by the door chimed, and a man stepped in—tall, dark-haired, crisp summer suit, sunglasses dangling from his hand. He paused, surveying the room, moving directly towards the Brymner painting.

Maya appeared from behind to greet him.

"Afternoon," Maya said, her voice quiet, just above the gallery's hush. "What do you think?"

"Beautiful."

"Maya Carson," she said, extending her hand.

"James Kilborn," he replied, his grip perfect, slightly firm.

He turned. "I love the light on the sails, the green on the boat's hull, just lovely colours."

"Different angle from the other Brymner painting, but this one has better light," Maya said. "On consignment from a private Toronto collection."

Kilborn nodded, arms crossed. "Always liked how Brymner handled sails. You feel them moving in the wind."

Maya smiled. "Brymner spent whole summers on the water. Painted the same boat from a few angles, bright sun to cloudy days."

He looked back at the painting. "I collect Brymner, some Cullen. Thinking of adding another Brymner if the price makes sense. Do you have room on the price?"

"A little, you probably know he bought it at public auction, but he's realistic. The market's gone up for this artist, collectors are looking for his better works. This is definitely one of them, don't you think?"

Kilborn stepped closer, examining the surface for cracks or missing paint, lips pursed. "Softer market overall, though.

A Brymner sold at Heffel for twenty-two last spring. A Morrice, for less."

Maya nodded. "True. But this is a great piece. Worth every penny. The owner isn't desperate."

Kilborn paused, then: "Twenty-five, that's the value. Money today by wire."

She didn't react. "I appreciate the offer, but it's low, he'd take a big loss after commission."

He shook his head, smiling faintly. "That's my offer. Can you get an answer."

Maya turned to call the owner in Toronto, hoping to connect. "Give me a minute."

The owner had a meltdown. Why bring such an insulting offer? Offended, he told her to go back at $34,000, full price, and "take it or leave it."

Walking back to Kilborn, Maya shook her head. "Sorry, he's firm at $34,000, he was little upset over the offer, thought it was out of line."

She watched for Kilborn's reaction. If he turned to leave the gallery, he wasn't bluffing; he wanted to steal it. But if he stayed and didn't make a fuss, he was haggling and wanted the painting, maybe desperately.

"Okay, no intention to upset the owner." Kilborn stood with his hand resting on his chin, his face expressionless, a neutral stance of a seasoned negotiator.

"Well, I'm not going to bid against myself. And you say the owner didn't budge from $34,000."

Maya let the silence hang, watching Kilborn's eyes stay on the painting. She never rushed these moments—let the quiet stretch, give it time and space for the negotiation to unfold. If a buyer stayed, there was always a path.

"If I could drag the owner down to $32,500, would you do that deal?" she queried, in a soothing, calm voice.

Kilborn had already made up his mind, "If you can get the owner there, I'll do it."

"But if I can, we have a deal, right?"

"Guaranteed, it's firm."

Maya left and dialled the owner, who didn't waste a moment and asked Maya: "So, did he take the $34,000?"

"He mentioned that he couldn't justify going there because of the recent auction prices and comparable sales."

The owner asked: "Then we are done for now?"

"I am just wondering, if the gallery drops it's commission by $500, then would you move down to $32,500? If we lose this deal, the painting might sit here for two months. Why lose it over a $1,000 net? We are trying to make it work here."

The owner paused, "Yes, agreed, that makes sense."

Maya walked back out to the gallery and extended her hand. "Mr. Kilborn, you own the painting."

Kilborn smiled broadly, mildly surprised, "Great job, I'll make arrangements to send the funds and I'll be back before you close."

"It will work for us. We'll wrap and box it."

"Perfect."

Kilborn's eyes lingered on the Brymner. He wasn't bluffing—he was already imagining it on his wall.

Maya let herself breathe. The deal was done. She let the feeling settle, just for a minute. She felt content, having achieved both the desired outcome and meeting the budget for the month.

A familiar pang of anxiety tightened in her chest. Tough in here, soft at home. Why was it so easy with strangers, so hard with Julian and Lucas?

She went to the window, glanced up at the Town Clock—steady, bright, keeping time as always. She made a mental note: get tougher.

And she smiled, knowing what she needed to do.

PART II

– 10 –

BY THE TIME I met them, nearly a year had passed since Lucas filed his lawsuit last summer against Julian, Maya, and her employer.

Maya's lawyer, Terrance Leeworthy, first called me in early April to ask if I'd serve as mediator—two properties, one expensive painting, and three people who no longer trusted each other. Now, in early June, I was finally on my way to the mediation session.

Halifax had a morning chill—the kind in early June where you'd want a coat at dawn but not by noon. The wind off the harbour made it feel colder than the forecast. I buttoned my suit jacket as I walked along Upper Water Street toward the office tower at Purdy's Wharf—sixteen stories of glass and steel, blue sky and clouds just beginning to reflect off the façade.

The city was waking up. A gull screamed over the parking garage. A delivery truck rattled past. People in suits hurried to their offices, eyes down, coffee in hand. I found myself outside the building, the wind picking up through the opening between the twin office towers.

My briefcase strap slipped from my shoulder. I caught it, pulled it back higher, hand slightly numb from the chilled ocean breeze. I crossed to the revolving doors, thinking about the case ahead. As the mediator, I was hired to help the parties reach an early, out-of-court resolution. They said they wanted to avoid spending a fortune on legal fees—hopeful, at least in theory, to end the dispute before the lawyers became locked in a full-scale battle.

A property dispute in Chester, one that started nearly twelve months ago. Maya Carson is in a dispute with the Barrett brothers, Julian and Lucas, over ownership of the renovated beach house and the adjacent vacant lot, which alone is valued at a million dollars or more. Additionally, there was an original Jean-Paul Riopelle painting, which could be worth as much as, if not more than, the land itself.

The Barrett family corporation had sunk money into renovating the Beach House and had allegedly purchased the Riopelle painting too, tangling the estate claim in a web of corporate versus personal ownership. The primary debate centred around who truly owned the valuable painting: was it given as a gift to the son and his common-law partner, or did the corporation still retain ownership? Everything was tangled—money, property, and the breakup of a long-term relationship, all bound up together.

There was a second lawsuit, though I wasn't mediating that matter today. According to one lawyer's mediation brief, this second lawsuit could dramatically lower the vacant lot's market value. A community group had started a lawsuit claiming decades of uninterrupted use had established their legal right to cross the vacant lot to reach the shoreline and beach. How might that influence the negotiations between the parties? There was genuine uncertainty—the property would be valued at a million if development was possible, but nearly worthless if it wasn't.

All of it hovered in my mind as I made my way to the elevators. A beach house, an empty oceanfront lot, and an expensive painting that sparked disagreement among everyone. Old family history running under the surface, feeding the conflict. Unfairness, resentment, entitlement, self-interest, and greed—each had a part to play in today's proceedings. These shadows tainted the facts, affecting every argument and every memory. No one in the room would see it from any perspective but their own. That's the funny thing about mediation. Everyone is sure they're right. Everyone else is wrong. It's just how it is—the facts and the law change in every case. Human nature doesn't.

As the elevator doors shut, I pressed the button for the ninth floor, sensing the weight of the task ahead pressing down on me. My mission was to navigate through it and help the parties get out of the court system—today.

Yesterday, I read each lawyer's version of the story and legal argument, trying to separate the posturing from reality. Pages of old emails, photographs—a house with pink walls, an abstract painting I didn't understand—all claiming that some or all of it belonged to them. The problems were never just about money. The real story was what you couldn't see: history, betrayals, hurt—the feeling that something had already been taken, or was about to be lost. Each was trying to shore up their position, make their best arguments, and persuade the other side of the strength of their case.

That was the work—sorting what mattered from what didn't. Coaxing sense out of chaos, reading what was missing in the spaces between the words, listening for what was happening below the surface. All the while telling yourself you were only here to hold the space, guide them through the conflict and out of an expensive court battle, let them find closure, and move on with their lives.

At the glass doors of the court reporter's offices, I paused, peering through the glass to catch a glimpse of who might already be waiting inside. Sometimes the parties arrived early, settling into opposite corners, tense and silent. Other days, I was the first to step into the mediation space, with time to gather my thoughts and plan the day's strategy.

Nine floors up, through floor-to-ceiling glass, the Halifax harbour stretched as a backdrop—soon to be filled with three people leaning forward in their chairs, voices rising and falling, lawyers shuffling papers beside them, all hoping I'd see things their way.

Mediators are supposed to be neutral, impartial—but can we avoid bringing any judgment or predisposition about how a case should be resolved?

That's the challenge: not to impose my solution or sense of justice, but to let the parties carve out their destiny. To allow them self-determination over their futures, not my version of how it needs to be.

I took a calming breath and stepped into the reception area. The aroma of coffee and pastries immediately greeted me. To my left, Maya and her lawyer, Terrance, were seated on a black leather sofa—Maya sat upright with her hands clasped, while Terrance was engrossed in his phone.

On the right, two oval green leather chairs flanked a low glass coffee table. A man sat in the left chair, his hair curly and dark, falling just a little too long at the collar, his expression gentle, almost innocent. For a moment, I didn't know if the man was Julian or Lucas. But then I saw he was seated beside a woman in a black suit—presumably his lawyer—in the right chair. So it had to be Julian, represented by Ms. Taylor.

I crossed first to the man and the lawyer in the black suit. She stood as I approached and offered her hand.

"Sandra Taylor," she said. "Counsel for Mr. Barrett—Julian Barrett."

Julian looked up, his eyes tired but steady. I shook Sandra's hand, then his—his palm cold and clammy with sweat.

"Good morning. Please, have a seat. I won't be long," I said, gesturing toward the green chairs.

Then I walked about ten paces across the reception to the sofa.

"Hi, Terrance," I said, knowing he was Maya's lawyer. "I'm Robert Coldwell." We shook hands—his grip easy, confident.

I turned to Maya. She stood to greet me, her handshake confident and self-assured, her gaze holding mine for a moment before she sat back down beside her lawyer.

Inviting them to make themselves comfortable, I asked them to wait in reception until Lucas and his lawyer arrived. "We'll begin once everyone is here."

The boardroom was the first one to the right off reception, entered through a big glass door, frosted for privacy. Inside, the long table dominated the room—nearly fifteen feet of polished wood, with four high-backed black leather chairs on each side and a single chair with arms at the head for me.

As I set my briefcase down, I considered the setup ahead. Who would sit where? Placement mattered—eye contact, proximity, which arrangement offered the most neutral ground, how to avoid alliances or body language that might spark tension. Already, I was working through the small choreography of the room: lines of sight, the occupant of each chair, how to keep everyone feeling safe but not too guarded, engaged but not on edge.

I took the seat at the head of the table, positioned exactly between both sides—not to claim authority, but to signal that I was there to facilitate, not to take sides. Everything was organised, designed to add comforts: a flat screen at one end, a tray of coffee and muffins on a credenza, pale green carpet softening every sound.

The harbour lay below, shimmering blue and silver in the morning sun. In the centre of the water, Georges Island stood out—mostly green grass, with a lone white lighthouse at its lower right edge. Through the floor-to-ceiling windows, a long rust-coloured vessel slipped across the view, its stacked containers piled high as it made its slow journey toward the Atlantic. The boardroom was silent, the case's drama on the verge of unfolding.

As I penned the names of each lawyer and client at the top of a fresh notepad, a voice cut through the reception area, too loud for the quiet of this place.

Lucas had arrived with his lawyer, his tone already occupying the space.

I stepped out to greet them. With everyone now present, I invited the group into the boardroom.

To minimize tension, Terrance sat to my immediate left, with Maya next to him, then Phil—Lucas's lawyer—beside her, and finally Lucas at the far end of the table. All four were in a row to my left. No one sat across from Lucas; just two empty chairs faced him. This was deliberate. I didn't want Lucas staring anyone down, especially not Maya.

On my right sat Sandra, then Julian beside her, both directly across from Terrance and Maya. By arranging the seating this way, I kept the likely combatants from facing off, using distance and space to help diffuse the room before we even began.

The air in the boardroom tightened as everyone found their seats. The parties moved stiffly, a little anxious, unsure where to put their hands or their eyes. Maya sat upright, scanning the table, her thumb pressed hard against her knuckle. Julian's gaze drifted past the table to the harbour beyond the window. Lucas leaned back, but his fingers drummed the armrest—a restless flicker he couldn't quite hide.

The lawyers, by contrast, were calm and practiced—pulling files from briefcases, uncapping pens, flipping through documents. They filled the silence with the rustle of paper and the muted clicks of phones and legal pads. Terrance checked the folder on top of his stack, while Maya arranged her papers into a perfect stack. Lucas's lawyer took a measured sip of coffee while his client tapped out a soft, relentless rhythm on the tabletop with two fingers.

For a few minutes, there was only the shuffle of preparation. The parties watched each other—and the lawyers—as if waiting for a signal, or a sign of how this would go.

I settled myself at the head of the table, feeling the weight of their attention. I looked from face to face, meeting each set of eyes.

"Good morning, everyone. Let's begin," I said—friendly, but with authority.

The silence after was like the hush before running a set of whitewater rapids—no telling whether we'd make it through in one piece or overturn before the finish.

– 11 –

"GOOD MORNING and thank you for introducing yourselves to each other. My name is Robert Coldwell, and I have the privilege of serving as your mediator today. I appreciate the opportunity to assist you in working toward a resolution. This is a voluntary process, and I want to acknowledge the spirit of cooperation you've already shown by coming together here today.

"Let me begin by stating that I am not acquainted with any of the parties involved in this dispute. As a neutral and impartial mediator, my role is to assist you in reaching a mutually acceptable resolution, enabling you to move forward constructively, avoid protracted court proceedings, and minimize unnecessary legal expenses.

"Participation in this process is entirely voluntary. If at any point you feel uncomfortable continuing, you are free to withdraw from the mediation. My goal is to support a process that is respectful of everyone's autonomy. However, I ask that I be allowed to discuss the reason for your concerns before the mediation process ends.

"As the mediator, I also reserve the right to end the mediation if, in my professional judgment, I determine that the process is no longer productive or cannot assist the parties in moving forward.

"As the mediator, my role is not to provide legal advice or guidance. Your counsel is here for that purpose. However, my job is to explain to each party why an out-of-court settlement is often preferable to the risks of litigation. If I raise concerns about going to court, know that I am doing the same with each party. I strive to be balanced and objective in sharing my perspective.

"One of the benefits of mediation is that you have greater flexibility than you would in court. Together, you can craft creative solutions that may not be available from a judge or jury. This flexibility is one of the primary advantages of choosing mediation to resolve your dispute.

"Today, the power to resolve this matter rests with you. You are the decision-makers. If you are unable to reach an agreement today, that power passes to someone else—a judge or jury—who will decide based on their interpretation of the facts and law. That decision may or may not reflect what you believe is fair or reasonable.

"As the mediator, I have no authority to impose a decision or determine how this matter is settled. My responsibility is to facilitate open and productive communication and to help everyone work toward a solution that meets everyone's interests.

"Mediation is focused on the future—on how you wish to move forward, not solely on the disputes of the past. I encourage you to participate with an open mind, to respect one another, and to listen actively—even when you disagree.

"Before I discuss the mediation process, are there any questions about what I've covered so far?

"Let me briefly explain the process. After this opening statement, I will meet with each party and their counsel privately for approximately 15 minutes. In these private meetings, you will have uninterrupted time to describe the problem from your perspective.

"What you share in our private meetings is strictly confidential, unless you specifically authorize me to share it. Confidentiality is fundamental to this process. There are rare exceptions—if information arises regarding a serious criminal act or a threat of harm, I may be required to disclose it. Otherwise, no one present today may disclose any settlement negotiations or discussions to anyone else, including family, friends, or neighbours.

"Regarding your lawyers' role: they are here because they have an ethical duty to seek early resolution and avoid protracted litigation. Even though your counsel may be working collaboratively today, please do not mistake that for weakness; I know they are all strong and capable advocates.

"If verbal offers are exchanged today and the terms of an offer are accepted by all parties, that constitutes a legally binding settlement. If an agreement is reached, it will be reduced to writing and signed by everyone, and each of you will receive a copy.

"I will meet with each party for the same amount of time, so the order in which I meet with you has no bearing on the process. I'll begin with Maya and Terrance, then meet with Sandra and Julian, and finally with Lucas and Philip Jenkins.

"We have three rooms, so I'll show you which private room you will be in for the day.

"Thank you for your attention. I look forward to assisting you all today."

Once everyone was settled, I stepped into Maya's breakout room.

Closed blinds veiled the glass wall at the front. Cream walls lined with old black-and-white photographs—schooners at anchor, a fishing village as the day's catch is unloaded, a sea horizon lost to fog. At the centre sat a table—dark wood, polished to a shine that caught what little daylight came through.

A lone stapler and a whole box of tissue, side by side. Spills, sneezes, and tears—these things happen.

A notepad and pen sat perfectly aligned with the edge of the table. Maya waited, posture precise, hands folded in her lap. She wore a navy dress and a single strand of pearls—businesslike, composed, everything held in tight. Terrance beside her, suit jacket still on, hands resting flat on his knees. In the introductions, he said to call him "Terry"—plain and simple, fitting his easygoing nature. He glanced at Maya first, then met my eye, waiting to see how this would start.

I closed the door and let the hush settle.

"Terry, thank you for your brief, you did an excellent job preparing me for today's session. What would you like to focus on?"

He opened a folder, found a spreadsheet, and pointed to the columns. "We've calculated Maya's investment in the Beach House. There's a column for every construction receipt she covered, all her labour hours, mortgage payments, taxes, utilities, and the rest. Over five and a-half years, the total comes to $188,875.42, to be exact. Julian, on the other hand, might have put in $5,000, at best. Maya says he spent the money he made from selling a few paintings on an expensive bike."

Terry glanced up, set aside the spreadsheet, and removed his reading glasses.

"We say she has a constructive trust, at minimum, for this amount, plus at least 50 percent of any equity growth in the Beach House property, which we estimate adds another $100,000 for her share. With legal costs, we're seeking a $300,000 payment from Julian or Lucas as a buyout on the Beach House.

"On the vacant lot, it could be worth $1 million, but she's prepared to take $150,000 to cover any interest she might have.

"Finally, the Riopelle—we say it was a gift to Maya and Julian from Julian's father. It's worth at least $1 million, maybe up to $1.25 million, so she'll want half of the low-end value. That's $500,000. Total claim is $950,000, all in."

Then Terry pushed a bound booklet forward labeled DAMAGES BRIEF. Inside, copies of every construction receipt and bank statement showing withdrawals from Maya's account for the mortgage, taxes, and utilities.

I paused. Jumping straight to numbers feels abrupt—almost a $1 million claim. My optimism for a successful outcome that day started to slip away. But I've been there before—sometimes, even when it feels hopeless, we get to a deal. No. Time to dig in.

"Terry, Maya, thank you for putting this together and providing such a detailed claim. Have you already given a copy to Julian and Lucas or their counsel?"

"No, we wanted to show you first. Do you think we should do that now?"

I paused, pen hovering over my notepad—almost a million dollars. The number hung in the air between us. I pictured the reactions waiting behind those other two closed doors—Julian's shock, Lucas's angry outburst.

I tapped my finger on the edge of the damages brief. "Let's hold off on sharing this for now. I think we might make more progress if we tackle these issues separately rather than all at once." I met Maya's eyes, then Terry's. "How would you feel about that approach?"

"We're in your hands. You are here to get us to a deal!" Terry commented firmly, looking at me to sell their demand to the others.

"Terry, I want to be candid—I can't promise any guarantees to you today. I don't control what the other rooms will do—no mediator does. My job is to bring you the best offer possible from the other side. Then it's up to Maya, with your advice, to decide if that deal is better than a long, stressful, and expensive court process. We likely won't know what's possible until later in the day. At this stage, it's about building some momentum and understanding where everyone stands."

Terry nodded, and Maya folded her arms, seemingly ready to do battle.

"Maya, have you had any discussions with Julian about how you may resolve this matter?"

"Nope." Maya's hands came up, palms open, a slight shrug. "Terry said to let the lawyers handle it. Julian and I haven't said a word in ten months, not since I moved out."

She glanced at the door, then dropped her eyes to the rows of numbers on her notepad, every figure underlined, exact. "Seeing him in the introductions..." Her voice trailed off. She cleared her throat. "I'd rather not have to see him today, if that's possible."

"Well, you're not required to do anything you're uncomfortable with. Years ago, we used to bring everyone into one room for a joint session—each side would make a formal opening statement, lay out their position. But in the last few years, especially in commercial and property cases, that's mostly disappeared. So you'll be staying in this private room for the duration of the mediation.

"I found value in a joint session, where everyone had a chance to speak face to face. But these days, most lawyers avoid it. They say it just creates hard feelings and makes people dig in deeper."

Maya sat back, arms crossed. "Well, as I said, I don't want to see Julian, so this suits me." She glanced at the door, then at her notepad. "And Lucas was sitting there in introductions, all smug and entitled. I have no interest in hearing from him or his lawyer."

I nodded.

Time to get into some specifics. "Terry, in terms of establishing rights as an equal owner in the Beach House, what would you want to point to, or what evidence might you be introducing?"

Terry offered a slight smile. "Well, I have this." He slid a piece of paper across the table—a screenshot of some text messages. "From Maya's phone. All from Julian."

The first message:

> Maya, can you cover the kitchen cost? Dad's company is tapped out at the moment. He's waiting to sell some of his condo units.

Another message asked her to pay for the decking and paint.

And then this:

> Don't worry, we are both building value here for our house. I promise. Dad's money for the renovations doesn't need to go back to him until we sell or refinance.

I looked up at Terry after reading. "Okay, I'm assuming the last text refers to the construction money—$200,000 from Howard's company. Have you provided a copy of these texts to the other counsel?"

"Nope. Maya just went through her messages the last few days and picked out the best ones. But there are others, similar in content."

"I see, thanks. May I have permission to share this with the other counsel when I think it might be helpful?"

"Of course. They're going to see it sooner or later."

I pulled the paper with the text messages toward me and slipped it into the side pocket of my leather notepad holder.

"What about the vacant lot and the Riopelle? Any relevant messages?"

Terry looked down, thumb tracing the edge of the table. "Not really anything for the vacant lot. We know we may need to be more flexible there, but with the community's claims—which we think are strong—we're not putting much of a dollar value on it. Maybe nothing, in fact."

"Okay, let's leave the vacant lot for later. But Maya, you feel the community's claim to the right of way is strong?"

"Absolutely. And I've got plenty to say about that."

"We'll need to get into that in more detail, but we've only got a few minutes left in this first meeting. We can circle back to the lot later."

I wasn't sure how to handle the issue in the other rooms. If Maya did have evidence that made the lot worthless, Julian and Lucas would likely fight harder for the Beach House and the Riopelle. I'd have to think it through before I opened up the discussion around the value of the vacant lot.

"All right, the Riopelle painting. Thoughts?"

Terry spoke up. "It was a gift from Howard to Julian and Maya. It's always hung in the Beach House. Besides, Maya found the painting herself—it was bought for next to nothing. I feel she just is entitled to something substantial in relation to the painting."

I nodded. "But my understanding is Howard's company paid for the Riopelle, and Lucas says the company owns it. Is that right?"

Maya cleared her throat. "Yes, Howard's company wired the funds directly from its business account to the gallery's bank account. But is that legally important, in terms of who owns the painting?"

Terry glanced over, waiting to see if I'd answer or let him take the lead.

I jumped in to fill the pause. "It's a bit complex. There had to be an intention to gift you and Julian the painting, for you both to own it. If the company paid for it, then that adds another layer, as Lucas says it was not Howard's to give. The company would have had to gift it to you."

Terry didn't hesitate. "Well, Howard owned the company. He could have directed it to gift the painting to them."

"Okay, that's an argument. But do you have any evidence of a gift to Maya?"

Terry shook his head. Maya cleared her throat again. "I don't have anything in writing, but once, when Howard borrowed the Riopelle for a Christmas party and didn't bring it back the next day, Julian and I went over for dinner—leftovers. Julian asked if we could take the Riopelle back to the Beach House. Howard said, 'Of course, I meant to tell you to take it back. It belongs in your house.'"

"How did you interpret that, Maya?"

"Howard meant it was ours. It was our house. It belonged to us."

"Terry, may I have permission to repeat that comment of Howard's in the other rooms?"

He nodded. "Yes. They've got a problem on the Riopelle. We'll need to see a strong offer for her interest in the painting."

"Noted. Let me work on this and see how things go."

I gathered my files and left for Julian's room.

– 12 –

I ENTERED Julian's room.

Sandra Taylor, his lawyer, was already waiting—maybe a year out of law school, young, hair pinned up, black suit crisp, a slim silver watch on her wrist. She looked up, mouth set in a small, professional smile.

Julian fidgeted in his chair, smoothing the sleeve of his plain white shirt. He had jeans and white sneakers on. A denim jacket hung off the back of his chair.

"Good morning," I said, taking the head seat. Julian sat to my left, Sandra to my right.

"Sandra, where would you like to begin today?"

She didn't hesitate. "I don't think the real fight is in this room."

"How do you mean?"

"Lucas is the problem. Honestly, I think Maya and Julian could work things out between them. But Lucas—his expectations—I'm not sure we can get it done, not with what he wants."

Julian gazed out the window, lips pressed thin, giving the slightest shake of his head. His shoulders edged back in the chair. He wanted to be anywhere but here.

"You know your brother better than anyone, Julian. Do you agree with Sandra? Anything you want to share?"

He shrugged and let out a brief chuckle. "Other than he's a total douchebag? Sorry."

"It's okay," I replied, pausing for a moment. "You feel like he completely disregards your needs."

"Exactly." Julian glanced at me and then straightened his posture a bit.

"So—explain your brother, if you can. How do we get him to offer a deal with enough value that it actually works for you too?"

"Let me think," Julian quickly sketched a box with vertical lines.

Julian tapped his pen on the paper pad, trying to find the right words. "When it comes to Lucas, you can't pressure him. He needs to believe it's his own idea or that he's getting the upper hand. If he suspects you're trying to outsmart him, he'll get angry and become totally unreasonable. I've always simply agreed with him. But that's the only way to get him to agree—he has to feel like he's won, that it's his deal that gets done."

Sandra broke in. "What would you suggest, then? How do we steer this?"

I needed to reply with care. While handling Lucas was like defusing a time bomb, I couldn't villainize Lucas either. Keeping a neutral mindset was key; otherwise, I'd be favouring one side over the other.

My throat tightened; I cleared it and looked straight at Sandra. "So, what you're saying is—he needs to feel in control. Right now, there's no way he'll accept any offer from you or Maya. That's correct?"

Julian perked up, leaned in. "Totally. He has to get his way, end of story."

Sandra nodded, settling back in her chair.

"So maybe the approach is to let him put his offers on the table. I can't push too hard or too soon. We need patience. You respond with your own offers. Let Lucas do what he needs to do, get where he wants to go. Then, before anything gets signed, you and Maya will have to agree on a split between yourselves. I don't see him ever agreeing to pay Maya what she wants, not directly. If he proposes a lump sum for both of you, you'll have to work out with her how to divide it."

Sandra glanced at Julian. He met her eyes.

"I think that works," she said. "Let's see what Lucas will actually agree to, then you and Maya can work out the rest."

Julian shifted in his seat. "Look, I want to be fair with Maya. I'm willing to take a little less to end this mess." He looked at me as if checking whether I knew how to handle this.

"So do you agree with that approach, to make a deal with Lucas, but subject to Julian and Maya agreeing to a split between them?"

Sandra leaned forward. "Would you mind if I had a word alone with Julian?"

"Of course. Take all the time you need. Just open the door when you're ready and I'll come back."

I walked out, pacing the corridor, my thoughts drifting to Lucas—how he evaluated every suggestion based on "What's in it for me?" His conviction that he's always right and entitled to everything was an attitude I'd need to manage carefully.

A minute later, the frosted glass door cracked open. I pushed it the rest of the way, then entered the room.

Sandra stood. "We're agreed. Let's work on Lucas. I think Terrance and I can work something out for our clients."

"Makes sense. I'll check with Terrance and Maya, see if they're on board. I'm meeting with Lucas and his lawyer now. Give me at least half an hour before I'm back."

Julian gave a crooked smile, playful but with an edge. "You'll need a hell of a lot more than that to get Lucas to budge."

Sandra grinned. "Good luck."

"I always accept luck. Thanks." I smiled, closed the door behind me, and headed toward Lucas's room.

Pacing down the hallway, I took a deep breath, smelling the air through my nose and letting it out slowly as my fingers touched the glass door, finding a place of calm and balance.

"Hello, Phil. Hello, Lucas," I said, offering them both a warm smile and meeting their eyes, as friendly as I could manage.

Neither smiled back.

Phil Jenkins occupied the seat at the table's end, partially obstructing the window. He was a large man, formerly muscular but now carrying extra weight around his midsection. His dark blue suit was broad through the shoulders and still buttoned, with ample room at the waist. With a square jaw and full face, his auburn curled hair was neatly trimmed, and he wore a bold red tie. His folders were arranged in a precise line beside his elbow. He didn't fidget or move, just watched with pale blue, steady eyes and a thin, hard mouth.

Phil's voice was low and precise. "My client doesn't want to be here all day. Let's cut to the chase."

I nodded, sliding into the seat across from Lucas, with Phil to my right. Already, I was calculating—reading the temperature, looking for an opening, knowing that with Phil, it would be all business from the first word.

Lucas leaned back in his chair, hands laced behind his head, elbows splayed wide, claiming more than his share of space. His blue blazer was unbuttoned over a crisp white shirt, collar open. A heavy gold rope chain caught the light at his neck, and a diamond-studded Rolex with a thick gold band gleamed on his wrist—flashy, impossible to miss.

Lucas looked at me, sizing me up, establishing his authority.

"Are you going to tell them not to waste our time? Don't bring me any bullshit offers." He glared at me.

With Lucas, control was the air he breathed. He watched me, eyes sharp for any hint of weakness, testing for the smallest give in my posture or voice. Nothing existed for him unless it passed through his hands. He saw the world his way—his interests the only ones that mattered, and if you forgot it, even for a second, he'd make sure to remind you.

I sat up straight, confident, my posture solid.

"I understand completely, Lucas. You want to make sure we're dealing with a real proposal and not wasting your time."

He brought his arms down to the table, relaxing.

"My job is to work on making that happen. I'm here to get you the best deal possible. You'll have every chance to lay out your terms, and I'll make sure they know exactly what it takes to reach an agreement."

Lucas didn't reply. He just watched, the faintest edge of a smirk on his mouth, as if the outcome was already decided and I would march to his tune. I was fine letting him think that—for now. But I'd be staying impartial, on my terms.

"Let's get an offer from them. You know our position from our brief. It needs to be realistic, they have a very weak case," Phil said, crisp as a judge.

I waited half a beat, refusing to rush. With Lucas, you learned to leave open space—sometimes he'd fill it, sometimes he'd let it linger, to see if you'd blink first.

Lucas spoke. "The numbers are straightforward. I've got very little room to budge."

He spoke in declarations, not compromises. I caught myself, careful not to answer in kind—he wanted the argument, the chance to push. The numbers weren't simple, but there was no use inviting a fight, taking his bait. Lucas cared less about consensus than about being right. "Fair" was whatever served him, and he changed the definition whenever he pleased.

I stood up. "I'll ask the other parties if they are willing to present an opening proposal to you. I'll need about 15 or 20 minutes."

Lucas said, straight-faced, "I want something good." Phil nodded.

"I'll see what I can do in that regard, though I don't control what they choose to do. I can express your concerns. Thank you." I left, not waiting to see their reaction.

I returned to Maya's room and got straight to the point.

"Lucas would like you and Julian to make an opening offer," I said, leaving space for discussion.

Terry pushed back. "I'm not sure we want to go first." Maya looked at Terry, then at me, clearly siding with her lawyer.

"Well, Julian's side thinks it's best not to push against Lucas's tactics. Let him feel in control. What do you think?"

Terry looked at Maya. "I agree, it has to be Lucas's deal, not ours. I get that. But how do we work this with Julian?"

"Negotiate with Lucas, get a deal with him—but make it subject to Maya and Julian working out their split on any final number."

"That makes sense." Terry looked at Maya for confirmation. She pursed her lips; eyebrows raised in agreement with a nod.

"Have you discussed an opening offer while I was gone?"

"Yes." Terry looked down at his notepad. "One million, all inclusive," meaning it included legal fees, interest, and any other claim or expense.

"Do you mean for Maya alone, or that's for Maya and Julian to divide by some agreement?"

"No, for Maya herself."

My heartbeat sped up, like the moment you brace for a slow car crash.

"How do you feel that offer will play in Lucas's room, even Julian's?"

"Well, they won't like it, but we need to start high. Lucas will work at getting us down, we need room to move."

I thought, maybe way too much room. Do I press them to lower their opening offer, or do I present it as they wish?

"I think there's a risk Lucas could end the mediation if I put that offer on the table." I wanted them to feel the temperature in his room, the stakes of pushing too hard.

"We understand. What do you suggest?"

"It's your mediation, your negotiation. But you might consider a joint offer from both Maya and Julian. Terry, maybe meet privately with Julian's lawyer and work out a joint opening number for both of them, but subject to an agreeable split between Maya and Julian."

Terry looked to Maya for confirmation.

I kept it direct. "Here's my thinking: if I present a million just for Maya, this could blow up. But if we offer a number for both Maya and Julian—even if it's higher—it might land better with Lucas. If you break out Maya's share, Lucas will see it as too much. Better to blend her claim with Julian's. Make sense? Julian has a solid interest as a beneficiary, so just fold Maya's claim in with his. Good?"

Maya nodded to Terry, and he turned to me. "Yes, good. That's why we hired you."

Their trust felt real. It mattered that this wasn't just my solution, but one everyone could stand behind.

I leaned against the hallway wall near the kitchen. The air was thick with coffee and pastry.

Terry slipped into Sandra's room to confer. Julian came out, pacing past me with a quick smile, headed to the kitchen, chasing espresso and free food, leaving the lawyers to their numbers and quiet calculations.

I waited for the lawyers to finish. In these pauses, you feel the weight of other people's hopes and disappointments grinding forward behind every word, every closed door. Nobody wants to go first; everyone wants to walk away feeling like they won. Maybe that's all negotiation is—a careful dance around fear, pride, and the stories we tell ourselves about what's fair.

The door creaked open. Terry stepped out, headed toward his room, and I followed. He glanced back. "Give me a minute with Maya."

He went down the hall to their room. A few minutes later, the door opened and he called me in. I closed the door, and he got straight to it.

"One million, three hundred and fifty thousand, all in. That's our number—pretty firm, not much room to move. Lucas keeps anything over that if he sells the Beach House and painting, and he gets the vacant lot too. Our clients want a guaranteed lump sum."

I made sure I had it right. "That's for both Maya and Julian to split, correct?"

"Yes."

It was a relief—a workable number, more grounded than a million for Maya alone. Finally, a step closer to something real.

I remembered one last step in the process. "I'll confirm that Sandra has also got Julian's buy in, then I'll present it to Lucas if that's the case."

"All good," Terry said, giving a thumbs up.

Julian agreed to the offer, as long as Sandra was on board. She said she was.

I paused at the frosted glass door to Lucas's room, took a quiet breath, and made sure my nerves stayed out of sight. Then I opened the door.

Lucas and Phil sat at the table. The plates and cups in front of them were empty, pushed aside. Lucas scrolled through his phone, lips pressed thin, one heel tapping a quick, restless beat against the floor. Phil sat back in his chair, arms folded, absently nudging a crumb around his plate. They both looked up when I walked in—Lucas's eyes narrow and impatient, Phil's gaze drifting, barely interested. The room smelled faintly of coffee and cold toast, the waiting that soaks into your skin.

I took my seat. "The opening offer is $1,350,000 all in—a lump sum covering both Maya and Julian's interest in the Beach House, vacant lot, and painting."

Lucas stood up, fast, buttoned his blazer, and shoved his chair in hard. "Let's go, Phil. No sense wasting our time or my money paying you to be here. What did I tell you, Phil? This mediation was a stupid idea."

– 13 –

I WATCHED the room. Lucas remained standing, fingers digging into the chair's leather back. His face was frozen, eyes wide and unblinking. For a moment, nobody spoke. In the corridor, laughter rose and faded. Inside, it was quiet as a waiting room. Lucas leaned forward, slowly, and picked up his notepad and pen. He didn't say anything. He just held them, his grip careful, telegraphing his next move. Phil watched him, then reached for his folder, sliding it off the table. No one had to say a word; the message was clear. If Lucas was leaving, Phil would follow. All of it played out in silence.

I softened my voice, aiming to lower the temperature. This wasn't the time to beg or scold—just to steady Lucas, keep him from walking out.

"Lucas, I can see this feels pointless right now. I just want to talk about where things stand. Let me ask you—do you believe they really want $1,350,000, or is their number lower? What do you think is their bottom line?"

"I don't know, but they should have just given me their bottom line. I told you not to waste my time." Lucas raised his voice on the last line—it hit like an accusation, meant to sting, as if I'd failed my job.

I felt the jab but didn't let it provoke. That was the point—he wanted a fight, to give himself a reason to leave.

I kept my voice level, steady, meant to calm, not inflame. "I acknowledge that you want them to tell you exactly what they want. However, it's a process to find that out. And your negotiating skill might change what they ultimately do. Even if this doesn't settle, at a minimum, you are gathering intelligence. You'll leave knowing more than when you walked in."

Phil nodded. "The mediator's right. Even if we don't settle, we still walk out with information—maybe something we can use later." He looked at Lucas, holding his gaze a moment longer than necessary, trying to keep him in the room.

Lucas glanced between us, calculating. He was intelligent. He saw the point.

He dropped his hands from the back of the chair, pulled it out, and sat down. "So we just play this stupid game and see what happens?"

"Well, that's one way to put it," I said, with a smile that gave nothing away. Whatever he threw at me, it wasn't going to shake me.

Lucas looked down at the table, then up at Phil. "Fine. But I want to hear a lower number from them. If they don't have a real offer, we walk."

Phil turned to me, reinforcing his client's demand. "Agreed. Yes, bring back a lower offer."

"Gentlemen, there's nothing wrong with your request. But in my experience, once a party puts out an offer, they won't come back lower. It just doesn't work that way. They'll say, 'We don't bid against ourselves.'

"It's your move.

"I'd suggest you send a counter. Even if it's one they won't like, I'll put it forward. That's my job.

"You decide what happens next.

"It's your call."

I wanted to give Lucas and Phil a sense of control, even if it meant letting their contempt show for the other side's opening offer.

"Here's another point. If you go back with an offer now, I'll watch how they react. Frankly, if their lawyers don't threaten to walk out after I present your number—what does that tell you? It means they want a deal today."

Phil spoke up. "Okay. Give me a minute with Lucas."

I waited in the hall until his door opened and then entered the room.

Phil looked down at his notepad.

"Three hundred thousand dollars, all in, for them to release all rights—Beach House, vacant lot, Riopelle painting. Payment comes from whichever sells first, the Beach House or the painting."

So they were sending back a lowball offer. In their minds, it was tit for tat. I cleared my throat. "I'll go present your counteroffer. But may I have permission to say—if they find this number insulting—that it's meant as a message? That you thought their opening wasn't workable, so you're sending back a similar counter?"

"Exactly," Phil said, hands coming up, fingers stabbing the air.

Lucas didn't smile. His voice came out cold, almost a threat. "They need to get real. Fast."

"Thanks. See you in a bit."

As I paced down the hall toward the other two rooms, I wondered who to see first—Maya or Julian?

Instinct took over. I stopped at the first door and went in.

"Sandra, I've got a counteroffer from Lucas's room to present to you and Julian."

They looked up, hopeful.

"It's their first move. They said they're sending a message—your opening number wasn't something they could work with, so they're starting at $300,000, all in. I appreciate that you will see this as very low."

Sandra turned to Julian. "You said Lucas would be impossible. That's not an offer, it's ridiculous."

Julian nodded.

"I get it. Let me take the offer to Maya's room. Sandra, you'll meet again with Maya's lawyer?"

"Yes. More likely than not."

"Fine. I'll tell Terry to knock when he's ready for you."

I pushed open the glass door to Maya's room. She was tapping out an email. So was Terry.

"Sorry—may I join you?"

"Of course," Terry said, offering a cordial smile.

"Well, I've got a low offer from Lucas. His lawyer says it's a response—a message—to your opening; they thought it was too high to work with. Three hundred thousand, all in, to release all rights."

"For both Maya and Julian to split?" Terry knew the answer but asked anyway.

Then Terry shook his head. "Well, we're over a million dollars apart. Doesn't seem like this is going anywhere today."

"True, it can feel that way. But I've been at this point in mediation many times. While there are no guarantees, I'm not ready to say this can't settle. Let's keep pushing forward. Why don't you send me back with another offer? Let's not quit, I feel we should keep the process going."

"Sure, we can do that." Terry leaned back in his leather chair; it squeaked.

"Terry, I'm wondering if you might speak with Maya about the vacant lot and Riopelle claims. I get that you need to see progress on the Beach House, but the other claims are layered with more uncertainty. I'm not sure Maya has a strong case on the vacant lot, at least not based on a constructive trust claim. She did put money and value into the Beach House, and that's something to push harder. With the Riopelle, proving a gift to Maya and Julian feels like a coin toss. Can you talk about the risks of taking those claims to court?"

"Yes, I hear you. We'll have that discussion, and we'll send you back with another offer."

Terry emerged and slipped into Sandra's room. Julian came out, caught my eye, then disappeared into the kitchen, leaving the lawyers to talk in private.

Twenty minutes crawled by. Terry and Sandra stayed closeted in a private conference.

At last, the door swung open. Only Terry's head appeared, scanning the hall for me.

I moved closer. He spoke quietly: "Can we see you?"

I took a seat, listening.

"We're thinking of making a big move, but then we'd have almost no room left to negotiate. We wanted to run it by you first."

"Go ahead."

"If we came down to a million dollars, all in, do you think they would counter with a number closer to that?"

I paused. "You might consider a number just under a million—say, $985,000. I call it my Walmart number. Sounds more reasoned than a flat million, less arbitrary. But in the end, they're almost the same."

The two lawyers exchanged a look, a silent agreement passing between them.

"We'll confirm that with our clients and let you know."

I went to the kitchen and looked over the buffet: sweet and sour meatballs, steam rising from a big white bowl; another with rice, platters of sandwiches, tossed salad, and a large chocolate cake. A senior lawyer was piling two slices of cake onto a small plate.

Terry appeared, walked toward me, and I met him halfway. "We're good with that number." He gave me a thumbs-up.

Lunch could wait. Back to work.

When I returned to Lucas's room, both men were eating, plates nearly empty. Phil wiped his mouth with a napkin.

"I can come back when you're done."

"No, no—join us. We'll talk and eat."

Lucas slurped his coffee, a half-bitten chocolate chip cookie resting on a small plate. He finished it in one bite, washed it down with the last of his coffee.

"They've come back at $985,000, all inclusive. They said there's not much runway left. Not a final offer, but they're signalling it's close to their bottom line."

Phil glanced at Lucas's sour expression. "Well, that's not good news," he retorted. "I'm not sure there's much point continuing."

I knew this was a critical moment in the mediation.

Time to push them on their risks.

I decided to dig deeper. "It seems to me the value of the Riopelle is the main issue—based on everything I've heard today. That's what's creating most of the gap between your numbers. Can we discuss the company's claim to the painting?"

Lucas leaned back. "The company paid for the Riopelle. What's not clear about that?"

"Have you produced the company's financial statements to the other side?"

"Not yet. We're working on a supplementary affidavit—maybe next month they'll have those numbers."

"Do you have the most recent financial statements here?" I asked.

Lucas nodded. "I sent them to you, Phil—late summer, by email."

Phil sifted through folders and pulled out a stapled document. "Southshore Developments Ltd.—year end 2023. Most recent. Want to take a look?"

I flipped to the balance sheet.

Under ASSETS—what was shown:

Cash: $3,344.
Inventory: $1,220,000.

Below LIABILITIES:

Long-term debt: $1,338,450.
Payable to related parties: $188,443.

"What's included in the inventory under the assets?" I asked.

Lucas answered, "We've got three condos left to sell in the Martin's Point development. Once those are gone, there's nothing left in the company."

The numbers raised more questions than they answered.

I pressed on. "Phil, you said the company paid for the Riopelle. But I'm not seeing the value of the painting showing anywhere on the balance sheet."

"May I?" Phil took the statements, scanned the pages, and then turned to Lucas. "Why isn't the Riopelle listed as an asset?"

Lucas froze, mouth open but silent. At last, he said, "There must be a good reason."

Phil looked at me. "Robert, we'll dig into this and let you know. But this stays confidential, right?"

"As always. What you say in your room stays here unless you give permission to share. But you know it'll come out eventually."

I left the room and had lunch standing at the buffet. Julian and Sandra were at the far end, eyeing desserts. Terry grabbed pie; Maya picked up an apple. I gave them a small wave but didn't engage further.

By nearly 1:15 P.M., I still hadn't heard from Phil and Lucas. After almost an hour, I gave the others a simple update: "We're waiting on Lucas's counteroffer."

At 1:38 P.M., Phil called me into their room.

"I spoke to Lucas's accountant. Seems Howard lent the company a large sum over the years. The Riopelle—and a few other paintings—were purchased with company funds, but then the accountant reduced the company's debt to Howard by the same amount, treating the paintings as repayment of his loan. In effect, the paintings were transferred to Howard to satisfy his loans to the company. As a result, there was no additional tax to Howard on the repayment itself."

Crucial information. I considered my response.

"With that in mind, I don't see how the company can claim it owns the Riopelle—not if the financial statements are accurate and signed by Howard, representing to the tax department that the information is true."

Phil didn't back down. "Maybe, but the painting was still owned by Howard, then."

"Yes, but that leaves only two possible outcomes at trial, doesn't it?"

Phil nodded. "Go on."

"If Howard was the sole owner, the painting falls to his estate. The value is split 50/50 between Lucas and Julian. But the court will also hear evidence that Howard gifted the painting to Maya and Julian. It hung in their home almost all the time. I have Sandra's permission to share this text message from Howard to Julian."

I slid a printed page from my notepad. Phil read it aloud:

> Jules, can I have the Riopelle for Saturday's party?
> I'll return it Sunday before I leave for Florida.

Phil handed the paper to Lucas.

"Not sure what that proves."

I kept my tone even. "Maya and Julian have more messages like that—Howard borrowing the painting for special occasions, always returning it. Their position is that he asked permission because, by then, it wasn't really his. He meant it as a gift to Maya and Julian. And remember, at the time, Howard had significant net worth—this was before any financial challenges."

Phil shook his head. "Howard was an art collector. He wouldn't gift the star of his collection. Plain and simple."

I nodded. "I understand. My only point is that, at best, Lucas owns half the Riopelle. At worst, he may have no claim if the court finds it was a gift. There's really no third option."

Phil's tone softened. "Okay, leave it with us. We'll go back with an offer."

I updated the others: it wouldn't be long before I had a counter to present.

At 2:16 P.M., Phil's door opened. I waited, not sure what was coming next.

"Seven hundred and thirty-five thousand dollars, all in. But that's our final offer."

I wrote down "$735,000" and underlined "final offer."

"But payment comes out of the Riopelle sale—there's not enough equity in the Beach House to pay that out."

"Got it." I wrote that down too.

"And there's one more term: Maya must agree to testify in the vacant lot litigation against the community. While she lived at the Beach House, she'll need to give evidence that Howard always gave permission to use the path to the beach. We'll want to go over her evidence, but that's the gist. Maya's evidence is especially important—she isn't family, so her testimony carries more weight. And here's the deal: if she won't, our final offer drops to $685,000. We knock off $50,000."

The number could drop by $50,000. That kind of cut might be a deal breaker.

But I nodded, keeping my voice neutral, despite my concern. "Okay, thanks. I'll take it to them."

I walked down the hall, feeling the weight of it all. Now to see if this would blow up the whole day.

– 14 –

I KNOCKED and stepped into Maya's room. It was warmer than the hallway, like the heat hadn't switched off from winter yet. Sunlight from the west-facing window pushed the temperature past comfortable, even though it was only early June.

"Mind if I close the blinds? It's a bit warm," I said, walking toward the window.

From the ninth floor, you could see the city in full late spring. The maples and oaks below were dense with new leaves, a deep green canopy spreading over the streets.

Maya and Terry had both draped their jackets over the backs of their chairs. I kept my jacket on despite the warmth and cleared my throat.

"I have Lucas's final offer. He's offering $735,000, all in, to be paid from the sale proceeds of the Riopelle painting. He's also requested that Maya support his claim in the vacant lot dispute with the community by providing helpful testimony. There is one more condition. If Maya doesn't agree to cooperate in that case, then the offer drops by $50,000, or $685,000 all in."

Maya leaned back, tears welling. I handed her a tissue. She dabbed at her eyes.

"Would you like a minute?" I said gently.

"No—no, I'm okay," she replied, forcing a smile.

Terry jumped in, frustration showing. "Those numbers are too low. We won't be able to settle on a split of monies with Julian—not $735 or $685. Maya will barely get more than what she put in, never mind her other rights and claims."

Maya held up a hand. "Terry, it's not the money." She looked at him, fingers tightening around the tissue.

"It's Lucas asking me to betray the community—betray Greta. How do I tell her she might never walk her dog on the beach again, because of me?"

I nodded. "I respect your priorities. I'm not pressuring you."

She let out an unsteady chuckle. "Honestly, I want to tell Lucas to take his offer and stick it where the sun doesn't shine. I can't be bought. You need to tell him that."

"Professionally, that's tricky to repeat," I said with a small smile. "But I will tell him you firmly reject it."

Terry glanced between us. "So—is that it? We're done?"

"There's still a $300,000 difference between your last offer and Lucas's." I let the words hang. "We're at a standstill, unless you'd consider a mediator's proposal. Would you like me to explain what that entails?"

"I know what you are talking about, but you can explain it to Maya." Terry looked at his client.

I turned my direction to Maya. "The mediator proposes a settlement figure. You would tell me, confidentially, yes or no. If everyone says yes to my proposed number, the matter settles. If anyone says no, there is no settlement and we're done for the day. No one knows who said what to my proposal. Only I know and that's why it is called double blind for that reason."

Terry looked at Maya, searching her face. "How would Maya and Julian split your proposed number, if it came to that?"

"This is what I'd suggest. Once I give everyone the proposed settlement number, then Terry and Sandra, with client approval, can work together to resolve how it will be split. If you can agree on a split and the number I propose works, you say yes. If not, you simply say no to my mediator's proposal."

Maya's voice held steady.

"I'm not supporting Lucas's case against the community."

She shook her head, pointing her finger into the room. "I'd rather walk away broke before testifying to help that snake."

Her eyes, unwavering with intent, seemed to be fixed on some distant goal, as if nothing could sway her from her decision.

"I understand. I promise you that I will not include that term in my proposal. Though, I'll need to explain that to Lucas and if he refuses to drop it, the mediator's proposal can't go forward, as it would surely fail."

Maya, then Terry, nodded.

Terry inquired, "Have you spoken about this to Julian's room yet?"

"Not yet. Heading there right now."

"Maya and Julian haven't reached an agreement on how to divide a settlement," Terry said, his brow furrowed. "I wanted to be open with you. We're still working through the numbers."

Terry provided me with a brief overview of the following: Julian proposed giving Maya 35 percent, keeping 65 percent for himself, if the settlement was just shy of a million. Terry, however, insisted that Maya needed 45 percent to ensure her claims to the Beach House were equitable, especially with a lower lump settlement.

Terry asked me, "Can you push Julian to 45 percent for Maya's share?"

"I'll see what I can do, and obviously I'll need permission to discuss this with Julian's room."

"You can. If you can get him there, we'll consider your mediator's proposal."

I thanked them, pushed the door open, and moved to the next room.

A couple of rooms down, I paused at their door and knocked. "Julian, Sandra—mind if I come in?"

Julian was sketching abstract shapes on a legal pad and then set his pencil down.

I explained: Lucas's offer, the impasse, the mediator's proposal. They listened quietly. But Maya wanted 45 percent of the settlement if it was under a million.

Sandra responded instantly. "But we told them 35 percent was our best offer. We aren't going higher."

"Could you help me better understand Julian's position on that split?"

Sandra's voice escalated, "Maya might not prove a 50/50 constructive trust. She had the benefit of low-cost housing with such a small mortgage—that needs to be factored in.

Maya has no viable claim for any interest in the vacant lot and we say Howard would never intend to gift Maya the Riopelle. He might have gifted it to his son Julian, to even up his estate between his two children. Remember, Lucas had received significantly more free money over his life."

"Sandra, the Court will weigh those factors. May I offer my perspective?"

"Please, we wanted your take anyways."

I reached into my leather pad and slid a copy of Julian's text across the table, the yellow highlighter marking the line:

> Don't worry, we are both building value here for our house. I promise.

"In my view, a court would find there's ample evidence that Maya invested significant money and labour into improving the shared home. This text stands as direct proof of her intent to share in the future value of the Beach House.

"A judge could see Maya's payment of nearly all the mortgage, taxes, and utilities as powerful evidence of economic integration—these are the foundational costs of any household.

"Asking for 45 percent wasn't unreasonable, given her contributions and the evidence of mutual intent. While not a legal argument, the court will also hear that Maya alone found and negotiated the Riopelle, securing the deal herself."

Sandra glanced at her client. "Let me speak to Julian."

Less than five minutes later, the door opened.

Looking down at her notepad for confirmation, Sandra spoke in a firm tone. "We'll entertain a mediator's proposal, but only at a 40 percent split to Maya and 60 percent to Julian. That's our final position."

I felt that was the reality. Before going to Maya's room to explain Julian's final position on the split, I decided to find out if Lucas would be open to a mediator's proposal. If not, then it was pointless to continue the discussion of a split with Maya. There was nothing more to do if Lucas was unwilling to consider my last-ditch efforts to find a resolution.

I had intentionally located Lucas's room on the opposite side of the suite of offices—less chance he'd bump into Julian or Maya.

Walking around to that side, I had a moment to reflect on my next mission.

I knocked. Then entered.

"All right, let me lay out where we are. Lucas, your final offer of $735,000 was not accepted, and Maya was not open to any settlement term requiring her to provide positive testimony against the community. I appreciate that your offer was $50,000 lower if she would not agree to that provision."

Lucas turned to Phil. "That's it, then. Are we done?"

Phil shrugged helplessly. "Any thoughts?"

I faced Lucas directly. "Leaving now means significant time and expense—years before you get to court. Everything tied up. No money flowing to you now. And think about the cash you'll need very soon, just to fund the legal costs. You might ask Phil if he's going to need a significant retainer from you."

Phil looked at his client. "I will."

"And Lucas, settling this case gives you the cash you'll need to fund your court fight over the community's vacant lot right-of-way. How do you manage that, unless you settle this today?"

Phil leaned in, voice direct and edged. "I still need to be paid, Lucas. We've been over that."

Lucas fixed his gaze on the table's edge, tapping his fingers once before clenching them into a fist. "You're not leaving me with any options," Lucas complained.

I explained the mediator's proposal again.

"If Phil advises you that your case can still be litigated without Maya's agreement to testify against the community, then I'll leave that term out of the mediator's proposal."

One last step. I needed to take Julian's offer to pay Maya 40 percent of the settlement.

Terry and Maya said they would discuss whether or not they could make that split work once they heard my mediator's proposal. It depended on my number.

By 4:00 P.M., all three rooms had agreed to consider my mediator's proposal.

Now I needed the correct number—the one most likely to get a unanimous "yes" from all parties. I wrote on my white ruled pad.

> *$845,000 all inclusive. No requirement for Maya to align with Lucas in the vacant lot court case.*

I delivered my number to the three breakout rooms. Each party would give me their answer confidentially: yes or no. Then I waited.

– 15 –

AS I SAT in the brown leather square chair in a small reception area, with a photocopier directly opposite, I couldn't help but wonder: Did I pick the correct number? Too high or too low? I walked down the hall, my leather binder in hand. The pad inside was marked with three names, a blank beside each—enough space to write one word, kept hidden as always. If I picked too low, Maya might not be able to agree with Julian. Too high, Lucas's stubbornness, that it had to be on his terms, might sink the deal.

Time to make the rounds, see if any room was ready. I approached Maya's door, I saw it was cracked open, my heart rate increased, and I felt a touch of anxiety, just like when I was about to hear a presiding juror stand and announce the jury's verdict. I tapped lightly and stepped inside.

Maya and Terry sat side by side, Maya's fingers shredding a tissue to tiny pieces, but arranging them in a careful, precise pile beside her water glass. Even her nerves were orderly. The atmosphere in the room was also charged, filled with anticipation.

"I need your answer to the proposal," I said. "A simple yes or no. It stays confidential unless everyone agrees."

Terry leaned forward before Maya could open her mouth. "Yes. We accept. We agree to the split with Julian if your proposal goes through." He sat upright, hands folded on the table in front of him, his voice even, businesslike.

I noted their response in my binder, angling it away from their view. "Thank you. I'll return shortly."

Maya's eyes locked onto mine, a silent plea in them as she tilted her head slightly upward. Her face held worry and a need for resolution. I met her gaze with a steady look, my expression a mix of strength and honesty. We both understood what passed between us—an acknowledgment of her anxiety, not a promise.

Further down the hall, Julian and Sandra's door was open a crack, waiting for me. I entered and found Sandra standing by the window, peering out. Julian sat hunched in his chair, shoulders drawn tight beneath his wrinkled white shirt, his right hand holding a pencil over a pad covered with a hundred abstract shapes, each shaded from empty to solid black.

"I want to confirm your answer to the proposal," I said, "and whether the 40 percent share to Maya is still an agreeable split at $845,000 all in?"

Sandra spoke, her voice clear but tired. "We are a yes. The split remains agreeable."

Julian's head moved in a slight nod, eyes on the tabletop. He pencilled a checkmark on his pad. I wrote it down, careful not to reveal a thing.

"Thank you." My voice stayed even. I slipped out, heart drumming faster. Only one room left.

When I reached Lucas and Phil's room, their door remained shut. I paused, clutching my binder. Muffled voices leaked through—Lucas's tone sharp with anger, though I couldn't distinguish his words. Taking a step back, I rested against the hallway wall, my shoulders finding momentary relief there.

Down the corridor, two staff members quietly gathered lunch trays and packed leftover food in the kitchenette, their movements absorbed by the thick carpet. The wall clock's hands approached five.

The noise behind the door didn't let up. I stood there, unmoving, waiting for the door to open, not knowing if they were moving toward a yes or a no. After ten more minutes, the voices went quiet. The door opened. Phil looked out, composed as always, and nodded.

I straightened and stepped inside.

Lucas sat sprawled in his chair, arms folded, one foot tapping a restless rhythm against the leg. He didn't look up. Phil stood by the window, face measured, watching us both.

I waited for their answer.

Phil broke the silence. "Lucas isn't happy with the number."

I nodded. "Okay." I left it open.

"But he's seriously thinking about it. We'd like to discuss this with you further."

Lucas cut in. "Did the others agree to this deal?"

I paused, choosing my words. "Lucas, as you know, this is a blind process. After everyone responds, I'll announce if there's a deal or not."

"But if you've met with them, then they must have said yes, or you wouldn't be here for my answer." Lucas stared at me as if he'd just cornered his prey.

My face stayed neutral. I smiled. "You might be the first room I've visited—correct?"

"Oh. Yeah, I suppose so." He realized the trap had failed.

Lucas picked at a thread on his shirt cuff, then shifted back in his chair, gripping the edge of the table with both hands. He looked at the floor, then up at me. "Do you think this deal makes sense, based on your views?"

I let the silence settle, glancing at Phil, then back to Lucas.

"Lucas, all I can say is I proposed this number because I believe it's the only figure with a real chance of everyone saying yes. It's my last-ditch effort to end this now, before years of expensive litigation. I can assure you—today is the only opportunity you'll have, for a very long time, to see money in your hands. And you're also facing the community lawsuit—and that's another cost you're dealing with right now."

Phil cleared his throat. "Could we have a minute?" His tone was calm, practiced.

I nodded and stepped back into the hall, letting the door close behind me. The low rumble of voices filtered out—a note of frustration, then quiet. I waited, binder tight in my grip, every muscle wound.

The door cracked open again. Phil's face was composed, but Lucas wouldn't meet my eyes.

Phil spoke. "It's a yes."

Lucas stayed at the window, shoulders rigid. "Convenient how the risk's all mine. Must be nice for everyone else."

He meant the house, the painting, the tangled title to the vacant lot—if any of it fell through, it was his problem now.

I wrote down their answer, my face not giving anything away. "Thank you, I'll be back to advise on the outcome." I wanted to remain faithful to my word; no one was to know the order of my room visits.

Only then did I let myself breathe. Three names. Three yeses.

Inside, a surge of relief. I pushed it down. My job wasn't to win—just to run a process that gave them the best shot at resolution, settlement or not.

I went first to Maya's room.

I knocked and entered. Maya's face was tight with expectation.

"All three rooms said yes. We have a deal."

She stood and came to me, hand outstretched, smiling now. I shook her hand. "Glad it's behind you."

She gripped my hand hard. "Oh my god, me too. Thank you, thank you so much."

Terry shook my hand as well. "Great job."

I left them and made my way down the hall to the next room.

Julian sat back in his chair, exhaling, his eyes on the floor. "Relieved it's over," was all he said.

I nodded, then moved on to Lucas's room. Both he and Phil were standing at the window, waiting.

"We have a deal. All rooms said yes."

Phil spoke first, calm but firm. "Good. I think this is the best outcome, Lucas."

Lucas turned, searching my face. "I hope you're right. This is a big risk."

I hesitated, not wanting to judge the result, to mark the moment. "Lucas, as Phil said, you have some control back now. I sense you're glad about that."

"True," was all Lucas said.

I shook their hands and stepped into the hallway.

Their outcome wasn't mine to wear. My job was to give them options—nothing more. I had to let it go.

—

ALMOST AN hour later, nearly 6:00 P.M., I walked down the hall; three stapled copies of the Minutes of Settlement pressed under my arm. The pages were still warm from the printer at the front desk—a faint scent of paper and toner trailing behind me. I paused outside Maya's door, squared the documents, then knocked twice and pushed inside.

Maya and Terry were seated already, coats folded on the backs of their chairs, as if they'd been waiting a while. Maya's fingers had stacked a second pile of shredded tissue beside her glass. Neither spoke as I set the stack of paperwork on the table and slid the copies in front of Maya.

I took my seat, feeling the weight of the last hours still in my bones. "Here we are," I said, voice low. "This is the final form with all the changes. Maya, you'll sign first."

Terry scanned the final document and said, "Go ahead and sign."

Maya nodded, wordless, her fingers tight around the edge of the page as she scanned everything one more time. When she reached for the pen, she hesitated just long enough for me to notice. Her pen moved across the page in measured strokes; each letter of her name was formed with precision. When she finished, she pushed the stack toward me and raised her gaze to mine. The wetness in her eyes caught the fluorescent light, but her face held steady.

For a moment, all the old noise—the arguments, the numbers—fell away, replaced by the dry shuffle of pages.

Maya stood and gazed out the window. "What a beautiful view. I feel like I can breathe again." Her voice was soft, almost private.

I gathered the papers with the signed pages, gave a last nod, and stood. "I'll take these to the other rooms. Then I'll be back with your copy."

Down the hall, Julian and Sandra were waiting. Julian had set his sketchbook aside and was drumming his fingers against the tabletop, eyes hollow with fatigue. Sandra had stacked the files neatly; her pen aligned precisely with the folder's edge.

I slid the documents across and explained the process. Sandra looked at the papers one last time. Julian reached absent-mindedly for his sketching pencil, turning it in his fingers as if about to draw. Sandra noticed and quietly handed him a pen instead. He took it, nodded once, and signed his name quickly but legibly. Sandra reviewed, signed, and witnessed. The silence was comfortable now—something released in the room, an old pressure gone.

Julian met my eye, his mouth twitching in something close to relief. "Thank you," he said. Sandra echoed it, quieter but sincere. "You didn't give up. That mattered."

I nodded, collected the papers, and moved to the last door.

Lucas and Phil were waiting. Lucas sat already, arms folded tight, his gaze fixed on the table. Phil stood by the window, the last of the daylight glancing off his glasses.

I set down the final set of documents. Phil reviewed them, then handed a pen to Lucas.

Lucas stared at the papers for a long time, not moving, as if he might push them away or get up and walk out. The silence stretched. My heart thumped. He looked at Phil, then back at the page. The room held still.

Finally, Lucas picked up the pen and signed—quick, almost defiant, his name slashed across the line. He slid the documents back and said nothing.

Phil extended his hand, tone measured. "Thank you, Robert. This was a hard case to settle. I didn't think it would, but you got it across the finish line."

I gathered the final set, the weight of all those signatures settling in my hand.

In the hall, I exhaled and let my shoulders drop. It was done.

PART III

– 16 –

MAYA LINGERED in the lobby of Purdy's Wharf, bag in hand. The sky was still bright in the early June evening. She stood for a moment, noticing how quiet it felt, how much space there suddenly was.

She stepped outside and let her feet carry her toward the waterfront. She didn't have a plan. The patios were crowded with people in their twenties, laughing, checking their phones, and talking too loudly over each other. Groups moved from restaurant to restaurant, looking for a table or just standing on the sidewalk, waiting to be let in.

The air smelled like salt, beer, and fried food. A busker played guitar under the awning of an old pub. Laughter came from a bar down the block. A couple sat on the railing, drinks in hand, talking close.

Maya kept walking. She passed a group in business clothes, friends out after work—someone in a suit shouting and waving to a distant friend. Every table on the harbourfront was full. Maya felt herself passing through it all—no one looking her way, no one noticing. For the first time in months, there was nothing for her to do, nowhere to be. She could hear her footsteps over the chatter, the scrape of chairs, the clink of glasses.

She moved through the crowd along the edge of the harbour until she stopped and looked out at the boats. She stood there, arms folded, just breathing, letting the sounds and movement wash over her. For so long, she'd been focused on what everyone else needed, what had to be done. Now, with nothing left to fight for, she tried to remember what it felt like to want something for herself—to imagine wanting anything at all.

The *Bluenose II* sat at the dock, tall and dark against the early evening sky. Her black hull was long and sharp, lines clean as a knife. The two masts rose high into the evening sky, rigging stretched tight, sails pulled in and stowed. Even at rest, she looked built for speed—something proud and stubborn in the way she held to the pier.

People filled the dockside, all noise and motion. They gathered to admire the schooner, posing for photos and selfies with her in the background. A few tourists pointed out details—the shine of the wood, the name on the stern. The crew stood by the gangway, some answering questions, others working along the deck.

Maya hung back, letting the noise and movement settle her nerves. There was energy everywhere—cameras snapping, bags slung over shoulders, the smell of the harbour: oil, salt, and something floral drifting from the planters along the walkway.

That's when she noticed Julian, off to one side on a low bench, sketchbook balanced on his knees. He was lost in drawing, elbows tight to his body, hair a mess, jacket draped across his knees for support. For a moment, she felt the urge to turn and walk away. But he looked up and caught her watching. His smile was small, tentative, but real.

He made his way over, moving slowly, sketchbook clutched like a shield. They stood, awkward at first, just watching the ship.

"You found the subject for your next painting?" she said, her voice a little detached.

He nodded, eyes never quite meeting hers. "It's beautiful, isn't it? Makes you feel small. But in a good way."

She waited, letting the silence stretch. For the first time in a long while, she felt the pressure lift a little, space opening between them, and in herself. Julian tapped the cover of his sketchbook, then looked at her straight on.

"I'm moving. Montreal. Art market is just bigger. I need to start over."

Maya nodded. She watched his hands—how they trembled just a bit, how he pressed his thumb hard into his palm, trying to steady himself. There was relief in her chest. What was left between them could finally end.

"I'm sorry, Maya," Julian said, voice barely above the wind. "For not being what you needed. For not listening. For letting it get this far."

She looked at the *Bluenose*, the easy tilt of the mast in the wind. "We both wanted something that wasn't there," she said. "You did what you could. So did I."

He tried for a smile, but it faded. "I wish I could fix it."

She shook her head. "Don't. Just let it be what it was."

He stepped closer, as if to kiss her cheek, but she turned just enough that his lips found air. He took the hint, stepped back. There was sadness in his face, but also relief.

"I hope you find what you need," he said.

Before she could answer, her phone buzzed—Greta's name on the screen. She held up a hand. "I have to take this."

He nodded, stepping back into the crowd, already part of the moving city.

Maya answered. Greta's voice was a warm anchor through the phone. "You sound out of breath, love. Is it done?"

Maya paused. "I can't talk about the deal, Greta. But I can tell you it's over."

"That's all right. Come to Chester on Sunday? I'll make some chowder for us."

Maya felt the weight in her chest soften. "I'd like that. Thank you."

Maya lowered the phone and looked around. The crowd had thinned. The harbour was quiet. She glanced back for Julian, but he was gone, nowhere in sight, as if he'd slipped away with the rest of the day. It was typical of Julian: present, but never really there. A ghost in her story, fading just as she turned to look.

A release settled in. The future was blank, but at least it was hers.

—

NEARLY THREE months had passed since the mediation settled matters. Maya left Halifax behind, heading west toward Chester. The road sliced through farmland and woods, red maples and white birch flanking her all the way. Traffic thinned as she turned onto Highway 3.

She hadn't been out to Chester since those first raw days after the mediation, and a slight guilt gnawed at her. Greta had invited her more than once; Maya always found a reason to stay in—Sundays spent baking for the gallery, scrolling her phone, drifting from one small task to the next.

Today, she was grateful she'd finally come. The long drive gave her space to think—room to let the past fall away and picture what might still come. She mourned the life she'd imagined, but under the sorrow, something else stirred—a sense of possibility, maybe even hope. For a while, she let herself drift: a real home, a family, children, someplace to belong. For now, the road and its quiet were enough.

The road hugged St. Margaret's Bay, twisting through spruce and stone, the ocean flashing between the trees. Early September—three months since the mediation. The leaves were still green, the air was cooler and drier, a warning. She rolled down the window and let the salt breeze wake her up.

She drove in silence. Radio off, wind rushing by, grounding her. Just her, the open road, blue sky, and the way ahead.

The road curved, and there it was—Queensland Beach, a pale crescent held between dark rocks, bright in the afternoon sun. Maya eased off the highway, tires crunching over loose gravel as she pulled in. She stepped out. The car door clicked shut behind her. The wind hit her, cold but not harsh. The beach was nearly empty—a few cars, a couple standing close to the water. She left her shoes in the car and walked barefoot over the gritty sand.

Waves slammed the shore, breaking hard and fast, each crash rolling up the beach before pulling away. The sound was everywhere—loud, steady, impossible to ignore. It pushed everything else out of her head. For the first time in months, she felt quiet inside.

She walked, letting the cold water numb her feet, eyes searching the tide line for something to keep. She'd always collected things—stones, bits of glass, driftwood worn thin. She picked up a grey stone, smooth and round, then a smaller one, pink with bright metal flecks. The stones would find a new home on the shelf in her office at the gallery—the old habit of making order out of nothing. The air was briny and fresh. Wind tugged her hair loose, stung her eyes, but she stayed until she remembered not to keep Greta waiting.

As Maya stood by the car, she took one last look at the water. For a moment, calm settled over her—then she realized she was trying to hold onto it, and it slipped away. The surf crashed, steady as breath, but each wave seemed to ask something new. Relief? Guilt? Freedom? Her mind kept circling back to Julian's face at the harbour.

She clicked the key fob with one hand and pocketed three stones with the other—one smooth, one jagged, one somewhere in between. Wiped her feet on an old towel from the trunk and got back in the car.

The drive picked up again. Villages shrank; houses dotted the curve of the bay. Boats lay moored offshore, the water glimmering and darkening as clouds drifted past. Maya breathed deep, each mile putting more distance between her and everything that came before.

Chester arrived quietly, the town sliding up out of the pines—houses with neat lawns, shops painted bright, flags shifting in the breeze. Maya found Greta's cottage by memory, not GPS: white clapboards, a low porch crowded with clay pots, late-season geraniums and pansies spilling colour everywhere. Through a gap in the trees, she caught a glimpse of the ocean, water shimmering in the early-day sun.

Maya parked and lingered, fingers brushing the cool stones in her pocket. The quiet felt expansive, unhurried. She drew a breath and got out, closing the door softly behind her.

Before she could knock, Greta opened the door. Short and sturdy, hair tied back with a blue ribbon, Greta's presence filled the doorway—her eyes direct, kind. Behind her, Sam, the old black Lab, thumped his tail against the wall. The air carried the scent of baking and lemon polish.

"How was the drive?" Greta asked with a smile.

"Heavenly."

Maya slipped off her shoes and her jacket, the stones in her pocket clicking together. She paused, searching for the right words. "Not much traffic. I stopped at Queensland for a while. The ocean was loud—the wind was pushing the sound right up onto the road."

Greta grinned and stepped back to let Maya into the hallway. "Best thing you could do, love. The ocean puts things in perspective. Reminds you how small you are and how big the world is. Good for the soul."

Inside, the cottage was just as Maya remembered—cozy, bright with sunlight, simple and well-kept. A pine table, a faded floral sofa, and an old armchair gathered near the window. Books and magazines were stacked everywhere. Late morning light poured through the bay window, washing over the muted colours of a braided rug on the worn pine floor. Sam stretched out on his bed, already drifting back to sleep.

Maya moved quietly, scanning the room out of habit. She always looked for disorder, even when she was a guest. But here, nothing felt out of place. Everything had been lived with, chosen for use, not show.

Greta bustled around the kitchen, filling the kettle, pulling out a plate of cheese scones, and a tin of shortbread. "Tea or coffee?" she asked.

"Tea, please." Maya took a seat at the table, hands curled around her knees, still feeling the leftover chill from the beach.

They sat at the kitchen table, steam rising from their mugs. For a while, they stuck to the small things—Greta's complaints about her garden, too many tomatoes this year, not enough basil.

"You'll take some home with you, won't you?" Greta said. "I can't eat them all, and I won't see them go to waste."

Maya agreed, grateful for the organic gift.

Greta set her cup down, her face settling into something more serious. "So, do you feel free now?"

Maya hesitated. She ran her thumb along the rim of her mug, tracing a small crack in the glaze. "It's over. All the paperwork, the meetings, the lawyers. Everything's settled. I thought I'd feel… lighter. Instead, it just feels empty. Like I don't know what to want."

Greta nodded, holding her gaze. "It's always like that after a long storm. You lose so much holding everything together, you forget what it's like to let go. Sometimes all you get at the end is silence. But that's not a bad thing. It's where you start again."

Maya traced the edge of the table, letting her thoughts catch up to her feelings. "I've always been the fixer. That was me with Julian, with everyone. If I kept everything in order, nobody could get hurt. But it didn't work. I ended up just as lost as anyone."

Greta leaned back in her chair, hands folded. "I know that story. I was eighteen when I fell for a boy in Halifax, in the Navy. Got pregnant, lost the baby, and the boy was shipped off. Never did marry. Had a string of men, but it was always the same.

"Most men want to be seen, but they never really see you—not what matters, not what hurts. They don't know how to listen, not the way women do. So you learn to find comfort elsewhere. Friends, work, a good dog. Or just a quiet room, with the right light."

Maya's eyes teared, but she kept her face still. "Feels like I've lived with my guard up so long, I wouldn't know how to put it down even if I wanted to."

Greta nodded, reaching for her mug. "Walls keep the pain out, but they keep everything else out too. If you want something real, you have to let yourself be seen—mess and all. Pick someone who listens, who's there with you when it's hard. And don't forget, women are the ones who hold each other up when men fall short."

Maya tried to picture what it would mean to let her guard down. To let someone see her flaws, her fear. She wasn't sure she could, but the idea felt less terrifying here, in Greta's kitchen, the air soft with tea and sunlight.

The dog snored on. The room felt suspended, safe. Greta reached across the table and squeezed Maya's hand.

Greta stood and crossed to the old writing desk in the corner. She slid open a narrow drawer and reached inside. "Oh,

I think I kept all the old letters Howard mailed to me..." She pulled out three envelopes, bound with a black binder clip, silver handles sticking out like wings. Greta glanced at them, checking they were still there.

"I'm saving these for the right moment," she said. "If it goes to court, these letters could matter for the community. The plan is to turn that lot into a park. These might help. Will you stand with us?"

Maya hesitated, then nodded. "I can't say anything about the settlement. But let's just say not everyone got what they wanted. When the time comes, I'll stand with you. That's a promise."

A quick spark of mischief crossed Greta's face. "Good. We need all the fighters we can get."

Maya sat back, the tea warming her chest. Window sunlight patterned the rug; the bay outside shone silver. She thought of the stones in her pocket, the cold sand, the miles of empty road behind her. For the first time in months, she let herself believe she might be allowed to sit, breathe, and let the day come as it was.

Greta glanced over, gentle but direct. "What about Julian?" she asked. "Heard he's left for Montreal. Sorry—everyone here gossips."

Maya nodded, a tightness loosening in her shoulders she hadn't realized was there. "He's there. He told me on the waterfront. I think he needs a bigger city—or maybe just somewhere he can disappear for a while. Honestly, I'm glad. I don't have to worry about running into him when I visit Chester. Sue McEachern and I are meeting for lunch at the Harbourfront Grill. It makes things easier, having some distance."

Greta smiled, setting down her mug. "Sometimes distance is the only way to find yourself again. He'll make his art, and you'll have room to grow."

Maya looked out the window at the bay through the trees. "I think I'd like to find a place here, someday. A cottage, maybe. Or a little house with a view like yours. Just somewhere I could come to be quiet, to feel the world again. I don't need much."

Greta looked at her with quiet, measured warmth—a look that held a hundred unspoken things. "There's always room for you in Chester," she said, her tone steady. "Maybe more than you think."

Maya glanced at her watch and stood, slipping on her jacket and reaching for her bag. "I might drop into the Chester Art Centre before meeting Sue—should run," she said, keeping her voice light.

Spending the morning with Greta was food for Maya's soul.

Greta moved to the counter and picked up a brown paper bag. "Take these with you," she said, handing over the tomatoes. "Too many for me."

Their hands brushed as Maya took the bag, both women holding the moment a beat longer than needed.

Greta gave a small sigh, glanced at the clock, then reached for her pills. "Think I'll lie down for a bit. The old ticker acts up now and then—doctor says it's nothing a rest and a pill won't fix."

Greta took two pills into her palm with the practiced ease of someone who'd done it a hundred times.

"Are you sure you're all right?" Maya asked, her voice gentle, worry threading through.

Greta waved her off. "Don't fuss. I've been through worse. My time's not up yet. I'll be fit as a fiddle after a nap. Go enjoy your afternoon."

Maya nodded, but the weight of the moment held her at the door, the brown paper bag crinkling in her grip. "Okay, but reach out if you need me."

Greta smiled, thin but steady. "Just getting older, that's all. You'll understand some day."

Maya let it drop, but the feeling lingered—a quiet warning she couldn't name, a thread she didn't tug, but felt all the same.

– 17 –

"**WE SHOULD** get going soon. It's a long drive, and the fog looks thick out there." Maya called impatiently towards the bedroom. Thomas's voice came back, "Out in a minute."

She was always like this on mornings she worried about the weather, about being late. It was mid-December, a Tuesday she'd taken off work, the early harbour outside frozen in fog, the city shrouded in a pale, cold mist. She'd already been to the window twice, checking for any change in the sky, hoping for a break in the cloud and the fog to lift.

Behind the closed bedroom door, he laughed—a quick, teasing sound. "Just one more minute. I'm nearly ready."

Maya let out a breath and sank into the modern leather chair, stretching her legs and glancing again toward the harbour. Below, the Dartmouth ferry edged away from its berth, the horn's low call drifting through the fog. For a moment, the boat vanished—swallowed whole by mist—then surfaced again, a pale ghost on the water. Winter made the world look different: blurred, uncertain, more monotone, hiding shapes that lived easily in summer.

She closed her eyes. The memory of last night flickered behind her lids—their laughter tangled in the sheets, the sweet, impossible way his body pressed against hers, the quick breath at her ear. The newness of it still charged her, a thrill every time he touched her, especially there, every time she heard his voice in another room.

The door opened. She heard the thud of size 10 dress shoes on the hardwood.

Thomas emerged. He saw her—standing in the main room, backlit by winter light, hair cut short now, grazing the edge of her jaw, tucked behind one ear. Her suit—a deep, chestnut brown—fit her perfectly, sharp at the shoulders, cut close at the waist. The silk scarf at her throat was a shade lighter than her eyes. Simple gold studs at her ears, a slim watch on her wrist.

She looked like a different woman from the one he'd met a year and three months ago, on that wet September evening at the museum gala. Then, she'd worn her hair long, her features quieter, her whole presence a little muted. Her voice had been cautious. She'd told him that night, with a half-shy smile, that she'd been single for less than a year. Her ex had just moved to Montreal after a messy court matter. She hadn't looked back since.

"Maya, you look gorgeous!"

She laughed again, that new, easy laugh, and ran a hand through her hair, smoothing it behind her ear. "You keep saying that," she said. "I might start to believe it."

Maya felt a rush of passion, electrifying her body, wanting him. She saw the lines of his face catch the morning light—sharp jaw, polished even teeth, a strong mouth always on the verge of a smile. Clear, dark eyes, framed by heavy brows, the kind that pulled her in. His hair, black and short, always a little wind-tossed no matter what he did. There was something striking and open in his expression—handsome, athletic, impossible to ignore. The kind of face women remembered.

He stepped toward her, the distance between them vanishing. Her breath quickened. She leaned into him, her palms finding the lines of his shoulders, the warmth under his shirt. She could feel the strength in him—muscle and heat, the restless energy that never quite left his body. She pressed her face to his neck, breathing him in, lips grazing his skin. The memory of last night still lingering in that embrace.

She pulled back first, breathless, eyes dancing. "Later—we can't be late," she said, laughing.

Thomas watched, the need for her still moving through him. He took her coat from the hook and held it out for her, steady as she slipped her arms inside. His hands lingered a moment at her shoulders, fingers pressing lightly through the fabric. She glanced up; he met her eyes with a quiet smile, something private passing between them.

He picked up her briefcase, held it out. "You have everything?" His voice softer now, a touch of concern in it.

She nodded. "I do."

He slipped into his coat, grabbed his keys. Together, they stood near the door, pausing as if neither wanted to be the first to leave.

She gave herself one last look in the hallway mirror—saw the newness, the self she'd worked hard to find, and the man standing behind her, ready to follow her anywhere.

They stepped into the cold together, the city blanketed in fog, the sound of the ferry horn echoing again from the harbour. Thomas's hand found hers, warm, certain. Six months ago, none of this had existed. Now it felt as if it always had.

—

THEY DROVE southwest along the new highway, fog pressed low, trees slipping in and out of the grey. On either side, narrow lines of melting snow edged the lanes—leftovers from last night's clearing, already fading. Maya sat beside Thomas, one gloved hand curled around her briefcase, the other in her lap, knuckles white. She watched the world blur past: exit signs for Chester, where Greta's cottage waited; stretches of highway she'd driven a hundred times, back when the Halifax gallery and the Beach House still belonged to her days with Julian.

She remembered coming home to Julian in the evenings, the ache of unfulfilled hopes—marriage, a family—filling the rooms, her heart always half-waiting for more. Now, with Thomas beside her, she let herself believe for the first time that what she wanted might finally be possible.

She leaned her head against the cold window glass, remembering Greta—a voice she would never hear again.

It had been seven months since the night Greta slipped away quietly, in her sleep, alone in her cottage on Shore Road. Maya remembered the phone call from Vivienne, her own voice breaking, the hush that followed. Grief rose like a swell, thick and raw, closing her throat for a moment.

Thomas noticed the quiet settle over her, the way she pressed closer to the window, eyes fixed on nothing. He eased his foot from the gas, slowing for a slick curve, matching his breath to hers without thinking. With one hand steady on the wheel, he reached over and rested his other hand gently on her knee.

"Greta would be proud of you, taking the stand today," he said, his voice low, breaking the hush. "You're giving her a voice."

Maya swallowed. Her voice was shaky, barely there. "She was supposed to be here, not me. Some days, I still wait for her to call. To tell me I'm overthinking. Or just send a message, something to make me laugh." She blinked hard, kept her eyes on the window. "It's not right, Thomas. She was the one who fought for everyone. I just…I just want to do what she would have done."

Thomas squeezed her knee, fingers warm and steady. "You're not alone in this. The whole community is with you. You'll do them proud—and Greta too."

Maya nodded, blinking to stop her eyes from welling up. She pressed the back of her hand to wipe a tear, steadied her breath. "I want to do this for her. For everyone." She gave a small, unsteady laugh. "Oh, god, I'm going to ruin my makeup."

As they neared the Courthouse in Bridgewater, patches of dirty snow lined the curbs, salt scattered all over the parking lot and walkways, and the sky held the same indifferent grey. Thomas slowed as they turned onto High Street, the courthouse coming into view—a solid block of stone and glass, flags flapping in the raw wind.

He pulled into the closest available parking space to the entrance and shut off the engine. For a moment, Maya didn't move. She looked down at her shoes, black leather, too delicate for winter. "I'm going to get salt all over these," she said, voice small, almost apologetic.

Thomas smiled. "I can carry you," he said, trying to lighten the mood. "Could make a dramatic entrance—carry you right up those courthouse steps. Though maybe I'll save that for our wedding day."

Maya managed a laugh, the joke landing just right. "You'd probably sprain your back—and miss your hockey tournament next weekend."

She walked carefully, heels clicking on the salted walk, eyes on the ground, focusing on each step. At the bottom of the courthouse steps, she paused, the weight of the day settling on her shoulders. Thomas turned to her, eyes serious. "You're ready. Just remember what the community's lawyer prepped you for, all the questions to be asked. Stick to that, you'll do great."

Maya nodded, drawing a breath. She looked up at the tall, pale façade, the big glass doors. "Let's do this," she said quietly.

They climbed the steps side by side; Thomas close beside her as they entered the courthouse. The doors shut out the cold. Still, the echo of Greta's memory followed them in.

Inside, the courthouse was brighter than Maya expected—high windows letting in early winter light, everything new with polished wood. Thomas led her down the corridor, past a cluster of lawyers in black gowns, to the second-to-last courtroom. A brass plaque by the door caught the light, black letters: No. 3.

Maya paused at the door and let out a breath. Thomas touched her elbow, steady.

Inside, the room was already alive with quiet voices and the rustle of papers. The second day of trial was underway; Maya could sense the slight edge in everyone's movements, the way routines had settled in but tension still lingered.

Blair Mosher, the community's lawyer, sat at the front table to the left, hunched over a sheaf of binders. Beside him was Vivienne, Julian's aunt, silver hair perfectly set, blue scarf at her throat, hands folded. Both looked up and smiled as Maya entered. She managed a nod and a small smile back, nerves steadying for a moment.

Across the aisle, at the right table, Maya spotted Phil—the lawyer from mediation—leaning in to say something to his client, Lucas. Lucas turned and met her gaze. His look was cold, jaw set, a flicker of old resentment in his scowl. Panic rose—her heart knocking hard—then she willed herself to breathe. Thomas squeezed her hand. She sat near the back, spine straight.

She let Lucas see her there with Thomas—her new man, her choice. The sight of them together would dig at him, she knew; it was a small satisfaction, a reminder she was no longer bound to Julian or to anything Lucas controlled. Having Thomas beside her wasn't just comfort. It was a quiet declaration—she had chosen her own ground, and she wasn't alone.

A sudden hush fell as the side door opened. The bailiff stepped in and called, "All rise. Court is now in session, the Honourable Madam Justice Pamela Green presiding."

Everyone stood. Judge Green entered briskly, her presence filling the room. Her robes—black, with a deep red sash and white collar—set off her short silver hair, her expression composed but not unkind. She moved with confidence to the tall bench and sat. Only then did the courtroom sit, the quiet settling around them.

She looked over the lawyers' tables. "Are counsel ready to proceed?" Her voice was clear, strong, with the command of someone used to being heard.

Both lawyers nodded. "Yes, My Lady."

She turned to Blair Mosher. "Mr. Mosher, you may call your first witness."

Blair stood, buttoned his jacket. "Thank you, My Lady. The community calls Maya Carson."

Maya felt the eyes of the room turn to her. She rose, heart hammering, and walked carefully down the aisle, stepping into the witness box. The world narrowed to the steady gaze of the judge.

She remembered Blair's final words to her: "We need to prove, on a balance of probabilities, that Howard did not give permission to people who crossed the vacant lot. We have to show they essentially trespassed, ignoring his warnings to stay off. That's what creates a prescriptive right of way in law. Kind of like getting squatter's rights."

It was clear—Maya understood. Now, on the stand, she vowed to get it right.

– 18 –

"CAN YOU, please, stand? Please place your right hand on the Bible and state your name."

"Maya Carson"

"Do you swear that the evidence you're about to give shall be the truth, the whole truth, and nothing but the truth, so help you God?

"I do."

"Thank you. You may be seated. And counsel, you may begin."

Blair Mosher, the community's lawyer, rose and stood at the front table holding a notepad in his right hand and asked several preliminary questions to explain who Maya was and her relationship to the case before the court.

The air in the courtroom was still as Blair Mosher approached the witness stand, a plastic-sleeved document in hand. "Ms. Carson," he began, "I'm showing you what's been marked for identification as Plaintiff's Exhibit 12. Do you recognize it?"

"Yes," Maya said. "That's the letter Greta Lindholm gave me. The one from Howard Barrett."

"I ask that the letter be entered as an exhibit," Mosher said, turning to the judge.

Phil Jenkins shot to his feet. "Objection, Your Ladyship."

Madam Justice Green looked over her spectacles at the defence counsel. "On what grounds, Mr. Jenkins?"

"Hearsay, Your Ladyship. Not admissible," Jenkins said, his voice resonating with confidence. "The rule against hearsay is fundamental. It exists to prevent exactly this: a trial by a piece of paper. The author of this letter, Mr. Barrett, is deceased. He cannot be sworn in, he cannot take that stand, and most importantly, he cannot be cross-examined."

Justice Green spoke to the objection, "Mr. Jenkins, can you provide more context please?"

"Certainly, my learned friend is attempting to introduce this document to prove the truth of its contents—that Mr. Barrett actually warned Greta about trespassing. But we can't test that assertion. Did he mean what he said? Was he prone to exaggeration? Were there times he gave Greta permission or was friendly? These are questions I would put to a living witness, but I cannot examine Howard, as he is deceased. The law doesn't allow testimony that can't be challenged, and that's what this letter is: an unchallenged, out-of-court statement from a man who isn't here to answer for it."

Justice Green nodded, then shifted her gaze to Blair Mosher, the community's lawyer. "Any response?"

"Your Ladyship," Mosher began calmly, "my friend mischaracterizes the letter's purpose. The rule against hearsay is only triggered when a statement is offered to prove its contents are true. We are not asking the court to accept that Mr. Barrett's legal threats were valid or that he had asked 'countless times before.' We are offering the letter for a much simpler, non-hearsay purpose: to prove that Greta received it. The critical fact is that she was put on notice. The letter is evidence of her state of mind, her knowledge that she was considered a trespasser. That is a fact, and it is directly relevant to what she told Ms. Carson next."

Mosher took a breath. "And even if it were considered hearsay, it would be admissible under the modern principled approach. The evidence is necessary because Mr. Barrett is deceased, and it is reliable because a formal letter threatening legal action carries its own inherent trustworthiness."

Justice Green steepled her fingers, considering the arguments. The silence stretched.

"Mr. Jenkins, your point is well-taken, but the objection is overruled," she stated finally. "Mr. Mosher is correct. The letter is admissible for the limited, non-hearsay purpose of establishing that a warning was sent and received. It speaks to Greta's knowledge, which is a central issue here. The letter will be marked as the next exhibit."

She made a note on her pad. "Proceed, Mr. Mosher."

"Thank you, Your Ladyship." Mosher turned back to his witness. "Now, Ms. Carson, please read the second and third paragraphs from the letter, which is now Exhibit P-12."

Maya cleared her throat and read the following in Howard's handwriting:

> I've asked you countless times before not to cross
> my lot for the purposes of walking your dog on

> the beach. You've ignored the private property signs and have climbed over the fence on the road and I consider this as a trespass.
>
> I am now instructing my lawyer to write formal cease and desist letters to not only you, but many other village residents who continue to flagrantly flout my private property rights. If you persist, I will have no choice but to commence legal proceedings against you to stop this and will seek damages and legal costs against you. You have been warned, AGAIN!

A murmur went through the public seating area filled with about thirty Chester residents, before being silenced by a sharp rebuke from the judge for quiet.

Blair Mosher let the words hang in the air for a moment before continuing. "Thank you, Ms. Carson. After Greta showed you this letter, did you have a conversation with her about its contents?"

"Yes, we did," Maya confirmed.

"And what, if anything, did Greta say to you about Mr. Barrett's warning?"

Jenkins was on his feet again, his chair rolling back and banging the rear wooden railing.

"Objection! Your Ladyship, this is of grave concern. Now counsel is asking the witness to repeat something Greta allegedly said. Greta is deceased. This is undoubtedly hearsay, and it's being offered to prove the very act in dispute."

Justice Green turned to Mosher, both eyebrows raised. "Mr. Mosher?"

"Your Ladyship, this is not inadmissible hearsay," Mosher countered confidently. "It falls squarely within one of the oldest and most reliable exceptions to the rule: a declaration against interest. The person who made the statement, Greta, is unavailable to testify because she is, sadly, deceased. The statement Ms. Carson is about to recount is an admission that Greta was knowingly and repeatedly committing a trespass—a civil wrong for which she could have been sued for damages. The law has long presumed that people do not make admissions that are contrary to their own legal or financial interests unless those statements are true. It is a powerful, common-sense guarantee of trustworthiness."

Justice Green considered this, her gaze fixed on a point just above Mosher's head. Jenkins stood, poised to argue further, but the judge spoke first.

"Mr. Jenkins, the court recognizes the exception for declarations against pecuniary and proprietary interest. The rationale is sound. The objection is overruled. The witness may answer the question."

Jenkins sat down, the frustration clear on his face.

"Ms. Carson," Mosher said, turning back to the witness stand. "Please tell the court what Greta said to you after you read that letter."

Maya took a deep breath, her eyes now laser-focused on Lucas's frozen, pale face. "She just laughed. She tossed the letter on her coffee table and said, 'I ignored that nonsense. I've been walking my dog on Howard's property for decades, first it was King, he lived to thirteen and then Sam. That's a quarter century. A silly letter isn't going to stop me now.'"

The words landed with quiet force. Mosher stood still for a beat. "Thank you, Ms. Carson. No further questions, Your Ladyship."

"Cross-examination?" The judge looked at Phil Jenkins.

"Just a few questions for Ms. Carson."

Blair Mosher sat down, and Phil Jenkins rose, approaching the witness stand with a deliberate, almost casual pace.

"Good morning, Ms. Carson," he began. "You were in a common-law relationship with Howard Barrett's son, Julian, for a number of years, correct?"

"Yes. We lived together for almost five years."

"And during that time, you lived with him at the Beach House, the property right next to the vacant lot in question?"

"That's factually correct."

"So you would have been there daily. You would have seen Howard Barrett interacting with his neighbours and other village residents frequently." Jenkins paused, letting the suggestion sit for a moment. "He was a friendly man, wasn't he? Liked to chat with people?"

"He could be, but it depended on whether he was sober or not," Maya answered thoughtfully, not trying to be cute.

Jenkins grimaced and gave a tight smile. "But you must have witnessed many occasions where he was present with residents on the property in question. People coming and going, crossing the vacant lot."

"I saw people on the public beach," Maya said, her tone even. "But on the lot, itself? No, I wouldn't say I saw many residents. Just one person with Howard, together, really, with any regularity."

Jenkins seized on the opening. "And who was that?"

"His friend, Teddy Haliburton," Maya replied.

"Ah, yes. Teddy Haliburton," Jenkins said, as if confirming a winning point. "He and Howard were old fishing buddies, weren't they? And you saw Mr. Haliburton cross that lot all the time, didn't you?"

"Yes, I did."

"And for what purpose?"

"Teddy had a boat tied up on Howard's dock at the beach." Maya said in a matter-of-fact tone.

"And Howard never stopped him. Howard gave him express permission to keep his boat on Howard's dock, isn't that right?"

Maya met his gaze, her expression unreadable. "I was never privy to their private conversations about permission. What I do recall, quite clearly, is that around the time Mr. Haliburton started using the path more often, Howard put up a new 'Private Property' sign. A big one, painted bright red, right on the fence post where people would climb over. He was quite particular about it."

The confidence in Jenkins' posture faltered. He had expected a simple confirmation, but instead, Maya had introduced a fact that directly contradicted the story his witness, Teddy, had been coached to tell. He saw the trap he had walked into. To press the point would be to highlight the sign; to abandon it would look like a retreat.

He cleared his throat. "But he still let Mr. Haliburton cross?"

"Like I said," Maya replied, her voice calm and steady, "he was a private man. I can't speak to what he chose to do with an old friend, and I'd say his only friend. He just cursed at the other neighbours who crossed the lot and used the beach. No permission there at all. I'd say the neighbours were there against his wishes and..."

Jenkins interrupted Maya, "That question I asked you was either a 'yes' or a 'no.' Please just answer my questions, not offer your opinions."

He stood for a moment, the silence amplifying Jenkins's defeat. "No further questions, Your Ladyship."

As Maya stepped down from the witness stand, a low buzz of chatter erupted in the public seating area. People leaned into each other, whispering behind cupped hands, their collective gaze following her.

At the defense table, Lucas Barrett fixed his lawyer with a stare that didn't blink. His lips thinned to a bloodless line. He leaned in close to Phil Jenkins, the words coming in a low, cutting hiss—inaudible, but the anger played out in the twist of his fist against the polished oak. Jenkins, refusing to meet his client's eyes, shuffled papers, face set and colourless. He had walked straight into the trap, and Maya's testimony about the red PRIVATE PROPERTY sign had gutted the value of their star witness, Teddy Haliburton.

Maya walked past the plaintiff's table, her steps measured and composed. Vivienne, seated beside Blair Mosher, looked up. She didn't smile, not in a way anyone else would notice, but her eyes, bright and clear, met Maya's. She gave a single, sharp nod—a silent, powerful acknowledgment that conveyed everything: you did it. Great job.

Maya returned the nod with a faint, fleeting smile of her own before taking her seat in the back, next to Thomas, who squeezed her hand tightly and gave her an affectionate shoulder bump.

Madam Justice Green surveyed the courtroom over her glasses, her expression impassive. She tapped her gavel once, a sharp crack that cut through the murmuring. "Order," she said, her voice calm but firm. The gallery fell silent. She turned her attention back to the plaintiff's counsel. "Mr. Mosher, you may call your next witness."

– 19 –

IT WAS Friday, July 12—seven months since the trial ended last December. The city was slowing down with the summer weekend coming, still warm at just past five. Maya stood on the corner, her back to the gallery's old red brick. She could see the Citadel clock from here, high above the city, its hands barely moving. She gazed at it, deep in thought as she waited.

The last client had been a hard close. Negotiations were tense, a line drawn between what was possible and what wasn't—the kind of talk that left her drained but satisfied. Then her mind turned to the auction. She kept seeing the flash of the Riopelle, the hammer coming down—1.1 million, US dollars, slightly more than she'd guessed. Even with the money—after Terry's voice on the phone, after all the numbers—she felt conflicted. More money than she'd ever had, her investment repaid and then some, but still second-guessing if she had fought hard enough. Not quite sure if she'd lost or won.

The Mercedes rounded the corner, top down, silver paint catching what was left of the intense afternoon sun. Thomas behind the wheel—hair all over the place, shirt sleeves up, jacket tossed behind him. He spotted her, smiled, and reached to open the door.

The seat's heat hit her back. She leaned forward, shrugged out of her jacket, and threw it in the back, not caring if it wrinkled. For a moment, she felt free again—but then the old pang of doubt returned, that sense that bliss never lasted, that something would come crashing down again.

"I hope you weren't waiting long," he said, his hand coming to rest on her thigh.

"Nope, all is good." He leaned over and kissed her on the lips—long, warm, exciting.

Maya laughed, shaking her head. "That's a nice way to start the weekend."

He drove off too fast for her liking, but she settled back, wind pushing her hair up and back. She let herself feel the ride, the grip of his hand, the rough sound of his laugh.

Halfway home, he asked, casually, "You meet with your advisor today?"

She nodded. "Catherine's got a plan. I'm going to invest the settlement money wisely, don't worry."

Maya explained the details, and he nodded back. "That's exactly what I'd do."

She felt it—his faith in her, the solid way he said it. The pressure in her chest eased, just a little. The city thinned out as they headed south on Barrington, tall trees blocking the sun, her stress lowering with each city block.

The Mercedes rolled onto Smith Street, slowing as Thomas found a parking spot right in front of his door.

Maya loved Smith Street, its pocket of the city, a single block of rowhouses lined up shoulder to shoulder—blue, grey, off-white. Victorian, nothing showy, all painted as pretty as the next. She gazed at Thomas's place. The soft pastel blue paint, the off-white trim.

Thomas pulled to the curb and silenced the engine. "Home," he said.

They climbed the steps together. The blue door opened, the house waiting, early evening slowly arriving.

As they entered, Thomas's duffel was sitting in the living room. He was grinning—too ready, like he'd rehearsed this moment. He had packed before work, ready to take her away for the weekend.

She eyed him, suspicious but amused. "You cancelled tomorrow's tennis game for me?"

He feigned being hurt. "What, you're not more important than tennis? Why don't you pack. We'll stop at Ken's for fish and chips before we hit the road for Chester."

Upstairs, she rushed to pack a small Coach bag from the closet. All the years leading up to this moment. Everything had changed—new driver, new plan, her life hanging in the small closet upstairs, jammed tight with all her clothes and shoes. His place was slightly larger than her condo, a place she was sad to say goodbye to. But his home offered new possibilities.

She smiled, slung her bag over her shoulder, and hurried down the stairs to Thomas.

Outside, the street was cooling, trees casting shadows across the house fronts in the setting July sun. She let herself feel it—a flicker of happiness, a note of suspicion, that old habit of wondering what comes next.

He nudged her playfully. "Ready, forget anything?"

She slammed the Mercedes door and smiled. "No, let's go!"

After the best fish and chips in town, the drive to Chester went fast. The highway was wide open, the sun low and blinding. Thomas pushed the speed with the top down, Coldplay pouring from the speakers. Maya let the wind take her hair, the music loud enough to drown out talk. It felt good to leave the city behind, the ocean and trees blurring past.

By the time they reached the edge of Chester, the air had cooled and the road narrowed, trees pressing in on both sides. Thomas slowed as they turned off the main road, tires crunching over the cottage's gravel drive. The cottage sat half in shadow, green roof and old shingles, the garden thick and wild around the front step.

Maya sat for a moment, eyes on the cottage. The engine pinged as it cooled. The driver's door opened, and Thomas reached for the bags in the back seat.

"Are you sure you're okay?" Thomas asked, not quite meeting her eyes.

She nodded, but her heartbeat was fast and strange, caught somewhere between grief and disbelief. She pushed open the car door, her right shoe sinking into the grass.

Maya walked up the porch steps first, and Thomas just behind. She fumbled the keys, nearly dropped them, then fit the brass one into the lock. It turned with a sound she remembered—old, sticky, familiar.

The door swung open. The cottage smelled faintly of cedar and must, the windows closed tight on a hot summer day. And something else—something that felt like Greta, like a voice about to call from the kitchen.

Maya stepped inside, Thomas quiet behind her. For a moment, she almost called out for Greta, then let the present come back in.

After four weekend trips in recent months, she still hadn't found the words. Greta—no children, no family left—had left the cottage to her. Not just the keys, but everything that mattered: the possessions, antiques, books, knick-knacks.

The rest—cash and stocks—had gone to charity. The cottage, though, was for Maya. Executrix. Trustee. The words still seemed foreign.

She turned. Thomas was watching her, a half-smile settling at the edge of his mouth, eyes crinkling. The tension in her shoulders eased.

"You still really miss her, don't you?" he said softly.

Maya nodded, a sadness pushing into her chest. "After this gift and I was so surprised, more than ever. She was one of a kind."

Thomas moved to the kitchen, and she heard the cork pop. They carried glasses out to the back deck, settling into two round, cushioned wicker chairs. Glasses clinked.

It all felt so deliberate, almost too loving—tennis quietly cancelled, dinner out, a bottle of wine chilling in the bucket, a mystery box, and food already packed in the cooler and placed in the Mercedes' trunk. It was almost too much care.

Was Maya dreaming? She kept glancing for the catch, waiting for something to go wrong, the way it always had.

It was habit, she knew—the old vigilance, the feeling that love always came with a trapdoor. She sipped her wine and tried to let herself sink back into the cushions, breathing in the salty air, lingering in the evening breeze. Nothing happened. It was just life and perfection.

Saturday morning came slowly and brightly. Sunlight slid over the garden, soft across the old cottage floor.

Maya woke to the smell of coffee and called out a loud, "Good morning!"

"I'm coming up," Thomas called back.

His quiet steps echoed up the stairs and down the hallway. He brought her a mug in bed—the blue one with the red heart—set it on the table beside her and brushed her cheek with his hand.

She pulled the sheet higher, feeling the slip of cool silk—lavender, almost translucent, the hem just grazing her thighs.

The memory of last night drifted in, soft and unhurried: the small white box, tied with a pink satin bow. She undid the knot slowly, the silk spilling out into her hands, soft as water. She slipped it on, caught her reflection in the mirror—Thomas behind her, watching from the doorway, his eyes dark with want. He stepped forward, hands cool and certain as he slid the fabric from her shoulders. His hands ever so slightly running down each arm, his lips softly tickling her neck. Then she inhaled his smell, skin to skin, his body pressing her onto the bed, the world shrinking to nothing but pleasure and touch.

She blinked, and there he was again—eyes wanting her. Maya lifted her coffee mug, sipped, and set it down. Leaning back on the pillow, she smiled at Thomas—a little wicked—then pulled him toward her. He grinned back, and for a moment they just watched each other, letting the tension build. The memory of last night's lovemaking still lingered in her body—then it was just all passion.

He cooked breakfast, cleared the dishes, and wiped the counter clean. She watched from the doorway, still in his shirt, the silk nightgown hidden underneath. It was almost too much—the perfect weekend, the attention, the ease of being wanted. She felt like a princess, and still, part of her kept waiting for the spell to break.

Around noon, Thomas asked her to walk. She changed into a sundress and sandals, twisting her hair up with her fingers and letting a few pieces fall loose around her face.

They left the cottage, the air warm and sweet with roses and cut grass and headed in the direction of the old Beach House.

It was still strange to pass it. Maya's chest tightened—a soft ache, old ghosts moving under her skin. She caught sight of two kids on the steps, maybe eleven and fourteen, one with a phone, the other with a popsicle, feet swinging above the gravel. The place looked happy, lived in, loud in its way. She felt something give and let it go, glad to be done with Julian, glad to have landed a real man, maybe even a future with her own family. She wanted to believe it. She was almost there, but not quite.

They kept walking, passing the old Beach House on their left and arriving in front of the vacant lot. Off to the right, in the distance, they could make out Howard's house, a FOR SALE sign posted by the road, its letters too small to read from here.

They paused at the edge of the lot where Lucas had tried to build. It was partly cleared now, the wire fence finally gone, the path to the water open and bright. Thomas led the way, towels in one hand, shorts and bare legs, Maya's sandals tapping on the new wooden walkway.

Down closer to the beach, a patch of brush and small trees had been cleared. Maya saw Vivienne and Linda talking, both waving as she and Thomas approached. Further down the beach, a cluster of neighbours gathered, calling out greetings.

"What's going on?" Maya asked, surprised to find old friends here, stepping closer to Vivienne.

Vivienne smiled, her face alive with excitement. "I'm guessing you heard that the town bought the lot from Lucas. Paid next to nothing. We're designing the picnic and play area, finally making it a real park. There's a committee meeting this afternoon, just planning it all out. Glad you could join us."

Then Maya realized—this was Thomas's surprise. Vivienne must have asked him to bring her to the meeting. She was Greta's stand-in now, stepping into the neighbourly role and carrying on Greta's commitment to the community.

Now his plan made sense.

Maya looked out across the sand, spotting a dozen more people down by the water—the heart of the community gathered together. She felt a wash of relief, old tension slipping away. The memory of the court case flickered through her mind—the public right-of-way secured, Lucas gone from town, Julian in another world, the future settled.

Thomas took her hand and led her down toward the far end of the beach. He stopped at the edge of the tide, shoes in one hand, looking a little pale, almost nervous.

Her old alarm went off, sharp and immediate. For a split second, she worried something was wrong with him. She turned to him, a laugh in her voice. "What's wrong?"

"I've got to tell you something." His voice choked with emotion. He couldn't find the words for a moment.

He dropped down, one knee in the sand, sudden and sure, holding her hand tight.

"Maya, you're the girl of my dreams. I can't imagine a life without you. Will you marry me?" His voice wavered. "I want it all with you, Maya—the house, the noise, the kids running barefoot through it. I want the whole damn thing."

She froze. He reached into his windbreaker, pulled out a blue velvet box, and opened it. The emerald-cut diamond caught the sun, glittering so brightly she had to squint, the facets throwing little sparks of white light.

Tears slipped down her cheeks. She couldn't speak at first. He waited, eyes searching hers.

Finally, she managed it, voice breaking with happiness. "Absolutely. One hundred million percent, yes."

He stood, and they hugged and kissed, holding each other tight in the sun. Then, friends began to jog toward them. Applause broke out—Vivienne, Linda, and the whole Chester crowd cheering and clapping, running up from the water. Maya realized, suddenly, that it had all been arranged. The meeting, the crowd, the perfect timing—Thomas had set it all up just for her.

She laughed through tears, turning to him. "It would have been awfully embarrassing if I'd said no."

Thomas grinned, kissing her again. "It was worth the risk."

A bottle of champagne popped, foam dripping onto the sand. Laughter spilled out with the waves, hands passing plastic cups, voices rising and tumbling across the beach. They toasted her engagement, the community's win, the park, and the right to be here, together, under the bright July sun.

Vivienne touched Maya's arm, pulling her gently to the edge of the group. Her voice dropped, calm but electric. "Council met last week. They rejected Lucas's condition of sale. He wanted it called Barrett Community Park."

Maya's breath caught, her eyes searching Vivienne's face. "Really? I thought that was part of the deal."

Vivienne smiled, shaking her head. "We said no. The sign will say—Greta Lindholm Public Park."

For a moment, Maya stood very still, the sound of the beach blurring around her. She heard Greta's name, felt it settle inside her—a rush of warmth, memories of letters tucked in drawers, late-night talks, the slow, steady courage that carried them here. She could almost hear Greta's voice, see her handing Maya the letter, remembering how Greta's words had been explained aloud in court—the way her presence still made all the difference, even after she was gone.

She turned, finding Thomas in the crowd. She saw her friends, neighbours, the sweep of sand, the sky gone wide and blue. Her chest felt open, full, and easy. For the first time in years, she stood with both feet on solid ground. She belonged. This was home. This was enough.

Maya reached for Thomas's hand, squeezed it, and let herself be held by the moment, everyone she loved close, nothing missing, nothing more to chase. Just sunlight, laughter, the sound of the ocean, and the future opening up in front of her.

About the Author

JEFFREY MORRIS spent twenty-two years as a lawyer before discovering he preferred peace to argument. For the past twenty-three years, he's worked as a mediator in court litigation matters. He divides his time between Toronto and Fort Lauderdale with his wife—and their two pickleball paddles. He is also the coauthor of *The Tao of Pickleball: Master Your Mind, Transform Your Game.*

Printed in Dunstable, United Kingdom

76819396R00119

Rule of Twelfths

J.M. Ozanne

Published in 2022 by Hollingwood Design & Print Ltd

ISBN 978-1-3999-3083-3

If you wish to contact the author Julia Ozanne, please email:
juliaozanne@rocketmail.com

Cover and design by Hollingwood Design & Print Ltd
01422 646720
07771 965063
hello@hwdap.co.uk
www.hollingwooddesignandprint.co.uk

For all lovers of the sea

My thanks to the following:

To my son James, for superb photography and local, maritime detail, my son Michael, whose quiet company and thoughtfulness kept me sane, my brother Michael and his wife Ruth, for technical support and help, and especially my sister Jane, for her ideas and sound judgement.

To Cathy Woodhead, Delfryn Publications, for her generous time and eagle-eye.

To Kathy Hopewell, The Freewriter's Companion, for her suggestions and encouragement.

To staff at the Ffestiniog and Welsh Highland Railways Company, for their time and kindness.

To all my family and friends for their love and support.
And to Mac, still with me in spirit.

"...fortune;
Omitted, all the voyages of their life
Is bound in shallows and in misery."

Act IV, Scene 3 Julius Caesar

William Shakespeare, 1564-1616

CHAPTER 1

The High Street was still busy with late-summer visitors, and I negotiated the elderly High Street shoppers with care. Coach parties of white-haired pensioners dallied outside shop windows and drank coffee at their leisure outside the restaurants and cafés, uninterrupted by the demands of bouncing, happy, holiday children.

I arrived at the doctor's surgery, sat on a cheerful, red plastic chair at the front of a few rows of others, equally cheerful in red, and faced a wall that was preferable than having to stare at the back of other people's heads; bald, mostly. I was the youngest by a long stretch, a mere twenty-one years of age, but felt worn-out and slightly unwell, light-headed and disconnected from everyday events, and wandered around the boatyard in a non-productive haze of tiredness.

I hadn't slept properly for weeks and the nights were long and restless, punctuated by nightmares that woke me in a hot sweat. I'd finally plucked up enough courage to make the appointment after I'd tripped over a mooring rope at the top of the harbour wall and only just saved myself from a terrible fall onto *Annie*, with her keel in the low-tide mud. I hadn't seen a doctor since I was a child and couldn't work out why the events of the last few months had affected me at all. Desperation overcame denial, so here I was.

A low table was pushed up against the wall in front of me, the surface stacked with neat piles of booklets offering therapies for all kinds of conditions. I scanned the posters on the wall in front of me; advice for vaccines against flu and shingles and pneumonia, help-lines for mental health, diabetes and heart conditions, osteoporosis, pregnancy and ante-natal clinics – chance would be a fine thing, but give that one a miss, anyway, I thought. Chipped skirting boards, which could have done with a coat of white gloss, completed the scene.

It was enough to make anyone ill, even if they weren't before. Add that lot onto the amazing, detailed information on the Internet for disgusting and rare illnesses and it wasn't surprising the NHS was overwhelmed. Perhaps some people liked being ill. Perhaps some people were unfortunate, poor, uneducated or just stupid. Was I one of those who brought this state of nervous anxiety and insomnia on myself? In shame, I squashed my predilection for the people-judgement I thought I'd left behind in adolescence. I was just grouchy from lack of sleep. And unkind.

Memories of my dad rescued me, diverted my thoughts and distracted me from having opinions I wouldn't much like to find in anyone. For the first time since he died, I wished he was here and I was a child again and could disappear into the comfort of the old sweater he wore when he was at home, be reassured by him in his practical no-nonsense way, that ups and downs of life have to be dealt with. He believed you should never make judgements before you'd put everything in perspective and then not take anything too seriously. Life comes and goes, he used to say. But that was an astronomer speaking, his head in far-away galaxies, his tuition to me a healthy take on the relative importance of humanity and its place in the evolution of the universe. Just passing through, he said. All was transient. I think I understood. A bit of it, at least.

I didn't want to be here in this surgery, trying to explain myself to a perfect stranger about the recurrent nightmare, the face of my drug-dealing neighbour, Doug Peterson, pasted on my eyeballs in the middle of the night with crabs crawling out of his eye sockets. It had been all round the pub, the gruesome details of his drowned and bloated body, told with relish by locals who were there on the beach when he was found by a child innocently wandering amongst the rocks with her bucket and spade. But it was the eyes when he was alive that haunted me, the steely blue eyes that narrowed, hardened, analysed and threatened more than words. The crabs came later.

I was the last patient for the morning.

"I've never needed sleeping pills," I said. I hadn't had to explain the story. He was local and it had been in all the papers. I explained about the nightmares and the fear of Doug Peterson rising from the dead to hunt me down in revenge. "It wasn't my fault he drowned. If he'd lived and been arrested and gone to prison, I could understand it. But he's dead, so why am I dreaming about it?"

"You've never put yourself in such a vulnerable position before, I'm sure," he said. "It's hardly unusual to be traumatised by big events afterwards, even though it seems okay and exciting at the time. It was a brave thing you did, alerting the police."

"Or stupid," I said. "He'd have known it was me. He was only a tiny part of something much bigger. He'd have talked about me, warned them I was being nosy, even the ones they arrested."

He sat back in his chair and studied my face. "It's not everyday someone so young gets mixed up in a major drugs haul. Dealers aren't exactly kind people when there are millions of pounds at stake."

I was conscious of taking up his time, but I needed to talk.

"I mean, suppose the people Doug Peterson worked for still want revenge, the ones who weren't arrested? I can't do anything about it, though, and I'm not going to run away from it. I just need some sleep." Why was I telling my GP all this? I'd gone way over my time. He'd been very patient.

"Sorry," I said.

"I'll give you one week's supply of pills, just to help you get your sleep patterns back. No more. Keep busy. Do the things you like doing. Sleep's a great healer. Come back if you need to. And I shouldn't need to tell you to inform the police if you are worried or harassed by anyone and not to tackle things on your own."

He was kind, sympathetic and understanding. The flood-gates opened and the fear and worry had poured out.

I snivelled into a tissue on the way out and bumped straight into Mark outside the surgery door. He looked at me quizzically, damp tissue in hand. It was no good hiding it, so I told him. He was young for a deputy Harbour Master, I'd thought, when I first met him, expecting another grizzled, stern old man like Will Roberts, his boss, but he'd helped me learn the ways of the harbour and never made me feel foolish when I didn't understand or made mistakes. He was married with a new baby. You could tell from the shadows under his eyes.

"Tell you what," he said. He'd listened intently with his head on one side, unfazed by my tearfulness. "What you need is a new experience. Get your confidence back. Take your mind off it. Done any kayaking?"

I idled my way back towards Madoc Yacht Club, the car-park nearly filled up by boat-owners able to sneak off from work early to join the weekend festivities, and stopped to chat to a few people I knew. They offered me congratulations on my press coverage of the power-boat being towed into Pwllheli and I was surprised how much I was comforted by the interest they showed in the future of the yard. I'd just shared my anxiety with an unknown GP and then Mark, in the space of fifteen minutes, and that helped as well. I leaned on the rail that overlooked the pontoons, returned a wave from the Harbour Master on the other side of the slipway and tried to accept that I'd let my guard down and that, actually, I felt okay about it.

It was the mixture of concern, acknowledgement and practical advice, I decided, and an element of trust. I was grateful for the GP's time and Mark, I hoped, wouldn't gossip, or at least he would be sympathetic if he shared the news of my tearfulness with his mates after too many pints in the pub.

I walked past the boatyards to the end of the path and unlocked the yard gate, opened the door to the Boat Shed and inhaled the comforting smell of oil and wood and paint, binned the soggy tissues, picked up a pair of scissors and went outside. The last of the rosebay willowherb drooped from the cliff-face behind the shed and I cut some faded blooms and arranged them in an old paint tin on the shop-counter I'd restored. The old oak top glowed rich brown and the paint tin was more in keeping than a flower vase against the background of planks of wood and coils of rope. The pink flowers and their wispy seed-heads gave me a quick flash of pleasure. Was this what the GP meant? I made coffee and a sandwich and sat in the sun outside the snack-bar and noticed that the fixings for the striped awning on the snack-bar were rusty.

Mark turned up after lunch with his kayak on the roof of the Harbour Master's pickup, gave me a quick lesson on how not to drown myself and how to do a sweeping stroke with the paddle when I wanted to turn round.

"I'd stay in the shallows today to practice, if I were you, then it won't matter if you fall in. Don't forget the buoyancy-aid and take your phone. It's got a plastic cover, yeah? See you in the pub tomorrow. I've got a night off nappy-changing." How practical and unfussy. That's why

I liked him.

"And don't go so far you can't get back before the tide turns. The current will throw you off-track."

I didn't mind the advice. He wasn't like my over-cautious solicitor, David, who seemed to see danger in everything I did and told me so at regular, boring intervals. I pottered around for the rest of the afternoon, doing very little and nothing unpleasant, as the GP had recommended. I had an excellent excuse to just think about the work ahead instead of actually doing it. But I did squirt some WD40 onto the awning tracks.

The warm September afternoon slipped into evening. I locked the gates, fetched a glass of wine from the caravan, pulled one of the plastic chairs off the stack by the snack-bar and took it over to the edge of the harbour wall. It was too early for the stars, but they were there, and would pattern the night-sky later, blaze in crystal pinpricks of light in the unpolluted darkness over the sea.

When I was eight, my dad took me star-gazing for the first time. He prepared the way with nightly homework and spared nothing in the instruction. The names of constellations rolled off his tongue as though he was giving a lecture, which of course he did all the time at the university when he wasn't chasing round the world to attend conferences. He settled me into the camping chair one cold, October night, adjusted the telescope, wrapped a rug around my knees and pulled the woolly hat firmly down over my ears.

"See the Square of Pegasus, Cassie?"

"Yes, I've got it. The horse with wings, wasn't he?"

"Good. Now, follow the star in the left-hand corner all the way to the Andromeda Galaxy. Remember her from the story? Those are her arms above her head with her wrists manacled to the rock."

"She nearly got ate, didn't she? Where's the one with my name?" I asked.

"Eaten, not 'ate'. Look up to the right. That's Cassiopeia, shaped like a big 'W.' You remember the story?"

"'Course I do," I said. I never forgot a good story. "Was she wicked to boast about her daughter? I mean, is it wrong to do that?"

"No," he said. "I do it all the time and if you become an astronomer, I'll be very proud of you."

"But suppose I want to be a ballet dancer, or a model?"

He bent down and moved the telescope.

"Now, see that constellation to the right…?"

I drank a toast to my dad, took a pill, went to bed and sank into blissful oblivion.

My night, devoid of nightmares, was followed by a perfect day of sunshine and no wind. I put the 'Closed' notice up on the gates after lunch, locked them firmly, carried the kayak down the slipway and paddled seawards out of the harbour into the shallows at the edge of the river. The sunlight caught the rippled sand beneath the surface, shifted and dappled the shadows and I knew that I could get out of the kayak and wade ankle-deep if it all went wrong.

I followed Mark's instructions on how to hold the paddle and splashed a lot in the warm water with little sense of time, no commitment and nobody to watch me, until I got the hang of it and set off up the channel. I smiled to myself as I imagined David, my solicitor, his face serious with concern and disapproval as his client flirted with danger once again. I still couldn't work out how he managed to be fearless crossing the Irish Sea in a yacht race and just laughed when it was rough. Funny bloke. Nice, but irritating.

Apprehension gave way to confidence as I moved into deeper water. It was the last two hours of the ebb and the flow of the tide had slowed. The outward journey became a rhythmic lift and dip of the paddle, the blades cleaved the water cleanly and quietly as my style improved. There was no need to follow the channel buoys as diligently as I would have done in

Annie. The kayak seemed to develop a life of its own and slipped effortlessly through an unreal landscape. There were no reference points, just the occasional flash of colour where the red and green buoys lay motionless in the channel or rested high and dry on the banks. Harlech Castle was now just a grey smear against the back-drop of the Rhinogs and the opposing castle at Criccieth, a black shadow against the sky-line. It felt like I could glide for ever and ever, with no ending, in a smooth, trance-like daydream.

Then the kayak rocked beneath me. I bounced into a ruffled line of white water that stretched from sandbank to sandbank, and directly in front of me, lay the No 4 Buoy that marked the bar. I hadn't meant to go that far out from the shore. The water peaked and broke in confused wavelets. The first niggles of panic broke my concentration, upset the fluid stroke I thought I'd just perfected and the kayak tilted, for one moment, onto its side. I sat very still and held my breath as it levelled out again.

Out there, in the late afternoon with the sun lower in the sky, a big expanse of water around me and not a soul in sight, I cursed my stupidity and knew I had to head for home. The thought of being out there in darkness was unthinkable but I had to turn the kayak first. I forgot Mark's instructions and my cursory practice in the harbour and the kayak's bow met the little waves at an angle, then beam-on for a brief second, the swell from the sea slight, but enough to unbalance it alarmingly as it rose on the crests and wallowed in the troughs. Then I remembered what I should have done, reached out with the paddle extended, dug the blade into the water with conviction, spun the kayak round to face home and paddled back into settled water, white-knuckled.

I'd had enough and headed back inland towards the North Bank and the safety of shallow water until the bow grounded on the sand. Then I climbed out and sat on the sand, sick to my stomach with my thoughtless daydreaming and misplaced confidence.

The phone bleeped in its waterproof case.

"Hi, Cass. How's it going?" I could hear the baby cry and the chink of dishes in the background.

"Absolutely fine, Mark," I said. "Lovely. See you later."

Black Rock Sands with the vast expanse of beach exposed at low-water, was empty now with just a few, late-afternoon cars parked up by the sand-dunes. It felt safer here and with shallow water under me, I paddled towards the golf course, past the rocky outcrop of Ynys Cyngar and the Powder House and into the off-shoot of the main channel round Samson's Bay. At the far end under the cliff, before it re-joined the main channel, I turned the kayak around, correctly this time, and looked back at the small bay which was now just a sand-bank with a ribbon of water separating it from the beach.

It was hard to imagine the scene as it would have been two hundred years ago. Before the harbour was built, ships anchored here in this tiny bay, waiting for their cargos to arrive. The slates were brought down in carts from the Ffestiniog quarries to the wharf at Gelli-grin on the Afon Dwyryd, loaded into small boats, then sailed down to Samson's Bay by the Philistines, as they called themselves. Those guys must have been tough, I thought, to transfer up to six tons of slate from each boat into the waiting ships.

The boats were then sailed or rowed back up the estuary to the wharf to wait and load the next shipment. Tough work. I'd even found models of two of the older ships in the Boat Shed, crafted by my great-uncle, down to the finest detail of spar and rig. There were other model ships, too, left to gather dust and cobwebs and in desperate need of attention. They would have to wait. I paddled back into the main channel, my mind full of things I would like to do, things I ought to do and things I had to do and came to no conclusion whatsoever.

Past Danger Rock and the sandy coves, I rounded Gomer Rock, inched into the dry bank opposite Borth-y-Gest, pulled the kayak up out of the water and sat down with my back against the hull and my toes in the sand. The current had slowed to a standstill and the water flowed dark green with a touch of blue sky reflected in the still surface as the sun sank lower in the sky. Congratulating myself for being back on familiar territory and only a stone's throw from the boatyard, I studied the village.

The fringe of sand under the sea wall merged with soft mud further out, dark greys and browns as the tide had receded to the channel and the bay had lost the full light of the late afternoon sun; clumps of grass and rushes sprouted in the marshy edges by the stream but were only visible now as faint, black shadows. At a normal high-tide, the sea reached the base of the sea-wall, kissed it briefly and retreated quickly, like a tentative lover and left the splashes of reds and blues and greens of the moored rowing dinghies abandoned on the grey mud. Small sailing boats leaned comfortably on their sides or upright on bilge keels.

With a high, spring-tide and a gale from the south, the sea could flood high up the wall and even splash over onto the road and into the car-park, but it was a rare occasion where the combination of tide and weather caused any grave concern with the residents. Predictions of rising sea-levels had, however, prompted new, stronger defences for the village and car-park and the residents watched, with differing views, as a new, higher sea-wall had been built with flood-gates at the top of the slipway.

The village had been busy all summer. Tourists flocked from far and wide, filled up the carpark and over-flowed onto the roads for the day, visited the beaches, walked part of the coastal path or just sat on a bench on the front. The café and restaurant had been booked up for days ahead, fed and watered the visitors with good fare and charming service and I'd told my London-based mother, who was only familiar with the east coast, that she didn't know what she was missing. I loved it, especially in a gale, the bay tucked safely out of the way from the rolling waves that marched down the channel.

A sudden chill in the air reminded me it was nearly autumn. I was cold, but unwilling to drag my eyes from the village, colourful by day with the houses festooned with hanging baskets and by night, lit-up with fairy lights above the café and restaurant. There was only one blot on the landscape, and that belonged to me.

Tai Pilots was built at the end of the seaward curve of the bay, a row of four, terraced houses with their frontages facing the road and their backs to the water. The one nearest the sea was mine; a dilapidated, virtually uninhabitable chunk of my inheritance with an interesting and practical history, now in a sorry state.

The houses had been lived in by the pilots who were paid to guide the ships waiting outside the estuary, navigate them over the bar and down the channel to the safety of the harbour. The slipway, down which the pilot boat had been launched, was hewn out of the rock just below my house and stretched far enough into the channel to allow access at half-tide. It was rarely used now, except by locals, and this evening, by others I'd rather not have seen.

A group of people hung around a fire on the stony slipway and shouts of laughter and the heavy thump of bass wafted over the water to me. My phone buzzed a text message – from Helen's Nain, of all people, from the Bed and Breakfast she ran on the front, facing the bay.

'Complaints about party and noise', it said. 'Jason's friends, I think. Could you deal with it?'

I stuck the phone back in the bag and tried to ignore the message. It was Saturday, after all.

Then my conscience got the better of me. I punched in Jason's number.

"What." Rude and not his voice.

"Is Jason there?"

"Jason, there's a woman on your phone."

"What do you want, Cassie?" slurred and irritable.

"Turn the volume down a bit, will you?"

"You spying on me?"

I sighed, "Just turn it down. People are complaining."

He rang off but the music faded to an acceptable level.

I'd tried to forget about the house during the summer while I was busy renovating the Boat Shed, but had become increasingly embarrassed by its shabby appearance. It hadn't mattered then, but with winter round the corner, I needed somewhere else to live. I'd allowed Jason, my young charge and helper to stay there for a few months, while I lived in my small, uninsulated caravan in the boatyard.

The house needed attention urgently and I wanted some detailed ideas to put to my solicitor to release some more money from the trust-fund left to me. I would visit after the weekend, I decided, while Jason minded the yard and I could make lists in peace. I didn't want to spoil the day thinking about it, but the familiar unease about my own life crept back. That needed sorting as well and I really didn't want to know about Jason and parties.

I dragged the kayak back into the water. It was the last hour of daylight and the last of the ebb, the quiet moment when the tide catches its breath briefly and time seems to hang heavy in the air. I'd been strangely comforted by the tides and their six-hour cycle over the last few months; that inextricable link between the moon and the sea and the only reliable thing I could trust to do what it always did; flood and ebb, repeatedly, unwaveringly and on time.

Rookie journalist turned boatyard owner, I was Jack of all trades, none of them too clever, or reliable, and master of none. I'd got to the point of questioning everything about myself, a babe in arms compared to most business owners and scarcely out of my teens, as Jason, only three years younger, reminded me on more than one occasion whilst telling him what to do and how to do it. I assured him that I was much more intelligent and therefore knew better.

The familiar banter had become second nature by now and neither of us was offended. He knew how hard I found it to fumble my way through the technicalities of an alien business and try to appear confident and capable, but he would never know how hard it was to be young and female and work in a predominantly male environment. I had to earn any respect the hard way, acutely aware of the career I'd given up. Any confidence I appeared to have, was like a house built on sand, unreliable and insubstantial like the estuary, where the channel chopped and changed with the vagaries of the wind and rain, much like some people I'd met who said one thing and meant another.

So, that's what I liked about the tide; the reliability. It had no choice, despite everything else going on around it. Its moods could change from pleasant and kindly, to ferocious and unforgiving; moods dictated by the strength and direction of the wind, by rain in the mountains, a spring or neap tide, high-tide, half-tide, low-tide and slack-water. There were times when a flood-tide with a following wind, could cover the sand in the estuary as quickly as throwing a sheet over a bed; then the ebb-tide at springs, with a strong wind against it that kicked up the bar into a maelstrom of confused, tumbling waves.

"To be avoided at all costs," Will Roberts, the Harbour Master said to me during one of his informal tutoring sessions. "It kicks up vicious short seas that'll toss a small boat like yours around like a child's toy. If a boat ever tries to enter and misses the top of the tide in those conditions, it should stand off or go to the marina in Pwllheli. You remember that, Miss Jones. No matter how badly you want to get home, don't do it. And preferably, don't get your tides wrong in the first place."

Once, in the summer, I'd seen a high-tide spill over the harbour wall and there were low-tides that were sometimes so low, and the sea so far out, one could be forgiven for wondering if it was there at all.

But my favourite time was at low-tide, just seaward from where I stood. The sea, as it receded, sculpted the sand into a landscape of scalloped hollows filled with crystal-clear water, separated by high, inter-connecting ridges of hard sand. Where these ridges dipped down in between pools, soft patches oozed water and quivered under the weight of your foot; not enough to be a serious quicksand that would swallow you up, but enough to be un-nerving. I avoided those when I was paddling. The fantastical horror of being sucked down and swallowed up, upkept me to the solid, sandy high-ground. In the pools, shoals of miniscule sand-eels, left by the tide, flashed and silvered the green depths and tiny white crabs scuttled below them, the unlucky ones stranded at the edges and baked to dry, crisp shells in the sun.

I dabbled my toes in the water and tried to make some sense of my lot in life. Twenty-second birthday in November, a career in journalism down the pan, and an un-asked for inheritance that posed ridiculous challenges. I was momentarily sick of my ragged nails, untidy hair, paint-stained dungarees and the constant nagging feeling that I didn't belong here. The cold filtered through my wet-suit. I was hungry, deflated after my epic on the bar and the complaints about Jason, and felt very alone.

Then the scene around me worked its magic as the last rays of the sun lit the beach at the end of Ballast Island and coloured the pebbles peach and apricot, ochres and browns. It darkened by the second as the sun disappeared behind the birches and oaks above the village on the other side of the channel. Then, little by little, light after light, the gloom of the gathering evening was dispelled by the necklaces of fairy-lights along the front of the restaurant and café and lamps were switched on in the bay windows of the Bed and Breakfasts and holiday cottages.

Behind me and over the other side of the estuary, the lighthouse on the headland was a pinprick of white, the village of Portmeirion itself hidden behind the promontory; a colourful, beautiful nonsense in white and turquoise and red with gilt-trimmed statues, fish in the pools and delicate fountains, terracotta roofs and arches leading nowhere. One man's dream; the perfect, Italianate village, famous for *The Prisoner* and a recent venue for the Festival 6 music event.

A flock of oystercatchers had settled on the sand behind me; red legs, red beaks and a stunning show of black and white when they flew off. For now, they could have been cardboard cut-outs, like the lone heron by the deep pool at the end of Ballast Island and the skeleton-timbers of the old quay pointing black and stark into the sky.

I saw all this and scarcely believed how much I saw, how much I'd learned in less than a year; a city babe with polished nails and a promising career, now beguiled by the sea and its ways. I paddled across to the slipway, carried the kayak into the yard and turned it upside down. It was infinitely easier than launching skiffs and dinghies and I'd liked the simplicity of it. Paddling seemed easier than rowing, despite my scare. At least I could pick a kayak up and drag it onto the sand easily and wondered if my solicitor would sanction the expenditure. Necessary transport, of course.

CHAPTER 2

The Ship that night was busy with the usual crowd and live music from the band. I bought Mark a pint, thanked him for the loan of the kayak and gave him a heavily-edited version of the day.

"Oh, yeah? Just up to Samson's Bay?" he said, and raised his eyebrows. "Glad you enjoyed it. Hang on to the kayak 'till you get your own." He didn't believe me but went off with his group of friends, easy and friendly. Accepted now by the regulars on nodding terms, I sat on my own at the bar.

I'd been too preoccupied to find new friends and surprisingly, I felt content with my own company, but happily chatted to those in passing. Tonight, though, I felt touchy, dissatisfied with my lot and not in the mood for small talk. Some guy I hadn't seen before, sat down at the stool next to me.

"Hi," he said. "Just come over from Bangor with Jake. He's my cousin, plays guitar in the band."

"I know Jake," I said.

"Not been in here before. You're the boatyard girl, aren't you? Buy you a drink? Vodka, is it? I'm Mike."

Boatyard girl?

"Owner, actually," I said, not even trying to keep the edge out of my voice.

But he hadn't noticed, or minded, and ordered before I could refuse. But then, I asked myself, why should I refuse? I didn't know him but he might be interesting; well-built, tidy, rugged, outdoor complexion. He knew who I was, of course. It seemed everyone did, being a newish novelty in the harbour and Jake, his cousin, being a local, knew who I was anyway. But a boatyard girl?

"Owner, are you now?" he said. "There used to be an old guy ran it. The Boat Shed, isn't it? I came over from Bangor once 'cos it was the only place sold odd bits of hard wood. Chandlers as well?"

"Sort of," I said, and made an effort to be pleasant. "There's a lot to learn."

"You own it now?" he asked. "Really?"

I nodded.

"You'll know your teak from your mahogany then?"

"Yes," I said, surprised. "I'm getting there."

"I'm a joiner, see. I work on wooden boats sometimes as well as houses. Off-cuts are hard to find. Haven't been for a while. Still around, is he, the old man?"

"He died," I said, deciding not to satisfy his curiosity with detail. "There's still some planks, though."

That set him off with a monologue of the properties of certain hardwoods for certain jobs in the building trade and those used in wooden boats. The difference between carvel and clinker-build wasn't what I wanted to hear tonight. He seemed to get it after a while. He downed his pint and studied the bottles behind the bar for a minute. He was still fishing. Nice guy, but he'd read me all wrong tonight.

"Another drink?" he asked.

I shook my head. "No, thank you. I need to go," and looked at my watch. "It was nice meeting you."

"Don't go just yet," he said. "Look, sorry if I bored you with planks and all that. Got to start somewhere with someone like you."

"I have a lobster to get back to," I said, then relented. "One more drink," and wished I hadn't.

He laughed, thought I was joking about the lobster, bought drinks, downed three pints to my one vodka and his inhibitions and tongue, predictably, ran away with him. His true colours began to show and he started on his life and loves and attitudes to women in general.

He leaned closer with each pint, slurred his words, his eyes hazy with drink.

"So, why's a girl like you running a boatyard? Must be a bit dull. Fancy a walk over to the *Australia* through the park? Short cut, like?"

"It's closed at night," I said.

"Come on, girl, lighten up. Few more drinks? You should be out clubbing and pubbing and having a good time."

He oozed beer and testosterone. His cousin Jake came to the bar and whispered something in his ear. I didn't need to translate it to get the drift. He nudged Mike's elbow, winked and went back to the group.

"I am having a good time," I said, quite politely, "and it doesn't include a quick screw in the park with a half-pissed joiner. Thank you for the drinks."

He muttered something in Welsh, glared at me, got down off his stool and shambled off to sit with the group.

I sat on my own at the bar for a while, wondered whether he was right or not and pondered over what people really thought of me and whether it mattered or not. My head was full of spiders; a confused, intermingled web of lists of practical jobs for the week ahead; *Tai Pilots*, what to do with Jason and whether I'd be able to eat for the rest of the winter, mixed up with emotions about my personal life which seemed to have been swallowed up in the summer's events. I'd had enough to drink and needed to be quiet and think, to re-evaluate all that had happened. I walked back to the yard along the path, the darkness and silence pierced once by the single cry of a heron hunting the channel.

I closed and locked the gates to the boatyard firmly behind me, changed my mind about the drink and unlocked the door to the Boat Shed. The now familiar smell of smoke and old timber, polish and oil greeted me, as always. It was embedded in the fabric of the place with its tin roof and burnished trade-counter I'd lovingly restored. A bottle of Glenlivet was tucked away on a shelf underneath. Much as I had disliked my great-uncle, my benefactor, grumpy old man as he was, I had reinstated one of his habits; a tot of whisky for important moments.

The logs in the wood-burner ignited with a stick or two and the comfy old chairs with their new plaid rugs beckoned cosily in the glow from the small light I'd placed in the window. I was beginning to understand why he spent all his time here during his last days. It was comfortable, undemanding, a small space that lent itself to reflection, which is what I needed. I poured the scotch into an old glass, curled up in one of the chairs and watched the flames dance in the fire-box.

Just to survive this male-dominated world of boats, meet so many new people, good and bad, and get my hands dirty with new skills, overwhelmed me at times. I needed to learn about tides and weather, the difference between a block and a cleat, iroko and mahogany, how to install an electric winch and whether I really wanted to do any of all this shit. How to make the business viable, was out of my experience. I poured another drink and dug deeper, deeper into the fantasy world of journalism that shaped my teenage years, the dreams of seeing my name in print, uncovering stories of injustice and unfairness with my name in by-lines at the top of the page. Not the astronomer my dad had so fervently wished for. Not even the journalist I'd so wished to be.

I shut the fire down for the night, locked the door firmly and stared at the outline of the Boat Shed in the dark. But it was not just a shed, not just an old, out-dated chandlery. It was a hub, where Jason and Angela and Hugh and Arnie and Denise, even Will Roberts, came and drank coffee by the fire or sat outside in the yard and gossiped and chatted, all of them with their own needs and difficulties. It had begun to feel like a family. I took a pill, despite the warnings about mixing it with alcohol and fell into the caravan bunk in an alcoholic haze. Before I drifted off, I decided, in a state of euphoria, I could run the yard and write stories as well, if there was something worth investigating. Doug Peterson and his crab-crawling eyes didn't bother me that night.

Hugh Phillips woke me on Sunday morning with the sound of the electric sander he used to perfect another plank on his boat. The wooden sailing yacht in process of renovation, was his pride and joy and he had taken great pains to inform me of its specifications, on and off, over the summer. Most of it had disappeared over my head; it seemed to me that one run-down wooden yacht was much the same as another, having glanced at a number of them in a section set aside for abandoned projects in the yard up the road. I told him so when I first met him, as diplomatically as I could under the barrage of information that he was determined to share with me, but had totally underestimated his passion and whether I was interested or not.

"All the same? Certainly not the case with my yacht, Miss Jones," he'd said, as he ran his hand lovingly over the teak planking. "She's a fine example of a *Vertue*, you know, designed by Laurent Giles back in 1951. *Vertues* were designed to cross oceans, this one built with teak planking on steam-bent, Canadian Rock Elm and caulked with red lead when she was built. Naturally, all her fastenings are non-ferrous."

Of course, naturally. I didn't dare ask. He continued the instruction.

"She's twenty-five feet and three inches on the deck, seven-foot on the beam and enough headroom inside for a person five-foot, ten inches to stand up in."

Hugh was hardly taller than me at five-foot, three inches, so that was irrelevant and in his own words, he had no intention of sailing it anywhere. It was simply the joy of restoring an object in which skill, time and love had been invested at its inception and which should be applied again.

"It's only right she should be able to sail the seas again. That was the whole purpose. It's disrespectful to allow something so beautiful to deteriorate for the want of work."

"Well, people do become ill, or poor, or die," I'd said. "It's not always deliberate. And fashions change. Everything's plastic these days and it's a lot of hard work, all this," glancing up at the partly-stripped hull. "Do you feel the same way about the railway and the engines you work on?" I'd asked, curious and surprised at his meaningful revelation.

"Oh, yes, indeed," he'd said, almost with reverence.

There was a lot more to Hugh Phillips than met the eye, I thought, with his old-fashioned sandals, striped socks and gentle formality. Not so good with people, preferred to be on his own when he could, but he held a deep-seated love for his toil that put me to shame. I hadn't forgotten that conversation and reminded myself, yet again, about ill-judged, hasty assumptions.

He greeted me with a friendly wave this Sunday morning, switched off the sander, ran his hand over the smoothed teak and put the sander carefully on the bench beside him.

"How's it coming along?" I asked, not entirely indifferent to the progress he'd made since I took over the yard. The hours he worked on the hull never seemed to make a difference at first glance, until I noticed the smoothness he'd attained in the preparation for painting. To sand

and varnish my great-uncle's skiff and a pair of oars with five layers, as I was advised, was my pinnacle of achievement and I was only just beginning to appreciate the effort needed to obtain a stunning finish. I studied the bare planks and only then did it occur to me that his boat didn't have a name and I'd never asked.

"Sanded off, of course," he said and graced me with a pitying look. "It's taken me a year to reach the wood under the coats of old paint and re-caulk the gaps. When she's had her coats of new paint, I shall replace it, of course. She's called *Capella*. I've been thinking, Miss Jones," he said. "Do you think we could have a talk?"

He took the Beanie off his head and turned it round and round in his hands, the bald pate now exposed to the sun, but it was a habit he had when he needed to talk. His greeting was as formal as ever, even after six months of seeing him most weekends.

"Hugh, do you think we could please drop the formalities? Can't you just call me 'Cassie,' now? It doesn't seem right when I call you by your first name. I wanted to talk to you anyway. Take a break and think about it while I make us some coffee."

We sat on an upturned dinghy in companiable silence. He had that effect on you, when he wasn't talking directly to your face. I'd noticed it over the summer when he was compiling the inventory of the stock in the chandlery on his own, revelling over the odd names for classic boat-bits he found stuffed behind empty boxes or tipped out of packets into untidy piles. He coiled ropes neatly and hung them on hooks, exclaiming when he found something he considered rare and unusual, like the original Yankee screwdriver he'd found in a box and proceeded to tell me snippets of its history. He was quite happy as he chatted to himself, until he had to talk directly to you.

"I've thought about it," he said, "but that's not what I wanted to talk to you about at all."

"What?" I asked, confused.

"How I should address you," he said. "I think, if I may, I'll call you 'Miss Cassie'. As a compromise."

"Why?" I asked, amused and curious.

"I can't explain," he said. "Because it feels right. One should always do the things that feel right, don't you agree?"

Helen's Nain once asked me if I could call her by her Christian name when I came back after uni. I tried 'Joan' as she asked, because I was grown-up. But, no, it didn't feel right. She was always going to be 'Helen's Nain', even though it was a bit of a mouthful. She'd laughed and said she didn't mind.

"I do agree," I said, "when it feels right. Miss Cassie it is, then. But I need to talk to you about the inventory of the stock you've done so brilliantly."

"That's what I need to talk to you about, as well," he said.

"Look, Hugh, you've easily cleared the debt we agreed over storage for that old caravan of yours and I can't afford to pay you for any more work on the inventory. It's nearly all ready for the website, now. I don't know what I'd have done without you," I said. "You know so much and I've learned such a lot."

Sitting side by side, he didn't have to look at me.

"I haven't started on the models yet," he said. "I couldn't possibly *not* do those, or finish the stock list, as well as *Capella*. The interior is complete now and another summer should see the hull finished."

"What will you do then?" I asked. "Sell it and renovate another one?"

I guessed he enjoyed his weekends in the yard, where he was able to work mostly in solitude and suspected he worked in the same way at Boston Lodge, where the engine-sheds for the Ffestiniog Railway were tucked into the old quarry at the end of the Cob. He polished and cleaned engines or parts of engines, or anything else they asked him to do, he told me, well away from the visitors. He hinted that he found it difficult sometimes to cope with the rough and tumble ways of the men who maintained the wind turbines and drove the ships out of Holyhead. They relied on his technical expertise, he'd said and left him alone to crunch figures and compile data. He must have been good at his job for them to tolerate him and his funny ways.

"Perhaps a small reduction in the yard fees?" he asked. "In exchange for completing the inventory?"

"Yes, of course. A good idea," I said. "Anything. That's fine. Please don't go, Hugh. I really need you."

"Thank you. Then I shall continue," he said and paused, quiet and serious for a moment. "However, there's a problem in the world that affects you more than you think."

"Just the one?" I asked. He didn't smile.

"It seems that restocking the chandlery and replacing specialist hard wood, is going to be far more difficult these days."

"But we've got loads left," I said, thinking of the planks of teak and mahogany stacked up at the end of the shed.

"Forgive me, but Mr Jones stocked wood years ago when people bought what they needed locally and there were still small, wooden yachts around. Like mine, of course."

"So, what's the problem?"

"The terms of your inheritance. If you get a buyer who wants it all and you can't afford the prices to restock, even if you can source the wood, what will you replace the stock with? Bits and pieces for the chandlery? For small outlets like this these days, you're competing with the big suppliers and Internet shopping. Mr Jones didn't have that problem when he first started".

"So, what's happened to the wood stocks?"

"Deforestation, indiscriminate felling to make way for food

production and now those terrible forest fires in South America. The prices have rocketed."

"Soya beans are more important than trees, now?"

He shook his head.

"I can't see how this is going to work," he said. "I think you'll have to talk to your solicitor about how much leeway you've got if you need to diversify to stay solvent, and keep to the terms of your inheritance as well."

"Can't we encourage people to come here and build wooden boats? Or fix them up, like you're doing?"

"Well, that brings me to the other issue I wished to talk to you about. Not many people wish to undertake such a project as building a boat, but I do have a proposal I have been asked to discuss with you in a moment. Let me finish, first.

'With respect, you're missing the point, if I may say so. Wood is the problem. Hard woods, specialist timber, properly seasoned. You can't compete with the bigger companies who sell kiln-dried timber as well as stocks of air-dried planks, which takes time, and of course they have the wherewithal to turn over a bigger stock. So much is plastic now especially for fittings. Mr Jones can't have realised how much life has changed when he made his will. He lived in the dark ages, from what people say."

I'd never heard him talk so much but had an idea that he was absolutely right. The terms of the inheritance were unsustainable, but it needed Hugh to tell me the facts and make me face the reality. I had been totally immersed in my days at work cleaning the place up, dressed in paint-stained overalls and grubby trainers and my hands, despite gloves, were roughened with cleaning agents and water. I just worked on the immediate and hadn't really faced the future.

I'd shared my worries with Jason, nineteen now, and foisted on me by his pleading father to keep him in work and out of trouble.

"Diversify, Cassie," said Jason, filled with youthful exuberance about the future when he first came back into town, hidden and protected up in the hills from the drug-dealers he'd unwittingly upset. "That's what Mr Roberts did with the farm when Mrs Roberts got sick. He did free-range organic chickens and eggs, sold them in the farm shops and just kept a few sheep, as well as his job. Why don't you do something different? There's still the smoke-house and the snack-bar to develop."

Diversify. I had ideas and both Jason and Hugh couldn't be wrong.

"I need more money," I said, "and I have to stay within the terms of the inheritance. I'm working on it. I'll talk to the solicitor." He made me promise. It seemed like ages ago and I had done nothing about it but Hugh's polite conversation reminded me. I needed to move on, make progress, put plans in place or go home to London with my tail between my legs. My mother would love that.

"The other issue I wished to discuss," Hugh said, as I picked up the mugs, "is on the subject of boats." I sat down again.

"I have a colleague in Holyhead, a young chap who works shore-based for the company but has a small wooden sailing boat, slightly smaller than *Capella*, in a state of disrepair. He lived on it in the marina, you see, to save costs. There were quite a few liveaboards at the time."

"Lived, as in past tense?"

"Yes, indeed. You must have heard about the terrible storm in 2018?"

"I'd heard the marina was damaged."

"Not just damaged, destroyed completely, along with all the boats that were left moored up for the winter; power boats, yachts, fishing boats, everything. We only managed to move the survey ships at the last minute and the lifeboats escaped to the fish-dock on the other side of the bay before it was too late."

If I'd seen Hugh solemn before, but it was nothing compared to the distress evident on his face.

"That's terrible," I said. "I didn't know it was that bad. I was still in London."

He stared over towards Ballast Island, as if seeing the images all over again.

"It was a north-easterly, you see, Force 12 in the gusts and it came right across the bay and hit the pontoons where our survey ships were moored. I'd never seen anything like it, or heard anything like it, screaming and howling with enormous waves breaking over the pontoons. It was truly terrifying."

"So, what happened to your friend?"

"Most of those liveaboards who were still on their boats, as well as owners who tried to reach their boats as the pontoons began to breakup, escaped back up the ramp before it became unsafe. There was nothing anyone could do except watch their boats. They were torn from their moorings as the pontoons disintegrated or swamped when they were pulled under the debris, still tied on and unable to move anywhere."

I was almost lost for words and he was still upset, but I was desperate for the rest of the story.

I asked, as gently as I could. "What happened after the storm blew over?"

"It was shocking," he said and stopped. I waited.

"Where the marina had been built, including the little bay behind it, was just a pool of floating rubbish, with the tops of masts and half-submerged boats sticking out of the water or washed up on the beach. I'll tell you what it was like," he said, thoughtfully. "It was a bit like old pictures you see of the World War Two convoys after they'd been attacked by submarines. Shocking," he repeated, "Just shocking. The polystyrene used for the floating pontoons broke up into chunks and tiny particles; they're still being washed up on the Anglesey beaches, you know."

"And your young friend?"

"His boat was washed up on the pebble beach in the bay before the breakwater. He was aboard, you see, when the storm broke and being on an outside pontoon, thought he could take the boat safely across to the dock after the lifeboats left. He managed to let go the mooring ropes and set off but his engine failed."

"How on earth did he get off?"

"He waited until the boat grounded on the beach, tipped on her side and jumped off. She was pounded for hours, but survived and eventually, after months of wrangling with insurance companies, re-floated and craned out into the yard."

A Sunday morning silence descended on the yard; even the gulls were quiet for a change.

"So," I guessed. "Is this the boat you wanted to discuss?"

"Yes, naturally. She is up and running with a new engine and sails and my friend is determined to restore her woodwork, much like this one. He wants a change from the yard in Holyhead for a couple of years. I explained about this one and as he now has accommodation in Holyhead and his job is now more secure, he would share the journey down with me at weekends and work on the boat then. Would you be interested? He asked me to ask you before he made direct contact with yourself."

"Can he pay the yard fees?" I said, trying not to sound too enthusiastic. "I don't want any derelict yachts and skint owners here, Hugh, but if it works out and he's genuine, it could be brilliant. He could be craned out with *Annie* in October. Even better, I can tell the solicitor I now have my second client."

I took the mugs in and decided I was not going to do any yard-work today. It was Sunday, after all.

Hugh returned to his sander and I went for a walk. Jason's ideas and

Hugh's concerns about the future dogged my steps all the way over the cliff path to Black Rock Sands, but the thought of a new client lightened them somewhat. I walked and paddled in the sea all the way to Craig Ddu, where the biggest cave in the headland was now accessible at half-tide, and wandered inside for the first time since I'd lived here.

The sand was cold under-foot, hard-packed and washed clean by the tide, the roof and sides formed by great folds of coloured rocks, in layers at different angles. I stood in awe and wondered at the immensity of the forces when the rocks were thrown up out of the earth, collided and settled into extraordinary shapes and colours; reds and green and bronzes hinted at the different geological times. Rain-water from the land above seeped through the roof and dripped into the pool by the entrance, where it rippled and radiated out in circles to touch the edges.

I padded to the back of the cave and left a line of perfect footprints. The headroom petered out and the space narrowed and ended abruptly. I felt a strong compulsion to return to the entrance, oppressed by the confinement of the cave with its roof now low over my head, the gloom and the thought of tons of rock above me.

Back at the entrance, the sides and roof to the cave framed the sky and sea like a picture with just a hint of disturbance along the beach where the waves met the empty sands and broke in a barely perceptible white line. Further out to sea, the colours graduated into gentle shades of grey and blue that blended with the sky and the horizon became just a figment of the imagination, a still-life canvas of pale, blended colours and far removed from the story Helen had told me when we first met.

A shipwreck happened here in 1907. She knew her history and regaled all the details. As if I hadn't heard enough horror sea-stories for one day, it was impossible to stand on this spot in the cave and not remember the story. She'd given me a guided tour from the bench on the promenade in Criccieth, and pointed to the east.

"That's Craig Ddu. Black Rock Sands is just round the other side," she'd said. "You can walk round the rock at low-tide, but when it's high-tide and there's a storm, the waves break right over it. You can imagine what it's like."

No, I couldn't imagine it then, but I could now. I remember how she'd sucked the ice-cream out of the end of the cone, crunched the rest of it and abstractedly wiped her hands on her jeans. I hadn't forgotten; so easy and natural, carried away in a burst of detailed story-telling.

"She was a three-masted, Porthmadog schooner, the *Owen Morris*, built in 1891, on passage home after a trip to Newfoundland and then to Italy. She was caught out in a storm in the bay and was driven onto Craig Ddu. The best bit," she went on, "was when the waves battered her so hard, her bows and bowsprit were pushed right up into the cave. The rest of the ship was pounded to pieces on the rocks."

"That's awful," I'd said, taken aback by her enthusiasm. "Did the sailors drown?"

"No," she said. "They were lucky. All six were saved by the Criccieth lifeboat."

She told the story with relish. I wasn't surprised, in hindsight, that her career and interests were in medicine. Death and disaster didn't seem to bother her much but at least, this time, I'd been spared the ghosts of drowned sailors.

I dug my heels into the cold sand of the cave floor and closed my eyes. It was hard to imagine a whole ship, hull and mast and sails, being destroyed by huge waves inside this cold cave and on a beach that most people only visit on benign, sunny days.

Once this summer, in a south-westerly gale, Jason and I had walked the footpath that climbs up onto the headland and overlooks the beach. We'd seen the breakers roll in, cover the beach in a welter of flying spray and break right to the edge of the sandhills. On Craig Ddu, the sea had burst against the rock and hurled white water high up the cliff-face and would have filled the cave. I shivered and was glad to walk out into the sunshine, back onto the open beach and leave any dark horrors behind.

Monday morning. I was beginning to feel more positive about life and had slept well for the third night. The GP was right. I had enjoyed the walk, and the talk with Hugh had been constructive and allayed my fears by coming to terms with where I was going and how I was going to deal with it. I'd also, in a bitter-sweet sort of way felt pleased with myself, having graciously declined the offer of a 'good time' on Saturday night, as the guy put it. I couldn't even remember his name. I checked my emails on the laptop, put the kettle on and stuffed the phone into my pocket. Ed had sent his reply to my write-up of the drug-traffickers' arrests and I wanted to read it on the harbour wall with a coffee in my hand and no distractions.

Edward Martin, or Ed, to those who worked for him, was the editor of the newspaper I'd abandoned after only six months apprenticeship. Considering I'd abandoned the job at short notice and considering he was a man who didn't suffer fools gladly, he understood why I had to leave, and in a fatherly way, offered to keep an eye on me by reading any reports I might want to write, unpublished of course, just to keep my hand in, he said. Just in case.

He had visited me during his summer holiday, feeding his passion for fishing trips out from Pwllheli to catch bass or tope or mackerel, or whatever was biting on the day. He'd been friends with the skipper of the fishing boat for years. I'd met the skipper, the obnoxious Mr Thomas, who was terse and unhelpful when I asked him about maritime drug-trafficking and couldn't understand their relationship. He'd dismissed me rudely the only time I met him, but then I was only an unemployed rookie journalist and chided myself at the time for having poked around too boldly and inexpertly to expect manners.

Ed was famous in the office for his sharp tongue, knowledge and wisdom. He was frighteningly well-informed politically, highly respected in press circles, had appalling taste in old-fashioned suits and wore creased shirts and mismatched ties which often betrayed his fondness for fried eggs and afternoon cream-cakes. He was dangerously overweight. I liked and respected him very much. He'd helped me out with contacts to submit the news photos I'd taken of the summer's big drugs event, and then, as he said he would, offered to read my unpublished coverage of the story, to be written in house-style, as it was the only house-style I was familiar with. I hadn't written it up and couldn't see the point. But then I did. He repeatedly said I should keep my interest and skills in writing alive; just in case.

Ridiculously nervous about the response to my article, it was almost as though I had to face him in his office. I made myself a mug of coffee, wandered across the yard to sit on the harbour wall, dangled my legs over the edge with *Annie*'s cabin roof below me and started to read.

'Cassie, what do you think you're doing? This is sensationalist, narrative writing that bears no resemblance to the style appropriate for this paper. You need to be able to adapt your work to your reading audience as requested by your editor, not indulge yourself in your propensity for writing thrillers more suitable for second-hand bookshops. Do it again. House-style this time, if you please.'
Ed

I laughed. I could have bridled, of course, but he was absolutely right. I'd missed writing so much, I'd just got a bit carried away, conveniently forgetting how close I had been to serious trouble. There were moments when Doug Peterson's piercing eyes, hidden threats and Jason's brothers, violent and unscrupulous, had troubled my dreams so badly, I had to wake up and convince myself Doug Peterson was well and truly dead, his running mate Gareth murdered and the twins arrested. Despite all that, it would hardly make a dent in the County Lines infiltration into the area, the police said, with the network so well organised. The drugs just arrived here by other means, what with winter coming and deliveries by sea being considerably more cold, wet and dangerous.

I'd write it again, as requested this time, was grateful for his trouble and had a sudden, uncomfortable moment when I missed his presence, the office banter with Tim and the buzz of a new incident to report on, no matter how mundane. Perhaps he guessed that I missed that part of it and wanted to keep me connected. Maybe he knew it would be cathartic as well, even therapeutic. Although I would have preferred to relegate the summer's events to history, the total pleasure of writing and working to improve the style and my need to please Ed, would absorb me quite happily on a rainy day. That was a promise I made to myself.

CHAPTER 3

The phone rang. Helen's Nain never rang. She sounded rather distant and by her own admission, didn't like the 'thing', as she called her smart phone, but her daughter in London had bought her one, set it up, and insisted she carry it with her at all times.

"I'm sitting on the bench, cariad, by the bus shelter."

"Oh," I said, "that's nice. Is there a problem? It's just that you never ring me."

"I need to tell you something."

"Oh." I said. "What is it?"

"That young man of yours."

"He's not my young man, Helen's Nain."

"Well, maybe not, but he left the house this morning about nine o'clock. I was walking back from the pillbox, saw him go past my house and up the steps and then a car drove up and a man went into *Tai Pilots*. He wasn't a nice-looking man, Cassie, with one of those hood things over his head. He didn't see me. I just thought it seemed a bit strange. And then I met Gwen."

"Who's Gwen?"

"Just a friend. She's sitting on the bench with me but I thought I'd mention it. She was the one who complained about the music."

"What else?" My throat tightened.

"People have been going into the house over the last few weeks while Jason was at work. They let themselves in, so nobody passing thought anything of it. It's just that this character was most… suspicious-looking. Could you have a word, cariad? Just to make sure he'd given permission?"

He might have done. I certainly hadn't.

"I'll check," I said. "Don't worry, I'm sure it's nothing. He'll be here soon. Has the car gone?"

"We haven't seen it go past."

I put the phone down on the harbour wall. That horrible, sinking feeling of bad news had coloured my day already and I turned round at the sound of the gates grating on the gravel. They'd been expensive, my new solid, galvanised gates with the security code that kept me safe and asleep at nights in my little caravan tucked up against the cliff behind the shed.

Jason, tall and still too thin for his nineteen years, wandered towards me, his weekend excesses evident in the lack of bounce in his walk. He stopped behind me, grubby trainers and bare legs below work shorts, the skin on his shins beginning to show signs of his eczema reappearing. I looked up at his face. He had dark shadows under his eyes and his cheekbones stood out against the faded, summer tan. For a few brief weeks in the summer when he'd gone to stay with Will Roberts, the hard work and fresh air had suited him and put some colour into his face. He'd put on weight, his skin had cleared and he'd looked well, cared for and cooked special foods for Mrs Roberts, like a professional, Mr Roberts said. She was now too sick to be at home and had been moved to a hospice.

Then he came back into town. It only took one music festival, the wrong connections and a severe beating to put the haunted look back in his eyes. I just wanted him to be normal, but normal meant going out and having fun. I couldn't stop him, neither could I put the wise head on his shoulders that suggested he choose his venues and friends more carefully. Today, he looked tired and twitchy. The text about the noise, and now the phone call, had to be handled with kid gloves, I was certain. To mention it without him flying off the handle was tricky. I wasn't his father, mother, not even a big sister, but I was his land-lady, however unofficial. I'd bide my time until it felt right.

"Hi," I said. "Have a good weekend?"

"Yeah, okay."

He shuffled his feet in the gravel and kicked a stone over the edge of the harbour wall. It dropped on the blue paint of *Annie's* cabin roof and bounced off into the water.

"You want the job of painting that?" I asked.

"Sorry. Can I borrow that boat you've been varnishing?"

"It's not just a boat, it's a skiff, and no, you can't. You've never rowed a boat in all the time you've been here and you said you couldn't swim. Anyway, you'd ruin it. I've only just finished the oars and they're still tacky."

"Just for show then, is it?" he said. "You haven't rowed much, neither."

"I rowed a bit when you were away. And it's 'either'," I said, "to be correct, I think. Your English is dreadful."

"And yours is too posh. Got to start somewhere. You only go out and play with the engine on *Annie* and you've only done that a few times and Mr Roberts came with you. Too scared to go out on your own, you are."

"Scared in case the engine breaks down, I agree. It'll get easier when I know a bit more."

"That's why I want to row, just to see if I can do it on my own. Just me and the boat, like. Just over to Ballast Island and back when the tide's slack, that's what Mr Roberts said, to start. And I wanted to go over there to look round. You said you'd slept out there once."

I looked round the yard at my collection of battered, old rowing-boats and wondered about the sudden interest.

"See that red dinghy over there? You can borrow that one if you glue and screw the seat on properly. There are spare rowlocks and oars in the shed and there's fibre-glass filler on the shelf. You'll need to glass the holes over. Then you can glue the seat on and let it dry overnight. It'll need screws as well. You can do that in the morning and then we'll carry it down the slipway tomorrow at high tide."

"What's rowlocks?"

"Metal horse-shoe shaped things for resting the oars in. You figure it out. And in case you ever need to write it down, it's spelt like 'row-locks', two words joined together but pronounced like 'bollocks.' Go on, fix it up and I can have a laugh at your efforts."

"Bollocks to you, then," he said, "and how come you suddenly know all this stuff?"

"Internet," I said, "and a bit of practice and help from Hugh Phillips while you were holidaying in the hills. Matter of having to."

He favoured me with a glimmer of a smile. We'd developed an easy-going relationship, but I still worried. He scuffed his trainers on the harbour wall, avoided my eye and tried to look nonchalant. I didn't trust him and he didn't fool me one bit.

"Oh, by the way," I said, "before you stun me with your expertise in boat renovation, do you think you could tone the music down next time you have your friends around? Also, pick up the beer cans from the slip."

"How would you know?" he asked, the momentary good humour

gone. "The good folk of the village spying on me, were they?"

"No, but you can bet your life they don't all appreciate your taste in music. I just happened to be on the sand-bank opposite *Tai Pilots* after my journey out in the kayak and back. I could hear the bass thud a mile off," I said, decided to keep Helen's Nain and her concerns out of it for the moment, while I thought hard about the implications if I confronted him with something he might have no knowledge of. Even worse, something he did know.

He grumbled a reply. I just hoped the friends and their cans of beer were the least of their habits and that the visits, if unknown, were innocent; going back to retrieve clothes or just somewhere to doss for the day. I thought somehow, it was unlikely. Unwelcome anxiety turned into worry and cast a yet deeper shadow over the morning. I didn't know what to do or who to ask. Certainly not the police; not yet. Not before I'd confronted him and not before I'd carried out some investigation of my own. It could wait for an hour or so, while I thought it through.

I headed for the Boat Shed and the morning's work, opened the lid to the post-box and recognised the type-face on the single letter. It had been lying there since Saturday morning when I'd been too busy planning my expedition to think about the post which was left in an old biscuit tin nailed to the wall. I picked it out, put it on the counter and spent five minutes prevaricating; washed mugs, polished the kettle and removed a new spider's web from the window. I knew what it was going to say.

"Please make an appointment to discuss expenditure and future planning."

I picked up the phone.

Mr Gerald Hughes, senior partner, was always immaculate in starched cuffs and tie-pin; he was formal and traditional with no sense of humour whatsoever and had reduced me to schoolgirl status in our regular, monthly, progress meetings. This time it would be different. I would go armed with a proper business plan, brandish my application of the food certificate needed to run the snack-bar and to refurbish the smoke-house ready for the following spring. I felt less inclined to be intimidated by him with a proper plan up my sleeve.

David, his son and junior partner, was so different, I'd thought when I first met him, with his easy manner, unruly black curls, green eyes and casual clothes. I'd liked him straightaway and relied on him for advice. He even took me sailing once, in a race to Ireland. I hated it and I swore I would never, ever, go to sea in a sailing boat again. But despite his obvious passion for adventure and danger when he raced his boat regularly through foul seas, he poured cold water on all my plans, questioned and usually disapproved of everything I did.

We'd had a row in the summer. I'd accused him of being more concerned with his reputation than caring about what was going on in the area. He'd been conspicuous by his absence since the drugs arrests, having warned me over and over not to get involved in issues that didn't concern me. But it did concern me and I did it anyway. It was a rift I wasn't sure would mend.

"If your father got killed by a cocaine addict, you'd want to be involved too," I'd said.

I think I'd shouted at him, or at least raised my voice.

"You're being really unfair," said Trish, my best buddy, when I told her over the phone. "He did all that organising for the new gates and Wi-Fi and stuff and he looked after that lobster and he rescued you from the nasty dealers when they came to the yard. You don't have to go to bed with him. Just make friends. You might need him. He's a solicitor after all. He'd be a good catch. Don't you fancy him?"

"No," I said, "emphatically no. I'd rather have a relationship with the lobster. At least it doesn't come over all paternal and protective. As for sleeping with a solicitor, he's probably got a list of conditions and a risk assessment policy."

"That's ridiculous," she said. "Just be nice to him. He obviously cares about what happens to you."

"Well, he just annoys me. I can't help it. That gentle, casual manner disappears when he doesn't agree with my ideas. Whoever he shacks up with will have to be someone a bit more malleable than me, I can tell you."

I'd heard that before from Trish, when she tried, earlier on in the summer, to advise me on how to approach Doug Peterson, my drug-dealer neighbour and yard owner. I didn't have a chance to be nice to him as he was hardly ever there during the summer, which was just as well. I thought I'd done a pretty good job of burying the electric attraction I'd experienced when I'd first met him but I was only seventeen at the time; he was hard, analytical, uncompromising and scary; definitely scary and scarily desirable. I put my initial reaction of knees-turning-to-jelly down to adolescent infatuation. As for sleeping with him then and even three years later, if he'd snapped his fingers, who knows? But after he'd been washed up on the beach, very dead and no longer a threat to me, I confided in Trish how I'd felt.

"He couldn't possibly have been your type," she said, shocked. "He was old enough to be your father. Not good, Cassie. A guy like that would eat you for breakfast and spit out the pips. Or maybe you like them tough and tender, if you can find both together. Good luck with that," she said, doubt in her voice born from long experience with a myriad of boyfriends she didn't keep for long.

But David Hughes was not my type, either. He was mild-mannered, respectable and boringly conventional. He questioned and then disapproved of my entrepreneurial ideas, even if he did enjoy dangerous sailing on sick-making seas. I couldn't work out how he could be both a kill-joy and a risk-taker. No, he was not for me. We clashed nearly every time we met. He didn't intimidate me as his father did; he just made me cross. I was looking forward to the day when the last of the trust fund left to me was finally handed over.

I prepared a list of jobs for the day, but was more interested in how Jason was coping with the latest project I'd given him. I watched him out of the door, re-drilling holes for the screws to fix the seat back on the dinghy. The rowlocks and oars lay on the ground. I couldn't wait, anticipating his first efforts on the water. I hoped he'd fall in, as long as he had a life-jacket on and stayed in the shallows. We could both do with a laugh.

I put the kettle on for more coffee and fed Neifion. The flakes settled on the gravel at the bottom of the tank and the bigger stones and pebbles had begun to show green algae in the crevices. It needed a thorough clean out, but I for one, was not going to do it. I couldn't face the thought of actually handling a lobster. Neifion didn't seem interested in the food but waved his antennae in the bubbles. I pulled the battered stool I kept behind the counter up to the glass and had my usual conversation with him.

Nobody had been sent to take over the yard next door. It was only a month since Doug Peterson's body, bloated and nibbled by crabs and fishes, was washed up and identified. We knew nothing more about him and his past; whether he owned the business or part of it, or if was owned by an unknown consortium. Denise, as his secretary, seemed to think that was the most certain choice.

He'd been active in drug-trafficking as part of a bigger set-up, with the business for cover, as we found out, not just the owner or manager of the yard which had never seemed right. He lived in an apartment over the showroom when he wasn't elsewhere and resented my presence, right from the minute I took over the yard. I was young and fit, not old and decrepit like my great-uncle, and I was naturally nosy. When I bought the caravan and lived on site, there wasn't much I could have missed. He had wanted my yard, with its own slipway and private situation to combine both boatyards tucked away at the end of the old wharf. In hindsight, his drug-dealing was evident in the flash cars and yacht he owned, the expensive Rolex and the lavish hospitality in the sailing world. I worried about the next owner, for Denise's sake as well as my own.

The lobster went to sleep, bored, and I shut up and put the stool away as Denise turned up for coffee. There was no need for her to visit on the pretence of a need to borrow sugar anymore; the events of the summer had thrown us closer together and we felt easy with each other's company. She was worried, too. The jet-skis usually stored for the winter were beginning to pile in. Their owners washed them down in the yard and booked maintenance and servicing, their machines treated just like racehorses, I'd thought, when I first saw the care and attention bestowed on them; glitzy, plastic machines my great-uncle had hated. He would only entertain wooden boats in his yard. I had to admit I fancied a ride on one. But it could wait.

Denise was beginning to panic over the lack of a boss, her future as an employee and the absence of a mechanic to carry out the winter work on the jet-skis and the more complicated power-boats.

"I suppose as long as they pay me," she said, "whoever they are, it doesn't really matter, does it? I just keep getting emails from 'Trade-wind Inc.' Carry on, they say. We'll let you know."

"I bet you could manage that place perfectly well," I said. "You've been doing it ever since I arrived. Doug was hardly ever there, was he?"

"No, but he still left personal stuff, clothes and that, in the apartment and I'm supposed to clear it out but I can't face it. Anyway, selling and managing were different. I did admin, he did the selling." She smiled and swept a wisp of blonde hair off her face and back on top of her head. "Wrong sex, Cassie. Try convincing the buyers. They're nearly always men. I can't talk about injectors and fuel-filters convincingly when I'm blessed with boobs as well as no knowledge, can I? I just don't know enough about this stuff, any more than you do and you can imagine how much I'd have to learn to get past the gender bug. Much as I hate it, that's the way it is."

"But their wives are interested in the interiors, aren't they? All that white leather and stainless trimmings? If you could find someone to do the mechanics and talk horsepower, bet you could do it. A double act and swallow the gender differences, if it sells boats."

"You're having a hard time doing it," she said, pointedly, "trying to make your mark in this world with the Boat Shed. It's difficult and you know it. I'd have to go and study engines and then spend years proving I could do it. And then, it would ruin my make-up and hair, all that grease and engine oil."

We laughed and I broke out the chocolate biscuits.

But I could tell the situation was beginning to affect her. Her blonde hair spouted out of the band on top of her head like a fountain, but more unruly than usual, the blue eye make-up now supplemented by puffiness under her eyes but I still had to clean the carefully-applied lipstick off the mugs when she came over to drink coffee in-between clients. She made up her face carefully for the customers every day no matter how she felt, showed them round, gave them what specs she could, dealt with the admin and ordered spare parts as asked for. She knew her job and was charming and capable. She deserved better.

She left and I wandered back over to the tank, stared at the bubbles rising and drifted off into a daydream. Without compromising the terms of the inheritance, I wanted to use part of the yard to store jet-skis for the winter, enough room for ten maybe, and a new electric winch. I was happy to think about that while Doug Peterson was alive, just to spite him and his arrogance, in a childish way, I suppose, but now wondered how to do it without hurting Denise. I'd have to find a mechanic but it would at least give me some rent.

The concrete slipway could be extended further out into the channel to increase access time around the tides but it was going to be a major piece of work. What Mr Gerald Hughes would think of that one, I wasn't sure. The conditions of the inheritance didn't actually say how much of the yard was to be maintained for classic boat restoration only.

My mind had run wild during the rare, optimistic moments for the future, usually encouraged by Jason and fuelled by several glasses of wine. The snack-bar could become famous for local, free-range produce and would include a gourmet fish-bar with 'catch of the day,' if there was one, fresh lobster and smoked salmon and mussels from the smoke-house.

I dreamed and schemed. The pump hummed gently in the quiet.

"Yeah. Get real, girl," I said to myself. Neifion agreed. I needed to write the plan ready for Mr Hughes on Friday and hoped he would approve the release of some more cash so I could at least eat for a while. I googled 'cold-smoking', and realised I knew nothing about smoking fish, nothing about jet-skis and nothing about stealing someone's business. I also knew nothing about how to fix my own state of mind, one minute up and the next minute down. I put my Marigolds on and cleaned the toilet. That I could do, at least.

CHAPTER 4

"Do you want to put that in the water yet?" I asked Jason the following morning.

He was on the phone. "I'll do it later," he said, and turned away from me.

"I have to go out soon."

"I can manage," he said. "You go. Don't want you watching me, neither. I'd rather do it on my own. I can keep an eye on the yard at the same time."

"Mind you do, then," I said. "Stay close to the slipway where it's shallow while you practice, then when you fall in at least you can wade back. There's a life-jacket under the counter. I wouldn't want to be in your shoes if Will Roberts catches you on the water without one."

He waved two fingers as he turned back to his work, nicely of course, with no malice intended.

I watched him, speculatively, as he continued to screw the seat down. For God's sake, he was nineteen and I had things to do, like a haircut for a start and a trip to see Helen's Nain and a check on *Tai Pilots* with a thought to selling it, if I had to. I'd only been back to the house a few times after I'd said Jason could live there for a short while and had respected his privacy, but I was curious, and now anxious to know the state of the place. I decided not to tell him I was going to see it in case he thought I was snooping. Which I was. I needed to have some facts straight before I had a chat with him.

I walked back from town after lunch, feeling good with a smart hair-cut in a swinging bob and newly-restored purple streaks which cost me all of my early birthday money, but I didn't care. My mother had asked me what I wanted, even though it was two months away.

"Streaks," I said. "Money for streaks and can I have it now, please? I'm desperate," followed by the inevitable lecture about London and salaries and proper jobs, but she'd sent the money. The lecture was a small price to pay and I needed to shed my scruffy self, particularly as the Friday appointment with my solicitor loomed closer. Even the nose-stud would come out, if it meant a favourable outcome.

"Play the game," Helen's Nain had said, before my first meeting early in the year with my elderly, and very formal solicitor. "Nose-studs and piercings don't give quite the right image, do they? It won't kill you for an hour or so."

I left Madoc Yacht Club behind, walked past the businesses and storage yards busy with jet-skis and power boats and stopped at the gates to the yard preparing for the lift-out of local boats for winter storage. It was mostly empty, apart from a few solitary yachts, their owners missing a season of fun for a variety of reasons ranging from refurbishment, illness and even death; boats long-abandoned with loose halliards, too stiff with green algae to even clack in the wind, crazed Perspex windows and the once-white hulls streaked with seagull droppings and water-marks.

I peered through the closed gates. A bright yellow digger worked to level the gravel surface while a fork-lift truck moved baulks of timber to be used as boat props. Smart, purpose-built galvanised boat-cradles for the deep-keel boats, were in stages of being erected. At least I understood a bit about yachts stored on dry land; I'd got used to the deep-keeled *Vertue* in my yard which was propped up with timbers in the traditional way, but never could find the confidence to stand under the hull in case they snapped or slipped and the boat toppled over. Hugh assured me it was unlikely and lectured me on downward forces but it made no difference. I never walked under the wooden hull in its various stages of renovation and gave it a wide berth.

Hugh had explained about the craning procedures for the lifting out of most of the yachts that spent the summer on the moorings or trots, as they were called, in the channel. Winter would likely bring more frequent gales and it was hard to believe on such a calm day as this, that large waves could roll down the channel and into the harbour. I'd only seen those conditions once during the summer when I first came here as a teenager to meet my great-uncle.

It was the day Helen and I had found Tomas's body, a full gale blowing and the harbour full of spray and heavy rain. The moored boats out in the channel had bucked and reared like badly-behaved colts, their ropes taut and snatched to their extremes as the waves rolled under their keels. I hadn't forgotten it. Craning out for the winter seemed quite a serious business and a sensible, safe option.

"Sounds like a big deal, this lifting out," I'd said.

"Well, it is," Hugh said, "with tens of thousands of pounds-worth of one's yacht swinging in the air on the end of a crane-jib. It is indeed a big deal, Miss Cassie, as you say."

The craning dates and times in October were posted on the gate, weather permitting, to coincide with high spring-tides when there was deeper water against the wall for longer. I'd never watched it, but after Hugh's explanation and a chat to Mark, the deputy Harbour Master who helped out on the day, I couldn't imagine trying to lift a yacht high in the air on the end of a crane. Got to be here to see that, I thought, and carried on along the road, up the path and down the steps to Borth-y-Gest.

At the bottom, I stopped and looked out across the beach to *Tai Pilots*. I still found it hard to believe I owned my own house, even if it was a wreck. A twinge of regret and longing for my old home in London passed through my mind, but then it had been mortgaged to the hilt. We never knew we were so badly in debt and we never really owned it. Dad kept it all secret while he lived. He didn't much care about material things, anyway.

The house felt remote from my ownership, unlike the Boat Shed of which I now knew every inch, with its cosy chairs behind the burnished counter and newly-cleaned chimney.

This was a stone and rendered, end-of-terrace, shabby and run-down, with its gable end to the estuary. It didn't feel like my home at all. I hadn't even said hello to it properly, just handed it over to Jason who had no doubt put his mark on it in the few weeks he'd lived there. But then I'd trusted his housekeeping after the glowing reports from Will Roberts. He'd have kept it neat and tidy.

There were decisions to be made. Should I move into it and abandon my caravan before the winter came and turn him out? I could no more live with a nineteen-year- old and his habits than fly to the moon. Neither could I see him living in a flat in Porthmadog or Pwllheli, where he had friends, but would be prey to all the dealers again. I ran down the steps and along the promenade to the car-park, knowing that snooping was an action not to be admired and wondered if I should have told him. But then, snooping comes naturally to those with journalistic leanings. I couldn't help myself and anyway, it was my house.

They say eavesdroppers never hear anything good about themselves, and I wouldn't have stopped normally, but as I crossed the grass verge at the end of the sea-wall to walk through the car-park, I passed close behind a bench where two white-haired ladies were deep in conversation. One turned and pointed towards the houses and I distinctly heard '*Tai Pilots*,' followed by 'disgrace' interspersed in the flow of Welsh; odd English words are not uncommon in a stream of Welsh dialogue.

I moved closer to the bench, stopped dead and turned away from them so they couldn't see my face but they spoke in Welsh. I couldn't understand any more. The word 'disgrace' was enough and I walked slowly through the hubbub of cars as they negotiated parking spaces and tried to mingle with the visitors. Some chance, if they turned to see me, of being anonymous with my hair newly-streaked and of course, being locals, they would know who I was. Borth-y-Gest was a small village after all and very little escaped notice. I ran up the path at the far end of the car-park, onto the road past the rest of the terrace and along to the house.

Slate steps led up from the road to the front door, the joints between the steps sprouted weeds and a few drooping, wild flower-heads. The door was half-glazed with a cracked pane; the once-white paint on the wooden lower part peeled off in places to show the wood underneath. The key jammed in the lock when I tried to turn it and the door was hard to push open against the tiled floor inside.

Jason had inhabited the front room. Net curtains, yellow with age, hung limply down over grimy windows. A mattress, dragged from one of the old beds, lay on the floor in front of a boarded-up fireplace, the surround and hearth hideous in beige, ceramic tiles. Sleeping bags zipped together were piled in a messy heap. On top, lay a grubby T-shirt and a pair of shorts partly hidden by one of the old rugs I'd given him from the Boat Shed.

I felt uncomfortable, even with one cursory look round; I had invaded his space, even though I owned it. The kitchen was as ancient as I remembered, the stained enamel sink and wooden draining board piled high with dirty bowls and mugs. An old saucepan with crusted food stood on the top of the cooker hob, its solid plates a testimony to its age. A box of empty cider bottles and beer cans filled a corner and take-away cartons overflowed from the rubbish bin. He'd been entertaining and whatever had happened, it was obvious either that he couldn't cope, or couldn't be bothered to clear up. I was cross before I'd even started. I didn't dare look at the bathroom, such as I remembered it, with its stained enamel bath and corroded taps. The toilet didn't bear thinking about.

To try and envisage the place as it could be, to impose some order, some idea for modernising it, was beyond me at that moment. My great-uncle had abandoned the house before he died, locals said, and slept and ate in the Boat Shed, 'keeping an eye on things' he told people. I was not surprised. Even cleaned and without Jason's disgusting mess, the house was old and cheerless, the battered old armchair and wood-stove behind the counter in the Boat Shed cosier than this. The state of the place just reinforced my suspicions about his ability to cope on his own and why he looked so tired and ill recently. I guessed that his dubious friendships with his mates had continued and that they had followed him here. Please God, it wasn't drugs again. I'd kill him.

Then I spotted the tin, empty and washed, lurking in the corner of the window-sill behind the curtain. Curiosity made me turn it around, only to be faced with the head of a happy pooch with lolling tongue. I didn't like dogs. Jason knew I didn't like dogs, legacy of a childhood confrontation, I'd told him, with a terrier's teeth. He would know I wouldn't want dogs in the house. He also knew I wouldn't have wanted other people in the house, unless they included a serious girlfriend and he would surely have brought her to meet me? I went back into the front room.

With another glance at the pile of clothes on the mattress, I buried my guilty feelings for prying and picked up the top T-shirt. A pale pink cardigan with pearly buttons lay underneath.

The front door buckled when I slammed it shut it, the lock stuck and the plywood shed flakes of paint on the steps as I pulled it tight behind me. I marched along the road above the car-park towards the bus-shelter, furious at the state of the place and concerned about his welfare at the same time. Of course, he'd have girlfriends...but a dog as well? And to keep it all secret from me?

Insulted and out of breath, I reached the bus-shelter on the way to see Helen's Nain as promised, the Bed and Breakfast house always welcoming. She would advise on how best to handle this. Then I walked straight into the path of the two, white-headed ladies I'd heard talking on the bench. I hurried past, but a voice stopped me.

"Excuse me."

I had to turn. There was no one else near me and I put on my best inquiring face.

"Are you the lady who owns *Tai Pilots*?"

I nodded.

She turned to her friend and back to me. "I told you it was, Gwen. Joan Parry said she knew you. Your John Jones's great-niece, aren't you?"

I nodded.

"Well, we don't like to tell tales but being as we've bumped into you by chance, we think you ought to know about the goings-on at *Tai Pilots*, being as you own it, you see. We've let Joan know already, as we thought you'd be worried."

I didn't want to hear this.

We sat on the seat in the bus-shelter after polite introductions. Gwen had a mild, rosy face and white curls and Gwennan, very different, had short, white hair in a stern, mannish haircut. She had a sharp nose and glasses with blue frames. They were close friends and long-time residents in Borth-y-Gest, they told me.

"Jason works for me," I said. "What exactly are these goings-on?"

I explained about Jason as a temporary lodger, how I hoped to rescue Mr Jones's business and was waiting to begin work on the house. They listened intently and the white heads bobbed frequently in approval.

"Yes," Gwen said. "We understand now. It's just that..." she faltered. "Shall I tell her Gwennan? I'm not comfortable with this."

"Just tell her. You have to. She can do what she wants after that," Gwennan said, her tone as sharp as her nose.

I sat like a stone and waited. God bless Milly and her mantra. Listen and wait, girl.

"People have been in and out of the house most evenings in the holidays, and during the day sometimes, coming in cars when the young man's gone to work. But what has concerned us, is about a young girl, on her own, just the last two days. All the others have gone now, back to school or college or work. We thought it was a bit strange she hadn't gone as well. Then yesterday, a man in a dirty car, one of those things that farmers drive..."

"A Land Rover," Gwennan said.

"Yes, that's it, Land Rover. Anyway, he was asking people, visitors mostly and then us, if we'd seen a young girl around, as he was supposed pick his daughter up from the car-park."

"What did you tell him?"

They looked at each other.

"We decided not to say anything," Gwen said. "Something wasn't right. He was very angry. He had a red face and filthy boots. Cow or sheep-muck, even on his trousers. He got out of the car, didn't he, Gwennan? You saw it."

The bus-shelter was quiet for a moment, the outside buzz of cars and voices and other people's lives on the periphery of the conversation.

Gwen cleared her throat. Gwennan sniffed and turned her head away.

"We spend a lot of time down here," Gwen said, almost apologetically. "Just people-watching and listening to snatches of chatter."

"We're not being nosy," said Gwennan, in defence. "But we do notice things out of the ordinary."

"And this man?" I asked. "What about him?"

They looked at each other again and shook their heads.

"That's why we're telling you," Gwen said. "It didn't feel safe."

"Safe?"

"He was angry and... she's very young. How were we to know he was her father, anyway? He could be anybody."

"How young?" I felt sick.

"Thirteen? Fourteen? Ought to be in school, anyway. Schools have started the new term, haven't they? She was definitely school-age."

"Young," Gwennan said. "Stick-thin. But you can't tell these days, can you? All that make-up they wear. And short skirts. And those tops that show their… well… stomachs. Not that we got that close. Did you see the make-up, Gwen?"

Gwen shook her head. "Oh, and there's a dog," she added. "A tiny dog, maybe a puppy. I saw her walk it up near the pillbox this morning. I couldn't see any make-up. She was too far away. Still looked very young, though. Under-developed, if you know what I mean."

I swear she blushed. "It didn't seem right, somehow," she said.

"Why didn't you phone the police if you were worried?" I asked.

"Well, the man said he was her father. If she was a missing person, we'd all know about it wouldn't we, from the news? It isn't our place to interfere with family matters, you know."

Really? I ran out of words to describe how I felt just then, except just plain sick. I said my polite thanks and that I would deal with it and would be grateful if they did not repeat it to anyone else until I found out what was going on.

"We won't," Gwen said, "but she will have been seen by others. People will wonder. It's the age, you see. She seemed like a child. And in the house with that young man, too, not to mention all the comings and goings. They weren't all youngsters like her."

"Yes, I understand your concern," I said. "I'll find out what's going on and thank you."

"I have to say, Miss Jones," said Gwennan, pursing her lips, "it's a disgrace to the village's reputation if things like that are allowed to go on."

Things like what? I arrived at Helen's Nain's. I was furious.

"They got to you first, I see," she said. "I was going to tell you the full story this afternoon. I did warn you. People are beginning to gossip. And that farmer man who said he was her father, left mud from his tyres all over the car-park. Gwen said he was very angry. There's been no news of a missing child or one of us would have informed the police. We haven't seen her today at all. Maybe she's just gone home."

We sat at the kitchen table, the inevitable brownies cooling on a rack. They were loaded with chocolate chips and oozed with best Welsh butter but I couldn't even face one at that moment. She poured tea. My anger was reinforced by the humiliation I felt, from the secrets kept from me, my own misplaced trust in Jason's behaviour and how it might reflect not only on me, but on Helen's Nain as a friend and someone I visited regularly. She knew what I was thinking.

"You don't have to worry about me," she said. "I've been around long enough to weather most things. It'll blow over as long as there's nothing to complain about. Nothing the village likes better than a bit of gossip."

I stared at her. She'd missed the point, the worst bit. I didn't want to have to point it out.

"I know Jason had a bad time with his brothers and the drugs thing," I said, "and then his mother leaving but I never thought he'd walk straight back into bad company. And as for having his mates in the house...it was a mess but Will Roberts couldn't fault him for his care looking after his wife. Even working in the yard, he's tidy and he's so capable."

"Well, you'll have to confront him with it and find out why he's changed," she said, pushing a brownie towards me on a plate. I couldn't resist it. "If it's only dirty dishcs, well, he's nineteen after all and a young man wants to spend time with his mates. He's not a saint, Cassie."

I shook my head and pushed the plate away, throat closed with the enormity of what she'd missed. I looked up at her kindly face, the sharp eyes that never missed a trick. But she'd missed this one.

"That girl," I said, picking at crumbs on the cloth, not wanting to meet her eye. "Your friends said she looked about thirteen, maybe fourteen." I looked up. "She's a child, Helen's Nain, and she's been staying with Jason. In my house. Under-age."

She looked at me blankly, then her eyes grew bigger as realisation dawned. She put her hand to her mouth.

"Duw Mawr," she said, and then whispered, "he wouldn't... he couldn't..."

"I don't know, let's hope it's nothing but I have to go and find out. I'll call you. Please don't talk to anyone about this."

I ran all the way to the Boat Shed. The gates were open and the door to the Boat Shed was pulled to, but there was no sign of Jason. The lifejacket I'd told him about was still in its packet under the counter. I ran to the edge of the yard and looked over the channel. The ebb-tide had picked up speed with a strong, visible current now and the sandbanks were beginning to dry out in the estuary.

The red dinghy I'd said he could borrow, lay pulled up by the pile of stones that remained from the derelict crane-driver's house on the island. A mooring rope was tied to one of the piles and the oars lay across the thwart. I called, but my voice drifted away with the tide and there was no sign of him. I phoned. The message I left wasn't polite and demanded his immediate return, or else. Or else what, I wasn't sure. I considered taking the skiff over to find him, but I didn't see why I should go to all that effort. He wasn't going anywhere. He would have to pull the heavy dinghy down to the water and wade through some mud to get back to the slip and I couldn't see him returning in the pitch dark. He'd have to wait for a flood-tide in the morning.

I decided he couldn't come to much harm over there. I was so angry with him I didn't care at that moment, if he drowned or broke his neck. He wouldn't have known about my forays to the house and the nauseating anxiety I felt about the young girl. There had to be a simple and perfectly acceptable answer. She'd been picked up by her father, probably and gone home. A silly girl who'd had a spat with her dad or mum. There were no reports on the news from worried parents and no-one had seen her that day. I tried to convince myself there was nothing to worry about, shut the gates for the night, poured an early glass of wine and sat on the edge of the harbour wall. And waited.

It was eight o'clock and nearly dark when I gave up watching. He wasn't coming back tonight. He said he remembered that I'd slept over there once. Of course, I thought, charitably, that's what he's doing before the weather turned and the nights were too cold.

"Right," I said, out-loud in the darkness. "You can look after yourself for the night. I hope it's cold and rains. Serves you bloody well right."

I was still angry with him, but it could wait until tomorrow. They say anger is a dish best served cold, so I walked back to the caravan and locked the door, heated my dinner in the oven and hoped he was hungry over there, communing with nature.

It was mid-morning when I heard the sound of a boat being dragged over pebbles. I stood in the caravan door and waited. He rowed over to the slip, climbed out of the dinghy, walked up to retrieve the launching trolley and attached the end to the electric winch. After the best part of a bottle of wine and a minor hangover, I wasn't in the mood to help him, or greet him with pleasantries, but I knew how I was going to handle it.

"I need to talk to you," I said. He followed me into the caravan.

I looked him straight in the eyes. "You're stoned."

"Yeah, sorry. I told you I wanted to go over there and see what it was like and yeah, I had a bit of blow and fell asleep. Then I woke up and couldn't get back until this morning. It was cold all night. Nothing wrong with that, is there?"

"Except you left the yard and shed open and you didn't answer the phone. Did it occur to you I might have been worried? The last thing you said was you'd keep an eye on the yard and wouldn't go far. How irresponsible is that? And you don't do drugs, remember? Or doesn't blow count?"

"No big deal. Not as bad as that bottle of wine you've consumed all by yourself." He glanced at the empty bottle by the sink. "Nobody comes here to buy stuff, anyway, so I can't see it matters. You're not my nursemaid, Cassie."

"And the other thing," I said, deciding to play it down a bit, "before you go getting all bolshy and defensive, there's been some talk about loads of people your age going in and out of the house, not to mention a dog and a new girlfriend staying there. You know how I feel about dogs and I don't know these friends of yours using the house. They could be anybody, like friends of the drugs-gang who now know where you live."

"I can have friends around, can't I?"

"Not when it raises eyebrows and causes gossip; drinking, leaving rubbish on the beach loud music and people in and out all the time. There are holiday cottages all around as well as residents and the holiday cottage firms won't be too happy if you upset their clients."

He was quiet for minute, picking at his nails, the eczema on the back of his hands more marked than I'd seen since I'd first met him.

"They won't be coming back," he said, "I told them I was moving out and the owner was moving in."

I poured tea. Not for him, I decided, but relented over his sorry state and gave him a large mug with two sugars. He looked dreadful.

"Hungry?"

He nodded and I put toast on the table. He was starving.

"New girlfriend, then?" I asked, quite casually, between mouthfuls.

"Who says?"

"Helen's Nain thought she saw you with a girl and a dog, a puppy. That's nice."

"Just a friend of friends. She's gone back to school. Only met her twice, when she hung out with the others during the holidays. She's just a kid. She won't be back."

"That's okay, then," I said, as casually as I could. "You can do without under-age girls having a crush on you. Nothing but trouble, teenage girls being what they are sometimes. Hopefully I can start work on the house if Mr Hughes releases some money. I need to talk to you about the smoke-house and the snack-bar. I've got some ideas."

"You're going to start on the cottage?" he said. "But where will I live?"

"We'll work something out," I said. "Eat your toast."

I wanted to believe him about the girl, that nothing had happened between them and gently reproved him for even innocently befriending her. I wanted to give him the benefit of the doubt but I'd given my warning shot and hoped that would be enough. I had to believe him. It would be too dreadful not to. I decided to let it lie. For now. He'd tidy up the house if I was to start work and plan to move in. Eventually.

"You can stay and do some work on the house," I said. "I'll survive a bit longer in the caravan, but no more gangs of friends, Jason, or young girls taking a shine to you, just friends or not. They should all be back in school or college or work, anyway. Got it?"

He nodded and pushed crumbs around on his plate. I desperately wanted to believe him about the girl. It was too awful not to.

"You'd better go and get some sleep," I said. "Come back into work tomorrow when you feel better."

I watched him scuff his way out of the yard, head down and shoulders stooped, surprised at all that sympathy I hadn't meant to dish out, but I couldn't help it. I never could; he was one of those stray lambs that tugged at your heartstrings, even when you're cross with them. I cleared up the breakfast dishes and tidied the caravan, the tiny space I called home and planned the day's work in my head. I wandered back over to the harbour wall and checked *Annie's* mooring ropes and the dinghy Jason had borrowed. He'd made a good job of mending the seat. I forgave him, just a bit, and headed for the Boat Shed to feed Neifion. But try as I might, I couldn't forget the pink cardigan.

CHAPTER 5

I knew he was dead as soon as I opened the door. It wasn't so much an obvious awareness of death, as the absence of life. A stillness pervaded the chandlery and settled on the newly-painted shelves and planks of mahogany and teak; a stillness above and beyond the hum of the pump in the tank and the gentle bubbles as they rose and broke on the surface of the water.

Neifion, my lobster and companion, was lying on the bottom of the tank. It was where he usually lay, but it felt different. Fronds of weed beside him waved in the current from the pump. I found a stick I'd used for stirring paint, lifted the tank lid and touched his shell, very gently. The antennae he'd greeted me with every morning did not respond. I closed the lid, gently, so as not to disturb him. How ridiculous was that?

Not so ridiculous when I considered he'd been my shed-mate for six months and seen me at my worst; in despair over my chipped nails and work-roughened hands, swearing over my ineptitude with spanners and screw-drivers, in tears from the sheer enormity of the work ahead and the anxiety about how to fulfil the terms of my inheritance. He listened, quite intently, when I needed to discuss problems with myself, like why I was being so bloody-minded to carry on at all.

Most mornings, I'd pull a battered old stool from under the counter, draw it up to the tank, throw some food in and discuss the day's work through the glass. It helped to set my mind in order, reading out the lists of chores that I could see for myself; and some I couldn't, like my great-uncle's collection of model ships, all Porthmadog-built ships used for the slate industry and spanning the whole of the nineteenth century. Hugh said it might be a treasure trove. All I could see was dust and cobwebs. The remnants of the model smashed in the summer were still on the floor.

"Those have got to be picked up carefully," Hugh said. "It could be valuable. I think it was an old model."

"Jason can do that," I said, "being as he broke it in the first place." Intricate work, I could see, and not for me to fix. I was more of a broad, brush-stroke person and hated fiddly things. Still, as my mother made a point of telling me on a regular basis, it was all my choice. Big or fiddly, it had to be done.

The lobster's death came as a shock. I knew he would die soon but it never seemed real. He was old and ugly, but he'd been a living presence in this old shed. A lump formed in my throat. I couldn't cope with this. Jason would be asleep back at *Tai Pilots* and I didn't expect to see Hugh until the next weekend. I swallowed my pride and picked up the phone.

"Are you sure he's dead?" David asked.

"Yes. I poked him with a stick. You'll have to get him out, David. I just can't. Please?"

There was a pause.

"Two thirty, then. I'm in meetings all morning. Turn the pump off."

I switched it off at the wall. The bubbles dissipated and the hum ceased. It was deathly quiet. I didn't like it, sat down on the stool and stared at the dead creature, sad and uneasy, not so much at the death of an old lobster and how to deal with it, but the end of one of the conditions of my inheritance. How would it affect me? I'd never asked and nobody had said. Just look after it, I was told. And I had, to the best of my ability. What would happen now? I missed his presence already, shook myself out of it and pondered what to do with him.

My great-uncle had retrieved him from a lobster-pot out on Sarn Badrig, the reef running eleven miles out from the land into the middle of Tremadog Bay. He was an old lobster, even then, and had lost one claw and for whatever reason, my great-uncle decided to keep it as a pet. Perhaps it was too old and too tough to eat. He gave it a name and 'it' became 'him; Neifion, the Welsh name for Neptune. Remembering the miserable old man I'd met as a teenager, his care for the creature had surprised me. The compassion he'd shown for the lobster and his reasons for his gift to me I would never understand. I wished I'd known him better and under different circumstances, but it was all in the past now. I owed it to him, and the lobster, two old crippled, grouchy creatures, to do the right thing.

"You're going to do what?" asked David, when he arrived after lunch, polite but not over-friendly.

"Bury him on the reef," I said. "That's where he came from. I'll do it tomorrow morning. The tides are right. And the weather looks settled. If you could just lay him in that piece of sail cloth, please, and fold it over, so I won't have to look at him. I'll stitch it up and put some stones in to weigh him down and then he can have a proper sea-burial."

"That's ridiculous, Cassie. He's only a lobster. I suppose you'll say a prayer as well."

"Of course," I said. "I looked up the correct words."

"But you've only been out to the Fairway Buoy once on the boat and the reef is further out. Can't you find someone to go with you, if you must go?"

"I'll be fine. Will Roberts told me he's going to be out to check on the buoys. I know what I'm doing. Really. And I am going to do it. Anyway, I need the experience, before the winter sets in and I lose my confidence and forget everything about tides and stuff. And I want to bury him properly."

He shook his head, lifted the lid of the tank, reached down and picked Neifion up carefully with both hands. I looked briefly, then turned away while he folded the canvas over into a neat parcel.

"Sometimes I think you're completely mad," he said.

"No, I'm not, and do you always have to bc so unkind? You never have a good word to say about any of my ideas. They're just creative, that's all."

"Well, I think it's too early for you to go gadding about out in the bay on your own. You know nothing about engines if it all goes wrong."

I stopped and thought for a moment, a moment of revelation. Why did he always make me angry? He was such fucking pessimist. Then, it occurred to me, it wasn't what I did, it was because it was me that did it.

"Oh, I get it," I said. "If I was a bloke, you wouldn't dare have said that, would you? It's because I'm a girl, isn't it? Girls in your family's world shouldn't do stuff like this, that's what you think. They stay home and cook and wash their husband's hankies in the old traditional way, don't they? Women in their proper place in the home? I'm perfectly capable of learning, just like any bloke, so what's the problem?"

His face tightened. I'd screwed up, opened my big mouth. He'd told me once, after I'd mopped up my tears with his own hanky he'd lent me, that his mother washed and ironed his father's linen handkerchiefs, folded to precision with the top corner peeping out of his suit-jacket pocket, a clean one for each day. I'd formed an opinion of his family life and slighted his mum. It was too late now.

"Sorry," I said. "I'm just upset," and too busy trying to justify my actions and prove myself, I thought. He just stared at me and by-passed the issue. Wisely.

"The problem is, Cassie, you haven't done enough sea-time to know how things go wrong. There's a saying; if it can go wrong, it will, and when you're at sea, things that go wrong get compounded pretty quickly. That's all."

He was too stuffy for words. I still thought the sea-burial for Neifion was a brilliant idea.

"Yes, I know, I'll be careful and Mr Roberts will keep an eye on me, he said. Anyway, do you always have to be so deprecating?"

"And do you always have to be so spiky? You should be glad someone cares about your welfare."

I didn't know what to say to that.

"You'll need to empty this water out. It'll stink. What do you want me to do with him now?" he asked, putting the lid back on the tank.

"Could you put him in the freezer, please?" I said, as though nothing had happened.

He left, tight-lipped, without saying a word.

The following morning while I waited for the tide, I kept myself busy with lists, cleaned and polished the counter in the Boat Shed until the fading flowers in the paint-tin reflected in the surface and wiped new spider-webs from the window. I needed to take my mind off the nervousness that accompanied my plans to bury Neifion. It was one thing to take a boat out to sea with Will Roberts on board in one of his tutoring sessions, but another to do it on my own. Of course, I could have backed out, but foolish pride had its way and Will Roberts would be out there anyway. I still had so much to prove, to myself as well as to all the locals who thought I wouldn't survive the year.

I wandered over to the wall and checked on the progress of the tide. No change there yet and still slack, low-water but there was a noticeable feel to the air; a cool, early morning edge to the tang of salt-marsh and the drying sands that stretched over to the Harlech side of the estuary. The sky was blue and cloudless, the promise of a warm day later, the only hint of autumn evident in the tired, muted green of the trees on the other side of the channel.

The trees on Ballast Island, with their flattened tops and stunted growth, had been shaped by the south-westerly gales which blasted them cruelly, especially in the autumn, so I was told, when the old apple trees and hawthorns gave up their dull leaves and bitter fruit to the sea, and bared their skeletons to the winter. I'd seen the trees last winter, black branches against grey skies and found it hard to imagine them in their summer dress with wild flowers at their feet and their branches full of the sound of nesting birds.

But I'd lived through the spring and the summer here and watched the island turn its face to the inevitable seasons with equanimity. It was time for it to show its autumn colours now and complete the cycle, my first experience of this change from bright, hot days to the dreariness and wildness of winter. The remnants of the old quay on Ballast stood proud in the early sunlight, black, wooden piles like sentinels rising up through the rocky foreshore, worn and jagged tops against the skyline, the wood as strong and dense in places as when first built. It looked as though it had always been there, a natural island at the entrance to the harbour but Helen's Nain had lent me the books she kept for guests and I knew that Ballast Island had not always been there.

It had been formed from stones brought back as ballast in the empty holds of the returning ships, their cargoes of roofing slates delivered all over the world and their holds re-loaded with goods for other distant countries before finally returning home 'in ballast'. Over the years, the stones, dumped on return, began to formed an island. Seeds from birds and the wind, even perhaps from the crane-driver's garden, if he'd had one, had grown from the stony ground into a scramble of vegetation;

apple trees and blackberry bushes, hawthorn, sloe, nettles and rosebay willowherb grew undisturbed, the only sounds the rustling of rabbits, the hooting of owls at night and the heron's cry. I'd slept out there once under the stars. It was magical.

I sat down on the harbour wall in my usual place, cup of coffee in hand. *Annie* lay below me with her blue cabin roof splattered with overnight seagull droppings and most of her keel in the mud. A shoal of mullet flashed silver in a pool of shallow water behind her stern, the outboard engine raised up and its propeller out of the water garnished with a string of seaweed. I reminded myself to clear that away.

It was just after low-water now and the current was sluggish and barely perceptible. I watched it as it began to creep up over the sand and the mud below me. It was on the rise.

I'd had to learn about the tides here from Will Roberts, in one of his most serious lectures. "This is not the Mediterranean, Miss Jones. You can't run a boatyard in this country without knowing your tides. This is an island with some of the most difficult and demanding waters anywhere. Take note."

The estuary and the beach at Black Rock often caught visitors out at low-water, as they wandered over the sandbanks in search of the sea. But it was at low-water when the tide seemed to stand still, sometimes for two hours longer than the book said, then rush in like a silver blanket to cover the banks in the flash of an eye. In the summer, the life-boat was often busy rescuing visitors.

Those who had paddled through the shallow water in the North Channel and out onto the North Bank to hunt for the fast-disappearing sea, were sometimes caught out on their return, not realising that the tide had sneaked in behind them. The fast-flowing current was sometimes too strong and deepened too quickly to wade through or swim safely. I'd been down there once when two kids had ridden their bikes over the shallow channel, turned to come back and found themselves stranded, panic-stricken and screaming as the water rose in front of them and cut them off. A couple of burly swimmers rescued them and their bikes and left them, lectured and contrite on the dry sand.

The tide crept slowly up the ladder rungs below me but not enough water yet for *Annie* to float. I thought briefly about my mother and what she would say if she knew what I was about to do, my anxieties about going out to sea on my own shifting to a more stable platform. It seemed everyone relished telling me I was too young and too inexperienced and I seemed to spend my time trying to prove I wasn't. Ed had been one of those. I wondered if he would return next summer and how he would advise me then if the business was flourishing and I had no need for journalistic tutorials.

When I went for my first interview at the newspaper, he had reservations about my capabilities and quizzed me about my age. As for being young, I explained, it wasn't my fault I got bored at school and was fast-tracked all the way through G.C.S.E.'s, 'A' levels and took my degree early.

"You're still very young," Ed had said. "Most applicants have an older head for this job."

"I've got one of those," I said. How arrogant was that? He employed me, anyway.

But today, going out to sea on my own, I was out of my depth and any confidence I thought I had, was shaky. Perhaps David was right. But I wasn't going to let him, or anyone else know. I pulled myself together.

I drank my coffee as the tide rose steadily up the ladder-rungs. I'd marked one with a piece of orange twine and knew that the water needed to creep up to it before *Annie* would float. It had an hour to go yet.

And I had jobs to do. I twisted around, swung my legs onto the top of the wall and stood up to survey my domain as the gates swung open, held by Jason. The Harbour Master drove through in his pick-up and parked by my side. The burly figure of Will Roberts leaned over the passenger seat.

"Good morning, Miss Jones. Are you still going out?" he asked, terse as ever. I nodded.

"I think so," I said, "if I don't get cold feet."

"As long as you don't get wet feet," he said, with not a glimmer of a smile. "I'll be out, as I said, checking the buoys this morning, so I suggest you go no further than the Fairway Buoy and see how you feel. You can always bury your lobster just there, you know. He won't mind. You'll remember your Rule of Twelfths, of course, for crossing the bar at the right time and also when you put your anchor down at the reef, if you decide to go that far."

"Of course," I said.

"Even with an echo-sounder, it's an old boat, remember, and it pays to be prepared, just in case you drop your phone in the water. I notice that young people use it for everything, tide data included. You have a water-proof case for it, I presume? And your tide-table to do your calculations? Nothing wrong with a bit of paperwork. It's good practice, even if you don't use it. You have enough time."

"Yes," I said. I nearly added, 'for the lecture' but thought better of it. "Thank you," and reached for the phone. Didn't know that rule.

He drove forward, turned the pickup round and came back.

"And Miss Jones, do keep the music down and leave your marine radio on, so you can hear it this time. I'd rather not watch you go astray out of the channel again."

I'd only done it once. He'd had to call me up on the radio to tell me, but I hadn't heard him and only just realised I was heading for the beach at Harlech in shallow water. I'd got away with it that time. He drove off.

There was no sign of Jason. I had two hours to kill and needed to check my list. The door to the Boat Shed was open and the smell of coffee and toast reminded me to eat and take provisions with me. Just in case.

"He's dead then?"

Jason emerged from the chair on the other side of my immaculate counter, mug in one hand and toast in the other. He still looked tired and strained, with even darker shadows under his eyes. Something wasn't right. At weekends, when he first came back from the hills, I knew he went off with his mates to do the rounds of the pubs, avoiding certain places, he reassured me, where he might bump into characters with grudges and long memories. Now with the concerns about *Tai Pilots*, I worried even more. I wished he was back with Will Roberts on the small-holding, tending sheep and collecting eggs, a safe-haven but not a life for a young lad. He needed excitement and people of his own age. I just wished he had a more sensible head on his shoulders.

"I'll empty the tank if you want. It'll stink otherwise. When you come back, can we have a talk?" he asked. "This afternoon, like?"

"Of course," I said. "Problem?"

He shuffled from foot to foot and wouldn't meet my eye.

"Should I come with you, what with you being on your own out there?"

"No, but thanks for the offer. I know how much you like being at sea. Not. Time you learned to swim. I need you here to mind the shop. Did you get some sleep? No more young ladies visiting, I hope?"

"I'll do the tank," he said and turned to wash his cup.

I took Neifion out of the freezer, the canvas parcelled up with string. I'd put a stitch through the edges, just in case, put him in the cool box and picked up the paper with the burial words I'd found on the Internet.

"You're not going to say prayers, Cassie," Jason said, shaking his head. "For God's sake, that's ridiculous. It's hypocritical. You're not even religious." He'd seen the paper on the counter.

"I am," I said, "going to say prayers, I mean, and you said 'for God's sake,' just now. Are you religious then? It might sound a bit theatrical to you, but it's a ritual, see. No worse than singing carols at Christmas. Bet you've done that, before."

"Yeah, maybe, but only when I was a kid. It doesn't mean nothing." I picked up the cool box and waved the paper under his nose.

"It's 'anything,' not 'nothing.' Can't do any harm. Give him a chance to go to lobster heaven. It's called hedging your bets. They say even hardened atheists pray to God when they think they're going to die, especially at sea. See you later," I said, "and don't you dare leave the yard unattended again. I'll be back about two-thirty."

I still had a while to wait and decided to do the calculations for the depth of water over the bar, not because I thought I needed to, but because if something went wrong and I went aground, I would never live it down with the Harbour Master after his advice. I googled the principles and did the maths on a scrap of paper, sitting in the cockpit with my back against the cabin bulkhead. I worked out the range of tide between high and low water, divided it into twelfths, as the screen said, and told the seagull sitting on the bollard above me what I thought was right; for the first hour of the tide, the depth would be one twelfth, the second hour, two twelfths, the third and fourth hours, three twelfths, the fifth hour, two twelfths and the last hour, the remaining one twelfth, taking local differences into consideration, of course, just to complicate matters.

"I got it," I said, finally to the gull. "More or less. Bet great-uncle John never did this, but then he knew this estuary like the back of his hand."

I knew enough already to judge when there was enough water under the keel to float *Annie*, and by the time I reached the bar, I should have at least two feet underneath me on the incoming tide. This should give me plenty of time to return from the reef before the falling tide got into its stride. There was a high spring-tide today and the ebb could kick up a sea over the shallow sand-bar for the middle two hours of the ebb. I planned it carefully, knowing perfectly well that I would be watched and my movements scrutinised from the harbour launch.

If I could get to the No 2 buoy two hours before high water, I worked out, and then motor for thirty minutes flat out to the reef, I would be back again just in time for the current to be slack for the last hour of flood or the first hour of ebb, if necessary and still arrive home when I said I would be, Neifion buried as planned. My plan also included the favourable comments from Mark that would fly around the pub. I knew he wouldn't gossip if it all went wrong but hoped he would sing my praises if I got it right, and was unashamedly anticipating the up-grading of my self-esteem and not the slightest bit bothered by it, if I was being honest.

The keel separated from the mud underneath with a gentle lurch. *Annie* rocked gently on the water and I remembered to scrape off the tangle of seaweed from the prop. I put Jason and his request for a serious talk out of my mind, slipped into the cabin and turned the power on. The battery lights glowed comfortingly. The engine lowered obediently and I checked the rush of cooling water as it spurted out underneath the casing, slipped the mooring ropes off the cleats and pushed *Annie* off the pontoon trying to look cool, calm and collected as I re-entered the cabin, took the wheel and steered into the channel. The harbour launch followed behind me. I concentrated and tried not to make a mistake as I approached the first harbour buoy and passed it within an inch.

I motored slowly past Borth-y-Gest, keeping well within the speed limit, which suited me fine and glanced up at the pill-box on the cliff with the church behind it. Although three years had passed, it was impossible to forget the memory of Angela, battered by the wind and rain as she screamed for her missing son in the terrible gale that night. A flicker of concern about Jason returned but I shook it off and negotiated my way past Danger Rock and Samson's Bay and then further out into the channel. Behind, the harbour launch followed my track unhurriedly from buoy to buoy and stopped at each buoy as Will Roberts leaned over the side. He had work to do.

I looked ahead. The estuary was clear of boats, the surface of the sea flat with a long stretch to the next buoy, bright red against the grey water and I pushed the throttle forward, further than I'd ever done before on my own. The boat surged ahead, leaving a white, wide wake behind and the bows began to lift above the surface. I pushed the throttle further, the boat sped faster and faster, my stomach in my throat with sheer exhilaration as I turned the wheel and rounded the red buoy so fast, I'd never have believed I'd have the nerve to do.

The conditions were perfect and I could see every buoy ahead clearly, bright red and green on the water. I followed the channel up the estuary to the open sea with still no other boat in sight. The No 4 buoy marking the sand-bar reminded me to slow down as I began to cross it, my mouth dry and palms sticky on the wheel.

The surface of the water on the bar was smooth but any doubts that the tide was flooding in fast were quashed by eddies and ripples that gathered around the buoy ahead. I remembered to glance back and take a fix on the buoy behind me, to keep my track in the rushing tide and stay in the channel.

"Leeway," Will Roberts had said, "don't forget your leeway. The tide will push you out of the channel without you noticing. Keep an eye on the buoy behind you at all times. Look behind, look in front, check the depth."

A list of things to remember, drummed into me by the Harbour Master who was no doubt still watching from a distance as he went about his business. I held my breath and then I was out and over the bar, into deep water. I turned to port at the No 2 buoy and headed for the reef. I laughed aloud, shouted to the sky, wound the engine up again and skimmed across the sea towards the reef at 30 knots, the wake like a broad, white ribbon behind me.

The black flags of lobster pots near the reef ahead brought me to my senses and I gave them a wide berth, left them to port, slowed and stopped where I could see the rocky bottom and turned off the engine. The boat lay completely still.

The water was so clear I could see the stones and pebbles that made up the reef. I crouched on the deck, lowered the anchor carefully over the bow-roller and fed the calculated length of chain out until it rested beneath the bows. The anchor lay to its own weight, the chain in a straight line down through the water. *Annie's* blue paint was mirrored in perfect detail, even down to its scratches and gouges; a surreal double image. Which was real and which was not? Could I dive into the image and surface to a parallel reality? My dad would have approved of that idea but then blast me with facts and figures to disprove any silly fantasies.

The thought was fleeting as a crab scuttled over the seafloor and reminded me why I was here at all, wondering about the piece of paper I'd down-loaded off the Internet with prayers and poems and I knew then I was being ridiculous. The phrase about 'committing his body to the deep', stuck in my mind from somewhere and had nothing to do with some of the nauseating poems I'd come across. The final act of casting the body into the water with a splash, sinking down for the fishes to feast on seemed to be enough. I wondered how long it would take the canvas to rot, but at least it was eco-friendly.

So that's what I did. I placed him in a bucket and lowered it by a long rope over the side until the bucket tipped sideways and he slipped out and sank, quite slowly, down and out of sight into the darker depths in the shade of the hull. I pulled the bucket back.

"Goodbye," I said, "and thanks."

The sun was hot on my back and I sat for a while in the cockpit, pondering briefly on the burial. It was done and it felt right. I remembered what Hugh had said about following instincts and doing the right thing. Not for the first time, I'd nearly embarrassed myself with fanciful notions about rituals and the stuff of stories. Then I put the kettle on the old gas-ring and waited until it whistled; a bizarre, homely sound out there on the sea in that vast space. I made some coffee and opened a packet of biscuits.

Sometimes it felt that my mind was in constant battle with itself; the factual side of journalism fighting the fantasy of story-land and I took the coffee back into the cockpit and sat with my back against the cabin bulkhead and my feet on the seat and disappeared into an unreal world, lulled by the calm expanse of solitude that surrounded me, sitting in 'a painted ship upon a painted ocean'. Coleridge knew what he was talking about but there wasn't an albatross in sight.

That feeling of surrealism wasn't something I'd ever felt on land, a sense of being suspended in an existential world where time and space merged into one and nothing really mattered except me. My dad would have understood that. I checked my watch and was comfortably ahead of schedule. There was no rush to leave for half an hour and I closed my eyes. I would be back over the bar before the tide turned.

The phone trilled and wrecked my peace. Jason.

"What," I said, irritated.

"Cass, you on your way back yet? There's this farmer guy came in the yard. He wanted to know if you were around. He wants to speak to you 'cos you're the owner of *Tai Pilots*. Someone in the village told him. He's going to the market with all these sheep. Says he'll call in on the way back. He was a bit scary. Angry, like. I need to talk to you, Cass. Urgently."

"I'll be back at two-thirty," I said, my whole day wrecked.

What was there to say? I'd find out soon enough, hoping to God that it wasn't the angry farmer looking for his daughter. I knew it was, deep down, I just knew it. But why was he asking now? Jason had assured me she'd gone when the others went and would be back in school by now. I knew nothing about any of it, I would say, and would stick to it.

I'd anchored in ten feet of water and laid out twenty feet of chain, the extra length coiled like a snake on the sea floor under the bows when I'd left it. I checked my watch and couldn't believe an hour had passed, just day-dreaming and drinking coffee, pleasantly relaxed, until now. I leapt forward and checked.

The chain was now taut as the tide rose and gathered pace. The water around the boat had lost its glassy surface and was now more disturbed as the current picked up. I turned the handle on the windlass and pulled in the last of the chain. The anchor lifted from the sea-bed easily, broke the surface and I lifted it up until it was snug against the bow-roller, fixed it in place and coiled the chain carefully in the well.

I stood up and turned around. That blissful moment, before the phone call only ten minutes ago, when life had seemingly no reference points, disappeared in a moment of terror as the black flag marking the nearest lobster pot I'd so carefully avoided, seemed to grow closer. The current caught the boat and it drifted, beam-on towards the first one. I ran to the cockpit, threw myself into the cabin, lowered the engine, started it up and in panic, pulled the throttle towards me; in reverse. The boat swung round, sped backwards, straight into the first pole with the flag. I pushed the throttle forward and surged ahead for a brief moment. Then the engine stopped, the pole with the pot attached lying sideways in the water.

It was too early for a controlled de-brief about what I'd done wrong. I just knew I had to free the boat and get out of here before I missed the top of the tide on the bar. I also didn't want to get caught by whoever owned the pots and looked around nervously for the sight of other boats. The sea was deserted. I tried the lift-control for the engine and hoped it might power itself loose. It whined against the pressure of the rope and I dropped it down again quickly. I swore a bit and remembered what David had said, 'When things go wrong at sea, one thing leads to another before you know it, and usually gets worse'. I sat down, thought it through carefully and tried to avoid a full-blown panic attack. I didn't want to drift again right into the forest of black flags behind me. I went onto the deck and let the anchor down with plenty of chain and kept an eye on the poles behind me until the boat settled, moored by its stern to the lobsterpot and the bows to the anchor. I had to free the line.

Will Roberts said to never leave your boat unless it is, literally, sinking under you. I didn't see that I had much choice. I'd never been keen on swimming in the sea and preferred the reek of chlorine and the safety of swimming pools with attendant lifeguards. I hated the thought of something unseen lurking below the surface. Mark said he fished for tope off the reef. He said that tope belonged to the shark family.

I pushed the image of *Jaws* to one side and rummaged for the old boarding ladder in one of the lockers. It was folded in half, courtesy of a rusty hinge and fixed with a clip, but it straightened out okay. I hooked the ends over the rail above the side-deck easily and the bottom rung reached just below the surface of the sea.

I stripped down to black bra and knickers, went back into the cabin and fetched the sharp, filleting knife in its case. I tucked it into the knicker elastic but the result was nothing like Ursula Andress emerging from the sea in *Dr No*, I thought wryly, her body scantily clad in a white bikini, knife in belt and a conch in her hand. There was no youthful James Bond either, to ogle my goose-pimpled white skin and M&S undies. 'Never leave the boat unless it's sinking under you,' sang in my head, so I tied a rope around my waist and fastened it to the cleat on the stern. Just in case.

I swung my leg over the side, felt for the rungs carefully and reached the bottom one below the surface of the water. It was icy-cold against bare, sun-warmed legs and naked belly and I looked back up the vertical ladder to the coaming and the safety of the side-deck, gauging my ability to climb back up. But it was flat calm today. I'll be able to do that, I thought, my arms strong from all the work in the yard.

I pulled myself along on the rope to the stern and the engine, held my breath, ducked beneath the water and felt for the offending rope, unravelled it from the propeller where it had wrapped itself around and cut it free. I surfaced, punched the sky in jubilation and shouted to a seagull who was sitting on the engine casing, totally unperturbed by my efforts. He watched me with one beady eye and flew off. The pole had sprung back upright. The pot on the sea-bed was now unconnected to it, but then the owner wouldn't find out until I was long gone. He'd never know.

I pulled myself back to the base of the ladder. The rungs towered above me like a cliff-face. I was cold now and could feel the energy leaching from my legs. I reached up with my right arm to the third rung, swung my leg up to stand on the first step and fell back with a splash. The bottom half of the ladder came away in my hand, the broken hinges and the top half still firmly fixed to the boat. Stunned, I trod water, held onto the bottom rung, swung my leg up through the water as high as I could but there was no way I could reach it with my foot. I grabbed the rung above with both hands but couldn't pull my body-weight up the remaining ladder and over the rail without any leverage for my feet. I thought I was strong, but it was impossible.

The jubilation in freeing the engine drowned itself in fear. At best, I'd miss the tide, at worst I'd drown, but the rope, my life-line, was still attached to my waist. I dragged myself back to the stern and felt around with my foot for the cavitation plate above the propellor. If I could stand on it and give myself enough leverage, I could pull myself up over the stern with the help of the rope. My bare knees might be bashed with cuts and bruises from the engine casing but it would be a small price to pay. A light breeze broke the stillness of the sea, skimmed over the water, chilled my already cold face as it ruffled the smooth surface into wavelets that broke and slapped against the hull. I hung on to the rope as my toes searched for purchase on the metal plate under the water. On board, the radio talked to fresh air and someone called the boat's name on Channel 6. I called back, ridiculously, and my words drifted away.

Then, as my foot slipped off the plate for the second time, a real voice called the boat's name, a real voice hailing me through a loudspeaker. A boat rocked gently in the swell a short distance away, an inflatable grey hull, white topsides and aerials bristling from the cabin roof. Along the side were large letters saying 'FISHERIES PATROL'. Two men stood in the cockpit, one with the loud hailer. I didn't care whether I was being arrested or saved. I waved. And shouted a bit.

They drifted close, threw a solid ladder over the side of their boat and helped me up. A man in a blue sweater handed me a towel, draped a blanket round my shoulders and another one thrust a cup of hot tea into my hand, not the slightest bit perturbed by my near nakedness. They chatted away as though this was an everyday event. Not for me, it wasn't, but they sat on the seat opposite and studied me. They knew what they were doing.

"Bit cold, love? At least you've got a cool head on your shoulders, trying to climb up that engine. Could have been worse. Can't see what else you could have done. Bit risky, though."

I didn't need to be admonished. I knew what I'd done wrong.

"I pulled up the anchor and hadn't started the engine first. The current took me. I'll pay for the damage," I said, once my teeth had stopped chattering, "if I know who owns the pots."

The skipper looked at me thoughtfully.

"Will Roberts asked us to look out for you when you didn't answer the radio. John Jones's great-niece, aren't you? We know the boat. He was a good fisherman, a good lobster man. Never went over his quotas, did he, Mike? Never took them under-size, not like some round here." He looked meaningfully at the poles. "Never took what he didn't need. Very gentle when he handled them. He was considerate. Very respectful."

Mike agreed.

"Tell you what," he said, taking the mug from me. "Being as you're still learning the ropes and know you made a mistake and you're a gutsy young lady coming out here on your own, we'll pop you back on *Annie*, make sure your engine's running and you'll catch the tide before it turns, no problem. We'll let Will Roberts know you're just fine, no detail, and that's it. He'll give you hell otherwise. Okay with you, Mike?"

"Thank you so much," I said, near to tears. "What about the pot, though?" I asked. "I need to pay the owner for the damage."

"What pot?" he said. "Come on, miss, let's get you aboard and on your way. Got any warm clothes with you?"

I let the reference to my gender go unchallenged, unlike my response to David. Now was not the time to discuss the difference between lads and lasses and their capabilities at sea when they'd probably just saved me from drowning. I held the wheel with white hands on the way back, still shocked by the ordeal and dreaded more problems with Jason and the angry farmer. Just lie, Cassie, I said to myself and he'll go away. But

Jason would be lucky to be alive after this.

I cleared the bar comfortably, and cruised down the estuary at half-speed with new resolve. Nobody but the patrol guys knew I'd made mistakes out there and I could handle the farmer. Water from my wet undies seeped through the tracksuit that I'd at least had the sense to bring with me but I still shivered, my hands sticky from the salt water.

I nosed *Annie* in gently towards the wall and the ladder as though nothing had happened, fenders flipped over the side ready, but I was cold and cross. Jason waited on the wall to take my ropes. The boat slowed against the ebb and came to rest. I grabbed the rung with the boat-hook and passed a line round it. At least that was perfect.

"Everything go okay, Cass? Did you say your prayers?" the false joviality not fooling me one bit. He looked even more stressed than when I left.

"Shut up and take the lines. And tie them on properly," I said, as I turned the engine off and lifted the prop out of the water.

"Okay, no need to snap. You look a bit pale," he said, as I reached the top of the ladder. "Can we have that talk now? Before that guy comes back, like?"

"When I've changed," I said. "I'm cold. Did you drain the tank?" He stared at the damp patches on my tracksuit.

"Yeah. The plastic ornaments are in a box on the shelf above the ropes. There's a ship's wheel and a treasure chest. Bit strange and dead tacky, especially for an old bloke. I had to scrape all the shit off the bottom. You should have cleaned it out, Cassie. It was disgusting. Oh, and there was a key; tiny thing under the chest, all covered in lobster slime. It's in the box."

He studied my hair, the ends clumped together, damp and still bedraggled.

"Been swimming?"

"I like swimming," I said. "Anyway, that talk will have to wait. What's that guy like, anyway?"

"Rude and angry. I don't want to be around when he comes back. Is it something to do with the house?"

I was not in the mood for a discussion and remembered that Jason knew nothing about the red-faced farmer who drove around the village to look for his daughter and what the two white-haired ladies had told me. I turned to face him.

"Now you listen. This is something to do with you and what's gone on at the house, isn't it? Before he comes back, you disappear into next door's yard and hide behind Denise. You spend enough time over there, anyway. I'll deal with it. I told you before, it was stupid of you to allow a young girl in the house with all those older friends but she's gone back to school now, I presume. I shall play ignorant about all of it and if he wants to take you to task, I'll reassure him that I shan't be allowing any more parties in the house as I shall be living in it. You stay out of the way. It's past now. Just a silly misjudgement of yours and I'm really annoyed about it. I'm not accepting the responsibility for your stupidity but I'll see if I can fend him off. Got it?"

His face clouded over.

"But that's the point, Cass. You know I said I needed to talk to you, two things, urgent, like."

"Not now. I can't face this until I've had a coffee and warmed up."

"No, now," he said and grabbed my arm as I turned towards the caravan. "You have to listen. She came back, early this morning. I let her in, in her school uniform, but she's got that bloody dog with her and she wouldn't go. Said she'd run away from home and hated school and wanted to stay there and she'd scream and shout if I made her go. She's in the house now and he's her dad, isn't he? What the hell am I supposed to do now?"

"Go," I said. "Go before I kill you," went back into the caravan and shut the door firmly to exclude the outside world for a few moments while I changed and composed myself. Then I moved into the Boat Shed and waited. Without the familiar hum of the pump, the silence was deafening.

CHAPTER 6

I heard the Discovery and its trailer before it appeared through the gates; the plaintive bleats of sheep echoed off the cliff-face and then more loudly in protest as the trailer came to a stop sharply in the yard. The tyres threw up a shower of gravel which spattered against the shed wall. I watched through the window as the driver got out, took off his cap and ran his hand through greying hair. He looked around then headed towards the shed. I met him on the step in dry clothes and tidy now and thought of 'Eleanor Rigby' as I picked up a polite, welcoming face from the jar by the door, heart thudding.

"Hello there," I said, as brightly as I could manage. "Cassie Jones," and held out my hand. He ignored it. "Sorry, I don't know your name but I heard you were looking for me. I was at a funeral."

I stood in the entrance and faced him square on. He faced me back, the colour ruddy in his cheeks and a twitch under one eye.

"How can I help you?"

"You can tell me where my daughter is, for a start."

"I'm so sorry. I don't think I know your daughter."

"You own *Tai Pilots*, don't you?"

"Yes, I do. Just about to start renovations on it, actually. It's been empty for a while since my great-uncle died."

He stared at me.

"Not what I heard," he said. "I was told my daughter was staying there, partying and that. She said she was at a friend's house for a sleep-over for a night last week but they hadn't seen her. I came to pick her up from the village but couldn't find her. She came home on time, alright, and we never knew any different. Said she'd forgotten I was to pick her up and got the bus. Now she's not in school. We sent her off this morning but she never turned up. Playing truant again, and on the first day of term? The school's not happy and I'm furious."

He ran out of breath.

"I'm sorry," I said. "I don't know how I can help you. I mean, are you worried, or does she do this often and then come home? A regular problem? Difficult creatures, teenage girls," I said with a smile. It didn't wash. "I'm really sorry," I said again, "but she's not here. I mean, is she missing? Should you inform the police?"

He coloured up even more.

"She's not missing," he said. "She's a little madam and she's taken one of my prize dogs. She's got to be somewhere local, obviously on a bus route and she won't be walking the streets with a puppy for long. I just want to know if she's gone to your house."

"It's empty," I said, "I can assure you, Mr….?"

"Gilbert."

"And she wouldn't be able to get in, Mr Gilbert. I did say renovations were due to start."

We stood in silence for a few minutes. The sheep in the trailer bleated, a bizarre sound in the boatyard with the cries of gulls overhead.

"I wonder if I can help," I said. "I'm sure you need to get back home with the sheep. I know lots of people in Borth-y-Gest. Would you like me to have a quick look around, perhaps ask a few questions? If we swap mobile numbers, give me a few hours and if I can't find her you can phone the police or if she suddenly comes home, I'll stop looking."

He stared at me, then nodded.

"I'm used to youngsters," I said. "Not so far from being one myself." Big smile. "If I find her, I'll bring her home, I promise."

There were no more pleasantries and he drove off, the throaty hum of the diesel engine disappeared down the road and the bleating gradually faded away, enough to know he was gone.

Jason poked his head round the gate.

"Now," I said, as controlled as I could be, "what was the other thing you wanted to talk about, before I have to go and bail you out. Apart from hiding young girls in my house?"

We stood in the middle of the yard in an uneasy silence.

"I have to go," he said.

"I agree. Now would be good. Phone your dad to come and get you. You can come back when all this has died down."

"No," he said. His eyes pleaded for understanding, cheek-bones too angular in the thin face. I lurched. Briefly. And waited

"No. I mean, go for good from here, Cass. Like, for ever."

Anger mixed with flashes of sympathy turned to disbelief.

"Go where, for God's sake – forever? Tell me quick. I have to find this girl and take her home and sort out the mess before it gets nasty. You need to be gone, just for a while, Jason. Now. Phone your dad. He'll understand."

"It's already done. A few days ago. I knew I couldn't get away from this after those parties and it all got out of control. They keep coming back and they won't leave me alone. And now that girl. She thinks I've left to get some food in. She wouldn't go and I don't know how to handle it. Nobody would believe me. It was all her doing."

"And has 'her' got a name?"

"Emily."

"So, what is that you've already done?" I asked.

"Dad got me an apprenticeship, well, sort of, with my uncle down south in Plymouth. I knew a week ago but I didn't want to tell you before it was definite."

"Doing what? Care work?"

"Learning about marine engines."

"What? You don't know a thing about engines."

"Yeah, well, I was doing a bit next door. Denise gave me an outboard to strip down, in my spare time, like. I got it going and thought it was just me and a bit of machinery that was fiddly and needed fixing. It was good. No people involved. I've had it with all these guys and parties and now that stupid girl. I'm out of here, Cass."

I sat down with a thump on an upturned dinghy.

"But what will I do without you?" It was pathetic, but it was the first thing that came to mind. I knew he was right but hadn't realised how much I depended on him. I'd thought it was the other way round. I sat there. He walked away and phoned his dad. I didn't listen, but knew he would come.

"Dad says he's on his way. He'll be a couple of hours. Will you sort Emily and take her home? Please, so I can go with a clear conscience that she's safe at least. And she needs to know she can't go round blackmailing guys. It's wrecked me."

"So, I'm her counsellor now, am I? Supposing she kicks off with me?"

"She won't," he said. "You'll know how to handle her. And can you bring my stuff back? Clothes, mostly."

"Right," I said, and pulled myself together. "I'll go and save your sorry arse and you need to hide until your dad arrives. Got it? Go next door. I'll phone Denise."

"… and don't let anyone find him," I said to her. "Not anyone, for any reason, except his dad and me."

I practically ran up the path to Borth-y Gest, down the steps, through the car-park, up to the road and stopped by the front door to catch my breath and gather my wits. And find the right words.

Yapping preceded the sound of the latch. The door jammed on the floor as it opened a few inches. I'd brought the key, just in case.

"Emily?"

Mousy hair hung loose and untidy round a thin face, pale blue cyes, a pert nose and a mouth set in a thin line, the stubbornness betrayed as she began to chew on her bottom lip. She clutched a fluffy bundle with a golden coat which wriggled in her arms and shed hairs on the navy blazer. It stared at me with black eyes and yapped, barked, whatever. I never did like dogs and was tempted to bark back.

"Who are you?" she asked, her voice too high for the belligerence on her face.

"I'm the owner of the house, Emily. Can I come in?"

"I don't know you," she said. "This is Jason's house."

"I'm sorry, but I'm afraid it's not."

She opened the door and the warped base scraped horribly on the tiles. She marched into the room ahead of me and sat down on one of the two shabby chairs. She clutched the dog so tight, it settled quietly in her arms. I sat on the other chair.

"Jason's gone away," I said. "He had work to go to, a long way from here. The house is about to be renovated. He won't be coming back."

"But he said he'd sort it out for me and the puppy. He said he was coming back with food and he never came. I'm starving." She faltered and buried her head in the dog's coat.

"It's a lovely puppy," I said Sit quiet and wait, Cassie, I said to myself. Milly, my parents' childhood Jamaican and mentor had instilled that into me at an early age. Settle the chatter in your own head and listen. And wait. People will talk, eventually and then you can get a better idea of what's bugging them. Don't keep asking questions. Difficult when you've trained in journalism. I didn't always abide by it but I did try.

She talked for half an hour, all the pent-up angst of a teenager who had rebelled against parental rules and wouldn't take 'no' for an answer. Then she stopped and hung her head.

"So, shall I take you home now? Before it gets dark. The puppy will want her tea. I'll explain to your dad. But I need you to listen to me first."

I waited until the head came up and the pale eyes focused on my face.

"If you want this puppy so badly, you'll need to convince your parents you can look after it. You said these puppies your dad breeds are expensive so he's not going to lose thousands of pounds over the sale of a puppy and watch you neglect it. It's a life-long commitment, Emily, not something you can just abandon when you fancy running away because you can't have you own way or things are tough at school. They certainly will be tough if you don't go to lessons and fall behind in your work. There are always people to help you if you don't understand something. If you're being bullied, that's another story."

"I'm not being bullied. No chance," she said, sharp as a pin. "I can look after myself."

"Good. That's fine at school. But the last thing, "I said, "lying to your dad about your sleepovers and coming here partying with all these older lads, is definitely not sensible. In fact, it's down-right dangerous and selfish and you could get yourself and them into a load of trouble. Do you understand what I'm saying? You're only thirteen. Under-age. Got it?"

She was silent.

"Got it?" I asked again, to make sure. "Or do you need a lesson in sex as well?"

She shook her head. I wasn't convinced she understood. I took a deep breath,

"Lads are not always as nice and respectful as Jason," I said, knowing she needed hard talk and not just an anatomy lesson, "and some of them might not be lads from school but a lot older than that. Grown men, Emily, and you have to ask yourself why they would want to be friends with young girls under the legal age for sex."

"We were only having parties," she said, sharp and defensive. "Nothing happened to me. Just music and stuff. It was a laugh."

"Well, that's alright then, but if you've been coming around here just for parties, you'll know what lads can be like if they've had too much to drink or even more dangerous, out of their heads on drugs. You've been lucky this time. Some men won't stop bothering you just because you ask them politely not to and the most dangerous time is when they encourage you to drink or take drugs and that's when you lose control. You wouldn't know what was happening to you or who was responsible."

Her head snapped up. "My mum and dad drink. They don't lose control."

"No, because they're adults and their bodies cope with it better. You're very young and very slim and you would be drunk and incapable very quickly. Even unconscious. Not good. Also, they could go to prison, you know, and you risk catching an infection, even pregnancy, if things got out of hand. You make the choices, Emily, when you're old enough to make the right decisions about what you want and are strong enough to withstand any pressure from others. That's not yet."

She was quiet for a moment, chewed her bottom lip and buried her face again in the puppy's coat.

"Got it now?" I asked, feeling like a social worker.

“Yeah, I get it.” She had the grace to blush. “Can we go home now?”

We drove over the Cob and turned down a lane at the back of Penrhyndeudraeth towards the river. I remembered, uncomfortably, about the scrape I nearly got myself into as a naïve teenager with the pervy salesman, and was glad to be distracted by the farm-track we turned into.

“You won’t tell them all that, will you?” she asked, biting her nails.

“I probably won’t need to,” I said. “They’ll have been worried sick, for the same reason I was. As long as you’ve listened, Emily.”

I stopped at a five-barred gate.

“Dad’s selling his sheep,” she said, as she opened the door.

“Why?”

“Because of the floods. That’s why he’s breeding dogs.” Dogs ran and barked on the other side. She got out and opened the gate.

“I’m not getting out with those dogs around,” I said, out of the window. “Do something.”

She didn’t need to. I pulled up outside the farmhouse door. Her parents were waiting and the dogs miraculously disappeared.

“You remember what I told you,” I said. “Apologies, promises and a little humility wouldn’t come amiss. I’ll come in and soothe the ruffled feathers if you like.”

A pannad and a scone later, delivered onto the kitchen table without any fuss by a strained but polite Mrs Gilbert, saw Emily suitably subdued and promises from her parents to discuss the puppy and from Emily, to mend her ways. It was uncomfortable and I felt I had no right to be there, despite the fact that I’d engineered it. It was personal, family stuff and I was glad when my phone buzzed. Jason.

“Dad’s here.”

“I’m on my way,” I said.

“Come and see me at the boatyard on a weekend, if you like,” I said to Emily, feeling she needed something to take her mind off herself. "Not with the dog, though. Boatyards are not really dog-friendly, what with long drops off the harbour wall into the sea."

She nodded her thanks. It was enough, and as much as she could manage, I knew.

"I'll bring her if she wants to come. We shop in Port on a Saturday," her dad said, "and we've yet to decide whether she's fit to keep a dog or not. We're not quite finished discussing it yet." He looked at her meaningfully and walked me to the door.

"Does your yard flood?" he asked, out of the blue as we walked down the path to a wicket gate. I looked out into the yard for the dogs. All was quiet.

"That's a strange question. I haven't been there long enough to find out."

"Right," he said, "well, we're only a week or so off the equinox. Let's hope it's not rain and gales again. You're right close on the water, aren't you? You've got the sea to worry about but rain's my problem. Played havoc with the grazing last winter, those floods."

I looked up at the fields at the back of the farm. They stretched steeply up-hill, the grass faded green from the hot summer and ended in a line of dark trees and dense woodland beyond.

"Floods?" I asked, as he followed my gaze.

"Not here. Down on the Traeth," he said. "The sheep graze on the salt-marsh. I specialise in salt-marsh lamb."

I looked at my watch, none the wiser, but curious.

"Sorry, I have to go. Please call in if Emily wants a visit. I'd love to hear a bit more. I know nothing about sheep."

And floods, and boatyards and just about anything else at that moment. I drove off

Arnie Blackwell's Range Rover gleamed as white as ever in the evening gloom of Denise's yard. There was no need for secrecy anymore, no reason for Jason to hide with the interesting Mr Gilbert out of the frame. I hadn't mentioned Jason specifically in the conversation at the kitchen table and I didn't think Emily would. Not for one moment.

Arnie emerged from the yard's showroom. He filled the door space with his shoulders, blocked out Denise and Jason behind him and walked towards me. His black hair, tied back in the usual pony-tail with a leather thong, was liberally salt-and-peppered, though it was only a couple of months since I'd last seen him. The gold hoop in his ear shone defiantly against the tanned skin and the Zapata moustache was now streaked with white. We shook hands, his paw as huge and gentle as I remembered. He looked tired.

"No Ben?" I asked, glancing in the back of the car to the empty car-seat.

"Left him with the nanny. Too late to bring him all the way over. It's his bedtime, anyway."

How should I begin to ask? So many questions, so many painful answers. Now was not the time and if he'd been talking to Denise, she would fill me in. She had a way of listening intently with her bright blue eyes focused entirely on her clients' faces. No wonder she was so popular. She knew Arnie well from the years of keeping his jet-skis in the yard. She knew Arnie's twin boys too, had experienced their rudeness and arrogance first-hand and suspected all along they were dealing drugs and that their mother covered for them. Spoilt brats turned criminal, Arnie had said, and he wanted nothing more to do with them, his own children and their mother. Ever. Prison or not. Jason and his five-year-old brother, Ben, were his life now, even if Jason had to go away. Scrap-dealing with his dad was not for him and never would be. But engines? I couldn't quite believe that and Plymouth was the other end of the world, it seemed.

There was no point in words. We hugged and he got into the passenger seat. I waved goodbye to the little brother I never had. Then I cried on Denise's shoulder and we drank a bottle of wine she kept in the office fridge.

"Considering the lad caused you so much grief, I'm surprised you're so upset," she said, handing me a tissue. "Although I must say he was pretty amazing with those outboard engines that I gave him to fix. Used Google and common sense and stuck at it. He'll come good, I bet. Eventually."

"We sort of had an understanding," I said, as I mused on our brief relationship. "I'd seen him at his worst and I'd got glimpses of him at his best, but I liked just having him around. Now the lobster's dead and gone as well. The place will be empty. I don't want to think about it."

"Don't then", she said. "Go back to the van and sleep. Tomorrow will look after itself."

"Tomorrow I've got to meet my solicitor. Oh joy," I said, and finished the wine.

She locked up and we stood briefly between the gates to the two yards before she pushed me through and checked I'd put the security lock on. We stared at each other.

"Well, looks like you, me and two boatyards, girl," she said through the bars of the gate. "As long as I'm still here, that is, and they don't sack me."

"How are you going to get home? You can't drive after all that wine." The sound of an engine cut through the silence.

"It's called a taxi," she said, cocking a thumb towards the road.

"But what will we do if you lose your job and I have horrible neighbours?" I asked.

"You'll think of something. About time you looked at the old smoke-house. You get that up and running for next year and just watch those customers flock to the door. Go and see Angela. She knows what you should do. After all, she was her running that snack-bar for a couple of years before you arrived on the scene and she lost Tomas. She's still working in Tesco. Don't forget to eat," she said, getting into the taxi, "and get yourself sorted out for tomorrow. You need to impress that solicitor of yours or there'll be no yard at all."

I sat on the bunk-bed in the caravan, ate a bag of crisps and a chocolate bar, uneasy in the intense silence of a quiet night with no wind and no rain to offer a gentle comforting pitter-patter on the roof. The absence of any other living creature on the premises, except perhaps rats, demolished any appetite I might have had. I took a pill, left my clothes on and hid under the quilt. Thoughts of sheep and floods and loneliness and threats from new, unknown neighbours and childhood ghosts in the night, plagued my mind. I drifted off with the image of Doug Peterson's face with black, empty eye sockets and tiny green crabs scuttling out over his cheeks.

A sharp, irregular, tapping on the roof woke me out of a drugged sleep. Not rain, more like hailstones. I lay half awake, then opened my eyes fully, the sound familiar, like the gravel Jason had accidentally kicked onto *Annie's* roof, followed by a clatter of bigger stones and a woosh of something soft. It stopped and I shot out of bed, put my headtorch on, all fear forgotten and went outside. There was no rain and the light from the torch wouldn't reach up and over onto the roof. The beam caught the rock-face above and right at the back of the caravan. A raw scar in the cliff where a ledge had fallen away left a tangle of dead nettles and brambles clinging to its surface. There was nothing I could do. No way was I going back in the van that night. I drew the two old chairs in the Boat Shed together, curled up in the new plaid rugs and lay sleepless until dawn, scared sick, twitchy with lack of sleep and as miserable as I'd ever been.

CHAPTER 7

I risked the potential avalanche of rocks and soil the following morning, glanced warily at the cliff behind the caravan and retrieved my sensible clothes to impress Mr Hughes. The rock-face was covered with a thick matting of brambles, faded nettles and the white, fluffy wisps of rosebay willowherb. The vegetation had been woven together with brambles, so thick in places, I couldn't see why just one ledge should suddenly collapse, showering dirt and stones onto the roof. I shuddered at the thought of a more considerable fall and knew the caravan should be moved further into the yard. I dressed carefully and quickly, took out my nose-stud and set off for the solicitors.

I was used by now to the ritual of tray and coffee-cups of the finest china, a selection of shortbread biscuits and Mr Hughes with his impeccable white shirt and cuffs. I sat, as usual, like a school-girl, with my knees together and waited.

"The lobster has passed away, I believe," he said.

"Yes. I looked after him as best I could," I said, "but he was very old. I gave him a decent burial at sea."

"I heard." He pursed his lips.

I bet you did, I thought, imagining what David had said and the general

disapproval for unnecessary risk-taking and fanciful ideas.
"Does his death affect my inheritance?" I asked, my heart thudding in my chest.

"I have a report from my son which states you have fulfilled your great-uncle's conditions satisfactorily. You are, now, of course, free to do what you choose with the business, apart from change the use, that is. There is still money in the trust-fund to continue as a classic boat chandlery, and, of course, to renovate the house, should you wish to. Although, I have to say, that a complete renovation would take considerably more money than the balance, which is approximately thirty thousand pounds. You have certainly been very frugal with personal expenses and the money spent on the yard has been sound investment, gates and so forth. Could we perhaps discuss your plans for the next few months to prepare for some further income next year?"

Was he being facetious? His face was as straight as a die. There had been no income of any note, apart from Hugh's meagre yard rental, and I'd cut that by half. I explained about the model ships and their potential value, pulled the folder from my briefcase and placed copies of my plans in front of him on the desk. I sat in silence while he leafed through the document. Why am I doing this, I thought? I'm free to go, free to sell and go back to journalism, to London or wherever. Then my mother's voice whispered in my ear. 'I told you so. Come back to a proper job, darling. A nice warm flat and all the delights of the city. And a nail parlour just round the corner.' I straightened my back and began to talk through the plans. Then I finished.

He folded his hands under his chin and the arms of his jacket rode up a fraction to reveal the gold cuff-links he wore. The little embellishments of tie-pin, white, starched handkerchief folded to perfection which emerged as a tiny symmetrical triangle in his top pocket and the glint of gold on his shirt-cuffs, made me wonder if he was OCD or just took care of his appearance as befitted his status. I was glad I'd taken the trouble to apply the same standards with my new haircut and Helen's smart jacket. She hadn't been back to Wales for over a year and worked for some international charity. She wouldn't have minded, her Nain said.

"I need money fairly urgently for a survey on the rock-face at the back of the yard and one for the house," I said. "I intend to start on the smoke-house first and the snack-bar, so it's ready for the spring. Then I need to find someone to help me start essential work on the house, just to make it habitable for the winter." Or saleable, I thought privately.

"It's nearly winter now, Miss Jones. That's a lot of renovation in a short time."

"Then I'll have to work twice as hard," I said.

I said nothing about the kayak I wanted to buy; a little craft of my own, and essential transport, naturally. I drank my coffee and placed the fragile cup down carefully. He consulted the file on his desk, then the one on the screen of the computer, a recent addition to his immaculate desk and hitherto on a separate desk in the corner of the room. I wondered briefly about his age and whether it was an indication of reluctance to leave the comfort of his chair any more than necessary.

"With your planned expenditure," he said, pursing his lips, "and the amount left in the account, and considering the main condition of the inheritance has been fulfilled, I think it would be sensible to credit you with the final amount. It stands to reason, of course, that the covenant requiring you to maintain and develop the classic-boat side of the business, still stands. However, there is nothing to suggest you cannot do what you wish with *Tai Pilots*."

I breathed a sigh of relief. Freedom, finally, and the last of the interviews having to justify my expenditure; my great-uncle's request to the solicitor to monitor my inheritance finally at an end.

"Thank you," I said. He escorted me out of the room into the reception area. We shook hands.

"The funds will be released into your account next week. I' m sure I don't need to remind you to take advice about reputable builders. Please ask David if you're unsure."

"I'd have to pay for that, though, wouldn't I?"

"Possibly," he said, and inclined his head so the skin on his neck crinkled and still stuck out of the starched collar, like an ancient tortoise, I thought, when I'd first met him. "We're always here for you and naturally will follow your progress with great interest. It's not every day someone so young is bequeathed such a gift and I do believe you have the mettle to make a success of it."

No pressure, then.

He opened the door for me. "Also, Miss Jones," a glimmer of a smile on his face, "there really is no need to remove your nose-stud if you need to come and see me again. My children have not always been as conventional as they are now. I am quite conversant with young people and their ways. Good luck with your next project."

He left me, open-mouthed, on the step. Children? Then I remembered Heidi, David's sister and sailing companion. Couldn't see her with a nose-stud, though, but she was a geologist and not exactly shy and retiring. Neither could I see David being anything but boringly conventional. I wondered if she would survey my rock-face. Dare I ask him? I walked back, deep in thought and plotted my way forward.

Denise rushed out from next door as I opened the gate to the yard and fixed it back on its tidy bolt.

"You'll never guess." She was wide-eyed and dishevelled. Wisps of blonde hair had escaped from their band on top of her head and stuck out in all directions. She stopped and as usual, without thinking, swept it back up and re-wound the band.

"Guess what? It can't be that bad," I said, detecting panic in her voice.

"It is. Well, not all bad. I had an email to say a representative of 'Tradewind Inc.' was going to visit. Soon."

"Okay. Well. Good. You were expecting it, weren't you? You'll find out who your boss is, at long last."

I waited patiently, while she fiddled with her hair, her blue eyes bright and earnest.

"But then, Cass, then he just arrived. No warning. He just turned up. And that's not all."

"What's not all?" I asked, amused by her enthusiasm.

"He's gorgeous."

I stared at her. Then I laughed. I laughed so much I had to drag her into the shed to sit down.

"So?" I said, still chuckling at her wide eyes, as though she'd had a shock.

"It's not funny," she said. "He was absolutely gorgeous, Cass, and oozed money. He turned up in this sparkly blue Porsche and he had on this grey suit, which was cut like you wouldn't believe, and a white shirt. With the neck open. I mean, no tie, but it all worked and he was so slim but you can bet he works out and he had a silver bracelet on one wrist… and he's got like, dark hair all slicked back and this designer beard, really close, and deep blue eyes and he spoke dead posh, not like the Queen talks but posher than you. Far back, you know?"

"Yeah, yeah. Slow down, will you? Have you still got a job?"

"Yes, can you believe? He just wants me to carry on, sales as well. They're going to send a mechanic to do all the servicing. But that's not all." Her eyes grew bluer and wider. "He wanted to speak to you."

"Me?"

"That's what I said. He's taken your mobile number off the gate."

The elation of the meeting with Mr Hughes faded away, the promise of money and projects and peace and something to get my teeth into. Why did I now think that something buried from the past was going to come back and haunt me? I stared at her and a grey mist seemed to form over my eyes as she yacked on to deaf ears.

"He was really nice," Denise was saying. "Charm itself. I mean, he's probably just being neighbourly but I got the feeling he really cared."

"Well, he would, wouldn't he? It's his yard."

"No, it wasn't just that. He was concerned about all that went on with the drugs and Doug Peterson. He sounded genuine, know what I mean?"

"Yeah, I'm sure you're right," I said, heart in my boots and didn't believe a word of it. "Really glad you're staying though. Really. It feels lonely already without Jason. What was his name, this guy?"

"Daniel Freeman," she said.

I needed to go and be by myself for a bit. I changed in the van after a quick glance at the rock-face, which seemed the same as it had when I left, and put work clothes back on; old denim jeans and a sweat-shirt, thick socks and work boots laced up tight, feeling at home and better within seconds. Keep busy, the GP had said, when the anxiety kicked in but I knew what the man wanted to talk to me about. I just knew. I also knew I hadn't the strength to fend off any unpleasantness when I said 'no' to his offers. If I ever needed a friendly face and sensible support, now was the time.

But nobody came near the yard on Saturday, not Emily, not even Hugh. By Sunday afternoon, I was desperate for company and something or someone, to occupy my mind and decided on a visit to Helen's Nain and another look at *Tai Pilots* without Jason around to worry about. A double-edged sword, I thought ruefully, care and affection, worry and annoyance all rolled into one, but I still missed him.

Then I remembered the key he'd found in the tank. It was wrapped in tissue in the box on the shelf; a tiny, brass key, the sort of key belonging to a small padlock. I couldn't think of anything in the Boat Shed that it would fit. I picked it up out of curiosity, reminded myself this was not a fairy tale with a hoard of gold stashed in a secret safe in the house, added the big torch and house-key and stuffed them both into a rucksack, locked the gates and made my way to Borth-y-Gest.

The front door scraped on the old tiles and left a ridge of dirt when I closed it behind me. The place still stank of damp and old material impregnated with dust and dirt and the sour, smell of old clothes that often permeates charity shops. The curtains in the front-room were hung from an old, metal track, pushed back against damp patches on the wall, the flimsy, once-white net yellowed with age, pulled across the window and held together with a rusty safety-pin. The two old easy-chairs sagged with ancient foam cushions and spilt their innards through holes in the seats and the over-stuffed arms. Jacob's nest of sleeping bags was still on the floor. I'd only picked up his clothes as he'd asked, and had no desire to go rooting through his sleeping quarters.

I wanted most of all to investigate the cellar, accessed through a wooden door under the stairs. I had no idea if he had opened it or not. There was an outside door to the cellar built into the wall at the same level as the beach. Hardly surprising it flooded at high springs, so I was told.

The door was stiff with damp but opened after a battle, followed by a hefty kick. It swung inwards into thin air on rusty hinges, creaked and stopped short of the wall. A rush of cold, musty air rose from below. I stepped back just in time, with one foot hovered over a black void. The beam from the torch picked out walls covered in peeling plaster and a flight of rough-hewn stone steps that led down into the dark. It was much steeper than I'd thought; the steps were narrow and sloped downwards with their centres worn away in soft-edged scoops from boots over the years and too far down for the torch-beam to penetrate.

I stood at the edge for a moment and thought it through. No-one knew I was here and I didn't know if the outside door was locked or boarded up. I could be stuck down here if I tripped and fell. Or, if cave monsters, like the ones in Robert Graves's poem that I'd remembered, came out and devoured me. A silly giggle formed in my throat and bubbled over in a mixture of excitement and fear, unsure whether I was blessed or cursed by the childish thought. Discretion being the greater part of valour, as my mother was fond of saying, I decided it would be foolish to launch myself into the unknown. And then I did.

The door had opened to the left and obscured a wooden pole fixed to the wall that disappeared at an angle into the darkness. The first step fell sharply away downwards, roughened and grooved at its edge; the rest were barely deep enough for me to place my whole foot without the toes of my trainers hanging over the edge. Sideways seemed to be the best option and by the second step I could put my hands on the top end of the make-shift banister. The wood was smooth, cold to the touch, covered with a pale green mould, almost iridescent in the torchlight, and left a powdery residue on the palm of my hand. I brushed it off on my jeans and tugged at the rail. It felt firm enough to rely on.

There were twelve steps altogether, my feet more secure sideways on the rough stone and I held onto the rail with both hands, the torch tucked under my chin until I reached the bottom, tentatively gauged the distance and |committed myself to flat ground. Hard-packed mud and shards of slate formed the floor, dry and solid with no obvious signs of damp or standing water.

I shone the torch around the walls. The room seemed to be the same size as the sitting room above. Ancient spider-webs hung down in swathes from the ceiling beams, grey skeins flecked with dust and old paint from the plaster-board in-between.

The outside door was set into the wall in front of me. It was criss-crossed with planks nailed to the door-frame, the bottom-half completely obscured by a galvanised, corrugated metal sheet fixed to a frame of stout wood. It was the same material as the roof of the chandlery and designed to deter anyone, or anything, from entering, especially high tides. Sea-water could seep through any tiny gaps, as water has a habit of doing, but then a cellar is a cellar and usually used for storage. It was geared up to stay dry.

I flicked the light onto the roughly-plastered wall to my right where three shelves with large boxes virtually covered the peeling paint; not mock-wood, flat-pack shelves, but wide planks of pine at least two feet wide and two inches thick, strengthened underneath with long lengths of wood screwed to the wall and held up by brackets fashioned from the same material. They were designed to withstand heavy weights, the punishment of damp sea-air and the rot of time.

The top two shelves supported wooden oblong boxes, the lids closed and fixed with simple metal clasps; long and low enough to allow the lifting of the lid to its fullest extent without it binding on the shelf above, but too high to reach. The box on the bottom shelf was locked with a small brass padlock. Tools, I thought, must be tools designed for heavy work, with metal, perhaps? I'd seen boxes like these in the builders' merchants but they were usually made of metal or plastic. I knew enough about wood by now to guess these were built from oak or mahogany. Great-uncle John must have stored them here when the chandlery became over-filled with stock.

The light from the failing torch flickered a warning. I made my way carefully back to the steps and crawled up on hands and knees to the open door and welcome light. The two top shelves had been too high to reach and it was too dark to try the tiny key in the padlock of the box on the bottom shelf, anyway. It would have to wait.

I pulled the front door behind me and stood at the bottom of the steps, dirty and disappointed. I hadn't done half of what I'd set out to do, like make lists of possible jobs I could do myself. The thought of living above that cellar with the front room only separated from it by floor-boards, and the sea if it ever flooded, the spider-webs that wouldn't have disgraced those in *The Hobbit*, and the task of getting rid of old tools I probably couldn't even lift, filled me with dread. I had no connection, bonding or even interest in the place. In fact, I hated it at that moment, with a passion that made me run all the way to Helen's Nain's.

I arrived out of breath, unlatched the garden gate, walked around the back of the house, composed myself and opened the door to the back porch. After all that had happened, the Bed and Breakfast was more like a second home now and Helen's Nain more like an elderly friend with her warmth and common sense; I couldn't remember my own grandmother.

My grandfather, stern and forbidding had lived on his own in London. Visits with my father were cold, tense and very short; no pannad to welcome us or interested chat about my father's work or my schooling. How my grandmother lived with my grandfather and his terrible guilt, I couldn't imagine. I found it difficult to relate to him; no shared history, or family get-togethers, or celebrations of births and marriages. Only deaths, it seemed.

I pushed the outside door open, tapped on the door leading into the kitchen and was met by a blast of warmth from the range and the ever-present smell of baking. Two heads turned from the table; Helen's Nain's, with her neat, grey curls and the other, with her soft, white waves, belonged to one of the Gwens, the one who reminded me of a marshmallow, her face soft and sickly sweet with pink cheeks and bright, acquisitive eyes. At least it wasn't the spiky one with the blue glasses, I thought, and wanted to turn and run. But it was too late. A chair was pulled out for me, the tea already poured and a slice of Victoria sponge placed on the plate.

"I've been to the house," I said, after the pleasantries and the reassurances about *Tai Pilots*. "It's empty now. I'll be starting work to renovate it soon," and explained that Jason had gone away to do some training. "He won't be coming back."

"But how will you manage? You can't do all that and the yard by yourself?" asked Helen's Nain, true concern on her face.

I fended off the questions, not having any answers, and listened politely to their chat, finished the light-as-a-feather cake, started to push my chair back and stood up to go.

"I know it was before your time," the marshmallow said, out of the blue, "but it was such a tragedy when those little children drowned. They would have been your second cousins, wouldn't they? And such a shame about the baby. Annie never got over any of it, did she, Joan? Three second little cousins, all dead. Terrible, wasn't it Joan, her losing it so soon after the children drowned?"

My chair stopped scraping, as of its own accord. I sat down again, heavily.

"What baby?" I asked.

I looked at Helen's Nain, abstractedly stirring sugar into her tea.

"I know you told me she died of cancer and a broken heart after the children drowned, but you never said anything about a baby," I said.

She added more sugar to her tea and carried on stirring. "No, I didn't, did I? She had cancer much later. She was unwell for a while, but nobody really knew what it was. She was sixty or so when she died."

They glanced at each other across the table. Was this a Gwen indiscretion? Was she being disingenuous and if so, why?

"I never heard anything about a baby," I said, again, even from my mother who probably didn't know either. I looked from one to the other.

It wasn't like Helen's Nain to keep secrets or gossip, but then, how well did I really know her?

"Why is it such a secret? Why wouldn't anyone tell me? Was she already pregnant when the children died? What happened to the baby?" Above the hum of the dish-washer and a clock ticking on the wall, it was suddenly very quiet in the kitchen.

"Nobody really knows," said Helen's Nain. "She just disappeared for a while after the children were buried. Gone away to get over it, people said. They were in my class, you know. It was terribly distressing, as you can imagine. All the village children knew each other and were growing up together. There was so much sadness. And blame, of course. People said awful things about your great-aunt and uncle, things about lack of care and responsibility. They didn't just blame your grandfather. They blamed Annie as well for letting them go with him. We couldn't understand what happened, either. Your grandfather was an experienced seaman."

"Just a terrible accident," Gwen said. "The village was shocked, you can imagine, and there was the inquest and everything and then your grandfather moved away to London with his wife and son; your father, of course."

"But surely people would have known what happened to her, I mean if she was obviously pregnant? Did she come back to have the baby or was she in a hospital? You must know."

"Not for certain," Helen's Nain said. "Nobody saw her for a month or so after the children's funeral, and then she just disappeared. People had left her alone, out of respect more than anything, so there was no-one to ask and it would have been difficult to approach your great-uncle. Not like these days when there seems to be support for everything. Your great-uncle was a solitary man by nature and often walked from the house to the yard without acknowledging anyone. There wasn't much anyone could do."

"But they were only in their thirties," I said. "She must have had friends."

Funny sort of respect, that, I thought, leaving a woman alone in those circumstances. How could a whole village just ignore someone after all that tragedy?

"So, did she come back after she disappeared and before the baby was born?"

Gwen picked up her teacup with a hand as soft and pink as the marshmallow face, an exterior she portrayed as so gentle and unassuming with her pleasant small talk. Was it just a remark she'd made, assuming I already knew or had she deliberately dropped it into the conversation to stir up old gossip? Was there a malicious side to her, a small-world lady with little but gossip to occupy her? Whatever it was, I couldn't let it go, despite my trying to distance myself from the past.

Helen's Nain got up and started to clear the table. She'd had enough, I could see. She picked up the empty teapot and stood for a moment.

"No," she said, "some people said she'd been in a psychiatric unit somewhere. Some said she'd gone to hospital in case she miscarried and had to be looked after for a while. Whatever it was, she came back after a few months, no longer pregnant and no baby. Nobody liked to ask. She just shut herself up in the house most of the time, came out to go shopping once a week when your great-uncle drove her into town, but she never invited people round or stopped to chat."

She shrugged her shoulders and clattered the cups and plates onto the draining board, opened the dishwasher and started to empty it. She was clearly uncomfortable. I should think so, too, I thought, bemused and angry at the injustice of it all. I needed to go before Gwen got up and I had to walk out with her. I could feel the sharp comments already on the tip of my tongue.

"I'll come back over the weekend," I said. "I need to bring Helen's jacket back. The caravan isn't safe anymore. I'll explain then."

I left, unsettled and as curious as hell, and climbed the steps from the bay, one at a time, and thought back to my dad's funeral and what little my mother had told me about the family tragedy. I remember quite clearly feeling sorry for my grandfather, to have all that guilt around with him. Was that the reason for Helen's Nain's discomfiture? Guilt? A whole community leaving a pregnant, recently bereaved mother to cope with one and then another tragedy because perhaps they couldn't cope with it themselves?

I would have offered support and friendship, whether she liked it or not. She would have been half out of her mind with her decision to let her children go sailing with their uncle and then having to cope with their father when he found out. She must have felt ostracised by neighbours, blamed and punished. I caught my breath with sheer emotion, tried to shake off the awfulness of it, stopped halfway up the steps and distracted myself with a last view of the bay

I looked back at *Tai Pilots*, shabby and grey and even from here I could see the broken line of the chimney-pot where ferns had clung on to the old mortar, where they flourished and survived, despite howling gales and baking hot sun. I wished the whole bloody place would disappear with the next tide, just crumble and sink into the ooze of mud and green algae that coated the bay at low-tide. My chest stopped heaving and I leaned against the rail, settled for a moment and chided myself for being critical of Helen's Nain, of all people, the wise and practical soul I'd come to rely on and then made judgements about her actions, or lack of them, all those years ago. Not for the first time did I feel I was on a roll of bad events. Was anything pleasant ever going to happen without an accompanying get-out clause? Not today, at least.

I locked the yard gates behind me, wandered around and checked

Annie's ropes, snatched bedding and my toothbrush from the caravan with a wary eye on the cliff-face above and settled down to prepare the Boat Shed for a more comfortable night. The two armchairs had fitted together with enough length for me to curl up in the quilt and pillows. There were sticks for the fire and I raided the snack-bar freezer for burgers and rolls, leaving them to thaw while I fired up one of the hot-plates.

Then I went back outside and looked at the caravan, tucked into the cliff with the small pile of stones and soil on its roof. There was nothing to suggest it would happen again and nothing to suggest it wouldn't. I needed to move it away from the cliff. I looked at the tow bar and couldn't see why I shouldn't hitch it up to the Toyota and pull it out myself. I could do that, if I could line up the van with the car. But I couldn't face it tonight, nipped back into the van for a bottle of wine and brightened up as I remembered it was Saturday tomorrow. Hugh would be in the yard for the day.

The wood in the stove caught with one match and I half-closed the air-vents carefully, went through the back door of the shed and into the rear of the snack-bar, parked only a couple of feet away. I'd closed it down to visitors a few weeks before; our little group were the last to sit on the white, plastic tables outside while we waited for news of Doug Peterson after the storm.

I flipped the burgers over, thinking about that storm as it raced through with torrential rain and gale force winds; it blew over as quickly as it arrived, born on strange, heavy, dark clouds like pleated cotton-wool that rolled ominously in from the sea. Weird and wild, the news called it, as we'd picked up chairs and tables afterwards and wiped off splatters of rust that the rain had washed from the shed roof. Tomorrow would be a better day, I hoped, as I spread ketchup liberally on the burgers, stood in the open doorway of the shed and ate them, without ceremony, off a paper napkin.

Evening descended over Ballast Island. Black-headed gulls cried and swooped over the sandbanks and flew off to settle for the night. A trickle of smoke from the chimney curled up into the cool air and I shut and locked the door, the warmth from the wood-burner and the mellow, headiness of oil and wood and paint, far more inviting than the caravan with its cold, plastic surfaces. I'd taken the last of the sleeping pills the night before, but nicely sleepy with a tot of whisky from the shelf under the counter and tucked into the nest of quilts and blankets, I watched the flicker of the dying fire through the glass door. And slept.

CHAPTER 8

Saturday morning and my first thought was of Jason; my second was accompanied by a pang of loss. He might have caused me grief, but I still liked his company and the easy banter we'd established, each taking the other's comments and opinions with equanimity, even if we disagreed and were sharp with each other occasionally. It never lasted. Sometimes we didn't need to say anything, just automatically knew what the other was thinking.

I couldn't ever achieve that with Hugh Phillips, who was calling for me outside the caravan in the yard, obviously in vain, but then he didn't know about the rock-fall. For the first time since I'd taken over the yard, I was so pleased to hear his formal, slightly diffident voice, I shot off the chairs and unlocked the door, dozy and still fully dressed from the day before.

"I am so pleased to see you," I said, "you have no idea how pleased. Coffee first and I'll explain."

After coffee and his second helping of chocolate biscuits, we went outside and stood at the foot of the caravan. He turned his Beanie round and round in his hands, which he did when he was thinking, or wanted to talk about something serious. The nearly-bald head, covered with the black Beanie come rain or shine, became paler where the ribbed edge rested on a high forehead but his face was smooth and tanned, a young man's face despite his fifty years, I guessed. He was not one to discuss personal life details, I just knew he worked as a technician on the survey ships based in Holyhead, on standby to ferry the workers who maintained the wind-turbines off the north Wales coast. Despite his formal way of speaking, strange pale-blue eyes behind rimless glasses, mild manner and slightly effeminate personality, he worked with a crew of Alpha male guys and never had any problems.

Will Roberts, who seemed to know someone from all professional walks of life and knew one of the crew members, told me Hugh was highly respected for his expertise and the crew looked after him like over-protective parents. God help any new crew members who arrived and decided to take a pop at him. I'd also seen him once wield a baseball bat with intent, to protect me against intruders. A strange man, one of those who radiated an air of confidence and self-reliance, despite his quiet voice, unassuming ways and obvious unease with face-to face conversations.

"I think, Miss Cassie," he said, turning his gaze to the cliff behind the caravan and the scar in the vegetation where the ledge had collapsed, "you would be advised to move the van. Not only away from the cliff-face, but right around to the other side of the chandlery and put it by the snack-bar where the tables and chairs are during the summer. After all, if you are going to move into the house, you will, no doubt, sell the van and it needs to be in good condition. I don't think that flimsy roof would withstand any bigger lumps of rock."

"I thought I'd get a survey done," I said, "in case it happens again and anything falls onto the back wall of the shed."

"As you wish, but I would move the van, now, if I may say so. If there is another fall, the open area between the cliff and the shed should contain it and prevent it from damaging the back wall."

"It's only a small gap and it's galvanised sheeting," I said. "It wouldn't take much."

"No indeed," he said, "but do consider that if you require the services of a surveyor, your insurance company might inquire why you hadn't informed them if you need to make a claim."

"Oh," I said, "so I take a risk either way?"

He nodded solemnly. "At least move the caravan."

"Will you help me?" I said, trying to keep the pleading out of my voice. "Jason's gone. If you just look out for me by the harbour wall, I think I can hitch it up and move it with the Toyota. I've done a bit with trailers…" I tailed off. The yard was littered with upturned dinghies and trailers, Hugh's boat up on its chocks and not much space for turning and reversing. The harbour wall was unprotected at the edge where it dropped away into the sea. The caravan was parked side-on to the cliff and would have to be swung round by hand to enable me to get to the tow-hitch. I couldn't do that by myself and I glanced at Hugh's slight frame and decided he couldn't do it either.

My mobile rang. The sound permeated the flimsy shed wall and I had a feeling it was the call I didn't want to take,

"Excuse me," I said, and dashed inside, took a deep breath and answered the phone.

"Miss Jones? Daniel Freeman speaking. From 'Tradewind', owners of Madoc Marine? I took your number from the yard gates after speaking to your lovely neighbour, Denise. Hope you don't mind me phoning on a Saturday but I'm in town and wondered if I could drop in and see you. Nothing formal, I assure you. Just to say hello. After all the trouble this summer, you must be wondering what will happen to the yard."

"When?" I asked, past being polite.

"In about half an hour?"

No, you can't. I don't want to see you. I'm a mess.

"I'm working," I said. "It's not really convenient."

I think my heart stopped for a brief second, the panic beginning to mount. I couldn't get my breath.

"Jolly good," he said. "I'll be with you shortly," and closed the call.

Cheeky bastard, I thought, and just what I'd expected. Angry, I picked the Toyota keys off the board and stood in the door for a moment to gather my wits. I knew what he wanted to talk about and knew I couldn't compete with a wealthy charmer who wouldn't easily take 'no' for an answer. Between his visit and the need to move the caravan, I was trapped and could not find the strength to tackle either. I was tired and hungry, hadn't washed and still wore yesterday's clothes.

I stepped outside, dazed, with the keys dangling from my hand. The tow-hitch on the caravan now faced the harbour instead of being tucked behind the shed. Hugh was nowhere to be seen, but I could hear scraping on the gravel as he moved tables and chairs around the other side of the snack-bar. He appeared by my side.

"If I may, Miss Cassie?" and took the keys from my outstretched hand.

Fifteen minutes later, he'd detached the Toyota from the caravan's tow-hitch, wound down the legs and parked the car by the side of it.

"Safe and sound here. That wall above is solid. Shall I put the keys back on the board?"

I should have known he would do it, quietly and efficiently. Why hadn't I just asked him?

"Thank you," I said, swallowing my pride. What else could I say?

"I'll get on now, if I may. It looks as though you have a visitor."

Denise had described the car perfectly. The Porsche Carrera in metallic blue, purred through the gate with hardly a whisper from the tyres on the pitted surface of the yard. It pulled gently to a halt and the window wound down to reveal the man Denise had described. He took his sunglasses off carefully and put them on the dashboard, opened the door, shut it, as carefully, and walked towards me with his hand outstretched.

"Miss Jones, I presume? Daniel Freeman." He tilted his head inquiringly; a studied pose, I thought, but not enough to make me judge him and taller than I'd expected. His eyes held mine for nearly longer than was comfortable, his hand touched mine, strong, smooth and warm with just enough pressure; mine grubby and a disgrace. At least I hadn't wiped them on my jeans. What you see is what you get, I thought, crossly; a working girl on a Saturday morning.

The suit Denise described had been replaced with designer jeans, white trainers and a pale-blue T-shirt. I glanced down at the gold Rolex on one, slim wrist, the silver bracelet on the other. It seemed history reared its head, repeated itself and memories flooded back. Was this another Doug Peterson back to haunt me? But his voice was as deep and as warm as his hand, the words perfectly enunciated. Denise had said 'posh', but his speech was without effort or ostentation.

"Thank you for seeing me at such short notice." There was no time for the comment I could have made. Get over it, I told myself.

"This is wonderful," he said, as his gaze took in Ballast Island and the estuary." A different feel altogether than next door. May I look round?" He'd already headed for the harbour wall and leaned over the edge above *Annie*.

"Is she yours? Nice engine. Out to sea in no time, I should think." Again, that smile as he turned to me. He headed for Hugh's wooden yacht, footsteps quick and light in the white trainers and before I knew it, had introduced himself to Hugh enthusiastically, almost as though I wasn't there. I stood back as they discussed the old methods of caulking, ran his hand over the smooth timbers and remarked on the rudder pintles.

Hugh didn't seem to mind at all, obviously over-joyed to share a passion for battered wooden boats, which I thought was a bit ironic considering my visitor's obvious financial status. It was blatantly evident in the car, astronomically expensive sun-glasses and clothes that hugged him to the point of perfection. I would have thought a sixty-foot *Oyster* would have been more his style and I only knew about that because David had pointed one out once in the marina, a visiting yacht from down south. His dream yacht, he'd said.

He took his leave of Hugh and spent a few moments at the top of the slipway where the tide had left a line of weed on the slope.

"Does the tide ever top this level?" he asked.

"Not in my time," I said, "but then I haven't been here long. I think you would need to have a combination of the worst conditions for it to flood the yard really badly. It's not unusual for the tide to reach the top of the harbour wall and spill over a bit, though."

I pointed up at the cliff of Yr Ogo. "If you look," I said, "the bluff juts out sufficiently to deflect the tide. The wind would need to be gale-force, and slightly east of south, a very high spring-tide and unusually low pressure. The estuary is relatively shallow and it's not as though the distance to Harlech over there would equate with the fetch from the Atlantic. It would be unlikely or an 'Act of God.' That's what the locals say, anyway. The perfect storm. Let's hope it never happens."

I tried to sound knowledgeable and hoped he didn't quiz me further. I'd picked up bits and pieces of information over the months but not enough to withstand scrutiny. I moved on and explained about the winch and my idea for extending the slipway to increase launch access for dinghies or kayaks, avoiding the fact that I'd fully intended to poach some of the jet-ski storage from his firm's business next door.

"Would you like coffee?" I asked, just to be polite, but charming though he was, I was irritated by his enthusiasm, embarrassed by my appearance and wished he would go away, or at least say why he'd come. The only thing I really wanted to know was how much he knew about the drug-trafficking from his yard. But he wasn't going to be honest about that, I decided so there was no point in asking. Not yet.

"Splendid," he said, and rubbed his hands together. "Can we sit outside?"

"There are some plastic chairs round by the snack-bar. If you would like to bring a couple over?" and get your beautiful jeans dirty, I thought spitefully and put the kettle on, as taut as a bow-string while I arranged my best chocolate biscuits and some custard creams on a plate, used the newest mugs and carried them out on a tray. Bad thoughts didn't include bad manners. I had my limits.

He'd placed the chairs either side of the old oil drum under the window. It had been used as a coffee table by my great-uncle John and I hadn't moved it. I had, however, taken the two disgusting old arm-chairs with their plastic covers to the skip. I put the tray down on the drum. He stood in front of the plastic chairs with his back to me and I watched him, seemingly unaware of my presence, as he systematically scanned the length of Ballast Island, the beach at the seaward end and the old wooden piles stark against the backdrop of the Traeth. It was half-tide and the sea glittered and sparkled in the morning sun as the tide receded and revealed the sandbanks stretching across to Harlech.

"Stunning," he said, as he turned to look further down the estuary towards the sea. "Just stunning."

We sat in silence. He sipped his coffee, surprised me as he dunked a custard cream, relaxed, quiet and absorbed in the view. I was still annoyed with his exuberant appreciation of the environment, the pretence at neighbourliness. As if. I'd had enough.

"What, exactly, do you want?" I asked. He ignored my question, turned liquid eyes on me and put his mug down carefully on the drum.

"Denise told me a little about you," he said, "and told me how you came to be here at all, a new journalist who gave up a promising career. Was that right?"

"She does like to talk," I said.

"She also told me how hard you've had to work, to learn about this nautical life. And keep your head above water, if you'll forgive the pun." He waved his hand vaguely around the yard. "It's very much a man's world, as you've no doubt discovered."

Was he being patronising? He was very direct.

"Yes," I said, unbending a little. "There's a lot to learn. But it's not entirely a male prerogative, you know, all this stuff, unless it's heavy and I can't lift it. I just have to work twice as hard to find ways of dealing with things. People are the worst," I said, and looked directly at him. "Not knowing whether they're genuine or not." I hadn't meant to talk so much.

He smiled, picked up another biscuit, a chocolate one this time and unselfconsciously nibbled the chocolate off the edges. Very endearing, I thought sceptically. If we were going to have this conversation, he needed to get on with it.

"So, you haven't stayed in town and come to visit me just to look at the view, or just be neighbourly," I said and repeated myself. "What, exactly, do you want?"

He finished the biscuit, put his empty mug on the tray, uncrossed his legs and sat forward in the chair. He placed his hands on his knees, looked me in the eye, leaned over towards me and said, "What I want, or would like…" He paused. "Would you like to join me for dinner tonight?" and sat back.

I held his gaze and looked hard, as though seeing his face for the first time, perfectly proportioned bone-structure, at his tanned skin, the dark, designer stubble that defined a strong jaw-line and a gentle, sensitive mouth, the newly-combed hair and searching, fathomless eyes the colour of a deep-blue sea. His shoulder muscles were stretched taut against the T-shirt. Denise was right. He was completely, and utterly, gorgeous. And was this what Trish meant? Tough and tender? I was completely taken aback. Then something stirred inside me. A gull screeched overhead and the halliards on Hugh's boat chinked in the light breeze.

"Yes," I said. "I think I would like that very much"

"Help," I said down the phone. "I need clothes, Helen's Nain. Can I come and raid Helen's wardrobe? I've got nothing that hasn't been packed in a suitcase for months. I haven't got time to wash and iron stuff."

I drove over to Borth-y-Gest late afternoon. Her bright eyes, full of enthusiasm and purpose followed me upstairs to Helen's room. I told her the bare essentials; dinner with a bloke, that's all.

"Now, let's see," she said, opened the mirrored wardrobe door, pulled clothes off the rail and laid them on the bed; blouses and shirts, trousers, skirts and jackets; I'd never have thought Helen was a clothes freak. And one dress.

"She had a very sociable life with the sailing club."

"But some of these are really expensive," I said.

"Apple of her daddy's eye, cariad, and he is a consultant, you know. Her mother too."

I'd forgotten.

"Classy, but not too dressy for *The Sportsman*," she said.

"Just shirt and trousers then? These?"

She stood back and looked at me thoughtfully, her head cocked on one side.

"Well, I think we can do better than that. Just because you do a man's job half the time, doesn't mean to say you have to dress like one. Take this into the bathroom and put it on. No bra. It's lined and shaped inside the top."

"You must be joking," I said. "Me in a little black dress?"

"Trust me. Not easy to choose when you've got purple streaks in your hair. Colours might clash. Black tights and heels as well. Go on. Try it out."

I did. The dress fitted like a glove, the shoulder seams snug against my skin, the neckline V-shaped in soft folds, beautifully cut and not so low it would need the bosom I didn't have much of. The hemline came to just above my knee. It was a simple dress, cut in at the waist and snug over the hips. She pulled up the long zip at the back and straightened the material on my shoulders.

"Now the jacket," she said, picking up a little box jacket with short sleeves, soft and black with a thin, black and white embroidered border edging the front panels and the sleeve cuffs.

"Wait," she said. She disappeared into the bedroom opposite and came back with a thin box covered in blue velvet. "Don't look."

She took something from the box, put it round my neck and fastened it at the back,

"Now look."

She shut the wardrobe door and turned me to face the full-length mirror, then handed me a tissue to mop up the tears. They trickled down my face without any prompting as I saw someone I didn't know. No, someone I used to know but hadn't seen for over a year, someone I'd nearly forgotten. I touched the choker she'd fastened round my neck, the tiny pearls threaded through the middle leaving an edge of black velvet.

"Shoes," she said, brisk as ever. "These, I think."

High-heeled sandals, black and strappy, and a plain black clasp-bag.

"Stud stays in," I said, tapping the diamond in my nose, trying to restore calm with humour. "That's part of me."

"Well, I don't know who you're meeting, cariad, but he's getting the best of both of you. Stylish and individual. Lucky man."

"But the choker…I can't, it's too lovely."

"Well, you're lovely too. My husband gave it to me way back in the sixties. Somehow, it's never dated. No opportunity to wear it, I'm afraid, and you can stop calling me Helen's Nain, please. Just 'Nain' will do. Now, go and take a shower, wash your hair and clear off and enjoy yourself. Who is he, by the way?"

"Oh, just a bloke I met," I said, as she turned to leave the room and my heart began to thud as I realised what I'd done. I'd re-invented all the teenage fantasies I'd spun over Doug Peterson when I'd first met him; strong, intense, hard, analytical, scary. The thought of just being touched by him had turned my adolescent knees to jelly. Until I learned better. But I couldn't ever quite shake off the feeling.

He'd been a world apart from the immature, groping, spotty-faced peers at uni, the pervy-sales man who tried to buy a blow-job and the half-pissed joiner who thought he could cadge an easy screw by plying me with vodka. But Doug Peterson was a bad guy and I had been out of my comfort zone with experience, only I didn't know it. Was that what this was? Another wolf in sheep's clothing? A softening-up before the inevitable pressure to purchase my livelihood?

I stared at my reflection. Nain was right about the clothes. I felt head and shoulders above the silly school-girl I used to be. I could handle this man. On my terms, except I wasn't sure what my terms were. At that moment, I almost looked forward to a confrontation; it felt risky, exciting and I couldn't wait.

"Come for tea tomorrow," she said. "Roast chicken and you can tell me all about it."

She stood at the gate and waved me off. She looked smaller, shrunken somehow, her back slightly bent, the grey curls blended with the backdrop of the house.

I took the Toyota. It wasn't quite the image I would have wished for; dressed-up and driving an old pickup, but not only did I not want to spoil my newly-straightened-to perfection hair, I doubted I could walk the length of the High Street in heels. Most importantly, I wanted a get-out clause if I'd made a terrible mistake. My own wheels meant I could only have, maybe, just one drink and keep my wits about me, as Millie used to say, and leave when I wanted to.

He was waiting in the lounge, welcoming and comfortable in front of the log fire that crackled in the old-fashioned fireplace. He stood up as I walked towards him. I held out my hand; formal seemed to be the way and I wanted to set the tone. He reached out to mine as confident and positive as he'd done that morning, a man who knew how to greet people. He touched it briefly, then raised it to his lips.

"As stunning as the view from your yard," he said, and held my gaze. I could have responded with a comment about scrubbing-up well but with the sincerity in his eyes and voice it would have been an insult. I think I blushed and mumbled my thanks. I wasn't used to compliments. He gestured to the chair opposite and we sat either side of the fire while a waiter materialised with menus and requests for drinks.

"One drink, only, thank you," I said. "I've driven down," and wondered if I could get through any of this without alcohol.

"They do have taxis here," he said, "on the firm, of course. Call it a research meeting. Besides which…"

The waiter placed an ice-bucket on the coffee table. "Was I being presumptuous?" he asked, eyebrows raised and a smile as the waiter uncorked the champagne.

Oh, what the hell, I thought, and reminded myself that I was in charge.

"What research?" I asked. Straight out with it, Cassie, so he doesn't waste his time. "I'd really like to enjoy the evening. I haven't been out to dinner for… well, ages, but can we get one thing straight? If you want to discuss the sale of my yard, then the answer is 'no'. Please, let's not discuss it."

I studied him carefully for a response as he poured the champagne, handed me mine and lifted his glass. His face was unreadable, as though he hadn't heard me, or chose not to reply. He was good at being evasive, following his own agenda. I'd remembered that from the morning.

"A toast," he said, "to entrepreneurs."

Interesting, I thought, but couldn't disagree.

It was late. The dining-room had emptied long since and our table, so prettily set, bore a nearly perfect resemblance to the curve of Tremadoc Bay, with the castles of Harlech and Criccieth represented by the pepper and salt. The spare cutlery served as borders for the beaches and the outline of Sarn Badrig.

"This is where most of the lobster pots are," I said, "and the reef runs out eleven miles into the bay. Did you know…" The waiter interrupted us; the restaurant was closing and would we like coffee or drinks in the lounge?

"Sorry about the table," I said, as he moved my chair back.

"…and the myths about the reef…" I carried on, "I just love stories. What do you read?"

It was midnight when the waiter opened the door, straightened tables and chairs and hovered meaningfully.

"Could you order me a taxi?" I asked, horribly aware I'd talked and talked. But then, so had he. He had told me of his childhood in Trinidad, where his parents lived and worked the business.

"My father started with one small boatyard here," he told me. "We now own boatyards and marinas at home. I'm the UK manager, these days. Madoc Marine was my first acquisition, so you can see why I have a particular care for it.

'I love boats and sailing. I'm an island boy, after all," he said, "One tends to grow up being half-in and half-out of the water out there. Holidays were spent sailing, fishing and swimming. The water's warmer than the UK, you know."

We hadn't even touched on his job – he preferred to touch on global issues, books, his public UK schooling supported by wealth and security, mine pretty poor after my dad died, but my minimal experiences in journalism had grounded me with the seedy side of people's lives. An advantage, I told him, in learning not to make generalised assumptions about people, so warned and lectured by those close to me, especially Millie, my Jamaican nurse and mentor. I hadn't always remembered to follow her advice, I admitted, thinking ashamedly of some of my worst moments.

"Do you think your early days at boarding school affected you?" I asked. "I can't imagine being sent away from home so young."

"It encouraged independence, I think, but I was lucky in having devoted parents when I was at home and the holidays were very long. I was brought up knowing I would be sent away to school so I suppose I was well prepared. It was a good school with caring teachers and a matron who was a battle-axe. She knew when you were swinging the lead with illness and knew when it was serious and then gave the best love and care possible. I was lucky and my parents chose well. No, I don't think I suffered."

I chose to skip over my uncomfortable bits; mother's drinking excesses and a clever father, mostly absent and disinterested in my difficult, teenage years when it was obvious that I was not going to follow in his footsteps. We swapped life-stories easily and naturally, mine carefully edited, and the conversation bounced from one topic to another. There was still a niggle in the back of my mind as to whether I was being groomed, whether there was a hidden agenda, but it hadn't stopped me enjoying myself. We drank and laughed and offered differing opinions without rancour.

The taxi arrived and parked outside the lounge window, the lights from the sign on the roof glowed yellow in the dark. It was very late. At the least I'd remembered my torch to see the security lock numbers on the gate.

I stood up. "Thank you for a lovely evening. I don't remember discussing any research, though."

"Listening to your story was enough, not to mention your plans for the future. I didn't toast you as an entrepreneur for nothing. It's my line of work, in a way, the development of business. It's always good to hear new ideas."

I didn't believe it for a moment. "Thank you again. I have to go."

"Do you?" he asked, his head on one side, as though considering my answer for me.

Did I? I was in charge, after all. Did I care if I was seen? Did I care about the morning? He held my gaze and gestured to the waiter. The taxi lights disappeared down the road.

At that moment, I didn't much care about anything else.

"Are you sure about this?" he asked, the lights dim in the bedroom. He touched the top of my arms with warm, strong hands, felt for the zip and slipped the dress off my shoulders. I shivered. It wasn't from cold.

"Oh, yes," I said, "I'm sure."

CHAPTER 9

I woke early, still tucked up into his shoulder; sculpted, tanned muscles a glorious shock against the white pillow. I slid out from under his arm and turned over carefully to sit on the edge of the bed. The champagne euphoria had died a predictable death and left me with a craving for a mug of sweet tea, in my own place in the yard with a much-needed time to reflect on the night. He was asleep, relaxed and peaceful and I studied his face for any sign of duplicity, my feelings a mixed bag of pleasure and anxiety, with just a touch of unwanted suspicion. Did I need his eyes to see the truth? I remembered Duncan's speech in *Macbeth* about 'no art to find the man's construction in the face.' He opened them, deep, almost dark-blue, and smiled.

"I need to go," I said, stepped into the dress and pulled it up to my shoulders. I couldn't reach the zip. I ignored the tights, stuffed them into my handbag and put my bare feet into the sandals. "I don't want the world waking up and see me sneaking out like a thief in the night."

"Does it matter?"

"A bit," I said, "I live here. It's a small place and I'm still quite new. Beside which, as a budding entrepreneur, so I'm told, one does have a reputation to maintain. Can you zip me up, please?"

"Of course." He sat up and pulled me down onto the bed.

"Just the zip," I said, and extricated myself to sit on the edge of the bed. He laughed and did as I asked. Still in charge, I reminded myself, but only just. He kissed the back of my neck and let me go.

"I have to travel up to Scotland today," he said, as he seemed to accept my decision with equanimity, plumped up both pillows behind him and reached for his phone. "Could I call in and see the model ships before I go? I have an inbred interest in old sailing boats."

"Mid-morning," I said, "I'll make coffee," business-like as well. I still hadn't asked him about the drug-trafficking, or the plans for the future of the business next door and whether it would affect me or not, apart from what Denise had told me. There hadn't been a moment when it was appropriate. He held out a hand.

"Do you really have to go now?"

"Yes," I said, and wavered, but only slightly. "Mid-morning."

I slipped out to the car-park through the side-door of the hotel, open for early risers and staff and drove up the deserted High Street back to the yard. I stood for a moment and looked over to Ballast Island, savoured the early bird-song as the tide slid in below me and smiled at the world.

In the caravan, I consulted my still-tingling body, washed and changed, folded Helen's clothes carefully and took off the choker.

"Leave it on," he'd said and ran his finger over the soft velvet.

"I feel like a high-class whore," I'd said, trying to joke away my lack of experience alongside his thoughtful competency.

Any inhibitions I had were thrown to the wind. The night flooded back in flashes of pleasure; a blend of wanton abandonment, warmth and gentleness. I chuckled to myself and wondered how much its owner would have disapproved. Not that I would tell her, obviously, and not that she would ask. An edited version would suffice for an elderly lady.

However, come Monday morning when Denise was back at work, I knew she'd possibly hear about my date on the grapevine, text, WhatsApp… - whatever. On reflection, I hoped she hadn't. It was too close to home and Daniel was her boss. She'd want details. Maybe my friend Trish, in London, was a better and safer bet for the sharing I craved. Then again, she'd probably give me a lecture about one-night stands.

I'd missed it all terribly; the fun and the buzz and the girly, aftermath chat. Wherever had my life gone to this past year? I consoled myself that absolutely nobody I knew would have had a night like that. With the brewed tea, I went back out to sit on the harbour wall, dangled my legs over the edge with the air cool on my face and the tea hot in my hand and basked in an overall warm glow of satisfaction. My yard, my business and one night of the most exquisite intimacy I could ever have imagined. No strings attached and I was still in charge.

He arrived as the kettle boiled, and any doubts I had, dissipated from the moment he closed the car door and held his face up to the morning sun and the light, fitful breeze off the sea.

"May I?" he asked.

He picked up the first model, the *Cadwalader Jones*, a sleek replica of the schooner with its figure-head tucked under the bowsprit and the colours still distinguishable despite the fading paint. He handled it with reverence, turned it round and held it up to the light like a precious jewel.

"Just look at the detail in that rigging and even the spokes in the ship's wheel," he said, almost with reverence. "This is amazing."

I was so used to looking at them now, I just stood back while he picked up one model after another. The pieces of the barque *Pride of Wales* that Jason had smashed during the summer were piled carefully in a basket.

"That's a shame," he said, picking up a tiny spar.

"Long story", I said. "Why are you so interested in wooden boat-building, anyway?"

"Same as your friend Hugh, I think. It's the skill in creating a vessel from trees, something that floats and moves with just the wind and how to use the sails to get the best out of the hull. Nothing like it. It's a basic thing."

"I sailed to Ireland once," I said. "I think that was in a yacht with a Bermudan rig. I didn't do much other than throw up, I seemed to remember. But you don't build wooden boats, as well, do you" I asked, confused by his obvious enthusiasm.

"No. More the development of marinas, now."

"Ah," I said, "I see." I was right, then. He caught my tone of voice. He looked over his shoulder and turned to me. "No, you don't," he said "You want to ask me if I've got designs on your yard but am not being truthful. Is that it? Don't worry. This estuary isn't really marina-friendly territory."

"Well, someone else you employed seemed to have designs on developing it," I said. "Didn't you know about that, or was he working for himself?"

"You mean Doug Peterson? I was waiting for you to ask me. No, we didn't know about his drug-trafficking and if he approached you for a personal sale, it would have been purely for the access and the slipway. Nothing to do with us at all. It was a bad business and I'm sorry it affected you."

"You'll choose your next manager a bit more carefully, then," I said. He put the model he'd been holding back on its shelf.

"Somehow, I find it hard to believe we were in bed together a few hours ago," he said. "I wanted to tell you I appreciated your company last night. It was… very enjoyable. And fun. Now you've gone all hostile." He smiled. "How do I convince you?"

How had I got to the point where I didn't trust anybody and made assumptions about people before the fact? Milly sat on my shoulder and wagged her finger.

"Sorry," I said. "I didn't want to spoil it and now I have. I just needed to know."

He lifted one warm finger and touched me under my chin, bent down and kissed me gently.

"That's to remind you. It's not about marinas," he said. "Can I come back and see you again when I've finished my calls up north? In about a week? We haven't finished swapping life-stories yet and I haven't answered all your questions. I would very much like to see you again. Besides, I have business in Holyhead."

"But surely…." I said, considering the improbability of anything more than one Saturday night.

He just shook his head. "Coffee? Then I have to go."

But he didn't, not straightaway. The blue Porsche filled the yard with colour as he wandered towards it and then stopped by Hugh's boat. I left them to it, whatever it was and busied myself with the mugs.

He was deep in conversation with Hugh. I went outside, stood back and listened to snatches about a 'vigorous, deepening low, tracking south. Probably Wednesday.' They walked around Hugh's boat, testing the props with a good kick.

"A couple more wouldn't hurt," Daniel said, nodding his head, "especially with all that loose gravel around."

"Hurt what?" I asked, with a gut feeling that I should know about this.

"Just a few more props under the boat, "said Hugh. "Bit of bad weather on its way, Miss Cassie, and unfortunately it coincides with the equinox. The boys at Holyhead are keeping an eye on it as we're due an inspection of a new turbine on Wednesday."

"Will it affect us here?" I asked, finding it hard to believe with the blue sky and warm, seemingly endless, sunshine. "Are you sure? How bad?"

Hugh shrugged. "One never knows, of course, but one should always be prepared. Mr Freeman is as weather conscious and knowledgeable as they come, I believe."

I looked from one to the other. Daniel put his phone away.

"I have to plan which marinas to visit first, so yes, it matters when inspecting them. Maybe batten things down a bit in the yard," he said. "Anything that's loose that might float away."

I laughed. "Float away? In the yard?"

"They're very high tides." he said to Hugh.

There wasn't much to say after that. I wanted him to go. And come back.

"I'll be in touch," he said, and drove off.

Hugh watched me collect the coffee cups from the oil-drum.

"What," I said, knowing he had something to say.

"I'll use those spare timbers round the back, Miss Cassie, if that's in order?"

"You're both serious, aren't you?"

"Yes, indeed. It pays to be cautious," he said, "I do think he's right about the props, at least, but our storms are not like the hurricanes I expect he's used to."

"A storm in a teacup?" I asked. He didn't laugh.

I folded and packed Helen's clothes and the choker into the rucksack, feeling like Cinderella after the ball. I'd felt special but couldn't see it happening again. I locked the gate at four o'clock and walked over to Borth-y-Gest. I'd put new batteries in the torch to investigate the cellar properly, the little key firmly in my pocket and looked forward to the roast Sunday dinner with Helen's Nain.

There would be no more discussion about my great-aunt, I decided, my indignation and disappointment at her treatment by the village, and that included Helen's Nain, had threatened our relationship and I was in no position to judge her. I focused instead on the contents of the boxes in the cellar and tried not to think about Daniel, not to be shortened to 'Dan', he said, and we laughed when I told him my full name; I didn't have such scruples and Cassiopeia was just too much of a mouthful anyway, but it set off questions about my dad as a well-respected astronomer. I hadn't talked about my mother.

The front door was just as difficult to open and the musty smell clung to my clothes. If it hadn't been out of curiosity, I would have turned round and gone away rather than force myself to descend in to the blackness of the cellar. I found a plastic crate, turned it upside down and could just reach the top two shelves. I decided to leave the secrets of the bottom box with the padlock until last.

The contents of the box on the top shelf were as predictable as I'd imagined. I could only just see into the box and any ideas I'd had of gold sovereigns or diamond tiaras, faded into the reality of a few old chisels, screw-drivers and spanners of every size, all heavy-duty and jumbled up in an untidy mess. I shut the lid.

The second box was full of hammers, nails and screws that had spilled out of old cardboard boxes and plastic containers without lids. Underneath, a set of wood-working clamps lay next to a small vice. I wasn't going to put my hands in there with loose nails and screws, closed it again and stepped off the crate.

The box on the bottom shelf I could reach easily. It was made from a different wood and one I didn't recognise with my limited knowledge of the planks in the chandlery; a pale gold with a delicate grain and perfect, almost seamless joints. I fished the key out of the rucksack and it turned easily in the padlock. The lid opened fully and settled on the brass hinges which locked it in place.

I didn't need the light of the torch to guess the material used for the lining; smooth and cool to my fingers, the pale-pink satin had been pleated into minute folds inside the lid and the sides and edged with pink braid. In the base was a cushion, quilted with pearl buttons. A small, gold-painted container lay in the middle of the cushion, an envelope by its side with faded lettering. I picked it up and an object in the shape of a tiny urn materialised in the poor light with the letters 'Catrin', in old-fashioned, copperplate lettering engraved on the side. I lifted it out, stood transfixed, and held my second cousin in the palm of my hand.

The cold from the dirt seeped through my trainers; the spider-webs above fluttered in the draughts and the walls and low ceiling hemmed me in; it was a mausoleum, a tomb of family tragedy and misery. I felt the beginnings of panic and knew I needed to get out of there. I picked up the envelope and put it in my pocket, then placed the urn gently back in its satin nest, offered a whispered apology for disturbing her, then I closed and padlocked the box. I couldn't take her with me, not then, not to Helen's Nain's.

"I'll be back," I promised. "I won't leave you here."

Tomas's face swam before my eyes, the memories of his death as clear now as they had been then. The death of a child seemed a violation of all that was right, whether unavoidable or not, and I would never forget his little body trapped under the pontoon and the waves breaking over his pale face. But this child's ashes, so few that they fitted into such a pitifully small receptacle, could have been no more than those of a new-born baby. I had to find out why. Then I needed to bury her. Properly.

The roast chicken dinner kept warm in the oven. "I can't do this," I said to Helen's Nain, who was as shocked as I was, the white envelope sharp against the blue tablecloth. I picked it up and turned it over and over in my hand.

"I can't bear to think of what might have happened," I said. "I mean, to lose that baby as well as their other two children. It's too awful."

"She must have been in hospital somewhere," said Helen's Nain, "and when she finally came back, she was no longer pregnant but without a baby. Your great-uncle was very controlling, quite formidable; a difficult man. No-one could get near her and I suppose as time went by, we in the village assumed she was coping. When she developed cancer some years later, it was only a short time before she was hospitalised and we only learned that through the local district nurse."

"Shall I open it?" I asked.

"I think we should eat first," she said, "perhaps it will help."

Catrin had only lived for two days. The birth and death certificates lay open on the table.

"She died of asphyxia, it says. That's a bit vague. Means she just couldn't breathe. How can that happen these days?" I asked, even more upset.

"It wasn't 'these days', then, cariad. We'll never know. Put them back in the envelope. I think we could both do with a drink." She opened a bottle of sherry and her hand shook a little; the neck of the bottle chinked against the glass when she poured. I put my hand on the stem of mine to steady it – and wondered.

"Stay and watch the forecast on *Countryfile* with me," she said, as we cleared away the dishes. "There's a gale brewing for mid-week. Will Roberts came this morning to check the new flood barriers by the car-park. It's also the equinox and very high tides. I want to take the hanging baskets down if it's going to blow. He asked about sand-bags. Have you got any for the Boat Shed?" distractedly, as though dead babies were inconsequential to the moment.

She walked me to the front door and tapped the barometer in the hall, as she always did.

"Falling," she said, "but then it's been high for ages." We crossed the road and looked out over the bay. "Hard to believe that the sea could even reach the wall when it's like this."
The bay stretched out in a greyness of muddy sand and grass, the tide well out and there were hardly any lights on in the holiday homes, so typical of a Sunday evening.

I waved her goodbye and set off for the steps. I needed more than a sherry, I decided, after last night with Daniel and the way I felt when I thought of him, not really knowing whether it was all a fallacy; just a one night-stand when I wished it wasn't. It couldn't possibly be any more, I convinced myself. He could have a choice of anyone he wanted to with money and charm and a body to die for. As well as being really nice and easy company. Well, chalk and cheese. Then there were the boxes and the remains of my tiny, hardly-breathing relative and the unthinkable unhappiness of my great-aunt and uncle.

I turned back at the end of the sea-wall, felt the envelope in my pocket and decided to put it back in the box, now, rather than let it fester in the caravan and disturb my train of thought; it would be best where it belonged. I walked back to the house, let myself in and put the lights on. I hated the thought of the cellar, but there was no-one else to do it.

I opened the lid of the box and placed the envelope on the cushion, deep down, and ran my finger over the tiny urn. Perhaps she should be buried with her brother and sister, another sad grave on the headland above Black Rock and rightly at home with her family. Of course, and felt better. I closed the lid and turned the key in the padlock.

I wanted to leave, then, but curiosity made me stop, reared its head and asked about any more hidden secrets. I shone the torch over the other two boxes. They were exactly the same size; length, breadth and depth, yet from what I could see then, there were only a few tools in the top one; the second was packed full. I climbed back on the crate, the torch under my chin and opened the lid of the top box. The tools were spaced out and I lifted out spanners, a set of chisels and a pile of cheap-looking screw-drivers and placed them on the lid of the next box down.

The torch-beam picked out a piece of plywood underneath, except it wasn't at the base of the box; it rested half-way up the sides. I shone the torch closer. One corner had been damaged and splinters of wood roughened the surface. I picked up one of the screw-drivers, forced it down the side, levered the base up and shone the torch inside. The base was packed with plastic bags, the powder inside, white and bright in the beam.

My brain in overdrive, I put the base back, placed the tools on top, shut the lid and stepped down carefully from the crate. I left the cellar as I found it, sank down into one of the filthy chairs in the front room and punched the number I'd been given into my phone.

For a Sunday night, the police were remarkably good about it all, almost enthusiastic, I thought, but I was still shaking after I'd listened to the instructions. I sat on the chair in the front room, alternately hot then shivering with cold. I wanted to throw up but couldn't face the disgusting bathroom. I was told to lock-up the house and go back to the yard as though nothing had happened, talk to no-one and not to leave until I'd been contacted. I was not going to argue. If the good folk of the village had been concerned before about the 'goings-on' as they called it, they'd had good reason to.

I now understood why Jason had to leave. It wasn't just about the girl. Dealing from my house? Did he know or had he been just a cover? I was horrified, then furious, locked the gates with meaning and drank several large glasses of vodka. Daniel seemed like a distant dream.

I slept badly, aware of every hour and woke hung-over on Monday morning, miserable and exhausted. My stomach rebelled against even the thought of a cup of tea. Any plans for the week would be on hold and I'd been told to carry on as normal and certainly not contact Jason, safely miles away. Someone would call to see me. Plain clothes, they said, so as not to alert anyone. Although I dreaded any accusation of my involvement by the police, it was unlikely and deep down, I knew it would be okay. What would not be okay, would be the dealers thinking differently.

I tried to distract myself with plans for the smoke-house. The smoke-house was my next project, a filthy job I would happily have passed over to Jason. He phoned me to say he'd started his new job.

"By the way," I said, as casual as you like. "Can you remember where you put the spare key to the front door? I forgot to ask you, being as you were in such a rush to leave."

"It was in with the spoons and forks and stuff, in the kitchen," and he changed the subject. "Buy some goldfish for the lobster tank for a bit of company, Cass. I've put the aquarium bits in a box on the top shelf – I told you, plastic ship's wheel and some coral stuff and a sea-chest and that little key. The old guy must have been watching *Pirates of the Caribbean*."

I could well imagine where the spare key to the front door had migrated to. Stupid, careless lad but I missed his banter already and the sharing of problems, swallowed the lump in my throat and made some toast. That stuck in my throat, too.

Was I going to have to spend all day here, not knowing anything? They'd put surveillance on the house, surely, but would the locals notice? They, whoever they were, were not going to leave that amount of gear behind for long, once they knew Jason had left. Maybe the stuff had been there all the time, before Jason even moved in; thousands of pounds' worth, but unlikely. They would come for it pretty soon, anyway. The police phoned, reassured me and insisted I do nothing and talk to no-one. I locked the gates.

I tidied the yard and worked out how to tie the small boats down. At lunchtime, the weatherman forecasted the storm with serious wind warnings, I stomached a banana and some toast, fell asleep in the van in the afternoon and woke in a hot sweat from a nightmare; the cellar at *Tai Pilots* had flooded, the door broken down from outside by massive breakers, the water level had crept up and the boxes on the shelves had been washed off. Catrin, dressed in a pink frilly dress and booties, had floated out of her box and drifted backwards and forwards in the swell. Her eyes were open and she looked at me. I stood on the steps and tried to grab her with a boat-hook.

I rolled out of bed, sick and disturbed, decided food and activity were needed, reached for a notebook and pen and made a list. Move models ships to higher shelves, I wrote, and should I move the Toyota out of the yard? What about *Annie*, tied up to the wall with her nose pointing down the harbour exposed to waves breaking over her stern onto the engine? What had Daniel said? Anything that floats. Was that really necessary? But then, I reasoned, if I didn't take all this seriously and something happened, I'd look like an idiot. And if I made all these over-cautious preparations, but then nothing happened, who would know? Err on the side of caution, prepare for the worst and hope for the best, they say. Still, I reckoned it was all scaremongering. Even during the gale when Tomas had drowned, the sea had only lapped the top of the ladder. I'd ring Mr Roberts in the morning. He'd know.

CHAPTER 10

Monday dawned bright and still warm and the nightmare of the dead baby with open eyes had faded into insignificance after the shock of that white powder, stashed in my house, my property. I should have guessed. I tucked it all in the back of my mind, the police instructions had relieved me from any involvement and I concentrated on the coming storm as I opened the gates to Will Roberts, the back of his pick-up piled with sandbags. He started to unload them and set six down on the gravel by Hugh's yacht.

"Just in case," he said. "You don't want to be caught out," and nodded with approval at the hull of the small yacht. "I see Hugh's already put in some extra props. I suggest you put these bags at the base of the shed nearest the slip. Those tin sheets won't keep much water out and a few sand-bags may help. Perhaps move the models to higher shelves, or even out of the room at the end of the shed altogether."

"I don't understand what all the fuss is about," I said. "This can't be the only gale this yard has seen. I can't see how Hugh's boat could be blown over."

He slung a bag over his shoulder and looked at me, undecided, I thought, whether to offer a scathing or patient reply. He ran his hand over greying hair.

"A combination of things, Miss Jones. It's not just the force of the wind. If high tide coincides with the peak of the gale, it could flood the yard. Do you see?"

Not really, I thought. It's only water.

"It happens occasionally; seaweed and all sorts get thrown up and washed into the yard, the sea picks up the gravel and it piles up against any solid objects – like boat props or cradles. It's hard to predict exactly. But the extra props look sound."

He carried some more sand-bags and propped them up against the shed wall. He'd picked them up as though they were made of feathers, dusted off his hands on his trousers and leaned against the pick-up door.

"This storm is the tail-end of a hurricane way out in the Atlantic," he said, "but the centre is deepening very quickly. Make sure you know exactly when high tide is and write it down. Then watch and wait. If you get past the top of the tide without any disasters then the ebb will take care of the rest. Nothing like the rules of nature to plan around."

"That's what my dad would have said. He told me that rules made by man can be broken but the rules of the universe were fixed and immutable – most of the time, anyway. Thank you for the sand-bags."

"Can't change the tides and their rules, Miss Jones. Which of course, you remembered on your trip to the reef and got back safely without going aground. Of course, it also helps, when you anchor, to gauge how much chain you need to put out." He knew. I swear he winked at me.

He turned the pick-up round and hailed me through the window.

"Call me if you're in trouble," he said, "and tie everything down. Oh, and make sure your phone is charged and move the Toyota out of the yard. If there's a power cut, use the engine to charge the phone," and drove off.

"What shall I do about *Annie*?" I called after him, but he'd gone. How did he know I'd got myself into trouble on the reef? Did the skipper of the patrol boat tell him, despite assuring me he wouldn't? Did it matter, anyway? I was getting past the stage of being annoyed and was beginning to recognise a feeling of gratitude; a warm feeling, like a gentle, soothing wave flattening out the prickly defences I'd had to put up to survive. They cared. Even old Mr Hughes. Even David. But Daniel? Probably not, I thought. He'd bigger fish to fry.

I did what I could in the yard, unenthusiastic about the six upturned dinghies awaiting renovation, some simply lying on the gravel and some on chocks of wood. I tipped each one on its side to thread a length of rope through the thwarts and bow-fittings and tied the whole lot to the solid steel machinery that housed the electric winch. I walked around with a bin-bag and picked up odd bits of rope and off-cuts of wood, a couple of rusty paint tins at the back of the shed, but Jason and I had worked hard to clean up the mess I'd inherited and only heavy timbers and a couple of steel I-beams were left. They wouldn't go anywhere.

I moved the models on to top shelves in the Boat Shed but making *Annie* secure, could wait until tomorrow. I thought that if I doubled up the mooring-ropes and tied a tarpaulin over the engine, that was the best I could do. There was no room further up the harbour for me, the yachts packed in to the pontoon after a good summer and not yet time for the lift-out. Will Roberts hadn't suggested requesting a yacht-club berth as he had done for last winter. He was distracted and anxious, I could tell, and had enough to think about. You're on your own girl, I thought, and turned back to the empty shed; no Neifion and no Jason.

Down-hearted and hungry, I knew I needed to eat and then do something constructive, not wait around for something that might not happen. Agonising over the drugs was a waste of time and energy. It was out of my hands and I knew I wouldn't be implicated. Jason would have to deal with it himself when he was questioned.

A text pinged on my phone. 'Food certificate granted.' I yelped and thanked whichever gods happened to be cruising around. My mood lifted and I decided to start work and prepare for the spring, made coffee, cooked up a bacon and egg bap in the snack-bar, donned gloves, mask and a cotton scarf tied tight over my hair and launched myself into the depths of the smoke-house. It was absolutely filthy.

The smoke-house, a single galvanised, steel box, stood at the rear of the chandlery, its back door opened to a small covered walkway where the chippings were stored. Some were still in undamaged bags and some were still scattered around the concrete floor where the firemen had doused the fire that Jason had inadvertently started in the summer. The soot and water had streaked the concrete black and small piles of burned-out chippings had piled up next to the wall. Along with all the other things to attend to, I'd just left it and hadn't the heart to make Jason do it. He hadn't started the fire maliciously and had been in a terrible state when Hugh and I found him hiding in the shed.

The walls to the smoke-house were covered in a black pitch. It stank from years of smoke and fish. I scraped the worst off and removed the racks from the roof beams and took them out into the yard for a proper scrub. The chippings were a mixture of oak and apple; only hardwoods allowed, it said in the book I'd bought from Browsers, giving details of length of smoking and instructions for vacuum packing.

My enthusiasm, despite the foul job, was easily maintained at the thought of my own smoked salmon, the best I could get and smoked to perfection; none of the nasty, slimy cheap stuff. Then there were all the flavours from the different woods; Angela would have a field day when I told her my plans for fillets of smoked trout, caught locally, not to mention the mussels from the Straits. I sang as my face blackened and the purple streaks in my hair crept out from under the scarf and were pushed back in smelling of fish. My mind wandered and I thought of Daniel, who said he would ring. I doubted it.

Then I thought of the storm as it brewed nastily out in the Atlantic and pushed it to one side, very briefly, until the phone rang. Will Roberts.

"Could I suggest that you turn *Annie* around tomorrow afternoon with her bows to the sea?"

"Why? Right, yes of course. I can see why. I didn't know what to do. Thanks."

"And double up the mooring ropes. Do you need Mark to come down and assist you?"

I thought about it for a nano second.

"Yes, please. I'd be very grateful. Is it really going to be that bad?"

There was a pause. "Probably, yes, is the answer. Tuesday night will be the start of strong winds with little rain, but check the high tide for Wednesday and write it down as I suggested. If the wind stays southerly and strengthens, you need to be in the yard to keep an eye on things. Do batten down. It's easy to forget the exact time of the peak of the tide when it's blowing and raining hard. An hour can make all the difference."

I left the scrapings from the smoke-house in black, watery piles and decided the racks I'd pulled out could stay where they were; I'd just rope them together, like the dinghies. I washed and changed, sat for a while in the late afternoon sun, then shivered as the sky hazed over, a milky-blue with the visibility clear and sharp over the Traeth to Harlech. The Rhinogs soared above and behind, silhouetted black, with the pass over the Roman Steps a distinct chunk out of the skyline.

I went to bed that night, uneasy. My mother rang with the usual bleating.

"You really should come home, darling, and get a proper job. London's buzzing just now and such nice people. You don't get out enough." Mother knew nothing about threatening depressions, barometric readings and cold fronts and I wasn't about to enlighten her; about weather - or recent liaisons.

"I'd like to come for a visit sometime in October. We're very busy at the moment," she said.

"Visit?"

"Yes, darling. Just dying to see all the improvements you've made."

I couldn't find an appropriate answer to that.

"Take care," I said, not 'love you,' to my mother, as my friends did. As for a visit, she'd have to stay in a hotel and as for her opinion on the yard… she'd hate it. I just knew she would.

The night was quiet, unnaturally quiet, but by early morning the shrouds on Hugh's boat had started to tap against the mast, then clack harder in a fitful breeze. Gulls wheeled and screeched overhead, dipped and swooped, turned and banked effortlessly in the rising wind.

Mark came mid-afternoon, took one look at the incoming tide, the surface calm one minute, the next ruffled by strong gusts and suggested we warp the boat round. I stood back and did as I was told. He attached ropes to the bow and a ring set into the wall, let go the stern into the current and *Annie* swung gently round to face the opposite way. He doubled up the ropes in her new position on the wall and checked the fenders. I was dead impressed and told him so.

"That's the best we can do, Cassie. She'll ride up over the swells but the hull might get a bit bashed on the wall. Nothing a bit of spit and polish won't sort out, though. Close the cabin doors tight and make sure the bilge pump is on. I've put an extra rope on the engine casing."

"Do you think it'll be that bad?" I asked. "Mr Roberts seems to think so, but nothing much apart from the odd gale has happened since I've been here. Could it all come to nothing?"

He looked up at the sky. Feathers of high, white cloud blown into curls and comma-shaped wisps began to streak across the sky from the west, the long tails reaching out into the pale-blue above us.

"Cirrus," he said, "you've heard of 'mares' tails?' But it's not just that. The depression is still way out in the Atlantic but the pressure is already low and falling quickly. They say if it falls five millibars in three hours, we could be in for something a bit more out of the ordinary than just a gale; we're talking storm-force winds and it just happens to be the equinoctial tides as well. Let's hope it changes its mind and buggers off somewhere else. Although somehow, I don't think so."

"What more can I do?" I asked, feeling small and helpless.

"Make us a cup of coffee," he said, and grinned. "By the way, did you have a good night on Saturday?"

"What?"

"I was in the Spar first thing Sunday morning. The baby got us up early so I went to buy some bacon. Saw you drive past. You looked very gorgeous, I have to say, for early morning."

He held up his hands. "Don't worry, my lips are sealed."

The sea had nearly reached the top of the harbour wall that afternoon as Mark had predicted, with an hour to go before high tide but not unusually so for an equinoctial tide, he'd said. The wind had been warm and gusty, and stirred up pockets of dust in the dry gravel. I listened to the Shipping Forecast at six o'clock, had no appetite for food and needed to get out of the yard. I couldn't stay behind locked gates for ever. Then, as though someone had read my mind, I had a phone call from the police. 'Carry on as normal but do not mention it to anyone and do not go back to the house.' As if.

I walked over to Borth-y-Gest. There were sandbags by the front gates of the row of houses that lined the front of the bay and the flood barriers at the top of the slip leading into the car-park were closed. Will

Roberts had been busy with signs to warn visitors not to use the car-park until further notice. The high-tide already reached about a foot below the top of the wall, but there was little wind in the shelter of the village and nothing yet to concern the residents. I scarcely believed it was possible for anything unusual to happen.

I stood at the bottom of the steps and looked out across the flooded bay, so different from the low-tide scene of mud and sand as though the sea didn't exist at all, and now at high-tide, a beautiful mirror of still water that lapped innocuously at the sea-wall. I glanced over at *Tai Pilots*, so tainted with the recent events, that I knew I had to sell it.

Helen's Nain was in the living-room. A cup of tea had grown cold on the coffee table and the television talked quietly to itself. Her glasses had slipped down her nose, her mouth half-open and her head rested to one side on the chair-back. She looked old and frail for the first time since I'd met her and a sudden lurch in my stomach reminded me how much I had relied on her, just for being there, comfortable and undemanding. She opened her eyes and caught me watching her.

"Will Roberts has left some sand-bags," she said.

"Yes, I saw them. He's put them across the gate. Should I move a couple by the front door?" I asked.

"I've never needed them there before. The water only splashes over the wall onto the road, usually."

"It's just that Mark was saying it could be really bad. I feel I ought to come and stay but I can't leave the yard."

She smiled. "We've had plenty of storms over the years. It'll be fine. I've got candles and a gas-stove if the power goes. Never had wet feet yet."

She levered herself out of the chair and the cup rattled against the saucer when she picked up the cup.

"Helen's Nain…" I started. She raised her eyebrows. "No, I can't call you 'Nain'. It's not right, I don't care what you say. Anyway, I just wanted to ask you… are you alright?"

"Why shouldn't I be?" she asked, a little sharply.

"I wondered if you were tired after a busy summer. That's all," I said, "and if there was anything I could do before I go."

She shook her head, bustled into the kitchen, clattered the cup into the sink, walked with me to the front door through the hall and stopped by the barometer.

"You need to see this," she said, tapping the barometer. "980 and still falling. In the lap of the weather gods, now, cariad, and the only thing you can do is be prepared. If bad things happen, at least you can say you've done everything you could."

She looked hard at me then, "and that applies to everything in life. Do the best you can at the time and no-one could ask for anything more."

I knew what she was referring to; my critical comments about my great-aunt. How could I judge her, not knowing the circumstances?

I gave her a big hug. "Will you be alright?" I asked.

"Of course," she said, "and you take care and don't do anything heroic in that yard. It's only property after all." She looked around, as though trying to remember something, settled on the geraniums that still burst with pinks and reds and hung in baskets either side of the front door.

"Can you just lift those down for me? Just put them on the ground under the table. They'll be fine. Seems a shame to let them be knocked around while they're still in flower."

I didn't want to go back to the yard. I didn't want to leave her, with the frailness I'd never noticed before, or the warm house and the security it offered. The Bed and Breakfast, like *Tai Pilots*, had been there a long time. Its owners would have watched from their windows as ships were built, launched and set sail, crewed by local people with families. Some had returned, some had not, their grieving widows and children a legacy of the sea and all its moods.

In a momentary dream, I stood half-way up the steps and closed my eyes, seeing images of ships in the making before the village, as it was now, was built, hulls constructed on the beaches with their new timbers like whale bones stark against the sand or half-clothed in timber as the bay rang to the sound of caulking mallets and saws. The only sound, at that moment, was the rustle of the dead leaves in the oak tree above me and the cry of the gulls.

The weatherman's voice on the six o'clock news said it all. They had been predicting the storm for several days as it raced across the Atlantic towards the west coast of Ireland, but the gravity of his words said more.

"A deepening depression," he said. "You can see how the jet-stream has dipped compared to the last few weeks."

Anyone could read the pressure at the centre, now 970 millibars.

"Frontal systems with storm-force winds will precede the centre, at present on track for Northern Ireland, Scotland and the north-west of England."

I knew very little about meteorology but had listened to Mark and Mr Roberts' general chat over the months. I googled a weather map, studied the isobars packed tight and the steep pressure gradient. It had been 980 at its centre only a couple of hours since. It was not so much the pressure, but the tendency over so many hours, Mark had said and he'd found my great-uncle's ship's barometer in the chandlery and set it.

If that was the tendency, I wished I was elsewhere. This was a vicious, nasty beast and amber warnings had already been issued for heavy rain later in the day. The Shipping Forecast would already have caused concern for those unfortunate to be in its track. The only thing I could do for comfort was to open a bottle of wine – and wait.

My last patrol of the yard at nine o'clock was a quiet affair, with an occasional cry from a stalking heron on Ballast. It flew off, slow and studied with its ungainly legs like sticks below the great wings. A late blackbird sang from the cliff-face, until he too flew away. I was left in the silent yard with an occasional gust of warm wind on my face and dust on my wine-glass. I shut the door to the caravan, checked my phone for charge and was startled when it rang. Daniel.

"Are you still in one piece?" His voice light and warm.

"Yes, and it hasn't started yet. This is horrible, all this waiting. I am so glad to hear a voice. Where are you?

"Just north of Oban. Where are you?"

"Sitting in the caravan with a glass of wine. I've done everything I can. I don't know what else to do now. It's like waiting for the end of the world. It can't be that bad, can it?"

I could hear the anxiety in my own voice and took a large gulp of wine. He laughed, a lovely deep laugh, full of comfort and acknowledgement.

"Well, they're predicting some serious winds for up here."

"What will you do with yourself if you can't work?"

"Oh, just sit around the hotel and drink whisky with the fishermen."

"Seriously? You'd like that?"

"No. I'd rather drink champagne with strange ladies who are more comfortable in overalls."

I laughed.

"I don't actually work on the marinas and I've plenty of paperwork to keep me going. This marina is fairly protected but the guys are out checking the pontoons and the ropes. Are you prepared, Cassie?" on a more serious note.

"We turned *Annie* round to face the sea and I've roped everything down. Now I'm drinking wine, tucked up in bed with my headphones ready. I don't want to listen to it when it starts to blow. I hate that whistling sound you get in the boatyards."

"That's what ostriches do, hide their heads in the sand. When it starts to moan in the rigging, that's when you know it's blowing. You'll need to keep your wits about you."

"How can you be so cheerful?"

"It's what comes of being brought up in a hurricane zone. You just learn to live with it."

"Well, you're not me, are you? I'm pretty scared."

There was a silence.

"I'd be scared too," he said. "I know what it feels like. As long as you remember, if it becomes dangerous, you get out of there and leave it to the weather."

"But it's my business," I said, "I can't just abandon it. I've got plans."

"You stay safe, that's more important," he said. "It's only property, Cassie."

"It's my property. There's no-one else to care about it."

"I care," he said, and hung up, just like that and for a few minutes, I stared at the phone like an idiot, then put it carefully on the bedside locker. I slept, despite the anxiety, too much wine and no pills, slept through the early morning high-tide and missed the dawn as it struggled to lighten the sky over the Rhinogs

It started to blow at seven in the morning. Not yet anything out of the ordinary and still warm and dry, but the gusts, although in short bursts, felt malevolent interspersed with eery lulls, as though the wind was playing with a threat of danger but couldn't quite make up its mind. The door to the van rattled and the noise of the shrouds on Hugh's mast brought me back into the real world, but despite the predicted storm and the drugs at *Tai Pilots*, I smiled to myself as I remembered Saturday night. I turned over in the bunk, and snugged down with the memory of hard muscle and warm hands. And tenderness. "I care," he'd said on the phone; me or the yard?

There was a mild thump from the roof. I sat upright in the bunk and stared at the plastic ventilation hatch above me. It rose half an inch as a gust caught the edge of the plastic, then fell back into place. I leaped out of bed and tightened the screws as far as they would go; it had never happened before and I tied my dressing-gown cord to the screw and tied it to one of the locker-door handles. The flimsy cover wouldn't survive much battering and if it was even fraction open, it might blow off, leave the inside of the van and my few precious possessions open to the elements. There would be no way I could fix it. It wasn't raining yet but they said it would do later. I sat down on the edge of the bunk and watched the hatch-cover safely through the next gust. It rattled but didn't lift. The van rocked underneath me, unsteady on its four legs but at least Hugh had pushed it so far back against the wall, it couldn't blow over.

I didn't want to stay in the van, which now seemed alarmingly flimsy and insubstantial, or go out into the yard and look over the wall to check *Annie*. I could see enough from the window and she rose and fell comfortably with her mooring ropes. The tide was now ebbing fast, as spring-tides do but there had been no rain in the mountains of any note for weeks to accelerate its speed above normal. Even so, with wind against tide, a short, choppy sea had kicked up over the gradually disappearing water. I opened the door in a lull; I had to check I'd done all I could to the shed; the sand-bags had been lined up against the base of the gable-end near the slipway and the model ships moved to the top shelves. Breakfast, forecast, phone charge, and then wait some more.

I made coffee and breakfasted mid-morning on cold sausage butties, blessed the snack-bar and fridge but promised myself healthier eating after the storm. The sky was cloaked in pale-grey with a faint shimmer of a halo around the sun as it struggled to shine through and mean-looking dark clouds scudded in from the sea. The wind was strong but I could stand against it and made my way to the harbour wall.

I'd missed the last high-tide but there was no tell-tale, top-of-the-tide-line; the sea had lapped over the wall briefly and left a few trails of sea-weed wrapped around the top of the ladder. *Annie* had settled back onto her usual place, the tyres that acted as fenders cushioned her comfortably from the wall and the mooring ropes were as tensioned as Mark had left them. I blessed the headphones for keeping me asleep; she would have floated near the top of the wall but stayed intact.

I didn't want to think about the tide later that day; the highest of the month, and left the miserable, grey, rushing river to its own devices. I shut the door of the shed firmly behind me and put the kettle on. There was nothing to be done except catch up with my lists and try to ignore the tinny clang when the roofing sheets lifted in the gusts and fell back into place.

The door flew open. Denise was a welcome sight, if unexpected. She burst through the door, a red sailing jacket borrowed from stock, presumably, over her smart, office jacket. A black thermal hat covered her hair with the ribbed edge dropped so low on her forehead, it threatened to spoil the blue eyeshadow.

"Well," she said, pulled off the hat and threw herself comfortably into one of the chairs. "You're going to love this."

"This? You're joking. It's horrible and dead scary," I said, and pointed out of the window.

"No, not that, it's only a storm. They come and go. Be alright. No, listen. Guess who I saw at the weekend? Haven't had a chance to tell you."

I pulled the tea-bags out of the mugs, added three sugars to hers without asking, handed her the mug and sat down in the opposite chair. And waited.

"Who's the most unlikely person to shack up with a blingy blonde?"

"The Harbour Master?" I said, not really wanting to play the game.

"Don't be daft. He's ancient. No, really. Guess."

"I have no idea. Shouldn't you be out tying things down before high-tide?"

"Yeah, yeah. Got ages yet."

"Go on, then."

"David Hughes." She slurped her tea. "Got any biscuits?"

It was impossible for the silence to be palpable above the wind, but it was, for a brief moment.

"David? My solicitor? So?"

"Yes of course your solicitor, son of what's his name, the old one. The one who drove you mad being all bossy and fatherly and you said poured cold water on all your plans. You had a couple of rows, I recall," she said, "not that I was listening. You just mentioned it."

"So?"

"Well, you said he was, like, dead stuffy, but you should see her. I mean, unreal, with a figure to die for, dripping with gold bangles and she'd got a posh convertible."

I sipped my coffee, not sure how I should react. Politely, disinterested possibly, I thought, then I just had to know.

"He's entitled to have a woman in his life, isn't he?" as curiosity got the better of me and I was glad of the distraction. "So, where did you see her…them?"

"I didn't, to start, but my brother who waits on at the *Plas Coch*, you know, that big country house hotel near Pwllheli? Anyway, on Sunday morning, he saw this car drive round to the front door and she got out to pick a guy up. He only mentioned it 'cos it was one of those cars he'd always lusted after, a Silver Mercedes and her all glam with blonde hair, all made-up and legs up to her armpits. He was full of it."

I laughed. "What? Her or the car? So, how do you know it was

David?" I asked, trying to unscramble the unlikely event.

"'cos I saw the same car he'd described outside his office yesterday and she was leaning against the driver's door when he walked out, gave her a kiss and got into the passenger seat."

She ended in a triumphant burst. "So there."

I had to get up and turn away, bottling up the laughter that threatened to bubble up and burst.

"What's the matter?" she said. "Don't you think that's a bit odd considering what you know of him? Conventional and all that?"

"Not really my business," I said. "Why should I care who he goes out with?"

"He likes you, though," she said. "I could see it in his eyes when he came to the yard to help. Real concern there, Cass. I could see it."

"Rubbish. Okay, I liked him at first and then he just kept telling me what to do. He wouldn't listen to any of my ideas and thought I was irresponsible and fool-hardy – that's exactly what he said. He was just looking after the yard until I took over. It was just business. He just went too far in telling me what to do, like he wanted to own me."

She drained her mug, took another biscuit and shrugged.

"Just thought you'd like to know about his girlfriend. Nothing like a bit of gossip to keep you sane. Right, now I've told you something to take your mind off the stupid weather, I'll go and tie things down though what the hell I'm supposed to do with power boats and jet-skis floating around the yard, God only knows.

'I'll tell you what, though, if it does flood, you'll get the worst of it being nearer the sea. It'll probably leave my yard dry. Doesn't really matter. The boss will have it all insured, you bet your life. He's not the sort of guy to take chances. Gorgeous, too. Can't believe he's actually human. You are insured, Cass, aren't you?"

She shut the door and I picked up the phone.

“Thank you for checking,” I said to Mr Hughes’ secretary, only seconds later. “Does that mean weather damage as well?”

“Up to a point,” she said. “You’ll have to read the policy, Miss Jones.”

CHAPTER 11

Jason texted. 'Big gale on the way. Job good so far. Bought any goldfish yet? Stay safe.'

Marigold gloves and cleaning were the only way to keep occupied. I couldn't leave the yard and my brain was on overload.

It had taken me a while to appreciate the therapeutic value of cleaning. When I was a teenager and we lived in London, Milly cleaned and cooked and scolded me for the mess in my bedroom; the dirty mugs, chocolate wrappers and occasional apple-core or banana-skin under the bed, but I rarely did anything about it. Then she taught me a lesson by flatly refusing to have anything to do with my room.

"If you want to sleep in a pigsty, my girl, that's up to you," she'd say, "but don't you come moaning to me when maggots come crawling out from under your bed. And don't you bring your dirty habits into my kitchen. And, you change your own sheets from now on."

The kitchen was a different matter and when I was allowed to play with pastry and make cakes, I followed her cleaning regime without complaint. The only thing I ever cleaned properly for myself, was as a rookie in the newspaper office, my coffee mug with 'Who's the best?'

written on one side and a picture of a grinning gorilla on the other, was sacrosanct, as was the keyboard on my desk, dusted with a soft paint-brush from Wilco. I'd dared Tim, my young, spotty and enthusiastic, desk-sharing colleague, to even touch it.

He emailed me with a keep-safe message, all the way from the office in Northampton, which was about as far away from the sea as he could be, for a fervent sea-kayaker. I thought he would have forgotten all about me. A sudden sense of loss at the lack of camaraderie and buzz with the newspaper stopped me in my tracks whilst polishing the counter. Then I was reminded me how bored I'd been with the daily grind of mundane stories. I took my gloves off and read it again.

'Big storm, Cassie. Bigger than most. Take photos, if you can safely and write it up for Ed. Don't forget the reporter in you while you're busy up to your neck in Marigolds and muck. Stay safe. Record it, write it up, take pics.' Tim.

How did he know I was cleaning? But he was right. I looked at the phone and my developing propensity for taking pictures with it instead of using the Canon, then thought about quality of image. I shot into the van and took the Canon from its case and checked the battery, a wave of focused enthusiasm taking over from the immediate worries. Perhaps I was really an anomaly of two halves; a grubby cleaner one minute, taking pleasure in the polished finish of an oak counter, or a glory hunter, always waiting for something momentous to happen, a moment to catch on film and a story to accompany it? Or happily both?

I put the camera carefully on the counter next to my phone and relished the fit of it as I cradled it in both hands, still human enough to be able to marvel at the technology to capture a moment in time at my fingertips, just with the click of the shutter. I picked the camera up again, re-familiarising myself with the knobs and buttons and the digital screen, a purposeful object that required a bit more thought than the phone, and felt a surge of joy. If the place fell about my ears in the storm, I could always go back to journalism. I'd dallied with the idea so many times and been pressured by my mother and then back-tracked at the thought of living inland, hemmed in by houses in a town or city with the constant hum of traffic and the joys of the rush-hour. It was good to remind myself of the option, though, if only I could get over the bloody-mindedness about staying.

Denise phoned.

"Mr Roberts says to go up to the headland past *Tai Pilots* for about two o'clock. He says it doesn't happen very often but the tide's as low as it ever gets and the channel's shrunk to virtually nothing. He says when the tide starts to come in today it'll come in like a tidal bore, you know, like they have on the Severn? Not as big, mind, but he says you can hear it coming."

I called Helen's Nain to tell her. She sounded tired and said she'd seen it before and to call in on the way back. "Only once or twice though. Don't miss it," she said.

I put the phone in my back pocket, then picked up the camera, slung the strap round my neck and tucked it into my jacket.

The wind was vicious on the headland, blowing hard from the south, the great expanse of sand over towards Harlech a flat, dun-coloured desert with low cloud obscuring the hills behind. There was little sign of the Dwyryd as it snaked its way to the confluence of the rivers and little sign of the Glaslyn as I would have recognised it; odd puddles left in the channels between the sandbanks were the only indication the rivers were there at all. We stood and looked over the wall at the end of *Tai Pilots*. I'd been told to act normally, so I did, chose to cast a quick glance at the front door and carried on. A small group of people had gathered, locals mostly, who'd seen it before. The channel below us had dwindled to a narrow stream.

"It'll be another thirty minutes yet," said a voice, as the group gathered around us, buffeted by the wind and holding hoods and hats on with both hands. "You the lady from the boatyard?"

I nodded.

"Seen this before? It's going to be one hell of a tide with this gale coming in. Your yard's right in the firing line as well."

"Thanks for that," I said. "Not much I can do about it."

We waited, the wind increased in the gusts, while the trickle below us seemed ever smaller.

"Never seen it so low," the voice behind me said.

"Oh, shut up," I mouthed to the empty estuary.

The wind dropped briefly, not completely but just enough to permit the addition of another sound. We heard it approaching from a distance, a faint sound at first, not born by the wind, a sound that grew imperceptibly louder and louder, then cries of 'Look' from the crowd. An unbroken wave-crest rolled from seaward into the channel below us. There was no precursor of dribbling water, no foam or froth, just one pure wave about two feet high. It filled the channel, perfectly formed from side to side; it didn't break, just rushed in with a quiet rumble.

Then it passed us and headed to the harbour, where it met the deeper water and dissipated to nothing. The silver sheet of the incoming tide spilled over the sandbanks and began to cover the estuary at a speed I'd never seen before. I took pictures, of course, with camera and phone but it was so fast, I didn't imagine I could have done it justice.

It was shocking in its intensity, an extraordinary event, and we walked back slowly, without speaking. I stopped at the gate to see Helen's Nain.

"I'm going to lock up the yard then go home," said Denise, her hood off and hair blown over her face. She brushed it out of her mouth. "Mr Freeman's just texted. He says to disconnect all the electrics from the power points in the yard and shut the gates. He said I've to go home.

What will you do, Cassie?"

"Stay. But I'm going to check Helen's Nain's okay first. I'll be fine. It's only a storm, as you pointed out this morning."

She didn't smile, all frivolity gone.

"Be careful. Get out if you need to. See you tomorrow." She turned to go then turned back and pointed at the camera. "Don't do anything silly, will you?"

I checked the sandbags piled against the front gate; one on top of the other and another two now, delivered by Mr Roberts and reassuringly placed at the base of the front door. I walked round to the back of the house and let myself in, the shelter from the wind more pronounced than the front.

She was sitting in the chair by the range; the kettle hissed gently on the hotplate and her feet were propped up on a stool, an open magazine on her lap. Her eyes were closed and the reading glasses had slid down her nose, her mouth open and slack. Again, I caught my breath as I watched for the rise and fall of her chest. I'd hardly seen her before in anything less than bustling activity but I'd noticed the shaky hands and the tiredness and had caught her asleep twice, despite the impending storm, and it worried me. It was easy to forget she was late into her seventies. She woke with a start and a smile.

"Interesting, was it?" she said. "Pannad? The scones are still warm from the oven. Make the tea, will you, cariad?"

I stayed for a while, reluctant to leave the warmth and security, not wanting to leave her on her own. The tide, even if it splashed over the wall onto the road, hadn't concerned me as much as the possibility of a power-cut lasting the night. She guessed what I was thinking.

"You need to go and keep an eye on your yard now. High-tide's not for a few hours yet. I'll be perfectly alright," and she pointed to the table where a torch, camping gas-stove and light, a box of candles, some tins of soup, a saucepan and a plate of bread, already buttered and covered with a fly-net were laid out. She'd done this before and I felt better for her preparedness.

I gave her a hug, with a promise to come back later. She held up her phone.

"All charged. Have you done yours?" she said, sinking back into the comfy chair.

"Of course," I said.

"Will you check the barometer before you go?"

The grandfather clock chimed four o'clock as I assimilated the ominous reading; 965, the black needle shrieked at me, and still two hours left to high tide. She just nodded when I told her.

"Take care," she said, as I shut the kitchen door, then the garden gate, walked to the front of the house, the wind so strong it caught me off balance. I gripped the top of the gate and stared at the scene in front of me.

I thought I knew this bay by now, but in just one hour, I hardly recognised it at all. Even in such a short space of time that I had lived here, I'd seen it in all its moods; high-tide and low-tide, in sun, wind and rain, its entrance flanked by the house of *Craig-y-Don* to the north, protected by a stout, high stone wall and Gomer Rock to the south.

The tide had already reached the top of the flood-gates in the car-park and lapped just below the top of the sea-wall directly in front of me. Waves born in on the swell broke and splashed over the top stones, the pavement now wet and a few trickles coursed down into the gutters and onto the road. The top stones of the wall that protected *Craig-y-Don* were awash as the rollers coursed down the channel; the main waves continued on their journey but the edges sprayed high over the top of the wall itself. It was hard to make out detail, even at this distance in the grey of the late afternoon as the wind whipped my hair over my face.

The electricity and phone wires between the poles whined in the gusts and, above the sound, I could hear the knock of the badly-fitted sash windows in Helen's bedroom above and behind me.

I looked at the sea-wall in front of me, checked my watch, remembered the tidal rules that Will Roberts had taken such pains to explain and took comfort in the fact that, according to the rules, the depth of the water in the channel would eventually peak, the rate of flow would slow down and leave the last hour of slack high water to the mercy of the wind alone. But that was under normal circumstances. I pulled my hood up and zipped the collar tight under my chin and ran all the way back to the yard. It would be okay, I convinced myself, and at least there was no rain. So far.

The yard seemed little different to when I'd left and the sea just splashed over the harbour wall and onto the gravel. I shut the gates behind me but decided not to lock them; there was no point and I felt more comfortable knowing I could leave easily if I needed to. Then I turned and looked at them again; heavy, galvanised steel that shook and rattled in the gusts, pushed them back open and fixed the bolts firmly in their housing set well into the ground. Will Roberts had said to move the Toyota. It was parked by the caravan, so quite safe from falling rocks but I fetched the keys out, started it up and moved it outside the gates to the parking area there, half-laughing at myself for the added caution.

Four thirty; an hour and a half left to high-tide. With growing confidence, I checked the hatches and the windows in the van, placed the Canon back on the bunk, opened and shut the door carefully against the gusts and walked around the Boat Shed, pushing the sandbags in further and tighter up against the rusty walls. A sheet of metal flapped at the back and I remembered the nails I'd hammered in to fix it and the drug dealers hunting for Jason. It seemed like only yesterday Hugh and I had discovered him, thin and desperate and hiding in the corner with the model ships and on the floor, in pieces, the one he'd smashed inadvertently.

I found the hammer and shoved some nails into my back pocket, the shed no longer feeling like a sanctuary as the roof sheets lifted and clattered back into place. The wind had eased and a strange lull had settled over the yard, whilst the trees on Ballast still bent under the onslaught.

In the estuary, white spindrift filled the air as the tops of the waves curled and broke against the shingle at the end of the island; they rolled in, high up on the beach and well into the trees and brambles, until only the very tops of the old wooden piles showed through in the troughs and were totally obliterated in the peaks. *Annie* bucked and reared like a mad colt and the waves broke clean over the cabin. She rose, higher and higher up the wall, the water-line now level with the top and the fenders, the huge tyres Arnie had brought from the scrap-yard, were well below the hull as she scraped against the wall. I gave Hugh's yacht, which shivered alarmingly on its props, a wide berth and headed back for the shed. Not much longer to go. I checked my watch, anxious, but not yet scared. I knew the difference.

I sat down but couldn't settle in there, the rattle of the tin sheets as they lifted in places and crashed back and the howl of the wind in the chimney, felt like being at sea in an ancient ark with the sea ready to sweep in and carry it all away. I opened the door and stood for a moment on the step, horribly aware that my trainers were now wet. The sea had poured down through the gravel from the top of the slipway, pooled around the sandbags at the end of the shed, and as I looked over towards Ballast, it started to slip over the top of the harbour wall, pushing *Annie's* hull with it. It flowed around the dinghies I'd roped together and the baulks of timber and steel I-beams that had lain in the yard since before my time, and surged down the yard towards the open gates.

I splashed through the water, past the gates, sat in the Toyota and reached for the phone in my back pocket to check the exact time of high-tide, and just to talk to someone; for comfort, reassurance, anything, just a voice would be enough to help dispel the terror. The water distracted me, fixed my attention in disbelief as it seeped towards the wheels of the pickup. I started the engine, backed up the slope to the road below the cliff. It surely couldn't come any higher, I thought, mesmerised by the rising level and the awful realisation it could cut off the whole road to the town and my only escape by road.

Will Roberts had said that if I could get beyond the top of the tide and into the ebb without a disaster, I'd be okay. High-tide at six o'clock, eighteen hundred, was fixed in my mind from the paper timetable he'd made me practice on and had calculated the height from high-water, Liverpool. I'd got used to doing the sums and knew to subtract two hours, forty-five minutes for Porthmadog, no problem. I'd quite liked the idea of the tide making its way up from the Western Approaches or down from St George's Channel, to see how long it took high or low-tide to arrive at one place or another. Then of course, there were all the local anomalies to take into account. But this was not the time for a lesson in tide-times and tidal streams.

My hand hit an empty pocket. I automatically checked the other one, then my coat. It was like losing a winning lottery ticket. A wave of physical nausea crept up my throat as I mentally retraced my steps, and guessed it had fallen out with the nails where I'd repaired the loose sheet. The back of the shed where I'd been working was now flooded. The phone would be underwater, but I desperately needed to check, to reassure myself that this flood would soon end and the tide start to ebb.

The tide-table with my exercise book for the homework Mr Roberts gave me, was in the caravan. I left the shelter of the Toyota, braced myself against the wind and stood outside the caravan door with my jeans soaked to the knees. Then there was a distinct lull, an eery silence, so brief it must have been seconds.

The next five minutes were drowned in a solid wall of rain, hurled in on a shrieking wind that knocked me off balance and back into the open gate. There was no more low threat from the whine and moan of the telephone wires and rigging on yachts, no more clack of shrouds and of tell-tale breezes, no memory of gentle zephyrs and ruffled, cats'-paws on calm seas or smooth, regular, unhurried swells. There was nothing, save a cacophony of sound, obliterating sense and reason with an elemental force that drove the air out of my lungs. A sheet of galvanised metal lifted and flapped at one corner of the shed-roof and with a tearing, grinding sound, broke off and hurled itself over the ridge of the roof to the cliff-face at the back, where it slid down and jammed between the shed and the smoke-house.

I'd nearly given up all thought of opening the caravan door to retrieve the tide-table, when I remembered Tim's last words. I opened the van door, squeezed through the smallest opening I could and shut it behind me. I picked up the camera and the tide-table, put my weight against the door again, slid out and turned to face the wind. It was like being in a scene from a movie. I felt as though I was apart, in a different existence, rooted to the spot not knowing what to do next, except get out of the yard. I didn't move, pinned to the caravan door with the strength of the onslaught and the sight in front of me.

The waves in the channel were even steeper; walls of grey flooded over the harbour wall, piled in one after the other in a confusion of different directions; some came straight up the slipway and those that were destined for further down the harbour, edged in from the channel where they broke in a welter of white water inside the yard. It seemed as though the yard had begun to be part of the channel itself. I watched as the water surrounded Hugh's boat and waves broke against the props, receded and scoured out the gravel from under their ends.

The hull shook and the mast vibrated as each wave broke but nothing more seemed to happen. Then in slow motion, the boat tilted, a slight shift at first and the angle of the three props on the port side and the hull began to flatten out, the ends no longer dug solidly into the ground. A wave broke directly on the hull and sprayed white water clean over the deck. A sudden lurch, and the boat shifted tilted a fraction further.

I don't know what made me react, but I lifted the camera up, held the view-finder firmly to my eye, and clicked the shutter, over and over, as it tilted further. The props slid out from underneath the hull, inch by inch and ploughed furrows in the gravel and slowly, the yacht, its supports now flat on the ground, slid onto its side on top of them with a crash that was barely audible over the wind. The mast shivered as it settled and the masthead hovered over the wall towards the channel, the rigging slackened in a mess of rope and steel. The waves broke relentlessly against the now-vertical deck and over the cabin roof.

I was still clicking the shutter, vaguely aware I had distanced myself from the scene, the reality in front of me framed in the view-finder, in another world where I didn't exist. Then the rain fogged the lens, obliterated the picture completely and I lowered the camera and faced it. Rooted to the ground in the terrible fascination of watching a disaster unfold, the adrenalin kicked in and the warnings from Daniel and Helen's Nain flooded back as another roof-sheet threatened to detach itself and fly towards me.

I ran then, photos and tide-table forgotten, as sheer terror moved my legs through the water and out of the yard, past the Toyota, up the pathway to Borth-y-Gest and to the top of the steps to the bay. I looked for the road below. There was no road, no car-park and no front garden to Helen's Nain's house, but I could see from there that the sandbags were still in place. Down the steps into ankle-deep water, I splashed around to the back garden where the water drained down the slight slope to the swampy area at the bottom. I opened the door and called her. The hall and kitchen floor were still dry inside. There was no sign of her.

"I'm upstairs, Cassie. Bring my glasses up, will you? They're on the table. And will you read the barometer?"

She sat in an old armchair in the bay window of her bedroom, a coffee table in front of her strewn with magazines and books. She'd stuffed old newspaper in the sash to stop it banging in the wind and a small bedside light helped to disperse the gloom from outside. I gave her the glasses, pulled up the dressing-table stool and sat down opposite. I was speechless, and my hand shook when I took my coat off and the Canon, tucked into the front, from round my neck. I couldn't face looking at the images. We sat in silence for a moment.

"Has something happened?" She seemed unperturbed that I had turned up, wet and out of breath. "Go and put on some of Helen's things and you can hang your jeans over the Rayburn."

"Barometer says 965," I said, dry and warm but not able to tell her what I'd seen, not able to say what I dreaded going back to. I had a feeling she didn't need to hear of anyone's disasters. "That's really low, isn't it? And it's dropped so quickly. But it's high tide in five minutes," I said, words gabbled in false, cheerful chatter. "You'll be alright. It hasn't come through into the house. In fact, it's not even up to the top of the first sand-bag yet," and tried to forget my own troubles for the moment. I couldn't even begin to think about the horror of Hugh's yacht on its side. Or my Boat Shed without a roof. My nervousness filled whatever silence could have been heard, had it not been for the screaming wind outside. She was not fooled.

She put on her glasses and picked up her copy of Laver's Tide-Table, open for the day and read for a few seconds.

"Has something happened?" she asked again, as the bedside light flickered. I just shook my head. "What time did you say high-tide is?"

"Six o'clock. I checked it yesterday. It'll start to ebb any minute." She put the tide-table on her lap and closed her eyes.

"I don't think so, cariad. We're still working on British Summer Time. You've forgotten to add the hour."

I snatched the tide-table from her lap.

"I can't have done," I said, "I've been using it all summer."

An unbelievable mistake, a calculation made in the stress of waiting, a fixed time in my head. It was wrong and I sat on the stool, sick and exhausted, the vision of the yard and Hugh's boat on its side and the horrible realisation that the waves would smash into it for yet another hour. As for the shed and my caravan and *Annie*, I didn't dare think about it. She knew.

"You can tell me about the yard when you're ready. Perhaps you could check those sand-bags at the front door," she said, "and shut the lounge and dining-room doors. There are some old towels in the airing cupboard. Push them up against the bottom of the doors to save the carpets. Just in case. The tiled floor in the hall and kitchen won't come to any harm."

Her head sank back against the chair.

"And don't plan on going anywhere, Cassie," she said, her voice firm and final. "You're to stay here until the morning. There's nothing you can do now. Heat up some soup while we still have the light and you can sleep in Helen's room. Go on, now."

I found a pair of wellies in the back-porch and waded through the running water outside and round to the front of the house. The sea had tipped over the low wall that separated her garden from the road and was half-way up the second bag by the front door and rising. The scream of the wind and the sight of the sea blasted my senses. Huge rollers swept up the channel and the swell surged into the bay and continued to pour over the sea-wall. All the front gardens and the car-park were flooded and even from where I stood, I could see the water had crept half-way up the steps to the bus-shelter. The hanging baskets I'd lifted down and put under the table outside, had been washed clean of soil and plants and were now a muddy mess against the front door and the table and chairs had been blown over and washed up against the house.

Although desperate to run back to the yard, her instructions to me were quite clear. She'd never forgive me if anything happened to either of us to make matters worse, simply because I couldn't help myself. I went back into the house, checked the hall floor – a dribble on the tiles, no more, heated up the soup and took it upstairs with the plate of bread and butter.

"If you look in the bedside cupboard, you'll find a bottle of brandy. I think we need a drink," she said. "Only half an hour to go. It'll be dark early tonight so at least we'll be spared the sight of the damage until morning."

Calm and collected, she ate her soup, sent me downstairs for glasses and then poured the brandy.

"We'll have a look at the news," she said, and picked up the remote control to the small TV on the chest-of-drawers. The lights went out.

"I'm surprised it lasted this long," she said, and reached for the camping light she'd brought up from downstairs. "Now we won't know anything."

I fetched an armchair from one of the other bedrooms and we sat in the bay window while the storm raged outside and the window rattled in the gusts.

"*Tai Pilots*," I said, out of nowhere, my brain intent on the yard, thinking of the cellar and the drugs and then the boarded-up outside door. It couldn't survive this intact.

"It'll still be there in the morning."

"Pity," I said.

"Oh? I thought you had plans for it, cariad."

"I did. Then that business with Jason and finding the baby's ashes and all that sadness – and other things. It's blighted, Helen's Nain. I can't explain. I hate the place."

"Perhaps you'll feel better about it when some work's been done and it's all clean and tidy."

I shook my head. Perhaps I won't, I thought. Perhaps I'll just sell it and go back to civilisation, sell the lot and write stories that had happy endings. Perhaps I should use Helen's Nain's phone and ring my mother. Then again, perhaps not. Would people be phoning me to see if I was still alive? What would they do when I didn't answer, my phone being dead and drowned in the mess at the back of the shed?

I ran through my list of favourite people. Jason would know I'd be okay, my mother knew nothing and cared even less about storms and weather, Mr Roberts would hope I'd listened to his advice, Denise would know I'd be here if the yard was dangerous, and Daniel? He'd be too busy rescuing his marina up north and besides, it was only a one-off liaison. Helen's Nain's phone rang, the ring-tone a strange sound above the elemental howling outside. The speaker-phone kicked in.

"Oh, yes?" she said with a quick look at my face in the half-light. "Are you the gentleman who took her out at the weekend? Yes, of course she's here. No, I'm not letting her go," she said, and handed me the phone.

"I'll be back when I can," he said, simply. "It's chaos here. Stay safe. If you've no power, save the batteries," and rang off.

"How did he know?" I asked, wondering into the phone. "How did he know your number and how did he know where I'd be?"

"Why is he coming back here? I thought you said he lived in London?"

"He does, but he's in Scotland on business. He'll be coming back to check the yard next door for damage, that's why. It's his property, after all. Let's hope Denise..."

I thought about it for a moment. He would have rung her and she would have guessed where I was, knew the address if nothing else. I'd mentioned it enough times and it was easy to find someone who knew someone, in a place like this. I didn't want him back here to see me in the state I knew I'd be in and I didn't want to have to tell him about the drugs. I hadn't forgotten how badly David had reacted and how unforgiving he was that I should be mixed up in something criminal. But he was a solicitor, after all.

"What's the matter, cariad?"

I hadn't meant to cry, especially here, where her needs were greater than mine and she'd seemed so frail recently.

"I think I've lost the plot," I said and wiped my eyes on my sleeve. "Sorry."

She poured me another drop of brandy, carefully in the poor light.

"You won't lose the plot, as you put it. You're tougher than you think. Is he nice?"

"Yes, no, I don't really know. Not really." I didn't want to talk about it. "Will you be alright? I know it's early but I need to go bed."

I lay there for a while, secure in warmth and comfort, while the insecurity of my wrecked business and my loneliness ate away at me. I tried to find comfort in childhood and teenage memories; mixed feelings about my dad with his outlook on life about why not to take life too seriously; we humans and our insignificant problems were just passing through, he used to say, but he was never there during my teenage years to discuss it with him. I'd learned to live with loneliness and worked out problems on my own. I still felt angry about the way he lived on a cloud and left us in a financial mess. As for my mother, she could only cope with the help of pills and gin when the going got tough. I hadn't forgiven her. I didn't want to be like either of them, I decided, and I'd face what I had to and get on with it. I wasn't going to run away from this.

I turned my mind to the day's events. With no phone, I couldn't see how the police would contact me and whether everything had come to a standstill during the storm. I hid from the world under Helen's quilt, vaguely aware that the wind had dropped to a low moan, checked my watch and knew that the tide had turned. There was nothing to be seen out of the window; no cheery fairy-lights, no comforting orange glow from the houses or from the street lights; just black nothingness through the rain on the window.

I slept through heavy rain, low-tide after midnight, and high-tide at dawn and woke up to the morning, still windy, grey and damp with the tide half-way out and the bay already dry but with white horses still to be seen in the estuary. Seaweed and silt littered the road and pools of water remained in gardens where the sand-bags had protected them from the worst.

I dressed, peeked in at Helen's Nain, still asleep, left a note in the still-dry kitchen and ploughed through a fine film of slippery mud to the steps. I turned with a sudden flash of guilt to look over the bay to *Tai Pilots* and imagined the mess if the cellar door had been smashed and the tide had flooded the cellar, damaged and waterlogged perhaps, but still there. Not for the first time, did I wish the whole house would just float away with the ebb-tide and vanish beneath the waves. Then I summoned up courage and walked back to the yard.

CHAPTER 12

Some things are hard to describe, those that wrench the senses from you and those that blind you from reality as your brain refuses to compute what your eyes see. Some things are so awful, you don't even want to talk about them for some time, pictures so shocking that the images hide behind a safety-net of denial, even false optimism.

I'd seen Hugh's yacht slide sideways onto the ground and lie to the mercy of the waves as they surged over the harbour wall and broke against the vertical deck; I'd seen one roof sheet from the shed torn from its fixings and fly over the ridge before I left, and I'd seen the gravel that covered the ground begin to sluice away with the receding waves. Those realities I could accept, but my brain refused to compute the thought of *Annie*, holed, broken loose and washed up in the harbour and the damage to the inside of my shed without its roof was unthinkable. It had rained all night.

I'd been told the yard had flooded many times before, maybe ankle-deep at the top of the tide on a storm, but I hadn't expected such chaos. Tangled seaweed, pieces of timber, odds and ends of rope and plastic bottles had been washed in by the tide and the yard's rubbish bin with its contents of empty paint-tins and used brushes had been carried through the yard to the entrance where it piled up against the gates of the yard next-door, shut and bolted as Denise had been instructed. I peered through the steel bars; her yard was wet but the power boats and jet-skis appeared undamaged.

I took a careful step onto the mud and sand that covered my own yard. The gravel, with its giveaway crunch when cars came through the gates and always my first indication that I had visitors, had been washed away completely and had joined the rubbish against Denise's gates. I could see the top of *Annie's* cabin below the wall. She had survived, still attached to the mooring ropes. She must have been washed back and forth on the wall and I couldn't imagine what the state of her hull would be like as the waves had battered and scraped her against the huge stones. She lay at a strange angle with her keel in the mud, listing towards the channel, the mooring ropes taut and feathered with weed.

I skirted around the dinghies, still roped together and tied to the winch at the top of the slipway. Silt covered the casing that housed the electric motor, ruined now, I supposed. I stepped over *Capella's* mast. The rigging was festooned with weed. Hugh had locked the cabin, as always, before he'd left the previous weekend, but the force of the hull as it hit the ground, had fractured the housing for the hatch cover and the boards had washed out. I could only guess how much damage the water had caused inside the cabin, the cabin that Hugh had refurbished so carefully and tastefully, a cosy den with everything in miniature.

It had been his first job in the renovation, he'd told me, and it had taken him years to replace the head-linings and re-make all the cupboards from scratch. The seats had been re-covered in new upholstery and the windows hung with tiny curtains he'd had made in Holyhead. The checked material and colours were co-ordinated, everything was bespoke and beautifully crafted. He'd made it all himself, even the wooden racks for mugs and glasses.

How could I tell him? As for the damage to the hull, there was no way of knowing until it was righted. I reasoned that the yacht had been built from hardwood, built to withstand ocean crossings with unforgiving seas, but to crash down on timber props? I needed my phone. The thought of it bashed and soaked and beyond repair and the isolation of having no communication with anyone, was unbearable. I couldn't tell him even if I wanted to. I now had to face the inside of the Boat Shed.

I'd never believed in God, any God, actually, and I didn't believe much in luck either, but when I opened the door, its familiar, comfortable darkness gone with the roof open to the sky in places, there was my phone, still charged and ready to go, lying on the counter by the paint tin with the now-dead willowherb. The roof-sheets above the oak-counter were intact, loose at the edge where adjoining sheets had been torn away, but the wind and rain had blown from the southwest and apart from a few spots on the polished top, it was dry.

I picked up the phone, kissed it and cradled it like a baby. Messages had been left, from Hugh, Daniel, Denise, even Arnie Blackwell back in Dudley: and from my mother, of all people. She could wait. I shouted with joy, then decided I needed help and I needed it now. I phoned Will Roberts. I didn't know what else to do and I needed to cover the roof.

"It's chaos in the harbour," he said. "I'll send Mark. There's no more rain forecast so you'll be alright for the rest of the day. See if you can find some tarpaulins. Ask Denise if there are some in stock next door."

There was no electricity, but enough daylight to see that the model ships were untouched. The snack-bar and my caravan had been protected by the shed but the sea had sneaked its way in through the gaps at the base of the back wall. The tin walls were a flimsy affair, fixed to baulks of timber set into the ground. My pathetic attempts at nailing the loose sheet at the back had failed miserably and the sheet itself hung by one nail. The narrow gap at the back of the shed between the wall and the cliff-face was littered with the debris from another fall of soil and rock. The roof-sheets that had torn loose had flipped over the ridge and wedged themselves in the gap.

There was nothing I could do but wait for Mark, make a cup of coffee on the gas hob in the van and find some courage to phone Hugh. I left a message. 'Phone me urgently', I said. A text would be unthinkable.

I went back to the Toyota and turned the radio on for the Welsh news. Cardigan Bay had been hit hard and part of Aberystwyth's promenade had disintegrated; near Aberdyfi, the main road to Machynlleth had flooded and the main railway track that fringed the estuary had been washed away in places. Even Holyhead had its problems when the wind had backed northerly. The swell compromised access to the moored-up Stena Line ferry and the harbour where the survey ships and fishing boats were moored, although nothing like the north-easter that had decimated the marina a few years back.

I was desperate for Hugh to phone, tried to formulate the right words and keep them ready in my head, but none of them seemed right. 'Sorry, Hugh, your boat fell over' was trite, but to the point; he would have worried, perhaps, but could never have imagined the reality. I needed to phone the police as well. They couldn't just leave me here with no news.

I moved the Toyota off the road, parked it outside the gates and lay on my bunk in the caravan. There was a text from Arnie; he would drive up from Dudley to check on his holiday-home static on Friday, would call in and hoped things weren't too bad. Ben wanted to say hello to the lobster. Another awkward one. I'd never had to explain death to a child before but then I wasn't his mother; not my problem. I phoned my mother, lied a lot and said it was all under control, vaguely aware that I was a mess, hungry, dirty and tired and couldn't see a way through any of this.

If I'd wanted to sell the yard before and go back to my so-called civilised life in London, I certainly couldn't sell it now and couldn't imagine the insurance company paying out for an 'Act of God', as they called it on the schedule. My last thirty thousand pounds would go nowhere, with *Tai Pilots* to renovate as well. Or sell it all as it was, wrecked and down-trodden, take what I could get and run? I could stop stressing about how to tackle the mess, put it in the hands of an agent and walk away. Dinners and nights out and lovely clothes. And nails, not the galvanised or roofing kind, but beautifully manicured, polished nails and a parlour just round the corner, as my mother had hinted. I thought of Daniel and the shadow of distrust that still clouded that night; I still couldn't believe he wasn't interested in the yard. He'd buy it for a song in this state and then double the business with the yard next door… Rubbish, I told myself, I really couldn't see why he'd be interested in a two-bit boatyard in a corner of Wales.

I needed food. The homely, comforting normality that accompanied the aroma of toast and coffee was a reminder of good times in the summer, sunny breakfasts discussing the day's work with Jason, but I picked at the toast, the coffee cooled and I put my elbows on the small table and my chin in my hands and stared at the plate, unable to think clearly. The police could wait.

I didn't hear the Audi pull up inside the gate; there was no gravel left for the tyres to warn me, and was startled out of my misery when the door opened and David stood there, shoes and the bottoms of his trousers splashed with mud. He ran his hand through his thick black curls.

"God, Cassie, I am so, so sorry. I came as soon as I heard. This is awful."

I just stared at him, his face was serious and concerned, without the usual hint of disapproval.

"Are you alright? Is the shed damaged? The models? And what about *Annie*? And Hugh's boat? Does he know yet and how the hell did that happen? I've never seen anything like it before." The words tumbled out.

I sat back from the table and pushed the toast crumbs around so I didn't have to look him in the face. Keep cool, calm and objective, I told myself or I'll get a barrage of lectures.

"It was the wind," I said. "Out of nowhere, like a mini-tornado and then it just picked the sea up in huge waves. It was only for a short time, but they came from all directions," I said, reliving the moment in a single image. "They just rose up over the wall and up the slipway and when they crashed back into the next ones, the force took the gravel away. I could hear it; it was horrible, like being on a shingle beach in a storm and each wave made holes in the mud around the base of the props until they started to slide and the boat tilted and then it …it just fell over. And, and… there are gaps in the roof of the shed…"

He crouched down by the table and looked me straight in the eye. It was enough. Tears welled up and slid down my cheeks. He'd seen me cry before, one of the few people who ever had, and through the mist I saw him take the neatly folded handkerchief out of his top pocket and put it on the table. I sniffed and blew my nose.

"Sorry. I'll wash it and bring it back."

He smiled, a moment of shared history soothing the moment.

"I know you will." He stood up. "Now, what can I do?"

"Advise me," I said. I'd had it with spiky comments about needing help. "I don't know where to start," and realised how much I cared about all of it.

The list was long, the phone calls endless. David pulled wellies out of the boot of his car and splashed through the mud and water without a care for his trousers. I could do nothing to help, so left him there and disappeared to Borth-y-Gest to check on Helen's Nain. It was a fleeting visit. The electricity in the village had been reinstated and she sat in the kitchen with a pot of tea between her and the marshmallow. I made polite enquiries, glossed over the disaster in the yard with a cheerful voice and fled back to it as soon as I could. A distinct antipathy for that woman with her silly pink face and artful innocence, grew stronger each time I saw her. If the drugs cache hit the news, it wouldn't be hard to imagine her reaction.

I stopped by the gate and watched David as he quartered the yard, phoned, moved on, busy and focused. No matter what the police said, I had to tell him about the drugs and Jason, and I would have to accept his reactions. He'd be furious. He'd hate me. And this time, I didn't want him to.

There was no sign of Denise. The gates were still locked and she hadn't answered her phone about the tarpaulins.

"Coffee?" David asked, seeing me by the gates. "There'll be some help here soon."

"What's that list for?"

"Insurance. I don't suppose you've made a claim like this before. You said you wanted advice. This is more up my street than yours."

"But I'm not your client anymore," I said. "You don't need to do all this, really."

"Just put it down to friendship," he said.

Not for long, I told myself.

I boiled the kettle in the caravan and we sat at the table while he studied his notes. I needed to tell him right then and swallowed some coffee. The words stuck in my throat. I couldn't. Then I did.

"I need to tell you something," I said, "and before I tell you, I know you're going to be angry and I'm sorry and you have to promise not to mention it to anyone."

He put his pen down and listened. When I finished and his beautifully laundered handkerchief was a wet ball in my hand, he got up from the table, pulled a piece of kitchen towel from above the sink and handed it to me.

"Blow your nose," he said. "There's work to be done," squeezed my hand and left.

The Harbour Master's pickup turned up outside with Mark and two other men. I stayed inside while they worked and cried and cried until I'd exhausted the self-pity. Nobody could hear me. I washed my face and went outside.

Mark took one look at me, the second time he'd seen me upset. He put his arm round my shoulders and gave me a hug.

"Take more than a trip in the kayak this time," he said. I recognised his mates from the pub and the builders' merchants. They'd thrown tarpaulins over the shed ridge, shrouded the gaping holes in the roof and tied them down to pegs in the ground.

"You're alright, love," one said, and shook his head when I asked how much I owed them. "Courtesy of the shop. Can't leave you on your own without a roof, yeah?" They drove off.

The phone rang. It was Hugh and I gulped, pulled myself together and was glad he couldn't see me. There was a stunned silence when I told him.

"Will you be down at the weekend?" I asked. "The yacht's okay for now, but we need to discuss what to do next."

He hung up. I sat down on one of the upturned dinghies, held the phone away from me and just stared at it.

"I don't get it," I said to David, who joined me, oblivious to the coating of silt we sat on. "He's normally so pragmatic and capable, about everything. He always knows what to do. He was so upset he couldn't speak."

“He’s been working on that yacht for years, “he said. “It’ll freak him out when he sees it. He’s a strange man.”

“I know. You’ve ruined your trousers.”

“No problem. My mother will deal with it.” He smiled. A joke, another bit of shared history, albeit an uncomfortable one. “It’s a funny thing, this relationship people have with old yachts,” he said. “It’s as though they know that their boats are designed to look after them at sea and the owners return the sentiment by bestowing love and care without sometimes ever putting them in the water.”

“That’s really stupid,” I said. “What’s the point?”

“The point is… it’s about care, I think. Just care and the pleasure of restoring something that someone has put love and time into building but may well end up as firewood.”

“Do you feel like that about your own yacht?” I asked.

“Like what? Caring? Yes, actually, I do. I met a man in Bristol Docks once. He was painting his anchor, not that anyone does that normally. It was the last thing to be painted after restoring the boat from scratch. I asked him how long it had taken him. “Eight years,” he said. “Too old to sail it now, but it doesn’t matter. It’s given me a lot of pleasure. Done a lot of dreaming, tucked up in the cabin safely on dry land in the boatyard, especially with a gale blowing down the Bristol Channel with foul seas and monstrous tides.”

I thought about Hugh and his obsession, not only with his yacht but as a volunteer for the railway.

“Did you know Hugh works at Boston Lodge as a volunteer?” I asked him. “Perhaps that will be enough for him, if the boat can’t be saved.” I looked at the smooth planking he’d spent weeks on and dreaded to think of the damage under the hull where it had fallen against the props. “I can’t see how hc can put all this to rights and hc hasn’t got much money. Will it be wrecked? Will they be able to crane it upright? What do you think?”

"I don't know. I really don't know." He looked at it thoughtfully. "The crane-in for the yachts in the harbour is booked for a couple of weeks but I can't see he would want it sitting on props again. He could do with a cradle. You did plan to have *Annie* craned out, didn't you? Perhaps they would lift the two boats for a reduced price. You can ask. It'll have to be righted to assess the damage."

"Not two, three boats. I nearly forgot, Hugh says he's got a new client for me as well, a friend from Holyhead. He's going to sail his boat down in the next few weeks. I haven't okayed it yet but I would hate to turn away another wooden yacht. It'll need to be craned out as well. That would be three boats in my yard for the winter."

"Well, that's good news. At least your great-uncle would be happy. Don't suppose you run to a bacon bap or a burger on your gas stove?"

My hands flew up to my mouth. "I'd forgotten about the freezer."

"Better eat some of the food, then," he said. "Insurance will cover it if the power stays off. We'll look at *Annie* after lunch, see if she floats on the flood. If she's holed, at least we can pump her out and do some repairs for the moment."

"I shouldn't be taking you away from work. I'm sorry," I said, still bemused by his kindness and the lack of comment about the drugs.

"It'll keep," he said. "Food?"

I nodded, exhausted, suddenly hungry and was so glad to have him here. I was worried about Hugh and wondered if I was ever going to sleep that night, alone in my drowned yard and makeshift chandlery. I was almost too tired to say what I wanted to say when he left, but 'thank you' had to do for now.

I ploughed through the rest of the week, cleaned and cleared rubbish and slept surprisingly well. I ordered more gravel and watched as the builders arrived and replaced the tin sheets on the roof.

"You could demolish this shack and put up a proper building," one of them said.

"You should see my plans," I said. "Just missing the lottery ticket." He laughed.

I filled in forms for the insurance company and the electricity came back on. There was one phone call from the police. Please carry on as normal. Do not go to the house. House? I hadn't given it a thought. Will be in touch, they said. I was desperate to share it with someone, trusted David implicitly and asked him on his last visit before the weekend what he thought would happen.

"Stake-out," he said. "They'll watch and wait until someone comes for it. You can bet your life they'll follow them back under-cover. It'll be part of a bigger operation. They'll be after the big boys. And," he looked at me meaningfully, "they won't want you giving any hints you know anything about it. So, no heroics, Cassie."

I didn't need to promise. I had no intention of going anywhere near the place. Until I could put it on the market.

Saturday morning and a Fiat Punto pulled up outside the gate. A young man got out from the driver's door, walked in through the gates and then back to the car. He opened the passenger door and Hugh emerged. He shifted his gaze into the yard, shook his head as I went out to greet him, turned on his heel and walked away, past the car and up onto the road.

"Hugh, Hugh, where are you going? Come on back, mate," the other man called, but he'd gone. His head shook from side to side as he disappeared round the corner.

The other man shrugged his shoulders and turned to me. "He can't cope," he said. "He's not been able to come to work and shut himself in the flat. I told him he had to come today. I said I'd help him to deal with it, being as I'm going to bring my boat here."

"Oh, right," I said, as realisation dawned. In your dreams, I thought, faced with an unshaven man in his twenties, pony-tail and an old donkey-jacket. A ring through one eyebrow and several studs in his ears, he didn't look as though he could afford tomorrow's dinner. I conveniently forgot my own nose-stud, but then it was a diamond and that didn't count.

"Paul," with a lovely smile and crooked teeth, "sorry, Paul Maguire, from Ireland. Originally. God, this is a mess," he said, and stared at the sight in front of him.

"Cassie Jones." We shook hands. I could at least be polite. "Hugh told me what happened to your boat when the marina was destroyed. That must have been terrible for you."

He shrugged. "These things happen. It's all fixed up now with a new engine. Turned out okay in the end."

"So why do you want to move it down here?" I asked.

"No marina, so no home. I've been staying on it in the yard until the insurers sorted things out but I want to work on the hull this winter. You specialise in wooden boats, don't you? Just fancy a change of scene, too. That's a hell of a mess," he said again, staring at Hugh's boat. "How are you going to fix it?"

"No idea yet. Would you like a coffee and we can discuss terms and conditions? I can't let you stay in the yard over-night at weekends, though. I'm still using the caravan as a site office and I'm not insured for anyone staying on the boat on land. Hugh stays in a B&B. I thought it best to meet first before we decide. Then we can work out where Hugh's gone and go and rescue him."

"He'll be in the sheds," he said, slurped his coffee and rested a leg over one knee, very relaxed and casual. I wondered how casual he was at sea. "He's done it before when things were difficult for him."

"What sort of things? What sheds?" Alarm bells started to ring.

"The engine sheds, Boston Lodge. When his mother died, he hid for a whole week. The boss was very good about it. He's a clever bloke, is Hugh, and we kind of look after him. Especially the crew on the ships. The guys at the railway are good with him, too. He just takes a job and tucks himself away into a corner where he doesn't have to talk to folk. Then when he's ready, he comes back out and faces it. We'll find him. Leave him for a couple of hours then we'll go and get him."

I remembered what Will Roberts had said about Hugh's colleagues and I thought about kindnesses. I also remembered about making assumptions. As long as he could pay his way. We agreed terms for a season, payment up-front.

"Will you sail the boat down on your own?" I asked.

"Oh yeah, it's only a small boat."

"So have you done lots of sailing?"

"Loads," he said. "Mostly with my dad. We used to sail out of Dun Laoghaire and cruise the Scottish Isles. I've picked a day when the tides are right, so if the weather's good, I'll leave in the morning and sail from Holyhead to Bardsey on the ebb, hit the Sound at low water and pick up the flood on the other side and be with you in the evening. The Harbour Master said I could use a mooring in the channel until the crane-out."

I nodded. It seemed like a good plan but it wasn't really my problem, except for a niggle of concern. He was cheerful and relaxed about the whole thing. Being at sea had always seemed so serious; he talked about it as an easy jaunt just down the coast. Perhaps it was. But what did I know? He appeared to know what he was talking about and no doubt Will Roberts would have spoken to him about the bar and the channel.

"What exactly do you do, job-wise?" I asked. He looked like a yard-hand.

"Oh, software stuff, you know," he said.

I didn't know but I'd find out.

"Can I wander round until we go for Hugh?" he asked, "I'd like to look at the estuary."

I sent him off to Borth-y-Gest for a couple of hours to study the channel from the headland beyond *Tai Pilots*.

"Now what?" I said crossly to a passing gull, as I phoned Hugh's number again and tried to digest the news about him. "Am I a car-park, or what?"

Arnie's Range Rover cruised through the gates. He was forgiven straightaway. He'd never shown anything except politeness and gratitude to me before, but he picked me up in a bear-hug and squeezed until I couldn't breathe. He looked well; less strained and tired, even though it had been only a week since he came to fetch Jason. He put me down and stared at the yard.

"Shit. What a mess. You never said this had happened, "he said. "Mind you, it was black over Bill's mother's, even down by us, when the rain came."

"Who's Bill?" I asked. Had I missed something?

"Just a saying," he said. He stood in the mud with his hands on his hips and shook his head. "Hugh will be gutted."

"He's run off. I hope to God he doesn't do anything silly. How's Jason doing?" I asked.

"Good," he said. "Good reports so far. It's only been a few days. Says he loves it down there. Not so sure about the engines, though. He's next door to a boat-builders, classic wooden yachts. Seems it's taken his fancy. Can't make up his mind. But you know what they're like at that age." I laughed. Jason was only three years younger than me. "No worries about Jason, Cassie, and Ben's with his mum for the weekend. Things are better with her, too. She's still a cow, but not quite so cock-sure of herself these days."

"When will the twins be in court?"

"November. That's what's shut her up. She's finally realised they'll do time."

He walked round the boat, over the mast and picked a piece of weed out of the rigging.

"Hugh couldn't face it," I said. "So, we have to go and find him but I can't say anything to reassure him, can I? Not until we know what damage has been done. He'll have to work on it all over again. I don't even know if he'll want to or be able to work with it, propped up on those stupid bits of wood. I never liked them, no matter how many times he told me they were safe. I'm being irrational, I know, but look at what's happened to it now, especially as they say we'll get more storms like that in the future."

We drank coffee in the caravan and he dunked one biscuit after another until the plate was empty.

"What happened to the lobster?"

I told him. "Will you explain to Ben?" I asked, "and tell him that I'm going to buy some goldfish, instead. I've got to have someone to talk to when things get tough. I miss Jason, but I know he had to go. Have you got fish to talk to?" I asked, conscious of the fact that he was on his own now and Ben was at school. Then I remembered he had a business to keep him occupied. But he understood.

"The evenings get a bit quiet," he said, "after Ben's in bed. Nobody to argue with over the telly and bloody *Cheshire Wives*." He tugged at the gold ring in his ear. "Mind you, no company's better than whining and bitching. Does that old lady you visit still do those chocolate brownies?"

He finished his coffee. "I'll go and have a look round, okay? See if there's anything I can do to help with Hugh's boat. What's it called? The make, I mean."

I told him. He walked round it with a notebook, made a few notes, sat on one of the plastic chairs outside and made phone calls. Then he left and Paul came back.

“The channel’s clear with all those buoys,” he said. “Piece of cake.”

CHAPTER 13

The car-park was as grey as the quarry behind it. Paul and I walked down a slope between old sheds, a mixture of brand-new and ones yet to be renovated, one with a perfect, newly-slated roof but the render over the slate walls had peeled off in places. A red-painted door relieved the greyness and led upstairs to an office where we were given permission to hunt for Hugh. A steam-engine chugged across the Cob and announced its presence with a whistle; a familiar sound to me that often carried on the wind as far as the yard, an unmistakeable, railway summer-sight and sound, with its immaculate engines and carriages full of happy people.

Paul was a familiar face to the staff. He'd worked as a volunteer as well for a while and rescued Hugh a few times when he was out of sorts and staff were worried about him. He was never unsafe, Paul said, just preferred to be on his own. So, he polished, cleaned, sorted or sanded whatever he was given to do until he worked whatever bothered him out of his system. Then he'd carry on as normal, courteous and quiet. Most people wouldn't even have noticed.

We were told he would more than likely be in the machine shop and picked our way through the acrid smell of steel and the sparks that flew from one of the grinding machines. A man lifted his mask briefly and pointed to the entrance to an adjoining room. Paul nodded a greeting to the grimy Churchill bull-dog above a balance machine and we pushed our way through the heavy plastic divider into the next area.

"You stay here a moment," he said and disappeared through another plastic curtain. He left me sandwiched between sets of storage cabinets; shelf upon shelf, box upon box of labelled parts, from pressure gauges to taper pins, split pins to thermo-couples, all heavy in their over-riding blackness. Everywhere I looked was grey and black, dirt and oil, parts purpose-built and practical, each component designed to fit a particular engine or coach, I presumed.

A paint tin on an old trolley with castors caught my eye, its lid rusty and hammered down hard but the letters on the label clearly said 'Vampire Green, by Pocket Rocket Lubricants.' I loved the name, a small reminder of fantasy and colour in amongst the old, rusted engine parts; stuff, I thought, stuff everywhere and all would have been of use, or still was.

The whole shed was imbued with the necessity for the small things that made the big things work, as boxes of grimy parts were transformed into a living, moving, part of history. I breathed it in; metal, oil, dirt, smoke, coal and the cold of inanimate objects. It was so very different to the Boat Shed with its pervasive, warm smell of wood. I closed my eyes, stood still and listened to the noise of the grinding machine we'd left behind. Somehow it failed to intrude on the silence and stillness of the room.

My phone pinged a text and startled me out of my reverie, surprised there was even a signal here. Arnie. 'Phone me,' it said.

"Now, Cassie," he said. "I want you to listen. Can you?"

"Yes, of course," I said. He sounded serious.

"Have you found Hugh yet?"

"No, but we think we'll find him soon."

"Well, when you find him, you can tell him this. Are you listening? I have arranged for a crane to lift his yacht and your *Annie*, out of the water. Also, the new boat from Holyhead, if it turns up before the day. I've spoken to Will Roberts about the lift-in for the yard and he reckons they won't have time to lift your boats as well as all the others. Now just listen, girl," as I started to protest. "You can tell Hugh there will be a new cradle for his boat as it's the biggest, *Annie* can sit on props, she's only got a shallow draft, and the new boat can have an old cradle that's sitting in the yard up the road. It's all arranged. I'll call in tomorrow before I set off home."

Paul pushed his way back through the plastic sheeting. I sat down on an old oil-drum, told him and stumbled over my words in disbelief.

"...and then he said the cradle's being made from bits of scrap steel he doesn't want and the lads who work for him can knock one up from the pictures and measurements he sent. He said Will Roberts thinks the hull will be okay with just a bit of work. He said... he said there was no cost for the crane, either. He was calling in favours. I don't know what to say. He said it'll help to get the yard on its feet again and used as it should be."

Paul leaned against the rack of shelves behind him. He put his hands in his pockets and we stood in silence.

"Bloody hell," he said, finally. "So, I'll need to bring the boat down the week after next. The tides will be right again."

"Can you?"

"I'll check with work, but it's too good an offer to miss. What a guy."

"He likes chocolate brownies," I said, irrelevantly, "and he's so gentle. I remember when Ben was only a baby and he cradled him in those enormous arms. He had the dummy in his own mouth, sucked it clean then stuck it back in the baby's. His wife shouted at him. Have you found Hugh? We've got to tell him right away."

"He's in there, sorting out a huge box of bolts. He's not talking yet. Best to tell him what's been arranged and not expect him to reply straight away. That's how he is. You figure it out."

He turned to lead the way through the curtain but stopped.

"You've got a strange set-up down here, haven't you? All these people seem to care about the yard; that Arnie and the Harbour Master? Lucky you," he said, and looked at me critically. "Or is it because of you?" and disappeared through the plastic. Not an empty-headed, over-chilled Bohemian, I thought, but couldn't see why he said that, well aware I seemed to do more taking than giving. I followed him in.

If it was cold before, then it was bone-chillingly cold in the old foundry. The shed stretched ahead with a line of arched windows set into peeling plaster; motes of dust danced and flickered as a stray sun-beam filtered through the glass panes. A dug-out section of the floor revealed old rail-tracks and the narrow plank over the gap wobbled alarmingly as we crossed it.

Chimney breasts where the forge fires had blazed were set into the wall on the right and the arm of an old crane and gantry hung from the ceiling, the massive blocks, hooks and chains still attached to it, black and still in the cold air. I'd been struck by the atmosphere in the previous room but in this one that had yet to be renovated, I could almost feel the history; ghosts of blacksmiths in leather aprons bent over coal fires, heated to extraordinary temperatures and the clang of hammers onto hot metal, bashed and bent to shape in showers of sparks.

Hugh sat on a paint-stained stool, tucked behind the forges with his back to us and a rusty bin in front of him next to a series of drawers on a makeshift table, his Beanie perched on his head, as always.

"Cassie's here," Paul said to Hugh's bent back. "I'll come back in a bit."

I walked around the stool and faced him.

"Hugh, I know you're upset but I need you to listen to me."

He listened and I left and waited outside. His cheeks were still wet when he emerged from the plastic sheet. He nodded briefly to Paul who gave the thumbs up to the grinder and we walked back up the slope through the greyness to the car-park.

"I have an idea," I said, vaguely aware I sounded like a mother hen. "As it's been a shit few days and it's Saturday and life has suddenly got better, I suggest we go back to the shed, I'll light a fire, raid the petty cash and treat us all to fish and chips and a drop of something to celebrate and toast Arnie. Okay, Hugh?"

"This Arnie guy," Paul said, as he drove onto the Cob, "you said he was gentle, sort of sensitive, but he's a scrappie? Doesn't seem to fit, somehow. I always think of scrappies as tough guys, not soft, like."

I heard Hugh chuckle from the back seat.

"Well," I said, "he just is. Mind you, I wouldn't want to cross him."

"Why not?"

"He's huge," I said.

They left after a convivial couple of hours, where Hugh, after a small whisky, chatted away about engines and classic, wooden boats. I learned nothing much about their jobs but had the over-riding impression, they were both computer geeks and it was hardly worth explaining anything to me. As for Paul's choice of life-style, he simply said he would prefer to live on a boat forever and wanted to finish the work on this one, sell it and buy a bigger one.

"Then what?" I asked.

"Round the world, maybe?" he said.

Hugh shuddered. "Could I trouble you for a drop more?" he asked and held out his glass. It was good to see him back to normal again. I also knew how little I'd really known about him.

The week hadn't finished with me yet. At an ungodly hour on Sunday morning, the police rang.

"We'd like you to drive up to your house this morning and go in as though you were cleaning. Take a bucket and mop or something. Someone will be watching, so there is no risk. We'd like you to check again for the second key you said was in the cutlery drawer. Behave as normal. Stay about half an hour."

"How long is this going to go on?" I asked. "It's a bit scary."

"Soon. We have some new information. Very soon. Are you happy to do that?"

Oh yeah, I thought. Ecstatic.

"Miss Jones, I know this seems a bit odd by phone but we don't want to risk anyone seeing a connection between you and the police. As far as we are aware, the ones who stashed the drugs at your house have no idea you know anything about it. You told us the young man who was living there warned his mates he was leaving and the owner was due to start renovations. Is that correct?"

"Yes, that's what he said."

"So, we are working on the assumption they'll want to retrieve the drugs ASAP."

"Yeah, I get that. So, if they see me going in to the house to clean, they'll move soon?"

"That's the idea. They haven't done so far, we reckon, because of the storm and the activity from the clear-up in the village."

I put a mop and bucket in the Toyota, front door key and fully-charged phone in my pocket and looked around the yard. Hard work and a lot of water would wash the silt away and apart from Hugh's boat lying like a dead whale in the muddy mess, I thought I could clean it all up in a week and make room for the crane. The dinghies could be moved with the launching trolley and I knew I could do that myself and spread the new gravel around. On a whim, I went back into the caravan, picked up the torch and drove to Borth-y-Gest.

I parked outside the house and carried the mop and bucket up to the front door. The weeds in between the steps had withered and blackened, swept over on their sides by the winds and lay forlorn against the grey stone. The key rasped in the front door and scraped its usual reluctancy on the tiled floor. The smell of damp was overpowering. I put the bucket down, checked my watch and headed for the kitchen and cutlery drawer. Jason had said 'in with the forks and spoons and stuff,' the stuff being mouldy breadcrumbs and a few bottle tops. Predictably, there was no key. He wouldn't even have noticed it had gone missing and his mates would have had free access at any time when he was at work.

I'd had no intention of cleaning and needed to kill an hour. I just had to go into the cellar to check on storm damage and most importantly, the box holding Catrin's ashes. The beam picked out the steep steps and the outside door to the beach. The floor glistened wetly in the light, but there was no standing water. My great-uncle would have known about storms, not that he could have imagined the ferocity of this one with its abnormal tide-heights and gusts of wind, but his carpentry had held and the door was unscathed. The sea had forced its way through invisible gaps, left water marks a few inches up the walls and the floor damp, but there was no other damage. The bottom shelf and box were untouched; I hadn't brought the key to the tiny padlock; there had been no need.

I shone the torch up and around the cellar. The spider-webs fluttered in the breeze as before; thick, disgusting grey curtains speckled with particles of dirt and the remains of dead creatures. I shone the beam round the floor. There was no evidence of any disturbance, but the crate I'd used to reach the top shelves was not exactly where I'd left it because I remembered the sharp edges had scuffed tracks in the hard-packed mud where I'd dragged it out of the way. The water must have been deep enough to float it a few inches to the left. I shone the torch up the wall.

The little devil that called itself nosiness, nudged common sense out of the way. How many packets? I hadn't looked long enough to count them and hadn't touched them. I'd been so shocked at the time. It would be easy enough to work out the current street value of cocaine and I assumed as it was being take so seriously, there must have been some indication how much had been stashed. The police had hinted at information. I just wanted to see for myself. Then I would know what level of worry to deal with. I stood on the crate with the torch under my chin as before, opened the lid and shone the beam in. The tools lay in a jumbled heap at the bottom of the box. There were no packets of any description. I shut the lid with a bang and fell off the stool.

I'd fallen sideways, put my hand out and caught it on the bottom step. It bent backwards and I got onto my knees, bruised and shocked, scrabbled around for the torch and picked it up. My left wrist hurt and I tucked my hand into my pocket and I scrambled back up the steps to the kitchen. The chairs in the front room were filthy so it didn't matter that I sat down with my jeans covered in wet silt from the floor. I punched in the number for the police contact.

I was not going to apologise for being nosy; if I hadn't looked, they wouldn't have known. The silence was palpable, the instructions when they came, quite clear.

"In half an hour, leave the house as normal. Drive to the Bed and Breakfast, the one that belongs to Mrs Parry, the lady you normally visit. Do not, repeat not, go back to the boatyard. Stay there until we phone you. Act as normal. And can we have the code for the gates to the yard?"

I let myself in through the backdoor. She was up to her elbows in flour, the storm forgotten and all back to normal. I couldn't explain to her, couldn't tell her any details. I said there was an issue that had reared its head from the summer and could I stay until I was told otherwise? She nodded, concerned but unperturbed, as always.

"Go and have a bath and give me your clothes for the wash. You can have Helen's room until you hear something."

There was nobody to talk to, nobody to confide in, nobody who would understand that none of this was my fault. I lay in the bath, my wrist too painful to soap myself with properly. I knew why I was here and forbidden to go back to the yard. The police would wait now until someone came for the drugs, find them missing and assume it was me who'd taken them. Then they would search the Boat Shed. It was going to happen today, I was sure. My level of worry shifted to anxiety, then to fear. Until they were caught, I was trapped in a situation I could only guess at, perplexed by how the drugs could have been removed if the house was under surveillance. Then it was obvious.

The power-cut provided cover and it would have been so easy to park out of the village and sneak through the streets to the house, remove the drugs and disappear, but why were the police so concerned about me? More than one dealer and a pact gone wrong? If one had tried to outdo the other and the other hadn't known he'd been betrayed and found the box had already been emptied, I would be the next choice; me and the Boat Shed. This was part of a master-plan by the drug squad, I thought, and they knew exactly who to look for and intended to get all of them. I was just piggy-in-the-middle.

I lay there in the bubbles and felt like the main victim in a crime drama. Only the actors went home at the end of the day. I couldn't believe I could be used like this but, on the other hand, as long as I was safe, the result could banish my problem once and for all.

Helen's Nain had washed my clothes and stuffed a chicken ready to go in the oven that evening. She poured me a sherry, set it down on the mat by a plate of cheese sandwiches and wrapped my wrist in a bandage soaked in iced water. I said I'd slipped in the mud.

"It's not broken, is it? It can't be broken. I've got all this work to do. Arnie Blackwell… you remember Arnie?" I told her about Hugh's boat and Arnie's plan.

"Well, I do remember him, now. That huge man. I've never seen someone eat so much cake at one sitting but that was a few years ago now. What a kind man. Don't you worry, cariad, it'll sort itself out. I don't think it's broken," she said, pouring more iced water over the bandage. "But you need to rest it. Here, these'll help." She gave me two paracetamol and a glass of water.

The phone was ominously silent.

"I can't bear this," I said, after lunch, as she loaded the dish washer. "I have to go and see what's happening. I need to check the Boat Shed. Supposing…?"

"But they said not to go under any circumstances. No, you must stay here and do as you've been asked, for once. Ring the police again, if you must, but stay here." She was very stern.

I didn't need to phone. We rushed to the front door as the sound of sirens filled the bay and two police cars sped past. She nodded. "Now just wait," she said and sat me down in front of the television. "Find a film. Stay in here until you're told. I'm sure there will be questions and statements or whatever these people do. I'm going upstairs for a sleep. The village will be buzzing after this. Let's hope it's the end of it now."

I watched her leave the room and noticed how she steadied herself on the door-jamb, helped myself to another sherry from the dresser cupboard, sat in the front room and stared out of the window. I could just see the stripes of one of the cars parked on the road. It was only three hours since I'd left the house. I could have still been in there. I drank the sherry and closed my eyes as the paracetamol kicked in.

It was late in the afternoon when I drove to Pwllheli for statements.

The Boat Shed had been broken into, but no major damage done.

"Did you get him?" I asked.

"He was still in the yard when we arrived, so yes. He left *Tai Pilots* in a bit of a rush. Must have had a shock when he found the empty box. We followed him. He'd left his car and scrambled through the bushes between the two yards, climbed around the security fence onto the harbour wall and broke through the door. Apart from a few planks pulled out, we got there in time."

"What about the drugs and the other dealer?"

"Indeed, yes. We'd had an idea who it was before but we had a useful tip-off that there'd been a falling out, so to speak. The informant, a previous addict known to yourself, I believe, sends his regards, by the way. Not to be mentioned outside this room, of course."

Pete, it had to be Pete. He said he'd gone straight. Maybe he'd finally had enough. Maybe the violence of the summer and the drugs haul had helped. But an informant? That was dangerous. I hoped he knew what he was doing.

The guy in charge said I'd done well and were sorry they'd put me in a difficult situation but thought I'd handle it okay after my involvement in the summer.

"You don't scare easy, do you?" he said.

"Depends," I said. I wasn't going to tell him, was I?

"I couldn't take photos this time, though," I said, to change the subject. "It's a bit different when they're alive and not drowned dead." I was almost afraid to ask. "Was there a lot?"

"Off the record again, being as you're a nosy ex-journalist, yes. It was a considerable amount and yes, they were rival dealers after the same stash. Thought they were good mates, as well."

"No honour amongst thieves, this time, then," I said. "Can I go home, now?"

"When forensics have finished, we'll phone you. How's the wrist?" and nodded towards the bandage. "Shouldn't go climbing on crates," he said, with a grin.

I drove back to the yard. The gates to next door were still locked, but Denise had texted the yard would be open the next morning. Mine were closed but without the padlock. I opened the caravan, checked in the shed and put the planks back in place. No way was I going to sleep there if I couldn't lock the gates and headed back to Helen's Nain's.

I stopped at the top of the steps and sat down. The typical Sunday evening stillness hung in the air; post-school holidays, post-drug and break-ins and the flood-tide yet to creep into the bay. I had a desperate urge to see Daniel and feel the strong warmth of his body, to look into those deep-blue eyes and take comfort in the care and compassion I'd felt in that short time. Even if I still didn't believe it. Did he hear me over the ether? The phone rang.

I decided not to tell him anything and it would be unlikely that national news would pick it up so early on. He'd been busy. Part of the marina he'd been assessing had been directly in line with the swell, some of the bolts had sheared, the pontoons were in danger of breaking free from the crossmembers and the staff had to replace them just before the height of the storm. In the local bay, a few small fishing boats had pulled away from their moorings and were washed up on the beach near the castle. It was messy, he said, but not too bad.

"What about you?" I told him about Hugh's boat and Arnie's generosity. Nothing more.

"What an amazing thing to do," he said.

"Isn't it," I said.

He was quiet for a second. "Are you alright, Cassie? You sound rather flat."

Flat, I thought? Flattened, more like.

"Fine, "I said. "Just tired. There's a lot to do in the next fortnight before the crane comes in. I'll be alright tomorrow. I…" I stopped.

"What?"

"I wish you were here," I said, and almost whispered it into the phone. I had no right. It had been only the one night, after all. Then, sod it, I thought. That's what I felt.

"I will be," he said.

I went to bed that night, safe at Helen's Nain's, cocooned in Helen's quilt and fell asleep with the distant roar of the waves on the North Bank.

CHAPTER 14

Monday morning dawned with a persistent drizzle. I woke from a deep sleep to the smell of bacon and toast and Helen's Nain calling me. There was a crash from the kitchen. I shot out of bed and ran downstairs. She stood in the middle of the floor surrounded by pieces of the teapot she'd been carrying to the table.

"It just fell out of my hand," she said, a bemused look on her face. "It was my best pot, too."

I sat her down in a chair. She was pale and her hands shook. She gripped the arms of the chair and sat upright and still.

"I'll make some more tea," I said, picked another pot from the dresser and swept up the shattered china from the floor while the kettle boiled. She never used tea-bags, always bought best Indian tea and poured it through a silver strainer. I buttered some toast and brought the plate of bacon to the table. She shook her head when I asked if she wanted some breakfast. I made a bacon sandwich for myself and watched her as she sipped her tea.

"Helen's Nain," I said, "I know you're going to hate me suggesting this, but do you think you should have a check-up with the doctor?"

The cup clattered against the saucer. She stared at it and folded her hands in her lap.

"Perhaps I should," she said. "I'm so very tired these days. I can't see how I could cope with guests next year if I was like this."

"Perhaps it's all my fault with all these 'goings-on,' as your friend puts it."

She smiled. "No, I think it's called old age."

"Do you think you should let your daughter know you're not too well? She lives in London, doesn't she? I haven't seen Helen for a couple of years and she hasn't been to visit yet. It's not really my place to suggest and I'll take you, if you like, but your daughter should say it's okay, don't you think? She'll want to know if you're unwell."

She snorted and got up quickly from the table, swayed, caught herself and sat down again.

"No," she said. "She won't care. We haven't spoken for months. We are somewhat estranged, Cassie. We were never close."

I know the feeling, I thought.

"I'm so sorry. Even so…"

"I'll make an appointment, and you can take me if you will and if there's anything wrong, I'll let her know then. Don't tell Helen, either. She's a loving grand-daughter but she'd make a fuss. And you can sleep here for the week, if you like, until you clear the yard and sort those boats out."

Fuss is what you need, I thought, and cleared the table, waited until she was comfortable in the chair by the Rayburn, put the phone on the coffee table by her side and left for the yard. I marched up the steps in a quandary; first Hugh, now this and I wasn't quite sure about the part I was being asked to play.

The week disappeared in a frenzy of work. I could manage to hold the hose with my right hand only and washed the silt from the dinghies, picked up the contents of the rubbish-bin and detached skeins of sea-weed from the winch and the rigging on Hugh's boat. Will Roberts rang and asked me if I needed help. I looked at *Annie's* ropes which needed adjusting. I'd tried with one hand and said 'yes, please', and I didn't know if he'd heard the news of the drugs yet. If it wasn't broadcast today, I'd be surprised. Of course, he knew already.

"Up to your adventures again, Miss Jones?" he asked, when he turned up, and looked pointedly at my bandaged wrist.

The gravel arrived with the same guys who'd fixed the tarpaulin. They spread it out without a word and left a pile to go under Hugh's boat when it was upright again. I hadn't asked them to, they said it was on the firm, just pay for the gravel, no worries, and left.

The Welsh news covered the story. It was minimised to 'a quantity of cocaine has been seized from a house in Pwllheli and two men have been arrested. There are indications the arrests were linked to the maritime drugs seizure in August.' That was it then. No details. Part of a bigger plan, I assumed.

On Saturday, a text arrived from Emily. I'd forgotten all about her and couldn't imagine why she would want to spend even five minutes in an old boatyard. It was another day of drizzle, grey and cold and I lit the fire in the wood-burner. She walked into the yard late morning, the puppy under her arm and stared at Hugh's boat. We sat in the Boat Shed out of the weather and I explained about the storm and the high tides. It hadn't affected the sheep, she said. There was no rain, hardly. Just the electrics went off for a bit.

"I fell off a crate," I said, when she asked about my bandaged wrist. "I see dad let you keep the puppy. Not a good place for it here, though."

"I wanted to bring her to meet you and to say thank you," she said, and chewed her bottom lip as I'd seen her do before when she was uncomfortable. "She's called Rosie. She's a Cavapoo," which meant nothing to me. I nodded.

"School good?"

"They give me some help now. I'd got behind with work." She looked embarrassed, "I'm not bothering with the boys. Not yet, right. I got it. Ta. Can I look round? I'll keep her on the lead."

By two o'clock, she'd cleared a space in the back room, laid out all the pieces of the broken clipper that Jason had demolished, sat on a stool and studied the rigging of the other models.

"Can I do this?" she said. "It's dead fiddly but it'll glue nicely and I can thread all those bits of string through. What are they called? It's alright," and didn't wait for an answer I didn't have, "I've got my phone. I'm good at stuff like this. Mum taught me sewing and stuff as well, embroidery, you know?" She whizzed through her ideas and comments so quickly, I had a job to keep up.

I drove her home late afternoon. Her dad said he'd heard that a boat fell over and offered the use of a tractor, if I ever needed one. Her mother took one look at my wrist and replaced the bandage with a Tubi-grip. I came away from the warm kitchen full of buttered scones, jam and kindness, locked up the yard for the night, walked back to Borth-y-Gest and ate lasagne hot from the oven. It was like coming home. Helen's Nain seemed better as we chatted over dinner. She cooed over the tale of the puppy but it didn't persuade me. I still didn't like dogs much; even expensive, fluffy ones.

Sunday, again, and I left the house to spend the day in the yard. I didn't even glance at *Tai Pilots* as I climbed the steps out of the bay. Paul phoned from Holyhead. He planned to bring his boat down on Wednesday with spring-tides due and plenty of water over the bar, if he arrived at the Fairway Buoy, a bit early or late.

"Fancy the trip?" he asked. "You could get the train up here."

Thank God for a sprained wrist. I declined; graciously.

"How's Hugh?" I asked.

"Out to the turbines collecting data for a few days. He doesn't mind being at sea for a short while as long as he's got stonking great engines to get him there and a crew full of heavies to look after him. He won't sail with me, no chance. Anyway, he's fine, now. Bit nervous about the damage to *Capella* but excited about the new cradle. At least you'll know how to handle him next time."

Next time? I hoped not.

Daniel phoned. I sat in the caravan and we said very little.

"I'm coming south at the end of the week but going straight to Holyhead for a spot of business first. Can I come and see you on my way back to London? I have to check on the yard and talk to Denise. I'll phone you."

He was coming to say goodbye and I tried to be philosophical about the inevitable parting, still confused about my emotions, laced with the mistrust about his motivation for any contact with me, other than sheer courtesy. Yet, the memories of that night overwhelmed me at times. I tried not to be miserable. Desire and mistrust were not good bed-fellows.

Monday morning and Arnie arrived with the new cradle loaded on a trailer, still in pieces, all newly galvanised with the adjusting pads for the supports wrapped in plastic and labelled.

"I thought you said this was going to be made out of scrap you didn't want," I said. "This is brand new. Hugh will be embarrassed. I'm embarrassed. It's too much," I tried to protest.

He smoothed his moustache with the thumb and forefinger of one big paw and considered the steel girders on the trailer.

"Well, it's like this," he said. "I got into it, tried it out as a protype, if you like. Bit of something new to work on – you know, to build something. Haven't done that for years. I'm always cutting things up in my line of work. I enjoyed it, too. Might make a few more. So, he doesn't have to be embarrassed. Or you. Also," he said, "you don't want tatty stuff around. New cradles give the yard a bit of class."

"What about the old cradle for Paul's boat, though? I know the one you mean. It's been stuck by the wall down the road, all rusty with grass growing through it. I'll need to paint that and how do I get it here?"

He cocked his thumb towards the gate as a tractor crunched through the new gravel, the newly painted girders laid flat across the fork-lift at the front.

Tuesday morning, and the doctor's surgery was much as I'd remembered. Helen's Nain sat upright on the red plastic chair, her handbag on her lap. She clutched the straps so tight that the veins stood out on the back of her hands. She unzipped the bag and fiddled around in it for a tissue, which she pulled out and put back in. I knew how she felt.

"Do you want me to come in with you?" I asked. She shook her head. We drove back in silence. The GP hadn't needed to tell her what she already suspected. I made tea and we sat in the kitchen by the Rayburn.

"I'd looked it up on the Internet a while ago. If it's Parkinson's," she said and her voice wavered, "I have to make plans. I couldn't cope with the house and guests. Not properly."

"Wait until you see the consultant," I said. "They can help the symptoms with drugs, I think, but that's all I know. You must tell your daughter, now. She would want to know, even if you…well…even if you're not close."

She sat back in her chair. I waited. She closed her eyes for a moment and sighed.

"She never had any secrets about how she felt about this place. She couldn't wait to leave school and home. She trained as a doctor in London, you know, and worked in the NHS for a while and then married Michael. He's a consultant as well. Then she started her own private practice and was so wrapped up in how much money she made, she sounded as though she'd almost forgotten why she was there at all. It's all she could talk about; the new practice with state-of-the art equipment, the renovation of the building, new staff, the type of clients. She sent expensive flowers on my birthdays but couldn't find time to visit. That was five years ago. She never wasted a moment telling me how much she hated this place; back of beyond, she called it."

"What about when you lost your husband? I mean, was she close to her father?"

She shook her head. "We were never close," and closed her eyes.

"What about Helen? She sounded as though she loved it here in her holidays."

"A very independent young lady, Helen, but she keeps in touch with long emails about her adventures. She spent as much time here as possible when she was a child, but now, I believe she's found a partner. They're coming for Christmas."

"How lovely," I said, "what's his name?"

"Hannah," she said.

I should have guessed. Helen had made no secret of her general feeling for men, but we were so involved with other things at the time; it was only one summer after all, laced with tragedy, and although we'd met up a few times in London, it was never a talking-point.

"Will you stay for Christmas, Cassie?" she said, "unless you're going home to London, of course."

Home? London?

"I don't know," I said. "I haven't got that far, but thank you for the offer."

I left her with the phone and the promise to ring her daughter.

"Or send her an email, if you find it too hard to talk," I said. "Helen will have her email address." She brightened at that.

The weatherman forecast light winds, drizzle and poor visibility for Wednesday, the wind due to pick up in the afternoon to Force 4 or 5 locally, by evening.

"Are you still going to sail the boat down?" I asked Paul over the phone.

"Sure, I am," he said. "I can get in a bit earlier than I thought, with it being spring-tides. I'll be with you about six, I reckon. I've down-loaded the changes to the buoys. Mr Roberts said the storm shifted the channel to run parallel to the bar for a short stretch with a sharp turn to starboard at the green."

"Oh, right," I said. I knew it would be cheeky to say what I thought, as he said he was an experienced sailor, but I did anyway. "Don't be hasty to come over the bar too early," I said, "especially if there's a sea running. It'd be right on the beam for you."

"Yeah, yeah," he said. "I got it."

I do hope so, cocky little sod, I thought, revised my opinion of him yet again and chuckled to myself that I thought of him as a wayward adolescent, when in reality he was probably not much older than me. I hadn't asked for his date of birth, had I? No need.

I spent the rest of the morning in the caravan studying the insurance claim David had helped with. He returned the paperwork I'd filled in and asked if he could poke around a bit more.

"I'm not sure about this," he said, "but I've been around the back of the shed and had a good look at the end wall nearest the slipway. I can't dig away at it, obviously, but it looks as though those freak waves that washed out Hugh's props have gouged out some of the mud under the beams at the bottom of the wall. The sheets are still nailed on but the ends of the beams seem to be resting on fresh air. Come and look. How it's stood up all these years, I don't know. But it doesn't look right. It'll be interesting to see what the surveyor says."

"Do you think they would buy me a new shed?" I asked. "Joking, of course."

"Who knows?" he said. "Any coffee on the go?"

But after he'd gone, pleasant, chatty and helpful, I started to think. Insurance claim, if they paid out, plus the money from *Tai Pilots*, plus the remains of my inheritance; I scribbled on my notepad and disappeared into a fantasy world that had nothing to do the daily grind of cleaning. It could all wait. Twenty minutes later, I held up the last drawing. That's what I want, I said aloud. Wow.

At three o'clock, the phone rang. Paul would be well on his way and I knew instinctively it was him, even before I looked at the screen. The breeze had picked up, as the forecast said it would, and I could see the dead bracken in the cliff-face begin to quiver.

"Cassie, I'm coming in." There was a tension in his normally, laid-back voice that I hadn't heard before. "I got to the Fairway Buoy quicker than I thought."

"No, it's too early," I said and checked my watch. "You'll have to stand off for another hour."

"I can't," he said. "I'm getting knocked around like hell out here on this swell. It's awful big, considering the wind strength. I can't stay here and the engine's running hot. It's like the sea's just gathering to rush in. I've taken the sails down and I'm coming in. It looks as though there's plenty of water."

"No." I tried not to shriek. "No, just wait. Another hour and it'll be okay. Wait. Go back out a bit."

"No. The wind's picking up. I can't turn round in this sea, anyway. See you in an hour," he said, and that was it.

I thought about it; four hours before high tide and he might, only might, just have enough water over the bar if it hadn't been for the swell. But that wasn't the problem. The channel now ran parallel to the bar and as the waves rolled in, they could push him out of the deeper water onto the sandbank and run him aground where he would lie with the waves breaking over him. It didn't bear thinking about. The swell would drop him off the crests and into the troughs, the force enough for his keel to hit the bottom only inches below him; shallow water and churned-up sand that his keel would dig into. He said he'd sailed a lot, but not in this estuary; deep water and marinas in Scotland, he'd said, with his dad and a crew. But this was different.

I tried to see the buoys from memory. Will Roberts had moved the green, he'd said, where if Paul turned at ninety degrees and followed through to the next red with the wind behind him, he could sail in if his engine failed. But I wasn't a sailor and knew very little about the art of sailing and wind directions.

"Paul, no, go back out and wait, or go to Pwllheli." I didn't need to put urgency into my voice; the panic was already there, but there was no answer.

Should I phone Will Roberts? Should I call the RNLI? I paced up and down. It wasn't an emergency just yet. What could they do anyway? Nothing brought those stupid tidal rules the Harbour Master had drummed into me more clearly than this. Wait, and you'll have your depth; a rule is a rule – mostly. Bit like life, I thought, but if you wait a bit after a bad thing happens, the worst seems to settle of its own volition, or maybe because it was simply that you'd given it time for a bit of rational thinking. Whatever, I couldn't see all the way up the estuary from the yard. I couldn't stand it, jumped into the Toyota and drove around to Borth-y-Gest. I abandoned the car outside *Tai Pilots*, grabbed the binoculars off the seat, checked the phone was in my pocket and ran up to the pill-box.

The visibility was good, despite the grey sky and drizzle but it wasn't a sight I wanted to see. Paul's boat, just a tiny sailing yacht, a black dot against the heaving grey sea outside the bar, lay tilted over in shallow water as the waves nudged it onto the bank. He was on the foredeck and clung on to the side-rail every time the boat lurched. I could see quite clearly as he freed the chain to put the anchor down and it slipped over the bow-roller into the water. Then he stopped, knelt on the deck and didn't move. I called the Coast Guard.

An hour later, cold and damp, with sore eyes glued to the binoculars, I watched the yacht finally right itself, float and lie to the anchor as the tide flooded in. The Criccieth lifeboat with Paul now onboard, sped down the channel below me and into the harbour. I had to be there to meet it.

An ambulance waited in the Yacht Club car-park and I watched as they helped him out of the RIB, onto the pontoon and up the ramp, a white bandage clearly visible on his right hand and his arm in a sling. He saw me and nodded before they bundled him into the ambulance and sat him down to take notes, his face chalk-white against the red sailing jacket.

I collared the cox and explained who I was.

"Is he alright? I didn't call until I saw he was aground. Did I do the right thing? Is he hurt badly?" The words tumbled out.

"He put out a Mayday straight after you called it in. He's lost a finger, love. Got it trapped in one of the chain links when the anchor was run out. He said it jammed in between the chain and the bow-roller as a wave threw him off balance and sliced it clean off. It was lucky he didn't lose the rest of his fingers, but his hand was crushed. Don't know how bad, but he's a bit shook up, as you can imagine."

I swallowed. "What about the yacht?"

"Will Roberts said he'd go and tow her in at high tide. The lad had put all the chain out so she should just float and ride pretty on the swell. All well, love," he said and looked at my horrified face. "Nobody's died and you did well to call as soon as you did. If nobody had seen him, or he hadn't been able to use his radio, I dread to think…"

He turned to go back down the walkway, swivelled round with a big grin. "Not skinny dipping today, then?" and disappeared through the security gate.

So much for secrets, but I just laughed.

They kept him in the hospital all Thursday, sewed up his finger stump and plastered his hand. I went to see him that night.

"Only little bones broken," he said, "but it's black and blue. Hurts like hell. I can't do anything about my boat. Mr Roberts said it's on the wall outside his office. There's no damage, except they had to cut the anchor off. I'm really sorry, Cassie. It went from bad to worse. I had no idea it could be like that." His voice broke.

Been there, done that, I thought and reassured him all would be taken care of.

"Which finger?" I asked.

"My forefinger. Dad's coming over from Ireland tomorrow to take me home for a few weeks while it mends."

Thank God for that. I thought. I'd enough on my plate with cranes and yachts. Not my problem. I'm not his parent and certainly not his nursemaid, I thought, uncharitably.

"I'll send you the bill," I said. "For unnecessary worry. Have you phoned Hugh?"

"He saw it on the Welsh news. Foolhardy, he told me."

"I agree," I said.

He smiled wanly and I left him to reflect on his future ability to put two fingers up to the world.

On Friday, the harbour bristled with nervous boat-owners. I could see the activity along the harbour wall while they waited their turn at the top of the tide and watched protectively as competent hands swung their precious yachts high into the air and settled them into their beds for the winter. Arnie, Master of Ceremonies, took over my yard and waved his arms around like a pro as he directed the crane-driver. Hugh watched, Beanie in hand, and hopped from one foot to the other until *Capella* was settled. I took a photograph of his face when the strops were finally removed and she sat sweetly in her new cradle, a few scratches and one small dinge in the planking where she'd toppled onto the wooden props. I took photos of Paul's little yacht high in the air and as it was being lowered into its newly-painted cradle and sent them off to him. Both yachts looked strange without their masts which lay neatly on trestles by their sides.

"Safer for the next storm," Will Roberts had advised. "Reduced windage, you see, Miss Jones. Also, the rigging can be repaired more easily."

Hugh pulled his Beanie firmly back on his head and wandered around *Capella's* hull. He ran his hand lovingly over the timbers, peered at the damage, walked over to Arnie, stood beneath his towering bulk and looked up at him. Arnie held out his hand and Hugh took it, his own, small hand lost in the big paw and was completely lost for words. Arnie understood.

"You're welcome, mate," he said, "and we'll use your old props for *Annie*, if that's okay?"

With the three boats safely on dry land, my yard now took on the semblance of a proper boatyard with two yachts; small, but they were still yachts, and one elderly fishing boat, lined up nice and tidy, the rearranged dinghies in a neat row ready for painting in the spring. I decided the Tubi-grip could come off my wrist; it was nothing compared to Paul's injury.

Hugh disappeared off to his engine sheds, Arnie to his static with thanks I could hardly utter and I picked up the sketch I'd finished the day before, as satisfied as I'd ever been. Despite the regular disasters that seemed to happen on a daily basis, I thought that if I was going to work and live with this maritime, nature-in-the-raw, that's the way it was and there was no use bleating about it.

I delved under the counter in the Boat Shed and pulled out the new bottle of Glenlivet I'd bought as a treat, poured a large one into a coffee mug and flung my tired body into the nearest armchair. I mused over the ritual I'd inherited and continued from my grumpy, great-uncle and thought that some people, including my mother, Helen's Nain, even Trish in London, definitely that marshmallow woman with the integrity of a slug, would think it most unbecoming for a young lady to celebrate on her own, and in whisky, of all things and poured another large one.

Then Daniel rang.

CHAPTER 15

"This may seem presumptuous, but can you spare some time this weekend? And can you come posh again?" he asked, very different to the short messages I'd received that week. I hadn't divulged any of the information about the drugs; I'd been asked not to and somehow, the whole incident seemed shabby. I raided Helen's wardrobe, found a respectable overnight case on the top of the wardrobe, packed trousers and two glitzy evening tops and told Helen's Nain I'd be back in the yard on Monday.

"I'll be fine," she said. "Gwen's coming around tomorrow and I'm blessed with good neighbours, you know."

Yeah, right.

"Can we have a proper talk next week, cariad?" she asked and rested her hand on my arm as I bent down to make sure she'd got her phone. "You don't have to go back to the caravan, you know. It's winter now. I couldn't bear the thought of you out there in the cold. You're welcome to stay here until you can fix *Tai Pilots* up. Also, my daughter's coming to visit. I'd like you to meet her."

I didn't want to experience a difficult relationship between mother and daughter, the very idea intrusive, but didn't see how I could avoid it.

Besides, I wasn't family and was increasingly uncomfortable about any help she needed that might be misconstrued. The business of duty, care and kindness reared itself in confusion; much like an anchor chain under tension when the tide rose and wrapped itself round your reluctant neck; a noose of care, I thought ruefully, put it out of my mind and set off back to the yard for a final check and to lock up for the weekend. I bounced up the steps to quieten the excitement and anticipation of the night ahead and arrived at the yard, hot, sweaty and dishevelled just as Daniel drove up to the gates and eased down the window.

"Hello, you," he said and smiled. It was a greeting of quiet intimacy and sent my pulse thudding. He was just as gorgeous as I remembered.

"Give me ten minutes," I said, and left him to wander round and examine the yachts in their cradles. I watched him run his hand over *Capella's* hull, as Hugh had done, and study the damage. I'd forgotten how tall he was and how he bounced off the soles of his feet like an athlete at the start line, his whole being full of caged energy.

"Excellent," he said. "You've done a good job here." For a fleeting moment, it sounded patronising. I climbed into the car and forgot about it.

The country hotel sat in amongst trees and mature rhododendrons that must have been planted when the house was a wealthy, private residence, the car-park tucked discreetly away from the front of the hotel which overlooked green fields dotted with sheep. Way to the south, the glimmer of the sea in late afternoon sun darkened and disappeared within minutes. I had a feeling it was the same hotel David had been seen at by Denise's brother and hoped fervently he hadn't planned to stay this weekend. That could be interesting.

It was now late October, and the clocks had already been put back an hour. The thought of long, dark evenings in the caravan, or even at Helen's Nain's, did not appeal, but tonight I had no intention of worrying about it.

I thought he'd come to say goodbye, but we picked up our easy chat over afternoon tea as easily as we'd left it; so much to talk about after the storm and how it had affected the marina he was assessing. I couldn't contain my enthusiasm about the yard, my amazement at Arnie's generosity and the kindness of Mark and the Harbour Master and the guys from the builders' merchants, who'd helped me without judgement or criticism.

"It counteracted the awfulness," I said. "Especially how it affected Hugh. I thought he might do something dreadful but for such a funny little man, people just understood and cared for him until he could cope and move on. It was quite humbling."

"You do seem to collect waifs and strays," he said. "And what about you?"

We left that until later, walked to the end of the long drive leading to the hotel, dressed for dinner in the sumptuous room, lingered over an exquisite meal and drank far too much champagne.

"Did you mind that I'd booked a room?" he asked, as we drank brandy in the lounge. "Truthfully?"

I shook my head. "Truthfully? No, of course I didn't mind. I could have refused but I wasn't going to pass up another night like the last, was I?"

He laughed. "That good, was it?"

"Passable," I said. "I could have said no, or been offended, but it was my decision. I thought you'd just come to say a polite goodbye, so this is a bonus." Still in charge, I thought. But only just. "I assume you'll be going to London and back to Trinidad for Christmas."

"I am. To both, in fact. I need to spend the day with Denise on Monday morning to discuss business. Then I have to go."

He was as tender as I'd remembered and then I let myself go with delirious abandonment, pleasuring the disasters and difficulties of the last few weeks out of my system. He turned over, propped himself up on one elbow and said, "Come with me."

I laughed.

"What's so funny?"

Nose to nose on the pillows, I said, "what's funny, is that I have a business to run. I can't just walk away and leave it."

"Even for a holiday? You can meet my folks. Sun, warm sea, blue skies and soft winds. I could teach you to sail. Just think, lying on the deck with a glass of cool white wine and nobody around to bother us."

"And it would be expensive," and looked hard at him. "I'm not blessed with unlimited funds. I have a plan for next year and I need every penny I can raise."

"Okay, okay," he said, and threw up his hands in mock resignation. "Not even as my guest?"

"No. But thank you. Besides which…" the devil called doubt filtered its way into my brain, "it would have to be serious. This can't be serious, can it? We've only met twice. Just because we're good in bed together and have plenty to talk about doesn't negate all the other things where we might not be compatible."

"Like what?" There was no rancour in his voice.

"More about getting to know you. The proper you under all that wealth. I've never had a serious relationship and I'd have to be very sure. I'm still learning about me. That's enough, sometimes. I'm not ready for a commitment, not happy to jump on a moneyed bandwagon for the sake of a life-style and I'm not tough enough to stand any big disappointments, even for just a holiday."

"Now we're getting to the truth," he said. "You want to make your mark on life and don't want a hand up the ladder. Even for love? With anyone?"

I had to think about that. It was one hell of a self-revelation.

"I suppose so. Not yet, anyway," and ran my hand down his chest, felt the contours of his muscles and the leanness and said, "but it doesn't stop me thinking you're the most beautiful man I've ever met. I'm just not ready to be part of someone else's life. Not even for a holiday. So can we stop talking, please?"

We drove to Morfa Nefyn on Sunday, parked on the cliff-top and ambled along the cold beach as far as the *Ty Coch*.

I paddled in the cold sea, its clarity and temperature quite different to the south side of the peninsula with its shallow, sun-warmed beaches in summer and laughed at his reluctance to test the water, even with his hand.

"Uncivilised," he said, shaking the drops off. "You really should come to Trinidad, Cassie," with a twinkle in his eye.

Could I be persuaded? As the day wore on, the importance of my familiar life seemed to shift. The yard and all my new acquaintances, faded away and I immersed myself in the enjoyment of leisure with no immediate responsibilities and shared Daniel's enthusiasm and appreciation of the scenery. We took the path from the *Ty Coch* and edged along the bottom of the cliff, crossed the sandy coves to the lifeboat station and up onto the headland and the National Coastwatch Institution look-out.

"That's Holyhead Mountain," I said, the Anglesey coast clear in the northerly breeze. The lighthouse on Llanddwyn Island stood out white against the green backdrop of forest and fields in the distance. I'd forgotten he'd been there on business and driven through the flat landscape to leave the island. I asked him, delicately, about the extent of his family business but he steered the question away with complaints about the cold. He was on a break too, I thought, and didn't want to talk about work.

We marched through the golf course at a brisk pace while he gave a running commentary on the excellent quality of the greens and the fantastic situation on the headland. I had as much interest in golf as flying to the moon, but even I could appreciate the immaculate, smooth greens and the work needed to maintain them. I just wasn't a perfectionist. Not at all. We drove back on narrow lanes to the warmth of the hotel.

"When are you flying back home?" I asked, vaguely aware he was good at avoiding answers.

"Before Christmas," he said. "I won't be back in the UK until the spring."

"That feels like a long time," I said, and we were quiet for a while.

That night felt like the end of something; a gentle exploration, unlike the passion of the other nights. In the morning, we were thoughtful and kind to each other, even verging on politeness as though we'd only just met and the short interlude of pleasure and luxury just a fanciful dream. I asked him to drop me at the end of the road. Denise would be at work already and I had no wish to be seen with him. I walked back to the yard past the quiet boatyards. Winter inactivity loomed heavily in the air, settled like a fog in my mind and the optimism I'd felt before the weekend, diluted in the drizzle, and disappeared entirely when I unlocked the gates to the grey yard. Is this it, I thought? My life?

"Shall I see you again, do you think?" I asked, when he'd finished his business with Denise and came to say goodbye.

He smiled. "Of course," he said. "I have a boatyard to keep an eye on. I'll be back in the spring."

We stood apart in the cold yard; the shrouds on Paul's little yacht tapped in the breeze and heralded the bad weather that was forecast; low cloud covered the sky and the trees rustled their dead leaves on Ballast Island.

"You could change your mind," he said. "Come with me," he said, "for a holiday, at least. You deserve it."

"I don't deserve anything," I said. "I don't see why you said that. It's not a good reason."

"Well, then, perhaps I could simply say I would like your company for a few weeks. I like your company. Very much. Think about it. I won't book tickets for another few weeks, at least. I have to spend time on the south coast."

He drove off, the engine so quiet I could hardly hear it.

November. Mother came and went, stayed one night at *The Sportsman*, and had to 'dash off, darling, to meet friends in Manchester'. I couldn't blame her and we managed to say as much as we ever needed to over a pleasant dinner. Our worlds were so apart and it was an unspoken agreement that really, we didn't need each other all that much.

"As long as you're alright, Cassie. You look well."

"Fresh air and hard work," I said, as I gave her a guided tour of the yard. It took all of five minutes and she hadn't brought boots. Thank God for new gravel, I thought, as she dusted off the edges of her shoes on the Boat Shed mat and accepted tea in the new mugs. I'd cleaned and polished the counter and taken the chair-rugs to Helen's Nain for a wash, bought some chrysanthemums and stuck them in a vase from the charity shop and lit the fire. It was warm and pretty and she thawed out when I showed her my sketches.

"Well," she said. "Very upmarket," and gazed round the Boat Shed with its stock of ropes and blocks and odd tools that only Hugh knew the names of, uncomprehending and unimpressed. "This shed should be demolished, anyway."

I didn't explain where the funds were to come from. It was only a dream as yet. She didn't ask about *Tai Pilots*, and I certainly wasn't going to take her there. Nor was I going to take her to Helen's Nain's; they would have hated each other and had nothing in common, except the tragic story of the drowned children, dead baby and their cousin who was to be my father, torn away from his Welsh home to live in London. No, I didn't want any of that. I think she was relieved when I said I would stay up here for Christmas. How could I not?

Helen's Nain's consultant daughter came, also for a short visit; just for one day, in fact. I made myself scarce after the introductions. She was smart and sharp and she couldn't wait to get out of there, I thought, once she realised that I was going to stay in the house with her mother; temporarily, I assured her.

"Great idea, mum," she'd said, "to let Cassie stay over and also to take you to see the consultant. The drugs are so good these days, you'll hardly even notice," she said, and breezed her way out of her responsibilities. "It's very kind of you, Cassie," patronising cow, I thought. "Of course, I don't mind at all if you can help out. You can't sleep in a caravan all winter and you'll never get builders to start on your house in this weather. Just look at this rain. Typical Wales," which it wasn't, most of the time. "Oh, by the way, I think I know of your mother's business. High-end décor for the Arabs, mostly, I believe? And flowers for big events. She's very well known."

Small world, when you've got money. I left them to it.

It rained. Day after day, heavy and persistent and the Traeth was a sheet of water as the Glaslyn broke its banks and flooded the pastures, just as it would have done before William Madocks built the Cob. The rain trickled through gaps in the roof of the shed where the sheets overlapped and I'd moved the lap-top to the caravan which was fast becoming a site office. It was still dry and warm and I could see all of the yard as well as the gates from the window. Denise popped over every day for natter as it was so quiet. I waited for the gossip about my liaison with her boss to reach her; I could have bet my life that someone in the hotel would have recognised me; even her brother, but he'd moved jobs, she told me, for no particular reason and I was relieved.

Daniel texted about the visit to Trinidad and the tickets; middle of December, he said. I said I wasn't sure. And then I was.

Helen phoned me. It was just before Christmas and still it rained. We hardly ever talked on the phone. Ever since she'd finished her training, she'd set off for far-flung corners of the world to work for charities and research into diseases I'd never heard of. It was strange to hear her voice after all the texts, 'WhatsApp' messages and the occasional email packed with details about poverty and illness; awful stuff, but she always sounded light-hearted and philosophical; she had to be, or she wouldn't do it, I supposed. She'd told me about her partner who she met in Thailand on a holiday. I was looking forward to meeting her.

"You know we're coming to Wales for Christmas?"

"Can't wait," I said, "and your Nain is so excited. She made me go up into the attic and find all the decorations."

There was a pause. "Listen, Cassie…" She sounded so serious

"I'm listening," I said.

Did I keep up with the news and did I follow any of the global news, she asked, and had I heard about the virus in Wuhan? A nasty, new virus causing chest problems, she said. Yes, I had and it was on the other side of the world, I said. Too busy mopping up water to worry about pneumonia in China.

"Don't joke, Cassie. It's not out in the open as such, but we work closely with other scientists, on global disease information, gathering data, you know?"

I didn't know; I'd lost track of exactly what she did after disappearing into the jungles of Africa on an Ebola study.

"There's some real concern filtering through from China. It's being played down by the Chinese authorities, so far as the public is concerned, but we're working with the World Health Organisation and gathering titbits. There might be more to this than we think, so…"

"Right, okay, but why are you telling me this?"

"Are you planning on going abroad in the near future? Like after Christmas?"

"I might be," I said.

"Don't," she said. "At least, don't plan anything just yet. Just in case."

"Just in case what?" I asked, intrigued and a shade irritated.

"We'll see you in a week. We'll know better then. Okay? Promise?"

I shrugged and finished the floor in the snack-bar, now scrubbed and clean and started on the stainless counter until I could see my face in it, ready for the spring and the new menu I'd devised. I needed to talk to Angela, who still worked on the till in Tesco. I couldn't run the snack-bar on my own and would need to spend time procuring the raw materials, locally, as much as possible. Emily and sheep came to mind; salt-marsh lamb, Mr Gilbert had told me about, and I hadn't yet followed it up. If Emily came again on Saturday, I could talk to him when I took her home in the afternoon.

We'd fallen into a routine on Saturdays. I was amazed she wanted to come back to see me, but she was so engrossed in mending Jason's broken ship and determined to finish it, I left her to her own devices in the back room and fed her hot-dogs at lunchtime. She'd blossomed in the few weeks I'd known her; the narrow shoulders had filled out and the lanky, scraped-back hair had been transformed to a soft curly mass that framed and softened her face.

She brought Rosie with her and we found a roll of fishing net on a shelf, wound it round some pieces of wood nailed to the wooden wall supports and fashioned a corner playpen for her. I sent Emily to the pet shop on the High Street to order some fish for the tank and ask for advice, and she took charge of that as well. She put fresh gravel in the tank, filled it up, planted new weed and clapped her hands in delight when I opened the box Jason had put the ornaments and the key in. She placed the plastic treasure chest and ship's wheel in amongst the plastic rocks and we waited a week while any chemicals dissipated and ceremoniously floated the gold-fish into their new home. They explored and darted in and out of the weed, gold flashes that brightened up the winter gloom of the shed and proved wonderful time-wasters. She named them, of course, never once asked if she could bring a friend or said she was bored, stuck her earphones in and just got on with the fiddly work.

"Not another stray lamb?" Denise teased, after I'd introduced her.

"She's easy company and very self-sufficient," I said. "Besides, how are you supposed to know what's going on with kids if you don't talk to them?"

Even I was surprised at the difference a few years made; she was only eight years younger than me; worldly, but only through social media. I hoped she'd learned one reality lesson, at least.

Helen and Hannah were due to arrive on Thursday and I'd put the Christmas tree up in Helen's Nain's front room, instructions followed to the letter. I'd shopped for the Christmas food and Helen's Nain had started the drug treatment prescribed by the consultant. The more I helped out around the house and the more she rested, the steadier on her feet she became. I had under-estimated how hard she'd had to work to keep the house in order and how she'd coped with the last paying guests in the late summer.

I helped to tidy, wash and clean the house every morning, but left her to do the cooking, which she enjoyed and could manage. Then I walked to the yard each morning with a renewed sense of anticipation. I yearned for the spring when I could open up the food business and start to restock some of the classic boat parts that Hugh had recommended. Income would have to come from food, mostly, and there simply wasn't enough room in the yard for any more than a couple more boats. I'd ditched the jet-ski idea.

Neither Hugh, Paul nor Arnie visited, the weather being so wet and farmers worried about water-logged land and floods. All the yards were strangely quiet, the yachts and jet-skis in hibernation for a few months and most of the caravan sites closed, as they usually were before the Christmas break. It was the dead time, followed by frenetic bursts of hard work before the spring preparation for the tourist season and the craning-in of the boats.

Life fell into the comfortable, regular, rhythmic pattern of the seasons, a reason to plan ahead and the necessity to adhere to targets; cold evenings in which to reminisce over sunny days of perfect sailing winds, or flat calms when powerful engines headed for the fishing grounds and trailed broad ribbons of white wake in the still water. That was my dream and I couldn't wait to do it all again and relive the thrill of the speed as the sea stretched ahead into nothingness as far as I could see.

Despite the relative, day-to-day peace, I still awaited the response to the insurance claim David had helped me with; the clauses described 'Acts of God,' and it was the company's interpretation that would decide the outcome of paying something, or nothing. The assessor had poked around under the foundations to the end wall the base to the beams that David had noticed, filled in a lot of forms and left. I didn't expect to hear anything this side of Christmas and pushed it to the back of my mind.

I'd also made tentative enquiries to an estate agent. Nothing definite, just a general idea, I'd said and would get back to them in the New Year. Perhaps for the spring market? Please ring after Christmas and we'll be happy to do a survey. Survey? Horror. The place was a mess, it stank, it was filthy and it housed the ashes of a dead baby, not to mention its dubious goings-on as a drugs-den. I put it all to one side.

Hannah and Helen and I sat around the fire in the front room on Christmas Eve. Hannah was funny, clever and caring and both she and Helen instinctively avoided all talk of disease, death and poverty which was their stock-in-trade. Hannah told tales that made us laugh; it was enough for Helen's Nain to cope with herself and the revelation of her own deteriorating condition without the woes of the world brought into the light-hearted chat. At nine, she took herself to bed, happy and smiling, pleased with herself that she'd provided a supper of roast ham, salads, crispy oven-chips, sherry trifle and cream.

"It's a traditional, Christmas Eve supper," she said to Hannah and myself. "Nothing else will do, will it, Helen?"

Her daughter should have been at the table as well, and I thought, sadly, that blood was not always thicker than water and sometimes strangers are your better friends.

Helen threw a log on the fire and I topped up the glasses.

"So, tell me," I said, "what's all this cloak and dagger stuff?"

The log crackled, spat, flamed eventually to ashes, succeeded by another one and yet another one. I fetched another bottle of wine from the pantry.

"So that's the worst-case scenario if it develops and can't be checked," Helen said. "Just think of global air-travel. Nothing's been published yet but info is being gathered. China has just fobbed the world off with news of a small cluster of cases."

"What about antibiotics?" I asked. "I mean, we can cure pneumonia now, though, can't we?"

"That's the problem. It's not bacterial, Cassie. It's caused by a new virus, a novel virus, we call it. Antibiotics don't kill viruses and we don't have vaccines for something we've never come across before. We haven't got the genetic code yet officially, but there are leaks. We're talking about China, remember. They're pretty hot on hiding stuff."

"Yes, but a pandemic? That went out with the Spanish flu, surely and that was a century ago. This is just you lot scaremongering, surely."

Helen shrugged. "Even so," she said, "we'll be interested in the data for the next two to four weeks. Let's hope it's nothing."

I caught Hannah's look as the doom and gloom threatened to overshadow a pleasant Christmas Eve.

"I'm just saying," Helen said, as the chill of the night crept into the room. "There's no smoke without fire. Unless it's gone out completely, which this fire has. I'm cold. Time for bed."

We left Helen's Nain asleep on Boxing Day afternoon and I took them to the yard. We needed to talk without her. Despite the fact that the weather was wet and grey, the solstice had been and gone and the sun crept a shade higher each day. The yard had an air of purpose and there were great plans afoot for the summer. I lit a small fire and made tea with a liberal glug of whisky and showed them the plans for the Boat Shed, just in case I won the lottery.

They loved the model ships, said hello to the goldfish and curled up in the chairs. I sat on the stool.

"We need to talk about Nain," Helen said.

"Yes, we do."

"My mum came to visit, didn't she?"

"Yes."

"Difficult, was it?"

I nodded. "I didn't stay. Your mum seemed quite happy to let me lodge at the house; temporarily, I assured her."

"I bet she did," Helen said. "Anything to save her the bother. Although it's not my mother's decision or opinion that matters. They never liked each other much. My mum never really needed parents, she once said, but Nain's her own person. I feel like a traitor even talking about her in her absence."

"I know."

She turned to Hannah. "How long do you think she's got before she needs care, Han?"

Hannah shrugged. "Years, with the right treatment and nothing else to make her ill. She looks very well at the moment. She'll become increasingly disabled though, and need extra help. There's no getting away from that."

"What are your plans, Cassie? I mean apart from this, which looks brilliant," she said, and picked up the drawings I'd brought back with me. "Would you go back to journalism if it doesn't work out? You must miss it, London and all that buzz you could get working on a big paper. I bet you're good enough. You're nosy enough, that's for sure."

"We'll see. I need to survive this winter just to see if I can do it." I decided to tell them about *Tai Pilots*. "If you and your mother are okay with me staying at your Nain's, I will, until I can move back into the caravan in the spring. If she needs help then, we can always advertise and I can keep an eye on her. I won't stay here, Helen. Much as I'm fond of her and she's been brilliant, I need some head-space, too. I've only just started. I can't be chained down."

"Not even to the right partner?" she asked. "Go on. Do tell. I can't believe you're celibate."

I raised an eyebrow.

"Okay, okay. Never mind that," she said. "While we're here," serious now, "I need to tell you something but it's not to be shared with anyone. Anyone," she repeated. Hannah nodded her agreement.

"Nain's left me the house in her will. Mother doesn't know. She would never have wanted it, anyway. She hates the place."

I nodded, unsurprised. "But you wouldn't want to live here either, would you?"

We walked back up the path and stopped at the top of the steps. The tide was out, the grey sand and mud dotted with spiky grasses in black winter garb, devoid of boats and people. The Scots Pines on the headland stood out stark and black against the sky but the houses around the bay brightened the scene in startling pink and yellow and shades of blue.

"You must come in the summer," Helen said to Hannah. "It's so pretty, isn't it, Cass?"

"Bit different to the Sahara and the jungles of Borneo," Hannah said, and linked her arms with mine and Helen's. "No lions and tigers and bears, ho, ho," and we skipped down the steps like three kids. I liked her very much.

December slipped into New Year, and still it rained. White water from the mountains gushed in torrents over the boulders in the Llanberis Pass and bounced over the road. The pass at Beddgelert roared with the angry river in spate as it tumbled over the rocks, the ferocity of which I hadn't seen before, and the Traeth disappeared beneath the Glaslyn when it continued to break its banks. The river water swept into the harbour, swirled dead grass, leaves and branches in the brown flood. The water level at high-tide rose almost to the top of the arches under the bridge and worried engineers were seen huddled together on the parapet. Mr Gilbert and the other farmers had long since herded their flocks of pregnant ewes to the upper fields and lambing was due to begin.

On the fifth of January, we listened to the news with concerned interest, as the World Health Organisation published their 'Disease Outbreak News,' the first public information to hit the world's press, about an unusually persistent, large cluster of pneumonia cases in Wuhan in China. Helen and Hannah and many others in their field had known and guessed correctly. Now it was out in the open but only mildly, played down by the authorities, as Helen had said. It hadn't stopped the thousands of people who jetted off to the Canaries for a winter break, or travelled to the West Indies to top up the tan.

Then it gathered pace. Only five days later, infection control guidance was published for droplet and contact advice. Two days later, the genetic sequence of the new virus was finally released and shared globally. The first case of the virus appeared in Thailand, China imposed its first lockdown in two provinces, Italy picked up cases, followed by the first in the UK. Helen emailed me from Nigeria, of all places.

"Watch the news carefully," she said. "Really carefully. And anything else you can find on the Internet outside the main news channels. Just because they tell you it's a low risk to the public, doesn't mean to say it's true, Cassie. Or anything else, come to that."

By the end of January, the WHO had sent a delegation to Chine to learn about the Chinese response to the outbreak and to offer scientific and technical assistance. Hannah was one of them. Helen was unconcerned; they'd often gone their separate ways in research. Then she phoned me again. "They're going to issue a PHEIC."

"What's that?" I asked, increasingly irritated by the intrusion into my daily planning. "Will you stop talking in acronyms. I'm not a scientist."

"It stands for Public Health Emergency of International Concern. Now will you take me seriously?"

The first Saturday in February, and Emily insisted I stay a while to see the new lambs in the barn. The place rustled and bleated with new birth, warm and surprisingly fragrant from the thick beds of straw in the bays, the ewes separated out in stages of lambing. She gave me an orphan to cuddle and feed. I put it down as quickly as I could.

"Not the motherly sort then, Cassie?" asked Emily's dad with a grin on his face. He leaned over the pen and picked up a lamb, turned it over gently in large, capable hands inspected it and put it back.

"Probably not," I said, "but I could be the butchering sort. Will you talk to me about the meat? I'm going to use local produce and put the names of the farms on a board in the snack-bar. Salt-marsh lamb has a good ring to it; made into a burger, or roasted and served hot with gravy and mint sauce in a baguette. What do you think?"

"Talk to my butcher in Penrhyn about cuts of meat," he said, "and it's always good when customers see the exact farm where the animal came from."

I went home with my head buzzing with ideas for the snack-bar menu. It was time I fired up the smoke-house, too; just an experiment with some best salmon the fishmonger said he'd keep for me and Helen's Nain had a recipe for gravadlax I wanted to try.

Two storms came and went in quick succession; the winds were ferocious, the seas were huge further down the coast and caused much damage and the rainfall was unprecedented; it ran off the ground already saturated and caused landslips, but the little yachts in my yard, snug in their cradles, sang and rattled in the howling gales and didn't budge an inch. Despite the Covid news, I cleaned and plotted and planned and Helen's Nain and I sampled the first smoked salmon from the smoke-house.

"Very, very good," she said and washed it down with a glass of chilled Riesling.

She seemed unperturbed by the crisis as it unfolded in the outside world and chose to confine her conversations to domestic issues. She'd finished documenting the inventory for the Boat Shed before Christmas and her laptop sat on the dresser and gathered dust. She listened to plays on the radio in the afternoon, took a nap before tea, enjoyed her food and went to bed early. The tremors in her hands were less apparent and we co-existed in a state of easy, regular routine. She seemed content. I was surprised how easily I was fooled.

"I hate this," she said, one morning and stared at the pills on the saucer in front of her. "I don't really want to go on until I'm useless, you know, cariad," and I was left with feelings of sadness and totally inadequacy. What could I say?

February's snowdrops finally drooped and faded and the first daffodils of spring nodded their yellow heads and brightened gardens and verges. But the March gales heralded more than the equinox. A pandemic was declared, and Boris Johnson, confident, positive, blustering, tried in vain to beat the virus into submission with rallying speeches, but had to explain to the nation the need for school and work closures due to spiralling hospital admissions. He announced a lockdown with travel restrictions. People must stay at home.

So, that's what I did.

CHAPTER 16

One Saturday early last summer, I'd packed lunch, swung the rucksack over my shoulder and set off for Black Rock Sands, down the steps to Borth-y-Gest, through the car-park, quickly past *Tai Pilots*, and up onto the headland by the pillbox. The tame robin at the beginning to the coastal path greeted me from his usual perch on the top wire of the fence, the path protected from the drop below to Danger Rock and the sandy coves. I walked the hot path surrounded by the coconut scent of yellow gorse and swathes of pretty pink campion and looked out from the cliff-top to the whole sweep of the estuary. The sea sparkled and twinkled diamonds in the bright sunshine, the tide at full flood and not a sandbank to be seen. It was a beautiful day.

After the turn to Carreg Wen, the path dropped down to Samson's Bay. Some of the risers on the steep steps had worn away and I held onto the rail, my legs almost too short for the stretch, then down onto the flat path again to the beach, ploughed through the soft sand and scrambled over the rocks below the Powder House. I thought I could hear the sound of music in snatches on the sea-breeze that had sprung up in the heat, and paddled along in the shallows as high-tide came and went, with hardly a mark to show it had visited at all. The sun flickered honey-comb ripples on the sand beneath the surface and in places, banks of fragmented weed surged black in the quiet swell. I walked in a dream of sand and sea, kicked and splashed through the bath-warm water up to my knees, and then I turned, slightly inland with the natural bend in the contours and stopped dead in the water.

Another sea, a black sea of cars filled the beach as far as the cliffs of Craig Ddu in the distance. The thump of bass music, the occasional tinny voice through a Tannoy and the whine of jet-skis on the water, broke the spell. I'd entered a different world: cars, vans, motor homes and campers, jet-skis on trailers, a crowd of bikers with brawny arms stripped bare of their leather gear rested on the sand, and their bikes, like prize race-horses, gleamed in the sun; pennants and flags drooped in the heat and there were tents and awnings and even a marquee as a reception area. The beach was covered with vehicles as far down as the Black Rock and as far up to the foothills of the sand-dunes.

Groups had corralled their cars in circles, erected gazebos with barbecues and a feast of fried onions and burgers filled the air; cans popped and children dug holes, built sand-castles and played cricket outside their compounds. Shaggy-coated dogs, tethered to car-bumpers, panted and slobbered over water-bowls under the shade of boot-lids or carefully-arranged parasols. I was transfixed, stunned with this seething mass of humanity in a space I'd only seen out of season and walked slowly along the tracks left by the cars as in a dream, as though I'd been transported to another world.

A big guy with tattoos on his arms and a fat belly squeezed into a wet-suit, stood by a trailer. He held a burger in one hand and a can of lager in the other. I asked him what was going on.

"Charity rally," he said, as grease dripped down his fingers. "Air Ambulance and British Heart Foundation."

I looked at his belly. Just as well, I thought.

Twelve months later, I stood on the same spot. I'd run and run and run along the tide-line in the shallows until I was out of breath, splashed warm water up to my waist and was soaked through. One hour in which to exercise per day? And only from home? The walk to the yard each day and back again, began to frustrate me. Common sense told me that if you didn't get close to anyone or any infected thing, you couldn't catch it; obviously. What would they do anyway? Arrest me? I was past caring what people thought. Helen's Nain had become quiet and withdrawn without the local gossip and I lived in a cocoon of silence, apart from Helen's anxious calls and Helen's mother's less anxious enquiries. I had to reassure them that I was well aware of my responsibilities and took precautions when I had to shop, to keep her, and myself, free from infection.

But out here, I could escape it all. There was no one to see me, no-one to offend, no-one to chat to, no-one to share the time of day with, and anyone else I met out here in this blissful tranquillity, would be doing the same thing and be on the same wave-length. So, I ran some more, then waded into the water, lay down and let the tide wash over me until it left me high and dry on the wet sand. I closed my eyes, and heard nothing; no cars, no dogs, no children, no sound of planes overhead, no distant sound of chain-saws or drills; only the gentle murmur of the waves as they broke in bubbles over my feet. I remembered the rally, then, and the cheek-by-jowl lives of folk from the cities denied the luxury of space in which to escape, the rising death toll of the elderly and infirm; even factors of obesity, colour and poverty, began to creep into the news.

I thought of Ed, in his office, back in Northampton; over-weight, unfit, unlikely to spare himself where news was concerned, and Helen's Nain, now my total responsibility now that no-one could travel and stay over. My mother and Felicity and Trish were furloughed, apart from providing a continual supply of flowers for funerals. Denise worked from home but there wasn't much work, she said, and the boss, now back in Trinidad, said not to worry, just check the security on the yard once in a while. She still didn't know about my fling. Or guessed.

"Tell you what," she'd said, after he'd gone back and left her in charge, "whoever snaps him up will be made for life, with that yummy body and all that money, and he's so *nice*, Cassie. Wonder if he's married already?"

"No, I don't think so," I said. "He doesn't look the type," and changed the subject.

Was he nice? Had he just used me? Or did we use each other? I preferred to think so. That evened it out. Curiously, he'd faded into a figment of my imagination, a vague recollection of warm gestures, kind thoughtfulness and wild passion but nothing lasting to make me yearn for his presence. There had been one thing I remembered, clearly, curiously; he'd commented on the improvements to the yard after the storm, orderly and tidy, with the boats in their smart cradles and suggested, with great enthusiasm, that concreting the yard, installing power points and water taps would be a splendid idea and would set the tone for the future.

I thought he'd sounded like a school-teacher tutoring a pupil, a top-down relationship, an appreciation of progress and perfection, an aspiration to all things lined up, in their place, managed and talked about the business 'going forward', which was an expression I hated. He was a business man after all, I reminded myself, the UK manager of some standing in a moneyed world I had no place in. Still, I hadn't yet dismissed his offer; it just needed to be on equal terms. More importantly, if he was the perfectionist I suspected, he wasn't for me. He was not going to tell me how to run my yard.

I turned over in the wet sand, put my chin in my hands and stared at the slopes and cliffs below the summit of Moel-y-Gest. The mountain shimmered in the heat, the ground baked dry and hard, an unadulterated freedom of human absence for the adders and grass-snakes in which to bask on the hot rocks. I walked back along the road and met Mark in the Harbour Master's pick-up on his way to check the locked barrier to the beach. He stopped in the middle of the road. The car window was wound down and he looked tanned and relaxed. The distance I'd walked from home was of no concern to him; he exuded common sense about rules and regulations and never made a fuss about anything unnecessary.

I leaned on the fence behind me, and I answered him back from across the road, having considered his close connections with family and friends, and aware of my responsibility to Helen's Nain. I kept my distance.

"Busy down there?" he asked, with a big grin and cheerful voice.

"It was," I said. "Packed. You couldn't put a pin between the grains of sand."

He laughed and drove off.

At two o'clock in the morning, I woke to the sound of Helen's Nain as she shuffled her way to the bathroom. Then I heard a cough. I lay awake and listened, but heard nothing more after she'd closed the bedroom door. In the morning, she wasn't in the kitchen, the kettle cold and the bacon still in the fridge. I made tea and took it upstairs.

"I think I'll have a lie-in, cariad," she said, propped up on the pillows, her face flushed and a distinct wheeze in her chest when she spoke, which set off a fit of coughing. I backed off, discreetly, went downstairs and put on one of her favourite cooking aprons, donned a mask and some gloves and picked up one of the lateral flow-tests on the dresser. I never thought, with her isolated existence, she'd ever need one and I'd tested regularly after each time I'd shopped.

I walked back upstairs and into the bedroom and sat down on the stool. She had her eyes shut.

"Now, don't panic," I said and her eyes snapped open as I opened the packet. She nodded. She knew.

"Positive," I said, "but I don't see how. You haven't been out to the shops or talked to people. Have you? It can't be me. I've tested negative this morning."

She turned her head away from me.

"She only popped in for a minute. Three days ago. I'd nearly forgotten. She was just passing and I waved. Then the next thing she'd let herself in through the back. The door was open, well, it always is, isn't it? We sat at opposite ends of the table, so I don't see… there was so much to catch up on. Just gossip, you know," and she waved it away with a feeble gesture. "We had a coffee and it was so good to talk to somebody. We laughed a bit. It did me good."

"Looks like it. Was it your friend, Gwen, by any chance?"

She nodded. "It was alright because she hadn't been near anyone, either. That's what she said. It can't have been her."

"Shops?" I asked. "She must go to the shops."

"I suppose so," she said, in a fit of coughing, then, "but it could have been you," with a hint of accusation between wheezes.

"Not me. I tested negative yesterday and today and haven't seen anyone. Sorry, but I think it must have been her. I'll need to let her know."

It was her and yes, she was positive as well. She wasn't at all well, but just a nasty cold and cough, she said. Silly cow. Didn't she know anything?

"I didn't think it would hurt," she said. "I didn't feel ill, then, just a bit of a sore throat and it cheered her up, you know, all that chat."

"But you know you shouldn't be visiting anyone, and particularly her. She's got Parkinson's," I said. "She's particularly vulnerable with all the drugs she's taking. She's not well at all."

I closed the call before I said exactly what I thought.

I watched Helen's Nain all day, propped her up on more pillows I'd fetched from the guestrooms and listened to the coughing fits. I saw her chest heave as she tried to recover from each one. I wanted to punch her friend's silly, pink face and disingenuous eyes. I found a thermometer in the bathroom cupboard and by four o'clock, it registered thirty-nine degrees, even with cold drinks which she could only sip. I gave her some Paracetamol tablets crushed up in jam. She settled, exhausted and dozed in short bursts.

I stayed out of the room as much as possible and doubled up the masks when I rearranged her pillows and washed my hands scrupulously. I didn't know what to look for, didn't know what to expect, didn't know at what point I needed to call an ambulance, if at all, just hoped this was as bad as it was going to get and she'd recover. The list of symptoms was quite clear but I phoned her daughter in London for advice.

"You'll have to use your own judgement," she said. "The hospitals down here are overloaded and I presume it's the same up there and there are only two hospitals for north Wales. Just keep an eye on her breathing."

I left my bedroom door ajar that night, opened the window and lay on the bed, fully dressed with the apron and mask on. She slept for short periods in-between the coughing fits. By six o'clock in the morning, the coughing subsided. I shot into the room and saw the panic in her eyes as her chest heaved in vain. Then, despite the terrible pressure on the NHS,

I rang for an ambulance.

I stood outside while they wheeled her out in a chair and lowered the ramp. She put her hand on my gloved wrist and squeezed it, nodded to me, almost a sign of acceptance under the oxygen mask. Then they shut the door and drove off; blue lights flashed and the sirens echoed round the bay and they were gone, up the hill and out of sight. That was the last time I saw her.

Visitors were not allowed. She'd been moved from the ward into Intensive Care and placed on a ventilator. I tried to put the image of her being alone, unconscious and with no family or friend to comfort her, out of my head; it was the only way to survive, and I worked hard enough to drop into bed every night exhausted, physically and emotionally. I cleaned the house from top to bottom, washed the bedding and aired all the rooms, scrubbed the kitchen floor and prettied up the paved area at the front with some geraniums from a neighbour. The bay was unnervingly quiet. I didn't even glance at *Tai Pilots* and I fled up the steps to the yard every afternoon and worked some more there. I sanded and painted the dinghies and taught myself how to use the drill.

I put up some new shelves in the shed, jet-washed the caravan, checked the two little yachts over and sent photos to Hugh and Paul. I filled and painted the gouges in *Annie's* hull and used T-cut on the scratches. I waited in vain for the insurance assessment for the damage to the shed's foundations, but Covid had slowed everything down.

I phoned the ward twice a day. Then they phoned me, instead, one morning. It was the phone call I'd dreaded. There was nothing more they could do. They were very sorry. A nurse had been with her until the end and held her hand.

I sat on the caravan step, numb with shock. Then I had a call from Tim, still a reporter on the paper in Northampton. Ed had died in hospital, also on a ventilator like Helen's Nain. The virus and his general health meant he hadn't stood a chance.

"We're gutted, Cass. The whole office. There was nobody like him."

I cleaned some more and cried into my bucket with only the seagulls to hear me and wondered what else could happen.

Helen's Nain's Bed and Breakfast was just an empty shell, much the way I felt, and I filled up the time as best I could but I couldn't bear to be in the house. I locked it up and moved back into the caravan to sleep and used the Boat Shed to give me the comfort I remembered; a cosy fire in the evening and the familiar, warm smells. Will Roberts arrived for a socially-distanced visit and with summer round the corner and a glimmer of hope for business to start again, I decided to go ahead with the estate agent and put *Tai Pilots* on the market.

But first, I needed to retrieve Catrin and bury her with her siblings and parents in the old church-yard high up on the hill overlooking the estuary. I didn't want to go into the house on my own this time and fished around in my list of people who could accompany me.

Past being worried whether he would be willing, or not. I picked up the phone and called David.

"You don't have to stand close to me," I said. "I've tested negative, anyway, and if you're still paranoid, just stay in the front room while I go into the cellar." I hadn't seen him since before Christmas. "Please?"

"I have to consider my parents," he said. "They're not young, as you know."

We sat outside the Boat Shed in the shadow of the cliff behind. He wore a mask, moved his chair further away from mine and declined coffee.

"You can't be too careful," he said.

"We're outside in the baking hot sun, for God's sake. Inside, yes, maybe, but not out here. Don't you read the data?"

"You're rather casual about all this," he said, disapproval evident. "I hear Mrs Parry died. I'm sorry. I know you were fond of her. How did she catch it?"

"A careless friend," I said, "with the brain of a parrot. There are rules to follow and rules to consider and personal risk assessments," I said, decidedly prickly, "and common sense."

We walked apart, up the path and down the steps to the bay, the car-park still empty.

"Did you manage to keep in touch with your girlfriend?" I couldn't resist it. "Lovely car."

He didn't answer.

"Sorry, none of my business," I said, thinking I'd upset him, that maybe she was sick or even died, kicked myself and sat down on one of the benches by the bus-shelter. He sat down at the other end. "I hope she's well?"

"I'm sure she is," he said and adjusted his mask so I couldn't read his face. He didn't look at me.

"Oh," I said. "Sorry. Shall we go?"

The house stank, as usual. I hadn't been in since the day I was asked to go by the police, the drugs found and the men apprehended, but my opinion hadn't changed. It was tainted for all sorts of reasons I found easy to explain; family tragedy, drowned children, dead baby, drugs and all the shit that went with their effect on youngsters, skinny Emily who could so easily have been a victim of her own ignorance and youth and Jason, hounded out of the area because he couldn't escape from the dealers; the grime and mould would have been enough. I opened the box in the cellar and took out the little urn and the envelope, put them in my rucksack and clambered back up the steps.

We walked up to the pill box and sat on the bench overlooking the estuary.

"Amazing what could be done with that place," he said. He was full of ideas. He sat well away from me at the other end of the bench. "It could be modernised like the other houses. It would make an ideal home for you."

Then I told him.

"So, the estate agent is coming next week. I'm going to put in for planning permission to build a new chandlery and boat store with living accommodation upstairs. Like the yard next door," I said. "I'll show you the plans. It's still within the conditions of the inheritance and I can run the snack-bar and smoke-house as extra income."

He was horrified.

"That's not very sensible, Cassie. You need to look ahead a bit more; investment, income in later age, it's not easy to find property round here. And if you're resident, it helps to keep the number of holiday homes down."

"Later age? Don't be ridiculous, David. I'm only twenty-two."

He flinched a bit. I was cross. He hadn't changed at all. If anything, the lockdown seemed to have heightened his irritating opinions. He adjusted his mask.

"And why don't you take that thing off, for God's sake? There's no Covid up here. Use your common sense and I can't see your face, either."

He ignored me and the mask barely disguised the frustration in his voice.

"I can't understand why you're so blasé about all this, Cassie; first Covid, which you seem to take so lightly, now all these ideas about living over the shop. It's ridiculous. You need a proper house, a proper home."

"Why?" I asked. "Why is The Boat Shed not a home? It's been a hub for more friendship than I've ever experienced in my life. Everyone who's come there has cared about everyone else. It's like having another family. You've no idea."

"But what will you do if *Tai Pilots* doesn't sell? What about planning permission?"

"I don't know," I said, truthfully, "but I'm not going to live in that gruesome place. I'd rather live in the caravan."

"But you can't do that forever."

We sat in silence. The incoming tide deepened in the channel below us and gradually covered the sand-banks all the way over to the Harlech side. The whole mass glistened and shimmered in the sunlight, the outline of the Rhinogs in the distance clear against the blue sky. Harlech Castle was just a grey impression.

"It's a shame," he said, out of the blue.

He detached the mask from his ears, scrunched it up in his hands, turned and looked at me.

"What is?"

"That we always bicker. I don't intend to be a killjoy but it upsets me to think you might lose more than you've gained. I can't help having a sensible head on my shoulders; it goes with the job."

"I don't understand you at all," I said and struggled with this sudden change. "One minute you're taking terrible risks in horrible seas when you're racing that yacht of yours, the next minute you're telling me to be careful and sensible and… and conventional."

"Well, you did ask me to advise you after the storm. You didn't mind that."

"That's different," I said.

He shifted in his seat, crossed his legs and leaned his arm on the back of the bench.

"We'd make a good team, you know," he said, quite conversationally. "I can be entrepreneurial as well; you with your big ideas and me with the nuts-and-bolts knowledge to navigate through all the pit-falls;

finance, legal, all that stuff. I have funds."

A seagull perched on the board with the speed-limit painted in large letters. He turned one beady eye on us and cocked his head to one side.

"Is that a business proposition?" I asked, and scarcely believed what I'd heard.

He smiled and looked me straight in the eye. "It's whatever you would want it to be."

For the first time in over a year, I saw him as he was when I'd met him at the gate to the yard; good-looking, tall, curly hair and green eyes and an easy manner.

But even then, he hadn't sparked something inside me. I'd seen the other side of him, when he'd not been able to acknowledge my desperate need for independence and my need to prove myself. For David Hughes, the sauce for the goose was not the same as the sauce for the gander, I thought, and he'd be in control before I could wink. Even if he'd hinted at a relationship on a more personal level as well, although I could scarcely believe that, and could hear Denise and Trish mutter in my ear about security and stability and money, but it made no difference. I couldn't imagine a fascinating conversation with him over dinner or a companionable walk on a cold, wet beach with a warm hotel and a night of wild passion to look forward to. No, he was not for me; either way.

The seagull flew off, banked over the pillbox and disappeared out to sea.

"Thank you for the thought, David, but I'm not ready to share just yet. It wouldn't work and we'd hate each other. Can't we just be friends, for once? And could you recommend someone to draw up plans for me? I've got the sketches."

CHAPTER 17

I submitted the plans for the Boat Shed. They said it would be many, many weeks, with the backlog of work and staff off-sick or self-isolating. I didn't mind; I'd set the plan in motion, at least. The vapour trails in the sky returned, the shops and hotels opened with limited hospitality and the tourists returned, slowly but surely, to the beaches. Daniel winged his way to the UK. My head was in a turmoil.

"When I've quarantined and finished down here," he said, from a London hotel, "I'll be going North to Scotland again and then back to Holyhead. I need to see Denise on business on my way south. Can I see you then?" He sounded hesitant, not as warm and exuberant as I'd remembered. Phone calls had become few and far between and emails laid out facts about business. What else was there to say? We had little shared history, after all.

Denise came back to work with a will, as the jet-ski owners gathered force and wanted everything done yesterday and to cram in as much of the remaining summer on the water as possible. The slipways opened and some boats, but not all, were launched and Hugh and Paul resumed their weekend-working breaks, sanded their little yachts and chatted about work over coffee.

I opened the snack-bar and moved the tables well apart for distancing and Angela swapped her Saturdays to work for me; the salt-marsh, lamb-baguettes were a true hit, the lamb roasted and sliced thinly with Angela's own, exquisite gravy made from real stock. The freshly-made mint jelly, courtesy of Emily's mother, bore no resemblance to the bottled stuff and I chalked the name of their farm and the butcher on the menu board. It was a small start, but worth it.

Arnie turned up one weekend with Ben in tow, still young enough to have ice-cream on his nose. He was a year older and had big shoulders for such a little lad, just like his father. He fell in love with Emily and followed her round the yard like a puppy. They sat on one of the upturned dinghies and she taught him how to fashion a cat's cradle with whipping twine, basic knots she'd learned on the farm and new, nautical ones on You-Tube. His fat fingers struggled and they laughed a lot whilst Rosie was happy in her new, doggie, play-pen that Hugh and Paul had built in the yard.

Emily asked about Jason, still down south and was impressed when I told her he'd started a proper course in wooden boat-building, as well as stripping down the odd outboard engine, and was glad he'd got all the bits of paper he needed to be accepted. Helen phoned me more than she'd ever done before. She was devastated about her Nain and that she'd died and been buried with no family around her and thanked me for looking after her. She didn't mention the house but said the family would arrange a memorial service when they were allowed.

I wandered around the yard in the evening on my own, with a glass of wine in hand as I used to do, excited about the plans but with a sense of loss and loneliness. I wanted someone I could share my optimism with, but above all, I wanted some money

David hadn't returned to the yard; he had no need to after he'd so kindly finished the insurance claim and I felt guilty about using him to bail me out, but we'd parted amicably. I knew that I'd upset him yet again with my fanciful ways and ideas and then my diplomatic refusal to even consider his proposals, even the business one which had possibilities, he'd thought. As for the rest, I must have misunderstood him. It was an incongruous offer, after all our differences and after the snippets I'd heard about his glamourous girlfriend, as far removed from my scruffy self as I could imagine and was itching to know about her. I asked Denise to keep her ear to the ground. I still couldn't fathom out his motives but felt a sense of loyalty to him, his proposal something that was ostensibly private, and just between us. But I still wanted to know. Had she dumped him? Or had he dumped her? Who was she, anyway?

"Why?" she asked, "I thought you didn't fancy him. He's been good to you though; straight here after the storm and that. He's always been here when you needed him. You're bonkers, upsetting him all the time. I bet he earns good money; solicitors do, don't they?"

"I don't do it on purpose," I said. "He's just…" I was going to say, so critical and he talks down to me like a wayward child, but I didn't. "Anyway, it's not always about money."

"Isn't it?" she said, "really?" and glanced at the copy of the plans I'd sent in. "You're an idiot, Cassie." I shut the biscuit tin and threw her out; nicely. I didn't tell her about his proposal and I hadn't heard anything from the planning department. No news is good news, I told myself.

Daniel texted to say he would be down at the end of that week. There was no mention of hotels or how long he was going to stay and ridiculously I hadn't tidied myself up and hadn't had my hair cut; it took weeks to get an appointment. I looked a mess but couldn't seem to find the motivation to do anything about it; no Helen's Nain to advise me, no access to Helen's clothes, no more warm homecomings and someone who listened to the day's events, no-one to share certain things with, remembering the beautiful choker she'd lent me. I felt the loss more than I thought.

My mother rang, as she did more often these days, furloughed during the summer and she had only just started the business up again. Felicity, her partner, had caught Covid on the Tube, but isolated herself in the house and soon recovered. Trish was bored to death with funeral flowers and finished with her boyfriend who'd 'gone off', she said, whatever that meant and when was I going to find a luscious man and get married? I nearly told her about Daniel but she would have waxed lyrical over beautiful babies and money forever.

Then he arrived, in the blue Porsche as before, the paintwork dusty from the journey. He looked tired and his smile of greeting was reserved but he walked towards me and enveloped me in a big hug, held me by the shoulders, studied my face and scraped a flake of paint off my nose.

"A bit battered," I said apologetically.

"Aren't we all?"

We sat outside, strained and uncomfortable, the relationship not stable or long enough to pick up the pieces easily. Out brief liaison had been a world away.

"So, how was your lockdown?" he asked. I told him and tried not to choke-up over the deaths, concentrated on the beach and how it rescued me, day after day.

"It was my fantasy world," I said. "I could stand and gaze at nothing, hear nothing, but my mind could wander wherever it wanted to. I could go where I wanted, when I wanted and how I wanted, declutter and breathe, then go back to work and make plans. Shall I show you?"

He flipped through the file with the copy for the planning application and studied the drawings.

"Very up-market," he said.

"That's what my mother said. Exciting, isn't it? Now tell me about your lockdown. You have this knack of allowing me to talk too much."

He got up from the chair, walked over to Hugh's boat and ran his hand over the newly -painted hull, turned round and leaned against the cradle.

"Did I tell you that the yard next door was one of my father's first enterprises?" he said, evasive as ever. "He started small in this country, bought up a couple of derelict boatyards and then moved on to bigger things and marinas. He ended up in Trinidad, met my mum and American money. We own and manage three marinas in the UK, as well as a few boatyards. He'd always hung on to this one, for old time's sake, I suppose. The company had plans afoot for developing a new one in Holyhead."

That didn't surprise me. Denise had said he wasn't going up there for nothing. I waited and listened. He sat down on one of the upturned dinghies.

"We held a board meeting two weeks ago," he said. "After the current crisis and looking ahead, when business seems, all of a sudden, very uncertain, it was decided that some of the international concerns need to be tailored. In short, drawing in our horns, to use the expression my father used at the meeting.

'Did you reconsider coming for a holiday?" he asked. "Coming back with me? It's going to be winter here again soon. The yard can look after itself for a few weeks, at least."

Restless, he got up and walked around again.

"Why?" I asked, "this time?"

"Because you're your own person," he said, "and I like that."

"Even like this? Poor and scruffy? In your world?"

He laughed. "You don't always have to be," he said. "You scrub up pretty well, I recall."

"Then I wouldn't be my own person if I had to scrub up all the time,"

I said, "just for show."

We stopped by the gates and he looked across at the other yard.

"We're selling up in the UK," he said. "That includes Madoc Marine which is on the market, with prospective buyers already. I've spoken to Denise and she'll stay and see it through. She's a bit upset, of course, and worried about a new owner and if she'll keep her job, or even want to. Will you come home with me, Cassie? See if you like it? It's not going to be the same here anymore and I won't have a reason to visit the UK if the marinas sell. We're going to develop more in the West Indies, nearer home."

He said he would call me before he flew back. I'd never been utterly lost for words, never completely confused for any length of time and never been so desperate to talk to anyone. But there was no-one I trusted to give me an objective opinion. I didn't have to commit myself to anything by taking a mere holiday but knew that there was a divide between us and it would be difficult. I still doubted his motives, wasn't sure whether he, or I, felt love clouded by lust but it certainly wasn't money.

I missed him as soon as he was gone but my confidence in establishing a relationship deserted me and I saw myself in his eyes; poor, with no aspirations to glamour, no great intellect or business acumen to bring to the table; I hadn't even written anything to challenge my brain since the feature I'd sent Ed, a sort of Cinderella or Eliza Doolittle who needed rescuing. Was that it? I couldn't believe anything else.

I worked away in a vacuum after he'd gone, amidst warnings of more lockdowns and mutation of viruses and was utterly miserable. Then, the morning post arrived and with it, an offer from the insurance company, and from the estate agents, a bidding war for *Tai Pilots*. The third envelope contained the refusal from the planning department.

I sat down in one of the old arm-chairs and stared at the rafters and the joints between the tin roofing-sheets, the spider-webs that crept onto the window pane and the dead flies on the sill and picked up the drawings from the counter. The two-storied, timber-framed building, like a log-cabin on stilts, had open-plan, modern living accommodation high above the yard in case of flooding and small-boat storage and working space at ground level; one small, enclosed area for a small stock of the classic chandlery I already had and a new computer work space linked to the rest of the world for the big stuff. If I couldn't stock it, I could at least find it. All for nothing. I picked up the phone to tell David and put it down again and I wandered around the yard, unsure of myself and decided not to tell anyone. I couldn't bear the sympathy.

Early on Friday evening, Hugh arrived on his ancient bicycle.

"I've finished work early," he said, "and thought I'd pop in. You've had a lot to deal with lately, Miss Cassie."

We discussed the chandlery for a few minutes. It was strange, and unlike him to offer a personal comment. Then he took off his Beanie and turned it round and round in his hands.

"What's up, Hugh?" I asked, dreading another problem.

"I think…"

"What?"

"I do think, if I may say so, that perhaps you should share whatever it is that's bothering you."

I stared at him, the most unlikely confidante I could have thought of. We sat on our usual upturned dinghy. Then I told him.

"In my opinion, if I may make a suggestion?"

I nodded.

"I think, perhaps, that you are better off without either of them. And as for the planning permission, I think all will become apparent. In time. Did you know, by the way, that Mr Blackwell owns the biggest scrap-yard in the Midlands? After his generosity, I looked him up, naturally. Shall I check around before I go?"

Saturday seemed a good day to celebrate. I'd thought it through and it seemed that the offer for *Tai Pilots* and the insurance claim would help me to renovate the existing Boat Shed and maybe that's what Hugh meant and that would be enough. As for somewhere to live, I'd think of something.

Hugh worked solidly and finished the last of the planks for the day and the late August sun had warmed the yard by the snack-bar and disappeared behind the cliffs. I closed the yard to visitors at four o'clock, Hugh and Paul finished work and I opened two bottles of chilled Cava, put some cold beers on the table and Angela cooked sausages and burgers. The Gilberts arrived to pick up Emily, stayed for a while and talked about floods and Covid and Will Roberts arrived with two sheepdogs caged in the back of the pickup and swapped sheep stories. I'd almost forgotten he ran a small-holding. I had a sudden urge to phone Jason.

We sat around the table, chatted and laughed and the sheep-dogs barked as the gate opened and Denise walked through.

"Sorry I'm late. I've only just shut the shop," she said, newly made-up with blue eye-shadow, bright pink lipstick and her hair piled on her head and fixed with a blue band. "Some of these jet-ski owners don't know when to go home. Actually, I had to bring one with me. He wouldn't take no for an answer."

Arnie's big frame towered behind her. He was dressed in a smart white shirt with the top buttons undone and the sleeves rolled up; the gold ear-ring winked in the sunlight and a heavy gold chain and medallion nestled against his hairy chest. She stood aside.

"I thought you'd like to meet the new owner of Madoc Marine," she said.

CHAPTER 18

Emily brought her English coursework to me. Schools were open part-time and she'd been asked to find a poem to analyse.

I looked out of the floor-to-ceiling window in the apartment above Madoc Marine's showroom. I'd started to get used to the new view and spent much of the day on the computer, impellers and gaskets as far removed from my knowledge as fids and baggy-wrinkles had been.

My new domain stretched out to the end of the slipway and I could see right down both boatyards to Hugh's yacht at the end of my yard, Ballast Island over the water and the sea of jet-skis and power boats below me. I remembered what Denise had once said, left on her own after Doug Peterson drowned, with no immediate boss to replace him and no guidance, and me on my own with no Jason and a dwindling purse.

"Just you, me and two boatyards, girl," she'd said, after a bottle of wine.

"You can manage it all between you," Arnie said, when I told him. "Live over the shop until your planning wins its appeal. Which it will. The new mechanic starts on Monday."

Rosie nosed her way onto my lap, the plush, leather settee installed by Doug Peterson now covered with pretty throws. I still didn't like dogs, pushed her off gently and Emily picked her up, sat at my feet on a cushion and handed me the book.

"It's called *Fern Hill.* Miss Thomas said we could pick what we wanted to get our heads back into gear. It was in mam's bookcase, and mam, she said it was a disgrace if I didn't read Dylan Thomas, same name as the teacher's, 'cos he's Welsh an' that. I like what he does with words," she said, "but I don't get half of it. Is it about being young and happy as a child? Enjoying it, like. And that end bit? You're going to get old and die, anyway. It's a bit sad, really. You can't escape from it, sort of stuck with it, like the moon and the tides. If that's right and it's miserable getting old, you might as well make the most of being young, I reckon. Whatever."

"Something like that," I said.